A World of Voice
Voice and Speech across Culture

Presented by the Voice & Speech Review
The Official Journal of the Voice and Speech Trainers Association

Voice and Speech Review Editorial Staff

Dudley Knight, **Editor-in-Chief**
University of California - Irvine, Emeritus

Lynn Watson, **Associate Editor-in-Chief**
University of Maryland, Baltimore County

Production Editor
Clayton Guiltner
Southern Arkansas University

Design Consultant
Alex Goodman
Wayne State University Theatre

Associate Editors

Ethics, Standards and Practices
Rena Cook
University of Oklahoma

Singing
Joan Melton
California State University - Fullerton, Emerita

Heightened Text and Verse
Ellen O'Brien
The Shakespeare Theatre

Voice Production, Voice Related Movement Studies
Dana McConnell
Viterbo University

Pedagogy and Coaching
Jeff Morrison
Marymount Manhattan College

Voice and Speech Science, Vocal Health
Ronald C. Scherer
Bowling Green State University

Private Studio Practice
Ginny Kopf
Voice and Speech Training

Founding Editor-in-Chief
Rocco Dal Vera
University of Cincinnati

Pronunciation, Phonetics, Linguistics, Dialect/Accent Studies
Erik Singer
Freelance Voice/Dialect Teacher

Past Editors-in-Chief
Mandy Rees
California State University - Bakersfield
Rena Cook
University of Oklahoma

Reviews and Sources
Tara McAllister-Viel
Central School of Speech and Drama

Editorial Assistant
Jessica Ruth Baker
University of Maryland, Baltimore County

Cover Design Stephen Milano

Citation Information
Title: A World of Voice: Voice and Speech across Culture presented by the Voice and Speech Review
Editor-in-Chief: Dudley Knight
Date: 2011
ISBN: 978-0-9773876-3-2
Publisher: Voice and Speech Trainers Association
Description: The official journal of VASTA containing articles on a wide variety of issues in professional voice and speech use and training, many centered on the integration of voice and movement studies as they relate to training actors and working with clients. 363 pages, 8.5"X11", 110+ b&w photos, paperback.

VSR is indexed in the MLA International Bibliography and listed in the Directory of Periodicals.

Correspondence
US mail shipping
Dudley Knight, Editor-in-Chief
19 N. 2nd St.
Easton, PA 18042
Telephone:
(610) 559-8464
Email:
dknight@uci.edu

Jeff Morrison, Editor-in-Chief 2013
jmorrison@mmm.edu

The Voice and Speech Review is an official publication of the Voice and Speech Trainers Association (VASTA), Inc.

VASTA is a non-profit organization and a focus group of the Association for Theatre in Higher Education (ATHE).

Editorial *by Dudley Knight*

Photo By: Stephen Ivey

Professor Emeritus of Drama at the University of California, Irvine, where he was Head of Acting for eight years and Vice Chair of Drama for ten; teaching engagements at many major theatre training programs throughout America; certified as a master teacher of Fitzmaurice Voicework; conducts workshops and lectures on voice and speech for actors and voice teachers nationwide and abroad. The author of articles and book chapters on speech training for actors, his speech textbook *Speaking with Skill* will be published by Methuen Drama in 2012. A founding member of the Long Wharf Theatre, his extensive stage career includes major roles in regional theatres along with hundreds of roles in film, television, radio drama and voice-over.

In retrospect, I consider it fortunate that, in deciding two years ago on a cover theme for this issue of the *Voice & Speech Review*, I chose the title *A World of Voice* instead of the more authoritative *The World of Voice*. That indefinite article, it turns out, has two qualities that I did not realize when I made the choice. The first quality is that *A World of Voice* recognizes and helps us celebrate the extraordinary variety of vocal use throughout the world: a world full of singing and speaking traditions that are both defined by culture and that also help us to define the most profound elements of our own cultures; yet, at the same time, an inclusive world that can reach across linguistic and musical differences to interact creatively with other languages and other music. The second quality that has become apparent in the collection of essays contained in this volume is that no single issue of this journal can hope to encompass *the* world of voice. Many articles in past issues of *VSR* already have offered impressive insights into vocal use across culture, so it is not as though the topic had been unexplored before now. On the other side of the coin, the excellent

and sometimes revelatory accounts of innovative practice and research by the authors of *A World of Voice*, while they explore many interactions of vocal traditions, in the end can only represent *a* world of voice, a selection from an abundance of possibilities.

At the beginning of my own career as an actor and teacher, there was little or no exploration of vocal and speech use across cultures, certainly not in American theatre training. Vocal production for the speaking voice, wa-a-ay back then, was based almost entirely on European classical singing techniques. Stage accents were conventionalized, even stereotypical, as a matter of course. One of my most gratifying life experiences has been to be able to hear the enrichment of our theatrical soundscape by the myriad ways in which vocal practice has become globally aware over the past half-century. Part of this dynamism comes from the discovery of artistic ties between cultures and part of it comes, paradoxically, from the discovery of artistic autonomies that help to define one culture from another. The creative tension between these two forces is one of the major factors that energize voice and speech training today.

Because culture is always reinventing itself within its own traditions, *A World of Voice* celebrates not only the contrasts between forms of vocal practice across cultures today, but also the changes in vocal use within cultures over time. Today's innovation becomes tomorrow's tradition, which often becomes next week's relic. And yet (here's that creative tension again) the valuable elements of vocal and verbal tradition seem to stay amazingly resilient through the years.

If our vocal world always changes, the world of voice and speech training changes also, inevitably, progressively and sometimes sadly. We continue to welcome young new teachers to our ranks, but it is a mark of the maturity of our field that we are starting to lose some of the visionaries whose pioneering work set standards for us all. *A World of Voice* mourns—but also celebrates—the lives of Mary Corrigan, Jo Estill, Arthur Lessac and Dorothy Runk Mennen. Their extraordinary contributions—to teaching, to research, to the Voice and Speech Trainers' Association itself, and to so many of us personally—are incalculable. They have left a record of accomplishment that invites our younger colleagues to emulate as these newer trainers carry their own efforts forward to ever deeper insights and new discoveries.

My editorial colleagues and I hope that *A World of Voice* captures the innovative spirit of our field with all its growing critical rigor, the interaction of differing ideas and intuitions, the contrast and even the clash of opinions and conclusions. I know that I have learned much from the peer-reviewed articles, essays and columns by our contributors. I know equally that I do not agree with all the assertions of all the authors. Then too, there are opinions expressed in essays that differ strongly from opinions in other articles within these pages. To me, this diversity and divergence is all healthy. The day that everybody agrees will be the day that a journal like this one will no longer be needed.

In the spirit of reinvention within tradition, there are new visual elements in *A World of Voice*. While much of the look of the journal will be familiar to the faithful—not to mention patient—readers of each biennial volume, there are changes of font and page layout designed to make the journal more reader-friendly. We hope we have approached that goal or, at the very least, started a process of reexamination of all elements of the *Voice & Speech Review* by subsequent editors. We know that we have set a path toward easier electronic access to past issues in *VSR* through the resources of University Readers. The next step will be to add audio illustration to our articles as the technology of e-readers and other portable devices improves. At the rate technology is accelerating, these goals may be at last partially realized by the time these lines reach their archaically printed form!

I am deeply grateful to the many colleagues—authorial and editorial—whose talents, intelligence and dedication have made *A World of Voice* a reality. I must add one individual acknowledgement. My Associate Editor-in-Chief, Professor Lynn Watson, has been an extraordinary collaborator in the process of producing *A World of Voice*. Her wisdom and keen judgment have not only contributed immeasurably to the positive qualities of this issue of *Voice & Speech Review*, they have often saved me from making even more editorial mistakes than our astute readers will find in these pages.

I hope that *A World of Voice* will help to open your world of voice, and through you, the voices of those touched by your skill and guidance.

Editorial Column *by Lynn Watson, Associate Editor-in-Chief*

Writing and articles have appeared in *VSR*, *Acting Now*, and *Teaching Breathing*. Extensive work as a voice, speech and dialect specialist at leading regional theatres including Arena Stage, Kennedy Center, Ford's Theatre, A.C.T. San Francisco, Mark Taper Forum and South Coast Repertory. Directing credits include the world premiere of Tina Howe's short comedy—*Milk and Water*. Acting credits: Off Broadway and leading classical roles in regional theatre. Professional affiliations: AEA, SAG, VASTA board member, and Fitzmaurice Voicework. She is an Associate Professor at the University of Maryland, Baltimore County.

One can't smell it, taste it or see it, except perhaps by way of synesthesia—when sensory messages overlap. But we touch it, or rather, it touches us via pressure waves. The touch of the pressure waves vibrates flesh, cartilage and bone, and is perceived by both the sound maker and those near enough to feel the waves as *voice*. So voice is experienced—heard—via invisible touch.

The oft-noted ephemeral nature of voice lends it a compelling sense of mystery, but also contributes to some essential misunderstanding. At the end of the first year of voice training in our acting program, I often ask students to think back to when they were just beginning classes and recall what they had expected to encounter. What had they anticipated doing in voice classes, and how did what actually transpired differ from their expectations? Their answers are revealing. *I thought you'd tell me what was wrong with my voice and speech, and I'd learn how to "talk better." I thought you'd correct my pronunciation and we'd learn accents. I thought you'd play recordings of "good speech" and we would try to speak like the recordings. I had no idea how much the entire body would be involved in our work. I thought the sounds of speech were formed just by the vocal cords alone. I'd heard it*

was important to use the 'diaphragm,' but had no idea how I was supposed do that. I didn't know breath was important, but now I understand that everything depends on it.

In a sense, every issue of *VSR* expresses a deep desire to reach out to the world beyond to share what we know and what we wish to learn more about; to share not just amongst ourselves, but with those outside our field. If my students are any indication, the ephemeral nature of what we do tends to obscure our tangible achievements, but this publication helps to remedy that predicament. It has been a privilege to work on this edition of the "moveable feast" that is *VSR*. Indeed, within the articles here you are sure to find ideas, methods, studies and theories that stay with you. An exciting and daunting proposition it is, launching into reading the newest volume of the *Voice & Speech Review*. How do you usually proceed? Flip through the pages and trust that serendipity will land you on an article topic that excites you? Scan the table of contents for something that catches your eye? Go straight to the section that covers your specialty? All perfectly reasonable approaches. I have some other methods to offer.

For a comprehensive overview, begin by reading through each associate editor's introduction to their section, where snapshots of the essays and articles are presented. Remember that in addition to essays and articles, *VSR* includes columns written by experts in the field who contribute writing to multiple issues. Be sure to spend time catching up on new publications and resources in the "Reviews and Sources" section. Or deliberately move outside your comfort zone and read an article that seems far from your area of interest. Science not your passion? Head for the "Voice Science" section and start reading. Don't be surprised if you find yourself lingering there. *VSR* editors and authors work to make articles accessible to a broad audience of readers with voice and speech backgrounds. Some performance voice pieces seem too "squishy"? Choose an essay or article with a "soft" performance focus and see if some "studio wisdom" contained within it triggers an idea for a research project. No matter how you choose to begin reading, your moveable feast will expand.

My thanks to the authors and editors who have contributed so generously to *A World of Voice*. In addition to their generosity and patience, I am grateful for all I have learned from them in the process of working on this issue. Thanks especially to Dudley Knight for his brilliance, unfailing wit and innumerable talents. He does as an editor what he does as an actor—brings out the best in all his compatriots. You, too, will benefit from that trait as you travel through these pages.

Contents

Contents

Ethics, Standards and Practices

Pedagogy and Coaching

Voice and Movement Studies

Contents

Pronunciation, Phonetics, Linguistics, Dialect/Accent Studies

Private Studio Practice

Contents

Voice and Speech Science, Vocal Health

Singing

Reviews and Sources

Contents

Cover Articles

Contents

VASTA Mission Statement

VASTA is an international organization whose mission is to advance the art, research, and visibility of the voice and speech profession.

Goals:

* SERVE the needs of voice and speech specialists, teachers, and students in training and in practice.
* ADVOCATE for those who work and study in the field.
* PROMOTE the vital role of voice and speech specialists for all professional voice users.
* BROADEN public understanding of the nature and importance of voice and speech use and training.
* CREATE opportunities for ongoing education, and the exchange of knowledge and information among professionals in the field.
* CULTIVATE diversity within our membership, and encourage a liveliness of thought and opinion.
* UPHOLD and advance the highest standards of voice and speech.

VASTA Publications
Available Online at www.vasta.org:
* Guidelines for the Preparation of Voice and Speech Teachers
* Promotion, Tenure, and Hiring Resources
    - Typical Job Responsibilities
    - Evaluation Guidelines
    - Recommended Models for Evaluating Teaching, Creative and Service Activities
    - Are You On the Promotion and Tenure Track?
    - Documentation
    - Suggestions on the Creation of a Teaching Dossier
    - Some Questions to Consider Before Accepting a Tenure Track Position
* VASTA Professional Index
* Diversity Bibliography
* Best Practices for Academic Theatre
* How to Use a Vocal Coach
* *VASTA Vision 2005-2014*
* Teaching and Learning: Educational Outcomes
* Online Newsletter Archive
* VASTA Bylaws
* Internet Resources for Voice and Speech Professionals
* Conference Information
* VASTA Online Bibliography

VASTA Voice - eNewsletter
published 5 times a year.
Members - free
Individual Subscription $10.00
Institution Subscription $20.00

Voice and Speech Review
published bi-annually
Members - free
Individual Subscriptions $35.00
Institutional Subscription $35.00

You may also order copies of *Shakespeare Around the Globe*, *Voice and Gender*, and *The Moving Voice* from University Readers at www.universityreaders.com.

Vasta.org - The VASTA Website
Visit www.vasta.org, the VASTA website. The site includes: News & Updates, Resources, Communication and Publications, Professional Index. Any VASTA Member may list contact information, resume, teaching philosophy in the Professional Index. The site also includes information on conferences and workshops, links to voice and speech related websites, the Mentoring Program, Newsletter Archive, Fellow Program, International Listserv, technology resources, grants & awards, website details, and organization Bylaws.

We are grateful to the following experts for their close and careful reviews of material submitted to the Journal:
Barbara Adrian
Eric Armstrong
Cynthia Barrett
Ana M. Carvalho
Pamela Christian
Dr. D. Robert Dechaine
Diane Foust
David Gardiner
Jan Gist
Julia Guichard
Jane Guyer
Allison Hetzel
Nancy Houfek
David Johnson
Nancy Krebs
Joan Lader
Gary Logan
Marya Lowry
Beth McGee
Carmel O'Shannessy
Pamela Prather
Marci Rosenberg
Karen Ryker
Mary Saunders-Barton
Christina Shewell
Philip Thompson
Phil Timberlake
Katharine Watts

The *Voice and Speech Review* accepts several types of submissions. While one of our primary missions is to publish peer-reviewed scholarship, we are also interested in presenting letters to the editor, opinion pieces, essays, interviews, reviews, poetry, and other forms of writing. Material may be submitted to:
Jeff Morrison
690 Fort Washington Ave. #5L
New York NY 10040
619-820-0953
jmorrison@mmm.edu

From the President

Patricia Raun's goal is to promote transformation by developing healthy and varied voices—both literal and figurative—in individuals, institutions, and communities. She carries out her goal in her position as founding director of the School of Performing Arts and Cinema, head of the Department of Theatre and Cinema at Virginia Tech, and as the current president of the Voice and Speech Trainers Association (VASTA). Raun has earned many honors for her leadership and teaching, including a 2010 Virginia Tech Excellence in Administration Award, and a 2011 College of Arts and Architecture Alumni Award from Penn State. Her recent accomplishments include merging Virginia Tech's cinema program with theatre arts; founding the School of Performing Arts and Cinema; and overseeing the renovations of the university's theatre buildings.

As we engage in the field of Voice and Speech we cannot help but engage in the difficult, yet intensely rewarding, pursuit of cross-cultural understanding and deep interpersonal exchange. I believe our highest aspiration as human beings is to transform our world by developing healthy and varied voices—both literal and figurative—in individuals, institutions, and communities. We do our work on stages, via media, in classrooms, in boardrooms, at conferences, and in personal encounters of all kinds. We know that with strong and supported voices individuals experience new and fuller ways of perceiving themselves. That change in perception leads to new ways of thinking, doing, and being in the world.

In these globally turbulent times when so many are desperate to have their voices heard, I have the sense that the connecting work we do has never been more important. We believe in the value of the human voice and in human communication. We resist the atrophy of verbal, physical, and imaginative powers. We are committed to the exploration of difference and of multiple perspectives among individuals and cultures. As artists and voice professionals we learn to synthesize ideas, empathize, take responsibility, evaluate options, imagine multiple outcomes, and we learn to put the well-being of the whole above our individual desires. We challenge society to hear things more clearly and we challenge individuals to explore who they might become. We listen. These are things that may see us through.

I remember the first VASTA conference at Pace University in 1987. There were only 14 or 15 of us in attendance. We focused on Alexander work — which was absolutely new to me at the time. I was deeply moved by the intelligent, committed, and caring women and men I met in this nascent organization. They put their hearts and minds into this work and their inspiration has sustained my own passion in the field. That week changed my life. Now, nearly 25 years later, I move toward the future and honor the past by remembering pioneers in our field, like Dorothy Runk Mennen and Arthur Lessac, who have bequeathed us so much. It is an extraordinary honor to serve as VASTA's president and to be allowed to provide these thoughts for our 7th biennial issue of the Voice and Speech Review. Look how far we have come!

On behalf of the organization I express profound gratitude to all of the contributors, the editors, and everyone responsible for giving birth to this important journal. Our special thanks go to our dear Editor-in-Chief, Dudley Knight, for his uncountable hours of work and his enormous intelligence and heart for this project.

I hope that you will relish and be challenged by the ideas and practices explored in the pages of *A World of Voice: Voice an Speech across Culture*. May you be inspired to increase your engagement, understanding, and growth in the world of voice. I believe your work is more important to the world than it has ever been.

Remembrance and Celebration

Mary Corrigan
Jo Estill
Arthur Lessac
Dorothy Runk Mennen

Every year, the voice and speech training world welcomes new trainers as more people in the English-speaking world and throughout the world in all its languages recognize the importance of the spoken word and the flow of song; even as speaking and singing, the most direct communications between one human being and another, seem to be threatened with obsolescence from the muffling march of electronic technology. Again and again, we experience that there is something astoundingly resilient in the human impulse to speak and to sing directly from one person to another; and however communications change, the human voice as its center will never be stilled. Indeed, there is reason to hope with confidence that vocal arts will continue to grow and prosper.

But the passage of time in our field takes as it gives. This issue of the Voice & Speech Review remembers and celebrates the lives of four colleagues whose contributions to voice and speech cannot be measured; immeasurable because the legacy of these teachers will continue long past the span of their mortal years. All of these people, in their own way, were pioneers.

Dorothy Mennen was the foundation, and one of the founders, of the Voice & Speech Trainers Association. Throughout a long and distinguished career at Purdue University, she shaped the development of voice and speech training in the theatrical context, starting at a time when this field hardly existed. To all who knew her, Dorothy was an inspiration, a guide and a stalwart friend.

When I first met Mary Corrigan in 1965, I was immediately smitten. This was, after all, back in the days when people could still legitimately become smitten. The beauty of spirit and person that she showed then is mirrored in the memories of those who knew her throughout her life, as the words about her that follow reveal so clearly. Her importance as a teacher and coach is inextricable from the extraordinary combination of qualities in her own personality.

I never knew Jo Estill, nor was she ever a member of VASTA, but it was impossible for any voice teacher in the last twenty years not to be influenced by her professional presence. The work that she developed has had—and will continue to have—a most profound effect on voice use, especially in singing; and her approach to voice science will remain an influential and astringent counterpoint to the dominance of imagistic teaching in voice practice.

Arthur Lessac was the first of us. Whether we follow his methodology or not, none of us would be in this field as professionals without Arthur. The many teachers that he trained over the years will continue his vision and his methods, but even beyond this rich legacy, he set a standard for all of us through his conceptual innovation, his extraordinary enthusiasm for voice and body work, and perhaps most of all, an abundance of spiritual generosity toward everyone with whom he came in contact. He was a hard-headed optimist and we all drew strength and inspiration from the sheer verve of his presence.

Some months before his passing, Arthur Lessac gave us permission to reprint his keynote address to the 2009 VASTA Conference in New York. We are deeply honored to present it in these pages as the ultimate tribute to the spirit that we remember in each of these four pioneers, an abundant commitment to the future. This is why we miss them and why we will continue to celebrate them.

Dudley Knight

Dorothy Runk Mennen

Tribute to Dorothy Runk Mennen
by Richard Stockton Rand and Richard Sullivan Lee

Dorothy Runk Mennen received her Bachelor of Science degree in Speech from Kent State University in 1938 and her Master's degree also in Speech from Purdue University in 1964. She was a pioneer in the teaching of voice and speech, served as vocal coach on over seventy Purdue Theatre productions, and was a founding member of the Voice and Speech Trainers Association (VASTA), serving as its first president in 1987. Dorothy had many accomplishments that spoke to her passion in education and equality. She helped form the Purdue Women's Caucus to study and implement gender equity and recognition of women. She was also the first woman to serve as the president of the American Association of University Professors and she was the first woman to chair the Purdue University Senate. Dorothy served on the boards of numerous regional and national arts organizations and was a role model for countless students, faculty and alumni. She received a College of Liberal Arts Distinguished Alumni award and a Sagamore of the Wabash award from the Governor.

Dorothy Runk Mennen

Dorothy served Purdue University for more than sixty years. She believed that you could do anything you set your mind to and she instilled that belief in her students. They carried that belief into their lives and work, and her former students established the Dorothy Runk Mennen Scholarship in her honor in 2006. Recognizing her impact beyond academics, this scholarship celebrates her unwavering enthusiasm and steadfast encouragement of students to pursue their dreams.

On a personal note: I first met Dorothy as a new professor in voice in the Professional Actor Training Program at Purdue University in 1991. In my first semester here I quickly realized my professional experience was limited when it actually came to developing a program in voice for the actor. I sought out an old friend, Marya Lowry for advice, and she wisely introduced me to Dorothy. From the day I met Dorothy I felt so blessed, and for the next twenty years I was rewarded with having her as my personal mentor and dear friend. She offered me her wisdom and guidance and I have been indebted to her ever since. Through Dorothy's assistance and vast knowledge in the field of vocal training, my education began. One of her first goals in my education was to introduce me to the VASTA, which has been an invaluable recourse in my growth over the past twenty years. Over the years she continually made an effort to know all of my students. When I needed assistance in diagnosing a particular student's vocal problem and trying to find a solution, Dorothy either knew what I could do or contacted the right person who could. Today I am the teacher that I am because of Dorothy. She has guided my training, taught me the true meaning of dedication and how important giving more of your self can mean to the success of a student. Before she left West Lafayette, not a month would go by that she did not check in to see how the new students were progressing or how the department was coming along with its new production, and always with a voice that said "I care." Meeting Dorothy was one of my great life changing experiences. Her mentorship guided me in my growth as a teacher in ways that are immeasurable. I do not start a semester's voice class without acknowledging her influence. She will remain in my thoughts and in my heart always.

Richard Stockton Rand has acted on and off Broadway; in regional theatres in the USA, Europe and Canada; and in film for public television. He has written and performed numerous one-person shows and is the recipient of an Indiana Arts Commission–National Endowment for the Arts Artist Fellowship for solo performance. His work has appeared in MONOLOGUES FOR MEN, BASEBALL MONOLOGUES (Heinemann Press), and numerous journals. He has been a guest artist at a hundred universities, and directed, choreographed or acted in more than a hundred productions at Purdue University, where he has also served as undergraduate coordinator and chair.

Richard Sullivan Lee has been a faculty member at Purdue University since 1991. His 40-year professional stage career has spanned both coasts. In addition to performing and directing, he has been on the faculty of Virginia Tech and Virginia Commonwealth University and has had guest artist contracts in a variety of college settings.

Tribute to Dorothy Runk Mennen
by Bonnie Raphael

Dorothy Runk Mennen was truly a queen among women, a fabulous role model for all members of VASTA, and a dear friend whom I sincerely miss. Second only to her family which was her primary reason for being on the planet, voice and speech were the center of her life and the focus of her energies during the course of a long and very productive career.

After leading and supporting the Voice and Speech program of the American Theatre Association, Dorothy was one of the founders and the first president of the Voice and Speech Trainers Association in 1986. During the course of the past 25 years, she grew this organization from a dozen or so members to a formidable presence in the world of voice and speech. She was there every step of the way—from the creation of a constitution to the formulation of professional standards and guidelines for tenure and promotion in our field; from a simple VASTA Newsletter to a highly regarded journal, the Voice and Speech Review; from VASTA-sponsored sessions at ATHE conventions to annual VASTA conventions, filled with presentations and networking and innovation and improving the practice of voice and speech training in the USA and around the world.

And Dorothy achieved all this with an iron fist enclosed in a velvet glove. Her leadership over a period of far more than 25 years was gentle but determined, formidable but without pretension, joyful rather than dictatorial, collaborative rather than hierarchal. Her sincere enthusiasm and belief that the whole is indeed greater than the sum of the

parts was absolutely contagious. Rather than attracting attention to herself or seeking recognition let alone fame, Dorothy's gifts lay in creating opportunities and circumstances for all of us to do our best, to surpass ourselves in what we believed we could accomplish, to achieve considerably more than we ever dreamed we could. She gave her peers the encouragement and support they needed to take their respective next steps; she provided newcomers to VASTA with opportunities to further their education and training and to add their particular talents and abilities to the organization she had originated. She rarely said no or turned down opportunities to interact and interface with other professional organizations like NATS or the Voice Foundation or ASHA and fostered the exchange of knowledge whenever she could.

Her twinkling eyes and hearty laugh and ability to take our work totally seriously without taking herself too seriously provided such joy and opportunity for those of us who were lucky enough to know her and build this organization with her. Her wisdom and determination provided such a solid foundation for those VASTA members who have become active since her most active years. She was a woman whose life and example have truly made a difference in the vigor and vitality of this unique organization. Hail and farewell to my mentor, my role model, my friend. With great love and deep respect, Bonnie Raphael

Bonnie Raphael has recently retired, after teaching and coaching professional voice users for over thirty years--at the University of North Carolina, the ART Institute at Harvard, the National Theatre Conservatory, Northwestern University, the University of Virginia, etc., acting as a voice consultant to well-known professional clients; and coaching hundreds of productions at major regional theatres.

Dorothy Runk Mennen: visionary, leader, founding mother
by Rocco Dal Vera

Vision, leadership — easy qualities to cite but harder to define. Often we can only understand them in retrospect. We can see looking back that a certain individual noticed a possibility others had missed. Hindsight makes it all look so obvious. We forget that the initiator of an idea had to think in thoroughly original ways, to struggle to enroll others, and to overcome their own and other's resistance, doubts and confusions.

The loss of someone dear to us invites retrospection. We may not experience as keen an appreciation of their impact until their absence invites us to wonder what our lives would have been like without them. As I write this on

Mother's Day, 2011, I'm thinking back on the life and influence of Dorothy Mennen, one of the founding "VASTA Mothers." I'm finding that, as I have done with my own mother, I only casually appreciated the extraordinary gifts I received from this great woman. VASTA didn't always exist. It had to be envisioned first. The time before voice and speech training was a recognized profession is well within the memory of many of us. There were no schools where you could major in the discipline. There was no agreement on what the job of a voice and speech professional was. There was no shared sense of how one was supposed to interact with colleagues, directors, actors, students, faculty, administrators, producers or critics. There was a poor body of research on methods, no commonly held set of ethics, standards, or the scope of one's practice, and no clear way to evaluate the quality and impact of the work. The great leap forward came from a small group of individuals who first recognized that voice and speech training was an independent profession. Dorothy was central to this.

Understanding that it is the responsibility of a profession to define itself and to elevate the common standards of the craft, Dorothy, along with a core of visionary women (Mary Corrigan, Carol Pendergrast, Bonnie Raphael, Lucille Rubin, and an expanding group of others) formed the first international association in the field, and in doing so established the field itself. At this point, everything was new and had to be discovered, debated, fought over, experimented with and concretized.

It's hard to hold up the torch of a vision while grabbing a shovel to dig the foundations. Dorothy did both. I sat in Board meetings for years observing her deep dedication to fairness, openness and professional standards, often in the face of a fractious membership holding divergent views and prone to grudges, gossip and intrigues. She was our mother throughout, and loved us equally.

And we grew up. And the landmark achievements were made: constitution, incorporation, conferences, newsletter, directory, tenure standards, website, listserv, peer-reviewed journal, endowment, scholarships, grants — all these happened under her determined encouragement, and all are a product of her original vision and her enduring leadership. The death of a parent is a critical passage in one's life. Dorothy brought us up right though and we'll be fine, thanks to her.

Rocco Dal Vera, *founding editor Voice and Speech Review, professor University of Cincinnati's College-Conservatory of Music, co-author with Robert Barton <u>Voice: Onstage and Off</u> (2nd ed.), with Joe Deer <u>Acting in Musical Theatre: a comprehensive course</u>, MFA Theatre Voice and Speech Coaching from the National Theatre Conservatory, certified Alba Emoting trainer with an interest in the voice and emotional extremes, resident vocal coach, Associate Artist, Cincinnati Shakespeare Festival, Cincinnati Playhouse in the Park, Ensemble Theatre of Cincinnati, Actor's Theatre of Louisville, faculty Xavier Leadership Center, and clay street project.*

Mary Corrigan

Visionary, Crusader, Ambassador, Mentor, and "Best Friend"
By Lucille Schutmaat-Rubin, Ph.D.

It was a warm August day in 1986 that the founding members of VASTA met in New York City to create an professional organization composed of voice & speech teachers, trainers, coaches and consultants. These members were: Mary Corrigan, Dorothy Mennen, Carol Pendergrast, Bonnie Raphael and myself. Dorothy became our President, Carol and Bonnie designed the Evaluation Guidelines and Code of Ethics. I authored the Training Guidelines and Mary Corrigan had her say in all of these endeavors plus addressing fairness in the workplace. Carolyn Combs served as secretary/treasurer and Evangeline Machlin, absent and retired, was our Advisor. Members came from different parts of the country, held diverse training methodologies and taught in unlike workplaces: university, conservatory, private practice and the media. Within one year VASTA was formed and we held our first conference in NYC 1987.

Mary Corrigan's contributions to VASTA were stellar. She was a fast talker and an active listener. She helped us find neutral ground on issues on which we differed. A born persuader and crusader, she eased us into agreement with her warm smile and hearty laugh. Her cup of ideas overflowed and her contributions to VASTA are many. Here are a few:

Helped Shape our Guidelines
Mary was a restless soul who continually searched for new ways to teach Voice and Speech. Having explored the work of Yoga, The Alexander Method, Rolfing, Feldenkrais, Progressive Relaxation, Bio-Energetics and Charlotte Selver's Sensory Awareness, she made sure that our Training & Evaluation Guidelines included body awareness training. Going one step further her training focused on the importance of mind/body connection as seen in her article, "Psycho-Physical Techniques and the Relevance to Voice and Actor

Mary Corrigan, Professor Emerita at the University of California, San Diego, was a member of the Theatre and Dance Department faculty for thirty years. An internationally known voice teacher, Mary Corrigan conducted numerous Master Voice classes and Workshops in Canada, Egypt, England, France and around the United States. Notably, also, she taught at Balliol College Oxford, England (BADA) for 19 summers. In her extensive acting career, she received the Best Actress Award at San Diego's Tony Award-winning Old Globe Theatre in 1979. One of the founders of VASTA, Corrigan coached and consulted on numerous professional theatre productions. She published in VASTA journals and authored chapters in each of the following books and tapes: *The Vocal Vision* (Applause Books), *The Complete Voice and Speech Workout* (Applause Books), *The Dancer's Handbook*. She also narrated Natl. Public Radio tapes on Chopin and George Sand.

Training" which appeared in *The Vocal Vision*, a collection of essays by VASTA members). Her M.A. degree in Theatre and Psychology reflects her interest in T'ai Chi, Chi Kung, Suzuki, Silva Mind Control and Transcendental Meditation. As Chair of the Theatre and Dance department at CU San Diego she was undoubtedly influenced by the work of their dance department.

Encouraged Study of Diverse Methodologies in USA & Abroad
Having studied with our American master teachers in the US, Mary looked abroad for new approaches to voice and speech training. In 1989 she was invited to teach for BADA (British Academy of Dramatic Art) at Oxford and moved to London for a period of 2 years only to return later for many summers. As co-director of UC San Diego Study Center for the UK & Ireland, she worked with actors, taught Shakespeare and classical text, attended performances with theater critics, and audited and took classes taught by actors and directors from the Royal National and Royal Shakespeare Companies. During her stay she taught in Scotland and at the American University in Cairo. These experiences moved her to encourage more of our VASTA members to go abroad and study new methodologies. In the VASTA newsletter of 1991 she wrote "Study Opportunities for Training in the UK" and gave details of every drama school and training center and how to contact them. Shortly thereafter, VASTA held its first Conference in London. Even though VASTA had its own liaison committee, it was Mary who became an ambassador for VASTA in that she encouraged our members to study abroad while also spreading the work of VASTA abroad.

Fought for Fairness in the Workplace: Promotion, Pay and Tenure
Mary's passion, fervor for fairness and her soft negotiation skills helped bring attention to workplace fairness. She served on both VASTA and CU San Diego Grievance/Appeals committees. In her report to our board in 1988 she

brought up several issues: "Do we have recognition in Theatre/Drama departments … directors, actors? What about protecting [our] copyrights? Do we have recourse and with whom?" These and related issues were later addressed in many on-going VASTA conferences thanks to Mary's initiatives. Many Voice & Speech trainers are using VASTA's website (vasta.org) for current information on Promotion and Tenure. This information is especially useful to those teaching in Higher Education Institutions.

Starred as Personal Mentor

I doubt that Mary knew how to teach without in someway making a deep connection with every student, teacher or client with whom she worked. VASTA has its own mentoring program but that never stopped Mary from making deep one on one connections with everyone. She made each of us feel as if we were her "Best Friend." Perhaps it truly was a magic breath connection she felt with others. In her "Breath Journal Exercise" in *The Complete Voice and Speech Workout* (containing 74 exercises submitted by VASTA members), she writes:

"If you think you are holding your breath, do two things. "First, be thrilled that you are becoming aware of your major saboteur of good voice production and a major deterrent to your spontaneous and immediate release of an acting text. (Lack of spontaneity can also get in the way of day-to-day interpersonal relationships!)." So like Mary to show how breath release can connect us all! And that she did.

Mary Corrigan marched to her own drum & heartbeat. Everything Mary did, she did with her heart: she acted with her heart, she taught with her heart and she gave to others with her heart. Now that heart is still but her beat goes on.

Fear no more the heat o' the sun,
Nor the furious winter's rages;
Thou thy worldly task hast done,
Home art gone, and ta'en thy wages…

Thank you, Mary, for you heart, gifts, contributions to VASTA and being "My Best Friend."

Lucille Schutmaat-Rubin, Ph.D. A founding, Honorary and Distinguished VASTA member, past president of the University & College Theater Association and world-wide workshop presenter, Lucille Schutmaat-Rubin, Ph.D. is a voice, speech, presentation & media coach serving the needs of executive speakers, Broadway actors, TV and radio reporters and hosts. She is President of Professionally Speaking in NYC and on the faculty of Circle in the Square Theatre School.

Our Mary, Ever Curious, Ever Generous.
By Ursula Meyer

I first met Mary when I was acting at the Colorado Shakespeare Festival in 1979. Bonnie Raphael was my voice coach - my first voice coach and the person who first made me curious about this wonderful profession - and Mary had come to visit during rehearsals. Mary was ebullient and passionate and gave me some very tough notes that I still cherish. I think that was what made Mary so marvelous. She was as bright as a star all day every day and relentlessly positive, but she never held back when things needed to be said. When I was called to come to UCSD , I knew I would have to produce some big sound in order to fill the void left when Mary retired. She welcomed me to UCSD with joy and laughter and we started a friendship. She included me in VASTA ideas, she supported me in new projects, she warned me about burn-out, she brought me into her circle with the wonderful Eva Barnes and Jan Gist and we became a little lunch party several times a year. And each time we met, Mary led us like a majorette to poetry, hearty full-throated hilarity, strong opinions, and a little dessert. She was passionately interested in every tiny facet of our lives, even though her life was incredibly full of family, community, her own teaching, and her plans for the future. That was another source of inspiration for all of us - she never wasted a minute - she demanded that we look forward - that we celebrate our work and each other - that we continue to make plans for the future. But that kind of child-like living in the present did not reduce her depth and wisdom. In Eva Barnes' lovely dedication to Mary at the memorial,

Eva outlined one of Mary's favorite exercises. Eva had done the exercise while working with Mary in graduate school. In my voice class this Fall , I decided to use it with my students. It is a very simple exercise, no bells and whistles , no props, no long-winded explanations in order to begin. It is a variation on Kristen Linklater's exercise using the phrase: "I am me". The students just have to stand in front of the group, breathe, and speak the words. I'm sure the voice teachers reading this will not underestimate the size of that thought. But of course, the students were very surprised at what it meant to simply let some air in and speak that truth. And I realized at that moment, it is still so difficult for me to reconcile the who in who am I. But Mary Corrigan was different. She was always ' Mary 'and never afraid to say it - proud and loud and fierce and smart and generous and firm and a fresh young girl and a wiser than wise woman and a friend and a hero and a shining light.

Ursula Meyer has been teaching Voice and Text and coaching for the theatre since 1981. She came in 1995 from the Yale School of Drama to UC San Diego to fill the graceful dancing shoes of dear Mary Corrigan. She trained at the Central School of Speech and Drama with David Carey and is a designated Linklater teacher.

Remembering Mary Corrigan
By Jan Gist

It's hard to conceive of the world that no longer includes Mary Corrigan. I get it, for a few minutes at a time—that she's gone. But then as I go about my day, my unconscious assumption returns that of course Mary is still in the world, flitting between her travels, attending San Diego theatre and concerts, and arranging her many activities with her many friends in so many different circles: her poetry and writing groups, women's walking group, her loved family, reading for the blind at KPBS, teaching her private students, rendezvousing with voice teacher friends from around the world. From when I first met Mary in the 1970s to our last lunch date a week before her stroke, Mary was a never ending fountain of enthusiasm and gusto.

Impressions:

~Her varying shades of red hair as bright as her personality

~Her laugh, from light giggles, to deep naughty chuckles, to loud, head-back guffaws.

~Her never ending compliments and advice for everyone from close friends, to VASTA agendas, to the waitress pouring coffee.

~Her effervescent joy and relish of life, people, food, drink, adventures, travel, theatre, training, art… she just kept on exploring and playing.

~Her naughtiness: a love and gift for gossip and the sensual sides of life, spoken in hushed confidence, and cushioned with empathy for human frailty, political savvy, and raw instinct.

~Her cars: elegant, comfortable, with the latest technology, and her delight in the convenience of her handicap-parking permit.

~Her insightful knowledge of voice, theatre, and training: She specialized in helping it all get more lively, fun, and free.

~Her generosity: she would focus her multiple energetic interests on one person or project and just keep pouring her time lavishly in that direction.

~Her insistence that work be balanced in life: she headed VASTA conference panels and discussions on facing our tendencies toward workaholism, and teach each other strategies for improving our life/work balance.

~Her homes: so gracefully decorated in whites and blues and sunlight, and also stuffed with books, recordings, and ever shifting piles of things to give away.

We voice/speech people live in an interaction with vibration. We influence all the voices we can, to reverberate and activate. Mary's presence did and still does vibrate, reverberate, and influence. So, of course it seems like she's still here. I wish she were really actually still with us. But then I'm greedy for her kind of aliveness.

Jan Gist, Professor/Coach Old Globe Theatre & USD Graduate Program since 2001. Prior to that, Voice/ Speech coach at Alabama Shakespeare Festival for 140 productions. Other credits include Oregon and Utah Shakespeare Festivals, The Shakespeare Theatre, Arena Stage, American Shakespeare Center, American Players Theatre. International workshops include The Moscow Art Theatre, and London's Central School.

Jo Estill

Josephine Antoinette Estill 1921-2010
By Anne-Marie Speed

In 1992, the Voice Research Society, the previous incarnation of the BVA, first brought Jo Estill to the UK to present her unique approach to voice training, based on an extraordinarily lucid and practical physiological explanation of vocal function. Those of us present at that first five day course were witness to nothing less than a revolution.

Josephine Antoinette Vadala was born in Donora, Pennsylvania on April 25th 1921. Her parents' families were from Italy and she was very proud of her Italian roots. Music was in the family and she always sang, even as a small child, accompanying her father who played guitar while she sang Italian folk songs. There is not space here for me to list her many achievements as a classical singer but after many years singing (including a tour of Europe in the 1954) and studying singing she decided to return to college to begin academic study of the voice before teaching. Despite reading all the literature available on voice and the teaching of voice, she remained unconvinced by the lack of physiological based instruction presented. I remember visiting her several times in Santa Rosa in the late 1990s and flicking through the books she had by other renowned teachers, and being amused as well as impressed by the pithy comments and criticisms in the margins. She was a woman of sharp and discriminating intelligence, questioning everything that wasn't backed up by sound science or practice based on physiological knowledge. There was not much that escaped her penetrating and disciplined gaze and she was fearless in her challenging of those who used the worst kind of fanciful imagery and avoided any awkward references to how the voice actually worked. She was the most well read teacher of other teachers' works that I have ever come across. I think that one of the most valuable gifts she gave me was how to think methodically and with much greater clarity and discipline.

Her great contribution to the study and understanding of voice, The Estill Model, is a peerless explanation of vocal function, connecting as it does physiology to a narrow range of predictable acoustic results, accessed through simple exercises that anyone can learn and practice. It gives not only understanding but control and with that the ability to produce the voice, either singing or speaking, 'on demand'. I am not the only one to mourn not just the loss of a true mentor and great teacher, but also a much loved friend. She had a wonderful sense of humour and one of my abiding memories will be how much we laughed together. However, I am sure that all of us also share a tremendous sense of privilege that we in turn have such an extraordinary legacy to give to our students and a very great debt of gratitude.

Anne-Marie Speed is a Voice Teacher, Vocal Trainer, Accent and Dialect Tutor, Performance Coach, and Professional Theatre Director, Royal Academy of Music, London.

Born on April 25, 1921, in Donora, Pennsylvania. Attended Oberlin Conservatory and then moved to Pasadena, California. From 1940–1947, she sang for the CBS Radio Network in Hollywood. Moved to Colorado Springs for further voice studies and subsequently married local businessman and arts enthusiast, Thomas Estill. Soon thereafter, she launched a European solo concert tour, cut short by her husband's heart attack in 1954. Received a BA in Liberal Arts from Colorado College in 1969 followed by an MA in Music Education from Case Western Reserve University. At the Upstate Medical Center, Syracuse, New York, she worked as a research associate under Dr. Ray Colton, and Dr. David Brewer, two of the top voice researchers in the United States and began her pioneering research on six voice qualities: speech, falsetto, sob, twang, opera, and belt. Subsequently published over 40 professional articles reporting on her scientific studies of the voice. Founded 'Estill Voice Training Systems LLC' in 1992. Retired at the age of 82. Awarded an Honorary Doctorate from the University of East Anglia and named Honorary Associate of the Royal Academy of Music in London.

A Transformative Pioneer
By Steven R. Chicurel

In 1985, I was out on the road performing when Kerrie Obert's and my former teacher-now-colleague, Julie Fortney, called me and said, "There's this person you need to meet. Her work will revolutionize yours." "Yeah, yeah, I'll try to find the time," said I…pretty much half-heartedly. It's not that I ever doubted Julie's assessment…but I was at the time an on-the-road performer/musical director with a career that was going well enough. I was completing my doctorate in music, and I felt I knew quite a lot to boot! Over the next couple of years, on chance meetings with Julie, she would remind me of this woman who was standing the world of voice on its ear and that, if I were smart, I'd find a way to learn from her. Scene change to summer, 1988. I was MD/pianist for a summer stock production of the musical "Cole." In what hardly EVER happens in the world of theatre, my show was actually ready to open about a week ahead of opening night! Because of that, daytime rehearsals were cancelled, and we would do only a run through in the evening. Fate intervened here….it happens that Jo was giving a 5-day workshop in the same town… Julie was there, and I was invited to come to the lectures/practice sessions gratis.

I can't tell you what went through my mind that week… in fact, I may have lost my mind in the best way possible that week. For, you see, I can honestly tell you, hand over heart, as good as I had assumed I was, I do NOT remember ANYTHING I used to do in voice lessons I gave or coaching sessions I'd hold BEFORE I met Jo. Revolutionize my work? She transformed me.

Now, some 23 years and two careers later, Jo Estill's teaching, counsel, and spirit inform the work I do every day in my position as a Professor of Theatre/Musical Theatre Voice Specialist at the University of Central Florida.

The past 23 years with Jo have had their share of serendipity – living 1 block from her in NYC in the early 90s, common interest – working NY Times crossword with Jo every day, and constant learning – engaging in creative arguments about artistry, culture, and, above all, voice.

Jo had always had a notion to write an opera. The setting is at the Pearly Gates of Heaven. In Jo's drama, St. Peter grants entrance to Heaven only to those who can sing in the voice quality he requests. Picture it…an opera with arias not only in 4 basic qualities (speech, falsetto, sob, twang), and opera and belting, but with all of those thousands of variations….it's an opera with no end, you see… If life (or death) imitates art, then Jo Estill may, in fact, be the only person in Heaven at the moment. Remember, she always was a renegade and a first.

Steven R. Chicurel, DMA, is Professor of Theatre/Musical Theatre Voice Specialist at The University of Central Florida. He is the co-author of Geography of the Voice: Anatomy of an Adam's Apple *and* Music Theory for Musical Theatre.

❖

Jo Estill: Our paths were meant to cross!
By Robert Sussuma

The course of my life as a performer and voice educator was forever altered when I encountered the revolutionary work of vocal visionary, Jo Estill. Although Jo herself had retired by the time I took my first course in 2004, I had the privilege of meeting and speaking with her several times and was always struck by her sharp intelligence, fearless vision, and sincere belief that ANYONE--given the right tools--could learn to sing and speak with refinement!

I thought I knew all about singing with refinement. I had just completed my Masters in Early Music Vocal Performance at The Longy School of Music (2003). As I started to build my private teaching studio I found myself challenged by singers interested in Pop, Rock and Musical Theater singing. I discovered that those sounds had been "trained out of me". Since I could not access them, I struggled to find skillful ways of working with them in my students' voices. This was somewhat disheartening. I started to feel that all my rarified classical training was useless in the real world and that what I needed was a new approach. I told a friend exactly what I wanted: "a voice training that is physiologically based and can teach one how to use one's voice to make different sounds in a concrete, functional way regardless of style or aesthetics."

Through a series of seemingly fated events, this friend encountered Estill Voice Training within the week at a Boston NATS panel presentation that included Mary McDonald Klimek, one of Jo's students. My friend called me immediately afterward, exclaiming with excitement, "Robert! Robert! There was this woman there (Mary) who made all these funny sounds. She could move her larynx up and down at will, move her vocal folds in different ways to change the sound from breathy to full-voiced and could even make these little flaps in her throat move--the false vocal folds! Here's her number. Call her now!" I called Mary the next day and the rest, as they say, is history.

I attended my first Estill Voice Training course as soon as possible. I found myself in voice nerd heaven! I learned more in five days than I had in ten years of conventional lessons and training. I caught the Estill "bug", and never looked back! Since then, I have risen through the Estill ranks and become a Certified Course Instructor. Using Jo's innovative approach, my voice training career has expanded to include actors, singers, and professional speakers in the U.S. and abroad. Students are continually impressed and intrigued by the capacity of Jo's system to break down the complexity of vocal craft into practical Figures (isolation exercises) that allow each vocalist (regardless of previous training and habit, or lack thereof) to understand and physically master the totality of her/his vocal potential healthily, easily and joyfully!

Thank you Jo! Your thinking was ahead of its time! May your ideas and discoveries continue to improve vocal understanding, education and performance throughout the world!

Robert Sussuma, MMus., is a Certified Course Instructor of Estill Voice and a Feldenkrais Practitioner. His teaching integrates a practical understanding of the voice and a passion for organic learning that brings the whole self back to the study of voice. Robert lives and teaches in NYC. ❖

Arthur Lessac

Ol' Man River and Me
By Nancy Krebs, Lessac Master Teacher

Arthur Lessac filled many roles in my life: teacher, mentor, inspiration, colleague, guide—and fortunately, also a dear friend and father-figure. I first became acquainted with, and fell in love with his work in 1972, when I was in graduate school at the Dallas Theater Center. I never thought I would actually meet him personally. But when I began teaching voice at the Baltimore School for the Arts in the theatre department, the Director of the school—David Simon, saw me carrying the Lessac voice text out of the school one afternoon in early 1991, and struck up a conversation in which I discovered that he had been Arthur's illustrator for the first printing of his book. One thing led to another, and soon David arranged for Arthur to come and conduct master classes with my students. When the time came, Arthur actually stayed with my husband and me for a night or two when we discovered that there were no available hotel rooms near the school for the first couple of nights of his stay. So I picked him up at the airport, and as soon as I saw him, I knew I was going to like him. He was about my size in height, with curly strawberry blond hair and sparkling blue eyes. We came back to my house and talked for half the night about the work, life, and every imaginable subject. His intelligence, (genius actually),

Arthur Lessac is among the most highly regarded teachers of voice, speech, singing and movement in the training world. His two books, *The Use and Training of the Human Voice: A Bio Dynamic Approach to Vocal Life and Body Wisdom: The Use and Training of the Human Body*, have become required reading for countless students and remain a lasting contribution to the field of acting and performing. Professor Emeritus at SUNY, he taught and lectured world-wide in both academic and professional programs. He was honored with numerous awards from professional organizations, published articles in many professional journals, worked with many well-known stage and film actors; and trained hundreds of teachers—celebrated in their own right—who carry on his distinguished legacy.

good humor, unflagging energy and effervescent personality kept me mesmerized for hours. Even back then he referred to himself as *Ol' Man River* because he never ran out of steam! He just kept rollin' along. Watching him teach over the next few days solidified my opinion of his genius and of his energized stamina; and I knew that I had to study more in-depth with him to advance my knowledge of this wonderful training that he so artfully presented to my students. That short visit began a relationship with him that only became more important to me over the next 20 years. I became certified in 1993, and was then invited to join the Summer Intensive Workshop faculty by Arthur in 1995. I learned how to teach this work watching him over the years, observing first-hand how he shared the fruits of his *labor of love* with participants, problem-solved, diagnosed vocal and physical issues, coached ever so gently to enable each person to fully realize his or her gifts. It was always a life-changing experience for those who attended the workshops—for Arthur taught people to teach themselves—to rely upon cues from their own inner environment for guidance. And he did that for me as well. I am a better teacher, a better human being for having had the honor of knowing him all these years.

I don't think I'll ever be able to refer to him in the past tense— for he will always be present with me in spirit. His spirit and love energy will always be with me. I'll hear his words coming out of my mouth and smile, knowing that *Ol' Man River* is still rolling alongside me.

Nancy Krebs is a certified Master Lessac Teacher, and received her graduate training at the Dallas Theater Center. She has been a professional actor/singer since 1975. She continues to work as a vocal/dialect coach for numerous professional and university productions in the Baltimore-Washington region and teaches in the Theatre Department of the Baltimore School for the Arts.

From Aross the Desk: Remembering Arthur
By Crystal Robbins

I remember meeting Arthur for dinner & a play in Los Angeles with my first voice teacher, Anita Jo Lenhart. I looked into Arthur's eyes, the exact color and life in them as my recently- deceased father. We three chatted on the long, crowded 10 freeway across town. No wonder it is so hard to see people regularly in this town. We picnicked at the theatre: salad, panini, pizza, sparkling water, chicken, cake; and never stopped talking & laughing. Arthur talked about his dream of playing King Lear. I talked about playing Cordelia. Jyo declared I'd be good for him to have around. Or maybe that he'd be good for me to have around. We sang as the sun began to sink and the night grew colder, even on a LA summer.

By the time I dropped them back off in Santa Monica, Arthur asked me to consider working for him in his office. I told him I didn't think I was the right person. I said it a few times. I was on my way to a travel-writing workshop north of San Francisco; capitalizing on my 3 years of backpacking around the world. I remember sitting on his couch trying to convince him I didn't know enough to teach him. He said that what we didn't know, we would learn together. Throwing in his lessons, how could I resist?

Every day I learned. I felt vibration on my hard palate in a palpable way that never again left me and began to guide me. I began to taste music. I began to move away from understanding the work as metaphor and move towards understanding it as music. I discovered the freedom and release of smelling the flower and in feeling the breath move around the back and up the spine. I liked the physical work and had fun and felt good. I liked feeling like a dancer again. I liked feeling like a singer again. Even when walking and talking.

When I found out I was pregnant, my workouts with Arthur took on the added dimension of exploring sound and movement with my pregnant self. Here was a place of wandering with real newness and experimental learning for us both. I remember explaining something I'd noted about the work in my own way, Arthur simply and quietly stated that I would be a good teacher. I fervently disagreed, said I had no leanings that way, no interest whatsoever. He just smiled.

Two years later & many hours of working with him privately, I was able to attend my first workshop, nursing daughter & husband in tow. What a wonderful immersion experience to exit the Intensive and immediately begin teaching, with Arthur as my mentor, visiting my classes, consulting and problem-solving as I grew. If you had told me that I would love teaching, that I would be on this path, I wouldn't have believed you.

I don't feel that I chose this work. It has consistently chosen me. And like the boy I ran into accidentally, crying on his shoulder, who now is my husband; and like the friend who was assigned to be my roommate in a London hostel and who became a sister of my heart; and like the old man from Corfu who ended up seeing through me on an Athens bench; and like the wild white horse that greeted me on hillside north of Dublin, some things just happen because they are supposed to.

Crystal Robbins, a Certified Lessac Trainer and Lessac Board Member, worked as Arthur's secretary and assistant for the past 12 years. She helped him research & prepare for every major workshop/project/event. But her favorite task was reading aloud to him his favorite book, The Hobbit. She teaches at Santa Monica College and was the co-creator of the first Lessac One-Week workshop, which she still leads at Woodbury University, in Burbank. Crystal is a founding director of the Burbank Youth Summer Theatre Institute, a Shakespeare camp for children 9-16 years old and of a salon reading group in LA, Bard In The Yard. A frequent contributor to the Lessac newsletter & VASTA publications, she is currently working on two Lessac-related books. www.crystalrobbins.com

Parts of this are adapted & previously published in Crystal's article about how she came to the Lessac Work in "Collective Writings on the Lessac Voice and Body Work: A Festschrift". Available at: http://www.lessacinstitute.com/resources.html

A Brief Remembering of a Father
By Michael Lessac

When my father died the loss was more than personal. It felt as if I had finally lost my grasp on time. It made me fear for my own mortality. Why you may ask, how can you worry about that? --- Are you nuts? The man was 101+ and dancing in the streets of Croatia two weeks before he died!

Yes…but with him, it felt like he had died prematurely. It

felt like I now had to rush to finish things.

Dad had made time another dimension for himself. He never considered time as an investment nor as something that had to be protected against or feared. In his work he fought against negative energy and looked for ways of making being optimally human an effortless thing. Politically he did not believe in choosing the lesser of two evils. As a teacher he did not believe in recognizing impossibility. Everything I ever started he expected me to finish. I always had him as a wind against my back. Having him around was a little like having Peter Pan genes.

I miss the wind against my back.

Time will tell about the genes.

He refused to age. Because he seemed to be living forever and because he never himself would ever recognize age as getting in the way of anything, he therefore never got old.

There was a trick to that. He just loved what he did. He loved teaching…he loved searching…he loved being curious.

To be sure he kept himself in superb and flexible condition almost without effort. This he did through his work. He stretched rather than pushed. He buzzed rather than shouted. He found what was familiar to the natural use of the body rather than accepting and pursuing limitations or defining abilities by the barriers we faced or by what tradition dictated.

Yes, his life force was helped by that uncanny ability to energize himself through the voice. Yes…of course he floated on the buoyant conviction that if we can walk we can dance, if we can talk we can sing. But what connected all this was something even more profound…something that crosses borders in this world of ours that threatens to destroy us through our own devices…. the overwhelming belief that if we can hear… we can listen.

He listened. He shut no one off. He never developed that academic/historic/art vs. science certainty that often threatens to choke new ideas. He listened to everyone and learned from everyone and his birth-given ability to stay young and vital was about that. It was about a child-like curiosity that blossomed with age. It was his weapon against fear…his weapon against depression…his shield against aging.

….and his belief that as humans we can break any barrier that others have set for us.
….and his belief that as humans we should defy any force that oppresses us.

He probably believed in magic, although he would never admit it.

I remember, one summer I spent time with him at one of his workshops. A fox got trapped inside the house. It ran at the walls and amazingly, like the iconic Donald O'Connor dance with Gene Kelly, literally ran up the walls in its attempt to get out of the place. It almost made it to the ceiling before it ran back down the wall. We were amazed. But dad had that toad-of-toad-hall look in his eyes. He came to the belief that if the fox could do it…so could a human… so could he. So for the rest of the summer he practiced. He practiced running up the wall perfecting back flips as he went.

To this day…well…to the last days in Croatia when he was dancing in the streets outside the new drama department he was co creating just a few months ago…to that day… he still believed he could have reached the ceiling if he had had enough time. It's been said the man was foxy.

The last ten years I have been working in theatre and film, crossing borders and working with music and humor and creating stories with actors who once looked down the barrel of a gun at each other. Dad came with us in the early years and taught and learned from a new nation being created by Nelson Mandela, Desmond Tutu and others. I am convinced they accepted us Americans easily because he was the white Elder who would not age. He was the white American who danced and sang and hoped. He was the elder who stared at a group of dancing children and simply said, "aren't they wonderful". He saw wonder in everything and wanted more. He liked being called "old man" because he still could stand on his head and roll out from a fall. Yes, he liked to show off. He was also a flirt. He became emblematic of a word The South Africans taught us. UBUNTU!

Ubuntu means "I am because you are".

He believed, he taught, he diagnosed by practicing around that theme…always trying to see the world through his students' eyes. This kept him alive because he never got bored because he always knew he *was* because you *are*". His work is being taught now in other cultures because it is about music and song in speech, it is based on optimizing being human and seeks to enhance the mystery rather than teach the form of our individuality and culture.

All you need is one human being to do one miraculous thing once and it becomes easier forever after. This is true of nations. This is true of the Four Minute Mile.

That is what I try to remember as I find myself missing that wind against my back. And when I feel it … I feel it again.

And one last thought to all of you…teachers as well as students…those who appreciated his work and those who couldn't…close friends and extended family of thousands around the world.

He loved learning from all of you.

Michael Lessac

Essay *by Arthur Lessac*
Keynote Address, VASTA Conference, August 3, 2009.

Thank you, Beth, for that very generous introduction.

Hello, everyone!

Since in four short weeks I'll be gently tip-toeing into the two zeros of my 100th year, I can think of no better birthday gift than this privileged invitation to address my fellow VASTAns, and I thank you heartily. This is an honor as well as an opportunity I shall not easily forget.

And speaking of forgetting…

Did you hear the one about the old man in the park?

An old man is sitting on a park bench, crying bitterly. A young man walks over to him and says, "Is something wrong?" And the old man looks up and says "I have a beautiful sexy wife, 30 years old…she cooks like an angel…we have sex every night." Young man says, "So why are you crying?" And the old man says, "I can't remember where I live!"

"Remembering" is a little harder these days. At 100, my memory is just not what it used to be. I have discovered that growing older is not for the faint of heart. I wear two very expensive hearing aids now, and neither of them are worth a damn. And as far as my eyes are concerned, I'm blind in my right eye, and I have only 20% vision in my left eye. I mean, any one-eyed pirate can see better than I can!

But for all that, my heart is good, my voice is strong, and I can still hold my breath underwater for 90 seconds! That makes me feel like a young man inside. And that's why I'm sorry I have to read this to you. I would rather talk to you. But that's the way it is. So I ask you, please, to indulge me a little if I forget what I'm going to say next, or if I lose my place in my speech.

The full title of this conference is "ORIGINAL VOICES: Voice Methodologies from the Source". And before I begin, I want to share with you my realization that all of us here are involved in training the voice, but for the next few moments, I ask you to think of just the first two words of that title: "ORIGINAL VOICES" and not about a specific way of training. Let's consider an ORIGINAL VOICE in a much broader perspective, as something which is innate, in need of protection, something that should always be encouraged to grow and thrive. Such a voice could help create a better world, a better world which honors communing instead of just communicating.

Let me tell you a story. It's a legend.

And this legend has it that in the very beginning of mankind (and womankind) human communication was carried on entirely through the singing voice, with appropriate melodies, body rhythms and facial expressions. Whenever groups of people got together, the communication process would evolve into original choral exchanges. Their bodies would move into dance forms, and ensemble harmony was a natural occurrence. But, as the many years kept racing by… "time" became more and more frugal and more and more economical and therefore, time itself became shorter and shorter until what was left was just barely enough time for consonants and vowels… and thus speech was born, leaving precious little time for meaningful melodies, for harmony, for expressive sharing… and certainly no time at all for supportive communing.

And that's where the legend ends. (And believe me I had nothing to do with that legend, I'm not that old.) But if we were to continue the story, more and more consonants and vowels would no doubt be eaten up by time. In other words, our ORIGINAL VOICE would get fainter and fainter and possibly could get lost altogether.

Now what do we really mean by "ORIGINAL VOICES"? Not original thoughts, not original words, but ORIGINAL VOICES!

I decided to look up the word "original" and I immediately got out my thesauruses (yes, I do have more than one!). Did you know there are over 60 synonyms for the word "original"? I didn't know that. There's "fundamental", "new", "unused", "native", and "basic", not to mention "cutting edge", "new wave" and "new age"! I was

Remembrance and Celebration
Keynote Address, VASTA Conference, August 3, 2009. By Arthur Lessac

overwhelmed. Finally, I came to "creative". That's it! I thought. Creative—fresh…yes. So I chose "creative" as part of my definition.

Now how about voices? Voice also has many meanings. It can mean freedom of speech, taking a stand, our unique imprint on the world. So, I asked myself the question: What can a voice really do? Any voice?

Well, it can….
> hum a lullaby
> call you in to dinner

But it can also……
> ring out in protest
> sing out in pure joy
> warn you of danger
> cry out for freedom….

Voice is so much more than tone or timbre, vowels or consonants. It is so much more than the apparatus. A voice that is free, that feels its inherent right to speak, will have no fear of calling out, whenever and wherever it is needed.
But most importantly, a voice can be a beacon in the darkness, something that lights the way for others.

And therefore, for my meaning of "voice", I chose "visionary"—someone who lights the way for others.

So, an ORIGINAL VOICE is a creative visionary, a remarkable energy. And here, at this very conference, we VASTAns are honoring four creative visionaries, four remarkable energies, who have followed their ORIGINAL VOICES and who have been beacons for others. However, I believe that all of us—all of us here in this room are ORIGINAL VOICES, capable of being a beacon for others.

In fact, I believe that everyone, everywhere, is an ORIGINAL VOICE. I mean, consider the newborn baby, fresh out of the womb. Talk about original! Every single baby born in this world is an original. Like a Stradivarius violin, no two are alike. (You do know, of course, the history of the Stradivarius violins? Stradivarius used only the finest and best woods and handcrafted the violins so that each violin, while essentially the same in appearance, produces an original, unique sound.) I think every baby is a Stradivarius violin, capable of producing unique music—with their ORIGINAL VOICE.

As a matter of fact, a baby's first cry is a perfectly placed clarion "Call"—it has all the qualities I believe to be part of an ORIGINAL VOICE—it's exciting, pure, healthy, fresh, singing, and strong.
Why is it, then, that many of us, as we grow into adulthood, suffer an adulteration of our "ORIGINAL VOICES"? What happens to that baby Strad? How does that ORIGINAL VOICE get lost or weakened or corrupted?

I believe the answer lies in a better understanding of our environments. And I'm using the plural, environments, intentionally.

So, at this point, I ask you to seriously consider that we are all, all of us, living, functioning, creating and problem solving in two separate, highly significant environments.

On the one hand, there is the huge Outer Environment:
* With everything and everyone in it.
* With all its ecologies, histories and mysteries
* With all its different NRG uses and NRG powers
* With its conditioning and patterning
* With its left brained, quantitative force ful influences
* And with its thousands and thousands of professionally trained ecologists.

On the other hand, we have our very own, vastly infinite, personal Inner Environment:

* With its own ecology.
* With its own mysterious wilderness.
* With its own multitude of personal NRG qualities.
* With its own right-brained qualitative and harmonic sensing.
* And, oh yes, with only one inner trained ecologist.

Every baby is born with this Inner Environment. But eventually the negative forces of the Outer Environment are over-powering. Pretty soon, the awareness of the Inner Environment has diminished so much that we lose touch with it, we lose our ability to feel it. But it still exists, it still exists inside us, inside a far vaster inner millieu or inner domain than anything conceivable in the outside world. It is in this Inner Environment that our ORIGINAL VOICE survives—that our ORIGINAL VOICE lives, though often unheard and unrecognized, even by us.

Too often, we become a "cog in the wheel" of the Outer Environment. Its patterns and its conditioning become our patterns and our conditioning, so much so, that we don't identify those patterns or conditions for the *poisons* they really are.
Now, friends, I want to make myself clear. You may think I'm being extreme. After all, poisons? Well, let's see. What are some of these poisons?

Well, there are the obvious ones: over-indulgence in food or alcohol, drug addiction, daily stress.... Stress alone causes negative emotions to accumulate in the Inner Environment. Current research indicates significant connections between emotions and disease—anger contributes to heart disease, anxiety causes panic attacks or heart arrhythmia, depression contributes to headaches and back pain. Stress creates more than discomfort in the body—it creates ill-health. It slowly *poisons*.

And then there are the larger, societal poisons which afflict all of us. For example, the Outer Environment asks us to accept "the lesser of two evils", but my inner voice says a life surrounded by the lesser of two evils still means living under evil. We don't want to live under the lesser of the two goods, either. Because our inner voices know that that particular 'good' just may not be good enough.

It is indeed the Outer Environment that seems perfectly content with half truths, quarter truths, honest truths. On the other hand, the Inner Environment tells us there "ain't no such thing" as a "half-truth" or a "quarter-truth" or a "perfect truth." A "half-truth" or a "perfect truth" is a contradiction in terms. The Inner Environment tells us: truth is truth; good is good…and poison is poison.

In our own Outer Environment today, right now, there is the poison of racism, the poison of thievery. Hunger is poison. Homelessness is poison. Being unjustly thrown out of a job is a nasty poison. Paying teachers with IOUs is a sneaky poison if there ever was one and there is no end to this list.

As far as I am concerned, it is the Outer Environment that seems to favor a left-brained democracy with a large, capital "D." Our Inner Environment, with its heart, gut, soul and spirit NRGs seems to favor an organic democracy with a small "d".

You know, we can go for our entire lives without recognizing all the kinds of poisons that exist today in our outer world. Take the economy, for example. Even with the recent downturn of the stock market, one could say that the average American lives in a fairly good economy. But, do we really know what kind of economy we are living in? We're not living in a capitalist economy. We're not living in a socialist economy. We're not living in a money or people's economy. But we are, I regret to say, living in a military economy. And all production is expected to feed and expand the worldwide military economy. And one of the most important products of that economy is war. And war, of course, is the greatest poison of all.

Our planet has been poisoned with continuous war for an awfully, awfully long time. And, mind you, war develops its own poisons such as killing, murdering, torturing, hating…

Clearly, as you might guess, I strongly prefer that the Inner Environment influence the Outer Environment rather than vice versa. *Because the Outer Environment stifles and starves the ORIGINAL VOICE that exists in our Inner Environment.* And I believe that we've been relentlessly losing our voices.

What can we do? Well, my experience tells me that the answer lies in our Inner Environment….and by developing our awareness of the feeling sense within us, we can become better ecologists for ourselves.

Now, what is the feeling sense?

Well, we all experience the Outer Environment through the five outer senses (touch, hearing, taste, smell, and sight)—which are quantitative (meaning they can be measured) and therefore, they can be limited.

But, in our Inner Environment, we do our experiencing and sensing through one sense only…the feeling sense… we call its workings "the feeling process". It is very close to that harmonic 6th sense and it also takes us a step closer to that elusive "Soul" NRG. Yes, for me, "soul" is the most delicate of all our body NRGs, and there are many of them, many NRG fundamentals and many NRG harmonics.

Now, you may ask, what do I mean when I talk about energy? Well, in very general terms, I am speaking of kinetic energy, the energy of motion. All matter in the universe is in motion; therefore, all of the universe is energy—including us. And in our Inner Environment, we also have definable energy qualities. I'm talking about body NRGs that can be felt neuro-physically.

For example, from my own research, I discovered that:

• There is an inner NRG quality that makes our bodies feel lighter, weightless, floating; we call this inner-felt sensing "buoyancy" NRG.[1]

• There is an inner NRG that gives us a new found strength, power and resilience; which we call "potency" NRG

• There is an NRG that helps us experience the various sensations of cheer-glee-exhilaration which we call inner-felt "radiancy" NRG.
• And there is an inner NRG that helps us feel

Remembrance and Celebration

Keynote Address, VASTA Conference, August 3, 2009. By Arthur Lessac

our vocal and verbal sensations and we call that "tonal" NRG. . . .tonal NRG that incorporates the music of tone –the music of consonants—the music of vowels—the music of speech. . . .a plethora of musical feeling that leads us to a livelier appreciation of random poetic expressions. . . .expressions such as "music is the universal language of mankind" or the expression "voice is the speech of angels".

We can also learn to feel the energy of courage, of awareness, of curiosity, or the energies of spirit and of love. And when I feel them, I sense a bit of questing, or better still, a bit of mystery. I believe it was Thomas Carlyle who said, "the perception of the mysterious is the origin of discovery", and I take that to mean the discovery of fascinating qualities and sensations within our Inner Environments.

And may I say that I am not alone in this recognition of the inner feeling process and its importance.

• It was the poet Yeats who said: "God spare me from men who think in their heads alone; he who sings a lasting song sings in the marrow bone."
Here is a person who recognizes the power of the energy found in the Inner Environment.

• And Neitzsche, the German philosopher said: "There is more wisdom in your body than in your deepest philosophy."

You see, he recognizes that it is our feeling process that holds the key to learning, not our thinking.

• And Henry Wadsworth Longfellow wrote: "How wonderful is the human voice! It is indeed the organ of the soul. The intellect of man is enthroned visibly on his forehead and in his eye, and the heart of man is written on his countenance, but the soul, the soul reveals itself in the voice only." (Bless his soul.)

• And then there's the story of Artur Rubenstein, the great virtuoso pianist. He had thoroughly prepared himself for a very, very special performance, but when he was on the stage performing, he found that part of his creative playing at this concert was outside his carefully practiced repertoire. Later, he said, "If my fingers hadn't done it, my mind would never have thought of it."

This is all Inner Environment percept-fullness…and what I hear Rubenstein saying is that this experience happened through a feeling process—not through an intellectual process. His preparation probably included both. But in that moment in performance, it was his feeling process that taught him more about his artistry than all his practicing had done.

My point here is that these artists and philosophers, themselves creative visionaries, perceived the mysterious feeling process within themselves and others, and held it up as a beacon to creativity, originality, leadership, and wisdom. This is ORIGINAL VOICE. It is only found in the Inner Environment. And when the poisons of the Outer Environment invade the Inner Environment, the ORIGINAL VOICE withers and even disappears.

But, here's the encouraging part (finally!): It is our feeling process that recognizes these poisons, and it is our inner body energies that give us the informational experiences that open the door to health and wellness and humanness and communing.
And the really good thing about this is that no poison can possibly co-exist or co-habit with any of our Inner Environment NRG qualities. One or the other must leave. They cannot live together. If, when we walk, we feel the rhythm of dancing and if, when we talk we feel the lilt of singing, our Inner Environment fills up with joy, pleasure, laughter, and spirit-fullness. In such an environment, it is impossible to also harbor hate, fear, jealousy, or rage.

And if, within these parameters, we recognize a poison, the wisest thing to do is to kick the damn thing out! If we don't, it will continue to do its dirty work. It's not difficult, either. We recognize fevers, rashes, and pains all the time. If we would recognize that jealousy, hate, or fear are poisons far worse than fever or rash, then we would immediately use our natural NRG resources to get rid of them and, yes, regain our health, regain our posture, regain our voice.

Our world, too, has pains, rash, and fever—but we call them poverty, hunger, and pollution, among other things. As long as those poisons continue to contaminate our Outer Environment, our Inner Environments are in danger. That is why it is in our best interest to combat all poison in the Outer Environment—so that we can all stay healthy. In fact, we must become selfish, very selfish—selfish about health! Individual wellness is very much at stake here.
When we are fully aware of our Inner Environments, when we can use our natural NRG qualities to combat the ever-present poisons of the Outer Environment, then we will feel the stirrings of the true ORIGINAL VOICE: a healthy voice, which, just like our baby Stradivarius voice, is exciting, pure, fresh, singing and strong.

This is the voice that is the beacon. This is the voice that 'sings from the marrow bone' in every nook and cranny of our globular planet regardless of the differences in pronunciation, accent or dialect. Peace, health, joy and spirit, work the same way, at any point in the universe. Universal communion may be bathed in different customs, different costumes, but the heart and soul and spirit is the same anywhere in our spherical world.

And while there are thousands of different languages in the Outer Environment, there is only a "communing language" for the Inner Environment, no matter what climate you are in; and most importantly, the fuel for that "communing" language is the feeling process. We should be interested in 'communing' rather than feeling that it is perfectly okay to just communicate. The truth is that communing always communicates fully but that communicating very often is inhumane. It is our ORIGINAL VOICE which speaks out for humaneness, and which recognizes all humanness.

We must ask ourselves: Do we want to live with the loss of this ORIGINAL VOICE? Do we want to live in a world community without ORIGINAL VOICES? We all want and need to live with freedom of speech--with ringing and powerful ORIGINAL VOICES. But, unfortunately, they have weakened. They have become tarnished, tarnished to the extent that freedom of speech is crippled, and we must have freedom of speech for—if we don't have freedom of speech—we have nothing.

Above all, we need that freedom of speech couched and housed healthfully, and wellfully….,and spirit-fully and colorfully voiced.
We are all born with ORIGINAL VOICES. Let us rediscover them, and then let us use them to create the promise and the potency and the peace of our world. Let us recognize the existence of poisons all around us lest they enter into our Inner Environments and rob us forever of our birthright—our ORIGINAL VOICE.

Our spherical world is currently spinning at a dangerous speed on the very cusp of nowhere, falling downward instead of rolling forward, like any ordinary ball. A ball never rolls backward—it keeps rolling forward—no matter what direction it takes. How can we get our globular planet rolling forward again?

This is where we, the members of VASTA, can play a unique and important role. We VASTA members understand better than anyone I know how important it is to celebrate and grow our unique and individual voices. It is incumbent upon all of us to look beyond the boundaries and limitations of specific styles of training—no matter how treasured or popular—to the far greater question of what we are doing to restore the world's ORIGINAL VOICES to their rightful strength and expressiveness. I challenge us to consider every cli-

ent, every job, and every coaching opportunity with this spirit--the spirit of communing, the spirit of health, the spirit of peace.

As I enter my 100th year, I am inspired by the endless contributions that our work can make to a sick and despairing world. We are not a large group, but each of us touches many lives through our work. Together, we can keep this earthly ball rolling forward. Personally, I believe that it's mostly a matter and manner of Inner Environment NRG, of Inner Environment courage, of Inner Environment soul and spirit.

So, I've asked the guy upstairs for 2 or 3 more years. I want to see where all this goes. I want to live, if only for a short time, in a world that rolls only forward. I want to experience the feel of that forward-rolling world. And I would love to see "VASTAns" help to "light the way" with our "ORIGINAL VOICES".

Meanwhile, I'll be like Ol' Man River, and I'll just keep on rolling along!

Thank you, and bless you.

Notes

1. At this point, Professor Lessac demonstrated the various Body NRGs as he described them in more detail.

Heightened Text and Verse, *Ellen O'Brien, Associate Editor*

Ellen O'Brien is Head of Voice and Text for The Shakespeare Theatre Company of Washington DC and The Academy for Classical Acting. Previous coaching includes People's Light and Theatre Company, Shakespeare Santa Cruz, Charlotte Repertory Theatre, Aurora Theatre, and The North Carolina Shakespeare Festival. A member of the Voice and Speech Trainers Association, she holds Advanced and Post-Graduate Degrees in Voice Studies from Central School of Speech and Drama (London) and a PhD in English from Yale University. Her essays on Shakespeare have appeared in *Shakespeare Quarterly,* *Shakespeare Survey, The Voice and Speech Review,* **and elsewhere.**

Each of the writers in this section has chosen to explore the world of voice created by Shakespeare's plays: a world distanced from us by four centuries of linguistic change, by its poetic form, and by the rhetorical nature of its language. How do we effectively give voice to characters defined by language often perceived to be remote from our own?

The question has given rise to a growing debate over whether it is time to translate Shakespeare into twenty-first century English. Given the constantly evolving nature of language, it seems inevitable that the time will come when Shakespeare will seem as foreign to us as Beowulf seems now.

> Hwæt! Wē Gārdena   in geārdagum,
> þēodcyninga,   þrym gefrūnon,
> hū ðā æþelingas   ellen fremedon.

While we can still appreciate elements like the play of sound and rhythm in listening to this language, it would be difficult to argue that entire plays in Old English could be spoken effectively onstage. (This and other passages of Beowulf can be heard spoken in Old English at: http://faculty.virginia.edu/OldEnglish/Beowulf. Readings/Beowulf. Readings.html.) Clearly, Shakespeare's language is far more recognizable to our ears than that of Beowulf. But has it become archaic enough to warrant translation? How do we know when we have reached the tipping point on change? Of course, selective translation of difficult words or phrases has long been a part of production practice: replacing 'ha' with the more modern 'he' or making substitutions for much-debated words like 'prenzie.' However there is an important difference between changing some words for a single *production* and putting a complete translation in *print*. The impact of the first is evanescent, disappearing from public perception at the end of the run; the second is enduring, lasting at least as long as the printed translation survives and often substituting for the original in the minds of those who read only the translation. In debating the question of translation, we would be wise to reflect on the impact of the cuts and wholesale revisions printed in eighteenth and nineteenth century acting editions. In many cases, those changes became nearly universal and lingered well into the twentieth century, limiting and re-shaping our perception of Shakespeare's characters and plays.

One group of our writers takes on the translation question. Linguist John McWhorter's call for great living poets to translate Shakespeare is countered by responses from linguist David Crystal and actor Ben Crystal. At the center of their exchange is the question of just how much linguistic change has actually occurred and how critical the specific changes are to understanding Shakespeare's language. Ben Crystal also alludes to the role of the actors in clarifying unfamiliar words and structures through their own fluency in Shakespearean language. While acknowledging the challenge of engaging four hundred year-old forms of language, verse, and rhetoric, he argues that it is the actors' work to use those very forms to reach hearts and minds through twenty-first century ears.

Implicitly opting for actor fluency rather than translation, David Carey and Erika Bailey offer tools for grounding modern actors in the verse and rhetoric of Shakespeare's time. David Carey's column explores an under-recognized and under-appreciated element of Shakespeare's prosody—the epic caesura. The need to scan Shakespeare's verse in order to speak it well is fairly generally recognized. Yet an overly simplistic knowledge of the meter can lead to dismissing difficult lines as simply "irregular". Too often, such a dismissal leads to speaking these lines as if they were prose or to imposing contemporary speech rhythms on them. Either tactic deprives actor and audience of rhythms which can help to shape meaning. The ability to recognize and use the lesser known elements of the verse can enable actors to bring more of Shakespeare's original rhythms into the way we voice Shakespeare today—and in so doing, to clarify the shape of the thought.

Erika Bailey addresses rhetoric as another of the shaping forces behind Shakespeare's often long and complex thought structures. Reaching back to the rhetorical training which was a fundamental element of education in Shakespeare's time, Bailey engages it as a tool for modern actor training.

While acknowledging the importance of verse and rhetoric, Michael Cobb takes a more modern approach to clarification, exploring a method for choosing operative words to carve out the shape of the thought.

How we talk *about* Shakespeare might be seen as yet another instance where time and change can prompt the impulse to translate. Tanera Marshall argues that shifts in the larger cultural structure of our thinking on femininity and gender make *feminine ending* a problematic term for discussing Shakespeare's prosody today.

Perhaps these essays can inspire us anew to nurture fluency in Shakespeare's English in the actors we train.

Translating Shakespeare into English: A Debate

In the January, 2010 issue of *American Theatre*, an issue focusing on the work of major voice teachers for theatre, there also appeared a provocative essay by celebrated linguist John McWhorter arguing on behalf of the "translation" of the plays of Shakespeare into modern English. *A World of Voice* obtained Professor McWhorter's gracious permission to reprint his essay and asked Professor David Crystal to respond to Professor McWhorter's proposal. David Crystal is famous both as a historian of the English language and also as a scholar of Shakespeare's language (see his interview by Paul Meier on "original pronunciation" in this issue). Crystal's reply led to a debate in sequential commentary by both eminent linguists. The final comment is by Ben Crystal, actor and co-author—with David Crystal, his father—of the glossary *Shakespeare's Words*. Ben Crystal assesses the translation issue from the performer's standpoint. (eds.)

Essay *by John McWhorter*

The Real Shakespearean Tragedy
It's been 400-plus years. Is it time to translate the Bard into understandable English?

John Mcwhorter is a William Simon Fellow at Columbia University and Contributing Editor for *The New Republic*. He is the author of *The Power of Babel* and *Our Magnificent Bastard Tongue*. His academic books include *The Missing Spanish Creoles* and *Language Interrupted*, and two anthologies, *Defining Creole* and *Linguistic Simplicity and Complexity: Why Do Languages Undress?* Beyond his work in linguistics, he is the author of *Losing the Race* and has written for *The New York Times, The New Yorker, The Washington Post* and elsewhere.

It's a Thursday evening and you've gotten home early to eat a quick dinner with your spouse before driving downtown for a night of theatre. A friend has given you tickets for *King Lear*. Freshly showered and nicely dressed, you slip on your coats, have a nice twilight drive, park, glide into the theatre and take your seats. The lights dim, the audience quiets down, you squeeze your partner's hand, and up goes the curtain.

The actors playing the Earls of Kent and Gloucester and Gloucester's son Edmund stride on in vigorous conversation, and you savor the finery of the costumes, the rich voices of the performers, the beauty of the set. And ah, the language, the language. We churls bumble around butchering the language with our *Billy and me*s and *hopefully*s and *Who did I see?*s, but here at last is the language at its most sublime. We have to remember to thank Maria for the tickets.

What a difference 20 minutes can make. Lear has made his first appearance and exited, and now his three daughters are discussing him. Goneril advises that:

> The best and soundest of his time hath been but rash; then must we look to receive from his age, not alone the imperfections of long-engraffed condition, but therewithal the unruly waywardness that infirm and choleric years bring with them.

Regan replies:

> Such unconstant starts are we like to have from him as this of Kent's banishment.

Goneril continues:

> There is further compliment of leave-taking between France and him. Pray you, let's hit together.

Isn't it great to be here at the theatre enjoying some of the mightiest drama civilization has to offer? Yet it has been a long day. It's going to take some concentration to follow this, well, to be sure, gorgeous and profound, but, if we may, rather *dense* language. It seems like we get thrown little curveballs every second line. What does *engraffed* mean? How about *therewithal*? Well, forget it—the line has passed. "Starts are we like to have from him as this of Kent's banishment"? Oh, she means "starts" like shocks, with the banishment being an example, I guess. "There is further compliment of leave-taking"? What compliment? What are they all going to "hit" together? And this is only three ordinary lines. Shakespeare!

We all esteem Shakespeare, but how many of us actually *dig* him? In 1955, Alfred Harbage beautifully captured the mood of most audiences at Shakespeare performances as "reverently unreceptive," "gratified that they have come, and gratified that they now may go." One is not supposed to say such things in polite company, but it is an open secret in America that frankly, for most people Shakespeare is boring. I, for one, as an avid theatre fan, will openly admit that while I have enjoyed the occasional Shakespeare performance and film, most of them have been among the dreariest, most exhausting evenings of my life.

It may be an overstatement to say that every member of a Shakespearean audience is wishing they had brought a magazine. But most of the people who truly get the same spontaneous pleasure and stimulation from Shakespeare that they would from a performance of a play by Edward Albee, Tennessee Williams or David Mamet are members of certain small subsets of the general population: people of letters (literature professors, English teachers, writers and Shakespeare buffs) and "theatre people" (actors, directors, producers, dramaturgs and playwrights). For the rest, the language of Shakespeare remains lovely in snippets, but downright tiresome as the vehicle of an evening-length presentation.

In response to this, many argue that Shakespeare's language merely requires well-honed acting technique. While it is true that inflection and gesture can clarify some of the blurry points in a Shakespearean passage, what emphasis, flick of the head or swoop of the arm could indicate to us what Goneril's "further compliment of leave-taking" means? No amount of raised eyebrows, bell-jingling or trained pigeons could coax, for instance, "The cod-piece that will house / Before the head has any, / The head and he shall louse; / So beggars marry many" any further from the Hungarian that it is to us today, and I have graciously giggled along with many an audience in utter bafflement at such witticisms from Shakespearean Fools.

It is true that Shakespeare's comedies are in general somewhat less of a chore than the tragedies. This, however, is in spite of the language, not because of it. Because comedy lends itself to boffo physical pratfalls, outrageous costumes, funny voices and stock situations, an evening of *Twelfth Night* or *The Comedy of Errors* is usually easier on the derrière than one at *Julius Caesar* or *Henry V*. However, a great deal of the language remains equally distant to us, and even the comedies would be infinitely richer experiences if we had more than a vague understanding of what the characters were actually saying while climbing all over each other and popping out from behind doors.

The common consensus seems to be that what makes Shakespearean language so challenging is that the language is highly "literary" or "poetic," and that understanding the plays is simply a matter of putting forth a certain "effort." Shakespearean language is indeed poetry, but it is not this which bars us from more than a surface comprehension of so much of the dialogue in any Shakespearean play. Many of our best playwrights, such as Eugene O'Neill, David Mamet, Tony Kushner and August Wilson, put prose poetry in the mouths of their characters, and yet we do not leave performances of *Long Day's Journey into Night*, *Glengarry Glen Ross* or *Joe Turner's Come and Gone* glassy-eyed and exhausted.

Some might be uncomfortable with an implication that the most challenge that should be expected of an audience is the language of the aforementioned playwrights, since after all, Shakespeare presents us with the extra processing load of unfamiliar vocabulary and sentence structure. But stage poetry can challenge us without being as dimly meaningful as Shakespearean language so often is to us. A fine example is David Hirson's *La Bête* (see *American Theatre*, *June '91*) set in 17th-century France and composed *entirely* in elegant, overeducated verse. Two-and-a-half hours of this certainly requires a close attention which Neil Simon does not—there is a challenge to be risen to here. Yet it is utterly delightful because the effort pays off in complete comprehension.

No, froufrou words and syntax, and the artificiality of meter, are not in themselves what makes Shakespeare such an approximate experience for most of us. The problem with Shakespeare for modern audiences is that English since Shakespeare's time has changed not only in terms of a few exotic vocabulary items, but in the very meaning of thousands of basic words and in scores of fundamental sentence structures. For this reason, we are faced with a language which, while clearly recognizable as the English we speak, is different to an extent which makes partial comprehension a challenge, and anything approaching full comprehension utterly impossible for even the educated theatregoer who doesn't happen to be a trained expert in Shakespearean language.

No one today would assign their students *Beowulf* in Old English—it is hopelessly obvious that Old English is a different language to us. On the other hand, the English of William Congreve's comedy *The Way of the World* in 1700 presents us no serious challenge, and is easily enjoyable even full of food after a long day. The English of the late 1500s, on the other hand, lies at a point between *Beowulf* and Congreve, which presents us with a tricky question. Language change is a gradual process with no discrete

Translating Shakespeare into English: A Debate
The Real Shakespearean Tragedy by John McWhorter

boundaries—there are no trumpet fanfares or ending credits in the sky as Old English passes into Middle English, as Middle English passes into Shakespeare's English, or as Shakespeare's English passes into ours. Thus our question is: How far back on a language's timeline can we consider the language to be the one modern audiences speak? At what point do we concede that substantial comprehension across the centuries has become too much of a challenge to expect of anyone but specialists?

Many readers may feel I am exaggerating the difficulty of Shakespearean language. However, I respectfully submit that Shakespeare lovers of all kinds, including actors and those supposing that Shakespeare simply requires a bit of extra concentration, miss much, much more of Shakespeare's very basic meanings than they have ever suspected, far beyond the most obvious head-scratchers.

In October 1898, Mark H. Liddell's essay "Botching Shakespeare" made a similar point to mine—that English has changed so deeply since Shakespeare's time that today we are incapable of catching much more than the basic gist of a great deal of his writing, although the similarity of the forms of the words to ours tricks us into thinking otherwise. Liddell took as an example Polonius's farewell to Laertes in *Hamlet*, which begins:

> And these few precepts in thy memory
> Look thou character.

We might take this as, "And as for these few precepts in thy memory, look, you rascal you!", conveying a gruff paternal affection for Laertes. Actually, however, *look* used to be an interjection roughly equivalent to "see that you do it well." And character—if he isn't telling Laertes that he's full of the dickens, then what other definition of *character* might he mean? We might guess that this means something like "to assess the worth of" or "to evaluate." But this isn't even close—to Shakespeare, *character* here meant "to write"! This meaning has long fallen by the wayside, just as thousands of other English words' earlier meanings have. Thus "And these few precepts in thy memory / Look thou character" means "See that you write these things in your memory." Good acting might convey that *look* is an interjection, but no matter how charismatic and fine-tuned the performance, *thou character* is beyond comprehension to any but the two or three people who happen to have recently read an annotated edition of the play (and bothered to make their way through the notes).

Polonius tells his son to "Beware of entrance to a quarrel; but being in / Bear't, that the opposed may beware of thee." We assume he is saying "Avoid getting into arguments, but once you're in one, endure it." In fact, *bear't* meant "make sure that"—in other words, Polonius is not giving the

rather oblique advice that the best thing to do in a argument is to "cope," but to make sure to do it well.

"Take each man's censure, but reserve thy judgement." Turn the other cheek? No—to take a man's censure meant "to evaluate." Polonius is advising his son to view people with insight but refrain from moralizing. "The French are of a most select and generous chief"? Another blob we have to let go by with a guess. *Chief* here is a fossilized remnant of *sheaf*, a case of arrows—which doesn't really help us unless we are told in footnotes that sheaf was used idiomatically to mean "quality" or "rank," as in "gentlemen of the best sheaf."

And finally we get to the famous line, "Neither a borrower nor a lender be." Have you ever wondered why the following line is less famous—the *reasons* why one shouldn't borrow or lend? "For loan oft loses both itself and friend / And borrowing dulls the edge of *husbandry*." So the reason one shouldn't borrow is because it interferes with the raising of livestock? Actually, husbandry meant "thrift" at the time. It does not anymore, because the language is always changing.

Polonius's speech is by no means extraordinary in terms of pitfalls like these. Indeed, almost any page of Shakespeare is as far from our modern language as this one. So shouldn't one simply read a Shakespeare play beforehand in order to prepare oneself to take in the language spoken? The fact is that one cannot simply "read" this speech without constant reference to annotations. How realistic or even charitable is it to expect that anyone but specialists, theatre folk and buffs will have the patience to read more than a prescribed dose of Shakespeare under these conditions? And ultimately a play is written to be performed, not read, and certainly not deciphered. A play that cannot communicate effectively to the listener in spoken form is no longer a play, and thus no longer lives.

The tragedy of this is that the foremost writer in the English language, the most precious legacy of the English-speaking world, is little more than a symbol in our actual thinking lives, for the simple reason that we cannot understand what the man is saying. Shakespeare is not a drag because we are lazy, because we are poorly educated, or because he wrote in poetic language. Shakespeare is a drag because he wrote in a language which, as a natural consequence of the mighty eternal process of language change, 500 years later we effectively no longer speak.

Is there anything we might do about this? I submit that here as we enter the Shakespearean canon's sixth century in existence, Shakespeare begin to be performed in translations into modern English readily comprehensible to the modern spectator. Make no mistake—I do not mean the utilitarian running translations which younger students are (blissfully) often provided in textbooks. The translations ought to be richly considered, executed by artists of the highest caliber well-steeped in the language of Shakespeare's era, thus equipped to channel the Bard to the modern listener with the passion, respect and care which is his due. (Kent Richmond, a professor at California State University—Long Beach, has been quietly doing just this with his *Shakespeare Translation Project*. (http://www.csulb.edu/~richmond/Shakespeare.html)

"But translated Shakespeare wouldn't be Shakespeare!" one might object. To which the answer is, to an extent, yes. However, we would never complain a translation of *Beowulf* "isn't *Beowulf*"—of course it isn't, in the strict sense, but we know that without translation, we would not have access to *Beowulf* at all.

I predict that if theatre companies began presenting Shakespeare in elegant modern translations, a great many people would at first scorn such productions on the grounds that Shakespeare had been "cheapened" or "defiled," and that it was a symptom of the cultural backwardness of our society and our declining educational standards. However, especially if they were included in season ticket packages, audiences would begin to attend performances of Shakespeare in translation. Younger critics would gradually join the bandwagon. Pretty soon the almighty dollar would determine the flow of events—Shakespeare in the original would play to critical huzzahs but half-empty houses, while people would be lining up around the block to see Shakespeare in English the way Russians do to see an *Uncle Vanya*.

Then would come the critical juncture: A whole generation would grow up having only experienced Shakespeare in the English they speak, and what a generation they would be! This generation would be the vanguard of an American public who truly loved Shakespeare, who cherished Lear and Olivia and Polonius and Falstaff and Lady Macbeth and Cassius and Richard III as living, breathing icons like Henry Higgins, Blanche DuBois, Big Daddy, George and Martha and Willy Loman, rather than as hallowed but waxen figurines like the signers of the Constitution frozen in a gloomy painting.

No longer would producers have to trick Shakespeare up in increasingly desperate, semi-motivated changes of setting to attract audiences—*A Midsummer Night's Dream* in colonial Brazil, *Romeo and Juliet* shouted over rock music in a 90-minute MTV video, *Two Gentlemen of Verona* on motorcycles, *Twelfth Night* at a 7-Eleven. Producers do this to "make Shakespeare relevant to modern audiences," but the very assumption here that the public needs to be reminded of this relevance is telling, especially since the assumption is so sadly accurate. A more effective way to make Shakespeare relevant to us is simply to present it in the English we speak.

Indeed, the irony today is that the Russians, the French and other people in foreign countries possess Shakespeare to a much greater extent than we do, for the simple reason that unlike us, they get to enjoy Shakespeare in the language they speak. Shakespeare is translated into rich, poetic varieties of these languages, to be sure, but since it is the rich, poetic *modern* varieties of the languages, the typical spectator in Paris, Moscow or Berlin can attend a production of *Hamlet* and enjoy a play rather than an exercise. In Japan, new editions of Shakespeare in Japanese are regularly *best-sellers*—utterly unimaginable here, since, like the Japanese, we prefer to experience literature in the language we speak, and a new edition of original Shakespeare no longer fits this definition. In an illuminating twist on this, one friend of mine—and a very cultured, literate one at that—has told me that the first time they truly understood more than the gist of what was going on in a Shakespeare play was when they saw one in French!

The glory of Shakespeare's original language is manifest. We must preserve it for posterity. However, we must not err in equating the preservation of the language with the preservation of the art. Perhaps such an equation would be the ideal—Shakespeare through the ages in his exact words. In a universe where language never changed, such an equation would be unobjectionable. In the world we live in, however, this equation is allowing blind faith to deprive the public of a monumental treasure.

We must reject the polite relationship the English-speaking public now has with Shakespeare in favor of more intimate, charged one which both the public and the plays deserve. To ask a population to rise to the challenge of taking literature to heart in a language they do not speak is as unreasonable as it is futile. The challenge we must rise to is to shed our fear of language change and give Shakespeare his due—restoration to the English-speaking world.

Essay *by David Crystal*

To Modernize or not to Modernize: There is no Question

David Crystal works from his home in Holyhead, Wales, as a writer, lecturer, and broadcaster, and is honorary professor of linguistics at the University of Bangor. His work on Shakespeare includes *Shakespeare's Words* (2002, with Ben Crystal) and its associated website, *Pronouncing Shakespeare* (2005), *Think on my Words* (2008), and regular articles for *Around the Globe*. He was Sam Wanamaker fellow at Shakespeare's Globe in 2003-4, and Master of Pronunciation there for *Romeo and Juliet* (2004) and *Troilus and Cressida* (2005). In 2010 he worked with the University of Kansas theatre department on *A Midsummer Night's Dream* in period pronunciation.

I really don't know what world John McWhorter is living in. It doesn't seem to bear any relationship to mine.

Most of the people who truly get the same spontaneous pleasure and stimulation from Shakespeare that they would from a performance of a play by Edward Albee, Tennessee Williams or David Mamet are members of certain small subsets of the general population: people of letters (literature professors, English teachers, writers and Shakespeare buffs) and "theatre people" (actors, directors, producers, dramaturgs and playwrights). For the rest, the language of Shakespeare remains lovely in snippets, but downright tiresome as the vehicle of an evening-length presentation.

Leaving aside the question of the aptness of McWhorter's analogy (I've often seen audiences leave modern plays with very long faces), his generalization is breathtaking in the way it ignores the Shakespeare world I know. Has he never been to a performance at Shakespeare's Globe, where, day after day, audiences interact enthusiastically and vociferously with the actors on stage, and packed houses cheer for several minutes at the end of the play? These are people

who would not take kindly to being described as members of one of his subsets. Nor evidently has he experienced the typical response seen even in the more refined atmosphere of the Royal Shakespeare Company in Stratford when crowds of youngsters, bussed in from their schools, cheer their way through several curtain calls, and leave chattering and enthusing about what they have just seen.

Not so long ago, I overheard (in an interval at the Globe) a group of inner-city teenagers furiously arguing about whether Lear was right to kick Cordelia out. Goneril and Regan were clearly prats in their eyes. Did they understand every word they had heard? No. Did this stop them having a great theatrical time? No. Had it turned them off Shakespeare? No. Should I have pointed out to them that 'John McWhorter says your experience must have been tiresome because you didn't understand Goneril's use of *long-engraffed*?' No. And why were some of these cool teens trying hard not to cry (and failing) when they heard Lear's final speech?

> And my poor fool is hanged! No, no, no life!
> Why should a dog, a horse, a rat have life,
> And thou no breath at all? Thou'lt come no more;
> Never, never, never, never, never.
> Pray you undo this button. Thank you, sir.
> Do you see this? Look on her! Look, her lips!
> Look there! Look there!

How does that relate to this?

> The problem with Shakespeare for modern audiences is that English since Shakespeare's time has changed not only in terms of a few exotic vocabulary items, but in the very meaning of thousands of basic words and in scores of fundamental sentence structures. For this reason, we are faced with a language which, while clearly recognizable as the English we speak, is different to an extent which makes partial comprehension a challenge, and anything approaching full comprehension utterly impossible for even the educated theatregoer who doesn't happen to be a trained expert in Shakespearean language.

Do you recognize Lear's speech from John McWhorter's description? Nor do I. And, while you're reflecting on the point, try turning that passage into an 'elegant modern translation'.

'Many readers may feel I am exaggerating the difficulty of Shakespearean language.' No 'may' about it. Of course we can cherry-pick difficult passages - especially those spoken by upper-class characters who use a high register of the language. But to go on to say, having selected some tricky lines in Lear, 'almost any page of Shakespeare is as far from our modern language as this one' is the kind of exaggeration that a linguist really ought to be avoiding. Linguists are usually able to see that there are two sides to a stylistic issue, and I don't understand why John McWhorter has been unable to do so in this case. Of course, he's not alone in trying to paint a black-and-white picture. For decades, modernizers have been using examples like 'super-serviceable, finical rogue' (*King Lear*) to make their case. Their opponents use examples like 'To be or not to be; that is the question' (*Hamlet*). To my mind, the question is straightforward: how much of Shakespeare's language is like the former, and how much is like the latter? Thanks to the studies of Shakespeare's grammar and vocabulary that have been made in the 2000s (such as Norman Blake's *A Grammar of Shakespeare's Language* (2002) and my own *Shakespeare's Words*, with Ben Crystal (2002)), I think it's now clear that only a relatively small proportion of the vocabulary would fall into the 'need to translate because the language has changed' category, and even less of the grammar.

Let's begin with vocabulary. The fundamental question is: how many *different* words are there in Shakespeare - that is, words which have changed their meaning between Early Modern English and now. Notice that, in any argument based on language change, the question is one of difference, not difficulty. Shakespeare uses plenty of words which haven't changed their meaning but are still difficult: Classical allusions are a good example. There is no linguistic problem in the sentence which Paris uses to explain why he has not mentioned his feelings to the grieving Juliet: 'Venus smiles not in a house of tears' (*Romeo and Juliet*, 4.1.8), but it make no sense until you know who Venus is. She turns out to be the same goddess of love today as she was 400 years ago. This is not a matter of language change. Similarly, Shakespeare gives us plenty of difficult and challenging thoughts, and these remain difficult and challenging today, but often this is nothing to do with the language they are expressed in. 'To be or not to be' is a case in point. Difficult thoughts are not a matter of language change, either.

So how many 'different words' *are* there in Shakespeare? Ben and I list about 3000 in *Shakespeare's Words* (2002). They include everything from really difficult items, such as *engraffed, incarnadine, and finical*, to words which would hardly give you a second thought because they are so close to modern words, and in some cases continue to be used in special contexts (such as poetry or religion) - such as *morn* and *bedazzle* - as well as those words where the metre has prompted a variant coinage, such as *vasty* instead of *vast* ('the vasty fields of France' in the opening Chorus to *Henry V*). So the really interesting question is: how many of these different words pose a *true* difficulty of comprehension. There are two types of candidate. First, there are words

which are totally opaque - like *finical*, where no amount of guessing will produce a correct interpretation. Second, there are words which look easy but which are seriously deceptive - the 'false friends' - such as *merely* meaning 'totally' or *ecstasy* meaning 'madness'. I don't know of any complete count, but I shall be very surprised if the combined total passes a thousand. That's about one in twenty of Shakespeare's total vocabulary.

However, I'm not sure that even this figure is very meaningful, because it ignores those cases where a word is intelligible at one level and not at another. Much of the insult-language is like this. When Kent harangues Oswald (*King Lear* 2.2) as being 'a lily-livered, action-taking, whoreson, glass-gazing, super-serviceable, *finical* rogue', we may not know what finical is, or several of the other words, but we jolly well know that Kent is not paying Oswald a compliment. The same point applies to modern English. If I call you a *blithering idiot*, you know the strength of my feeling - but if I were to ask you what *blithering* actually means, you probably wouldn't be able to answer. Can you tell me what *fell* means in one *fell swoop*? And what about *hurley-burley* (from the opening scene in *Macbeth*)? Few could define this, but at a pragmatic level we can easily guess what it means.

It's crucial to take the pragmatics into account, because we need this perspective to help explain the notion of 'level of response'. Any lines from Shakespeare can be responded to at different levels. The more we know about the detailed meaning of every word in the text, the more we are likely to get out of the play, of course. But it does not follow that the only legitimate response to a play (or any use of language) is at this level. If 'full comprehension' is the only criterion of legitimate language use, then we'd all better stop talking to each other right now. The crucial point to appreciate about the interaction between Lear and his three daughters, in the opening scene, is that Goneril and Regan are hiding behind insincere words, whereas Cordelia is not. It is simplistic to think of their high-blown waffle as just a matter of language change: the groundlings wouldn't have been able to understand much of it either. The two daughters' rhetoric is there to make a contrast with Cordelia, whose simple 'Nothing' is soon to follow, along with her explanation with its effective lines:

> Why have my sisters husbands, if they say
> They love you all?...
> Sure I shall never marry like my sisters,
> To love my father all..

Which bit of that did you find tiresomely unintelligible, exactly?

Translating Shakespeare into English: A Debate

To Modernize or not to Modernize: There is no Question by David Crystal

Another example of a variable level of response comes when we find ourselves grasping just part of the meaning of a sentence. Take Toby Belch's offer to Maria, 'Shall I play my freedom at tray-trip ...?' (*Twelfth Night*, 2.5.183). We may have no idea what *tray-trip* is (many such Elizabethan practices are shrouded in mystery), but the collocation with *play* shows that it must be some kind of game. Collocations provide major clues to meaning - something that modernizers regularly forget. Translators well know that meaning does not lie only within a word, but actually comes from an examination of a whole sentence. It is the sentence that, literally 'makes' sense of words. This point is often lost sight of when modernizers talk about Shakespeare's 'difficult words'.

It's also worth noting that Shakespeare himself was well aware that some of his words were difficult, which is why he often glosses them, or paraphrases a sentence to get his meaning across. 'No, not a grise', says Cesario (aka Viola) to Olivia, talking about pity being akin to love (*Twelfth Night*, 3.1.121). Turning *grise* into 'step, whit, bit', or some such word is something that directors often do anyway, without anyone (bar a few scholars) noticing, and I don't have a big problem with that. But we mustn't forget that often Shakespeare himself does the translating for us: the Duke says to Brabantio, 'Let me ... lay a sentence / Which as a grise or step may help these lovers / Into your favour' (*Othello*, 1.3.198). Well, thank you, Will. And if you're having a problem with *incarnadine* (*Macbeth*, 2.2.62), be patient for another line and you'll learn what it means: 'making the green one red'.

At sentence level, similarly, we often see Shakespeare approaching a point in a number of different ways. When the Friar explains to Juliet about drinking the potion, he describes the effect thus (*Romeo and Juliet*, 4.1.93):

Take thou this vial, being then in bed,
And this distilling liquor drink thou off;
When presently through all thy veins shall run
A cold and drowsy humour.

Modernizers would stop us there, point triumphantly to *humour* and say how unintelligible it is. But we must listen/ read on: 'For no pulse/Shall keep his native progress, but surcease.' *Surcease*? Another possible difficulty, if the listener fails to make the link with *cease*. But keep listening/ reading:

No warmth, no breath, shall testify thou livest.
The roses in thy lips and cheeks shall fade
To wanny ashes, thy eyes' windows fall
Like death when he shuts up the day of life.

Wanny, another problem. But anyone who carries on like

this, failing to read the whole passage before sounding off about the comprehension of individual words, is going to miss the point. I have used this passage as an exercise with students, some as young as 10, and none of them ever fail to understand what is happening. I generalize: I defy anyone to hear this passage, presented well in the context of that part of the play, and be unable to give some sort of explanation about what is going on. And if that turns out to be the case, then the argument for universal translation evaporates.

Based on the counts done for *Shakespeare's Words*, I estimate that the case for modernization is supported by only about 5% of Shakespeare's vocabulary. Even if we included all 3000 differences (i.e. including such cases as *morn* and *vasty*) we would still only reach about 15%. Turn this on its head. Modern English speakers already know 85% or more of Shakespeare's words. This is not a very strong case, it seems to me, for a general modernization policy.

The same approach can be applied to other domains of language. How many differences are there between Early Modern and Modern English grammar? A useful source for making a rough calculation is G L Brook's *The Language of Shakespeare* (1976), in which he conveniently sets out points of difference between Early Modern and Modern English in numbered paragraphs. He identifies about 250 points in his chapters on syntax and accidence. This sounds like a lot, until we reflect on just how many grammatical points there are in English - about 3500 described in the large grammar compiled by Randolph Quirk and his associates, *A Comprehensive Grammar of the English Language* (1985). So less than 10% of Early Modern English grammar is likely to cause a comprehension problem. The vast majority of the grammatical rules found in Shakespeare are the same then as now. I do not know what John McWhorter can be thinking of when he talks about 'scores of fundamental sentence structures' being different to the point of incomprehensibility.

There are indeed islands of difficulty in Shakespeare which arise from a combination of lexical or grammatical unfamiliarity and metrically influenced word order variation; but they are islands within an ocean of accessible meaning. The impression we have to the contrary, I think, arises from the glossarial approach itself, so prominent in the notes to edited texts and a focus of attention in the classroom. This can actually *cause* the lack of comprehension, by stopping us mid-flow and making us concentrate on individual lexical trees, thereby distracting us from the sense of the overall semantic wood. It is a trap that can be avoided by going to see a play before reading it, and then going to see it again after studying it.

As this last remark suggests, nothing in my argument

reduces the value of studying the plays and learning the meanings of the words that are unclear, so that we refine our response to them. The more we understand whole lines, and sequences of lines, the more we will develop our appreciation of character, plot, and atmosphere, and value their status as poetry. There is a phonaesthetic as well as a semantic response which can be achieved only from an awareness of each line as a rhythmical entity, and word-meaning plays its part in that response along with sentence meaning. For example, I've heard an actor 'milk' the three [s] sounds in *surcease* to great effect, reinforcing its sense of cessation. And obviously, the more we understand what *humours* are, the more we will appreciate the all-encompassing power of Friar Laurence's drug. But 'full comprehension' of the words *humour* and *surcease* is not a *sine qua non* of understanding what Friar Laurence is saying to Juliet.

The basic error in John McWhorter's argument is his view that Shakespeare's language is more like Beowulf than Congreve. Look again at my examples above and tell me that's true! The period between 1600 and the present-day is actually one of the slower-moving periods of English linguistic change. So, rather than modernize Shakespeare, in my view our efforts should be devoted to making people more fluent in 'Shakespearean', by devising appropriately graded Early Modern English syllabuses just as one would in any language-teaching world. All modern English speakers have an immensely powerful start, in that they already know some 80 to 90 per cent of the language. That remaining 10 per cent or so is admittedly an impediment, but it should be seen as an opportunity and a challenge to be overcome, not as a barrier to be evaded. We only have to learn what *bootless* means once, and we have removed 22 instances of that barrier at one fell swoop. The sense of achievement, once the energy has been devoted to the task, is tremendous, and yields a reward which is repeated every time we encounter one of the poems or plays.

Response *by John McWhorter*

Professor Crystal's response to my article is refreshing in actually grappling directly and sustainedly with my main point, which is not that Shakespeare is difficult, but that we can no longer comprehend the basic meaning of an alarming number of the words he uses. The problem is such, I argue, that we are not in a position to be able to even appreciate the difficulty and poetry except in a foggy way, especially when we receive the plays in live performance.

Crystal notes that only about ten percent of Shakespeare's vocabulary is opaque to us in this way, a useful observation. However, the money quote in Crystal's reply is "That remaining ten percent or so is admittedly an impediment." Who is to say that the decisive barrier that I describe would require more than a ten percent discrepancy in vocabulary? Spoken language goes by very quickly -- if we heard someone dropping a nonsense word into their speech even every fifteen words rather than ten, we would quickly start losing the thread of what they were saying. They would wear us out, fast. The live Shakespearean experience can be seen as analogous.

Crystal notes that "modernizers" such as myself might "cherry-pick" especially opaque passages – but then, as he also notes, so might people of his mind. Here, then, Crystal may well choose a passage that happens not to contain any toe-stubbers such as the one from Lear's final speech. However, in response to Crystal's implication that my opinion on this issue is irresponsible coming from a linguist, I submit that he is neglecting what entire running scenes of Shakespearean language are very often like.

"How does that relate to this?" Crystal insists, "this" being my argument, after the relevant passage of Lear's final cry. Well, how does this passage from the beginning of *Measure for Measure* relate to Crystal's implication that I am off my rocker? This is Vincentio – and this is at the beginning!

> Of government the properties to unfold,
> Would seem in me to affect speech and discourse;
> Since I am put to know that your own science
> Exceeds, in that, the lists of all advice
> My strength can give you. Then no more remains,
> But that to your sufficiency ... (end quote)

and a bit later:

> What figure of us think you he will bear?
> For you must know, we have with special soul
> Elected him our absence to supply,
> Lent him our terror, dress'd him with our love,
> And given his deputation all the organs
> Of our own power.

The problems with now distant word meanings – how many people will immediately process that to Shakespeare science still meant "knowledge" -- just pile all over one another here. No amount of Globe or Barbican acting smarts could get the meaning of these passages across in real time – and I do not see Shakespeare providing us with "glosses" here, either. Say that the solution is just to cut this part and I simply propose an alternate universe where we alter it in line with how modern English words have evolved.

This sample from *Measure for Measure* is, in fact, typical of a problem Shakespeare scholars have traditionally noted in his late plays, an increasingly dense, inverted, listener-unfriendly form of phraseology. This vein in the Bard's writing is thought to have been written even over the heads of ordinary playgoers of his time. If most Globe patrons had trouble with this brand of the late plays' writing style, then I doubt the inner city kids Crystal refers to would have much more fun with it. Upon which I submit – if we are to relate to it four hundred years later, is it an insane proposal that the words that no longer mean what they did to Shakespeare be revised? After all, in a passage like the one above, all it takes is a single word to throw a listener for good, never mind "ten percent."

What world am I living in? (as Crystal asks). Not one devoid of theatrical experience – I am, in fact, quite the "theatre person" as a spectator as well as performer (I have even acted with yeomanly competence in a Tom Stoppard play, complete with dense language and a British accent). As such, I am well aware of audiences enjoying Shakespeare, including young people. Here in New York there were lines around the block for *Hamlet* (or really, Jude Law in *Hamlet*) and (Patrick Stewart in) *Macbeth* most recently.

What worries me is that so often what the audience is taking in is such an abridgement of what Shakespeare meant, or of what one can process only having read the play beforehand. This comes from, in fact, my being a linguist – I seek an ideal of fuller understanding of the words than is possible given the four-plus centuries' remove. Crystal gives a perfect example in the scene where the Friar explains to Juliet about taking the potion. Of course audiences know what is going on in a general sense. My claim is not that Shakespeare is "closer to Beowulf than to Congreve" in terms of comprehension, and I submit that Crystal is falling into straw mannism here. Does he really think I am claiming that Shakespeare may as well have been writing in West Saxon?

I am, simply, wishing that *more* people could get more of Shakespearean text in live performance, and I'm not sure my point classifies as "carrying on" as Crystal puts it. Is he truly able to distinguish between being a virgin listener and being a Shakespeare-loving expert on the English language? Quite simply, the line "For no pulse shall keep his native progress, but surcease" is exactly the kind of thing I am calling attention to. Catching the *cease* part of *surcease* and processing that the meaning is "stop" is, for one, something that the untutored listener will quite certainly "fail to make the link" on in real time. And there is more opacity of this kind in the line. *Progress* in modern English most spontaneously has an abstract sense rather than the more literal one of "go on" as applied to a pulse. One gets this having parsed the line on the page – but what about hearing it for the first time? The *his* is a remnant of Old English's gender marking that could apply to objects as well as people – but to a layman, is one more thing to trip up the listener.

Which he is referred to? Oh well – we move on.

Crystal may even agree here, but suggests better education in Shakespearean language. I understand that, but given the nature of education in the America we live in, it would seem a bleak prospect. Opinions will differ on how realistic or fair it is to expect spectators to attend Shakespeare having done the homework of carefully reading the play first; I, for one, see this, too, as a prescription unlikely of success in a world ever less oriented to print. For these reasons I suggest translation, with all due respect to David Crystal's reply and awesome body of work.

There is, however, in Crystal's reply an air of pique that I have frequently encountered in response to my suggestion. My impression is that this pique is more visceral than intellectual, despite my sincere gratitude for Crystal and his son's quantitative approach to the issue and the line on my bookshelf of Crystal's books.

And in that light, I find myself thinking of two experiences I have had recently. Two friends of mine, one an actor by trade and the other an occasional performer like me who loves the Bard – as I do – were years ago quite dismissive of my insisting that overall, Shakespearean language is alarmingly opaque to modern listeners except in careful excerpt. (Note I mean listeners, not readers.) One of them even got a little snippy as Crystal has.

However, it would seem that the matter was one of an initial irritation which passed, followed by a more temperate reception over the passage of time. Quite by chance, both of those friends have told me without my asking them in the past year – and neither were aware of the article Crystal and I are sparring over now – that upon reflection they understand what I mean.

Is the testy response from people like Crystal more a matter of impulsive recoil at any questioning of the worth of Shakespeare as an artist? Or, to push it a bit, are those who have mastered Shakespearean language so proud of the effort this took that they bristle at a suggestion that the language be rendered such that they could no longer look to it as a mountain they climbed?

If so, I get it. But I also cannot see that I am deaf to poetry, a poor linguist, or out of my mind.

Response *by David Crystal*

As Elbert Hubbard once said: 'If you can't answer a man's arguments, all is not lost; you can still call him vile names.'

So, after a promising start in his response, John McWhorter resorts to name-calling. I am, evidently, piquey, snippy, and testy. I think I must be getting somewhere.

Let me try to restore the debate to a polite level and focus on the main point. What I'm charging John McWhorter with is harmful exaggeration. It's exaggeration because he is seriously overstating the amount of difficulty in Shakespeare. And it's harmful because this can make people even more scared of the bard than they were before.

Make no mistake about it. McWhorter is arguing that there is hardly anything in Shakespeare that can be understood. Two quotes from his original piece: 'we cannot understand what the man is saying'... 'the language of Shakespeare remains lovely in snippets.' I take precisely the opposite view, that the language of Shakespeare is difficult in snippets. Moreover, the difficulty isn't spread evenly over the whole canon, as McWhorter seems to think:

> Spoken language goes by very quickly -- if we heard someone dropping a nonsense word into their speech even every fifteen words rather than ten, we would quickly start losing the thread of what they were saying. They would wear us out, fast. The live Shakespearean experience can be seen as analogous.

If it were so, indeed we would. But it isn't analogous. The difficult words in Shakespeare don't appear like that. They occur in clusters, or are isolated points of contention. In previous writing I've called them 'islands' of difficulty. The clusters are things like insult strings (as between Hal and Falstaff or Kent to Oswald) or character-related obfuscation (as between Poor Tom and Lear) or topic-related moments (as when Hamlet comments on the nature of man) or plot-related moments (such as a heraldic announcement in a history play) or poetry-related moments (when the metre prompts an unfamiliar word order).

In relation to isolated words, McWhorter doesn't address my point that there are levels of difficulty. For example, 'science' meaning 'knowledge' isn't as difficult as might be thought, because both words share some semantic features, and these are enough to suggest a sense that carries the direction of the speaker's thought. It isn't the 'full comprehension' that he wants, but it's a start. In any case, there's no such thing as full comprehension in a literary work (and it's chimerical even in everyday conversation, as all those books on men and women misunderstanding each other illustrate). Every time I study a piece of Shakespeare, I learn something new (as my regular articles for *Around the Globe* illustrate) and deepen my understanding. This is a general experience for Shakespeare scholars and neophytes alike.

Note that the real issue isn't one of translation, as such, but

I think I already know what the thousands of words are - they're listed in *Shakespeare's Words* - though what 'basic' might mean isn't at all obvious. But 'scores of fundamental sentence structures'? I have no idea what is being claimed here, and this shouldn't take too long to substantiate. So, let's have a list of scores of fundamental sentence structures, please.

Or, try this. Let's accept, for the sake of argument, the necessity of translation. How are these translations to be achieved?

> The translations ought to be richly considered, executed by artists of the highest caliber well-steeped in the language of Shakespeare's era, thus equipped to channel the Bard to the modern listener with the passion, respect and care which is his due.

That sounds good. OK, so do it. Which artists does McWhorter have in mind? And, having found some, let's see some examples of their work. I'd love to see a translation which retains the poetic quality of the original, avoids banality, and approaches the 'full comprehension' demanded in his original piece. I have to say that, having read a number of translations into modern English, I find them pretty poor, focusing on plot rather than character, turning characters into stereotypes or pastiches, and losing any sense of poetry. So, my second challenge is to provide a quality translation of one of those difficult pieces of text that he cites. Full comprehension, mind.

Response *by John McWhorter*

I think most readers will agree that in my response I did respond to Crystal's points quite directly. My point that Crystal's response was piquey, snippy, and testy was not levelled as a flimsy substitute for argumentation but as an additional observation, because his response was indeed all three.

And overall, his second response would seem to indicate that we have gotten down to issues of degree and "Where do you draw the line?" regarding which there can be no conclusive resolution in the formal sense.

Except -- Crystal's challenge for me to provide someone who has provided an adequately artistic Shakespeare translation misses the subjunctivity of my point. I wrote that such translations OUGHT to be done / tried. The fact that such translations by proven artists do not exist at present cannot be taken as refutation of my argument.

However, it's a straw man point to note that the translation could never equal Shakespeare's text itself. Of course it wouldn't. The question is whether more immediate comprehension of the language would be worth a degree of dilution of the excellence of the original. Opinions will differ -- and likely usually fall on Crystal's side, to be sure -- but again, the particular argument I made stands.

The Translation Debate: an Actor's View

Ben Crystal studied English Language and Linguistics at Lancaster University before training at Drama Studio London. He co-wrote *Shakespeare's Words* (Penguin 2002) and *The Shakespeare Miscellany* (Penguin 2005) with his father David Crystal, and his first solo book, *Shakespeare on Toast* (Icon 2008) was shortlisted for the 2010 Educational Writer of the Year Award. His workshops developing fresh approaches to acting Shakespeare are given around the world and can be found at www.passioninpractice.com. In autumn 2011, he will be playing Hamlet in the first Original Pronunciation production of the play for 400 years, at the University of Nevada, Reno.

I've spent much of the last ten years acting and working on Shakespeare's plays and poems with people from a variety of backgrounds and a spectrum of cultures, languages and abilities. They've ranged from professional actors and drama students through teachers and pupils in high school to neophyte youngsters in Kolkata who simply felt they had an interest in Shakespeare.

The main obstacle I've found across the board has never been one of understanding the text. On the contrary, the barrier that needs to be taken down is what I'd call 'permission'. The blocks surrounding Shakespeare have less to do with comprehension, and more to do with the literary tradition that states these works are there to be read and studied, rather than for the common masses to hear, speak and perform.

Once people have been given this permission - once they realise that these works are crammed with real emotions, difficult decisions and heart-breaking encounters - I've never known the meaning of the words to be a permanent

obstacle. They are thrilled by the lofty heights Shakespeare takes them to. Gradually, the complex ideas unravel. When one stands back and lets the speeches flow, they begin to make sense. Great Shakespeare actors often say that the instinct with poetry is to slow down, whereas the more you make the words your own and 'speak the speech trippingly', as Hamlet says, the easier they are to understand.

It was the same for audience members in Shakespeare's time. When Macbeth utters the words 'If the assassination / Could trammel up the consequence', the Elizabethan audience's collective brain would have sparkled to hear the new and unfamiliar word, *assassination*. They would not, though, have struggled with the meaning, already being familiar with the word *assassin*. Shakespeare knew they'd be able to make the leap, and his audience would know that in going to see one of his plays, such leaps would most likely have to be made.

I've just finished performing Edgar in *King Lear*, in a castle in south-west Austria. The audience were primarily second-language English speakers, from all walks of life, but we performed entirely in English - aside from a German prologue who introduced the characters at the beginning of the show. Comprehension was not a problem. When it came to a more difficult speech of Edgar's, I certainly had to work harder:

> Yet better thus, and known to be condemned
> Than still condemned and flattered, to be worst.
> The lowest and most dejected thing of fortune
> Stands still in esperance, lives not in fear:

In isolation, this is tricky to understand. In performance, when 'thus' clearly refers to Edgar's physical state (covered in dirt, wearing a filthy, torn blanket); when *known to be condemned* refers to him, as he's still in disguise and on the run; when *still condemned and flattered, to be worst* refers to Lear, whose company Edgar has just left; when I can express notions of 'dejection', 'hope' and 'fear' by my face and body - what is there to be translated?

But if one does translate, which version does one translate from? This speech differs wildly depending on whether you head to the Quarto or the Folio. The vocabulary choice of *esperance* over *experience* will lead you down different paths, as will the various punctuation differences. Many people disregard the Quarto texts, some worship the Folio (being the product of two of Shakespeare's lead actors and colleagues), and some disregard the early-modern English punctuation altogether. Shakespeare has left us enough choices to make, before we start modernising words.

The next problem facing the translator is obvious: which meaning of a word to choose? Here is Kent Richmond's

Translating Shakespeare into English: A Debate
The Translation Debate: an Actor's View by Ben Crystal

version of Edgar's speech:

> Better like this, to know that one's despised,
> Than still despised and flattered. For the worst,
> The lowest thing, the most cast down by fortune,
> Is always hopeful, never fearing loss.

To take the last word of the first line: *condemned / despised.* *Contemned* (both the Folio and Quarto spell the word with a t rather than a *d*) is indeed defined in the OED as *despised,* which a modern audience would probably understand to mean *hated.* But Edgar is not simply 'despised' - he has actually been condemned - to death, if caught. The translation has narrowed the sense of what Edgar is saying, and in so doing has lost half of Edgar's point. And the latter half of this version is more a reinterpretation than a translation. I struggle to make sense of it, in relation to what has been happening by this point in the play.

The best example of endless interpretation is perhaps the most famous: Hamlet's 'To be, or not to be, that is the question' speech, on which I had someone email me this very week. The meaning of the line is, at first glance, very simple, and requires little thought. Scratch at the surface, or begin to explain the line to someone else, as I tried to do in my response to my correspondent, and it becomes a very different matter.

The speech is an onion, with many layers of meaning (talking about life and death, action and passivity, endurance and submission) which will all change depending on how the actor playing Hamlet has interpreted the character up to that point in the play. This, surely, is one of the principal joys of Shakespeare. Certainly there are specific words in that speech whose meaning is unclear to a modern listener, but if actors are worth their salt they will have discovered this meaning in rehearsal, and will be able to convey it through the way they express themselves - through their body, voice, and intention.

I don't know anyone who can say they've 'mastered Shakespearean language' - and I include myself in this. Surely one of the most wonderful aspects of encountering Shakespeare is the way the meaning will slip and slide out of your reach. I personally don't relish the idea of 'full comprehension' of the language. One of the reasons we're even having this discussion is because the plays, the characters, and the things they say are open to endless interpretation, to peoples and cultures around the world.

A few years ago I met the late and great comic actor Ken Campbell. He also thought that there were bits of Shakespeare that were so impenetrable as to be unperformable. I challenged him live on radio to pick any piece of Shakespeare, and claimed I would not only perform it a few days later to a full house at the reconstructed Shakespeare's Globe, but that it would present the audience there with no comprehension problems. He agreed to pay me £50 if the audience response showed I'd done it.

He picked Touchstone's lawyers speech, towards the end of *As You Like It* (Penguin text):

> I did dislike the cut of a certain courtier's beard. He sent me word, if I said his beard was not cut well, he was in the mind it was: this is called the Retort Courteous. If I sent him word again it was not well cut, he would send me word he cut it to please himself: this is called the Quip Modest. If again ' it was not well cut,' he disabled my judgement: this is called the Reply Churlish. If again ' it was not well cut,' he would answer, I spake not true: this is called the Reproof Valiant. If again ' it was not well cut,' he would say, I lie: this is called the Countercheck Quarrelsome: and so to the Lie Circumstantial and the Lie Direct.

Certainly not the easiest speech for any modern actor to tackle - but then, where did this idea come from, that Shakespeare, one of the greatest dramatists, who often deals with incredibly complex ideas, should be easy? It *should* be hard work. It *was* hard work. But it was hard work for *me*, to find a way to speak Touchstone's speech and make it clear to the audience, to make it accessible without dumbing it down. (I got my £50.)

Dumbing down is a problem. It's all too easy to add lewd or inappropriate visual jokes, as many modern productions of Shakespeare do, in lieu of working hard to make sense of what is actually being said. An alternative, of course, is to forget all that, and celebrity-cast the lead parts: then the audience won't give two hoots about the production they're watching, as they're more excited to see Captain Picard (Sir Patrick Stewart), Gandalf (Sir Ian McKellen) or Jude Law a few metres from them (all a producer's joy, as doubtless the show will sell out). How hard do we need to work as theatre practitioners, if a full house is pretty much guaranteed, and the lead could just as well be reading the phone book?

The theatrical profession needs to work harder at Shakespeare. We need to stop thinking his plays are easy to bring to a modern audience, or that we should make them easier. Modern audiences must learn to work a little bit, not expecting everything will be handed to them on a silver platter in bite-size pieces. If easy-to-swallow drama is looked for, watch a soap-opera. If challenging, powerful and intelligent drama is sought, come to Shakespeare - and the way *he* wrote it.

The modern Shakespearean actor's objective is to take as much of this work off the audience's shoulders as possible.

back, a scientist in Liverpool discovered that, when you read Shakespeare, the extra work that the poetry and the unfamiliar words require makes part of the temporal lobe of your brain light up. Taking the time to work at Shakespeare, evidently, makes you smarter.

Scanning Shakespeare: The Epic Caesura

David has been a voice teacher since 1977. In 1986, he became director of the Voice Studies course at Central School of Speech and Drama, and during his tenure trained over 200 voice teachers. He has been a Senior Voice Tutor at the Royal Academy of Dramatic Art (2003-2010). He is currently a Resident Voice and Text Director with the Oregon Shakespeare Festival. In 2007, David was awarded a National Teaching Fellowship by the UK Higher Education Academy. David and Rebecca Clark Carey have published two books: "Vocal Arts Workbook and DVD" (2008) and "The Verbal Arts Workbook" (2010).

In our new book, *The Verbal Arts Workbook* (Methuen Drama, 2010), Rebecca Clark Carey and I briefly touch on the metrical phenomenon known as the epic (or feminine) caesura. It wasn't our goal for the book to deal in depth with all the variations of iambic pentameter found in Shakespeare, but I became so intrigued by this particular irregularity that I decided to investigate further. For the uninitiated, the Latin term "*caesura*" literally means "a cutting" and in classical poetry it refers to "a break caused by ending a word within a metrical foot" (McArthur, 1992, 173), usually indicated in the scansion by //. In English poetry, however, it refers to a pause or sense-shift in the middle of a line, with one of the most famous and memorable examples being Hamlet's "To be, or not to be, // that is the question..."

It is possible to distinguish between two main types of caesura: i) the masculine caesura, which is a pause or sense-shift following a stressed syllable, for which Hamlet's line would be a good example; and ii) the feminine caesura, which is a pause or sense-shift following an unstressed syllable. Although the American scholar, George T. Wright (1988, 25), seems to use the terms feminine caesura and

epic caesura interchangeably, some writers sub-divide the feminine caesura into two further categories: i) the lyric caesura, which is "a feminine caesura that follows an unstressed syllable normally required by the metre"; and ii) the epic caesura, "a feminine caesura that follows an "*extra*" unstressed syllable..." (*Encyclopaedia Britannica*, my emphasis). An example of the former can be seen in these lines of Hamlet from the same soliloquy:

> The heartache and the thousand natural shocks
> That flesh is heir to. // 'Tis a consummation...

An example of an epic caesura from the same speech is:

> Or to take arms against a sea of troubles
> And by opposing end them: // to die, to sleep...

The epic caesura is like a hiccup in the flow of the pentameter, an extra syllable that disturbs the pattern. As Samuel Beckett's character, Balacqua, in *Dream of Fair to Middling Women* says: "I have a strong weakness for the epic caesura.... I like to compare it...to the heart of the metre missing a beat..." (Brater 1994, 144).

George T. Wright gives full consideration to the epic caesura in his book, *Shakespeare's Metrical Art*. He says that the epic caesura "may feel like a feminine ending of the first half-line" (1988, 29) and points out that the additional syllable "often seems a mere extension of the previous stressed one" (1988, 25). He goes on to observe that "the pattern usually invites a pause before the second half-line resumes a more regular meter" (1988, 25). According to Wright, over 1600 lines of Shakespeare's dramatic verse contain an epic caesura, while none of the poems do. And, while it occurs in every Shakespeare play, it is most frequently found in the plays of Shakespeare's more mature period from *The Merchant of Venice* onward, particularly in shared lines of verse where "the extra syllable either allows the line's first segment to draw to an off-beat finish or insures a longer-than-usual pause at the midline, or both" (1988, 166). He notes (1988, 167) that the epic caesura can occur earlier or later in the line than we might expect, and can even occur twice in the same line. In all, he says, "[t]he increasing use of epic caesuras helps Shakespeare's later dramatic verse secure special effects of variety and tension and an extraordinarily dense poetic texture" (1988, 167).

The epic caesura is thus one of the common metrical irregularities which Shakespeare uses to heighten the dramatic effect of his verse. As Wright says, the extra syllable of the epic caesura "is almost always followed by punctuation, and the resumption after the implied pause seems like a new beginning, often restrained, hesitant or deliberate.... [Sometimes] the extra syllable seems to provoke as well as to express increased agitation. In all cases, the line with such an extra syllable changes the procedures a little, ruffles the current, modifies the pattern" (1988, 165-166). He also notes that such metrical deviations were a means of making dramatic verse "sound like speech as well as like verse" (1988, 281). Shakespeare chose a type of versification for his plays "whose departures from pattern can better convey the unpredictable vitality of human beings talking to one another in English" (1988, 282). For Wright, such departures from pattern are the very essence of character.

To explore this notion further, I've selected a few examples from *Macbeth* and *King Lear*. First, there's this moment in *Macbeth*, Act I Scene 4:

DUNCAN:
> Sons, kinsmen, thanes,
> And you whose places are the nearest, know
> We will establish our estate upon
> Our eldest, Malcolm, whom we name hereafter
> The Prince of Cumberland: which honour must
> Not unaccompanied invest him only,
> But signs of nobleness, like stars, shall shine
> On all deservers. // From hence to Inverness,
> And bind us further to you.

Although there are other caesuras within this speech, it is the marked epic caesura which creates a change of focus and tone: Duncan changes from a formal proclamation addressing the assembly of thanes to a more informal directive addressing Macbeth, whose castle is at Inverness. Dramatically, in this speech Duncan provides Macbeth with both a motive to kill him–naming Malcolm as his heir–and the means to do it–placing himself in Macbeth's trust. The epic caesura acts as a turning point in the plot.

In the following scene (Act I Sc 5), Shakespeare gives Lady Macbeth two epic caesuras in the same speech:

LADY MACBETH:
> Glamis thou art, and Cawdor, and shalt be
> What thou art promised: // yet do I fear thy nature,
> It is too full o'th'milk of human kindness,
> To catch the nearest way. Thou would'st be great,
> Art not without ambition, but without
> The illness should attend it. // What thou would'st highly,
> That would'st thou holily; would'st not play false,
> And yet would'st wrongly win.

Again, there are other caesuras within the speech, but the first epic caesura clearly marks a shift from Lady Macbeth's excitement at the news of the witches' prophecy to a more anxious consideration of Macbeth's shortcomings. The dramatic shift at the second epic caesura is open to interpretation, but suggests to me a sudden deepening of insight into

Macbeth's nature on the part of Lady Macbeth: an insight which produces a double antithesis in the following lines. It certainly provides the actress with psychological material for exploration.

A key moment at the beginning of *King Lear* (Act I Sc 1) is occasion for another epic caesura:

KING LEAR:
> Meantime we shall express our darker purpose.
> Give me the map there. Know that we have divided
> In three our kingdom: // and 'tis our fast intent
> To shake all cares and business from our age,
> Conferring them on younger strengths, while we
> Unburthened crawl toward death.

To adapt Wright's words above, Lear is changing the procedures a little, ruffling the current, and modifying the pattern by his decision to divide up his kingdom, and it seems very apt to mark this with an epic caesura. And there is a deliberateness to Lear's language following the caesura, perhaps in response to some unscripted reaction on behalf of the court at the announcement which the extended pause of the epic caesura might provide for.

Finally, here is Edmund in Act I Sc 2, expatiating on bastardy:

EDMUND:
> Thou, Nature, art my goddess, to thy law
> My services are bound. Wherefore should I
> Stand in the plague of custom, and permit
> The curiosity of nations to deprive me?
> For that I am some twelve or fourteen moonshines
> Lag of a brother? // Why bastard? Wherefore base?
> When my dimensions are as well compact,
> My mind as generous, and my shape as true
> As honest madam's issue? // Why brand they us
> With base? With baseness bastardy? Base, base?

Shakespeare seems to be trying to capture the anger and anguish, envy and jealousy of the illegitimate human being in all his vitality. He achieves this through a powerful compound of questions, repetitions and metrical irregularities. Each of the epic caesuras seems to occur at a moment when the emotional heat is intensified, leading to the increased agitation that Wright refers to. Before the first epic caesura, Edmund only hints at his illegitimacy; after it, he uses the word "bastard" for the first time. Before the second epic caesura, Edmund sounds reasonably rational; after it, he becomes almost incoherent. In this we begin to see the essence of his character: unlike Macbeth, Edmund does not lack the illness that attends ambition.

Rebecca Clark Carey and I have both found in our teaching that when students are first learning to scan the iambic pentameter in Shakespeare's dramatic verse they can easily tie themselves in knots if they are unaware of the epic caesura and will try to resolve the irregularities it produces by looking for hexameters or trying to elide syllables. It is my hope that this short article has demonstrated how common the epic caesura is in Shakespeare's plays and how beneficial to an actor's process an awareness of it can be.

Bibliography

Brater, Enoch, *The Drama in the Text: Beckett's Late Fiction*, New York: Oxford University Press, 1994.

McArthur, Tom (editor), *The Oxford Companion to the English Language*, Oxford: Oxford University Press, 1992.

Wright, George T., *Shakespeare's Metrical Art*, Berkeley: University of California Press, 1988.

Encyclopædia Britannica Online, s.v. "epic caesura.", http://www.britannica.com/EBchecked/topic/189668/epic-caesura (accessed 06 Sep. 2010).

Essay *by Erika Bailey*
Classical Rhetoric and Heightened Text: Creating an Introductory Class for Actors

Erika Bailey teaches vocal production, text, speech, and dialects for the MFA program at University of Missouri, Kansas City. Among her projects as a dialect coach, Professor Bailey has coached *Syringa Tree, To Kill a Mockingbird,* **and** *Bus Stop* **with Kansas City Repertory Theatre, and** *A Christmas Carol* **with Princeton, New Jersey's McCarter Theatre. Professor Bailey also served as dialect coach on the Broadway production of** *Mary Stuart.* **She received a BA in Theatre from Williams College, and an MA in Voice Studies from Central School of Speech and Drama. She is an Associate Teacher of Fitzmaurice Voicework®.**

Introduction

Heightened text proves a stumbling block for many actors. Since Greek and Roman times, the discipline of rhetoric has provided a method of understanding the structure of language, both heightened and prosaic, and of speaking it persuasively. At VASTA's 2007 conference, I attended Rebekah Maggor's excellent presentation on rhetoric and oratory within the Harvard Curriculum, "Teaching Speaking in a Pluralistic Society: Oral Communication in the Harvard College Curriculum," (Maggor 2007) and was inspired to explore the subject of rhetoric further. I teach voice, text and dialects in the MFA Acting program at the University of Missouri-Kansas City. Some of my most talented students struggle with speaking complex text. They can be emotionally connected to the story and pursuing strong actions, and yet the details of the text fall flat. Rhetoric had proved useful to speakers and actors in the past, what were the specific concepts in the field that my students would find beneficial and how could I introduce them effectively? Using the discipline of rhetoric and oratory, how could I shape a class that would challenge my students to speak the words of Shakespeare, Moliere, Shaw, Stoppard, and

McDonagh with more passion, clarity and nuance? Rhetoric is the art of persuasion. Aristotle, one of the first great thinkers on rhetoric, defined it as "the faculty of discovering all the available means of persuasion in any given situation." (Corbett and Connors, 1) The use of rhetoric and the variety of rhetoric chosen by the speaker or writer must meet the needs of the situation, the context in which the persuasion occurs. In an interview for the Harvard Writing Center (Zarefsky 2010), David Zarefsky, a Visiting Professor at Harvard and an expert in presidential rhetoric, describes what is fundamental to rhetoric as "the relationship between a message, a text, a discourse, and audiences who understand it, respond to it, create it." This active and practical definition of rhetoric, involving a speaker, a listener, text and clear awareness of circumstance, felt rich with possibilities for use in an acting training context.

In the vast field of rhetoric that includes everything from composition manuals to literary criticism to political analysis, I discovered several books and articles that addressed the subject in a practical way for actors. Jacqueline Martin's *Voice in Modern Theatre* describes the history of rhetoric and its influence on styles of speaking within the theatre. She encourages an examination of the history of rhetoric, asserting that in order

> to examine the principles which have guided the way actors have spoken on stage from the time of ancient Greece to the nineteenth century, one must first look closely at rhetoric. This is a practical art based on concrete advice and rules together with a general theory about what really happens in the process of speech and how people react generally to different means of expression, intellectually, aesthetically and emotionally. (Martin 1991, 1)

Sister Miriam Joseph's *Shakespeare's Use of the Arts of Language* takes a detailed look at Shakespeare's application of the structures and devices of classical rhetoric. In this work she asserts that a knowledge of the 'language arts', which includes rhetoric as well as logic and grammar, is necessary to appreciate the detail and mastery of Shakespeare's use of language. And Ellen O'Brien's *Voice and Speech Review* article "Re-empowering Rhetoric: Performing Language-driven Plays in a Language-deaf Culture" examines methods to help actors activate the rhetorical structures of Shakespeare's text. O'Brien states that often for contemporary actors "the rhetorical potential—for shaping and sharing thought, proving a point, persuading at an intellectual as well as an emotional level—lies dormant."(O'Brien, 105) According to these authors, an understanding of rhetoric will enrich an appreciation of the artistry of heightened dramatic literature and challenge actors performing in these plays to activate the language more dynamically.

Heightened Text and Verse
Classical Rhetoric and Heightened Text: Creating an Introductory Class for Actors by Erika Bailey

A Brief History of Rhetoric

Taking inspiration from these authors, I studied the history of rhetoric in order to gain a clearer sense of the overall concepts addressed in the field and to see how they might be effectively introduced to contemporary acting students. Rhetoric as an organized school of thought began in the first half of the 5th Century BC in Sicily. The story goes that after a cruel tyrant, Thrasybulus, was overthrown, and "a form of democracy established, the newly enfranchised citizens flooded the courts with litigations to recover property that had been confiscated during the reign of the despot."(Corbett and Connors, 490) History credits Corax with having created a system whereby any citizen could persuasively argue his case for his property in court.

Corax was followed by a long line of Greek and Roman orators and philosophers who put together written manuals and created schools to train men in the art of rhetoric, the art of persuasion. Some of the most famous Greek and Roman thinkers on rhetoric were Isocrates, Aristotle, Plato, Cicero and Quintilian. Their philosophies and training systems grew and developed, becoming integral to organized education. "By the middle of the fourth century BC rhetoric had become the central discipline in Greek education, affecting 'all public utterances' and indeed all intellectual activity."(Vickers, 11) Rhetoric continued to be central to the educational system from Plato through the Romantics. (Vickers, 12)

Major Tenets of Classic Rhetoric

Classical rhetoric contains five major subjects or canons:
- Invention
- Arrangement
- Style
- Memory
- Delivery

Invention is "concerned with a system or method for finding arguments"(Corbett and Connors, 17) that would support an individual's chosen cause. Aristotle divided the types of arguments a speaker could use into three groups, those arguments based on logic (*logos*), those based on emotion (*pathos*) and those that set out to prove the character of the speaker, (*ethos*). A good oration could use all three or remain purely in one category.

Arrangement provides tools to effectively and persuasively organize the ideas discovered in *invention*. Traditionally, an oration is organized into six parts: 1) Introduction (*exordium*) 2) Statement of Facts (*narratio*) 3) Outline of the points or steps in the argument (*divisio*) 4) Proof of the case (*confirmatio*), 5) Refutation of opposing opinions (*refutatio*), and 6) Conclusion (*peroratio*).(Corbett and Connors, 20)

The study of *style* looks at the kind of communication being used: is it straightforward, elevated, poetic, and does that *style* serve the goal of the oration? *Style* encompasses word choice, the arrangement of words in phrases, rhythmic patterns of words, the sounds of phrases in terms of vowel and consonant use, and the use of rhetorical figures and tropes. (Corbett and Connors, 21)

The fourth canon, *memory*, explores mnemonic devices to aid in the memorization of speeches. It also covers researching material to support the main point of the speech through appropriate quotations and improvisatory speech. (Silva Rhetoricae, 2007)

Delivery covered the management of voice and gesture.

> Precepts were laid down about the modulation of the voice for the proper pitch, volume and emphasis and about pausing and phrasing. In regard to action, orators were trained in gesturing, in the proper stance and posture of the body, and in the management of the eyes and of facial expressions. (Corbett and Connors, 22)

Delivery and *memory* are the least discussed of the canons in written texts on rhetoric though they were an integral part of the practical education of an orator, practiced through exercises and declamations. (Silva Rhetoricae, 2007)

The manner in which students of rhetoric studied these five canons also proved interesting. Beginning with rhetorical analysis, students followed a three-step process. First, students analyzed exemplary texts and orations for their use of grammar, logic and rhetoric.

> A passage would be analyzed logically for its arguments or topics of invention …some analyses would be of a purely rhetorical character, including the identification of tropes and figures, as well as other rhetorical dimensions such as the arrangement of the entire discourse, or matters of rhythm and style. (Silva Rhetoricae, 2007)

Following this analysis, students would begin exercises in imitation. "Imitative exercises consisted either of copying some type of form within the original, but supplying new content; or, of copying the content of the original, but supplying a new form." (Silva Rhetoricae, 2007) In the final stage of training in a rhetorical education, students would write and present their own orations in their own style, having, ideally, absorbed all the lessons on effective invention, arrangement, style, memory and delivery that had been exemplified in the works they had studied and orators they had observed.

Core Concepts

From this history, several concepts appeared particularly helpful to focus on when introducing acting students to classical rhetoric:

- An understanding of the larger structure of speeches: the introduction, the statement of facts, the outline of the argument, the proof, the refutation and the conclusion.
- An exploration of the argument in the piece in terms of *ethos*, *pathos* and *logos*.
- A recognition of the smaller rhetorical devices used in heightened text, such as various forms of repetition, antithesis, and metaphor, and how those support the argument. And most importantly,
- a focus on the *argument* of the speech or monologue, the idea of building a case through language.

The class would also employ traditional rhetorical pedagogy, a pedagogy that focused on imitation of style or structure.

Class Plan

While rhetorical skills can certainly be applied to an exploration of dramatic scenes, most of the texts referenced in rhetorical works are political or legal orations given by individuals. Because of this, political speeches seemed an excellent segue to applying rhetorical skills to dramatic text. Political speeches have clear persuasive goals and would give students practice in focusing on this mode of analysis. The students worked on two political speeches.

The whole class worked on the same first speech, Obama's inaugural address. (Obama, 2009) The assignment was to analyze the organization and style of the speech and then replicate Obama's speaking style. This challenged the students to listen carefully and match effective vocal patterns that were distinct from their own speaking habits. It also gave them an opportunity to motivate vocal shifts that would bring rhetorical devices alive, as Obama does so smoothly.

Students chose their own speeches for the next project. I asked them to choose speeches that interested them and were written before 1960. As John McWhorter writes in his compelling book *Doing Our Own Thing: The Degradation of Language and Music and Why We Should, Like, Care*, "It is in the 1960s that the space for high language starts wasting away."(McWhorter, xx) As a result, language in public speeches before 1960 was likely to be more complexly structured and benefit from rhetorical analysis.

The outline of class work for the six weeks was as follows:

Week 1	• Introduction to Rhetoric • Recording of initial monologues
Week 2	• Vocal variety - Delivery • Ethos, pathos, logos - Invention
Week 3	• Larger organization of speeches - Arrangement
Week 4	• Obama speech
Week 5	• Student-chosen speeches
Week 6	• Final presentation of political speeches • Final recordings of monologues

Four of the five canons would be explored in this plan. Students were not required to memorize any material and as a result we neglected this canon. Under *delivery* we focused on vocal variety as, in this course, flexibility of expression was valued above a particular style of presentation. Under the canon of *invention*, the class analyzed works in terms of *ethos*, *pathos* and *logos*. For *arrangement* we examined the larger structure of the speeches we worked on and under *style* we explored the variety of rhetorical devices used within speeches.

Plans for Assessment

Assessment needed to occur on two levels: had the spoken language skills of the students improved and had the structure of the class and the material used proved useful and effective? We used political speeches for the major assignments, but the goal of the unit was to improve the students' ability to speak heightened dramatic language, so it was necessary to use dramatic texts and not political speeches for the final assessment. For this assessment, students recorded two monologues before class work began and then the same two monologues at the end of our work on rhetoric. They were assigned a Shakespeare monologue, Antony's 'friends, Romans, countrymen' speech from *Julius Caesar*, and a modern piece of text, the coin-tossing monologue from Stoppard's *Rosencrantz and Guildenstern are Dead*. These two monologues employ complex rhetoric and could benefit greatly from a focus on argument and an understanding of rhetorical structures. Students received no faculty coaching on these monologues in between the two recordings, which would hopefully reveal what skills they were processing without direct intervention.

Heightened Text and Verse

Classical Rhetoric and Heightened Text: Creating an Introductory Class for Actors by Erika Bailey

The rubric below illustrates the specific skills I wanted the students to strengthen.

RHETORIC RUBRIC			
SKILLS	EXCELLENT	GOOD	EMERGING
Persuasiveness/Strength of Argument	Student has demonstrated a clear point of view and attempted to persuade the audience of their argument through a variety of tactics.	Student's point of view is not consistently clear. Student works to persuade but without a variety of tactics.	No clear or consistent point of view. Student does not actively work to persuade audience.
Audible Structure of the Piece	Larger structure of the piece made clear.	Some of the larger structure of the piece is audible but not consistently clear.	Structure of the piece is not audible
Audible Structure of the Thoughts	Operatives, antitheses, parentheticals, parallelism, and other rhetorical devices made clear through a use of vocal variety.	Student is aware of the rhetorical devices but not activating them clearly.	Student runs through rhetorical devices without awareness.
Vocal Variety	Variety in pitch, volume, pacing, rhythm and resonance used throughout.	Student uses vocal variety but not consistently, and not always in service of the text.	Very little vocal variety is used.
Power with Ease	Student was able to achieve vocal power when necessary without physical strain or pushing. Student used breath to support his/her thoughts and maintained an appropriate and intelligible speaking pace.	Student understood when the text called for vocal power but achieved it without breath support. Student rushed or maintained a slow pace too often, leading to moments where it was difficult for the audience to follow the argument of the text.	Student's choice to use volume or speed not motivated by text and not supported by breath. Many moments where argument of the text was unclear.

I used this rubric to guide my teaching but it later proved useful in assessing the students' improvement, as well. The basis of this rubric was created prior to the beginning of class, and while the class discussed all of the concepts included in it, I did not share it with them in this form. This was a lost opportunity. Had I handed out copies of the rubric at the beginning of class we could have used it as a basis for class discussion and self-assessment.

As another tool for assessment, the students wrote feedback at the end of the class, responding to the following questions:
1) What skills have been explored in class during this unit on rhetoric?
2) Do you feel these are useful skills for an actor to learn?
3) Do you feel your ability to use these skill has improved over the course of the unit? If so, which skills in particular do you feel you have greater mastery over?
4) Which assignments or exercises did you find particularly useful?
5) Which assignments or exercises did you not find useful?

Responses to these questionnaires and analysis of the two sets of recordings would allow for assessment of student improvement and of the strengths and weaknesses of the class plan.

Students

There were seven students in this second-year voice class, four men and three women. As a group they had varied performance backgrounds, from musical theatre to oral interpretation. Three of the students were already very comfortable speaking and analyzing complex text and the other four had varying levels of confidence in speaking plays written in heightened language.

Vocal Variety

After introducing the idea of rhetoric and recording students' initial monologues, class work began in earnest with exercises to expand vocal variety. Speakers can bring the structure of language alive as a persuasive tool more easily with a voice practiced in nuanced vocal variety. Increasing the students' abilities to use vocal variety was, therefore, integral to our study of rhetoric.

In my rubric I defined vocal variety as "variety in pitch, volume, pacing, rhythm and resonance." In class warm-ups we played with all of these concepts, extending pitch and volume range as we released sound, and experimenting with rhythm and pacing shifts while speaking tongue twisters or articulation drills. As we started to apply vocal variety to text, I asked the students to work with playfulness and curiosity in speaking poems and short quotations from speeches. As a result, students were breaking from habitual speaking habits in entertaining ways, but the sense of the texts became muddy.

When I asked them to link the use of vocal variety to operative words and rhetorical devices, a playful use of sound began to support the meaning of the text. It was clear, however, that my students had a very narrow range of vocal variety, particularly pitch variety, that they could use and still feel that they sounded 'truthful'. I looked for authors whose writing invited the use of vocal variety.

Dickens' language provides great material for playing with vocal variety and connecting it to complex structure. In class we explored the sentence structure of the first paragraph from *Bleak House*. Here is a section of that first paragraph:

> London. Michaelmas term lately over, and the Lord Chancellor sitting in Lincoln's Inn Hall. Implacable November weather. As much mud in the streets as if the waters had but newly retired from the face of the earth, and it would not be wonderful to meet a Megalosaurus, forty feet long or so, waddling like an elephantine lizard up Holborn Hill. Smoke lowering down from chimney-pots, making a soft black drizzle, with flakes of soot in it as big as full-grown snowflakes--gone into mourning, one might imagine, for the death of the sun. (Dickens, 1)

At each punctuation mark a new student spoke. After the first phrase, they had to decide if their section was subordinate to a previous section and if it was they touched the person who spoke the independent clause. So the person who spoke "forty feet long or so," and the person who

spoke "waddling like an elephantine lizard up Holborn Hill" were both touching the person who spoke "and it would not be wonderful to meet a Megalosaurus." This process started over at every period. This gave the class a physical experience of the structure of the sentences. Hearing different voices speaking different phrases helped to wake their ears up to the possibilities for vocal shifts at these transitions. It also highlighted the shifting rhythms from short, sharp thoughts, to long, winding thoughts. At the end when we had created our physical chain of each sentence, each student spoke the entirety of the paragraph.

Rhetorical Devices Project

As we began to look at speeches, the students researched rhetorical devices. Miriam Joseph states that there are anywhere from 90 to 180 rhetorical tropes and figures. The devices cover everything from grammatical structure (*asyndeton* – lack of conjunctions between words or phrases) (Lanham, 182), to stylistic tone (*irony* – implying a meaning opposite to the literal meaning)(Lanham, 92), to techniques of argument (*enthymeme* - an abridged syllogism in logic) (Lanham, 65). The twenty-three assigned devices were ones that could be particularly useful for the students to understand as they tried to build language toward an argument. Through an exploration of rhetorical devices, the students would hopefully learn to see heightened language as having patterns and structures that could be used as tools towards winning arguments or moving audiences. Each student needed to research three terms. The assignment ran as follows:

> For each device, please come in with a definition (look in more than one place), an example from literature or a speech, and an example you've written. Two good sources are:
>
> http://www.americanrhetoric.com/
> http://humanities.byu.edu/rhetoric/Silva.htm
>
> If your word comes up in the list on American Rhetoric you will have the opportunity to listen to several examples of the use of the device spoken aloud. From listening to these, what are some tools we can use to make these devices come alive when speaking aloud? Is there anything you can generalize about rhythm, volume, pauses, pitch?

Alliteration	Enthymeme	Parallelism
Anadiplosis	Epanalepsis	Parenthesis
Anaphora	Epimone	Polysyndeton
Antithesis	Epiplexis	Rhetorical Question
Aposiopesis	Epistrophe	Syncrisis
Apostrophe	Climax	Syllogism
Asyndeton	Irony	Symploce
Assonance	Onomatopeia	

Heightened Text and Verse

Classical Rhetoric and Heightened Text: Creating an Introductory Class for Actors by Erika Bailey

Each student presented the definitions and examples of their three terms to the class. These were then combined into a class rhetorical dictionary that provided a resource in analyzing the political speeches the class took on next.

Student feedback provided a good suggestion for improving the effectiveness of this exercise. Four of the seven students listed learning rhetorical devices and applying them to their monologues as among the most useful exercises introduced over the course. Two of the students, however, felt that dividing up the responsibility for researching definitions left them without a solid understanding. "Breaking up the various types of rhetorical devices made me a little more confused because I felt that I was not totally understanding the information people were giving me. It's not that they didn't know, I just felt I'd have a better understanding if I had looked them up myself," wrote student C. In future it might be more beneficial to spread this assignment out over several classes and have everyone research each of the devices. This would solidify the students' understanding of the terms and create more dynamic discussions of meanings and examples.

First Speech Project

With definitions of rhetorical devices in hand, the class began work on Obama's inauguration speech. In a three-minute section of the speech, the students were asked to listen carefully for Obama's use of vocal variety, to note where he paused, where his pitch changed, or tempo sped up, and to consider the effect of these vocal shifts. They would then present their imitation of Obama's speech to the class. They were also required to go through the text and mark it for rhetorical devices and to find the introduction, statement of fact, outline, proof, refutation and conclusion of the speech as a whole.

As we listened to Obama's speech phrase by phrase, we came to the realization that though Obama uses rhythm and volume with great nuance and dexterity, his pitch range does not travel far. This was neither a good thing nor a bad thing but something we noted and the students worked to emulate.

What I also wanted them to emulate, and which they did with less success, was Obama's easy but energized speaking. He does not push or strain to speak powerfully to large groups of people. In class I worked to help everyone in the group adopt that level of speaking energy. This was a great reference point when asking the students to achieve vocal power with ease in their next project.

The students responded to the Obama assignment enthusiastically. Five of the seven students listed it as an exercise that was particularly useful. The fact that everyone in the

group was listening to the same speech helped the class members to comment constructively on each other's work. Student C wrote that, "Listening to the Obama speech and having to mimic certain inflections was invaluable. I really turned on my ear to that and was able to pick out specific moments and understand why he inflected or drove through the way he did." This response confirmed my sense that the students were not only noting and emulating Obama's technical vocal shifts, but were understanding the effect of those shifts. They were sensing that certain pauses caused the listeners to move forward in their seats or that an increase in tempo heightened the excitement of the audience. With this knowledge, an increase in technical vocal variety could be filled with persuasive action and avoid becoming vocal decoration.

Second Speech Project

For the second project each member of the class chose their own speech. My hope was that allowing the students free choice in this assignment (with the proviso that the speech had to be written prior to 1960) would allow them to pick speeches that inspired them, thus helping motivate the action behind the rhetorical structures. As a class, we had practiced finding the larger structures in speeches by Martin Luther King, Jr., John F. Kennedy and Hillary Clinton and we applied these findings to their individual speeches. It was necessary to edit the speeches down to five minutes or less to give us time to work carefully through the text and this complicated the overall structural analysis and the students' ability to activate the structure they found. Within their speeches, I also asked each student to name what they were arguing for and to examine whether they were using *pathos*, *ethos*, *logos* or a combination of these to win that argument. Each student worked through the speech in class twice with an individual tutorial with me between the two readings.

In my tutorials with students, I stressed the relationship between speaker and audience as key to the rhetorical style of the piece. One student working on a 1916 anti-war speech by Carrie Chapman Catt had trouble accessing the rallying cry inherent in the text. I pushed her to infuse more *pathos* into the speech. Another student was working on one of FDR's fireside chats; his tendency was to make the speech big and heroic, and we worked to find more vocal intimacy and the argument that he was to be trusted, the *ethos*, to make this gentler radio style work.

Certainly students were learning to fit the vocal style of the piece to the context in which it was given, but it was difficult, given time constraints, to explore the overall structure of the edited texts the students had chosen or the details of rhetorical devices within the speeches. The students as a group had trouble remaining engaged during this project. "Although I loved my speech, I had trouble giving much insight into my fellow classmates' speeches. I had trouble understanding their speeches as they were from such a wide time period and spanned such a variety of topics," Student G wrote in his final feedback for the course. Clearly, more time would have been helpful in exploring this project further. Perhaps, also, assigning students specific speeches rather than letting them choose for themselves would have given me the ability to analyze the piece carefully before students worked on it and thus shape my coaching more specifically to bring out the rhetorical elements of the project beyond the speaker/audience relationship.

Assessing the Students

The students recorded the second round of *Julius Caesar and Rosencrantz and Guildenstern are Dead* monologues after finishing the political speeches. While they did not receive coaching from me on these texts, they did work in pairs to coach each other using the concepts they had been working on in the previous weeks: persuasiveness and clarity of argument, clear use of the larger structures of the text and the smaller structures of the rhetorical devices, vocal variety, and vocal power with ease. Here is the text of both monologues with several of the rhetorical devices annotated:

Rosencrantz and Guildenstern are Dead
Tom Stoppard

Guildenstern:
The scientific approach to the examination of phenomena is a defense against the pure emotion of fear[i]. Keep tight hold and continue while there's time. Now —counter to the previous syllogism: tricky one, follow me carefully, it may prove a comfort. If we postulate, *and we just have*[ii], that within *un-, sub- or supernatural*[iii] forces the probability is that the law of probability will not operate as a factor, then we must accept that the probability of the first part will not operate as a factor, *in which case the law of probability will operate as a factor within un-, sub- or supernatural forces*[iv]. And since it obviously hasn't been doing so, we can take it that we are not held within un-, sub- or supernatural forces after all; in all probability, that is. Which is a great relief to me personally. Which is all very well, except that---we have been spinning coins together since I don't know when, and in all that time (if it is all that time) I don't suppose either of us was more than a couple of gold pieces up or down. I hope that doesn't sound surprising because its very unsurprisingness is something I am trying to keep hold of. The equanimity of your average tosser of coins *depends upon a law, or rather a tendency, or let us say a probability, or at any rate a mathematically calculable chance*[v], which ensures that he will not *upset himself by losing too much nor upset his opponent by winning too often*[vi]. This made for a kind of harmony and a kind of confidence. It related the fortuitous and the ordained into a reas-

suring union which we recognized as nature. The sun came up about as often as it went down, in the long run, and a coin showed heads about as often as it showed tails. *Then a messenger arrived.*[vii] We had been sent for. Nothing else happened. Ninety-two coins spun consecutively have come down heads ninety-two consecutive times. (Stoppard, 17)

i. Through its use of logic and argument, this monologue appears to use *logos* more than *pathos*. Yet it begins with a discussion of 'fear' and the pathos of the piece cannot be denied. The monologue can be seen as a struggle between the fear, *pathos*, and the defense against it, *logos*.
ii. *Parenthesis*: a word, phrase or sentence inserted as an aside in a sentence complete in itself. (Lanham, 108)
iii. *Parallelism*: similarity of structure in a pair or series of related words, phrases or clauses. (Silva Rhetoricae 2007)
iv. *Syllogism*: a deductive scheme of a formal argument consisting of a major and a minor premise and a conclusion. (www.merriam-webster.com)
v. *Polysyndeton*: employing many conjunctions. (Silva Rhetoricae 2007)
vi. *Syncrisis*: comparison and contrast in parallel clauses (Silva Rhetoricae 2007).
vii. Change in style from long complex thoughts to a short succinct statement. This shift in rhythm illustrates how the arrival of the messenger marks a shift in the rules of the universe. An ominous arrival.

And
Julius Caesar
William Shakespeare

ANTONY:
Friends, Romans, countrymen[viii], lend me your ears;[ix]
I come to bury Caesar, not to praise him.
The *evil that men do lives after them*;
The *good is oft interred with their bones*;[x]
So let it be with Caesar. The noble Brutus
Hath told you Caesar was ambitious:
If it were so, it was a grievous fault,
And grievously hath Caesar answer'd it.
Here, under leave of Brutus and the rest--
For *Brutus is an honourable man*;[xi]
So are they all, all honorable men--
Come I to speak in Caesar's funeral.
He was my friend, faithful and just to me:
But Brutus says he was ambitious;
And Brutus is an honorable man.[xii]
He hath brought many captives home to Rome
Whose ransoms did the general coffers fill:

Did this in Caesar seem ambitious?
When that the poor have cried, Caesar hath wept:
Ambition should be made of sterner stuff:
Yet Brutus says he was ambitious;
And Brutus is an honorable man.
You all did see that on the Lupercal
I thrice presented him a kingly crown,
Which he did thrice refuse: was this ambition?
Yet Brutus says he was ambitious;
And, sure, he is an honorable man.
I speak not to disprove what Brutus spoke,
But here I am to speak what I do know.
You all did love him once, not without cause:
What cause withholds you then, to mourn for him?
O *judgment*![xiii] thou art fled to brutish beasts,
And men have lost their reason. *Bear with me*;[xiv]
My heart is in the coffin there with Caesar,
And I must pause till it come back to me.
 (Shakespeare, William. 2010)

viii. Parallelism
ix. This appeal uses all three modes of persuasion, *ethos*, *pathos*, and *logos*. Logically impressing the audience with Caesar's character and ending with an emotional charge to mourn for him.
x. *Syncrisis* and *Antithesis*: juxtaposition of contrasting words or ideas. (Silva Rhetoricae 2007).
xi. *Epimone*: frequent repetition of phrase or question. (Lanham, 68)
xii. *Irony*: implying a meaning opposite to the literal meaning. The repetition of the phrase builds to a sense of irony. (Lanham, 92).
xiii. *Apostrophe*: when one turns speech from one audience to another, often turning to speak to an abstraction such as judgment. (Silva Rhetoricae 2007)
xiv. Possible *Aposiopesis*: breaking off suddenly in the middle of speaking, often due to emotion or the appearance of emotion. (Silva Rhetoricae 2007).

The group's performance on the second round of monologues was markedly better. Vocal energy and vocal variety both grew substantially from one recording to the next. In assessing the difference between each student's recordings, I listened carefully to how they dealt with the rhetorical devices annotated above and found that overall they used the devices more clearly in the second round. An awareness of the use of *ethos*, *pathos* and *logos* was also clearer. Ashlee LaPine, a lecturer in theatre in my department, reviewed the recordings. I gave her the final recordings first and after hearing the second set she had no doubt as to which was the final group. "The first batch was stronger. There was a lot more vocal variety and freedom. They were also more energetically involved in the text. And for the most part I felt a greater understanding of the text." (Ashlee LaPine, personal communication). To get a clearer sense of improvement, each recording was assessed against the class rubric. A numerical score was then added to each column. An 'emerging' level received a score of 1, work in the 'good' column scored a 2 and 'excellent' work landed a 3. With five areas being assessed a student could receive a score anywhere from 5 to 15. The scores ran as follows:

	First Round	Second Round
A	7	10
B	9.5	13
C	11	13
D	6.5	10.5
E	6.5	11
F	10	13
G	11	11

All but one of the students improved according to this method of assessment and that matched the first impression Ashlee LaPine and I had on listening to the recordings. Quantifying student improvement in this way is still a very rough method of analysis. To specify the analysis further and to ascertain how students were improving on the speaking of specific rhetorical devices, I chose two sentences from the Rosencrantz and Guildenstern monologue to focus on in detail.

If we postulate, *and we just have*, that within un-, sub- or supernatural forces the probability is that the law of probability will **not** operate as a factor, then we must accept that the probability of the first part will **not** operate as a factor, in which case the law of probability **will** operate as a factor within un-, sub- or supernatural forces. And since it obviously hasn't been doing so, we can take it that we are **not** held within un-, sub- or supernatural forces after all. (Stoppard, 17)

In listening to the students speak the short, italicized *parenthesis* at the beginning of the passage in their first and final recordings, I looked to see if the student had improved the clarity of their phrasing. Improvement could mean a change in tempo, pitch or volume to signify that 'and we just had,' was a less important phrase than the surrounding language. Several of the students made this clear in their first recording but all seven of them had strengthened the clarity of that aside by the second recording.

The complex logic and argument of this passage cannot be made clear without strong use of the four operative words that have been bolded in the passage above. Operative words are not included in lists of rhetorical devices. A clear use of operatives, however, will lead to a clear argument, and I was looking to see if the students were improving in their ability to activate the structure of language to make a clear argument. On each set of recordings I scored the students on a scale of 1-4 depending on how many of these key words they stressed. 'Stress' could come in any form of pitch or volume change. Pacing shifts seemed a less effective tool when lifting a single word.

Operative Use		
	First Round	Second Round
A	1	3
B	1	3
C	1	4
D	1	3
E	0	0
F	1	3
G	2	1

For five of the seven students, the use of these operatives became much clearer in the second round of monologues and this made Stoppard's bewildering argument understandable. The two students who did not increase their number of stressed operatives, stressed the verbs instead.

Student E, in particular, interested me. When scoring her against the rubric she had shown the greatest improvement of anyone in the class. Of all the students, she was the least confident of her abilities to handle heightened text. In her first recording of the monologues, she had pressed vocally and barreled through the text, missing new thoughts and rhetorical devices, and clearly struggling to understand the *Rosencrantz and Guildenstern* piece. In her second set of recordings, she found much more sense in the language and ease and support, which allowed her more nuance in using the rhetorical structures. Before listening for her use of these specific operatives, I assumed she was now using them on par with her classmates; this was not the case. This careful, word-by-word, analysis can therefore lead to a deeper understanding of student performance and comprehension. Unfortunately, this detailed listening hap-

pened after the class was over; it could have proved useful to have her listen to the recordings and hear where she was still missing key words. Her progress had been impressive despite her missed operatives; a specific example of where she still needed more specificity could have improved her use of language further and given her more confidence in her ability to speak heightened text.

In a final analysis of the change between the two sets of recordings, the majority of these students made clear gains in their ability to bring the structure of the heightened text alive as a persuasive tool. I have attempted to quantify this improvement in two ways, through scoring the rubric and through close listening to individual phrases. I want to continue refining these methods of assessment to make them more exact and useful. I realize that given the small number of students in the class and the lack of outside evaluators, the specific numbers are not statistically significant. There are other factors, as well, that could have positively impacted students' improvement; work in acting classes or rehearsals, increased familiarity with the recorded texts, for instance. Nonetheless, the results are encouraging. This class successfully introduced ideas from classical rhetoric that proved useful in activating heightened text.

Assessing the Class

Student feedback supported my confidence in the usefulness of the skills introduced in this unit. In answer to the question "do you feel these are useful skills for an actor to learn," all seven of the students responded positively. The next question provided a more complicated response. When asked "do you feel your ability to use these skills has improved over the course of the unit?" five of the seven wrote yes, their skills had improved. Of the two that didn't feel their skills had improved, Student D wrote, "The usage part is very vague to me. I believe awareness has grown greatly, but I don't know about how it has affected my sound." The student had gained useful tools for analyzing text through our unit on rhetoric but needed feedback that his new awareness was translating into an audible change in how he spoke complex language. I will need to go farther when I teach this class next, and ensure that students can hear themselves speaking the text with more nuance and clarity. If the second set of recordings had been made a class earlier, it would have allowed us all to listen to the first and second set together. The class could have listened to and discussed particular examples of improved use of heightened text or moments where students still struggled to make the text clear.

Along with using the recordings and the rubric as teaching tools, not solely as analytical tools, several other possible improvements to the course surfaced. In scoring the students against the rubric, I noted that none of the students had received an 'Excellent' in making the overall structure of the piece clear. When the whole class had difficulty with this concept, it was worth examining the way the idea was presented and how I asked the students to apply it. Not surprisingly, the classical rhetoric model of introduction, statement of facts, outline of argument, proof of argument, refutation, and conclusion had proved difficult to apply in a helpful way to speeches and monologues not necessarily written with this structure in mind. To make the task more difficult, the class used edited versions of the speeches, thus disrupting the original structure of the text. We had also spent more time looking at the structure of speeches on paper than discussing and practicing how to make the written structure translate into an audible experience of structure for the audience. Discovering the overall structure is a vital element to analyzing speeches and monologues but I need to create a way to make it more applicable. Suggesting a simpler structure of three, introduction, argument, conclusion, for instance, might make it a more useful tool, or allowing students to create their own vocabulary for structure could provoke fruitful discussion and experimentation.

Overall, the exercises that proved most elusive were ones that tackled larger sections of text: the final speech project lost focus and analyzing a speech for larger structures and making those structures audible was discussed in class but never fully realized. The exercises that proved most helpful in activating language were those where the whole group looked at spoken text in detail: creating vocal variety in Dickens' sentences, emulating Obama's rhythm and vocal energy, exploring the possibilities for activating rhetorical devices through defining the terms and listening to examples. In all of these assignments, the entire class was focused on one short piece of text. This allowed detailed work, with opportunities for students to listen and learn from their classmates' interpretations of text that they themselves were exploring, creating a rich learning environment.

Conclusion

This class took key concepts from classical rhetoric and applied them to analyzing and speaking political speeches with the goal of improving students' abilities to speak heightened text with clarity and commitment. We then looked to see if the skills practiced in the political speeches translated easily to the speaking of heightened dramatic text, and indeed they did. Through this process, the majority of my students demonstrated improved abilities to activate complex language. In teaching classical rhetoric to acting students, three things were particularly helpful: a playful attitude, close group-listening and the idea of the text as an argument to be proved. The playful attitude, established through the early exercises on vocal variety, helped the students explore language with curiosity and imagination. The

playfulness lessened the sense that there might be a 'right' way to speak an introduction or a *polysyndeton* and kept the focus on an exploration of what the clearest way to speak these structures might be. The close listening and speaking we employed as a group, looking phrase by phrase at text and speakers, proved particularly fruitful. Through it the class not only gained an understanding of the structure of text and the musicality of individual speakers, but increased their awareness of their own habitual phrasings and musicality. And, finally, keeping all the work tied to the argument of the speech or monologue gave the specific vocal shifts and modulations we were playing with a purpose. This kept the work from becoming purely technical and decorative and created a useful bridge to the idea of playing an action. These three concepts are central to the new rubric and syllabus I am developing as I prepare to teach the class again.

Through the process of creating and assessing this class, I hope to inspire other teachers of voice and text to re-explore classical rhetoric and discover ways to include the subject in their classes. The discipline of rhetoric has the potential to activate language in exciting ways and to awake in actors a passion to explore the building blocks of language and verbal argument. In a culture and, increasingly, a theatre dominated by visual communication and the truncated phrasings of text messages, we need to champion muscular language and complex verbal expression and to hone the skills needed to make heightened text thrillingly clear and persuasive.

Bibliography

Corbett, Edward, and Robert J. Connors. *Classical Rhetoric for the Modern Student.* New York: Oxford University Press, 1999.

Dickens, Charles. *Bleak House.* New York: University Society, 1908.

Joseph, Miriam. *Shakespeare's Use of the Arts of Language.* Philadelphia: Paul Dry Books, 2005.

Lanham, Richard A. *A Handlist of Rhetorical Terms.* Los Angeles: University of California Press, 1991.

Martin, Jacqueline. *Voice in Modern Theatre.* New York: Routledge, 1991.

Martin, Jacqueline. "Rhetoric Goes Full Circle: Voice Pedagogy in Sweden." *Voice and Speech Review* (2009): 281-285.

McWhorter, John. *Doing Our Own Thing: The Degradation of Language and Music and Why We Should, Like, Care.* New York: Gotham Books, 2003.

O'Brien, Ellen J. 2005 "Re-empowering Rhetoric: Performing Language-driven Plays in a Language-deaf Culture." *Voice and Speech Review* (2005): 100-111.

Stoppard, Tom. *Rosencrantz and Guildenstern are Dead.* New York: Grove Press, 1967.

Vickers, Brian. *In Defense of Rhetoric.* Oxford, UK: Oxford University Press, 1998.

Websites

American Rhetoric. 2010. http://www.americanrhetoric.com

Shakespeare, William. 2010. The Complete Works of William Shakespeare. http://shakespeare.mit.edu/julius_caesar/julius_caesar.3.2.html

Silva Rhetoricae.. http://humanities.byu.edu/rhetoric/Silva.htm, Last modified 2/26/2007

Essay *by Michael Cobb*
"Two-and-a-Half to Start": A Structural Device for Unlocking Shakespeare's Verse

Michael is currently in his sixth year as Head of Voice, Speech, and Text at the National Theatre Conservatory/ Resident Vocal Coach at Denver Center Theatre Company under Kent Thompson. He has served as coach under directors Mark Wing-Davey, Dominique Serrand, Robert Woodruff, and Martha Clarke, and has taught at the American Studio of the Moscow Art Theatre School, St. Lawrence University, SUNY Potsdam, and Rhode Island College. Michael holds an M.F.A. in Voice Pedagogy from the Institute for Advanced Theatre Training at Harvard, an M.A. in Theatre Studies from Brown University, and is a graduate of Trinity Rep Conservatory.

Some years ago, after I'd finally been given a thorough grounding in the nature and use of operative words, I found myself, both as a teacher/coach and performer, still seeking some sort of guide to help me make sure I neither under- nor over-identified operative words in a verse line or text. I found, and still do find, the technique of selecting operatives the way one might select words in a telegram, in which one has to pay for each (and therefore choose as efficiently and economically as possible) extremely useful. Perhaps as a result of my experience in those instances when I felt I really had succeeded at unlocking a text, it still often seemed, however, that I hadn't quite gotten as far as I might. Then, while preparing text for a rotating rep of two Elizabethan plays, Hamlet and Antonio's Revenge, I noticed a relatively common pattern in the number and degree of operative words occurring in each pentameter verse line—a pattern of two full operatives and one half operative, in varying order.

In what follows I will first, through referring to others' descriptions of what an operative word is (including what kinds of words are typically not operative), seek to approach a definition of the term "operative word" sufficient for this discussion. I will next describe this device I'm calling "Two-and-a-Half to Start" and then apply it to several iambic pentameter text selections, in order to demonstrate both its basic and more sophisticated possibilities in practice.

A definition (derived from an actor-training setting but to date unclaimed) which I find helpful as a place to begin describes an operative word as being "the word or words without which the phrase has no meaning; the word or words which make up a 'thing image' or an 'action image'; the skeleton of meaning of the phrase; the word or words which give enough information that the listener can guess the rest." Nancy Houfek has further honed the first element of this definition by adding that the operatives are "the essential word, or words, upon which an image phrase depends for its [i.e. particular] meaning." [italics mine] (Houfek and Delorey, 3) And Sabin Epstein assists in stating that operative words "carry the information of the text; they reveal action, meaning and intent." (Epstein, 1)

The kinds of words helpful to consider as one's last candidates to be operative are:
-Articles ("a", "the", "an", etc.), prepositions ("of", "to", "from", "on", "in", etc.), and conjunctions ("and", "but", etc.)
-Particularly in classical texts: negative words and prefixes ("not", "no", "un-", etc.) and pronouns ("she", "he", "it", etc.), including possessive pronouns ("my", "your", "her", "their", etc.)
-Verbs of being ("am", "are", "is", etc.)
-A repeated word or image. If something is repeated, look for the new information ("I went to the store on the corner. It was a <u>great</u> store.")

Also, any given modifier is probably going to be less operative than the thing it's modifying ("the <u>red</u> house") or held together with it as a single image ("the <u>red house</u>"). The important caveat in classing the above as less or least likely candidates to be operative is—in the absence of a construction that specifically and unavoidably calls for them to be so. The clearest response to the question "Which house?" would obviously be along the lines of "The <u>red house</u>"—the construction, common sense, and the implicit goal of clarity trumping the rule. Finally, good writing is constructed in a way that prompts us to stay with it, so when seeking operative word choices, always consider whether the writer might have put them towards the end of the verse line or thought unit (sentence, clause, phrase) in a way which will keep the listener engaged.

Hopefully, the foregoing can prove sufficient to support the topic at hand. One doesn't have to look far to find varying perspectives on operative words; e.g. some tend to favor verbs as full operatives to a greater/lesser degree than others. My hope is to communicate this Two-and-a-Half device clearly enough that, even where views on operatives differ significantly, anyone may be able to benefit from its application.

By "Two-and-a-half to Start" I mean, in a nutshell, that when designating operative words within a Shakespeare or other pentameter-based line, it is useful to start off looking for two and a half operatives per line. If two and a half operatives should not prove workable because of a construction either within or extending beyond the line, then try to fulfill the particular construction as economically as possible still seeing if you can use no more "operativeness" than would be in two and a half operatives.

So, borrowing and adapting the methodology used in Edith Skinner's *Speak With Distinction*, when scoring a pentameter-based text for operatives I use a double underline [══════] to denote a full operative, a single underline [─────] to denote a half operative, and an intermittent (I say "dotted" in teaching) underline to denote a quarter operative (represented here by a line with a single break [── ──]). Start by assuming that you'll find two and a half operatives per verse line, in any order. In the event that can't work, see whether, however you divide it up, you can still end up with the same amount of operativeness in each verse line (something adding up to five full underlines total, such as exists in two and a half [══════ + ══════ + ─────] = five). With relatively little practice, this approach can begin to feel like a game in efficiently and effectively unlocking meaning.

To begin this process of trying to find two and a half operatives per line, I've found it helpful to start by choosing the three candidate words in each line, marking each with a single underline, before going on to decide their degree of operativeness. Take Ophelia's Act II, scene 1 description of Hamlet's visit to her chamber. (I've provided one possible scansion for each of the following lines, as the relationship between meter and operative choices can be relevant and interesting)

˘ / ˘ / ˘ / ˘ / ˘ / ˘
Ophelia: My lord, as I was sewing in my closet,

˘ / ˘ / ˘ / ˘ / ˘ /
Lord Hamlet, with his doublet all unbraced;

/ ˘ ˘ / ˘ / / ˘ ˘ /
Pale as his shirt; his knees knocking each other;

˘ / ˘ / ˘ / ˘ ˘ / ˘ /
And with a look so piteous in purport

˘ / ˘ / ˘ / ˘ / ˘ /
As if he had been loosed out of hell

˘ / ˘ / ˘ / ˘ / ˘ / ˘
To speak of horrors, he comes before me.

The advantage in considering such a basic narrative at this point in the discussion derives from its freedom from any preceding context or construction ("Which house?"). Ophelia's simple goal here is to describe (and assumedly evoke) Hamlet's appearance as clearly as possible. In the more common case where context does bear on operative choice, the context being brought to bear should always be firmly supported by the text as a whole.

In the first line the word choices are relatively clear:
˘ / ˘ / ˘ / ˘ / ˘ / ˘
My lord, as I was sewing in my closet,

The two and a half parameter calls for three operatives, which have already been selected. Assuming that some combination of two full operatives and one half operative will suffice, try each of the following by engaging changes in pitch and length (the commonly recommended approach to activating operatives, instead of volume or punch):

˘ / ˘ / ˘ / ˘ / ˘ / ˘
My lord, as I was sewing in my closet,

˘ / ˘ / ˘ / ˘ / ˘ / ˘
My lord, as I was sewing in my closet,

or
˘ / ˘ / ˘ / ˘ / ˘ / ˘
My lord, as I was sewing in my closet,

Each possibility represents a different choice in terms of what exactly and essentially is being said. The effectiveness of any process for choosing operatives depends on the degree to which it remains an exercise in discovering and clarifying the sense of what's being said; this as opposed to the target being to evoke or score an emotional, predetermined, or "dramatic" value or delivery. To maintain a focus on sense as derived specifically from the text/context avoids the risk of descending into a Monty Python-esque sketch of merely how one might say it to achieve "Great Acting," and brings one closer to having information which can be very helpful in approaching the real thing.

The first two words of this line ("My Lord") represent a form of "direct address", a common mechanism best activated by a slight drop in pitch, and "Sewing" and "closet" most clearly describe the event; this fact, and the pitch drop for "Lord", effecting its half operativeness in relation to the others, lend support to the third marking choice.

"Two-and-a-Half to Start": A Structural Device for Unlocking Shakespeare's Verse
by Michael Cobb

˘ / ˘ / ˘ / ˘ / ˘ /
My <u>lord</u>, as I was <u>sewing</u> in my <u>closet</u>,

˘ / ˘ / ˘ / ˘ / ˘ /
Lord <u>Hamlet</u>, with his <u>doublet</u> all <u>unbraced</u>; [...]

In this following line "Hamlet" is obviously of primary importance. As for "doublet" and "unbraced", Polonius and the audience would certainly receive the intellectual information if these assignments of operativeness were reversed. The proposal here is that this choice (which follows the earlier suggestion regarding the relationship between modified and modifier) transcends the linguistic or emotional scoring level and works more effectively to evoke the image being described. The final word in the line remains operative (as is often the case), but in a secondary capacity. In terms of "Lord" and "all", the question is whether including them will support or encumber "Hamlet" and "unbraced" in the actual activation/utterance.

/ ˘ ˘ / ˘ / ˘ / ˘ /
<u>Pale</u> as his <u>shirt</u>; his <u>knees</u> <u>knocking</u> each other;

The existence of four operatives here raises the possibility of a relatively common construction worth early consideration whenever there are four operatives.

/ ˘ ˘ / ˘ / ˘ / ˘ /
<u>Pale</u> as his <u>shirt</u>; his <u>knees</u> <u>knocking</u> each other;

This construction also breaks the otherwise very useful guideline of maintaining the equivalent of two and a half operatives, five total underlines, with a total of six. This construction can often be useful; it generally occurs in this sequence of gradation, and is characterized by the middle two operatives being of the same degree.

Each of the next three lines can be scored with the standard two-and-a-half pattern of two full operatives (with two underlines each) and one half operative (with one underline). Leaving each to be completed by the reader, with a brief consideration to follow—

˘ / ˘ / ˘ / ˘ ˘ / ˘ /
And with a <u>look</u> so <u>piteous</u> in <u>purport</u>

What's modifying what here? What choice helps carry the action of the text forward?

˘ / ˘ / ˘ ˘ / ˘ / ˘ /
As <u>if</u> he had been <u>loosed</u> out of <u>hell</u>

˘ / ˘ / ˘ / ˘ ˘ / ˘ /
To <u>speak</u> of <u>horrors</u>, --he comes <u>before</u> me.

One refinement of the advice to steer clear of prepositions occurs when they are coupled with a verb. In that case, they may sometimes carry the operative potential, as in

"stand up", "pass on", "come about", "follow after", etc. In this case, "before" helps to evoke the immediacy of Hamlet's presence.

The following Act III, scene 2 soliloquy of Hamlet's, which I've fully marked with choices I and a student came up with together for a recent production, provides an opportunity to consider more variations on, and sophistication in the use of, the Two-and-a-Half device.

˘ / ˘ / ˘ / ˘ / ˘ /
Hamlet: Tis <u>now</u> the very <u>witching</u> time of <u>night</u>,

Three words and degrees of operativeness adding up to five lines total. This construction serves to manifest his being in the middle of a night that's been going on for some time.

˘ / ˘ / ˘ / ˘ / ˘ /
When <u>churchyards yawn</u> and <u>hell</u> itself <u>breathes out</u>

In reviewing this we questioned whether to borrow a quarter operative/dotted line from "breathes out" and shift it to "hell itself", but stayed with this; obviously, also choosing in each of those instances to join words into a single image.

˘ / ˘ / ˘ / ˘ / ˘ ˘ /
<u>Contagion</u> to this world: now could I <u>drink</u> hot <u>blood</u>,

My sense is that "world" and "now" (established in the first line) are implicit. This marking choice is also influenced by the scansion, which joining "hot" with "blood" as a single image would challenge, suggesting that "hot" falls on a strong rather than a weak beat. Working from a regular metrical foundation, making only those changes which seem necessary, and recognizing the importance that "drink" holds in the essential statement being made, all suggest the possibility that "hot" is not part of the operative. In which case it becomes implicit to "blood" and thereby potentially strengthens rather than diminishes the statement (i.e. of course it's hot, it's from a living creature).

˘ / ˘ / ˘ / ˘ / ˘ /
And do such <u>bitter</u> <u>business</u> as the <u>day</u>

This choice bets that "do", being both on a strong beat and a relatively neutral verb, can take care of itself. Note the development from "<u>night</u>" in the first line to "<u>day</u>" here.

˘ / ˘ / ˘ / ˘ / ˘ /
Would quake to <u>look</u> on. <u>Soft</u>! now to my <u>mother</u>.

˘ / ˘ / ˘ / ˘ / ˘ /
O <u>heart</u>, <u>lose</u> not thy <u>nature</u>; let not ever

One might consider tinkering with this further if one thought that "ever" (also noting its position at the end of the line) calls for something more; in this pass and case we didn't.

⌣ / ⌣ / ⌣ / ⌣ ⌣ / / ⌣
The <u>soul</u> of <u>Nero</u> enter this <u>firm bosom</u>:

The single image choice for "firm bosom" potentially strengthens the intended meaning of solidity.

/ ⌣ ⌣ /⌣ / ⌣ / ⌣ /
I will be <u>cruel</u>, <u>not</u> <u>unnatural</u>:

The inclusion of "not" results from the this-not-that construction and is supported by its falling on the strong beat.

/ ⌣ / / ⌣ / ⌣ ⌣ / ⌣
I will <u>speak</u> <u>daggers</u> to her, but <u>use</u> none;

Such an act as using daggers would be "unnatural" (as her son). The daggers, therefore, have in a sense already been mentioned in the previous line, and the new information and distinction of the statement is between speaking and using.

⌣ / ⌣ / ⌣ / ⌣ / ⌣ /
My <u>tongue</u> and <u>soul</u> in <u>this</u> be <u>hypocrites</u>;

"This" lightly serves to hold things together; the rest develops naturally.

/ ⌣ ⌣ ⌣ / ⌣ /⌣ / ⌣ /
<u>How</u> in my <u>words</u> <u>somever</u> she be <u>shent</u>,

⌣ / ⌣ / / ⌣ ⌣ / ⌣ /
To give them <u>seals</u> <u>never</u>, my soul, <u>consent</u>!

Here the Two-and-a-Half device provides a handle on a difficult construction, helping the actor to mine the difficulty in the making of the pledge, and also to fulfill the rhyming couplet.

In using this approach to teach/coach students, I tend much more towards discussion than demonstration (on either of our parts) when it comes to helping them make a choice, with each of us working it out in our own "mind's ear". It's worth noting that a growth in facility with this device is often accompanied by an increased temptation to exceed the two-and-a-half/three word starting point in the interest of fine tuning. To do so, in my experience, unnecessarily runs the risk of doing more to straitjacket one into an overly careful and restrictive reading than to help discover and activate a living and breathing manifestation of what the text is saying, flexible and adaptable even to shifts in objective and action choice.

A further development in the approach, consistent with its primary goals of effectiveness and efficiency, involves the potential for borrowing operativeness between adjacent lines within a speech or longer thought in order to score a construction, when it would prove helpful. However, more often than not the simple formula of finding two-and-a-half operatives per verse line, and limiting oneself to the equivalent amount of operativeness, even when exceeding three words, can serve to unlock the potential for a sophisticated outcome with economy and ease.

Works Cited

Epstein, S. E. 2010. Operative Words and Images. Photocopy. 1.

Houfek, N. and Delorey, P. 1999. Language Structure Terminology. Photocopy. 3.

Essay *by Tanera Marshall*

Re-thinking Terminology: A Look at the Connotative Profile of "Feminine Ending"

Tanera Marshall is head of Voice and Speech at the University of Illinois at Chicago. She earned a BA from Oberlin College, an MFA from DePaul University's Theatre School, and is an Associate Teacher of Fitzmaurice Voicework®. Her professional voice/speech/dialect credits include numerous Chicago productions, major motion pictures, and Broadway. She is a member of SAG, AFTRA, and VASTA, and is an Associate Editor for the International Dialects of English Archive online.

A sensitivity to word connotation is a hallmark of our work as voice and speech professionals. We encourage discussion of a playwright's choice of one word over another and enjoy mining that word for clues to character and motivation. Those of us who teach in actor-training programs no doubt find that an actor's dexterity with words on stage begins with developing a sensitivity to them in the classroom. I, for one, initiate such word sensitivity in my university students' very first semester of voice instruction. Though they spend the early days *doing* (breathing, imaging, feeling, reflecting) without talking, I eventually lead them to the articulation of their experiences after the conclusion of class exercises. I ask them to find words that describe a feeling or an image as best they can—not because a description can be right or perfect, but because 1) the act of reflection serves to clarify a student's perception of his or her experience; and 2) the process of finding language to sufficiently describe that experience is a first step toward sensitivity to words, because the student is forced to distinguish apt words from those that are not.

I myself strive for word specificity in the classroom. I recognize that young students often want to be good students and get things "right," so with words I steer them hard toward a mindset that gives priority to process rather than product. I respond to their ideas and experiences, for instance, as being "meaningful," "fruitful," or "interesting" rather than "wrong" or "bad." I invite them to "wonder why" and "how," and encourage them to "acknowledge experiences without judgment." Because of the language I use or do not use, students quickly perceive that our studio is more of a laboratory than a classroom. I like to think that this emphasis on exploration gives them permission to value their own experiences—another critical component of developing their sensitivity to language. By giving word to their unique experiences, students are "owning" them, a skill without which it is difficult, I would argue, for students to own the experiences and words of characters they portray.

This journey toward specificity and owning words has led me to question the continued use of the prosody terms *masculine* and *feminine* to describe an ending to a word, foot, or line of verse. I recognize that these terms refer, respectively, to stressed and unstressed endings and not to gender identity, sex, or grammar. But they are heavy with multiple connotations, some of which can be perceived as sexist or derogatory, and I have found that their use in the classroom is problematic. I have chosen not to use them and instead refer to stressed and unstressed endings or identify the foot by its precise name: trochee, iamb, dactyl, amphibrach, and so forth.

Some may argue that the definitions of these terms are devoid of judgment, and their contexts—in grammar, prosody, and sex/gender—are clear and commonsensical. Here is how the *Oxford English Dictionary* (OED Online) defines them:

masculine, *adj.*

Of sex: male. Of a person or animal: belonging to the male sex; male.
Grammar. Designating the gender to which the majority of words denoting male people and animals belong. Of a word: belonging to this gender. Of a suffix, inflection, etc.: used with, or in forming, words of this gender.
Prosody. Of a rhyme: occurring between lines ending in a stressed syllable; esp. in masculine rhyme.

feminine, *adj.*

Characteristic of, peculiar or proper to women; womanlike, womanly.
Grammar. Of the gender to which appellations of females belong. Of a termination: Proper to this gender. Of a connected sentence: Consisting of words of

this gender.

Prosody. feminine rhyme: in French versification, one ending in a 'mute e' (so called because the mute e is used as a feminine suffix); hence in wider sense, a rhyme of two syllables of which the second is unstressed…

The definitions of these terms are devoid of judgment, and their contexts—in sex/gender, grammar, and prosody—are clear. At issue, however, are their connotations. The line between definition and connotation can become blurred in class discussions about the significance to actors of masculine and feminine endings. As we delve into the effects that these endings—and the contrast between the two—can have on speaker and listener alike, students seek out clarification by means of synonyms. Together we contrast words such as *confident, steady, emphatic* with words such as *gentle, unsure, urgent* (to name a few). Indeed, sometimes even the words *strong* and *weak* are used interchangeably with *masculine* and *feminine*. Of course we don't mean to equate masculinity with strength or femininity with weakness. A masculine ending may not feel strong at all and a feminine ending may not feel weak. But despite my attempts to countervail reductive conclusions, I cannot ignore the fact that a connection between our prosody terminology and a negative connotation of an otherwise descriptive, even useful, word may have been made. Have I inadvertently reinforced an outmoded ideology of gender? What other unintended connotations were heard by my bright but young students, for whom gender and identity are doubtless intensely personal issues?

A range of scholarship on the subject suggests we might be right to seriously consider this question. The gap between what a speaker means and that which a listener hears is one explored by philosopher Janice Moulton, who states, "One cannot account entirely for the meaning of a term by the intentions of the speaker" (Moulton, 109). A listener's understanding of a word can inform what is heard, thus complicating the use of that word.

A word's many layers of meaning make up what one semiotician, Marcel Danesi, calls a *connotative profile* (Danesi, 27). This profile is informed by the word's social, political, and historical context; it is, as Danesi says, "constrained by culture." A word or term's connotative profile is complex and often in contradistinction to its definition—an elasticity that makes language wonderfully nuanced but also very powerful. Consider the impact of language on thought and behavior. In the early part of the twentieth century, the anthropologists Edward Sapir and Benjamin Whorf explored the relationship between culture and language. After conducting field research with the Hopi tribe of the Southwestern United States, Whorf concluded that "our behavior … can be seen to be coordinated in many ways to the linguistically conditioned microcosm…. [P]eople act about situations in ways which are like the ways they talk about them" (Whorf, 75–93).

Now known as *linguistic relativity*, the idea that language affects thought and behavior is generally accepted. Much has been written on this topic across many disciplines. Musicologist Susan McClary, who in 1991 argued for the discontinuation of the terms *masculine* and *feminine* in regard to musical cadences, acknowledges that "it is in accordance with the terms provided by language that individuals are socialized: take on gendered identities, learn ranges of proper behaviors" (McClary, 21). And linguistic relativity has of course influenced feminist thought, of which the philosopher Sara Shute's work is typical: "[T]he elimination of sexist language is necessary for the elimination of sexism in any society. . . . [P]eople necessarily help to eliminate sexism by replacing sexist terms with nonsexist ones, and cannot totally eliminate sexism until they do" (Shute, 32).

Contemporary writers and artists seem to be distancing themselves from the term *feminine ending*. The term has been put in quotes (Fabb and Halle, 122), preceded by "so-called" (Wright, 161), and disclaimed: "there is seldom any need for [it]" (Boulton, 45). Informal conversations I have had with voice and speech instructors reveal that while some use the term without reservation, there are others who eschew it, often not using it all. A number of those who use the term claim to do so only after qualifying the term as the industry standard, or as what was taught to them as students. The term seems to be used interchangeably with any of a number of other terms: *irregular, eleven-syllable,* or *falling* line; *soft, weak, offbeat,* or *paroxytonic* ending.

None of these is ideal, however. *Soft, weak,* and *irregular* are judgmental, implying inferiority, and reflect the negative elements of *feminine's* connotative profile. The term *eleven-syllable line* is not only clumsy, but does not necessarily refer to an unstressed final syllable. The term *paroxytonic* is useful—referring to a stress on the penultimate syllable. However, it refers specifically to words in either poetry or prose, rather than to poetic feet. In poetry, then, it may be useful to identify trochees (X –), dactyls (X – –), amphibrachs (– X –), iambs (– X), anapests (– – X) but my students get a little cross-eyed at all that. In my own experience, I've found that the terms *stressed ending* and *unstressed ending* are both the most effective and most appropriate. The potential for confusion is great in university classrooms and rehearsals— where personal perspective is integral to discussions about text and character —and is the reason I ask for specificity from my students in class discussions and their written work. It is also why I choose to use terms that are unencumbered by rich but complicated connotative profiles.

Re-thinking Terminology: A Look at the Connotative Profile of "Feminine Ending"
by Tanera Marshall

Bibliography

Boulton, M. *The Anatomy of Poetry*. London: Routledge & Kegan Paul, 1953.

Danesi, M. *Of Cigarettes, High Heels, and Other Interesting Things: An Introduction To Semiotics*. New York: Palgrave Macmillan, 1999.

Fabb, N. and M. Halle. *Meter In Poetry: A New Theory*. Cambridge: Cambridge University Press, 2008.

McClary, S. *Feminine Endings: Music, Gender, and Sexuality*. Minneapolis: University of Minnesota Press, 1991.

Moulton, J. "The myth of the neutral 'man.'" In *Sexist Language, a Modern Philosophical Analysis*, ed. M. Vetterling-Braggin, 100–115. Huber Heights, Ohio: Littlefield, Adams & Co., 1981.

Shute, S. "Sexist language and sexism." In *Sexist Language, A Modern Philosophical Analysis*, ed. M. Vetterling-Braggin, 23–33. Huber Heights, Ohio: Littlefield, Adams & Co., 1981.

Whorf, B. "The relation of habitual thought and behavior to language." In *Language, Culture, and Personality, Essays In Memory Of Edward Sapir*, ed. L. Spier, 75–93. Menasha, Wis.: Sapir Memorial Publication Fund, 1941. Accessed June 19, 2009. http://sloan.stanford.edu/mousesite/Secondary/Whorfframe2.html.

Wright, G. T. *Shakespeare's Metrical Art*. Berkeley: University of California Press, 1988.

Ethics, Standards and Practices, *Rena Cook, Associate Editor*

Editorial Column *by Rena Cook, Associate Editor*

in her article entitled "A Call to Action: Embracing the Cultural Voice or Taming the Wild Tongue."

Rena Cook is Professor of Voice at the University of Oklahoma. She holds an MA in voice from the Central School of Speech and Drama and an MFA in Directing from OU. She has coached such productions as *Beauty Queen of Leenane, The Real Thing,* and *Cosi.* She was Editor-in-chief for the *Voice and Speech Review* 09 issue and co-edited *Breath in Action* with Jane Boston. Her new book *Voice in Action: A Young Actor's Guide to Vocal Expression* is set for publication by Methuen in 2012. She has presented workshops throughout the US and the UK.

Introduction

In the six previous issues of the *Voice and Speech Review*, there have been a total of twenty one articles in the area of Ethics, Standards and Practices. These articles explore a range of issues - gender identity, cultural voice, racial identity, bilingual Shakespeare, standard speech, and touch in teaching. Over half deal with the topic of diversity, a subject which VASTA agrees is one of our most crucial areas of concern and action. As part of the VASTA vision 2004-2014, the VASTA Board created a Committee on Diversity which remains one of the most vital aspects of VASTA's profile in the voice training profession. With the announcement of this VRS's cover topic, *A World of Voice,* Editor-in-chief Dudley Knight invited us all to reflect on where we have come and where we have yet to go in the journey toward inclusion of all voices into our pedagogical rubric.

Micha Espinosa has been a champion of diversity, focusing her research, writing and practice in the area of cultural identity, particularly the duality experienced by Latinos/as in progressing through acting and voice training. In this issue she gives us a deeper look into the problem and provides recommendations for a more inclusive pedagogy

A Call to Action: Embracing the Cultural Voice or Taming the Wild Tongue

Micha Espinosa, Professor of Voice and Acting for the School of Theatre and Film at Arizona State University, holds a BFA from Stephens College and an MFA from the University of California, San Diego. She has taught voice, speech and movement workshops nationally and internationally including: Japan, Canada, Mexico and Chile. She is a member of AFTRA and SAG and has performed in film, television, commercials and regional theatre. She is also a certified yoga instructor with extensive Feldenkrais training. She is an associate teacher of Fitzmaurice Voicework and a trainer for the Fitzmaurice Voicework Teacher Certification Program.

"Those of us who want to make connections, who want to cross boundaries, do." bell hooks

"Cuando vives en la frontera, people walk through you, the wind steals your voice." Gloria Anzaldúa

Introduction

At the intersection of Border Theory and contemporary voice training we find highly skilled voice trainers who embrace the concept of cultural voice and their Latino/a[1] students who often feel that their trainers would rather tame them than free their "wild tongues."[2] It is my hope that, if acknowledged and examined, this intersection can aid in effective intercultural communication and effective self-determination for individuals who struggle to maintain their cultural voices in an environment that unintentionally and at times intentionally denies, ignores, transforms, or confuses the identities associated with the cultural voice. Throughout this article, cultural voice is described as the self-constructed, emotionally bound, non-dominant performer's identity and identification with the social-historical values and principles of one or more cultures.

The concept of cultural voice can be further explored in the works of O'Connor (1989), Mills (2009), and Dunn and Jones (1994). However, it is Gloria Anzaldúa, the leading scholar in Chicano cultural theory/border theory, who passionately explores linguistic terrorism of the "authentic wild tongue," the internalized beliefs of illegitimacy, and the feelings of duality that Chicanos/as face:

> *Nosotros los* Chicanos straddle the borderlands. On one side of us, we are constantly exposed to the Spanish of the Mexicans, on the other side we hear the Anglos' incessant clamoring so that we forget our language. Among ourselves we don't say *nosotros los americanos, o nosotros los españoles, o nosotros los hispanos.* We say *nosotros los mexicanos* (by *mexicanos* we do not mean citizens of Mexico; we do not mean national identity but a racial one). We distiguish between *mexicanos del otro lado* and *mexicanos de este lado.* Deep in our hearts we believe that being Mexican has nothing to do with which country one lives in. Being Mexican is a state of the soul–not one of mind, not one of citizenship. Neither eagle nor serpent, but both. And like the ocean, neither animal respects borders. (84)

As a Chicana voice trainer who has lived a life where I have crossed both physical and psychological borders, I am heavily invested both emotionally and professionally in the ethics and pedagogy of the voice profession. In an attempt to understand my own experience with identity and Euro-centric theatre practices, I have invested much of my career in researching and exploring educational models that will alleviate the emotional pain Latino/a theatre students too often experience. To further explore the contrast between the perceptions of a largely Anglo voice profession and Latino/a students, I will reference border theory and the first-hand experiences of Chicano/a students reflecting on the personal cost of taming their authentic "wild tongue." Finally, I will explore one teaching model that embraces and builds on the concept of cultural voice in real and lasting ways.

The key questions I will investigate are: How do we develop and embrace a border-sensitive pedagogy? How do we incorporate teaching savvy and cultural sensitivity in our practice to support students' efforts as they navigate the complex changes we ask of them? How does one enter a community, join that community, be a part of that community, help develop the future voices in that community without requiring, conveying, or exemplifying a Euro-centric voice?

I will use my own history as a Latina theatre artist—a history of transitioning into a predominantly Anglo-dominated Euro-centric society, of leaving and returning to a Latino world, and of entering but not being at home in an

Anglo world and belonging and not belonging in the Latino world—to illuminate the experience of students and teachers who encounter this simultaneously porous and binding border. I will use my own border narrative as well as border theory to describe the struggle of which I speak.

Border Theory

Political and cultural subordination characterized Arizona and much of the Greater Southwest long before current borders were established.[3] The political, legal, social, and cultural landscape that is created when two cultures collide is magnified on the border. The current battle over Arizona Senate Bill 1070, coupled with the official state policy to terminate English teachers with heavy accents and eliminate ethnic studies programs within public schools, underscores the importance of border theory and border studies. In this political context, it is vital that border students' voices be heard and acknowledged.

Border theory is the examination of multi-cultural/bi-cultural identity when the non-dominant culture bumps[4], collides, and grinds against the dominant culture. Over the last twenty years as border issues have become more visible and volatile, border theory, an interdisciplinary paradigm with its roots in sociology, education, politics, literature, history, geography, and economics, has blossomed and flourished. Students, artists, or scholars who examine borders, borderlands, and their complex and unique issues are adding to this growing field. At Arizona State University, for example, we offer a PhD program in Theatre Performance in the Americas and a Performance in the Borderlands initiative that promotes the cultures and traditions of the Borderlands. Foundational texts for the study of border theory include but are not limited to literary writers Américo Paredes and Gloria Anzaldùa, cultural theorists Sonia Saldivar Hull and José Davis Saldivar, anthropologists Renalto Rosaldo and Carlos Vélez-Ibáñez, and scholars Alfred Arteaga and Ruth Behar. The arts are no stranger to this paradigm; Latino artists such as Culture Clash, Guillermo Gómez-Peña, and Teatro Campesino are rich examples of artists who use border identity politics to frame their stories.[5]

In her book, *Qué Onda*, which examines border identity and urban youth culture, Cynthia Bejarano widens the definition of border identity:

> Border theory does not reside and was not created within one rigid strict academic discourse, but grew from people's border narratives and from the streets and geopolitical spaces that describe the daily experiences of people on the borderlands. It is an organic theory that originated from the local and subaltern communities. As such, it is a theory linked with

praxis, which transcends the boundaries of academic thought and disciplinary locations. (25)

She further identifies why border theory is the ideal framework for analysis of Latino/a issues:

> Border theory helps explain how Latina/o youths are impacted by structural inequality, cultural hybridity, social hierarchies, and the legacy of colonialism that overshadows life on the border. It draws upon, integrates, and sharpens numerous theories that can be carefully packaged into what border theory offers.
>
> Border theory helps interpret my experience and that of the other Mexicanas/os and Chicanas/os on the borderlands as one of getting lost and finding ourselves in a labyrinth. It is a labyrinth filled with languages and competing cultures, of ethnicity and the differentiation in hues of "brown," of forbidden, exotic "Latin" accents and choppy, foreign "anglicized" ones. It involves a search in the thick *acequias* (canals) where muddied rivers of our "brownness" merge to create border people negotiating multiple marginalities. (28)

I employ Bejarono's concept of border narratives to give voice to acting students from "historically ignored populations."[6] I use the paradigm of border theory to describe and interpret the non-dominant performer's voice, herein referred to as the "cultural voice," and the objectification and deprivation of those voices in the classroom. I propose that the cultural and class divisions between students and teacher comprises a borderland, and the training in performance constitutes a fragile territory where linguistic experimentation, class divisions, commerce, industry, cultural emergence and cultural conflict meet.

Being Mexican or of Mexican origins in the United States requires responding to the negative identity, whether that be cultural, linguistic and/or class associations imposed by the dominant Anglo culture. Latino performance artist Guillermo Gómez-Peña, in his 1988 essay *Documented/Undocumented*, validates this assertion with his description, corroborated in findings by Morris, Masud-Piloto (1995), Jorge J. E. Gracia (2000), Bejerano (2005), Vélez-Ibáñez (1996) and Omi and Winant (1994):

> In general, we are perceived through the folkloric prism of Hollywood, fad literature and publicity; or through the ideological filters of mass media. For the average Anglo, we are nothing but "images," "symbols," "metaphors." We lack ontological existence and anthropological concreteness. We are perceived indistinctly as magic creatures with shamanistic powers, happy bohemians with pre-technological sensibilities, or as romantic revolutionaries born in a Cuban poster

from the 70's. All this without mentioning the more ordinary myths, which link us with drugs, super-sexuality, gratuitous violence, and terrorism, myths that serve to justify racism and disguise the fear of cultural otherness. (132)

The cultural otherness that Gómez-Peña describes also includes suspect patriotism, low socioeconomic status, resistance to speaking or learning English and laziness. The investment in these associations is integral to the border identity and evident in the over-representation of Mexican poverty, crime, illness, drugs, and war in film, television, and theatre. The Mexican voice fares even worse: signaling a lack of education and language such as the Taco Bell advertisements featuring a Chihuahua. Anthropologist Carlos Vélez-Ibáñez describes this phenomenon as the "distribution of sadness":

> For Mexicans, our participation in each of the categories of sadness is over-represented….Nevertheless, this population has always faced the difficulties of economic inequality, commoditization, discrimination, miseducation, and all their attendant ills with ideas and behaviors adaptive to becoming human and humane. However, even these have to be buttressed by educational institutions and opportunities that support them. Unless these appear in significant numbers, there is no doubt that more of us will fall by the wayside to become the next casualties of all the "ills" present in Northern Greater Southwest. In so doing we all become casualties. (206)

At the 2009 Association for Theatre in Higher Education Conference in New York City, I experienced this "distribution of sadness" phenomenon. I attended three presentations related to Latinos and theatre with a focus on gangbanging criminals, homeless youth, and gang violence. Thus, even within the academy, the prevailing critical discourse rarely includes the complex and varied history and culture of Latinos in the United States. The predominance of these stereotypes forces Latino/a actors to choose between working within the "categories of sadness" or unemployment.

As one of the actresses in the Broadway production of *In the Heights*[7], reports,

> The agent I had sent me out on lots of interviews, but they had all been for either housekeepers or people who were trying to get across the border, and swimming the Rio Grande, and I had grown up in Los Angeles, I grew up with my mom, I spoke like I speak, and I was having to say, "Señor, please don't hurt me, I am just here for my family." And I was like, "Fine, fine, I'm actress, but is this it? Is this what's going to happen?" So I signed with this other agency who promised me, "Oh no, we don't think of you like that at all." Liars. So, they send me out for nothing but housekeepers, which I played about fifteen of them, and it was when I was pretty successful as a television actress that I was shopping in Beverly Hills one day and feeling like a lot of myself and I walked by this window. I was just dreamily window shopping, I stopped, I was thinking about something else; it ended up that I was standing in front of the Beverly Hills Uniform Store. And then I became very conscious, I looked at all of the uniforms and I realized I had worn every one: the gray dress, the black dress—those are the dress uniforms for the party scenes, or the high-rent houses—and then I had worn the blue and the pink, the little bric-a-brac one, and every Mexican actress I know in L.A…. they know those uniforms.

This actress's career and her frustration with the television industry and writers who rarely thought beyond stereotypes echo similar experiences among the numerous Latino/a students who I interviewed during my research for this article. Latino/a students enter conservatory programs with dreams of expanding identities but instead they confront the same subtle and overt one-dimensional representations. The reality of this gross stereotyping within the industry may be difficult to change but one would expect a broader and more nuanced narrative within educational settings. Stephen Bender dissects Latino stereotype, Hollywood, the media, and the law in *Greasers and Gringos*:

> Related to the public's view of Latinas/os as unwilling or unable to assimilate is the widespread perception of Latinas/os as foreigners. This perception encompasses even those Latinas/os born in the United States to immigrant parents, as well as Latinas/os of later generations. Speaking Spanish, whether by monolingual or bilingual speakers, is assumed to signify recent immigration. Speaking English with an accent similarly triggers the assumption of foreignness. So pervasive is this view of Latinas/os as foreigners that physical appearance alone may be used to signal national origin. Many later generation Latinas/os have fielded the question "where were your parents born?" implying they are a mere generation removed from foreignness. (84)

Bender challenges his reader to re-invent American education and life. He is one of many scholars[8] who outline the effects of how media, film, and television continue to create and perpetuate the damaging views of Latinos. More importantly he demonstrates how internalized negative social images create psychological inferiority to the dominant Anglo culture. Imagine the distress of the actress mentioned above when she realized that even though she was making a living she could only do so by adding to the derogatory stereotype, thus adding to the "distribution of sadness" for her culture.

Of my research, I have been asked the question, "How is the Latino student experience distinct from other students'?" The answer is that, to succeed, Latinos and Mexican students have to negotiate an identity with the psychological and physical realities they have been given. Both students and teachers often find themselves working with unexamined and opposing sets of external and internalized beliefs. These include beliefs about the acculturation process, Mexican-American identity formation, and privilege as it pertains to being part of the dominant culture. For Latino/a students those beliefs and how they experience those beliefs might differ dramatically from their Anglo instructors. When the place students come from is stigmatized and when their ethnicity and their language are considered foreign or substandard in both worlds, then it is not surprising that they carry internalized beliefs that they are somehow illegitimate, outsiders, a mish-mash of cultures and identities.

Anzaldúa's words reflects this border identity in her landmark book, *Borderlands/La Frontera*:

> I am a border woman. I grew up between two cultures, the Mexican (with a heavy Indian influence) and the Anglo (as a member of a colonized people in our own territory). I have been straddling that *tejas*-Mexican border, and others, all my life. It's not a comfortable territory to live in, this place of contradictions. Hatred, anger, and exploitation are the prominent features of this landscape. However, there have been compensations for this *mestiza*, and certain joys. Living on borders and in margins, keeping intact one's shifting and multiple identity and integrity, is like trying to swim in a new element, an "alien" element. (18)

Understanding the transitional state that Anzaldúa refers to is a critical first step for students and teachers, who need to recognize and become adept at border crossing and together create a new border pedagogy. In order for teacher and student to become healthy border crossers, I believe a cultural shift is called for, one which includes a pedagogy that is sensitive and cognizant of border identities. If we do not embrace this shift, we risk the possibility that the training we provide and its history become not only a border, but also a fence that keeps some students physically and culturally out.

My Narrative

The use of personal narrative is regularly employed by border theory scholars[9] to construct and view history and experiences. I draw upon my own experiences to inspire others to share their stories.

I was born on the border. We were living in Mexico and my mother—an Anglo married to a Mexican national—crossed the border to give birth to me. From the moment of my birth, I have been a border crosser. As someone whose ethnicity is not easily identifiable (my phenotype is European), physically crossing ethnic borders was relatively easy for me until I entered the world of theatre. There cultural and monetary capital was acquired by entering the dominant culture. To gain entrance, I abandoned my voice.

The goal had been assimilation, a severing from my cultural voice. I was twenty-four and studying in London at Patsy Rodenburg's[10] professional voice instructor's intensive. During that intensive, David Carey, acclaimed vocal coach, teacher, and educator, conducted a workshop discussing aesthetics of voice with the multicultural participants representing numerous countries. I had never discussed the aesthetics of voice. I had adopted my Anglo teacher's aesthetic. The voice teachers all agreed on the benefits of a clear tone and a healthy instrument. But one of the voice teachers, a non-native English speaker, liked a voice with a little dirt in it. A voice that sounded like it had life. Maybe that life was hard? Maybe that voice had imperfections? If I were really truthful, so did I. I do believe that a voice should be free of those pesky glottal attacks and/or have the ability to sustain throughout a run of a show, but it was at that moment that I became aware of the cultural voice. A voice that has endured the dirt and struggle of constantly crossing borders might not be as aesthetically pleasing to some, but it was a lot more interesting to me.

It was then that I began to develop my own voice as it pertained to my culture, politics, and values. And now that I have returned to the borderlands as a voice professor encountering faces and voices that look and sound like mine, I am aware that it is this history, this training, this tradition that I have struggled to overcome. As a student I was often told, "You don't look Mexican and so you shouldn't sound Mexican." It is only now in the current hostile political climate in Arizona that I have become conscious of the racism inherent in these kinds of remarks.

I also experienced some wonderful mentors and teachers who showed me the power of teaching voice and how, if done right, it can empower students regardless of their ethnic, linguistic, or class background. For example, Catherine Fitzmaurice[11], my primary influence, taught me about healing and encouraged me to teach "from my wound." At the 2009 Voice and Speech Trainers Association conference diversity panel, Catherine said, "Much can be done to honor and move on from difference, especially any difference that is inherently unequal, by working with breathing in its physical and spiritual dimensions. Let's celebrate where we have come from, and let's also ask where are we going." Studying with nuanced teachers like Catherine Fitzmaurice and Patsy Rodenburg gave impulse to my curiosity and inspired me to embark on a journey of re-discovering my own voice.

Good Work

In addition to Fitzmaurice Voicework, the work of Dudley Knight and Phil Thompson[12] took many in the profession from prescriptive voice and accent training to descriptive voice and accent training. Knight's scholarship on Standard American speech and the Knight/Thompson[13] practical workshops have done a tremendous service to the voice and speech profession, ensuring that new teachers forego the historical white colonizing speech practices and instead approach students with a much more nuanced approach to speech training.

As a voice profession, we have taken multiple steps to engage in the diversity discussion. As an organization, the Voice and Speech Trainers Association has created both a diversity statement[14] and a diversity committee, and holds annual diversity panels. In fact, the work of the Voice and Speech Trainers Association has contributed significantly to addressing the problems of diversity within our ranks and in the classroom. And yet, through my discussion, research, and practice, I find that the same struggles with identity, belonging, and training of our non-dominant culturally diverse students persists and that our well intended practices continue to alienate.

My research, personal and professional experience, and my origins in and understanding of the Borderlands, lead me to conclude that the bumping into and the border crossing with Chicano/Latino/a students and their predominantly Anglo, Eurocentric teachers and directors will continue unless a clearer understanding of cultural and political experience— one that includes artificially created challenges to identities—is achieved.

Below are reports of two theatre conservatory students documenting their struggles within an overwhelmingly Eurocentric environment, their "other" status, and the lack of understanding from their teachers, peers, and the institution itself.

The Student Experience: Taming the Wild Tongue

This research evolved from a 2009 Association for Theatre in Higher Education (ATHE) panel that examined the practices of a small successful theatre company in the Borderlands. Panel presentation and discussion were then amplified by a series of subsequent semi-structured interviews, which took place between September and December of 2009. The two student respondents are both of Mexican heritage and attending the same well-regarded theatre conservatory. At the time of the interviews both Victoria and Barbara, pseudonyms, were academically successful students in their early twenties. Their voice and speech teachers reported that both young women were excellent students and were unaware of their emotional distress.[15]

Victoria:

> English and Spanish are the languages that I grew up with. There wasn't a first language. So, what I'm noticing now, and I'm aware of now, is the reason why I'm having so much difficulty, was because, first of all, my dad was the one who taught me how to speak, which wasn't very good English, or Spanish. It was slang. So, I grew up speaking slang. I think that's one of the reasons I'm having so much difficulty. Teachers said, oh, well maybe you just learned Spanish… Spanish was your first language. I told them that doesn't have anything to do with it.

Victoria is not an immigrant: she was born in the United States; her father is Mexican; her mother an American who grew up in a border community. She identifies herself as an American, but in the predominantly white environment of her conservatory training, her nationality is assigned and her linguistic confidence is severely injured in the process:

> My peers focused a lot on the differences of others, my differences…. So I felt like this isolation and hostility between my peers, and the more and more I tried to relate and understand them and tried to communicate, I felt more rejected. I would try to hang out, and they would push me away, so that kind of made me really, really angry and that was starting to hinder my work in class, and I was starting to notice that my evaluations came back, "Oh, you need to become more vulnerable." You're closing off a lot; be more open. And I think the reason why I was being closed off was because I was feeling very angry of the way I was being treated. I was the only Latina in my year and I didn't have any support. I wasn't in the dorms, I was about thirty minutes away from school so that even made it more hard, because the first year we're supposed to mingle and get to know everybody and create friendships, and I wasn't doing that because I lived so far away. Well, how am I supposed to be open when I feel rejected by all these people? How am I supposed to trust them, when, when I feel like…I felt like this big neon sign above my head, like, "Mexican Mexican." At times, I felt really stupid because I was the only one in my class constantly asking questions, my reading comprehension was lower

than everybody else's. I felt inferior to everybody else because of my vocabulary and my accent.

Victoria's comments clearly demonstrate the stark contrast between her experience of college life and of being part of the school's theatre community and that of her Anglo peers. Her experience was one where she felt alienated from her culture and an alien to the dominant culture. Near the end of her comments, one can see that Victoria directs her feelings inward towards her sense of self and her vocal identity.

Michelle Halls Kells, professor of writing and ethno-linguistic identity, clarifies:

> Speakers of stigmatized language varieties internalize the social norms and linguistic value judgments of the dominant group. Grammatical forms that are reflective of low socioeconomic status or low-prestige, working class speech are judged inherently bad or wrong. Linguistic insecurity or ambivalence among members of subordinate social groups is reflected in negative self-perceptions and language attitudes; members of these social groups display a high regard for the language varieties that signal the elite class and concomitant low regard for their own linguistic varieties. (11)

Anzaldúa further clarifies this phenomenon of sadness:

> Chicanas who grew up speaking Chicano Spanish have internalized the belief that we speak poor Spanish. It is illegitimate, a bastard language…Peña. Shame. Low estimation of self. In childhood we are told that our language is wrong. Repeated attacks on our native tongue diminish our sense of self. The attacks continue throughout our lives. (58)

Over the course of my interviews and discussions, Victoria's attitude toward her voice and her identity became more positive. Anzaldúa refers to this growth as a "new consciousness," a new *mestiza* consciousness:[16]

> The new *mestiza* copes by developing a tolerance for contradictions, a tolerance for ambiguity. She learns to be an Indian in Mexican culture, to be Mexican from an Anglo point of view. She learns to juggle cultures. She is a plural personality, she operates in a pluralistic mode–nothing is thrust out, the good, the bad and the ugly, nothing rejected, nothing abandoned. Not only does she sustain contradictions, she turns the ambivalence into something else. (101)

Victoria continues:
> I've been so appreciative of the way I speak, in a way, because it's so unique. And I don't ever want to move

back, but also I don't want to leave it. I want to live in other voices with my whole being. So, I acknowledge that this is my voice and this makes me who I am, or this is who I am right now, but I can also explore and expand myself even more, and that's what I want.

Victoria's expansion of self in relation to her training is the common goal for actor training. In modern training, vocal trainers hope that the physical, mental and emotional aspects of self are well functioning and integrated. For cultural voice students this new consciousness does not come easily.

> The ambivalence from the clash of voices results in mental and emotional states of perplexity. Internal strife results in insecurity and indecisiveness. The *mestiza's* dual or multiple personality is plagued by psychic restlessness. (Anzaldúa, 100).

Victoria began to embrace her cultural voice, her *mestiza*, and her ability to cross and straddle the borders of her worlds. A second student, Barbara, is a native Mexican and an immigrant to the United States. She struggles as she balances the different sociolinguistic messages she is receiving from the dominant culture:

> I completely understand how you can be changed (modify accent), but when it's thrown at you all the time, especially in an environment where there aren't that many Latinos, you hold onto your language because it's a part of your identity, your character. You can't lose it because then you'll lose yourself.

> I was constantly being told in every single critique from all my teachers, that I was not being understood. I never quite understood what they meant. At first I thought, I'm not articulating right. Then, I realized I'm not pronouncing the word in English how it's supposed to be. Then, I thought, it's in my language. Is it because I have an accent? Then it was brought up that maybe I should try an American accent because that will open up my possibilities, expand my range. In my second year, I auditioned for a play with a "large equity theatre in United States." I got cast in it, and it was an incredible experience and, and all of the reviewers never mentioned that I couldn't be understood. I had a small role, but yet I was mentioned in every review, and in good light. I was completely shocked that I was understood.

Repeatedly, at university auditions, directors told Barbara that they couldn't cast her because they were afraid she would not be understood. The roles she was given had very little text thus limiting her ability to exercise her skills in the same way as her classmates. Ironically, when she worked professionally her voice was embraced as part of her talent. This was frustrating and confusing for the student, "I don't get to explore because I'm the only one. Will I not be able to explore what it's like to be a sister, a mother?"

She asks these questions of her academic setting because Barbara came from a high quality, multicultural theatre community. She knows what is possible. She was also aware that her classmates, who themselves spoke regional dialects, were given the opportunity to expand while her Mexican accent, her foreignness, her cultural voice was treated as an insurmountable wall.

A visiting casting director echoed the sentiments of Barbara's academic directors, telling her she would need to eliminate her accent if she was going to work in the industry. When academics bring well-meaning industry professionals who are insensitive to issues of class, race, and culture into conservatories, then consciously or unconsciously we demoralize and marginalize the Latino student. When we unconsciously continue to cast that one Latino student as a spirit, or "other," we again propagate Eurocentric dominance and the student's social marginalization.

In my research of the Latino students' experience while studying theatre, inequality of opportunity to learn was a major complaint. In *The New York Times* video segment celebrating the revival of *Fences* starring Denzel Washington and Viola Davis, Ms. Davis eloquently adds to a fiery discussion on being an actor without white privilege, "You get to be humanized with August. Usually I'm a function, I service, I'm a facilitator, and I'm there to illuminate the Caucasian character. With August, you get to have a voice. You get to go on a journey."

Often, well-meaning directors in good programs make decisions about cultural students without realizing the effects. For example, a director once asked me to record the one African-American student I was working with at the beginning of the semester, and he expected that by the end of the semester this student would speak in a Standard American dialect. When I rejected his advice, the director felt that I was not teaching this student the skills he needed. He had no knowledge of the emotional carnage that following his advice would have inflicted.

I highlight this because I hope that we can examine our own departments and see how we are treating our cultural voice students. Taking advantage of their "other" status in casting, giving them parts that only allow them to experience playing "other," and inadvertently imposing colonizing voice attitudes are some of the ways that we continue to create borders between cultures. Barbara graduated in spring 2010. Sadly, she remembers parts of her training as

a place where she was continually treated as "other." Her training was a place where, to succeed, she needed to strive to become whiter. To get roles, to be able to transform, to be successful in the dominant culture, she needed to take on "whiteness." This is an example of the oppressive attitudes that increase tension and self-hatred for cultural voice and acting students across the nation.

Frustración

It is not only students who experience frustration; teachers also report frustration in negotiating across borders. From the many diversity conversations, committees, papers, and panels in which I have been a participant, I have learned that we could all use more skills when it comes to cross race/cross cultural conversations. For example, at the 2009 Association for Theatre in Higher Education (ATHE), an audience member attending the Working Classroom Panel reported:

> I am a white chick and I teach at a small school where there's 12% people of color with much fewer faculty and so I'm known on campus as one of the teachers who students of color can come to and it will be a good environment for them, which I'm honored. But I'm constantly feeling like I'm not doing a good job, because I'm sort of this outsider looking into things and thinking what this student would want from me, this person who doesn't truly understand them except that I'm a human being, and whatever I might understand about that condition is what I might understand about them. I teach acting, voice, movement, and gender in theatre classes. In my acting and voice classes, I try to, when I see students who are Latino or African American or Asian and I say, "Would you like to work on a play that deals with your ethnic story?" And some of them, they look at me (and this is where I don't know if I'm doing the right thing), they look at me like I've just slapped them, and I've asked some of my students, "What did I… I'm sorry, did I say something wrong?" And they're like, "No, but it's just that nobody's ever asked me that. Are there plays about me?" How do I understand and help a student who might not have an African American faculty or a Latino faculty to go to? How can I be a better teacher to a student that I might not fully understand? I don't even understand the white Jewish kids, because they're eighteen and I am not anymore. So I'm doing the best I can with all my students.

The teacher above returns us to our original question. How do we teach when there are borders, and how do we bring cultural sensitivity to students in transition? How do we recognize our colonized Eurocentric thinking? As educators, we have a tremendous amount on our plate and with tightening budgets and diminished resources, our roles, subjects, and jobs continue to expand. We are counselors, academic advisors, diversity officers, scholars, and voice, speech, and acting coaches all rolled into one.

Patsy Rodenburg, Director of Voice at the Guildhall School of Music and Drama and author of *The Right to Speak*, offers the following advice to teachers. Although she is referring to the borders between Received Pronunciation (the accent of Standard British in England) and other regional English dialects, there is a clear correlation to the teaching of Standard American:[17]

> What I believe is that if you teach an accent that has painful historic resonances you must teach that accent with grace and sensitivity. You must also understand that the student has a right not to master or even speak that accent without the fear of failing a course. Of course, not speaking certain accents will affect an actor's potential casting—Received Pronunciation is still very important for British actors' careers—and that fact has to be very clearly communicated to the student. Most of my students, who have emotional problems with Received Pronunciation, when given the above option and having their pain honored, do learn and own Received Pronunciation. (Personal Communication)

Rodenburg acknowledges that some students come to the classroom experiencing pain. I believe she is describing the "distribution of sadness" phenomenon. When cultural voice students studying in the United States learn Standard American, the clear historic resonances must be honored and respected. I contend that as teachers we must become familiar with this phenomenon, examine it, and observe its subtleties and implications.

When Borders are Embraced

In 2008 I was a guest voice and speech instructor for Working Classroom, a street conservatory and intergenerational theatre company based in Albuquerque, New Mexico, founded by Nan Elsasser and Moisés Kaufmann.[18] Their community is primarily Chicano, which provided me the opportunity to develop classes in both Spanish and English. I had absolutely no idea of the impact this experience would have on me. Not only was I developing curriculum, but also along the way I began to investigate my own fears. The practices of Working Classroom are examples of the commitment, activism, and cultural sensitivity required to empower students of "historically ignored communities," and a working model of what happens when borders are embraced.

According to Nan Elsasser, the founder and community activist artist of Working Classroom:

> We prepare young actors and artists for the future by offering long term, tuition-free professional training. During the 4-6 years students participate in Working Classroom, they work with artists who share their cultural and ethnic backgrounds, those who don't, and many from other countries. Our students grow up connected to a multicultural network of people with careers in theatre and the arts. We supplement artistic training with academic tutoring. We have a college scholarship program, and we offer students counseling if they need it, legal representation if they need it, a place to stay if they need it, whatever they need to be able to focus on their art and to forge a career. We are not a recreational program, a program to save the children or keep them off the streets. Our mission is not drop-out prevention, pregnancy prevention, gang prevention or drug abuse prevention. (Interview)

The Working Classroom company looks like America. The students are Hispanic, Mexican, Native American, Anglo and African American; they are middle and high school students, young and older adults. Elsasser attracts and hires teachers of extremely high caliber, thus blurring the lines between professional and non-professional theatre. They work in a modest, funky, storefront building. The students and program are multifaceted.

Since 2008, I've returned to Albuquerque six times to teach voice/speech/acting workshops for Working Classroom. Typically, I work with a class of twelve students ranging in age from eleven to sixty-five. I had never worked with a company that was so complex and devoted to its members regardless of age. I jumped in, and in the short intensives we covered speech, vocal production, vocal health, and text. I offered the students the exact same materials, principles and ideas that I teach my MFA actors at Arizona State University. We easily moved from English to Spanish. My Spanish is conversational, my Spanglish is good, but we faced our fears of working in different languages together. We tasted vowels, consonants, and ideas in our own unique way. I provided materials in both languages. The results were amazing: actors who froze under the pressure of developing their voices in a second language would unfreeze when being invited to explore in Spanish first; when asked to repeat the exercise in English most performed much more successfully.

I've incorporated this practice in all of my classes at Arizona State University. I also introduce tongue twisters in Spanish and challenge the non-Spanish speakers to explore them. "Switching tongues" is a valuable exercise for the identity development of my cultural voice students who, for once, enjoy the position of power. The English-speaking students also benefit from experiencing the linguistic rustrations that cultural voice students negotiate on a daily basis.

Another typical voice and speech exercise I employ, which when introduced at Working Classroom had surprising results, is the metaphorical exploration of voice. I have always begun my voice classes by distributing crayons and paper and asking students to draw their voices. There were dramatically different images from those at the Midwest University where I had previously taught. Instead of pictures of notes and flowers and stress anxiety, these border students depicted voices that at times feel stuck or trapped, images of boxes and parallel universes.

The Working Classroom classes were a riveting and moving experience—¬my own language acquisition, assimilation challenges, and fears were reflected in my students. One of the students, a very talented thirteen-year-old immigrant, eloquently described how his voice lived in a nowhere land. He drew his voice as a desert, and of course there was a fence. He didn't belong in Mexico and he didn't belong in the US. This physical and metaphorical description of the actor's voice and his identity awareness resonated with me and inspired me to begin this research. Anzaldúa explains:

> For people who are neither Spanish nor live in a country in which Spanish is the first language: for a people who live in a country in which English is the reigning tongue but who are not Anglo: for a people who cannot entirely identify with either standard (formal Castilian) Spanish or standard English, what recourse is left to them but to create their own language? A language which they can connect their identity to, one capable of communicating the realities and values true to themselves–a language with terms that are neither español ni inglés, but both. We speak patois, a forked tongue, a variation of two languages. (77)

Anzaldúa's description reflects the liminal identity of the immigrant student above. Because of the importance for students of working with instructors and mentors who have a shared or similar experience and/or language, Working Classroom bylaws require that the majority of their board, their staff, and their guest artists be from "historically ignored communities." Successful role models from similar ethnic and class backgrounds have the cultural capital to say, "You can do it. I did it. *Mira*, this is how it felt. Here's what you might experience."

Another fundamental principle for Working Classroom founder Nan Elsasser is that art alone does not provide students from economically, ethnically, culturally or racially oppressed communities the support they need to overcome the challenges they confront. Working Classroom sets extremely high expectations and then provides students with intensive mentoring and a range of support services to support their ambitions.

The Working Classroom model made me realize that recruiting and accepting culturally diverse students into a program without this kind of strong support and commitment to their success is misguided. Experiencing the Working Classroom community propelled me to examine my own practices, my university's policies, and the steps that I have taken to be an advocate for Latino/a students.

Working Classroom exemplifies what students and teachers can achieve when borders are erased. By removing the barriers of age, culture, language, and class and blurring the lines between professional and non-professional, the distribution of sadness lifts. Working Classroom students enter highly regarded arts programs and build successful careers. They return to the community, therefore creating a healthy cycle. Over time, Working Classroom alumni are creating/participating in a vibrant multicultural arts community.

Practical Solutions

Below, I outline practical solutions inspired by my teaching at Working Classroom:

1. Work in the native tongue first.
For example, when working on dialects, if the students' primary language is Spanish and they have an understanding of International Phonetic Alphabet, allow them to work on multiple Spanish dialects before attempting English language dialects. They will gain a sense of accomplishment and experience less stress when they attempt the English dialects.

2. Honor the wild tongue.
Allow Spanish-speaking students to explore Spanglish. Honoring Spanglish allows students to violate linguistic borders and is especially effective in addressing code switching.

3. Become knowledgeable about culture on campus and within the industry.
A knowledge of and relationship with Latino organizations and professors on campus can help the Latino/a voice student find support in a predominantly white institution. For performance students, this practical step is often overlooked. The demands of training for theatre or film make it very difficult to be involved in anything else; however, that is not always healthy for those students who could

benefit from having a community and support system that reflects their cultural heritage.

4. Become knowledgeable of culture-specific playwrights, theatres, and professional organizations. Be prepared to direct students to opportunities outside the Eurocentric mainstream theatre. As teachers, we may need to seek resources to improve our knowledge in this area.

5. Avail yourself of the latest discourse and theory that explores race, class, gender and teaching. Become familiar with current academic discourse and theory that explores race, class, gender and teaching. I have attended multiple NCORE (National Conference on Race and Ethnicity) conferences and have always been grateful for the knowledge and range of perspectives attained. I highly recommend this conference for those who are interested in improving inter-cultural relations within the classroom.

6. Help students navigate cultural expectations. Respect the multiple responsibilities students have to *la familia*[19] and work. The culture of college for Latinos is one that also includes complex responsibilities and obligations to home, including contributing financially.

Conclusion

It is our job as voice and speech educators to empower students' voices within their communities. Our goal should be to create artists who could return to their communities to tell their stories. Our goal should be to create artists who tell their stories on a global stage. The culture of racism and prejudice toward Latinos/Latinas and Latino/Latina voices is endemic in the United States of America; therefore, voice and speech trainers should take responsibility for cultural voice students' emotional health as they navigate these complexities. Voice and speech trainers are in an excellent position to contextualize the prejudices that students will experience within the profession. We must begin to challenge the ethnically and racially limited mindset of casting directors, film and theatre directors, and the industry. bell hooks, expert on race, class, gender, and culture, writes:

> Dominator Culture has tried to keep us all afraid, to make us choose safety instead of risk, sameness instead of diversity. Moving through that fear, finding out what connects us, reveling in our differences; this is the process that brings us closer, that gives us a world of shared values, of meaningful community. (197)

The shared values and diverse community that hooks envisions is attainable, but first we must embrace the cultural voice and stop trying to tame "the wild tongue." While the inequalities I speak of may not be endemic in every program, without close and honest examination of our practic-

es we may be perpetuating the inequalities and reinforcing the hidden artistic and cultural borders.

Notes

1. Throughout this paper I will use the term Chicanos/as for Mexicans and/or Mexican-Americans who identify with border culture and politics. I will use Latino as an umbrella term, to identify the socially constructed, market-driven identity that encompasses numerous national and cultural identities.

2. In her book *Borderlands: La Frontera*, Gloria Anzaldúa titles Chapter Five, "How to Tame a Wild Tongue." I borrow the concept to best describe Latinos/as and their relationship to identity and language.

3. In 1848, Mexico lost half of its territory to the United States — when the countries signed the Treatry of Gualdeloupe Hidalgo. A full account of what Chicano historians call an "act of imperial agression" can be found in *Occupied America. A History of Chicanos* by Rudolfo Acuña.

4. From *Border Visions* by Carlos Vélez-Ibáñez. Vélez-Ibáñez traces the intense "bumping" from before the border was created to the present.

5. The list of writers, scholars, and artists that use border theory is not exhaustive but is meant merely to provide a reference for those new to the subject and to show the range of lenses that border theory encompasses.

6 "Historically ignored communities" is a term coined and used by Albuquerque-based art and theatre organization, Working Classroom.

7. *In the Heights* was created by Lin Manuel Miranda and Quiara Alegría Hudes, winner of four 2008 Tony awards. The show features salsa, hip-hop, and merengue music and tells the classic story of chasing the American dream in the primarily Latino neighnorhood— Washington Heights.

8. The 2001 study by Rocio Rivadeneyra, *The Influence of Television on Stereotype Threat Among Adolescents of Mexican Descent* (University of Michigan, 2001), shows how watching Spanish language television led to better school motivation while watching English language television led to lower school motivation. Also see Charles Ramírez Berg, *Latino Images in Film: Stereotypes, Subversion, Resistance* (Austin: University of Texas Press, 2002) and Clara E. Rodriguez, *Latin Looks: Images of Latinos and Latinas in the U.S. Media* (Boulder, CO: Westview press, 1998).

9. See for example Vila (2000), Bejarono (2005), and Salivar (2006). Salivar's description for novelist Américo Paredes' border narratives summarizes my decision to use this device: "The epistomological crisis of the borderlands subject can be most meaningfully resolved only allegorically, in narrative as a problem of social aesthetics." (164)

10. Patsy Rodenburg is Director of Voice at the Guildhall School of Music and Drama and the former Director of Voice at the Royal National Theatre. She is also the author of *Speaking Shakespeare*, *The Actor Speaks*, and *The Need for Words*.

11. Catherine Fitzmaurice is considered one of the most influential voice teachers of our time, creator of the Fitzmaurice Voicework (a comprehensive approach to voice training often referred to as De

12. Dudley Knight is Professor Emeritus from University of California, Irvine, and a master teacher of the Fitzmaurice Voicework. Philip Thompson is Associate Professor and the Head of Acting at University of California, Irvine and a master teacher of the Fitzmaurice Voicework. Founders of the Knight-Thompson Speechwork.

13. Knight-Thompson Speechwork has a physical focus which allows actors and others to approach the learning of accents kinesthetically with a strong focus on articulatory agility.

14. VASTA diversity statement can be found at www.vasta.org/vision/diversity.

15 . Minimal changes in grammatical structure were done for clarity in reading.

16. *Mestiza* refers to the racial mixture of European and Amerindian peoples. Anzaldúa claims the new *mestiza*—a feminist perspective and a reclaiming her identities—white, Mexican, and Indian. She describes, "I want the freedom to carve and chisel my own face, to staunch the bleeding with ashes, to fashion my own gods out of my entrails. And if going home is denied me then I will have to stand and claim my space, making a new culture—*una cultura mestiza*—with my own lumber, my own bricks and mortar and my own feminist architecture." (44).

17. Terms such as: General American, Good American Speech, Theatre Standard, and Standard American are not universally accepted. For purposes of this research, I will refer to the teaching of these accents as Standard American.

18. Moisés Kaufman is a Latino writer, director, and the founder of Tectonic Theater Project. He is best known for his works *The Laramie Project*, *Gross Indencency: The Three Trials of Oscar Wilde*, *33 Variations*, and *I Am My Own Wife*.

19. *La familia* means "the family," and I use the term to define the Latino customs, traditions, and value system that inform identity development. Authors and psychotherapists Gil and Vasquez, *The Maria Paradox* (New York: G. P. Putnam's Son, 1996) give excellent advice to Latinas trying to navigate family and community expectations and life in North America.

Bibliography

Acuña, Rodolfo. *Occupied America: A History of Chicanos*, 2d ed. New York: Harper & Row, 1981.

Anzaldúa, Gloria. Borderlands =*La Frontera: The New Mestiza*, 2d ed. San Francisco: Aunt Lute Books, 1999.

Bejarano, Cynthia L. *Qué Onda?: Urban Youth Culture and Border Identity*. Tucson: University of Arizona Press, 2005.

Bender, Steven. *Greasers and Gringos: Latinos, Law, and the American Imagination*. New York: New York University Press, 2003.

Ethics, Standards and Practices
A Call to Action: Embracing the Cultural Voice or Taming the Wild Tongue by Micha Espinosa

Berg, Charles Ramirez. *Latino Images in Film: Stereotypes, Subversion, & Resistance*, 1st ed. Austin: University of Texas Press, 2002.

Dunn, Leslie C., and Nancy A. Jones. *Embodied Voices: Representing Female Vocality in Western Culture*. Cambridge: Cambridge UP, 1994.

Elasser, Nan. "Working Classroom Panel." ATHE 2009 Risking Innovation Conference. New York Mariott Marquis, New York City. 09. Aug. 2009. Speech.

Fitzmaurice, Catherine. "Diversity Panel." VASTA 2009 Origins Conference. Pace University, New York City. 05 Aug. 2009. Speech.

Gil, Rosa Maria, and Carmen Inoa Vazquez. *The Maria Paradox: How Latinas Can Merge Old World Traditions with New World Self-esteem*. New York: G.P. Putnam's Sons, 1996.

Gómez-Peña, Guillermo. "Documented/Undocumented." In *The Gray Wolf Annual Five: Multi-Cultural Literacy*, edited by Rick Simonson and Scott Walker, eds. Saint Paul, Minnesota: Graywolf Press, 1988: 127-134.

Gracia, Jorge J. E. *Hispanic/Latino Identity: A Philosophical Perspective*. Malden, Massachusetts. Oxford: Blackwell Publishers, 2000.

hooks, bell. *Teaching Community: A Pedagogy of Hope*. New York: Routledge, 2003.

Kells, Michelle Hall. "Linguistic Contact Zones in the College Writing Classroom: An Examination of Ethnolinguistic Identity and Language Attitudes."
Written Communication 19.1 (2002): 5-43.

Masud-Piloto, Felix. "Nuestro Realidad: Historical Roots of Our Latino Identity." *Beyond Comfort Zones in Multiculturalism: Confronting the Politics of Priviledge*, Jackson, Sandra and Jose Solis, eds. Westport: Bergin and Garvey, 1995: 53-63.

Mills, Liz. "Theatre Voice: Practice, Performance and Cultural Identity." *South African Theatre Journal*, January 1, 2009, http://www.thefreelibrary.com/Theatre voice: practice, performance and cultural identity.-a0224102076 (accessed November 24, 2010).

O'Connor, Terence. "Cultural voice and strategies for multicultural education." *Journal of Education* 171, no 2 (1989): 57-74.

Omi, Michael, and Howard Winant. *Racial Formation in the United States: From the 1960s to the 1990*, 2d ed. New York: Routledge, 1994.

Piepenburg, Erik. "Video: Denzel Washington and Viola Davis." Video blog post. http://artsbeat.blogs.nytimes.com/2010/04/15/video-denzel-washington-and-viola-davis/. New York times, 15 Apr. 2010. Web. 16 Apr. 2010.

Rivadeneyra, Rocio. *The Influence of Television on Stereotype Threat Among Adolescents of Mexican Descent*. Ph.D. Diss. University of Michigan, 2001. In Dissertations & Theses: Full Text [database on-line]; available from http://www.proquest.com.ezproxy1.lib.asu.edu (publication number AAT 3029418; accessed November 23, 2010).

Rodenburg, Patsy. "Quote." 05 May 2010. E-mail.

Rodriguez, Clara E. *Latin Looks: Images of Latinas and Latinos in the U.S. Media*. Boulder, Colorado: Westview Press, 1997.

Saldívar, Ramón. *The Borderlands of Culture : Américo Paredes and the Transnational Imaginary*. Durham: Duke University Press, 2006.

Vélez-Ibáñez, Carlos G. *Border Visions: Mexican Cultures of the Southwest United States*. Tucson: University of Arizona Press, 1996.

Vila, Pablo. *Crossing Borders, Reinforcing Borders: Social Categories, Metaphors, and Narrative Identities on the U.S.-Mexico Frontier*, 1st ed. Austin: University of Texas Press, 2000.

Pedagogy and Coaching, *Jeff Morrison, Associate Editor*

Jeff Morrison currently serves on the theatre faculty of Marymount Manhattan College, where he teaches voice, speech, and dialects. He is a Certified Associate Teacher of Fitzmaurice Voicework and has assisted Catherine Fitzmaurice at numerous workshops and certifications since 2002. He has taught at the American Repertory Theatre, the Moscow Art Theatre, San Diego State University, the Old Globe at USD, Tufts University, the University of Northern Iowa and the Heifetz International Music Institute. He has coached for stage and television in New York City, Los Angeles, Boston, and San Diego. He is a Member of the Board of VASTA.

The cover title of the 2011 *Voice and Speech Review, A World of Voice*, is highly evocative to me as someone who double-majored in Folklore and Theatre as an undergraduate and traveled to places like Sri Lanka to study ritual performance. The title suggests crossing boundaries of culture, language, ethnicity, performative tradition…. *A World of Voice* makes me want to go somewhere obscure and bring back evidence of an amazing vocal technique that nobody has ever heard of. And in fact, some of the articles in this year's Pedagogy and Coaching section do just that. Other articles, however, offer other perspectives on how our voices and voicework inspire and enable travel through geographical space, cultural space, and (read aloud in the voice of Carl Sagan) *time itself*.

Rinda Frye's article on Elsie Fogerty takes readers back in time to the origins of contemporary voice and speech work in the British theatre at the turn of the last century. Anne Schilling's latest article on keening also has a go at time travel (as well as the more mundane kind one can do on a plane) as she attempts to follow the practice of keening back to its roots in Ireland.

True to the cover theme, several articles likewise explore little-known nooks and crannies of the work of voice and speech professionals who are doing remarkable things in unusual places: Karina Lemmer and Marth Munro explore how to use Arthur Lessac's work to aid Zulu-speaking acting students in South Africa to effectively shape English phonemes; Marlene Johnson chronicles an international collaboration that marries Frankie Armstrong's work (with which many VASTA members are familiar) with the work of the DAH Theatre and Eugenio Barba (something that most Americans, at least, know very little about); and the peripatetic Lissa Tyler Renaud records her travels through the theatrical voice-scape of Eastern Europe and the Baltic States.

Other pieces address the cover theme in more indirect ways: Anne Harley uses her experience with singing instruction from three non-Western traditions to interrogate contemporary singing pedagogy in America; and Daydrie Hague begins to build a bridge across one of the widest divides in America by taking her university acting students into a rural Alabama grade school for a service-learning project to explore African-American praise poetry and create a performance with the grade school students.

And last but not least: some of you may remember Paul Ricciardi's paper from the Mexico City conference last year; it is edited for print and included in this year's issue. He interviewed a variety of voice and speech professionals and examined the process of mentorship in the development of voice and speech trainers. His article captures something essential about what voice and speech trainers do. It's about the world of the voice and speech trainer. It's about our world.

Happy Reading!

Elsie Fogerty and Voice for the Actor

Dr. Rinda Frye teaches acting and stage voice at the University of Louisville where she is Director of Graduate Studies for the Theatre Arts Dept. She was named Distinguished faculty in the College Arts and Sciences for her artistic and professional work. Her publications include scholarly articles, the most recent of which are a series on Grotowski's Paratheatrics workshops in Portland, Oregon and transcripts of his conversation about Paratheatrics soon to be published in *The Soul of the American Actor*, **a newspaper available in NYC and on-line, and a book,** *William Poel's Hamlets: The Director as Critic*. **A member of Voice And Speech Trainers of America, she frequently coaches stage dialects at Actors Theatre of Louisville, among other theatres in the Louisville area. She recently directed** *Measure for Measure, As You Like It* **and** *Hamlet* **at U of L and played Titus in** *Titus Andronicus*, **directed by Dennis Krausnick. She co-founded and was artistic director of the Utah Shakespeare Players in Salt Lake City.**

Elsie Fogerty may be the least famous great woman of the English Stage. Although she was considered the most important voice teacher and acting coach of her day, her name now scarcely produces a glimmer of recognition (particularly on this side of "the pond") unless coupled with her most famous pupil, Sir Laurence Olivier. There is an oft told anecdote about their first meeting when he nervously auditioned for her. She recognized his talents immediately but also pointed out a "weakness" in the center of his forehead and nose. Many have assumed this was the source of his penchant for wearing false noses on the stage.[1] But to be remembered for such a strange lesson is a dubious honor at best. And Fogerty's anonymity is undeserved. Her pioneer work in actor training alone should have ensured her notoriety. Fogerty's accomplishments are still remarkable: she founded the Central School for Speech and Dramatic Art in 1906, pioneered speech pathology in England, and taught many of the most famous actors and voice teachers

of her generation and the next.

At the beginning of the last century, the new realism of the Edwardian stage required a new kind of acting, sufficiently natural to withstand the close scrutiny of an audience no longer forced to squint through the glare of footlights. At the same time, a renewed interest in Shakespearean production demanded technically precise and flexible actors while opportunities for training under the old repertory system were swiftly disappearing. In response to this need, Fogerty offered private elocution classes at the Albert Hall. Many of the techniques she used were gleaned and from her work with Shakespearean producers William Poel and Sir Frank Benson, who later became the first president of the Central School.

During her almost forty years with the Central School, Fogerty had a phenomenal effect on the new generation of British actors. Olivier was not her only famous pupil. She worked with Sir John Gielgud, Dame Peggy Ashcroft, Dame Edith Evans, Dame Sybil Thorndike, and Sir Lewis Casson, among many others. And the sphere of her influence extended far beyond her own classroom. For instance, two of her pupils, Ruby Grinner and Irene Mawer, inspired by Fogerty's ideas about Greek choral movement and *eurhythmics*, developed the influential Grinner-Mawer school of dance.

Her innovations in speech education have had perhaps the most long-lasting effect on the English-speaking theatre. In 1912 she established a Central School speech clinic in conjunction with St. Thomas's Hospital, a symbiotic relationship that continued for many years. Through the 1980s Central School student teachers interned at the clinic and the professional speech pathologists were available for consultation at the School. By 1923 she had convinced the University of London to accept her curriculum as the basis for a Diploma of Dramatic Art, one of the first degrees of its kind in England. Achieving a respectable academic recognition for the always disreputable art of drama was no small accomplishment, but even more important was her special three year training course for teachers of speech. Fogerty-trained voice teachers worked in public schools, universities, and theatres throughout England, and even traveled to the wilds of the United States, Canada, and South Africa. Sir Herbert Beerbohm Tree had beaten Fogerty to the punch by founding his Academy of Drama just a few years before the Central School; but within twenty-five years, voice at RADA was taught by Amy Rean, Nancy Brown, and Clifford Turner, all Fogerty-trained teachers.

Given such a wide array of accomplishments, one might expect to discover that what Fogerty taught was as sound as whom she taught; and indeed, such was the case. She seemed to have a facility for bringing together the best

Pedagogy and Coaching

Elsie Fogerty and Voice for the Actor by Rinda Frye

people and ideas of the time and she had the good sense to rely on their expertise without interference. Her vocal technique was founded on the most up to date scientific, physiological and psychological information available at that time. Consequently, much of her methodology still seems startlingly modern, partly because so much of it was kept and passed on by her students.

Her own early training involved an eclectic admixture of techniques gleaned from two countries. She studied mime from Felicia Mallet in Paris and the art of acting at the Conservatoire with Augier, Delaunay, and Coquelin. Fogerty paid tribute to Coquelin's genius in her translation of his *Art of the Actor* but she had found the Conservatoire training lacking in "definite technical principles." Everything was taught on an *ad hoc* basis: "voice, articulation, gesture, even the history of the theatre, were dinned into the pupils during the study of an actual part" (Coquelin 1932, 15). Despite such illustrious teachers, it was Russell Wakefield, the Vicar of Lower Sydenham, whom Fogerty considered her true mentor. Elsie's father had refused to accept the stage as a proper *métier* for a young woman of breeding and only through the intervention of the eminently respectable clergyman was she allowed to continue studying drama after leaving the Conservatoire. The bishop held "at home" readings of Shakespeare and coached the young Miss Fogerty for several years in the niceties of verse speaking. Later, after the family's financial reversals and Mr. Fogerty's consequent death, Wakefield suggested his *protégée* as an elocution teacher for the Crystal Palace School.

Elsie's training in verse speaking was crowned by her work with William Poel, the innovative Shakespearean director who in the 1890s had started the Elizabethan Stage Society. Poel revolutionized the then "current idea of speaking Shakespeare—which had alternated between a sonorous rant and a pleasant chattiness not unsuited to comedy, but definitely comic in tragedy" (Fogerty in Cole 1967, 29-30). Poel's method involved keeping some of the chattiness by means of identifying equivalent modern vocal inflections (what he called tunes or tones) and applying those to Shakespeare's words. To avoid sonority, he identified what he called the key words in a speech. By emphasizing those, the actor could achieve a rapid-fire delivery without sacrificing meaning. Fogerty played Viola in Poel's *Twelfth Night* and worked as his assistant director and stage manager on other productions. Some time later she told Lillah McCarthy that "she had attended the rehearsals of all Poel's productions making notes of emphasis, speed, and rhythm which he insisted on" and that had given her "excellent groundwork for her own teaching" (Cole 30).

But probably the greatest influence on her work came from William A. Aikin, a medical doctor and early phonologist. With the invention of the laryngoscope in the mid 19th

century, medical practitioners and voice people alike were able actually to see what happened with the vocal folds during speech and singing. Aikin was a pioneer in the study of the voice. Fogerty, always ahead of her time, offered him a room while she was teaching at the Crystal Palace in 1889 and made her students available to him for his experiments. Aikin's books are now out of print, but still excellent reading. He strongly influenced many of her notions about breath, rib reserve, vowel pronunciation, and the use of the *bone prop*, which Aikin invented to create the ideal mouth shape for resonance. The bone prop was originally a chicken bone that he used to keep the mouth open while the pupil formed vowels. It is still used by Cicely Berry's students, though now in the more sanitary form of a cork.

The vocal method that Fogerty passed along to her own students was remarkably comprehensive, especially so given that the very notion of actor training was a novelty at the time. Fogerty's was a holistic approach that combined both movement and voice. Much of the early work at the Central School centered on developing a technique for breath that would allow the actor "to speak on the run, to combine poetry of movement with poetry of sound; to be completely relaxed, yet perfectly controlled" (Cole 35).

She achieved this by insisting that breathing exercises utilize the natural rhythms and normal muscular actions of the body. The philosophical underpinnings for this approach were based on the ideas of Emile Jaques-Dalcroze, who worked with such theatre greats as Appia and Copeau. Dalcroze eurhythmics were designed to release and augment the natural and expressive rhythms of the human body in response to both music and poetry. Actually, Dalcroze intended his *eurhythmics* not simply as an expression or interpretation of musical language, but as a language in itself, a physical transcription of sound. The aim of *eurhythmics* was

> To strengthen the power of concentration; to accustom the body to hold itself at high pressure in readiness to execute orders from the brain; to connect the conscious with the subconscious…to create more numerous habitual motions and new reflexes, to obtain the maximum effect by a minimum of effort… (Dalcroze in Pennington 1925, 77).

For the *eurhythmist*, breath, like pulse, was one of the natural forces that predisposed humanity instinctively toward the perception and execution of rhythm.

Eurhythmic concepts permeate Fogerty's ideas on voice production. She insisted that "vocal tone" required the rhythmic movement of the breathing musculature, or "the practice of equally balanced inspiratory and expiratory movements, in a relaxed position" (Fogerty 1914, 23). She conceded that the light, easy breathing that occurs when the body is completely relaxed was not sufficient to the needs of strong voice production. Speech requires a "modification in the rhythm of respiration, substituting a light, rapid inspiration and a slow, controlled expiration for the equal normal rhythm." But any modification must take place "without any disturbance to the normal action of the muscles concerned; briefly, without forcible inspiration or rigid expiration" (Fogerty 1936, 83). She concluded that since breathing and phonation involve a series of muscular movements, like all movement, it could be improved. When designing exercises for that purpose she asked:

> What sort of work really improves a movement? First, anything that makes the movement flexible and free; secondly, if the movement is a conscious one, anything which gives us control over this movement (1931, 26).

She cautioned, however, that not all of the movements involved in voice production can or should be consciously controlled. Pitch, for instance, is regulated by the indirect control of hearing, not by conscious manipulation of the vocal folds. Some aspects of breathing are deeply unconscious and Fogerty warned that

> ...it is never a good thing to try to make yourself conscious of a movement which is naturally unconscious; it tires you, and often you will jerk and twitch where the unconscious movement would be perfectly smooth and easy. As a matter of fact, if you try to control an unconscious movement you generally do something quite different from what you intend... Whenever you try to move an involuntary muscle over which you cannot get control, you will almost certainly stiffen the voluntary muscle nearest at hand (1931, 27-28).

She also backed her ideas with sound scientific research. In 1909 she asked the University of London to investigate the problems of speech training. One of the results was Sir Charles Sherrington's discovery of the "Law of Reciprocal Innervation" which governs all muscular contraction. In terms of breath control, this meant that because "the inspiratory and expiratory muscles are mutually antagonistic," when "the motor centres of the inspiratory [muscles] are inhibited," (Fogerty 1914, 524) expiration will likewise be inhibited. Sherrington's experiments with rabbits showed that in order to function normally and to avoid exhaustion, the diaphragm must relax with each exhalation.

Fogerty's work in this area was and still is extremely sophisticated, especially when compared with the prevailing notions of the time about the virtues of "deep breathing" on elocutionary technique. Fogerty fought valiantly against the barbarisms of the Swedish drill, a rigid form of calis-

thenics equally popular in the grade school classroom, on the armed forces drill field, and in most manuals for public speaking. The breathing component of Swedish gymnastics involved the hyper-expansion of the ribcage, accompanied by a contraction or bowing of the lumbar region, stiffly turned out legs, and rapid arm movements to the side or over the head. These were usually done in the open air with the intention that as much air should be gotten into the lungs and held for as long as possible. Photographs of the period show schoolboys, deformed by abnormally distended chests, holding their collective breaths like so many little puffed pigeons (Alexander 1918). Fogerty abhorred such practices, complaining that jerky, stiff movements led only to exhaustion and that "antagonistic muscular movements using forced inspiration" could only "injure vocal tone." As to the puffed-pigeon look, she insisted that "beyond a certain point, every additional gain in expansion of the chest is at the expense of control, and is liable to lead to permanent deterioration of the muscles and injury to the lung" (Fogerty 1914, 523).

Fogerty's exercises began with an awareness of body length and balance. She advocated a relaxed stance, the weight balanced between the legs, but shifted slightly forward onto the balls of the feet. The knees were straight, but not locked, the shoulders down and back, and the head and neck carried in a straight line above the feet. Sometimes, when deep relaxation work was needed, the students would perform her exercises lying on their backs on the floor, "like corpses in Hamlet, but straight and tidy," while Fogerty moved amongst them urging them to "Breathe iiiin… Ooooout…Iiiin…Ooooout," (Cole 1967, 191) while sometimes poking them to make certain they really were relaxed.

Breath work centered immediately on rib expansion. The hands were placed on either side of the rib cage to direct attention to the rise and fall of the ribs while the student inhaled and exhaled, each on a count of eight. When this was successfully accomplished, the next exercise strengthened the abdominal muscles, which Fogerty thought could be safely brought under conscious control. With one hand three inches below the waist, on a voiced "one, two" count, with each "one" the muscles under the hand were "softly and firmly" contracted, then relaxed on a whispered "two." The final step, when the first two stages had been mastered, was "rib-reserve" breathing. With the rib cage expanded, air continued to move in and out of the body, controlled by the diaphragm and abdominal muscles alone. The idea was to have absolute control over the exhalation, steady air pressure for a clear tone, and a little air always in reserve for difficult passages. Ideally, in practice, the rib cage would expand at the beginning of a poem or a long soliloquy and would remain so through to the end of the passage when the rib cage would momentarily relax to take in fresh air. It's interesting to note here that Fogerty and later Gwynneth Thurburn, who headed the Central School for many years, both taught pupils to relax the ribs at the end of the breath, while Clifford Turner advocated keeping the ribs expanded throughout.

Rib-reserve breathing is a little old-fashioned now; few voice teachers use this technique any more, though it was still being taught at LAMDA in the 1980s. But, tellingly, the contemporary rationale against rib-reserve—that "it is unreal and makes for a great deal of tension," (Berry 1973 27)—comes directly out of Fogerty's hundred-year-old philosophy. Likewise, some eyebrows might raise over the forced contraction of abdominal muscles to control the breath, particularly given Fogerty's concern over the tension produced when interfering with involuntary processes. Other voice practitioners, however, will see no conflict here; the relative merits of the soft versus the firm center is still a lively debate among voice experts. In years past, many voice and speech teachers like Turner, for instance, advocated a firm abdomen to help push the voice. Far fewer would support that notion now, though certainly the firm center is still advocated by many singing teachers.

Fogerty often compared the human voice to a wind instrument with bellows, vibrator, and resonator, with the majority of her exercises focusing on the resonator. She recognized that proper phonation "demands the most exact possible synchronization between the emission of air and the approximation of the vocal cords," (Fogerty 1934, np) but expended very little energy on the vibrator itself, since the vocal folds are not subject to direct conscious control. Instead, she concentrated on the breath when faced with phonation problems. She vigorously protested against the adverse affects of "glottal shock" at a time when some voice teachers encouraged it. The Delsarte system, for instance, advocated a glottal attack for vocal power. Fogerty attributed glottal shock solely to breathing issues. Fogerty believed that too sharp an attack of breath violently forces apart the vocal folds; therefore, she concluded that controlled breath should remedy the problem.

Fogerty's resonation exercises were based on a resonator scale devised by Dr. W.A. Aikin. Her work with Aikin led to a reliance on resonance rather than force for the carrying power of the voice. This allowed for greater relaxation of the throat and abdominal muscles with the result of greater power and more natural vocal tone. Aikin realized that the three resonating cavities, pharyngeal, mouth, and nose, resonate on certain pitches, independent of the phonated pitch. He dismissed the nasal cavity as an accessory resonator, which has a fixed shape and is therefore not subject to control. According to Aikin, the mouth and pharyngeal cavities, however, change shape as the lips and tongue move to shape vowels and consonants, though the sum total of the two spaces remains constant. Aikin showed that as these

cavities change shape in the formation of vowel sounds, the resonant notes of the cavities also change. Fogerty suggested the following short experiment to demonstrate this phenomenon: with a loose jaw, and using only the tongue and lips to shape the mouth, whisper, "Who's to know small frogs pass up, where landsmen wade in reeds?". If whispered in a received British accent, this sentence contains the vowel sounds /u ʊ o ɔ ɒ ɑ ʌ ɜ ə æ ɛ e ɪ i/. A careful ear will hear a distinct octave between the /i/ and the /ɑ/ and a fifth between the /ɑ/ and the /u/, with the rest of the vowels falling on notes in between. The resonant pitch of the pharynx is much lower, and can be heard by placing the fingers along side of the windpipe and tapping them lightly with a pencil while performing the same whispered exercise. These observations on vocal resonance properties of the voice led Fogerty and Aikin to two fundamental realizations: first, that the throat, tongue and jaw must remain as relaxed as possible so as to encourage pharyngeal resonant undertones; and second, that the precise but relaxed formation of vowels could vastly increase resonance in the mouth cavity and decrease nasality.

Fogerty's main vocal exercises, comprised of variations on these combinations of vowel formations, were designed to facilitate the maximum possible resonance. The pupil worked for flexibility of lips and tongue while keeping the throat relaxed, the tip of the tongue at rest behind the bottom teeth and the jaw loose but open at least an inch. Fogerty recommended the use of a bone prop (a ¾ to 1 inch bone, which Aikin invented to help keep the teeth apart when practicing the movement from /ɑ/ to /u/). The tendencies to depress the back of the tongue on the /ɑ/ or to widen the lips on an /i/ were firmly discouraged as unnecessary tensions that dampen resonance. The beginning student whispered the scale, which allowed Fogerty both to check any inclinations toward glottal attack and to reinforce proper placement in the front of the mouth. More advanced students sang the basic vowels and diphthongs with accompanying consonants, moving up and down the scale, combining resonator work with diction drills.

Interestingly, in the early days of his experiments while in residence at the Crystal Palace, Aikin was very taken with the notion that resonance could be greatly improved simply through proper shaping of the mouth cavity. He actually insisted that some of his singing pupils should give up singing altogether for at least two years and instead spend their time whispering while practicing vowel drills. He was certain that this would lead to perfect singing resonance; his students were not convinced.

The resonator scale also provided a rationale to justify the need for standardized speech. For Fogerty, Cockney nasality, for instance, was not simply a regionalism, but patently wrong since it corrupted the proper shaping of vowels for maximum resonation. The vowel drills freed her

> ...from the necessity for the irritating type of correction which amounts merely to the demand, "Stop talking your way, and talk my way." Being constructed on the principles of vocal sound, and in accordance with its natural properties in resonation, it is equally helpful to every form of dialectical or individual mispronunciation (1936, 87).

Her intentions were highly egalitarian: to establish as a standard, an English dialect that could be understood by all who speak the language and that betrayed no class or regional restrictions. However, her standard for beauty was itself a product of certain regional and class biases, which she occasionally inadvertently let slip. For example, she deemed the conversion of a final "y" into an /i/ instead of an /ɛ/ as in "get" a "very unpleasant vulgarism." The word "beauty" would then be pronounced, somewhat affectedly by today's standards, "beauteh" rather than "beautee." Similarly, the speaker who slipped into a colloquial "yuss" or "yepp" had not, by her standards, simply betrayed class or educational background, but had expressed "a personality which would be likely to bore and annoy sensible people" (Fogerty 1931, 6).

Still, her overall methodology was sound, and miles ahead of the old-fashioned elocutionists and deep-breathers who preceded her. Her voice work was only one part of a remarkably full curriculum of training that included verse-speaking, prosody and poetics, several kinds of dancing, fencing, drama, costume history, and mime, among other aspects of acting. Voice teachers were required to study a year longer than actors and their program included phonetics, anatomy, psychology, and speech therapy. Through her ministrations Central School developed its well-deserved reputation as one of the best actor training programs in the country.

Many of us who are voice and speech practitioners will recognize aspects of her work that we may have thought original to our own methodologies. One can easily draw a direct line of teaching practices from Fogerty to Clifford Turner, Gwynneth Thurburn, Cicely Berry, Barbara Houseman and Patsy Rodenburg, all of whom, among many others, studied at the Central School. The greater influence of her work can be attributed in part to the fact that the Central School focused so strongly on teacher training for voice and speech and many of these teachers worked at various schools throughout England. In his brief essay on the history of voice training in the United Kingdom, David Carey notes that Rose Bruford and Greta Colson, who were trained by Fogerty and Aikin, became principals of drama schools with strong voice and speech training (Carey). Iris Warren, Kristin Linklater's teacher at

LAMDA, did not train at Central School[2]; however, she was strongly influenced by Aikin's books.[3] Certainly Linklater's "Zoo Woe Shaw" exercise, like much of her resonator work, is reminiscent of Aikin's resonator drills.

Fogerty's renown evaporated as the next generation of voice teachers—people like Clifford Turner and Gwynneth Thurburn—came into their own. Fogerty was the harbinger of change in attitudes toward acting and actor training, and like most pioneers, her ideas were often as rooted in the old as in the new. Her several books make for rather dull reading, partly because she takes so much for granted with her reader and partly because her writing is often riddled with the vestiges of antiquated Edwardianisms. Her sentimental worship of all things Greek is quaintly reminiscent of the ladies' Grecian urn posturing in *The Music Man* and her patronizing attitudes toward people of African descent (the implication that their voices are more open because they were somehow simpler and more primitive) echoes too much the doctrine of vocal imperialism to sit comfortably with modern sensibilities. She was also quite disappointed that most of those who followed in her footsteps to become voice teachers were female (with the exception of course, of Clifford Turner, whom she adored), echoing the misogyny of John Knox by referring to them as "that monstrous regiment of women" (Cole 1967, 120). Sybil Thorndike, who praised Fogerty for helping her to recover her lost three-octave voice, once said of her,

> She had a wonderful technical knowledge of the voice. She was often extremely tiresome and we could have blown her head off; but she knew what she was up to. I've never known anybody quite like her (in Burton 1967, 58).

However "tiresome," this tireless woman has earned her place in the history of the theatre and deserves acknowledgement as the pioneer of modern voice training. Voice and speech practitioners everywhere are indebted to her work. Her influence on modern voice training cannot be denied.

Notes

1. Olivier told the story on countless occasions. It appears in several biographies and can be found in Marion Cole's book *Fogie* and in Hal Burton's edited anthology *Great Acting*.

2. Gwynneth Thurburn, an unpublished 1986 interview with the author. Thurburn had met Iris Warren many times as they had been on boards together to adjudicate public school speech, but Thurburn saw Warren as an outsider to the Central School group.

3. Sybil Beresford-Pierce, a British speech therapist, introduced me to one of Iris Warren's protégées who was teaching at LAMDA in 1986. I cannot recall her name and have misplaced my old notes from that interview. She told me that Iris had given her a book that Iris considered to be the most important book about voice that she had ever read. It was Aikin's The Voice: Its Physiology and Cultivation.

Bibliography

Aikin, William Arthur. *The Voice: Its Physiology and Cultivation*. London and New York: MacMillan and Co., Ltd., 1900.

Aikin, William Arthur. *The Voice: An Introduction to Practical Phonology*. London, New York: Longmans, Green and Co., 1920.

Aikin, William Arthur. "The Principles of Vowel Pronunciation." *Journal of the Royal Musical Association* Volume 30, Issue 1, (1903): 1-14.

Alexander, F. Matthias. *Man's Supreme Inheritance*. New York: E.P. Dutton & Co, 1918.

Berry, Cicely. *Voice and the Actor*. New York: MacMillan and Co., 1973.

Burton, Hal, ed. *Great Acting*. New York: Bonanza Books, 1967.

Carey, David. *History of UK Voice Teaching* (pdf). Accessed February 2, 2010, http://www.vocalprocess.co.uk/resources/HistoryofUKVoice-Teaching.pdf

Cole, Marion. *Fogie*. London: Peter Davies, 1967.

Coquelin, C. *The Art of the Actor*. Translated by Elsie Fogerty. London: George Allen & Unwin Ltd., 1932.

Fogerty, Elsie. *Rhythm*. London: George Allen & Unwin Ltd., 1936.

Fogerty, Elsie. *Speech Craft*. New York: E.P. Dutton & Co., Inc., 1931.

Fogerty, Elsie. "The Harmony of Psychological and Aesthetic Standards in Speech." *International Conference in Speech Therapy*. Budapest (1934): np.

Fogerty, Elsie. "The Training of the Faculty of Speech, its Place and Method in General Eduction." *Fourth International Congress on School Hygiene*. Transactions 3, (1914): 523.

Pennington, Jo. *The Importance of Being Rhythmic*. New York: G.P. Putnam's Sons, 1925.

Thurburn, Gwynneth. Personal interview with the author. Sussex, England, July, 1986.

Lift Every Voice—Vocal Performance and Civic Engagement

Daydrie Hague (AEA, SAG, AFTRA) has worked Off Broadway and in regional and repertory theatres in the U.S. and England, including the Alley Theatre, New Dramatists, The Vineyard Lab Theatre and Alan Ayckbourn's Stephen Joseph Theatre in the Round. She is the Co-Director of the BFA Performance Program at Auburn University, where teaches acting and voice. Hague is an Associate Teacher of Fitzmaurice Voicework, Associate Editor for IDEA, and theatre consultant to the NSF Advance Program. Her most recent article "The Human Voice: Celebrating Diversity and Creating Community," was recently published in the International Journal of Diversity in Organizations, Communities and Nations.

Introduction
Like You

Like you I
love love, life, the sweet smell
of things, the sky-blue
landscape of January days.

And my blood boils up
and I laugh through eyes
that have known the buds of tears.

I believe the world is beautiful
and that poetry, like bread, is for everyone.

And that my veins don't end in me
but in the unanimous blood
of those who struggle for life,
love,
little things,
landscape and bread,
the poetry of everyone.

Roque Dalton (2000, 129)

This poem by the Latin American poet and revolutionary Roque Dalton was one of two works that captivated me with their passion and perception, inspiring the development of a service-learning project that engaged BFA performance majors and rural Alabama school children in the study, rehearsal, and performance of African-American praise poetry. Dalton's assertion that "poetry, like bread is for everyone," (2000, 129) suggests that our human need to love, thrive, and express our deepest desires through poetry is universal, crosses cultural boundaries and connects us one to the other.

In generating a community and civic engagement effort that brought together white undergraduate acting students with African-American grade school children, we used poetry to bridge the racial and cultural divide. Praise poetry, a ritual in many cultures, has served as a means of passing on community history, language, poetry, and ethics to the next generation (Fountain). This keeps oral traditions alive and strengthens a sense of cultural identity. In bringing these two groups of students together, we hoped to "instill new visions of self and community" (Dolan 2001, 5) in both. The Auburn students stood to gain a new sense of themselves as teacher- artists, passing on their knowledge of theatre and performance. The African-American children could claim this poetic heritage as their own, identifying with its themes of endurance, spiritual unity, and cultural pride. Poets belong to everyone, and Dalton's fervent language, while informed by a different cultural experience, served as a touchstone and catalyst for our efforts.

If Dalton served as our muse, Jill Dolan and her article, "Rehearsing Democracy: Advocacy, Public Intellectuals, and Civic Engagement in Theatre and Performance Studies" provided the ideological spark and pedagogical underpinnings for our project. Dolan writes about the need to train our theatre students, not only to learn the technical skills associated with performance, but to participate in theatre as informed scholar-artists with empathy and a concern for social justice (Dolan 5). As an artist, I recognize the need for an actor to be empathetic, knowledgeable, and skilled. As a teacher of undergraduate students pursing performance training within a Liberal Arts curriculum, I want my students to understand the myriad forms theatre can take, and the many ways it can impact our lives. This would include participating in outreach theatre that fosters social awareness through community and civic engagement. Engaged activities involving universities and communities provide learning opportunities for everyone involved. The potential exists to create exciting collaborations between diverse partners—establishing new communities and strengthening existing ones, and creating theatre does precisely that. I wanted my acting students to witness that first hand, discovering something about themselves and their place in the theatre in the process. My hope was that by inviting my students and the rural community students to create a production around African-American poetry, they could teach each other something about theatre, acting, poetry, and citizenship.

As the project unfolded, my goal was to assess the academic, social, and cultural value of engaged learning for both sets of students: the development of language and communication skills, multicultural perspectives, and the promotion of empathy and social responsibility. I also wanted to see if this work could enrich the training of undergraduate actors.

Background

Our project focused on a small Alabama community of roughly one thousand people with an agriculturally based economy, no central business district, and a campus that serves grades one through twelve. Eighty five percent of the students qualify for the subsidized lunch program, and there is no arts programming in the elementary grades (Lee County). The school is, in fact, the community center. Auburn University, with its land grant mission of "improving the lives of people in the state," (Auburn University) supports outreach efforts to underserved communities. The College of Liberal Arts at Auburn, through its Community and Civic Engagement Initiative, is committed to "creating a culture of faculty and student engagement both within and outside the university that will address and solve challenges facing communities" (AU College of Liberal Arts). Civic engagement has been defined as "actions that make a difference in the civic life of our communities and developing the combination of knowledge, skills, values, and motivation that make that difference"(Erhlich 2000, vi). In 2008, Auburn's College of Liberal Arts instituted a Community and Civic Engagement Summer Academy to provide faculty training in the best practices for developing civically engaged programming, the policies and procedures involved in these activities, and the resources available to fund them. It was through this facilitation that I was able to identify the ways in which my theatrical training and the growing communication skills of my vocal performance students could be put to use in amplifying the voices of these minority children through the study, rehearsal, and performance of African-American praise poetry.

According to the *Imagining America: Artists and Scholars in Public Life* "Curriculum Project Report on Culture and Community Development in Higher Education," the most effective university-community partnerships are "reciprocal and collaborative, producing knowledge through jointly designed activities that serve communities as well as students" (Goldbard 2009, 56). Mindful of these directives, we worked closely with our community partner, the Director of the Extended Day Program at the county elementary school, establishing a series of learning outcomes for our students related to voice, performance, language, interper-

sonal and intrapersonal skills, and cultural sensitivity. We set up a schedule of twelve vocal performance workshops to be taught by the AU performance majors, which would culminate in a public performance of African-American praise poetry.

We hoped that these interactive sessions would engage both sets of students in an exploration of the rich and powerful language of our major African-American poets, discovering together what is both unique and universal in their work. We hoped that the Auburn students would concretize their knowledge of voice, speech, and text by teaching it to others, widen their multicultural perspectives, and strengthen their sense of social responsibility as both artists and citizens.

Preparation

Gregory Jay, in his article "What (Public) Good are the (Engaged) Humanities?" insists that community engagement requires "critical reflection on diversity and multiculturalism since it almost always involves asymmetries of power in relationships among individuals who may have had little or no contact because of continued segregation" (Jay 2009, 20). My students, who were all white, were understandably hesitant about teaching African-American poetry to African-American children; they wondered what kind of authenticity they could bring to this process. I could only tell them that we had been invited to teach the skills that would help the children bring the poetry to life in performance—skills that they had been developing for the past four years in their BFA performance program. The children would no doubt be teaching *them* about the experiences the poetry described. All of the poems we chose for the presentation focused on themes of racial identity and unity, underscoring the community building efforts so critical to the objectives of civic engagement. In an attempt to broaden our awareness of issues related to racial and cultural identity, and to take steps toward confronting our own implicit biases, we read Linda Christensen's *Unlearning the Myths that Bind Us*, which uncovers the subtle and overt stereotypes hidden in children's media and literature.

Christensen, a writer and educator, asserts that American popular culture—comics, cartoons, and animated films—teach us simplistic and demeaning associations about racial and ethnic groups from a very early age (Christensen 2000, 20). She notes that children see and hear images that present an "other"—with darker skin, exotic features, or accented speech—that is less than heroic in their motives and behavior.[1] The Chilean writer Ariel Dorfman calls this our "secret education," which he says leads us to accept the world as it is represented in these distorted social blueprints (Dorfman 1983, ix). By encouraging my students to look more closely at the ways in which we may have been encouraged to "legitimate social inequality," (Christensen 41) I hoped they would approach their teaching with a new awareness of any assumptions they might be holding about the children.

Because we also needed to address the place of the artist in the multicultural landscape, I required each of my students to read Jill Dolan's "Rehearsing Democracy: Advocacy, Public Intellectuals, and Civic Engagement in Theatre and Performance Studies." This essay challenges theatre instructors to train their students to be informed, engaged theatre artists and scholars. Dolan contends that our students "need to look beyond the classroom's walls into the larger culture because theatre and performance help shape and promote certain understandings of what America looks like and believes in" (Dolan 5). As artists in an increasingly multicultural nation, our students need to make informed artistic choices as performers, but they won't be able to if they are unaware of, or insensitive to, our continuing national challenges with the ways in which race and economic inequality continue to divide us.

Dolan's theories have sparked discussion about the aesthetic tension that exists in academic theatre communities between those who would educate the whole student and those who focus specifically on performance skills. While some may contend that our theatre students come to us with expectations of being trained to become employable actors, my own view is that the undergraduate student and aspiring artist who is well informed and socially aware will ultimately have far more to contribute to the theatre—wherever they choose to create it.

In preparing to lead the workshops, the twelve Auburn students were divided into teams of four. Each team was responsible for leading two workshops and staging two of the poems we had selected for the presentation. The teams developed a series of age-appropriate warm-ups that would introduce the basic principles of alignment, breath support, vocal production, clear articulation, and exercises for embodying language. They researched the work of Langston Hughes, Marie Evans, Maya Angelou, and Alexis de Veaux, as well as the cultural roots and purposes of praise poetry. They reviewed the terms and techniques they had discovered in their own study of heightened and poetic texts: metaphor, simile, antithesis, and rhythmic patterning. Together we identified a series of basic skills that we hoped the extended day students, aged nine to thirteen, would be able to master: skills related to vocal production and speech, language and movement, and working cooperatively. Each team built their lesson plans around developing those skills.

Finally, my students and I completed the Collaborative Institutional Training Initiative Certification process. CITI's on-line tutorials serve to educate researchers about the ways in which one can responsibly recruit, interact with, and process information about human subjects to insure their safety and privacy (CITI).

Completing the Collaborative Institutional Training was one of a number of requirements we had to fulfill to secure our Institutional Review Board's (IRB) approval. I needed this because I was, in effect, conducting human subjects research on both sets of students. I had to assure my institution, in writing, that all parties involved had been apprised of the risks and benefits associated with the project, that the subjects' privacy would be protected, and that identifying words or images would not be presented in research venues without express permission from parents or the university students themselves (AU IRB). This was an exacting and tedious process, often frustrating and discouraging, but I respect those who serve on the IRB and their efforts to protect the students, the institution and those of us working with human subjects.

Process and Performance

In the early workshops, which involved theatre games to develop team building, vocal exercises, and analysis of the poetry, the twelve extended day students were engaged and enthusiastic. A typical session at the elementary school would include gathering all the students together in a circle and "spelling in"—a little ritual of sound and movement that identified us as an ensemble. Each student created a unique sound and accompanying movement, and eventually we performed these in sequence, as a group. This was our "spell" and we used it as a way of bringing ourselves together into the creative moment. We then would do some kind of aerobic activity: jumping jacks, running in place, or something we called "crazy dancing"—expansive free form dancing in the style of Steve Martin, involving all parts of the body. These exercises would energize the group and give them a physical release from sitting in the classroom all day. It also challenged their breath to the point where they could be instructed to ground themselves and use their hands to feel where their breath was moving in their body, focusing particularly on the ribs and the belly. Sometimes we would practice what the Auburn students had dubbed "puppy panting." This involved getting the kids to drop their jaws and pant like a puppy, pulling in their tummies on the out breath. We then asked them to add voice to that abdominal action, which helped them to feel how their sound was being supported. My students constantly reinforced the idea of alignment and its connection to breath and presence. We defined presence as "being aware, relaxed, focused, and proud." The elementary kids particularly enjoyed the silly characters my students and I created through demonstrations of less-than-optimal posture, illustrating the ways in which breath and voice could be squeezed and compromised. After practicing alignment and releasing breath into sound, we would create little improvised scenes in gibberish in which the characters had to move away from each other in the space while maintaining sufficient volume to communicate with each other across the distance. Early on in the process, we encouraged the extended day students to think of the audience member in the last row of the auditorium as the person who really wanted to hear what they had to say, and then asked them to go on stage and tell that imaginary person about something in which they took great pride. This helped them to understand that intention was as important to communication as breath support. Over time, their ability to fill the space vocally grew significantly.

We tried to follow a logical progression in the warms ups: releasing the body to release breath and sound, expanding the sound in range and volume, adding speech to sound, and finally singing, which synthesizes all these elements. To loosen the articulators, we made scrunchy faces, fish lips, floppy tongues, burbled like babies, and recited tongue twisters. We then would put the whole thing together with a series of African call and response songs that focused on using all these techniques to communicate something meaningful to partners like "welcome" or "I'm proud of you."

As I had hoped, the poetry became the bridge between the two groups. The elementary children vied for the chance to read aloud and offered sophisticated insights about the imagery, the ideas, and the music they identified in the poems. One rather silent young man, who spent much of his time daydreaming on the floor, surprised us one day by offering his interpretation of the Langston Hughes poem *The Dream Keeper*. Upon hearing "Bring me all of your dreams, you dreamers…/ that I may wrap them / in a blue cloud-cloth / away from the too-rough fingers / of the world" (Hughes 2004, 20) this student piped up with: "that means your dreams are *sacred*, you can't let people mess with them." Our experience reinforces what educators and writers have always believed: that poetry can help us to develop a sense of community because "if we use words well, we can build bridges across incomprehension and chaos" (House of Poetry). The American poet Georgia Heard, author of *Awakening the Heart*, reminds us: "We read poetry from a deep hunger to know ourselves and the world" (Heard 1999, 19). The sessions in which the two groups were engaged in speaking aloud and sharing their responses to the poetry were among the most fruitful, connected and harmonious.

Making the transition from understanding a poetic text, and communicating it clearly, truthfully, and imaginatively is a challenge for experienced actors, let alone ten-year-olds. Children tend to find a single pitch and rhythmic pattern and repeat it, particularly if they are speaking in unison. In an attempt to inspire spontaneous speaking inspired by the text, we asked the kids to breathe in a word, and whisper it back out into the space in a way that expressed their image of that word. We asked them to sing what they thought were the important words in a given poem, exploring pitch as a way of inviting the audience to listen to the operative word in a phrase. They took turns literally embodying the words to see what kinds of shapes the words created in their bodies, and how those shapes affected their vocal delivery. Together the ensemble looked at the patterns of the words on the page to see where the breaths or silences might be. We had them identify the long and short words, and experiment with tempo and duration to express the mood or intention of the narrative voice in the poem. Sometimes these exercises produced surprising vocal choices that illuminated the text, and sometimes they didn't. I think we planted some seeds, though, because when we began to stage the poems, the students began to contribute ideas that revealed their budding understanding of spoken text. For instance, one child suggested we hum the /m/ sound in the word "music," and make the /u/ sound long. She said it would sound more like a song that way. In effect, we incorporated the voice, speech, and text approaches we used in our studio classes, keeping the concepts simple and the language direct, but working toward the same aesthetic goals: free voices that express ideas and images in a varied and spontaneous way.

As we began to rehearse our presentation, we encountered some significant challenges. For all of our idealistic intentions, we still had to "put on a show." After-school attendance was erratic, making it difficult to stage the presentation. Some of the children struggled to learn their lines, inviting criticism from their peers and undermining the sense of ensemble we had been trying so hard to build. Some of the Auburn students struggled to establish their authority with the children in the face of some uncooperative behavior. We dealt with each obstacle as it occurred, learning as we went. When children were absent from the rehearsals, and this happened regularly, my students would have to reconfigure the staging they had created for a particular poem on the spot, or reassign lines to the children who were present, so we could proceed with the rehearsal. They had to do this in a way that would incorporate the absent children upon their return. When this first happened, my students looked to me solve the problem. They eventually learned to build a contingency plan into every workshop session. We also had to learn, through trial and error, how to establish a positive but authoritative relationship with the extended day children. We experimented with a rotating buddy system and assigned one Auburn student to one elementary student each week, thinking we could build relationships more quickly that way, and draw out some of the more introverted children. In some instances this worked well, but some youngsters would get very attached to their Auburn student and totally shut down when they had to work with someone else the following week. We discontinued that practice, and just tried to make sure every child got our attention and support. I could see that some of my students were uncomfortable asserting themselves when the children became unfocused or disagreeable, so we devoted one of our planning sessions to this issue. We developed "scripts" we could use in these difficult instances, praising the children's positive contributions to the production, but clearly communicating our expectations of respectful behavior toward their peers and their instructors. In the workshops, we continued to reinforce the idea of cohesion, and reminded the children how strong our production could be if we worked together. Many times this approach worked, and the younger students applied themselves more enthusiastically to the rehearsal process. Sometimes it didn't—especially if a kid was just having a bad day. A number of the children in our project were living in unstable domestic environments and occasionally they would have an emotional melt down or act out in aggressive or defiant ways. We all struggled to understand these behaviors and to deal with them in an appropriate manner. If a child was crying, one of my students would take them out of the room and just be with them until they could collect themselves and rejoin the group. In one instance, when a child's behavior had been consistently provocative, the Director of the Extended Day program and I made a decision to remove the child from the project—which was disheartening. We moved doggedly forward however, inspired by these kids who had so many challenges in their lives and still managed to show up most days with energy, a sense of humor, and a willingness to play. This perseverance paid off; members of the elementary school, the university, and the local community enthusiastically received the production "Lift Every Voice—A Celebration of African-American Praise Poetry". It seemed clear that both sets of students were visibly proud of what they had accomplished together. In a little ceremony after the performance, my students presented each one of the extended day students with an acting award. We called them Peet Feet, named for our Telfair Peet Theatre at Auburn University. They are little wooden feet made from pieces of our old sets, representing a passage from our theatrical community to this new one. Each child received a special commendation: "most energetic", "most professional", etc., and they each were very pleased to be recognized, and to be a part of the group.

Assessment

The goals of civic engagement revolve around the transformation of those involved. Engaged scholars insist it is most beneficial when students have what is termed a *discontinuous experience*, one that is "distinct from their every day

experiences so that they are challenged to broaden their perspectives on the world" (Cone and Harris 2000, 27-41). In evaluating both student learning and community benefit, I had to determine what new knowledge was created and what new skills were mastered. What kind of intercultural dialogue took place? What was the impact of engagement on the attitude and knowledge of students in the area of diversity?

Our community partners confirmed that providing students and parents with an exposure to the performing arts filled a significant need in the school and the community. The performance, a public affirmation of African-American values of family, strength, and unity convinced those assembled that this work was worth continuing. The Extended Day Director described this response: "for many of the parents, this performance was their first opportunity to view live theatre. They were impressed with the children and the production and wanted to see more" (Davino). While we did not directly interview the county children because of limitations imposed by the IRB, we were able to witness their evolving focus and commitment to the work, as well as their evident pleasure in being part of a project that received so much positive attention in a very public arena.

We have committed ourselves to refining, strengthening, and sustaining this partnership over a three-year period, with the intention of institutionalizing the program and maintaining our ties with community.

To maximize the educational benefits for all involved, our community partners intend to establish a more rigorous vetting process in selecting the children who participate in the workshops in order to secure those with a sincere interest in performance. We have agreed on the necessity for on-site staff support at the county school to discourage disruptive or uncooperative behavior. This will free the AU students to focus on teaching and directing. We will encourage parents to support this initiative by making sure their children attend the workshops as regularly as possible.

Assessing the value of the service-learning work for the Auburn University students was more complex. Acting students in the last semester of a BFA performance program are understandably more focused on their future careers than civic engagement. While the workload was manageable, we spent more than half the semester on the project, more than the course syllabus originally outlined. To address this imbalance and enhance our ability to establish and reinforce keys skills, we plan to restructure the workshop schedule to conform to a three-week intensive, meeting the children every day, rather than once a week.

We hope this will facilitate ensemble building, memorization of text, and the children's ability to retain movement sequences as we move towards performance.

My observation was that while the AU students individually demonstrated varying degrees of commitment to the project, their group dynamic—built on the principles of ensemble theatre training—carried them through. While we reviewed each workshop in class, and the students were submitting lesson plans and reflective journal entries regularly, they each completed a final summary and analysis of their engaged learning experience. In this final report, they evaluated what they perceived to be the relative effectiveness of their teaching and communication skills, the progress they observed in each of the children based on the educational goals we had identified together, their new understanding of diversity issues, and their view of the ultimate value of the community and civic engagement experience. These summaries almost uniformly articulated a clear assessment of each component of their engaged experience—reflecting significant growth in their critical thinking skills and their verbal acuity.

There was a collective sense from the Auburn students that the majority of the children grew in their performative and cooperative skills. Their reports indicated that while they found the project extremely challenging, they felt they had grown through the experience, and were proud of the fact they had followed it through to a successful conclusion. One student concluded: "Sometimes you have to draw on the experience as a whole to get the value out of it. Even though I [was] really stressed some days we were working with the kids, educationally it was a great experience because it made us, even for the briefest moment of the day, think about someone other than ourselves. It was remarkable the way I watched my peers turn off their personal issues for the sake of doing something great with these kids" (Riley 2010, 6). Some of the student comments revealed the implicit biases they continue to hold around race, but many of them seemed to grasp the idea that by grappling honestly with the lessons of this experience, and by placing themselves and their skills in service to others, it was actually their own lives that were enriched.

One uniquely perceptive student observed: "Watching these students progress and discover, allowed me to progress and discover. I found glimpses of myself in their bad and good moods, in the pride and joy they exhibited in their final outcome. They taught me lessons about life and creativity, how to embrace others and myself—lessons of human understanding" (Rule 2010, 7). The intellectual, cultural, and humanizing benefits of a project that combines language, performance, and community would seem to provide a powerful training experience for any actor.

There is a singular moment from this entire experience that stays with me and encourages me to continue this work.

Notes

1. Rosina Lippi-Green, the writer and linguist, discusses the ways children are taught to absorb stereotypes by linking the character accents they hear in Disney and other animated films, with social status and power. English with an Accent: Language, ideology and discrimination in the United States discusses, among other things, the relationship between language and social identity.

Bibliography

Books

Christensen, Linda. *Reading Writing and Rising Up, Teaching Social Justice and the Power of the Written Word*. Milwaukee, WI: Rethinking Schools, 2000.

Cone, Dick and Harris, Susan. "Service Learning Practice: Developing a Theoretical Framework." *Introduction to Service Learning Tool Kit*. Providence, RI: Campus Compact, Brown University, 2000.

Dalton, Roque. "Like You." *Poetry Like Bread, Poets of Political Imagination*. Ed. Martin Estrada. Evanston, IL: Northwestern University Press, 2000.

Dorfman, Ariel. *The Emperor's Old Clothes: What the Lone Ranger, Babar and Other Innocent Heroes Do to Our Minds*. New York: Pantheon, 1983.

Erlich, Thomas. *Civic Responsibility in Higher Education*. Phoenix: Oryx Press, 2000.

Lippi-Green, Rosina. *English with an Accent*, Language, Ideology and Discrimination in the United States London: Routledge, 1997.

Heard, Georgia. *Awakening the Heart: Exploring Poetry in Elementary and Middle School*. Portsmouth, NH: Heinemann, 1999.

Hughes, Langston. "The Dream Keeper." *Poetry for Young People*. Ed. D. Rampersad and D. Roessel. New York: Sterling Publishing Company, 2004.

Articles

Dolan, Jill. "Rehearsing Democracy: Advocacy, Public Intellectuals and Civic Engagement in Theatre and Performance Studies." *Theatre Topics* 11 (November 1, 2001) :1-17.

Fountain, Bonnie, M. "The Praise Poem: History and Construction." National Park Service, The U.S. Department of the Interior. http://usasearch.gov/search.

Jay, Gregory. "What (Public) Good Are the (Engaged) Humanities?" Imagining America: Artists and Scholars in Public Life, http://www.imaginingamerica.org, 2009.

Reports

AU Institutional Review Board for Research Involving Human Subjects, Research Protocol Review Form #09-346-EP 1002, 2010.

Goldbard, Arlene. "The Curriculum Project Report: Culture and Community Development in Higher Education." Imagining America: Artists and Scholars in Public Life; http://www.imaginingamerica.org, 2009.

Riley, Kara. "Summary and Analysis: Civic Engagement Project." Auburn University, 2010.

Rule, Heather. "Summary and Analysis: Civic Engagement Project." Auburn University, 2010.

Websites/Email

Auburn University Website: http://www.ocmauburn.edu/welcome/visionandmission.html.

Auburn University College of Liberal Arts/ Community and Civic Engagement Website http://media.cla.auburn.edu cla/civicengagement/index.cfm/.

Collaborative Institutional Training Initiative Website: https://www.citiprogram.org/.

Davino, Cindy. Retrieved from email, July 10, 2010.

House of Poetry: Boyds Mill Press. http:// boydsmillpress.com/poetry. Lee County, Alabama Public Schools Website: http://www.lee.k12.al.us.

Many "Right" Ways: Honoring Diverse Teaching Methods and Learning Modes

Robert is professor emeritus in acting at the University of Oregon. He is the author of the books *Acting: Onstage and Off* **(now in its 6th edition),** *Voice: Onstage and Off,* **with Rocco Dal Vera,** *Theatre in Your Life and Life Themes,* **with Annie McGregor, and** *Style for Actors* **(all in recent 2nd editions). His newest text is** *Acting Reframes: Using NLP to Make Better Decisions in and out of the Theatre.*

The United Nations of Dialects

My teaching of dialects used to be uninspired. I was assigning scenes actually written for the dialects and guiding students to avoid stereotypes in creating characters. I was trying to do the right thing. It wasn't fun.

Then one day I woke up and went in the opposite direction. I realized what I was avoiding might actually be a great place to start the training. None of us want our actors to succumb to stereotypical choices when honesty and complexity are required, but in the acting classroom types can be a pedagogical tool.

Actors need to master stereotypes in order to be able to play them or ignore them, as needed, in which case they need to know exactly *what* they are ignoring. In their careers, they may be asked to do a very thick, highly clichéd dialect character for satiric sketch comedy, improv company work or a commercial, a modified but still bright one for farce or musical comedy, all the way down to something delicate, subtle and nuanced for naturalistic drama. They need to be able to take a dialect and thicken it up to a heavy

chowder or thin it down to broth. The accompanying attitude needs to move from playing way into the obvious to gradually circumventing it.

So I started asking students to begin, as they studied the technical aspects of dialects, to develop the broadest, most outrageous alter egos possible. These creations attend various sessions of The United Nations of Dialects as delegates and share with others how to pass in whatever culture they are representing. This requires considerable research into those cultures, an understanding of predominant values, influences of climate, geography and various living conditions, as well as the effects of history and tradition.

The class gathers in a configuration similar to the General Assembly at the U.N. with various delegations, each presenting brief lessons to the others represented. This has the effect of gradually building confidence, because in early sessions each actor only has to speak the dialect briefly as the team shares: basic introductions of themselves, dominant cultural images, strong physical life/movement choices, managing social encounters, the three most important characteristics of the dialect, and the announcement of scene choice selections. I serve as the UN Secretary General, gavel in hand, to keep things moving, cutting off those going overtime, making sure the agenda is served. Actors work in delegations of three and are asked to embrace the polarity of cultural types between them with as much area for conflict as possible. So a Russian team might include a KGB officer, a Babushka bread line peasant, and a diva prima ballerina. An Irish team might include an IRA fighter, a nun and a leprechaun.

There is a lively interface between the research and presentations. The outrageousness of the creations decimates any tendency to seriously generalize about an entire people, while also making it vividly clear that stereotypes do not just magically appear, but are based on many persons making similar decisions. It is also great fun as absurdity reigns. The dialect itself is more quickly learned in a full out attack on the sounds with a strong sense of play. Once mastered in broad extreme, we do exercises to gradually reign in both sounds and character elements, taking them all step by step down to nuanced believability. The team members eventually teach their classmates how to thicken and thin the dialect in which they are specializing.

I also discovered that the most enlightening and enjoyable scene for any dialect group to study is not necessarily one that perfectly suits it, but can be one that is an absurd choice, completely inappropriate and wildly in contrast to our assumptions about the dialect or the people who speak it. Teams are asked to pick material that is first of all highly familiar, so much so that audience members already know many of the lines. Film scripts are fair game as is any show mounted recently in our theatre season. In this case, obscure material will work well because it is highly familiar to the participants. Actors are asked to "think silly", finding a scene where actual tension is created between the script and the dialect. If the dialect is heavy and consonant driven, the scene might be light, frothy and airy. Or the dialect may be melodic and spirited while the scene is depressed and turgid. Actors are encouraged to embellish the text with lingo and key phrases from the dialect.

Here are some examples of incomparable juxtapositions students have shared:

Cockney: *Electra and Romeo and Juliet*
Bronx: *Cyrano de Bergerac* and *Les Liaisons Dangereuses*
Russian: *A Streetcar Named Desire* and *The Breakfast Club*
German: *Blythe Spirit* and *Mary Poppins*
Italian: *The Importance of Being Earnest* and *Brokeback Mountain*
British: *The Godfather* and *Sexual Perversity in Chicago*
Irish: *Who's Afraid of Virginia Woolf* and *Fiddler on the Roof*

What happens is that the familiarity of character and lines makes everyone in class listen more carefully. Because we all know how the words have traditionally been spoken, every speaker and listener hears more acutely how they have been altered to suit the scene. Notes and feedback on the precision of technical changes can be highly acute and everyone is actively engaged in the process.

When the scenes are first announced, it is at a U. N. session where each country or region's delegation is claiming to honor another delegation and expand their own worldview by selecting a scene that had its origins elsewhere than the assumed identities of the team. While scenes are first presented and critiqued in class, actors then take that feedback back into rehearsal, preparing for a second showing the last week of the term. This is a late afternoon showcase with an open invitation for anyone interested to attend. No one used to come to these when we did sensible dialect scenes. Now the entire department shows up, with some always turned away. The theatre is packed with eager audiences. There is considerable buzz within the department the week before, once the particular dialect/scene combinations are announced. Audiences generally respond with howling laughter during and tumultuous applause after each scene. The incongruous juxtaposition of elements seems particularly to appeal to the Gen Y sensibility since these performances are certainly postmodern. Actors feel rewarded for all the hard, sometimes tedious work mastering the dialect by the overwhelmingly celebratory audience response. Audience members constantly leave quoting lines with relative accurate mastery of the dialect and debating over favorite choices. So observers and participants are fully engaged.

I would welcome anyone reading this to try your own United Nations and silly scene assignment. And if not these particular choices, then ones of your own that welcome surprise and delight.

Essay *by Dr. Anne Harley*

Orality overlooked: What can be learned from oral pedagogies of music?

Canadian soprano Anne Harley D.M.A. (Boston University, 2006) specializes in performing contemporary music and music from early oral and written traditions (www.anneharley.com). She has appeared as a soloist across North America and Europe with *Handel & Haydn Society*, *Boston Camerata, Opera Boston, American Repertory Theatre, Banff Centre for the Arts,* and *Bang-On-A-Can.* In 2000, she co-founded the early Russian music ensemble, TALISMAN (www.talismanmusic.org). Subsequently, the group has recorded several more CDs in collaboration with Russian Roma musicians. Her solo performances appear on Naxos, Sony Classics, Dorian, Canteloupe, BMOPSound and Musica Omnia. She joined the faculty of Scripps College in 2009.

Teachers of singing in oral musical traditions have a lot to teach teachers of applied music in what is commonly termed the "West," especially in the context of conservatory-style applied lessons. The examination of orality (vs. literacy) and how it operates in culture has historically been the domain of anthropologists and researchers of folklore, but I feel that the results of these studies can fruitfully be applied to the pedagogical strategies of voice teachers in North America and Europe. In many cases, the application of teaching techniques from oral musical traditions can also be supported by scientifically based investigations of the musical learning process. In some cases, these techniques already exist in an atrophied form in the conservatory applied voice lesson, and could usefully be consciously re-invigorated. However, current ideology regarding literacy, individualism, artistic originality, and other traditions favored by post-Enlightenment industrial society may throw up resistance to these changes in pedagogy.

This article springs from a number of experiences I had over the course of the last two decades, during which time I attended graduate school in voice and opera performance at Boston University (M.Mus., Opera Certificate,

D.M.A.), and started teaching applied voice in institutions of higher learning in the United States (first in the context of a public state university and then in a liberal arts college). During this time, I took lessons from master voice teachers in several different traditions that rely extensively on oral transmission: Northern Hindustani, Russian Roma and *flamenco.* The comparison between those modes of study and my institutional training bore valuable fruits in my performance and teaching practices, and leads me now to recommend that every singer in a conservatory program study at least one semester with a master teacher in an oral tradition. This recommendation is also particularly relevant for all those who intend to teach applied voice, as well as, to a lesser degree, teachers and students of theatre, and instrumentalists.

Commonalities in voice lessons from three oral traditions

Each lesson usually started with the teacher performing the song that was to be the focus of study that day. This performance both inspired me, the student, and laid out the style and overarching shape of the song. After this charismatic performance, the teacher then sang shorter phrases that I was expected to imitate immediately as closely as possible. A family of acceptable gestures was established by trial and error as I repeated what I was able to hear. This process involved a refinement of listening skills as much as technical ability. This mimetic process continued, over and over again, until I got it "right." The adequacy of my performances was defined by a set of rules that were rarely overtly explained by the teacher, but rather derived by trial and error. I knew I had sung the phrase correctly when the teacher moved on to learning the next phrase. Often I scribbled down notes to myself: the words to the song, and neumatic markings very similar to the kind of *neumes* found in medieval musical manuscripts. I remember being desperate to furnish for myself some tools for my own learning process, since very little instruction took the form of technical or conceptual commentary between iterations. This forced me to take responsibility for my own learning process. I noted that this was also the process for my Russian Roma colleagues as they learned new songs. Over the course of the lessons devoted to the song, the master teacher sang a large set of possible renderings of each line, thereby outlining a set of expected variations permitted in that tradition.

Human vs. textual authority

As a Western student of voice, I was thrilled by the new immediacy of the musical experience in this learning environment, but despite my many years of training, I was completely unprepared for this kind of lesson. The aural repetitions challenged me to develop into a much better listener. The intimate contact with a master performer who sang for me *in performance mode* taught me to be a more charismatic performer. Learning the song as transmitted by the human body, rather than as printed on a piece of paper, dramatically changed my approach to the work of music, and presented it, from the very beginning, in an encultured relationship with another human being. Since the proliferation of printed music, the Western classical tradition has presented a piece of music to the student as an immutable, printed ideal, written by a master (often dead), to be served by an all-too-human servant, who will inevitably make errors. As part of entering into conservatory training, the student implicitly agrees to a relationship with works of genius before which he or she will confirm the feebleness of his or her own humanity. As McLuhan wrote: "the printed book added much to the new cult of individualism. The private, fixed point of view became possible and literacy conferred the power of detachment, non-involvement." (McLuhan 1967, 50) In the conservatory, the authority of text precludes any modification by a human, be it the teacher or the student, except in the name of "performance practice." The use of a printed score also orders the educational experience: correct pitches and rhythms must be reproduced first—only then may possible divergences from the score be taught. Since the expressive gestures of *rubato* and ornamented cadenzas require a deep knowledge of the limits of "tasteful" divergences from the score, they are exceptions to the rule of print that are reserved for the practice of advanced students only.

Instead of decoding an idealized, printed score that abstracts a physical and acoustic experience into visual space, the source of music for the student in the oral tradition is the active connection of the student to the teacher. In the oral traditions I experienced, humility before the teacher substituted for servitude to the text, and expressive gestures were an inseparable component of vocalism from the very beginning. While this might be expected to be true for improvising modes of vocalism (for example, in Northern Hindustani *raga*), it also held true for those genres where pitch and rhythmic improvisation are not central to the structure of the music (Russian Roma song). My teachers seamlessly transmitted styles of musical gestures and a physical connection to the performance of the song to me that are impossible to learn from a written score, and they did so starting with the first lesson. In addition to teaching the pitches and rhythms of a "correct" performance, they taught me a way of being in music, and the centrality of relation to other human beings through music, that is de-emphasized in the score-driven model of Western education.

The Western academic model and literacy

Applied voice lessons in the West are firmly embedded in the academy, and perhaps because of this heritage, are firmly tied to a written score. Literacy is a prerequisite for progress in all applied music lessons, and none more so than classical voice, which involves not only musical notation, but four or more foreign languages. Music programs in higher institutions of learning typically include both applied music and the more textually dependent subdisciplines of musicology, ethnomusicology and music theory. One might reasonably expect more text-based learning in the latter disciplines. Indeed, with the exception of a few annual conferences, transmission is extremely text-centered. What is striking is how much textual learning dominates the applied lesson. Although the end-goal of applied lessons is usually a musical performance without visual aids, the score is present in most of the teaching moments in a Western lesson, especially with beginning students. In the beginning it is a vital document, taking most of the student's attention. Then it becomes a memory crutch. Finally it becomes the document against which the student's performance is checked for errors, and a handy way of referring to these errors quickly ("The C at measure 5 is flat."). In the trajectory from first exposure to performance, the amount of time that the student spends looking at the score far outweighs the time they have spent in a purely aural learning mode. This phenomenon is so prevalent, that at least one classic tome on the art of the song recital (Emmons 1979, 197-8) cautions the student against memorizing the words in such a way that the score reappears in the visual imagination during recital.

If the dominance of print in an essentially aural discipline passes without special notice, it is partly because literacy and playing music have been inextricably connected in an elitist culture, since the printing of music arose in the late fifteenth century:

> Over the last centuries of European history written modes have been taken as the paradigm for education, scholarship and artistic activity, a dominant cultural view widely accepted. . . What was written was to be valued and analyzed; and what was not written was not worth scholarly study. (Finnegan 1988, 124)

The majority acceptance in the West of the inferiority of the "direct modeling methods" (rote learning) continued well into the second half of the twentieth century. But in 1967, one of the largest arts education organizations in the United States, the National Association for Music Education, published *The Study of Music in the Elementary School —A Conceptual Approach* which valorized the conceptual teaching method over others, including the direct modeling method. Significantly, the suggestion to question the conceptual approach in music education came from the newest musical field to become professionalized: ethnomusicology. A little over twenty years later, in 1991, ethnomusicologist Patricia Campbell's *Lessons from the World: a Cross-Cultural*

Pedagogy and Coaching
Orality overlooked: What can be learned from oral pedagogies of music? by Dr. Anne Harley

Guide to Music Teaching and Learning drew on oral traditions of music from across the globe in order to present compelling arguments for placing greater emphasis on "aural skills and creative musical expression" (Shehan Campbell 1991, 305). Disenchanted with academic Western musical education, she argued that while these two qualities are "widely accepted as fundamental attributes of thorough musicianship, both are frequently overlooked in practice…. The absence of any of these components means that a thorough aesthetic education has probably not occurred." (Shehan Campbell 1991, 305) She warns "without conscious attention to developing the aural sense…they may pursue their art from a linear perspective without injecting it with the refreshing and creative spirit that comes from knowing the aural essence of the music." (Shehan Campbell 1991, 307)

The modeling approach may be philosophically more appealing, but it also has very pragmatic and quantitatively demonstrable benefits. In 1986, Rosenthal experimentally evaluated three different teacher strategies in the applied music lesson: verbal-description only, modeling-only, combination of verbal-description and modeling. Rosenthal compared gains in performance scores against a controlled practice-only group: ". . . the highest scores were consistently attained by subjects in the model-only group on all variables." (Rosenthal 1986, 269) In one study of teacher/student interaction in instrumental private lessons (Hepler 1986), the leading six behavioral categories listed by percentage of lesson time showed a very low percentage of teacher modeling in the medium:

1. Student Performance in Medium 25%
2. Teacher Conceptual Statement 16.35%
3. Teacher Unclassified Lesson-Related Statements 10.66%
4. Teacher Technical Statements 10.50%
5. Teacher Performance in Medium 7.61%
6. Teacher Performance in Outside of Medium 7.33%

Optimistically, the ready availability of the voice would suggest that categories 5 and 6 would combine to total a little over 15% in a voice lesson, as opposed to the listings above in an instrumental lesson. Even this 15% is still below the 25% of student performance and the 16% devoted to teacher conceptual statements. Rote learning also improved some aspects of general musicianship, as noted by Shehan ("Effects of Rote versus Note Presentations" 1987, 118):

> "In a discrimination test of meters and rhythms, Stockton (1982) found that college non-music majors exposed to rote learning of rhythm patterns over a 12-week period performed significantly better on a meter identification test than did students exposed to an instructional sequence based on notational analysis of recorded musical excerpts."

However, despite the philosophical and pragmatic arguments for the modeling approach, most teachers of private applied lessons have yet to make modeling the most substantial part of the lesson, if my experience is any indication. This may be because a teacher who teaches in this manner "does not seem to teach, certainly not from our ["Western"] standpoint." (McPhee 1970, 232) McPhee, the Canadian ethnomusicologist and composer describes the Balinese music teacher further: "He is merely the transmitter; he makes concrete the musical idea which is to be handed on, sets the example before the pupils and leaves the rest to them." (McPhee 1970, 232) For the Western teacher, perhaps, the act of modeling is somehow too simple and too physical to qualify as teaching in the academy.

Applied music in higher education

The faculty at a university in the United States has, for the most part, developed a textual consciousness, and therefore is culturally resistant to teaching using the newly reinvigorated sources of oral tradition (such as the internet, or the recording device). Unique among disciplines in this regard is music, which has, since the ancient *quadrivium*, struggled with its identity as an academic *doppelganger*: it is both an intellectual liberal art *and* an applied embodied performance experience. These two modes of music are vastly different and require different skill sets. During the Renaissance and Baroque, composers (the theorists) and performing instrumentalists (the applied musicians) belonged to different echelons of society, and instrumentalists were often treated as a sort of musically talented animal that could materialize the abstract creations of the thinking composer. Along these lines, Louis XVI established a permanent group of musicians that he named "*La Grande Écurie*," literally "the big stable," who were commanded to physically realize compositions by court-sanctioned composers such as Lully. Post-Enlightenment, the aforementioned mind/body split further exacerbated the distance between poles of the musical profession. In some music departments, this inheritance is discernible in the uneasy partnership between theoretical and practical musical disciplines. In these faculties, a tension between D.M.A.- and Ph.D.-holders can cause applied teachers (usually M.Mus.- or D.M.A.-holders) to be wary of their devaluation by the university or college administration, should they venture too far from literacy-guided methods of instruction. Generally, the ensuing streaming of applied and non-applied faculty tracks result in general differences in salary and benefits that disadvantage applied teachers. The resistance to the oral transmission of repertoire therefore prevails among applied music faculty, even though the end product of study will be an embodied sound performance, which, if successful, will not bear any trace of written text (except possibly in the program note for a recital). In fact, the accomplished performer creates the illusion of spontaneous expression, within the restrictive parameters of style, language, timbre and physicality that mark a song recital. Given these goals, the question we should ask is not: "should applied teachers teach music by modeling sound and physical gestures more than by using visual texts?" but, rather: "How can the textualized teacher gain access to the mind-set associated with orality that is necessary for good teaching?"

Issues that arise in teaching vocal performance from notation

Although instrumental teachers might gain from the inclusion of oral transmission methods in their pedagogy, it is teachers and students of voice and opera who stand to benefit the most. Non-notational aural and kinesthetic methods are all the more relevant to vocal performance training, where the performance "product" will often include a large kinesthetic performative aspect: in opera, the singer may even dance. The score unhelpfully flattens the essential musical instructions onto the page in a visual, two dimensional medium. Students who depend exclusively on visual musical cues for their learning process are handicapped by the additional task of a translation of consciousness. According to Ong, writing is a technology that restructures consciousness both directly and indirectly. "More than any other single invention, writing has transformed human consciousness." (Ong 1982, 216) Learning repertoire via oral tradition liberates the brain from the activity of translation from the visual space of text, freeing up the student to experience the physical and aural space of the performance right away. Oral methods of learning also have implications for the process of memorization that must take place for a successful performance. Emmons clumsily expresses an intuitive concept that is obvious for anyone who has memorized a song:

> Rote learning is in the long run most efficient, because for best results during performance the material that is memorized must reside in the subconscious. A singer who has memorized intellectually is put into a position during performance where he must sacrifice part of his valuable concentration in order to assure the correct notes and words. This is not only a waste of his resources, it may well prevent his memory from functioning at all. It is far better that the music and words should be lodged in the subconscious, programmed to reissue at certain stimuli; memory must *allow* itself to be revived during performance. (Emmons 1979, 179)

Emmons makes an error in contrasting "rote learning" with "memoriz[ing] intellectually" thus opposing oral transmission methods with intellectuality. In fact, it is the linearity and disembodied flatness of print, rather than its intellectuality, that makes it unhelpful for memorizing for performance. Likewise, oral transmissions do not lack in intellectuality. In fact, along with his commendation of "rote learning" Emmons later recommends that memorization be based on analysis of the music and text, thus combining intellectuality with "rote learning." Despite this blunder, Emmons does valuably point to an experience every voice student has had: it is generally true that a student who eidetically reproduces a line of musical notation will not give as convincing a performance as the student whose memory is constructed of deeply meaningful images (imaginary, visual, sensual, aural, kinesthetic) that, seamlessly connected, lead the performer on a compelling internal imaginary journey. Mnemonic memory devices which pull the singer out of the physical gesture of song and back into the disembodied experience of print are counter-productive to performance. Likewise, the singer of oratorio, in which the performer may hold a score, must always struggle to avoid the temptation to read their part from the score, in order to enter more deeply into the communicative work of performance.

Motor learning and singing

Notation is an invaluable tool that enables transmission of the instructions for extremely beautiful music-making abroad and into the future. It equips musicians in our Western tradition with powers to reproduce an enormous quantity of music quickly and accurately. Musical literacy should be taught as part of the curriculum, but in this article, I question its centrality to the applied lesson. My deliberations are not only based on personal or ethnographic evidence, but also on recent scientific studies in the motor basis of language learning and its connection to the function of mirror neurons which may, in fact, recommend a return to features common to oral pedagogies:

> Mirror neurons are motor neurons that get activated when an animal performs an action, *and when that animal sees that same action performed by another* [emphasis added]. Thus, they provide a means by which gesture-signs can be made and identified. Second, mirror neurons in nonhuman primates are found in the area of the premotor cortex homologous to Broca's area, which underlies human language: not surprisingly, mirror neurons have been linked to the origins of language. (Skoyles 2000)

If singing can be considered a heightened form of speech, then it makes sense to speculate that kinesthetic imitation may also be one of the primary pathways for learning to sing. In another study by neuroscientists (Fadiga, Luciano, et al. 2002, 399-402), listening to speech specifically modulated the excitability of tongue muscles in humans, who responded with imitative movements of their own tongues when hearing strongly pronounced consonants that involved the tongue in pronunciation. Again, since the tongue muscles of listeners to speech were responsive, we might also expect that hearing the correctly sung musical gestures may also stimulate articulatory muscles in a mirroring pattern. Gruhn claims that neural development in the brain begins by an arousal pattern that is initiated by movement and that musical understanding follows when a student feels the experience of music. The research suggests that actual physical experience of making sound is more necessary to learning music than we had previously imagined. This close interaction of kinetic and aural elements also happens to be the primary method by which oral traditions often pass on their music. Ethnomusicologist Michael Bakan points out that major research studies on applied music instruction in the West have shown that demonstration-only methods of teaching are significantly more effective than either verbal-descriptive-only methods, or methods which combine demonstration and verbal description (Kennell 1992, 7). The same study also points out that music teachers talk four times as often as they play when they teach. These scientific studies in fact recommend an imitative model of learning that many applied teachers may dismiss out of hand as illiterate, and therefore not worthy of attention.

Synchronous mimesis

Some oral traditions of transmission take imitation one step further and encourage the student to sing or play *with* the teacher at the same time (Bakan 1993, 10). Typically, in my experience teachers discourage students from "jumping in" during demonstrations, believing that the students cannot listen as effectively. That may be so, however, teachers who ask the student to wait their turn before joining in may miss an important pedagogical advantage. In this extremely efficient experiential method, the student imbibes the model that the teacher provides, immediately and without linguistic intervention. The attentive student notices, as well, the moments at which he/she is diverging from the model. By repeating this process several times, if the teacher wisely chooses limiting models of performance (varying in style, dynamics, rhythm etc.), the student quickly learns the ways in which the musical phrase may change and yet remain within the bounds of acceptability. Again, this method is at odds with current practice in several ways. The ideal of the performing musician as a uniquely creative, original artist has been popular since the Enlightenment. The cultivation of the arts as a means of individuation is a common goal of liberal arts colleges, and in conservatories, expression of that individuation at the highest virtuosic level is the goal. The cult of the individual is therefore expected to express itself with particular intensity in the "private" applied lesson; the regular individual attention is unduplicated elsewhere in the university. However, by asking the student

to blend their sound into that of the teacher, the teacher encourages the student to temporarily abandon that ideal and by extension, an entire approach to music education. Looking to other cultures, we find that the cultivation of individuality is not considered a necessary part of the successful music lesson. In Confucian society, quite the opposite is true: "The student emulates the teacher, and measures his success by the completeness of his imitation." (Shehan 1987, 3) The same is true in Balinese musical practice as reported by Bakan (1993, 8).

Even cases where the end goal of musical lessons is a solo performance, implying an expression of individuality and originality, students need to imitate some sort of model, be that a teacher or a recording, in order to learn new forms. In my opinion, guiding the student as he or she tries on these models, learns from them and discards them, is one of the functions of a good teacher.

Mimesis vs. originality

Strongly contradictory messages about originality abound in Western schools of music. Conservatories are expected to conserve traditions, but also, at the same time to produce original performers who embody the cult of individual genius. The tension between these two contradictory goals produces a pedagogy that is fraught with contradictory messages. Many times, during the course of my education, I was encouraged not to imitate models from recordings, and not try to sound like another vocalist. At one point, during a master class, one well-respected soprano and teacher warned us not to listen to recordings of arias newly assigned to us, because we would lose our ability to develop original performances. At the same time, musical gestures that were appropriate to one period were not allowed in another, and certain vocal timbres were preferred over others. These judgments were certainly based on an aural corpus of experience that was available and conserved primarily via recordings, even in the pre-internet 1980s. There is a tension behind the remarks I heard on freely creative vocalism that is conducive to the development of neurosis in the singer: although we students heard many times that the voice, once released in its naturally free form would become the classical operatic instrument, the actual range of permitted sounds and gestures in an operatic aria (especially one from the canon) is remarkably formalized, highly circumscribed, and hardly natural. Thus the student must strive to find their original performance in this very formalist art form, carefully avoiding elements of the recordings of masters of their tradition: hardly an enviable position.

Private vs. open lessons

The term "private lesson" in the context of Western musical education carries with it a subtext: what goes on in that weekly interaction requires privacy. I believe that it is an attitude towards the body in Western society that has anchored that nomenclature in our institutions. Although the illicit romantic relationship of a music teacher with a young female student has furnished the plot for more than one opera, the concentration on the physical body during voice lessons need not be sexual to require privacy in our society. The structure of the "private" lesson implies that certain sounds and negotiations of one's sound with one's surroundings must be made in private. Presumably, privacy is necessary because the student's lack of control over his body and the sounds coming from his body, in combination with criticism by the teacher is highly shameful. Remembering the many conservatory-style lessons I have taken or given, I remark upon how many times the teacher (here I am also including myself) stopped the student mid-phrase to remark upon a digression from the score, a mispronunciation, a technical vocal issue or a problem with intonation. Indeed the intensely self-critical mindset practiced in those lessons is exactly the opposite kind of mindset required to enter into the "flow" of solo performance.

In contrast, in the oral traditions that I experienced, teachers gave intense personal attention to my musical development, but lessons were almost always "open." Family members and other students would come and go during the lesson as a matter of course. This holds true of most of the oral music pedagogies that have been studied to date. They diverge again from the Western model by commonly opening the studio to several students at once, or holding lessons in a public space (Rice 1996, 9 and Bakan 1993, 7). While the conservatory curriculum insists on private lessons as the best preparation for its performing majors, the open studio asserts nothing of the kind. To the contrary, the music and lesson are social spaces in which community *and* the best performers are formed. During one Russian Roma music and dance lesson my teacher unexpectedly suggested we have our lesson out on the street because our apartment was too small to accommodate my full dance skirt. In another example, passers-by were invited to join in at the open-air drum lessons reported by Bakan (1993, 15). Other benefits of an open studio include learning to work with an ensemble immediately, simultaneously improving listening skills and responsive musicianship, and lessening the oppositional dichotomy between practice and performance identities of the student musician.

Literacy, orality and class

Musical literacy is associated with upward mobility. In popular forms such as folk, rock, jazz and hip-hop, a musician's good ear and ability to play are primary, while on the other hand, in classical music, musical literacy is essential. Meanwhile, in the musical theatre industry, the genre that mediates between "high" and "low" cultural aesthetics, a performer's ability to read music is desirable, but optional, if they have the necessary musical, vocal and dramatic chops. Thus, in higher education (which has traditionally been a ladder to membership in a higher social class) the applied teacher who openly advocates "learning by rote" as a substantial part of the lesson can expect to be stigmatized for this strategy and for advocating a supposed devolution to illiteracy. The mandate to teach from text is true even when a student's musical ability far outpaces their literacy, or when deficits in literacy are remedied in another part of the curriculum. The applied teacher is expected to teach literacy as part of the process of learning to play or sing, so that, as Taruskin puts it, high art can continue to engage in its "traditional business of creating social division by creating elite occasions."(527) There is, therefore, considerable historical and social resistance to adopting an oral pedagogical strategy based in sustaining class difference.

Other obstacles to change

Private applied lessons are remarkably difficult to study because few teachers are willing to allow researchers into their lessons. The long and rich tradition of the private applied voice lesson has occurred largely behind closed doors, since the introduction of an observer raises complex educational and ethical issues. This long tradition of instrumental/vocal teaching tends to lead to deeply held convictions that resist challenge and change. The latter holds all the more true, since there is no research tradition to complement and advance the teaching practice of applied instructors. Indeed, most instructors of voice are performer-teachers who learn how to teach not by observing lessons, but from their own experience as students (Haddon 2009, 57-70), observing master classes, vocal pedagogy textbooks, and ancillary professional literature. However, these methods are indirect, and the instructors lack feedback about their effectiveness as teachers (Haddon 2009, 57-70). There is some consciousness of the need for more direct forms of training in the profession, evidenced by the fact that The National Association of Teachers of Singing offers an annual summer teacher-training program in a response to this deficit. It is my hope that this article will encourage ethnomusicologists as well as performing scholar-teachers to study the tradition of the "private lesson" and to bring universally beneficial teaching methods into the Western tradition, even if they are not based in music literacy.

Extending teaching and enculturation using non-literate methods

The youth of today are not permitted to approach the

the traditional heritage of mankind through the door of technological awareness. This only possible door for them is slammed in their faces by a rear-view mirror society (McLuhan 1967, 100).

Although McLuhan wrote this well before the age of the Internet, his words are uncannily prescient. Despite the prevalence of recording devices, astonishingly, some teachers still do not allow recording of the lessons by the student, and do not extend their teaching to include musical experiences the student encounters outside the studio. It is my belief that this creates a split in the student's approach to music that exacerbates the already apparent divide between classical music and modernity. Our traditional heritage originates from previous centuries, but it is itself not obsolete. It is the pedagogical framing of classical music that needs constant renewal in order to survive transmission to the next generation. Teachers need to design and build the new "technological door" that serves their discipline and the new world of technology in which their students live. To strengthen their teaching, teachers should assign and discuss recordings the student listens to outside the lesson hour. This could include commercial and non-commercial recordings of professionals and amateurs, as well as recordings of students in the studio. The new influx of recorded performances available to each student and teacher on the internet, via YouTube, iTunes, and any number of electronic databases of recordings (e.g.: Naxos) offer opportunities for valuable enculturation, but only if teachers embrace and encourage in classical music, the kind of voracious listening our students seem, so far, to reserve for pop music.

The main argument that teachers raise against the inclusion of recordings available freely on the Internet is that they are uneven in quality. It is true that students are as likely to encounter a bad undergraduate performance online as they are to encounter one by a master performer. However, students are subject to a rapidly exploding profusion of choices of performances on the Internet, which promises to accelerate. "At the broadest level, the musical exposure of the average person today is greater than it has ever been." (Smith 1996, 210) Training students to listen for what makes an acceptable, excellent or masterful performance and how to select models for emulation, should be part of the applied music lesson. To paraphrase McLuhan (2004, 1): "The electronic revolution of television has made the teacher the provider no longer of *information* but of *insight* [emphasis added], and the student not the consumer but the co-teacher, since he has amassed so much information outside the classroom."

Teachers can also now tap into the rapidly growing popularity of social networking applications and strengthen studio (and alumni) community by setting up a private channel of videotaped performances. The channel might host performances by the teacher, studio members, as well as videos of master classes and other performances there for the student, his/her peers and their family to listen to and to watch. A teacher might also build studio community and critical skills by giving commenting privileges to members of the studio and grading comments. To protect all concerned, students should receive a full explanation, in writing, of how their recordings will be used and sign a release before any video is released.

Professional performing musicians at the top of their fields are leading the way in terms of both technological and aural renovations of the learning process. As reported in the New York Times on Jan. 14 2011, the prestigious Borromeo String Quartet flaunted their use of recordings before each performance:

> Musicians have listened to themselves since recording became possible, but the Borromeo players take it to an extreme. Before every concert they run through a program and immediately listen to it, "with the rule that nobody should talk while they're listening" (Wakin 2011).

Conclusions

The world is now transitioning from a period characterized by the linear bias of type to an era that Marshall McLuhan characterized as richer in an audile and tactile field (1967). The vast array of video and audio recordings and availability via Internet of professional as well as amateur performances are witness to this change that started with television in the 1950s and accelerated with the Internet in the 1990s. Every day, our students of voice move and extend themselves in a sea of highly proliferated auditory stimulus, much of it musical, much of it recorded, which performs the work of enculturation. This shift could bring with it enhancements to studies in applied voice and live performance of all kinds, if teachers embrace it. The alternative, if teachers reject or ignore this change, is that students of voice will live in a fractured world, in which literate performance is, at worst, a stilted emotionless translation of a printed score, and illiterate performance is a thoroughly felt, but thoroughly disrespected act of disparaged "rote learning." Oral transmission is often associated with the remote past in the West, and (incorrectly) with backwardness, and with a lack of progress. I would suggest that we actively claim its associations with the future and with the recent findings from our own scientifically grounded tradition. It is on those grounds that I propose for consideration the following lessons from music teachers in oral traditions, collected by ethnomusicologists:

Lessons from the world for Western music teachers
(adapted from Bakan and Campbell (1991)):

1. Increase the amount of time spent in direct model-and-imitation teaching with both advanced and beginning students. Since one hour per week is not sufficient modeling time, integrate recordings of teacher, student and other performers into learning process.

2. Provide demonstration models of the entire piece of music during the lesson and in recording form.

3. Model performances for your student as you might perform them, at full tempo and with all ornamentation.

4. Have students play/sing along with your modeled performances. Encourage capturing overall style, rather than individual notes.

5. Model performances that incorporate as much kinesthetic information as possible.

6. Compel students to become self-reliant by not offering guidance and advice in every situation.

7. Have the student play from the beginning to the end of the work as often as possible.

8. Create an ensemble environment whenever possible. Invite students to observe each other's "private" lessons.

9. Make music more and talk less.

Notes

1 . In the Indian tradition, this is part of a national tradition of respect for teachers. To mark the sacredness of the teacher, the student arrays him/her with garlands and gives gifts of sweets on *Guru Poornima*, the annual summer holiday honoring teachers.

Bibliography

Bakan, Michael B. "Lessons from a World: Balinese Applied Music Instruction and the Teaching of Western 'Art' Music," *College Music Symposium* 33-34 (1993): 1-20.

Duke, Robert A., Patricia J. Flowers and David E. Wolfe. "Children Who Study Piano with Excellent Teachers in the United States," *Bulletin—Council for Research in Music Education* 132 (1997): 51-84..

Emmons, Shirlee. *The Art of the Song Recital*. Schirmer Books: New York, 1979.

Fadiga, Luciano, et al. "Speech listening specifically modulates the excitability of tongue muscles: a TMS study," *European Journal of Neuroscience* 15, no. 2 (2002): 399-402. Academic Search Premier, EBSCOhost (accessed November 15, 2010).

Finnegan, Ruth. *Literacy and Orality: Studies in the Technology of Communication*. Oxford: Basil Blackwell, 1988.

Frielick, Stanley. "Winged Words/Caged texts: Oral tradition and teaching African literature" in *Catching the winged words: oral tradition and education: selected conference papers*, eds. E.R. Sienaert and A.N. Bell (Durban: Natal University Oral Documentation and Research Centre, 1988), 203-212.

Pedagogy and Coaching
Orality overlooked: What can be learned from oral pedagogies of music? by Dr. Anne Harley

Gruhn, Wilfried. "Body, Voice, and Breath: the Corporeal Means of Music Learning," *The Orff Echo* Vol. 42, Issue 3 (2010): 34-37.

Haddon, Elisabeth. "Instrumental and vocal teaching; how do music students learn to teach," *British Journal of Music Education* Vol. 26 Issue 1(2009): 57-70.

Hepler, L. E. "The measurement of teacher/student interaction in private music lessons and its relation to teacher field dependence/independence." *Dissertation Abstracts International*, 47, 2939-A. (University Microfilms No. 86-27848) 1986.

Kennell, Richard. "Towards a Theory of Applied Music Instruction," *The Quarterly Journal of Music Teaching and Learning*, No. 2 (1992): 7.

McLuhan, Marshall. *Medium is the Massage*. New York: Bantam Books, 1967.

McLuhan, Marshall. *Understanding Me*, eds. Stephanie McLuhan and David Staines. MIT Press: Cambridge, MA, 2004.

McPhee, Colin. "Children and music in Bali" in *Traditional Balinese Culture*, ed. Jane Belo. New York: Columbia University Press, 1970.

Ong, Walter J. *Orality & Literacy : The Technologizing of the Word*. Routledge: New York, 1982.

Rice, Timothy. "Traditional Methods of Learning and Teaching Music in Bulgaria," *Research Studies in Music Education* 7 (1996): 1-12.

Sienaert, E. R. and A. N. Bell eds. *Catching the Winged Words: oral tradition and education: selected conference papers*. Durban: Natal University Oral Documentation and Research Centre, 1988.

Shehan, Patricia. "The oral transmission of music in selected Asian cultures," *Bulletin – Council for Research in Music Education* 92 (1987): 1-14.

Shehan Campbell, Patricia. "Deep Listening to the Musical World," *Music Educators Journal* Vol. 92 No. 1 (2005): 30-36.

Shehan Campbell, Patricia. *Lessons from the World*. Toronto: Schirmer Books, 1991.

Shehan, Patricia K. "Effects of Rote versus Note Presentations on Rhythm Learning and Retention," *Journal of Research in Music Education* Vol. 35 No. 2 (1987): 117-126.

Skoyles, John R. "Gesture, language origins, and right handedness," *Psycoloquy* 11:024 (2000).

Smith, Thérèse. "The challenge of bringing oral traditions of music into an academic teaching environment," *Crosbhealach an cheoil [The Crossroads Conference]* (1996): 206-210.

Tannen, Deborah, ed. *Spoken and Written Language: Exploring Orality and Literacy* Vol IX of *Advances in Discourse Processes*. New Jersey: ABLEX, 1982.

Taruskin, Richard. *Music in the Late Twentieth Century*. Oxford University Press: New York, 2009.

Wakin, Daniel J. "Bytes and Beethoven" *New York Times* Jan. 14, 2011 (Accessed Feb. 12. 2011).

Walker, Robert. *Musical Beliefs: psychoacoustic, mythical and educational perspectives*. New York: Teachers College Press, Columbia University, 1990.

Essay *by Marlene Johnson*

Double Directions in Serbia and Greece: Blending the Methods of the DAH Theatre and Frankie Armstrong

Marlene Johnson was named a 2011 National Teaching Artist by the Kennedy Center American College Theatre Festival—one of six such awards in the country for 2011. She acts and directs for City Equity Theatre recently playing Mrs. Gabor in *Spring Awakening*. She has vocal directed shows at Pennsylvania Shakespeare Festival, Orlando Shakespeare Theatre, Alliance Theatre, Theatre Virginia among others. Marlene has taught Acting Shakespeare at University of Westminster, London. Training includes American Repertory Theatre with Bonnie Raphael, National Theatre with Patsy Rodenburg, Kristin Linklater, Frankie Armstrong, Alexander Technique certification work. Marlene has served on the boards of VASTA and SETC. She teaches at University of Alabama Birmingham.

Martha Curtis performing Chi Gong at the Temple of Poseidon at Cape Sounion

Photo by Martha Curtis

"The core of a method consists of a nebula of impulses which have to be unearthed and awakened in us.'"

On Directing and Dramaturgy by Eugenio Barba

In May and June of 2010 I accompanied Janet Rodgers to Serbia and Greece for three weeks of immersion into the creation of Greek theatre using the methods of Belgrade's DAH Theatre and the voice training of Frankie Armstrong. Previously, Rodgers, Professor of Theatre and Head of Performance at Virginia Commonwealth University, had taken several groups of actors to work with the DAH theatre both in their home in Serbia and to the Sibiu International Theatre Festival in Romania where the DAH had taught workshops. The trip to Belgrade in 2010 allowed Rodgers to explore these diverse methods of training and theatre creation but included Frankie Armstrong's voice work onsite in Belgrade for the first time. This resulted in an exciting piece of theatre which the actors presented in an ancient Greek theatre in Thorikos near Cape Sounion. My part in this project was to accompany Armstrong to Belgrade from London and to assist in the teaching of her traditional voice work.

What I discovered in these diverse methodologies was a powerful and unique way to explore voice and performance training. This was my first visit both to Serbia and to Greece. I had witnessed the DAH's work in Richmond, VA in 1999 when Artistic Director Dijana Milosevic and actor Maia Mitic shared their process in workshops and performance at Virginia Commonwealth University. I had worked with Frankie Armstrong in 2002 and 2006 in Kinnersley, Herefordshire, and I have been teaching workshops on Armstrong's Voices of the Archetypes with Janet Rodgers since 2003.

In 2009 Rodgers co-authored a book with Armstrong entitled *Acting and Singing with Archetypes* which included exercises based on explorations inspired by Rodgers' work with the DAH. Rodgers wanted to experiment with finding a way to get the Armstrong vocal training combined with the DAH training in the same place at the same time. Both Rodgers and Armstrong were keen to investigate Greek text with some of the voice work, and Janet wondered if they could put on an entire Greek play combining DAH methods with Armstrong's.

In an interview Rodgers said:

> I had seen my first DAH performance, *The Legend of the End of the World*, in 1996 at the Sibiu International Theatre Festival and then worked with them alongside my actors during Summer Study Abroad trips to Romania in 2002, 2006, 2007, and 2009. In 2010 I decided to observe the training and process. What

113

Double Directions in Serbia and Greece: Blending the Methods of the DAH Theatre and Frankie Armstrong by Marlene Johnson

struck me first about their work in 1996 was how it was able to absorb me completely as an audience member. In addition, I was thrilled by each actor's physical and vocal dexterity and how, by using metaphor and imagery, their theatre resonated so strongly in my being. I determined to learn more about how they trained and how they created their devised performances. During my years of exploration into how the DAH worked I learned about "Double Direction", "Edge of Balance", and other training processes which the actors in the DAH, through daily practice, use to keep their bodies, minds, and imaginations alive, strong, and focused. (Rodgers)

On each of these trips to Sibiu or Belgrade in which Rodgers worked with the DAH, she also took the same group of actors to work with Frankie Armstrong at Kinnersley Castle, Herefordshire in England. Actors were getting training in both methodologies. However, Frankie Armstrong had never met or worked with the DAH, and the DAH had never known Armstrong's work. Janet decided to bring them together in 2010.

DAH Influences and Training:

DAH Theatre's training and theatre creation descends from the work of Jerzy Grotowski and Eugenio Barba of the Odin Teatret and the International School of Theatre Anthropology [ISTA] in Holstebro, Denmark. Barba's mentor was Grotowski with whom he trained in Poland for three years. Barba later became the editor of Grotowski's *Towards a Poor Theatre*. Both Grotowski's and Barba's methods are grounded in a strong physical approach to actor training and play creation, and both explore the voice differently from American traditions of voicing. Barba's many writings on acting and performing—such as *Paper Canoe* and his most recent *On Directing and Dramaturgy*—are both dense and profound.

The DAH's Dijana Milosevic in turn studied with Barba in Holstebro, Denmark for three years. It was during the Bosnian War that Milosevic started the DAH theatre. The theatre has now been in existence for 20 years and has recently begun an International School for Actors and Directors intensive where artists can come to the theatre and observe and participate in their training and theatre creation.

Jeff Morrison, who teaches theatre at Marymount Manhattan, has traveled to Holstebro and studied with Barba and several of his leading actors. What he said to me about Barba's work reflects what we see in the work of the DAH. Said Morrison:

Both Barba and Grotowski highly value "actor dramaturgy"—meaning that the creative material that makes up the final performance originates with the actor. In actor's dramaturgy, the actor creates dramatic material or interprets a text in rehearsal by creating a sequence of actions or behavior that can be repeated and learned. That actor's work is then valued just as highly or even more highly than a playwright's. There's a kind of act of faith that the actor's impulses as an artist in and of themselves will be true and valuable. The director's job is to sculpt, shape, and montage the material that the actors generate into something coherent. But the fact that the actors make what they later perform is supposed to give that performance material an extra spark of life and presence—because it's theirs, all the way down the line. They aren't trying to interpret a role; they create the role and then refine it. (Morrison)

Key to the DAH's creation of a piece of theatre is the idea of the actor developing not one, but several scores. This idea, taken from Barba, plays with developing several layers in which the actor is working simultaneously. These layers create a multi-leveled, complex theatre piece with depth. Barba compares these "levels of organization" to the different systems in the human body; the respiratory system, the vascular system, the muscular system, the nervous system: all function separately yet are needed to work together to allow the full organism to function.

Barba sought to create an "extra-daily" focus of heightened awareness and physical engagement. He referred to this hyper-awareness as "sats." Barba speaks of working to develop in the actor the energy that holds a readiness for action. This energy state engages the whole body. It is similar to Patsy Rodenburg's "Second Circle" energy that embodies "presence." Barba's word for this, "sats," is defined as an energy that can be suspended, holding the potential for acting on impulse and "counterimpulse." He links this energy state with what Meyerhold calls "preaction" and with similar ideas in embodying energy in both Balinese dancing and in the Peking Opera. In *Acting and Singing with Archetypes* Rodgers quotes Barba:

Sats is the basic posture found in sports—in tennis, badminton, boxing, fencing—when you need to be ready to act. There needs always to be a dynamic in stillness, however long that stillness lasts. (Rodgers and Armstrong)

In *Beyond the Floating Islands* Barba further explains this word:

I use a Scandinavian word, "sats," to describe energy gathered unto itself, the starting point of action, the moment in which we concentrate all our forces before directing them towards an action. Whatever the action might be, the sats corresponds to the runner's starting position. The sats is characterized by a charge of energy which goes in the direction opposite to that of the movement to be carried out, as when one directs one's weight downward in order to jump or when one gathers up all one's energy by moving the arm slightly backwards in order to then strike a blow forwards. (Barba)

The theatre piece has "bios" or life when these moment to moment "sats" are strung together. For each of these layers the actor develops a score. In stringing together these individual moments, the actor develops many different scores simultaneously. The word "score" is used slightly differently from the traditional Stanislavskian use of the term. The actor may have a physical score, a vocal score, a text score, an image score, a sound score based on song and music, and other scores that are rehearsed separately and then woven together. At some point the director will work with the actor to condense these scores into shorter and shorter sequences, while keeping the germ of the original score.

Morrison further elucidated the ideas of "score" and "sats" from his own work with Barba:

> ISTA was and is, in many ways, an attempt to demonstrate that performance forms all share something in common—the property of bringing the performer to a higher, "extra-daily" level of physical engagement in a task and heightened awareness. Western theatrical aesthetics largely lack the forms of Balinese, Indian, or other traditional performance, so you have to create it by creating a score—a memorized physical sequence that the actor is constantly refining and exploring through repetition. There is a mental aspect to this as well that has to do with sats. I remember the Odin actors saying that sats was the moment before action—the moment of readiness before something happens. I think this might be a uniquely Danish word. Keeping the score alive is done by learning to move from sats to sats—you discover nuance in the "drawing back of the bow," and then releasing it for each impulse. And then you do it again and again. (Morrison)

To train the actor in the development of this sats "extra-daily" awareness, the DAH works with two primary principles taken from Barba: "Double Direction" and "Edge of Balance." Double direction seeks to embody opposite directions within the actor simultaneously, for example, leading forward with a right arm yet feeling the pull in the opposite direction backwards with a left leg or experiencing "up-ness" in one body position while simultaneously experiencing "down-ness" in another body part. This metaphor of double direction--feeling or experiencing two energies

in opposition simultaneously--is at the heart of everything the DAH does. On the letterhead of Barba's Odin Teatret appears the phrase: "Opposites are complementary."

The principle of "edge of balance" can best be embodied in putting the actor's body into any unbalanced position where he is right at the edge of where he might fall. In the moment of being on the very edge of balance, there is an electric aliveness or focus that arises in the actor. Thus, the sought-for sats emerges from within the actor. The DAH explores these two key principles both in training and in their theatre creation. The primary methods they use to explore these principles of double direction and edge of balance, as well as developing this hyper-focused awareness, are Chi Gong, Drum Work, and Three-Step. In seeking to awaken and unearth this dynamic energy, the actor embraces the concept of opposition in the form of double direction while seeking to clarify her movements with exact precision.

Chi Gong:
For half an hour in the morning actors in our group would learn and develop the form of Chi Gong with Maja Mitic. Maia led Chi Gong exercises playing with double directions such as "fingers strong, but soft in the hand." The hand can hold both strength and softness. Working to keep shoulders down while hands are raised up in the air is another example of feeling this double direction in oneself simultaneously. Maja urged the actors to work with 70% of their energy rather than 100% in order to avoid overeffort. The actors quickly noticed small ways in which they were not being precise and thus made adjustments. By the end of the time in Belgrade the actors embodied more detail and precision.

Drum Work:
Following Chi Gong the actors worked with Milosevic while she beat on a drum. With the beating drum actors investigated a variety of movement sequences including "Stop and Balance," "Edge of Balance," "Double Direction," and "Drop/Jump." These are all used by Barba as well. When the drumbeat became suddenly loud and stopped, the actors froze into a position that incorporated the "edge of balance" while experiencing some double direction in the body: an arm reaching up while a foot is pointing down or hips poking left while rib cage pokes right. At the stop of the next series of drumbeats, the actors dropped to the floor, freezing in a "fully-filled," energized position. The drum resumed, and when it next stopped, the actors jumped high in the air and upon landing froze in yet another body position. The frozen body position always incorporated double direction as well as the edge of balance.

Double Directions in Serbia and Greece: Blending the Methods of the DAH Theatre and Frankie Armstrong by Marlene Johnson

Milosevic side-coached while doing the drum work:

> We are trying to get you to be in the present, so that thinking and impulse become one thing. If something is too easy, add more layers, more tasks. When you do something for a longer time, the brain gets lazy and we lose presence. How can the brain keep present in action? Feel the space. We need to be reaching for change at all times. Go everywhere! Don't send your energy into the floor. One part of the body is exploring "upness" even when you are on the floor. While moving backwards, something reaches forward. (Milosevic)

Photo by Marlene Johnson

At the DAH Theatre Actors perform Three-Step

Three Step:
Sanja Krsmanovic-Tasic next led the group in a movement form of stomping called "Three-Step." Energy builds within the body as the actor stomps in time in beats of three: "ONE-two-three, ONE-two-three, ONE-two-three," changing the foot that stomps on the strong ONE-down-beat as the internal dynamic energy (sats) builds within the actor. This continues for quite some time. Eventually the external stomping lessens while the internal energy created by the stomping continues to emanate from the actor in a dynamic stillness. Sanja side-coached: "Bring the 3-step to the smallest size you can. Let the whole impulse be in the body. Each step is a new direction. Your task is to find double direction as often as possible. Keep the 3-step in your body" (Krsmanovic-Tasic). Sometimes the emphasis would be on the first beat, sometimes on the second and sometimes on third. The Three-Step would continue for up to 40 minutes.

Frankie Armstrong's Vocal Collaboration:

After working with these three forms in the morning train-

ing, Frankie Armstrong then stepped in with her vocal training. Armstrong has developed an approach to voice based in folk singing styles from around the world, in archetypes of myth and story, in mask work, and in Feldenkrais physical explorations. She regularly gives workshops around the world.

Rodgers first met Armstrong in Philadelphia in 1993 when Armstrong, as one of the VASTA conference presenters, demonstrated samplings of her archetype and folk singing work. Rodgers met up with Armstrong again in 1999 at the Giving Voice Festival in Aberystwyth in an archetypes workshop Frankie was leading. At the time Rodgers had been cast as Lucifer in a production of Marlowes's *Dr. Faustus*. When Frankie began the workshop by having participants voice and embody the devil archetype, "Lucifer," Janet found an aid to getting quickly inside a character which no amount of "given circumstances" or "magic if" method work had been able to prepare her for playing the role. Rodgers then began taking students and voice professionals to work with Frankie in England. Participants there found the archetypes training to be transformative.

Armstrong taught the actors her signature "ornamentations" of drones, bleats, slides, twiddles, and lamentation and grief calls found in various folk singing traditions. She often began with explorations designed to open the throat and then used a group setting: we moved into circles in which we imagined ourselves as a community working together, singing and doing physical labor like swinging forkfuls of hay or digging dirt. Armstrong also did a lot of articulation warm-ups which were crucial for the actors in order to be understood in these huge outdoor sites in Greece that we would be visiting later in our trip.

To prepare the actors for the droning which was the basis for two of the songs she taught the group, Armstrong had them roll /r/'s, rolling the sound on the lips and had them hum and trill "dddrrrrrum's" softly. Then they warmed up facial muscles and then played with more droning. Actors partnered and then "hunkered down" by lowering their centers/pelvises and bending the knees while pressing thigh to thigh against their partner, trying to move the partner. This lowered the breath support and gave the actors great power in voicing. (This exercise is similar to Patsy Rodenburg's "Readiness" exercise where the actor either pushes against a wall or pushes against another actor's hands.) Next the group walked slowly like elephants, swaying from side to side while singing "Hey mama hey mama hey mama hey," and then with "nonsense" or improvised "folk syllables."

Armstrong then taught the group songs which included a Macedonian song of greeting, a lullaby, and her own creation of a song based on a piece of Greek chorus in *Iphige-*

nia in Aulis, the piece that the whole project was based on. All of these were incorporated into the final presentation of the piece in Thorkis. The greeting song was used as troops were returning home to Greece from Troy, the haunting song from the text was used in the middle, and the lullaby was sung by a chorus of women lamenting their dead children as they left the orchestra in the exodus. Milosevic took Armstrong's songs and wove them into the theatre piece in a powerful and surprising way.

Frankie Armstrong and Janet Rodgers at Agamemnon's Palace, Mycaenae

The Project of Play Creation:

After training in the morning, Director Dijana Milosevic, along with other core DAH members, worked with the actors in developing the scores that would become the text and other theatrical elements for the final presentation. The objectives were to expand the actors' training using the highly physical energy work of the DAH, to develop a piece of theatre using these methods, and to come away with a performance piece with scenes of text consisting of three main units plus choral interludes. These scenes were often referred to as "shards" as in the shards of a piece of broken Greek pottery. This is consistent with the ways in which Odin Teatret creates theatre. Presenting in an ancient Greek theatre was crucial in Rodgers' mind to the final project.

In the afternoon Milosevic directed the piece with Rodgers assisting. Sonja Krsmanovic Tasic choreographed the stage move-

ment, with VCU Dance Professor, Martha Curtis assisting her. Maia Mitic led text and voice explorations. As previously mentioned, actors developed a physical score, a vocal score, an image score, and a sound score. Though this may sound unwieldy and overwhelming, it is in keeping with the DAH's techniques for theatre creation.

To prepare, actors read *Iphigenia in Aulis* in advance of traveling. Then the actors condensed selections from the Greek text—interweaving it with "found" contemporary text from sources such as magazines, blogs, pictures, and newspapers which dealt in some way with the themes of war, soldiers, suffering, etc. From these contemporary sources the actors selected simple lines to form a contemporary monologue. They now had two texts that they would be drawing from—one classical Greek and one contemporary. Milosevic instructed the actors to choose a character from *Iphigenia* and memorize some of their lines before arriving. Then actors were assigned an animal and prepared the character's lines while physically embodying the imagery of this animal. Next they created a movement score for their character from *Iphigenia*, and then made a separate movement score for the found contemporary text.

Each actor brought sandals that suggested Greek footwear. For training, they dressed in all-black clothing adorned with colored lengths of stretchy fabric—about 6 feet long--in red, yellow, purple, light blue, dark blue, and brown. These fabrics were used as belts, blindfolds, regalia, mourning scarves and other costume and set pieces. The group also brought simple tunics of neutral colors—mostly white, tan, beige—which ended up being used primarily as set pieces such as babies and dead bodies. In one instance the tunics were used in a ritualized action of dressing singer Alyssa Davis. The tunics weighed her down and enlarged her size as the actors layered 16 tunics over her one by one allowing her to serve as a kind of larger-than-life narrator while singing one of the three verse songs. As Davis later peeled the tunics off one by one while singing, she spread each one on the ground across the stage, suggesting dead bodies slain in the Trojan War.

Actors condensed selections from the Greek text.

Davis created a song to accompany her chorus lines in the play. Another student, Tony Sanchez, developed musical accompaniments with his mandolin and incorporated these into the scenes based on lines from the play:

> Out of the East
> All gold and shining
> A prince of Troy
> Came sailing, sailing
>
> Out of her house
> Came Helen, smiling,
> And both their loves
> Were burning, burning
>
> Out of that fire
> Many good men
> Will sail to Troy
> And lie there dying
> Dying, dying, dying.

Separately, Frankie had also created a song to go with these verses. Since there were already two versions of this choral ode, Armstrong considered that her song might not be used, but was pleasantly surprised when Milosevic placed the song in an unusual part of the play. Each song resonated with what was happening in the individual scene in which it appeared, creating a different tune and mood. But because the audience heard the repetition of the words, these words resonated from scene to scene establishing a throughline of story, mood, and theme. In addition to these improvised songs, Frankie taught the group 2 other songs—one a Macedonian song of joyous greeting welcoming the soldiers home from the war sung with a lot of frontal resonance and one a lullaby that was sung as the chorus made its exodus.

Following the training and play creation in Belgrade, the cast performed the piece *in situ* at ancient theatre sites, setting the play about key characters from the Trojan War in an original context. Sites selected were Epidaurus, Mycaenae, Argos, Delphi, Sounion, Athens' Theatre of Dionysus, and Thorikos. Because of restrictions in some of these theatres, students visited all of these and tested the acoustics but were only able to present in some of them. The

Actors performing Chi Gong at Sounion

Photo by Martha Curtis

most fully realized production was presented at the ancient theatre near Cape Sounion called Thorikos. This theatre is not in most guide books and is rarely visited. But it allowed the team the greatest freedom to produce the play. At Epidaurus and at Mycaenae (in "Agamemnon's tomb") the cast was able to sing Armstrong's songs from the production, and at Argos students were free to sing and speak Shakespeare, Greek, and other texts.

Synthesis and Reflection:
Following the performance in Thorikos Rodgers reflected on the experience as a whole:

> I found that the more I trained with the DAH, the further I could push beyond my perceived limitations and the stronger I felt on stage and off. At the suggestion of Dijana Milosovic, I read some of Eugenio Barba's writings and learned more about his ideas of the kinds of skills that the actor needs to embody in order to do this very different type of theatre. I can best describe this theatre as imaginative, metaphorical, and actor-centered. It requires tremendous focus, strength, and commitment. (Rodgers)

Martha Curtis, Professor of Dance at Virginia Commonwealth University, has accompanied Janet Rodgers twice to work with the DAH Theatre, including this trip. When asked what it was that she found compelling about the DAH's work she said:

> I found the DAH's work and process to be inspiring and deeply relevant to my creative investigation. Performance and the creation of work are drawn from a physical experience or state of being. Dijana's montage method of creating work is both choreographic and cinematic. She is able to excavate truth by weaving together micro and macro moments of material that is generated through a complex process of creative investigations. This is like editing in film; this is like combining movement ideas to make a dance; and this is like the way some American choreographers like Joe Goode are working. (Curtis)

In articulating what the training seeks to do, Curtis went on to say:

> The training makes the performer develop levels of awareness which enables the performer to embody numerous layered objectives simultaneously. One must be completely in one's body/mind. It develops the ability to think with one's body and respond with spontaneity. The principles of double direction and being on the edge of balance are woven throughout the DAH's training. (Curtis)

Tiza Garland, Assistant Professor of Movement at University of Florida, has worked with the DAH on several occasions. She found the work to be appealing and important because of the physicality of the acting:

> The work causes the actor to recognize that the power of the actor is in being engaged with the entire body at all times. This includes the voice. A body that is engaged in each moment with a high degree of specificity influences the voice. (Garland)

In describing the vocal work, Curtis offered:

> The DAH Theatre works with vocal scores and movement scores that are created and deeply investigated by the performers. These scores are often created with physical obstacles such as speaking text while also climbing on and over a structure of five chairs or exhaling while speaking until the actor totally runs out of breath and only then being allowed to continue speaking. These scores are then deconstructed and layered with other movement or vocal scores by Dijana Milosevic to create a visual and auditory non-linear narrative. (Curtis)

The defining ingredient which Frankie Armstrong's work brought to the DAH's work and the Greek Theatre Project, according to Curtis, was:

> Frankie Armstrong brought the element of song. The vocal quality of the Greek Chorus was developed with attention to the tonal qualities of folk music of the regions once occupied by the ancient Greeks. To me these sounds gave the final work its heart and made it deeply moving. (Curtis)

One of the actors in the group, Kerry McGee, had this to say about the Greek/Serbia/DAH/Armstrong experience:

> Frankie, like Janet before her, helped give me confidence in my voice and in my singing. I liked that there were alternatives to singing the melody to the songs that we learned. Singing is not my strong suit; however, I learned that I'm actually a very good droner. S he made all of the vocal lessons very accessible. I never would have thought to try some of the ornamentations that she demonstrated, but since she allowed for a sense of play, I felt comfortable experimenting with them. Her instruction made me feel very capable. I really enjoy the DAH's use of incorporating multiple texts and source material into one cohesive story, and for that story to resonate so much with a variety of people in multiple languages. I think that their theatre really has a power—which is something that I find lacking in much of the theatre that I see. The thing that I took away with me was the idea of precision. I admired how precise and economical every move that they made on stage was. I found myself really admiring it and wanting to devote time to it in my training. (McGee)

Janet Rodgers talked about what was positive about the whole experience.

> The students brought themselves into the inner life of these contemporary texts. The students were creating what was important to them. Dijana Milosevic and I decided that it was too much to do an entire play as they had originally planned. (Rodgers)

Rodgers continues: "The piece wasn't finished. It was a bare sketch. With more time we would have further developed the specificity of some of the voice work, more playing of action with less emotion." In some ways the experience far exceeded expectations. Rodgers said: "Where we ended up was back at the beginning. It was an unfinished piece. But it could have used more inner story elements from the students in terms of detail and refinement."

The total time period with the DAH Theatre was eight days of training in the morning and creation of scenes in the afternoon. The training and the theatre creation are two very separate things. Rodgers stated: "We tried to hold on to the training in the afternoon. It was a trade-off." Both Janet and Dijana felt that the training was crucial to the whole project rather than simply putting a play together. Training without the play creation experience would not have achieved the goal. The piece by itself would have defeated the educational goal of using the DAH training to create a Greek theatre piece.

Rodgers felt that what was unique about the work was that students got an opportunity to visit two countries and to meet with people from those countries. They were also able to create and develop an acting piece as a way of learning about two very different methods of training. It was an extraordinary pedagogical experiment.

Rodgers summed up:

> In addition to the artistic work and on another level, the DAH's commitment to creating theatre through very difficult political times has always reminded me of resilience and perseverance, two qualities that I believe are absolutely necessary in order to survive and thrive as an artist in any society but particularly in a fascist dictatorship such as Serbia's in the 90's and during wartime. Students whom I have brought to study with the DAH have returned to the USA with new commitment to their art and artistry. Some have gone on to create their own theatre companies. I strongly believe that international pedagogical and artistic experiments of this type create real bridges between artists, audiences and communities of the world. (Rodgers)

Bibliography

Barba, Eugenio. *Beyond the Floating Islands*, New York: Performing Arts Journal Publications, 1986.

Barba, Eugenio. *Land of Ashes, Land of Diamonds: My Apprentice ship in Poland*, Aberystwyth: Black Mountain Press, 1999.

Barba, Eugenio. *On Directing and Dramaturgy*, New York: Routledge, 2010.

Curtis, Martha. Personal Communication, December 3, 2010.

Garland, Tiza. E-mail message to the author. January 6, 2011.

Krsmanovic-Tasic. Workshop at the DAH Theatre with actors and with author. June 2, 2010

McGee, Kerry. E-mail message to the author. December 6, 2010.

Milosevic, Dijana. Workshop at the DAH Theatre with actors and with author. June 2, 2010.

Morrison, Jeff. E-mail message to the author. November 4, 2010.

Rodgers, Janet and Armstrong, Frankie. *Acting and Singing with Archetypes*, Milwaukee: Limelight Editions, Hal Leonard Corporation, 2009.

Rodgers, Janet. E-mail message to the author. December 5, 2010.

Photo by Marlene Johnson

Janet Rodgers with Sanja Krsmanovic-Tasic and Dijana Milosevic of the DAH Theatre

Photo by Marlene Johnson

Maia Mitic of the DAH Theatre

Peer-Reviewed Article *by Karina Lemmer and Marth Munro*

Lessac's Structural NRG as an Aid to Zulu Performers' Production of English Vowels – A preliminary exploration

Karina is a Lecturer at the Department of Drama and Film Studies at Tshwane University of Technology, in Pretoria South Africa, where she teaches voice and speech. Karina holds an M A from NWU and has completed several projects working actors and other professionals as a voice and dialect coach in South Africa, Kenya, Namibia and Botswana, in her former position as Director at the I. E. Group. She has also been actively involved in research projects that examine voice and language in the African context, in preparation of a PhD.

Marth Munro is Professor Extraordinaire at the University of Pretoria, South Africa. In her PhD she investigated the acoustic properties of Lessac's Tonal NRG and the "Actor's formant" in the female performer's voice. She is a Certified Laban/Bartenieff Movement Analyst, a Certified Lessac Voice and Movement Teacher, a Qualified Hatha Yoga Teacher, a Bio- and Neurofeedback practitioner, a NBI whole-brain practitioner and a Sound Therapy Intern. She was editor-in-chief of the Festschrift on the Lessac work which appeared in 2009, and co-editor of the 2010 edition of the *SATJ*. She was an associate editor for several *Voice and Speech Reviews*.

Introduction

In *The Actor Speaks* Patsy Rodenburg states "…I'm regularly asked, 'What is a good voice?' I often answer 'One that I don't notice.' I would also add, one which makes me notice things about a spoken text" (Rodenburg 1997, 163). This statement could be interpreted as achieving cohesion between voice and speech that is connected to communicative intent and lends itself to creative expression. Such creative expression should be the goal when coaching student performers. However when performance is applied in a second or third language, non-deliberate creativity becomes challenging. Working with student performers in the South African context, where eleven official languages are embraced, this is a daily reality. English has been adopted as a lingua franca in South Africa, despite the fact that first language speakers of English constitute approxi-

mately ten percent of the population (SA Census 2001). Although mother-tongue material is applied in training and performance, work opportunities in the local theatre, television and film industry are significantly increased for performers who are able to work in English. As a result voice coaching that applies explorations and texts in English is relevant in the student performers' training, and often the only practical consideration as a single class may include students from eight different language groups. This implies conscious accent acquisition that inevitably leads performers to a stage where they become acutely aware of "how" they produce the English sound systems. In this process it is important not to prescribe correctness as this may inhibit impulses and expression. The performer should be guided to trust his/her impulses, to release habitual tension and

Pedagogy and Coaching

Lessac's Structural NRG as an Aid to Zulu Performers' Production of English Vowels – A preliminary exploration by Karina Lemmer and Marth Munro

to enable the articulators to function organically. Aspiring to a perceived notion of correctness may increase tension and reduce creativity. This is compounded by auditory perception skills. Studies such as Wissing, Selebeleng and Stander (2000, 45) investigated the listening perception of Sotho and Zulu speakers and concluded that these speakers experience difficulty in correctly identifying the length and quality of English vowels. Considering that imitation and focus on sound production may create articulatory tension and challenge auditory perception, a kinesthetic or "kinesensic" approach could potentially assist second and third language speakers to produce English effectively for performance purposes.

The concept of kinesthetic awareness of sound production has been explored by several approaches to voice and speech development. Berry (1982, 27-29) asserts that voice can only function organically and naturally when the performer becomes aware of the muscular sensations involved. Linklater (1976, 35) refers to a "touch of sound" implying the conscious awareness of the sound vibrations that are released from the body. Alfred A. Tomatis, founder of auditory stimulation by means of Audio-Psycho-Phonology, refers to "listening" versus "self-listening" (1991, 54). He defines "listening" as the awareness generated by the external passage of the ear that may be contaminated whereas "self-listening" generates awareness by means of bone conduction. Tomatis' work with singers that applied bone conduction by means of a device called an Electronic Ear enhanced the vocal performance of singers in a manner that impacted positively on tone and their production of phonemes (Tomatis 1991, 55). This potentially indicates that a sensory awareness of sound production could elevate the performer's vocal output. This resonates with Lessac's *kinesensics*, which he describes as sensing through movement training that employs whole-body learning that applies an intrinsic sensing where vocal energies are "felt" rather than "heard" (1997, 2). It is "organic" instruction (Lessac 1997, 5) that heightens awareness and therefore promotes self-teaching through embodied learning rather than prescription and imitation. Turner (2009, 380) offers that Lessac's notion "to discard the ear" provides the student with the freedom to "learn through experimenting with bone conduction and muscular sensations".

This article will investigate the potential of applying the Lessac kinesensic voice and body training, with specific focus on the Structural Energy (NRG) component, to assist Zulu speaking performers with the production of English vowels for performance purposes. This will be illustrated by firstly exploring the Zulu vowel system to establish a base for the challenges that Zulu performers face when producing English. Lessac's Structural NRG will then be examined with a view to applying its core philosophy and explorations to the coaching of Zulu speaking performers.

Finally, Zulu and English text samples will be employed to briefly illustrate the shifts required by Zulu speaking student performers in training.

The Zulu Vowel System

45.7% of the South African population is first-language speakers of the Nguni language group which includes: IsiZulu, IsiXhosa, SiSwati and IsiNedebele (SA Census 2001). Zulu is the largest speaker group of the Nguni language family and for this reason it was decided to isolate Zulu as the language of focus in the article. Like all Nguni languages, Zulu is characterized by a complex consonantal system that includes phoneme clusters and its signature "click" sounds. As a result Zulu speakers create sounds that are not found in English (Adendorf & Salvini-Beck, 1993, 239). In contrast the Zulu vowel system consists of five basic vowels (van Wyk 1981, 59; Adendorf & Salvini-Beck 1993, 234). These directly reflect the five vowel letters in the Roman alphabet as listed below:

/i/ in "lima" (plough)
/ɛ/ in "thenga" (buy)
/ a/ in "thanda" (love)
/ɔ/ in "bona" (see)
/u/ in "funa" (seek)

The tongue positioning and placement of the Zulu vowels is illustrated in the vowel chart below:

(1)

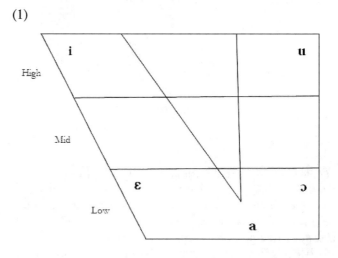

Chart one (1) reflects the production of the Zulu vowels as depicted by South African linguists (see van Wyk, 1981, 69). It displays the peripheral positioning of Zulu vowels and indicates specific articulation and tongue positions that occur, For example the /a/ in Zulu is produced with the tongue in a more central position than the English /ɑ/. It could be noted as a closer resemblance to the English /ʌ/ than /ɑ/.

In chart two (2) below the Zulu vowels are superimposed on an illustration of the English vowels to depict the differences. Zulu vowels are highlighted for easy reference. Since variations occur in vowel production, exact plotting of vowel production is not always possible (van Wyk 1981, 69). Chart two (2) should therefore be viewed as an approximation of the English vowels used for illustration purposes. The vowels as applied in South African English by first language speakers were used as base for plotting the phonemes in chart two (2).

(2)

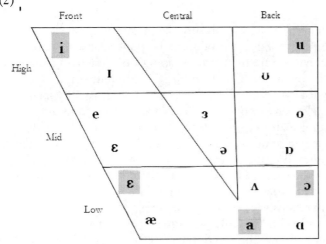

The following core differences between the vowel systems manifest:

1. Zulu contains a significantly smaller number of vowels and several cardinal English vowels do not exist in Zulu. This implies that Zulu speakers are required to produce phonemes in English that have no counterpart in their own phoneme system. The Zulu speaker is then likely to subject the phonemes produced in English to the phonetic rules of Zulu. The result is approximations that could impede clarity (Heny 1994, 62, Gleaser 1995, 2).

2. Zulu vowels are positioned peripherally as no central vowels exist in Zulu. This factor would likely result in adjustments as Zulu speakers would approximate central vowels in English towards their closest counterparts in Zulu.

3. English vowels are spread in articulator positioning and appear in clusters. For example /ʌ/ in "ton", /ɔ/ in "taught", /ɒ/ in "top" and /ɑ/ in "tart" are positioned in the lower back right corner of the vowel chart. In the top right the /ʊ/ in "cook" and /u/ in "cool" can be cited as examples of clusters (Adendorf & Salvini-Beck 1993, 237). Such clusters are not present in Zulu and could lead Zulu speakers to produce all the phonemes in an English cluster to reflect the one sound present in Zulu.

4. In English certain vowels are inherently longer or are lengthened to communicate meaning. The minimal pair /ɪ/ in "it" and /i/ in "eat" is such an ex ample. No pairs that signify meaning adjustments when lengthened occur in Zulu. In fact, in Zulu any vowel can be lengthened when it appears in a penultimate position in a word or when it is used to indicate a remote past tense form in verbs (Adendorf & Salvini-Beck 1993, 238).

5. In Zulu, all vowels are produced with agile muscular activity, thus Zulu never employs neutralization of phonemes as noted in English. For example in a two-syllable word such as "alone" the vowel in the unstressed initial syllable is usually neutralized as /əloʊn/. When produced by a Zulu speaker however, neutralization is not applied and it is articulated as /ɑlon/. Such production of inherently neutral sounds is also likely to affect the overall rhythm of the Zulu speaker's English which may inhibit both clarity and confidence.[3]

6. Lastly, although not depicted in the chart, Zulu contains no diphthongal sounds, in contrast to English, which contains several diphthongs.

The above brief exploration of the English and Zulu vowel systems reveals significant differences as an illustration of the complexities that Zulu performers face when working with English text. In order to empower these performers an awareness of the English vowel system needs to be cultivated. Instruction applying the IPA could instill awareness of the English vowel system. Methodologies such as Louis Colaianni's work that applies the IPA in a manner that promotes connections between phonetic signs and the embodied sound experience opposed to learning that relies solely on logical and linear thinking (Anderson & Colaianni 1997, 4) could benefit the Zulu speaking performer significantly. However, IPA training when usually applied in South Africa constitutes a cognitive and analytical approach (see Adendorf & Salvini-Beck 1993, van Wyk, 1981). It could be argued that the solely cognitive instruction methods largely prevalent in speech training in South Africa such as phonetic transcription may emphasize the vast differences and leave Zulu performers focusing cognitively on technical elements that could inhibit and impede creativity. Theoretical instruction may also result in Zulu speakers striving to produce the English vowels "correctly" based on external models. Ideally, the embodied discovery of the English vowel system should be part of the Zulu performer's voice building and creative vocal exploration. Since Lessac's Tonal NRG explorations are applied as part of the Zulu performers' voice building in our classes with undergraduate student performers in South Africa, extending their exposure by applying Structural NRG with a view to aid vowel production is deemed a workable approach as it facilitates integrated experiential learning.

This does not imply that IPA based approaches will poten-

Pedagogy and Coaching
Lessac's Structural NRG as an Aid to Zulu Performers' Production of English Vowels – A preliminary exploration by Karina Lemmer and Marth Munro

tially not yield positive outcomes, but following the current bodymind tendency in education that moves from primarily cognitive approaches towards kinesthetic and proprioceptive learning strategies, we argue that that cohesive instruction that explores voice building and vowel production *simultaneously* could benefit the Zulu speaking performer in training. Therefore, for the purpose of this article, the Lessac work's implementation of kinesensic learning will be explored as a means to enhance awareness and production of English vowels in an organic and non-descriptive fashion, while enabling integrated learning.

Exploring Lessac's Structural NRG approach as a means to enhance vowel production

Lessac kinesensic voice and body training[4] promotes a kinesensic[5] awareness that seeks a synergistic relationship between body, breath and voice by means of three vocal energies (NRG) (Tonal NRG[6], Consonant NRG[7] and Structural NRG[8]) as well as body energies[9]. Its global goal is to achieve a balanced state that promotes vocal health and expression (Kur 2005, 14). The Lessac kinsensic training's positive impact as a voice-building tool and a means to enhance vocal performance and general well-being has been documented (for a compilation see Munro et. al. 2009).

The explorations[10] applied in the Lessac work are aimed at generating a familiar event (Lessac 1997, 2) that recalls a positive comfortable event, always experienced as spontaneous and accessible. Additionally, it shifts focus from hearing perception to a deliberate organic sensing, relying on three principles of the work itself namely; *body esthetics, inner harmonic sensing and organic instructions* (Munro 2002, 16; Hurt 2009). Lessac refers to "overriding the outer ear" (1997, 18) implying that auditory feedback and the resultant judgment of the sounds' perceived correctness is replaced by a more intrinsic response and awareness. This tactic stimulates the face, lips and tongue areas of the somatosentory cortex (Dowling 2004, 86) and actively accesses embodied learning. The resultant organic self-awareness that promotes enhancement through kinesensic self-monitoring rather than self-judgment based on an external perception of correctness is considered as a potential means for Zulu-speakers to acquire English sounds. It could be argued that it may be particularly relevant in the training of Zulu performers as their auditory perception may initially be reduced due to the limited nature of their first language's vowel system. Further, Lessac's philosophy of applying focus on inner feel rather than outer ear (1997, 19) could be considered a more educationally conducive approach as awareness is focused on the inner-self, thus fully embracing personal uniqueness in a process orientated manner. Lessac refers to exploring the music of the vowels (1997, 160). This paradigm has a universal accessibility that potentially transcends linguistic boundaries. Such an angle could be of significant value in a culturally and linguistically diverse and complex environment such as South Africa.

When reflecting on the impact that the Lessac training's explorations may have on the English vowel production of Zulu speakers, it is important to note that the three energies applied in the work should not be separated. However, for the purposes of this article focus will be placed on the Structural NRG component that explores vowel phonemes. Application of Tonal NRG and Consonant NRG forms part of the Zulu speaking student performer's training and is implied.

Structural NRG explores the shaping of the oral cavity as different vowels are produced. It applies the sensing of the phonemes from the largest shaping with AH /ɑ/ to smallest lip opening OO /u/. While the different vowels and oral cavity shaping is explored, cavity size is gently maintained to ensure optimal space capacity for sound in the oral resonator (Lessac 1997, 161). This process develops resonance and vowel awareness simultaneously in a single, integrated action and could benefit the Zulu performer's self-awareness. The fact that the explorations range from largest to smallest lip rounding position, also implies a comprehensive and organic sensing of oral cavity shaping, thus allowing the Zulu performer to experience the full extent of vowel production in English. It could be argued that this could generate valuable awareness to speakers who apply a limited vowel sounds in their mother tongue.[11]

Each sound explored in Structural NRG is described and processed in an accessible manner highlighting lip opening and oral shaping, with an emphasis on what is felt (Lessac 1997, 164-168). Describing the vowels with the constructs of "form" and "feel" generates tangibility that could heighten the kinesensic awareness and is potentially less cognitive than traditional phonetic transcription. Symbols are assigned to each vowel phoneme or structural shape. Kur (2009, 437) describes Lessac's depiction of vowel sounds as tono-sensory phonetic transcription that emphasizes the physical awareness of the sound's production. Numbers are used and assigned as follows:

# 1	OO as in "cool" or /u/
# 21	ō as in "boat" or /oʊ/
# 3	*AW* as in "call" or /ɔ/
# 4	ŏ as in "not" or /ɒ/
# 5	*AH* as in "father" or /ɑ/
# 51	*OW* as in "now" or /aʊ/
# 6	Ă as in "add" or /æ/
# 3y	*OI* as in "boy" or /ɔɪ/
# 6y	ĭ as in "why" or /aɪ/
# 3r	R-derivative as in "bird" or /ɜ/

Although this could be deemed as broad transcription if compared to the International Phonetic Alphabet, it allows for flexibility within the individual sound's duration, tone and pitch enhancing creativity in vocal performance (Kur 2009, 437). These tono-sensory transcriptions contain only three sounds present in Zulu: # 1 /u/, # 3 /ɔ/ and # 5 /ɑ/., although the tongue position and articulation area of these sounds may differ in Zulu, as is the case with the /ɑ/ that is produced as a more central /a/ closer to the English /ʌ/. The remaining sounds could all be considered "foreign" and structural exploration could potentially assist Zulu speakers with attaining these sounds, by means of sensing. Five diphthongs are also included and an exploration of these could aid Zulu speakers as no diphthongs are present in their mother tongue. Diphthongs are not always depicted as double sounds and this may instill an overall awareness of the phoneme's sensation rather than a cognitive awareness of double sound production. Additionally, the three Zulu sounds that are reflected in the tono-sensory transcriptions are mostly applied as short sounds in Zulu. Exploring these sounds by means of sensing the oral structure in cohesion with tonal awareness could enhance awareness of vowel length. Lessac's Structural NRG explorations categorize the remaining English vowels as neutrals. These are described as sounds that are produced with a neutral facial posture (Lessac 1997, 197) or rather a neutral facial orientation and include:

N1   as in "took" or /ʊ/
N2   as in "tick" or /ɪ/
N3   as in "tech" or /ɛ/
N4   as in "tuck" or /ʌ/

Lessac describes the neutral vowels as short staccato sounds (Lessac 1997, 197). In IPA based description, the term "neutral" is assigned to the schwa /ə/. Kimble-Fry (2001, 32) terms the schwa the neutral vowel due to the neutral resting tongue position. This description is also used by Spencer (1996, 26). Lessac's use of the term "neutral vowel" therefore differs from its depiction in the IPA as Lessac does not specifically use tongue positioning as base but describes the "neutrals" as "sounds representing the shortest distance between two consonants" (Lessac 1997, 184). It could be concluded that Lessac's tono-sensory markings apply the term "neutral" where phonetic description of the English vowels may refer to "short." Lessac also states that the "neutrals" constitute sixty five percent of vowels used in formal communication as "weak-forms" or what he terms "familiar" forms (Lessac 1997, 184). This could be interpreted as Lessac's description of vowels applied in "weak" or "unstressed" syllables, thus vowels that are applied with reduced articulatory energy in connected speech. As stated above in point 5 above, all Zulu vowels are produced with agile muscular action despite their short duration. Therefore, no distinction is made in Zulu between "short" sounds

and "neutral" sounds, as is the case in English. It could be concluded that Zulu speakers never apply a neutral facial orientation or tongue position when producing vowels and are therefore likely not to employ neutralization when producing connected speech in English. Exploration of what Lessac terms "neutral" vowels could potentially assist Zulu speakers with reducing the articulatory energy applied in weak syllables therefore establishing greater contrast between "long" and "short" phonemes as well as "weak" and "strong" production of syllables. This has the potential to elevate the clarity in connected English speech. Zulu speakers are likely not only to shorten longer sounds but also tend to shorten and approximate "neutral" vowels towards the resonator shaping of Zulu vowels.[12] Generating a kinesensic awareness of "neutral" facial orientation towards producing the "neutral" sounds in English could potentially generate a sense of familiar comfort, that could assist Zulu speakers with vowel neutralization which tends to be a challenge is traditional accent acquisition coaching. Additionally kinesensic explorations that focus on the sensing and feeling and as such deliberately engage with somatosensory activity could elevate awareness of length-variety as "neutral" vowel explorations are contrasted with the other Structural NRG vowels. Such contrasting explorations may assist in the stimulation and development of auditory perception skills as length perception has been cited as a challenge for Zulu speakers (Wissing, Selebeleng & Stander 2000, 45).

As indicated, Zulu contains no central vowels. This may imply that central vowels /ɜ/ and /ə/ could be particularly challenging for Zulu performers to perceive and produce as no counterparts exist in the sound system of their mother tongue. The concept of the forward facial yawn[13] could aid Zulu speakers in sensing the central vowels. The forward facial yawn is a core element of tonal energy, and is used at the initiation of Structural NRG explorations (Lessac 1997, 160) to generate awareness of vocal tract shaping and the vibrations that result. Sensing, recalling and ultimately managing the size and shape of the oral cavity and the muscles in the jaw and cheeks could assist Zulu speakers in the acquisition of central vowels. This process is reflective of what Lessac refers to as "Sensation-Perception-Awareness-Response" or SPAR. Hurt (2009,108) unpacks SPAR as "…the body and all of its senses act[ing] as filters taking in sensory information that creates gestalt, perceiving its harmonic resonances, and guiding awareness for instantaneous response."

Kur (2005) applies the Structural NRG as a kinesensic approach to accent/dialect acquisition. This integrated approach views accent/dialect acquisition as a continuation of the development of the vocal instrument and not an isolated task (Kur 2009, 434). Sensory awareness of the changes in the vocal tract provides an immediate and

Lessac's Structural NRG as an Aid to Zulu Performers' Production of English Vowels – A preliminary exploration by Karina Lemmer and Marth Munro

uniquely personal awareness of vocal behavior that could not only assist the Zulu speaking performer to gain access to his inner life but also that of the character that he is portraying. This implies that the Zulu-speaking performer could learn to respond to his/her own immediate and personal perception, rather than reliance on external feedback. Finally, establishing a link between vocal and inner expression may lead to more authentic expression (Kur 2009, 435) and this could be viewed as vital when the Zulu performer is required to apply a language or accent that is significantly different from his own.

Illustration and Exploration

This section will attempt to illustrate how Lessac's Structural NRG could potentially assist the Zulu-speaking performer in effective production of English vowels as a depiction of the argument posed.[14] Explorations and the basic strategies of the coaching process will be discussed and illustrated by means of shorts extracts from a Zulu and an English text. The application illustrated in this section is based on the conclusions drawn from the analysis of the Zulu vowel system as well as the authors' experience applying Structural NRG explorations with student performers in a training context. This article is written from the perception of reflective expert practitioners and is as such experiential and ethnographic and not merely speculative. Before explorations are examined, it is vital to state that Structural NRG should form part of broader vocal coaching that employs all components of the Lessac voice training (Tonal NRG and Consonant NRG) in combination with the body work and breath explorations. This is important as all aspects of the performer's vocal development could contribute to heightening kinesensic awareness in the student performer, which could potentially elevate the impact yielded by the application of the Structural NRG. It is also essential that solid knowledge and sensory awareness, thus a bodymind understanding, of the Lessac work exists before text explorations are attempted (Maes 2007, 264). This will generate awareness and kinesensic sensitivity that could ease the exploration of English text for the Zulu-speaking performer. As a result this could provide the Zulu-speaking performer with a sense of ease and an organic awareness rather than a pure cognitive analysis of the phonology of the text.

Before explorations are discussed and illustrated, the sound system as applied in Lessac's Structural NRG is imposed on the vowel chart (3) that illustrates the Zulu vowels. This Structural NRG symbols are placed in circles indicating the general area of articulation rather than a distinct position.

(3)

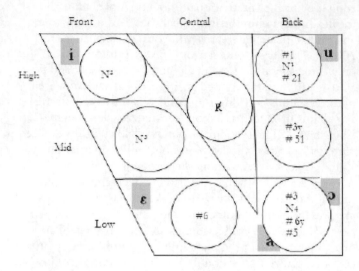

Chart three (3) illustrates the general area in which the sounds applied in Lessac's Structural NRG are produced, imposed on the Zulu vowel chart. It reveals that the explorations applied in Structural NRG span all areas of articulation. It could therefore be argued that exploring Structural NRG would provide Zulu speaking performers with exploratory sensory awareness by means of resonator shaping in positions where their mother tongue does not provide exposure. This is of particular relevance in the mid and central areas of articulation where Zulu contains no vowels. Continued awareness by means of structural explorations could generate a familiar event that would aid the Zulu speaking performer to produce the mid and central vowel phonemes with greater ease and potentially greater efficiency. In return this could also facilitate ear training.

From a practical standpoint, some degree of kinesensic awareness should precede explorations that consciously adjust phonemes. If the Zulu speaking performer's kinesensic awareness is heightened to a level that is comfortable and free of tension, application of the Structural NRG sounds or resonator shaping would be less foreign, thus enabling the performer to apply phonetic shifts with a greater level of confidence. For this reason it is suggested that body work aimed at release and centering is followed by Tonal NRG explorations that will initiate kinesensic awareness. Explorations such as the Y Buzz, +YBuzz and finally the Call[15] would assist the Zulu-speaking performer in cultivating kinesensic awareness, body esthetics, inner harmonic sensing and organic instructions (as defined above) as a highly personal experience. When such awareness is firmly established, the Structural NRG tono-sensory symbols or markings that depict the sounds can be introduced. It may be advisable to introduce the Structural NRG sounds or resonator shaping to the Zulu speaker working from the most familiar to the least familiar. This suggests for example that it could be more effective to start with the sounds that are positioned in the general articulation areas where the Zulu vowels are produced. This would imply that #1, #21, #3, #6, and #6y may be an effective starting point as it is applied in the general area of articulation where the Zulu vowels are produced. In contrast, #3r, #3y, #5 and #51 are applied in the mid and central areas where no Zulu vowels exist, and should potentially be applied once a sense of comfort has been generated exploring the other sounds. This is however an analytical strategy and practical exposure has revealed that the reaction to the exploration of Structural NRG is experienced in different ways by individuals and as such the student's personal uniqueness should determine the order of the explorations. Certain Zulu-speaking performers find exploration of the central vowels easier as it constitutes a "new" sensation. I t is therefore impossible to formulate a clear-cut sequence; it is rather suggested that the voice coach is acutely aware of each individual's uniqueness and applies a flexible approach.

Once sensory awareness of the resonator shaping is established, the sounds/resonator shaping is applied to words[16] as suggested by the Lessac kinesensic training. When working with second and third language speakers of English, we have found it useful to not limit the explorations to the word lists provided in the Lessac voice text (1997) but to encourage student performers to devise and apply their own word lists containing the target sounds. This reinforces their understanding while simultaneously serving as a vocabulary activity that raises awareness of the spelling. We have noted that this activity assists Zulu speaking students with linking the sound to the word, an activity that English speakers take for granted but that can be challenging when one's mother tongue employs limited vowels and applies phonetic spelling. This activity also initiates a link between the pure kinesensic awareness[17] and a more cognitive task,[18] which prepares the Zulu speaking student performer for text work.

Exploration at a word level is extended to application of the target sounds/resonator shaping in sentences or phrases. This allows for greater integration of the different sounds in combination while linking Structural explorations to other "familiar" elements such as Consonantal NRG that ultimately promotes application into connected speech for text. Additionally exploration of sentences generates awareness of stress patterns towards meaning and intent, drawing on the prosodic patterns of the English language. This is useful for the Zulu speaking performer as it will lead to an awareness of emphasis on longer vowels and reducing muscular activity for neutral vowels. Exploration of sentences is followed by text exploration. The first challenge Zulu performers generally have is identifying the sounds/resonator shaping when they are confronted with the written word. It often requires revision and an element

of analysis. We have also found that applying Structural NRG to mother tongue text eases second and third language speakers into the process while reinforcing kinesensic awareness that is generically true to all languages and as such, provides them with a process that is more organically true to them. Since the Lessac tono-sensory markings are approximations, it lends itself to application in multiple languages which is incredibly useful in a multi-lingual context.

Application of the Structural NRG to text will be briefly explored using short extracts from a Zulu text *uNosilimela*, created by Credo Mutwa and produced by Workshop 71.[19] This illustration depicts the process suggested to aid Zulu speaking performers with acquiring effective English. (However, elements of this illustration could also be applied to achieve the reverse, should an English speaking performer need to acquire a Zulu accent.) The first extract from *uNosilimela's* opening chorus indicates phonetically how a Zulu speaker would produce the vowels, followed by application of Lessac's tono-sensory markings to the same text. A second illustration draws from Tony Kushner's *Angels in America: Part One* as an illustration of a contemporary English text. Although this is an American text, the illustrations reflect application in South African English as the dialect that Zulu speakers are likely to use in performance.

Velani   velani   batwana *(come out my*
ɛ a i   ɛ a   a a a   *children)*

Maye   kumnandi   ukuba   izingane
a ɛ   u a i   uua   i i a ɛ   ɛ a a
zelanga *(how lovely it is to be children of the sun)*

N³#5N²   N³#5N²   #5 #5 #5
Velani   velani   batwana *(come out my*
                                              children)

#5N³   N¹ #5 N²   N¹N¹#5   N²N²#5N³   N³#5#5
Maye   kumnandi   ukuba   izingane   zelanga
(how lovely it is to be children of the sun)

As depicted above in the marked Zulu text, approximated as it would be produced by a Zulu speaker, all the vowels are vocalized equally even when a sound is repeated in a word. Although the "neutral" markings are used, as applied in Lessac's Structural NRG, these vowels are not produced with a neutral facial posture/orientation, tongue position or reduced articulatory energy as all Zulu vowels are produced with agile energy and limited contrast. Zulu is produced with agile lip spreading, lip rounding, and tongue position adjustments. However, depicting Zulu text in this manner heightens the Zulu speaking performer's awareness of

Lessac's Structural NRG as an Aid to Zulu Performers' Production of English Vowels –
A preliminary exploration by Karina Lemmer and Marth Munro

vowel shaping in general and the distinct pattern present in his mother tongue. This establishes awareness before applying the tono-sensory markings to English text. Before that commences the Zulu speaking performer may be encouraged to deliver the Zulu text, marking only one significant vowel in each word as illustrated below:

#5   #5   #5
Velani   velani   batwana (*come out my children*)

This illustrates and allows the Zulu speaking performer to experience the energy generated by the selected vowels as Structural NRG is applied. It is experienced more distinctly, as an element of neutralization will organically start to emerge. Such an awareness enforces kinesensic awareness of the vowels and prepares the Zulu speaking performer for application in English text. Most of the Zulu speaking student performers have also reported that it elevates the meaning and intent of the word, which, in turn, aids characterization and overall performance.[20]

In applying the tono-sensory markings to English text, the Zulu speaking performer will firstly be encouraged to indicate and then "experience" the structure of the vowels that carry tone and convey meaning. This assists in reducing their spontaneous tendency to indicate all vowels as applied in Zulu. Sensing the structure of the sound will by default extend to more energy being exerted on certain sounds, thus enhancing the meaning and intent. In illustrating the application, the vowels in a line delivered by Prior in *Angels in America: Part One* will be transcribed (using IPA symbols) below, in the manner a Zulu speaker would produce it without any application of the tono-sensory markings or awareness of vowel structure or length, thus first language transfer in its true form.

It's   something   you   learn   after   your
i   a i i   u   ɛ a a ɔ   ɛ ɔ   i
second   theme   party:
a i
It's   All   Been   Done   Before
i   ɔ   i   a   i ɔ

As illustrated above, in the English approximated to resemble how a Zulu speaker would produce English text, the Zulu speaker is likely to produce most vowels with equal energy while replacing longer sounds with short counterparts and replacing sounds that are not present in Zulu with approximations, such as the /ɜ/ in learn that becomes /ɛ/. When indicating the vowels in the text with tono-sensory markings the Zulu speaker is likely to mark more vowels than a mother-tongue speaker would. As illustrated:

N²   #5   N²   N¹   N³   #5
It's   something   you   learn   after

#3   N³ #3   N¹   #5
your   second theme   party:

N²   #3   N²   #5   N² #3
It's   All   Been   Done   Before

If a Zulu speaking performer has a strong personal kinesensic awareness of the sounds and the Structural NRG has been applied to an extent that it has facilitated a familiar event, adjustments in the tono-sensory markings can be suggested. Linking the markings to the sensory awareness of the related oral resonator shaping should enable adjustment of the articulation of that phoneme to a degree that potentially facilitates greater clarity. Additionally, the sensory awareness of the sound and shaping is likely to organically increase the duration of certain sounds, thus elevating meaning. For example, by adjusting the above text to the sample text below:

N⁴   #3r   #5
It's   something   you   learn   after   your
N²   #5
second   theme   party:

#3   N⁴   #3
It's   All   Been   Done   Before

This may not resemble the manner in which a mother tongue speaker would produce the text, yet it would potentially enhance meaning while allowing the Zulu speaking performer to apply his/her kinesensic awareness of the marked sounds, thus heightening self-awareness and free expression rather than conscious adjustment of phonemes. It is through this process of inner harmonic sensing and organic instructions that the process of accent acquisition is facilitated by using Structural NRG. It is through deliberate and channeled structural shifts that the Zulu performer will be able to change from his/her own Zulu accent towards a required English accent as a role demands.

Conclusion

This article provides a subjective reflection on the use of Structural NRG in the holistic performer training of the Zulu performer in South Africa. It propagates embodied learning through accessing the Lessac kinesensic strategies. It serves as a preliminary investigation based on experience and observation.

Lessac's Structural NRG explores the form, size, shape and function of the oral cavity in a manner that is flexible and linked to inner experience (Kur 2005, 1). Although this flexibility lends itself to application in a multi-lingual context, it complicates a direct and cognitive comparison with the IPA as attributes such as specific lip shaping and tongue positioning in the production of vowels are not defined. The kinesensic process, allowing each Zulu performer to work from his/her personal uniqueness exploring organic shifts towards other vowels that might be foreign to the mother-tongue, ensures embodied learning which activates somatosensory processes that in turn provide an exploratory instead of corrective approach. This is of vital importance when the performer has to not only acquire required vowel shifts but simultaneously create a character.

In-depth controlled testing would be required to determine if kinesensic exploration could influence the Zulu performer's production of English vowels as proposed by us. Related elements such as Zulu's complex consonant system and the impact it possibly yields on vowel production are beyond the scope of this article. Another consideration is that fact that the phonemes described in Lessac's Structural NRG reflect General American English and relevant nuance differences may need to be examined in greater detail to fully empower Zulu speaking performers. Working with student performers, the researchers have observed positive results in all aspects of vocal development, including production of English vowels, using Lessac kinesensic voice and body training.[21] A comprehensive study that employs pre- and post-testing of vowel perception and production is planned to further this investigation.

Notes

1. Both authors of this article have spent time teaching accent acquisition in undergraduate drama programs in both the University of Pretoria, and the Tshwane University of Technology. This article draws from and reflects on these experiences.

2. For the purpose of this article the Zulu "a" sound is depicted with the symbol /a/ as applied by South African Linguist E.B van Wyk (1981, 69), and the English counterpart is depicted with the symbol /ɑ/.

3. The stress pattern of Zulu influences the Zulu speaker's production of English as Zulu does not employ neutral vowels. However this is not examined to its full extent within this article.

4. For the reader not familiar with Lessac terminology, short descriptions of cardinal concepts will be provided as footnotes. As the Lessac work is an integrated "bio-sensory approach that uses body and vocal energy states to awaken a largely untapped reservoir of knowledge, spirit and perceptive awareness" (Munro et al 2009, back cover), none of these concepts stand alone and, although defined here as separate entities for the sake of clarity, they are, in teaching, accessed in an holistic manner.

5. Lessac (1981, 5) defines kinesensic as a 'kinesthetic understanding and appreciation." Hurt (2009, 100) posits that "kinesensic training (is) an intrinsic training process where energy qualities are physically felt and perceived and then tuned and used for creative expression."

6. Krebs (2009, 305) describes the Tonal NRG as "the concentration of vibration that enables us to possess power without pain, strength without strain." Acker (1987); Raphael and Scherer (1987); Munro et al (1996) as well as Barrichelo and Behlau (2007) all wrote about the enhancement of the acoustic output of the performer's voice through Tonal NRG.

7. Kur (2009, 437) frames consonant NRG as "a combination of tactile and vibratory perception and the expression of the individual qualities of the consonants." He further offers that the "purpose of the consonant energy is intelligibility…. The association of these physical sensations with instruments (and sound effects) of the orchestra adds to that purpose musicality, contrast, variety, tempo and rhythm" (Ibid).

8. Structural NRG implies sensing, feeling and organically adjusting the "form, size, shape and function" (Kur 2009, 436) of the oral cavity as the main resonator area for vowel and diphthong shaping. The deliberate and integrated shaping heightens the somatosentory awareness of shifts between various vowels.

9. The body energies (Buoyancy, Radiancy, Potency and Inter-involvement—see Lessac (1978); de Oliveiro (2009, 413-417) and Hurt (2009, 104))—fall outside the scope of this article but form part of the integrated approach.

10. Within the Lessac work the term "exploration" is preferred rather than "exercise." Exploration relates to the concept of continuous experiencing and experimenting with the gestalt. As Hurt (2009, 101) offers "(I)n gestalt, sensations are measured against ongoing happenings of the body, gaining deeper meanings when they are considered as part of the entirety of the actor's experience."

11. This falls outside the scope of this article.

12. The lack of neutralization of vowels in Zulu can be contributed to several factors including the voicing of voiceless consonants and the glottal attracts applied in the complex Zulu consonant system. The scope of this article did not allow for exploration of the complex consonantal system and its impact on the production of Zulu vowels. It is however an important consideration for future research.

13. The concept of "forward facial" refers to the spatial orientation of the facial muscles. The forwardness provides a longer resonator and as such a lower F1 formant (see Raphael and Scherer 1987). The "yawn" refers to a muscle stretch but this term is preferred in the Lessac work as it implies a gentle organic orientation towards lengthening of muscles.

14. The first section of this article introduces the theoretical underpinning of the argument and is presented in speculative form. The application that follows concretises the conclusions and addresses the speculative.

15. These explorations are the primary explorations of Tonal NRG. Subjectively viewed, the sensing and feeling pivots around the bone conduction of the sound (Munro et al 1996). The Y-buzz is both a vowel-like /i:/ and consonant-like /y:/ elongated sound. It is "explored and developed only in the lower third range" (Lessac 1979, 125). The +Y-buzz starts with a neutral schwa and then accesses the Y-buzz in the second syllable. The +Y-buzz "starts with a tiny ping or gentle tonal impulse, …" (Lessac 1997, 131) to emphasize the awareness of the bone conduction: Yey…Yey…Yey. The Call "requires a fuller facial…. (orientation), a more definite yawn feel, and, therefore, a wider space between the teeth" (Lessac 1997, 137). Influenced by the pitch of the call the oral cavity shape organically shifts from an inverted megaphone for the lower pitches towards a megaphone for the higher pitches.

16. In the field of linguistics this notion would perhaps more accurately be referred to as "at a word level".

Pedagogy and Coaching
Lessac's Structural NRG as an Aid to Zulu Performers' Production of English Vowels –
A preliminary exploration by Karina Lemmer and Marth Munro

17. Actively accessing somatosensory activity.
18. Neo-cortex activity.
19. Workshop 71 was a theatre company established in South Africa in 1971, whose primary purpose was to engage with theatre in South Africa that would confront the awfulness of Apartheid. Its approach was participatory, multicultural, multilingual, democratic and progressive. The 1976 uprising brought the company to an end. The introduction to the volume from which this text is drawn (written by Robert "Mshengu" Kavanagh), sheds much light on the company.
20. The results reported here are informal and reflective of our teaching, and are not sanctioned by research ethics clearance (or IRB clearance), as is standard practice in South Africa. As such we cannot be more specific.
21. Articles in this regard have been published in previous Voice and Speech Reviews and other Journals.

Bibliography

Acker, Barbara. "Vocal tract adjustments for the projected voice." *Journal of Voice* 1, 1 (1987): 77-82.

Adendorf, Ralph. & Salvini-Beck, Marina. "The teaching of English vowels and consonants in the New South Africa." *Journal of language teaching* 27, 3 (1993): 232-247.

Anderson, Claudia & Colaianni, Louis. *Bringing Speech to Life — A Companion Workbook to The Joy of Phonetics and Accents.* Anderson & Colaianni, 1997.

Barrichelo-Lindström, Viviane & Behlau, Mara. "The Contribution of Lessac's Y-buzz from Two Brazilian Voice Therapists' Perspectives." In *Collective Writings on the Lessac Voice and Body Work, A Festchrift*, edited by M. Munro, S. Turner, A. Munro, K. Campbell. Coral Springs, FL: Llumina Press, 2009.

Census 2001, S.a. Accessed December 12, 2010. http://www.statssa.gov.za/timeseriesdata/pxweb2006/Dialog/ Saveshow.asp.

De Oliviero, Maria Regina Tocchetto. "The Body Energies in the Actor's Performance." In *Collective Writings on the Lessac Voice and Body Work, A Festchrift*, edited by M. Munro, S. Turner, A. Munro, K. Campbell. Coral Springs, FL: Llumina Press, 2009.

Dowling, John, E. *The Great Brain Debate: Nature or Nurture.* Washington, DC: Joseph Henry Press, 2004.

Hurt, Melissa. "Building the foundation in Lessaac's Kinesensic Training for Embodied Presence." In *The Moving Voice: Essays on Voice and Speech* edited by Rena Cook. Cincinnati, OH: VASTA, 2009.

Glaser, Robin. *An investigation into the effects of Nguni first language interference on the identification of vowels by English and Nguni listeners.* B. Sc diss. University of Cape Town, 1995.

Heny, J. "Learning and Using a Second Language." In *Language: introductory readings*, edited by V. P. Clark, P. A. Escholz, and A. F. Rosa 160-163. New York: St Martin's Press, 1994.

Kavanagh, Robert. *South African People's Plays, Plays by Kente, Mutwa, Shezi and Workshop 71.* Johannesburg: Heinemann, 1992.

Kimble-Fry, Alison. *Perfect Pronunciation.* Sydney: ClearSpeak, 2001

Krebs, Nancy. "Acoustic Properties: The 'Ring' of Truth." In *Collective Writings on the Lessac Voice and Body Work, A Festchrift*, edited by M. Munro, S. Turner, A. Munro, K. Campbell. Coral Springs, FL: Llumina Press, 2009.

Kur, Barry. "Lessac Kinesensic Dialect Acquisition." In *Collective Writings on the Lessac Voice and Body Work, A Festchrift*, edited by M. Munro, S. Turner, A. Munro, K. Campbell. Coral Springs, FL: Llumina Press, 2009.

Kur, Barry. *Stage Dialect Studies: A Continuation of the Lessac Approach to Actor Voice and Speech Training.* West Fairmount: Kur, 2005

Kushner, Tony. *Angels in America, Part One: Millennium Approaches.* London: Royal National Theatre & Nick Hern, 1992.

Biliography (continued)

Lessac, Arthur. Body Wisdom, *The Use and Training of The Human Body*. San Bernardino California: L.I.P.Co, 1981.

Lessac, Arthur. *The Use and Training of the Human Voice*. McGraw-Hill, 1997.

Linklater, Kristin. *Freeing the Natural Voice*. New York: Drama Book Publishers, 1976.

Maes, Kathryn. "Examining the Use of Lessac Exploration in Shakespearean Text" In *Voice and Gender and other contemporary issues in professional voice and speech training presented by the Voice and Speech Review*, edited by Mandy Rees. Cincinnati, OH: VASTA, 2007.

Munro, M., Turner, S., Munro, A., Campbell, K. eds. *Collective Writings on the Lessac Voice and Body Work, A Festchrift*. Coral Springs, FL: Llumina Press, 2009.

Munro, M. *Lessac's Tonal Action in Women's Voices and the "Actor's Formant": a comparative study*. PhD diss., PU for CHE, South Africa, 2002.

Munro, M., Leino, T., & Wissing, D. "Lessac's Y-Buzz as a Pedagogical Tool in the Teaching of the Projection of the Actor's Voice." *South African Journal of Linguistics* Suppl. 34 (1996): 25-36.

Raphael, Bonnie & Scherer, Ron. "Voice modification for stage actors: acoustic analysis." *Journal of Voice* 1, 1 (1987): 83-87.

Rodenburg, Patsy. *The Actor Speaks*. Great Britain: Methuen Drama, 1997.

Spencer, Andrew. Phonology. Cambridge Massachusetts: Blackwell, 1996.

Tomatis, Alfred. *The Conscious Ear*. Station Hill Press, 1991.

Turner, Sean. "Pedagogical Explorations and Other Applications" In *Collective Writings on the Lessac Voice and Body Work, A Festchrift*, edited by M. Munro, S. Turner, A. Munro, K. Campbell. Coral Springs, FL: Llumina Press, 2009.

Van Wyk, E.B. *Praktiese fonetiek vir taalstudente, 'n inleiding*. Pretoria: Heer Drukkers, 1981.

Wissing, D. Selebeleng, Zakia. & Stander, M. 2000. "Acquiring the English Vowel System by Sotho and Zulu Speakers: A Perception Experiment." Paper delivered at *International Conference on Linguistics in Southern Africa*, Cape Town, South Africa, 2000.

EarWitness: Some Theatre Voices in Eastern Europe[1]

Photo by Karim Iliya

Lissa Tyler Renaud, a master teacher of acting and voice at InterArts Training in California, has taught and given workshops throughout the U.S. and at major theatre and voice institutions of South Korea, India, Taiwan, Singapore, Mexico (for VASTA) and Russia. A recipient of Ford Foundation and National Science Foundations grants, among others, she is an award-winning actress, and a recognized director and alignment practitioner. Renaud is English language editor for *Critical Stages*, journal of the International Association of Theatre Critics (UNESCO Culture Sector). Her co-edited book, *The Politics of American Actor Training* (Routledge, 2009) was called "an important contribution."

Many people have had the experience of attending a theatre performance in a language they don't know, and finding themselves engaged by the voices themselves. That is, it is sometimes satisfying enough to sense what the voices mean, even without understanding what the words mean.

I see this phenomenon in action in good performances overseas: "foreign" audience members often turn off their simultaneous translation devices, preferring to listen to the actors speak compellingly in their native language, rather than to understand the translated "meaning" they hear on their headsets. Or, they may switch channels on their devices among several languages they don't know, content instead to find an appealing or expressive translator's voice in any language.

This ability of the voice to capture the hearer beyond the word-definition aspect of language has interested me for a long time. In the somewhat dizzyingly multi-cultural San Francisco Bay Area, I have trained many actors with whom I just barely shared a language. I have also lived and trained actors in countries where I don't speak the language at all.

Over the years, the part of my work that focuses on these matters has developed into workshops I teach about Speech Melody. These workshops give performers a chance to consider how they can use aspects of the speaking voice to communicate directly with audiences who don't share their language. I have given such workshops in many states in America, in many countries of Asia and, most recently, at the 2010 joint CEUVOZ-VASTA conference in Mexico City. Being able to think in terms of the sound of language rather than the meaning of language is a great boon for the actor who wants to participate in today's global culture.

In September and October of 2010, I had an extraordinary opportunity to listen to voices in languages I didn't understand. Because I am a board member and English language co-editor for the French-English *Critical Stages*, Web-Journal of the International Association of Theatre Critics (IATC, UNESCO Culture Sector), I was invited on a five-day group tour to the national theatres of Sweden, Latvia and Estonia, where I saw—and heard—productions in each country's language. This tour was followed by five days in St. Petersburg at the prestigious Baltic House Theatre Festival, where I attended performances in Lithuanian, Polish and Russian. Following my stay at the Festival, I lectured and taught a master class over three days as the guest of Russia's oldest theatre school, St. Petersburg State Theatre Arts Academy. In addition to engaging with my eminent international theatre colleagues, of course I couldn't help traveling with my Voice Teacher ears wide open! But aside from the performances themselves, some of my most wonderful voice-related experiences came upon me by surprise: on a long bus ride, in a café and in a teachers' lounge.

* * *

When Europeans look back into their history, they see civilizations and empires, kings and queens, cathedrals and armadas. When Americans look back, they see open ranges and tribes, chiefs and deer, teepees and canoes. Excavations around Europe uncover the villas, baths and gardens of ancient Rome; excavation for a shopping area near my home in California uncovered a sacred Ohlone Indian burial ground thousands of years old. Europeans may trace many of their place names to the Greeks, the Celts and the Vikings; many Americans live where place names come from the Sioux, the Choctaw and the Iroquois. Inescapably, these differences in our pasts surface not only in our national characters, but also in our theatres. No matter how "global" the world becomes—people sharing access to travel, internet and rap music—Europe will still look back and see the Spanish Golden Age, and we will still look back and see the Golden Age of the American musical.

Thus, the trajectories that our theatres have followed over time have landed us in different theatrical sensibilities today. Dr. Kim, Yun-Cheol of South Korea has offered a succinct overview of European theatre trends:

> Since the 1990s, "new European theatre"—or "in-yer-face theatre"—has become one of the predominant phenomena of Western theatre: it originated in Great Britain, and then spread throughout Western and Eastern Europe. This banal and violent form of theatre has been pouring blood and sperm onto stages, relying heavily on the aesthetics of the ugly. Logocentric language has long disappeared from this new stage, which has become the representative theatrical form of this post-dramatic era.[2]

Kim's description also features graphic representations of gore, uninhibited violence, homosexual brutality, rape and body parts.

Today, theatres across America are doing musicals, as well as classics and original plays, and they are also exploring new forms. But even our most venerable avant-garde theatres—such as Mabou Mines, La Mama, The Wooster Group, Robert Wilson, Bread & Puppet—are not working directly in this vein.

It is a truism that the theatre is always the last to absorb any art trend. But in America, we find this "in-yer-face" impulse not on our stages but in Andres Serrano's photographs involving bodily fluids, such as his infamous *Piss Christ*; in the homosexual eroticism of Robert Mapplethorpe's controversial photographic series; in the self-mutilation of performance artist Marina Abramovic; and, it can be argued, in the video-taping of psychedelic guru Timothy Leary's death.

The performances shown in conjunction with the Europe Theatre Prize in Poland in 2009 were distinctly of the "new European theatre" ilk: the killing of a lobster, masturbation, mental incapacity, nudity, etc. And although the plays I saw on this 2010 trip had none of these, these were still the critical context, the touchstone for what I did see.

European and American theatres are largely different in terms of subject matter, production style and audience expectation, but the non-European voice teacher can both recognize and learn from the vocal challenges their contemporary productions pose for the European actor.

BALTIC HOUSE TOUR: THE "THEATRE ARK" PROJECT[3]

I. Stockholm, Sweden: Dramaten [Royal Dramatic Theatre]

August: Osage County, by Tracy Letts (U.S.); directed by Stefan Larsson (Sweden)

It is easy to see the appeal: a play with suicide, addiction, pedophilia, incest. Plum roles for high profile, talented actors. An American drama that shares the theme of family dysfunction with Scandinavians Ibsen, Strindberg, Ingmar Bergman and the contemporary Lars Norén. Although the production got its share of rave reviews, strictly from the listening perspective, it was far from dynamic.

Vocal challenge: Style

Behind-the-scene talk had it that the play was selected as a kind of novelty offering for audiences for whom the Nordic take on disastrous families has long been a crowd-pleaser. But one has to wonder whether this American script really offered the right opportunity. Noting the play's relatedness to Eugene O'Neill's *Long Days Journey Into Night* and Sam Shepard's *Buried Child*, critic Charles Isherwood gave this evaluation of the play:

> It is, flat-out, no asterisks and without qualifications, the most exciting new American play Broadway has seen in years…. Mr. Letts infuses his dark drama with potent energies derived from two more populist forms of American entertainment. The play has the zip and zingy humor of classic television situation comedy and the absorbing narrative propulsion of a juicy soap opera, too.[4]

In the event, this production seemed to want to take from the script those qualities that would appeal to the Swedish audience, but this left them with the problem of what to do with the rest of it. Neither the sitcom nor the soap opera being indigenous to Sweden, to my ear, the vocal style of the play never stopped feeling uneasily suspended between a Universal backlot and the wall over Ibsen's desk where hung a portrait of Strindberg.

Vocal challenge: The set

The set was an encumbrance for the actors. The original production's big, angled, TV studio-type set was brought downstage to give it a "chamber play" feeling. The result was an abundance of heavy furniture, arranged in several flat rows nearly from the lip to the farthest upstage plane. Much of the actor's physical and vocal energy was expended in negotiating impenetrable clusters of furniture pieces. And it has been said of Shakespeare's theatre that the round stage space made round characters; here, the flat set made flat voices.

Pedagogy and Coaching
EarWitness: Some Theatre Voices in Eastern Europe by Lissa Tyler Renaud

Vocal challenge: The stereotype

In the U.S., we have our hands full just deciding how to do plays from different cultures within our own country. Are we tied to the drawl for every Southern play we do? Does every Bronx street crook have a Bronx accent? Is use of the Valley Girl lilt demeaning? Is foreign-accented English classist? And for a responsible production, such questions multiply when we do a foreign play: When an Irish play is performed for an Irish audience, the speech of the people onstage and of those watching is essentially they same; would we use an Irish accent when doing an Irish play for an American audience, for whom the sound of the Irish speech is foreign? When we do a Russian play, should we try to sound like Russians, or create a sound that allows us to pronounce the multi-syllabic names without being distracting but essentially matches the speech of our audiences? What are the guidelines for the Euro-American attempting an Asian script, or an African one? Is it arrogant to do such a play, or not to?

August: Osage County is set in Chicago. For this Swedish production, the admirable vocal task they set for themselves was to distill some qualities that could reasonably be recognized as Chicago-esque, and then to make those qualities part of the characters. Unfortunately, this translated widely throughout the cast into an aggressive, overly-emphatic delivery; a pushed, flat-tongued pronunciation pressed into a pitch range slightly below what was optimal for each actor: a kind of "gangster" voice, replete with wide stance and hands on hips. The beloved actress who played the mother had the added problem of how to play someone anesthetized by addiction without sounding vocally anesthetized; again, although her performance was very enthusiastically received, it cannot have been for her monotonous vocal work. Other actors tried to get some traction with being "American" by walking with straight legs and talking with lowered chins in a cowboy sort of way, or by using a brassy Lucille Ball voice for comic effects. And I am afraid that all around the world, actors playing characters much younger than themselves may adopt a high-pitched voice of a sort not found in nature. Taken all together, the vocal landscape of the production gave me the impression that the likeable actors found the material to be much weaker than the Swedish treatment of the same themes—a Scandinavian colleague called it "O'Neill Lite"—but that they were willing to make a go of it if it was good for their theatre.

All this said, the production was presumably intended for Swedish audiences, who doubtless read many of the signals coming from the stage differently from how I did. I understand the Swedes have had their own "home-grown" sitcoms since the early 1990s. So perhaps the vocal stereotypes I heard were not actually American, but were all their own.

II. Riga, Latvia: New Riga Theatre

The Grandfather, written and performed by Vilis Daudzins; directed by Alvis Hermanis

This three-hour monologue was written by the actor about his search for information about his grandfather, who was never accounted for when World War II ended. This material gave the actor the juicy chance to play himself and the three men he met along the way who shared his grandfather's name: one who had fought on the German side, one on the Russian side, and one on both sides. As a writer, it also gave him a chance to address larger issues about what transpired in Latvia during the war.

Vocal challenge: Multiple characters

With a text this long, it would be natural to begin by considering how to keep the vocal work varied and surprising. A way into this task would seem obvious: the narrator and each of the three men he meets would require the actor to use a different part of his voice. By this I don't mean "character voices," but a different basic range, resonance, pace, emphasis and anything else one could think of or discover to make them distinct. It's difficult to think why the actor didn't take this path, instead choosing to use a virtually uniform vocal quality in spite of changing characters and subject matter.

To a native speaker, Latvian critic Valda Čakare, the actor seemed to be doing enough other things to make his performance interesting that she didn't miss what I missed in his limited vocal work. In her review, in which she compared this actor warmly to the ancient Homer, who both wrote and spoke his epics, Čakare observed:

> The actor provides the performance with an impressive rhythm, solving problems such as how to find a balance between comic and tragic scenes; how to use repetition in the performance; how to generate both specific information and general insight in one performance. ...Each of [the characters] clearly belongs to a specific social class and comes from a definite region, communicated through a slight shift in accent and the use of specific place names in each story.[5]

Indeed, the actor, Daudzins, did have slight accent changes that even I could hear, and someone who understood the Latvian language was sure to hear in the text that the location of the character speaking had changed. The actor also sat a little differently to change characters—now straight ahead, now with one foot under him; but his almost complete lack of engagement with the set—piled high with evocative bags of potting soil and other gardening-related items, all begging to help him with his transitions—was puzzling. He also changed his clothes to mark a new character (sleeveless undershirt to button down, for example);

but he did this onstage, showing more skin than necessary for the play, doing more to confuse the style of the performance than to clarify who the characters were.

In any case, I noted that at least that one critic-audience member easily found other aspects of the performance that helped her get a handle on what she was watching. Because of this, the sadly impoverished vocal imagination of the actor did not trouble her.

Vocal challenge: A somber subject

The three men whom the narrator met on his search had all gone through terrible experiences during the war. And both the younger narrator and the actor speaking the narrator's part felt their three stories deeply. It was unfortunate, vocally speaking, that the production adopted a small range of tones that suggested trauma, grief, condolence, respect and reverence for the dead. The actor's face remained nearly immobile, with the frozen forehead one sees so often on young television actors, his facial muscles in concert with his very narrow pitch range. This was apparently a choice, and not from lack of ability: well into the second hour, one of his characters broke briefly into a high range when imitating someone in the telling of an anecdote, but this level of expressivity was not heard again. And since the actor was working with director Alvis Hermanis, considered by many to be among the leading directors in Europe today, a listener has to assume that the three-note, pressed sound of the actor's voice was a conscious artistic choice.

I also thought it was a conscious style because I had encountered it before, in a production I saw in Poland entitled *Sunken Red*. This was also an extremely long monologue, also about horrifying World War II experiences, also performed with nearly no contact with the set on which it was being played. It was also performed with an immobile face and in an entirely uninflected voice. Here, Dirk Roofthooft, the well-known Belgian film and television actor could be heard just above a whisper in spite of the microphone taped to his face. Assuming it wasn't a technical glitch, his low volume might have been meant to be confessional, or to challenge the audience to lean in to listen. However, in combination with his foreign-inflected English full of errors, and with very dim stage lighting, this sustained murmur took its toll on the drowsy audience.

The *Sunken Red* press page invites us to appreciate Roofthooft's performance according to criteria that were unfamiliar to me:

> Every movement, every word is timed to the nanosecond. His performance takes perfection to a whole new level.... Roofthooft has understood the text, better than the audience. So your experience of *Sunken Red* is like nothing you have experienced before. He

knows better than anyone the effect of the words he utters. Rarely have I witnessed such control and concurrence of performance and content.[6]

Time will tell whether, for the current generation, words "timed to the nanosecond" and understood better by the actor than the audience will be able to replace the persuasive voice that has ruled the stage since hundreds of years before Cicero.

Both *The Grandfather* and *Sunken Red* were performed by admired actors and directed by respected directors, on sets into which much thought had gone. When I saw them, they had already played to large houses in more than one country or won prizes, and received outstanding reviews. It is a testament to how little audiences have come to expect in the way of vocal interest that so many seemed not to notice how dull the shows were.

Vocal challenge: Simultaneous translation

Among the shows I saw on this trip, *The Grandfather* was unique in providing simultaneous translation for the audience. This would seem to be a thoughtful gesture, requiring extra planning and a financial commitment on the theatre's part. And it is a complex matter to add this additional layer to the audience's experience. What is the right relationship of the translator to the action on the stage? Obviously the translator can't "act" all the roles, changing his voice with each character whose lines he speaks; that would sound ridiculous. Can the translator even be expected to have a theatre background, or a voice that is pleasing to listen? Or should the voice the audience hears over the headset be neutral, as if it were reading a subtitle? If so, should it be during or after the line?

Unexpectedly, the closest I got on this trip to the "aesthetics of the ugly" was the voice contribution of the man reading the Latvian stage text into my ear in approximate English. It was a surly voice, full of contempt for—what? The play? The English-speaking spectator? Or: he hadn't been paid his salary? At all events, the fellow not only rattled the lines in an aggressive drone, but also pointedly let us hear him light and smoke his cigarettes, and even burp whatever he was drinking! Surely the impression he made is not the one the actor-playwright was working so hard for simultaneously onstage.

Having read the great reviews for this show, I have to wonder if the critics are really doing the job of evaluating, or whether they have other tasks in mind. I was seated in about the fifth row, and I easily counted 25 people sleeping just in the rows in front of me. The imaginative ways people tried to keep themselves awake were the most compelling acts taking place. It reminded me of the story of an earnest young playwright who chided Carl Sandburg for falling asleep when he'd invited Sandburg there for an opinion of his new play. "Young man," Sandburg replied, "sleep *is* an opinion."[7] And all would be forgiven if one thought that at least the play was bringing out of the darkness some tragic aspects of World War II heretofore unknown to the Latvian public, however widely known elsewhere. But as it was, a critic among us who is knowledgeable about theatre in that part of the world said firmly on the way out, "That was an insult to our intelligence." How confusing it was to see people who'd been asleep sit bold upright at the end, or even stand, and clap loudly! When did audiences become so docile, so cowed by the critics' appraisal? I propose that we re-institute the throwing of rotten tomatoes as a general strategy for upping the quality of the theatre.

III. Tallinn, Estonia: Tallinn City Theatre

I Loved a German, adapted from A. H. Tammsaare and directed by Elmo Nüganen[8]

This lovely, delicate production was based on a 1935 novel that Estonians hold dear, and it was sensitively adapted for the stage by an actor-director who has earned the love of his colleagues and his audiences. The story is about a sincere young Estonian man and a pretty young woman of German descent, and the ways that history and prejudice conspire to defeat their chance at love. That is, it is a fairly conventional story of star-crossed love, with the requisite severe parental figure who keeps them apart, and who comes to regret it when the young woman's untimely death ensues and destroys the nice young man who loved her.

Küll Teetamm (Erica) in *I Loved A German*. Dir. Elmo Nuganen, Tallinna Linnateater (Estonia). Premiere 12/12/2009.

Photo: http://www.linnateater.ee/en/repertory/maarmastasinsakslast.html

Vocal challenge: The playing area
Director Nüganen made an unconventional choice for the playing area, and the voice work of the actors benefited from them. First, he selected a stark, concrete space under the theatre, not meant for performance and yet perfect for it. The voices leapt off the concrete surfaces, which gave them now a ringing quality, now an echoing sadness. Every word was easily audible, even perhaps amplified by the hard walls and the emptiness. The audience members were seated so that the playing area was diagonal to them, divided by three very large square pillars that actually supported the building, one near, one in the middle distance,

one far. Aside from cleverly providing depth, these pillars were transformed into a room, a tree or an imposing front door by not much more than a telling gesture or a glance. This stark, set-less setting provided a metaphor for the stark realities that intruded on the love story and, with really nothing to distract the viewer, brought the acting, the beautifully tailored period costumes and the voices absolutely to the fore.

Vocal challenge: A well-known book
On the whole, the adapted text was extremely spare. Our Finnish colleague had been kind enough to bring us a scene-by-scene synopsis so we could follow along, and the basic dynamics of each scene were very clear from the performances. The young man punctuated the action with several longish explanatory monologues, filling in narrative that was provided in the original novel. Not an especially elegant device, but I understand the Estonian audience was likely to know the book well. The script simply brought to life through dialogue the two- and three-person scenes that occurred in the book. On this point, the actors gave the uncanny impression of both reading aloud from a book they had in common with the members of the audience, and embodying their roles at the same time.

Vocal challenge: Character development
The weak link in an otherwise wonderful chain was that the voices struck one note from the beginning and essentially stayed there for the whole piece. The actor who played the young man, who opened the play with one of his narrative monologues, can't have had an easy time animating the literature-based language. He had a pleasing mid-range voice, earnest and ardent, and that got me about halfway through the play, when I started to hanker for a different vocal texture as the action darkened, and the pleasing, smooth quality started to draw attention to itself. The actress was older than the young woman character was at the beginning of the play, and she used a very high voice. She moved around somewhat within that high range, but I still thought she overshot a bit, since after all her character wasn't five years old. Then because the voice sounded so artificially high, I wondered if the pitch was a character statement: She was not authentic? She was cut off from her body? She was feigning immaturity? I was prepared to give her any of these. Then twice, at emotional moments, her voice plunged into a low range that was very exciting and prom-

ised great things as her character grew and deepened from opportunistic schoolgirl to beleaguered, doomed heroine. But although the median pitch of her voice came down an interval or two later in the play, the swooning dark timbres of the Baltic voice were never fully discernible in the fine performance of this fragile character.

Regarding an older actress playing a younger role, I had encountered this high-pitched vocal strategy at a theatre festival in South Korea in 2006. Along with productions that featured gorgeous heightened voices (*Three Beautiful Soulmates*, by Lee Yun-Taek) and endlessly nuanced contemporary voices (*Kyung-Sook; Kyung-Sook's Father*, by Park Keun-Hyung) there was also an older actress, much loved by the public, who played a little girl (*Fairy in the Closet*, Korean adaptation by Bae Sam-Shik). During the war, her father was forced to hide in the wall of their home, and the little girl had a sweet relationship with the mysterious voice coming from there. In terms of the distractingly high voice, I was willing to wait for it to come down as the girl got older, but it never did. To make it worse, the back of the actress's tongue was lifted in the "baby voice" position. No doubt there were layers of cultural meaning that weren't making it through the barrier, and I didn't have what I needed to make sense of that choice; my only associations with a mature woman's speaking in a baby voice are distasteful ones. As a result, I wasn't able to sympathize much with the play, directed by Sohn Jin-Chaek, whom I admire very much.

Both *I Loved a German* and *Fairy in the Closet* took place in times of dangerous political upheaval, during tragic periods in their respective nations' histories; for these reasons alone the plays must have been moving for audiences. I am certainly eager to see more acting work by these two delightful young Estonian actors, to understand more clearly whether either the melancholy nature of the script, or its literary source, might have had a limiting effect on their voices.

* * *

Up to this point, we had taken boats between Helsinki, Stockholm and Riga, and then a bus to Tallinn. Now, five days later, we started on the long bus ride to St. Petersburg.[9] It was finally on this leg of the trip that my Romanian colleague, Ludmila—who had kept mostly to herself as if harboring a splendid secret, who was forever swathed in great layers of a stalwart black shawl, who wore a tightly-secured bun as if it were a warning of something—finally let her hair down, like a fetching librarian coming out of her shell. More on Ludmila to come. Voice-wise, there were two things of note on that bus ride.

First, there was the singing from the Russian group in the back, hour after hour: the international sound of someone suggesting a song, everyone laughing in recognition,

starting in with great gusto and then trailing off as people get iffy on the lyrics. They could have been a busload of children on their way to summer camp, except that there was vodka involved, that even here the voices were glorious, and that the singers were a delegation of the some of the foremost figures in Russian theatre. Over the miles, a pattern seemed to develop: the lone voice, the swelling of group voices and the drifting off, then quiet, some scattered chatter: the sound of Chekhov.

SPECIAL ACCOUNT #1: Roman Gromadsky[10]

I heard the great Roman Gromadsky before I saw him. A liquid, spacious *basso profundo* that caught my ear and held onto it as it careened casually through an anecdote, a cheerfully ironic comment, a playful rejoinder to something shouted in the back of the bus, his voice handling them all like a race car driver steering with one finger. He was

Photo by Yuriy Bogatyrev

Roman Gromadsky [L.] in *The Master and Margarita*. Dir. Jona Vaitkus (Lithuania), Baltic House Theatre Festival (Russia).

sitting with his petite wife, kitty-corner behind me across the aisle, a solid, big-boned man with a powerful, expressive face and twinkling eyes. As the end of the bus trip approached, I spoke with him with the resourceful translation help of Alexey Platunov.[11]
When did you begin your training?
At 13, in the 7th grade, and I continued into high school.

How did you find your teacher?
We have a different system: here, teachers choose their students. And then they become like family.

Were you allowed to sing and continue your vocal training through your voice change?
[He replied about a change in his voice.]
I was in the army at that time, and my voice got stronger and stronger from shouting orders. (Here he did a funny imitation of a naïve young person taking soldiers through their paces.)

Pedagogy and Coaching
EarWitness: Some Theatre Voices in Eastern Europe by Lissa Tyler Renaud

How has your voice teaching changed over the years?
[He replied about voice teaching in general.]
I studied in the 1960s and '70s. Those teachers were geniuses—now they are not so good.

Do you teach the same way your teachers taught?
Much of vocal technique is like learning the multiplication tables. There are the basics. I teach those fundamentals to my students.

But everyone doesn't agree on what the basics are. What are yours?
Our system is different from the American one. Here, everyone is required to study voice, acting, gymnastics, fencing… [some discussion with the translator].

My students work on those basics in their first year. Then, their end-of-year shows get more and more fully produced until their last one, which is performed with full lights and costumes. This last one may be the most elaborate production they will ever be in, since they all get to play leading parts—Juliet and so on.

You are blessed with a Chaliapin-like baritone voice. Do you ever use your upper register?
(He replies in a lovely, high, woman-like voice—very supported and rich. And funny!)

[Returning to his teaching:]

To train the voice, you have to train the imagination. I have my students do exercises for this. One example: I have them touch each other's hair and guess who they are touching. I teach them the importance of touch. Another example: I ask a student, "What do you imagine on the other side of the moon?" He replies, "An elephant." "How did it get there?" "Some astronauts took it there, but when they were leaving they couldn't lift off so they left the elephant there." And there are thousands of such exercises. There are also exercises to learn how to relax the body.
[At some point he had referred to his teacher as "she." I asked:]

Have you ever had a male teacher?
No.

[After consultation with the translator:]

Now I have a new teacher, because my 70th birthday jubilee is coming up and I am preparing for that.

What do you do with your teacher?
I read to her; we are selecting the pieces for my program. You have to keep studying for your whole life.

[Here we were interrupted, and we never had a chance to return to our conversation. In any case, Roman Gromadsky insisted that all my questions would be answered if I came to observe him teaching at the St. Petersburg Humanitarian University, where he is a professor in the School of Acting and Directing. We got close to arranging this, but finally schedules did not allow.

After our exchange, a friend of his who had been listening approached to tell me: if Mr. Gromadsky's answers seem more general than personal, it is out of a sense of modesty. He doesn't want to appear to think he is some kind of Stanislavsky; he feels his experience isn't that important. He is just… himself.]

* * *

BALTIC HOUSE THEATRE FESTIVAL: ST. PETERSBURG

I. Othello, by William Shakespeare; directed by Eimuntas Nekrosius (Lithuania).

Vocal challenge: Voice without language
In non-English speaking countries worldwide, there is a long tradition of Shakespeare productions that bypass the thorny problem of translation by simply using the storylines as a point of creative departure.[12] There is also an international theatre festival culture that encourages the creation of productions without language so they will be accessible to all audiences.[13] This production was at the intersection of these two phenomena: a Lithuanian production of Othello just right for non-Lithuanian festival audiences. The well-known tragedy unfolded in image after striking image, each one without a literal relationship to the action but rather inhabiting some hyper-intuitive dimension skewed by urges, anxieties, violences one might have known in a dream and worked hard to forget. For long sections, there was an unnerving soundtrack of a simple chord that refused to resolve, standing in for the foreboding usually provided by dialogue. The Desdemona was an accomplished ballet dancer, which reinforced the visual emphasis of the production.

Occasionally, a character made a vocal sound such as laughter, a mouth sound such as "phew." Some of the actors were more skillful at this than others, and since there wasn't much voice overall, the problem was magnified when a voice sound wasn't coordinated with the thought it was meant to express. Toward the end of the play, Othello raised his chin and gave a series of lines in a hoarse, flat roar that might have had a primeval kind of impact for any audience member who was not disappointed by the lack of speech melody.

II. The Crucible, by Arthur Miller; directed by Andrzej Bubien (Russia)

Vocal challenge: embodying a text-based character

People go to the theatre for many different reasons; for example, some go to stay abreast of cultural goings-ons, some to see a specific play or actor, some to see work by their friends, some to be seen in the lobby. I go to hear the voices, especially voices that are translating a dramatic text from two to three dimensions—or four, if we include Time. And this production had the voices I love to hear.

How rare and what a treat. Each voice—for large roles and small— was beautifully placed, was wonderfully audible without microphones, and achieved crystalline diction without being prissy. Each voice had a range and timbre right for the role, and each actor was attentive to using his voice in a way that complemented and contrasted with the others. Each new character that entered the stage made a new vocal contribution to the ensemble. All thought was connected to all breath, each actor's breath connected to every other's. The scenes played like musical duets, tri-

Yurii Itskov as Danforth in *The Crucible*. Dir. Andrzej Bubien, St. Petersburg State Theatre Na Vasilievskom (Russia). Premiere 12/12/2009

os, chamber groups, with everyone working together to create a vocal score that was integral—not extraneous, distracting or parallel—to the telling of the story. Each actor took his character's part with sincerity, not irony, delving into difficult experiences in a way that expanded the emotional lives of the people watching. The actors transformed those experiences into speech, voice and breath sounds along an enormous spectrum of qualities and urgency.

The standout in this remarkable cast was the brilliant Yurii Itskov, a tremendously experienced actor who has appeared in a steady stream of award-winning films for years. *Variety* refers to him as a "vet thesp," or veteran thespian. He played Deputy Governor Danforth, entering the story midway and setting the stage aflame with a ready intensity. He spent much of the role in a tenor range[14], and used it with great elasticity to move through moments of incredulity, accusation, exasperation, insistence—all as if he were on the threshold of a barely contained explosion of shrillness. Within and around this: infinite tonal variety, every line beginning somewhere on the scale that was surprising and exciting. Skillful control of volume, where control freed the text. A voice both rough and refined, used with passion and intelligence.

I have never been so little concerned about the cultural translation of a play: here was 17th century Salem in its true spirit, given marvelous, terrifying voice.

III. Persona. Marilyn, directed by Krystian Lupa (Poland)

To make a sweeping statement: during roughly the same period that America's "contemporary" theatre has been pre-occupied with generating new plays, with exploring matters of identity and fulfilling the nation's multi-cultural project, European theatre has pursued a course that was in some respects laid before the two world wars effectively dismantled it: it looked for something to do with the stage besides tell stories on it. The results: texts that are extra-lingual and non-linear; stage work that uses multi-media to underline its fragmentation; "performance art" collaborations with sculpture, experimental poetry or new music. Along with these go the "in-yer-face" and "aesthetics of the ugly" theatre described above, of which the crowning glory is perhaps the "provocation," or stage action with no other purpose than to piss people off, such as drowning a hamster or appearing to defecate. This production, *Persona. Marilyn*, hangs within this large constellation of trends.

http://satira.spb.ru/

Vocal challenge: the post-dramatic voice

An unarticulated task for today is to explore the vocal equivalent of this "post-dramatic" or "beyond theatre" impulse in the theatre. What can it sound like, or otherwise *be* like? What is the speaking voice without inflection, aesthetic or human qualities? The first half of this performance suggested some answers. Using Marilyn Monroe as the starting point for a meditation on stardom and loss of self, purposeless phrases unfurled lazily and repeated, leading to nothing and arriving nowhere. The director's charmless version of Monroe stumbled histrionically and slurred incoherencies at intervals that never tried to achieve a Beckettian rhythm or other pattern that would render it "artistic." Mechanical squealing; repetitive shouting. On a set angled for the camera lens rather than the spectator's eye, she lay on a table with her nude bottom turned to us, trying less to communicate with the character sharing the stage than to co-exist with the video and photo images of herself on the flat screen. These served her for an audience and rendered the live audience nothing but prurient. Pauses were not fraught, but were simply silences, as if a television had been turned off.

Having responsibility for my lecture the next day, I could not stay, but hope to see the second half another time. I understand it was much denser, faster paced and, if not quite dramatic, at least thematic in a way that was rewarding, with increased focus on Monroe's "healthy obsession" with starring in Chekhov's *Three Sisters*.[15] On my way out, I thought how important it is to go to a performance ready for anything, and not to see what a production is not, but what it is. I also thought back to the beginning of my trip: in a stylish museum café in Helsinki, my cohorts and I had lunched with a Finnish critic who confessed she would often rather write about the theatre than attend it.

SPECIAL ACCOUNT #2: Ludmila Patlanjoglu[16]

There had been little time to talk with colleagues, so before *The Crucible* when I stopped at Ludmila's table in a café to say hello, we fell into a burning, extended conversation from which Ludmila emerged as a delightful companion and surely a fierce ally to have in any campaign for an enhanced vocal culture in the theatre.

The thrust of our discussion was this: the human voice is a metaphor for the larger project of connecting people. The breath provides a bridge between the mind and the body and then, in the theatre, between minds and bodies. As such, it is critical for the aesthetic voice to be unmediated by technology, and the increased use of microphones constitutes a terrible loss for the organic exchange between the stage and the house. There is a power inherent in being able to breathe fully, in being able to use the breath, the voice, to know the interior surface of your body, surfaces no one can touch but yourself, and then to reach out of the body with the artistic voice to make contact with others. Microphone use promotes reduced vocal capability, so that actors are now using microphones even in very small performance spaces, and theatre dialogue has come routinely to be heard with an electronic sound, more machine than human. In addition, the microphone doesn't improve a voice or substitute for training; it simply amplifies poor diction, or other voice or speech problems.

This situation has had terrible consequences for the progress of the theatre. Many productions with an adventurous sensibility have not made their way into audience's hearts, and no one recognized that the problem was the untrained voices. Even "new theatre" productions at the highest levels—earning rave reviews and winning prizes—are rife with poor posture and weak diction, vocal strain and lack of awareness of basic speech principles. How many more tools the performance artist, the theatrical provocateur,

the multi-media poet could have to work with! In theatrical terms, this lack constitutes an international emergency. The international theatre will not move forward in its development until performers have the breath, voice and speech means to support their performance efforts.

* * *

ST. PETERSBURG STATE THEATRE ARTS ACADEMY
SPECIAL ACCOUNT #3: Elena Kuzina, Liubov Mochalina, Olga Samokhotova

My lecture on the theatre work of the painter, Wassily Kandinsky, came about through the invitation of Nikolai Pesochinsky, Vice-Rector for international relations and Professor of Theatre Studies at Russia's oldest acting school, founded in 1779. Following the lecture, the lovely Elena Kuzina invited me to demonstrate the practical application of Kandinsky's work to students of the Advanced Directing studio. When that session ended the next day, Elena invited me to the faculty lounge to talk further with her and two of her colleagues, in particular about the practical application of Kandinsky's work to voice training. We spent two intensive, tea-drinking hours together: they saw video and a power point of my work, and generously answered my many questions about their work. Elena Kuzina teaches acting, and has a special interest in the application

Photo Critical Stages WebJournal,
http://www.criticalstages.org/attach/1/1353409432.jpg

Ludmila Patlanjoglu (Romania)

of Meyerhold's Biomechanics to contemporary theatre. Olga Samokhotova is deeply connected to Grotowski's work and to those who carry it on. Liubov Mochalina is an actress and Associate Professor in the Voice and Speech Department at the Academy. The basic transcription that follows is from my notes about the part of the discussion that focused on Liubov's very copacetic voice teaching, with the participation of all and able translation by Elena.

Lissa Tyler Renaud: I find the problem of speech melody in the theatres of every country, including Russia.
Liubov Mochalina: (nodding vigorously): The television voice!

LTR: The actors are speaking while holding their breath.

LM: Yes, I don't like that sound [does a parody of a low-pitched, declamatory voice]. I like the voice in the body. When I found the body, that's when the voice work became really interesting for me.

LTR: Do you teach voice the same way your voice teacher taught?

LM: My approach is much more physical; my teacher was more traditional.

LTR: Oh, I would say the same about my own teaching compared to my teacher's; maybe it is our generation. How did you find the voice work you do with the body?

LM: (laughing) I don't know! It came from… (She looks at the "heavens").

LTR: Nowadays, many Western teachers are combining a voice technique with a body technique. Do you know Feldenkrais? (They all nod.) Alexander? (They all nod.) Pilates?

LM: He is new for us.

LTR: Well, you will find that there is a spectrum of Pilates teachers—from organic to superficial. I mean, some teachers of Pilates' work are very profound, and others are just for fashion.

LM: Yes, we know that.

LTR: These days, there is also a trend for teachers to show their students what the larynx looks like with a camera, or to show videos about them.

LM: (General hilarity.) No! No! If someone is sick, the doctors can do that. But for general voice students, I think it doesn't help them.

LTR: Also, some voice teachers now focus on teaching dialects. Do you teach dialects?

LM: No. Russia has a lot of dialects. Our job is to remove them.

LTR: And if a student needs a dialect for a play?

LM: Then of course the student will have special training. But this is not the goal for the whole class.

Elena Kuzina: We also work with the stick (she shows an exercise from Meyerhold, manipulating a long stick with great fluidity). We learn to move with the whole body.

LM: Yes. And the ear! We have training to use the ear.

EK: And we use balls. We throw the ball, with the sound. We put the sound on the ball, and throw it.

LM: Yes! I learned: we can put sound on objects, and the objects will move our voices. When we are on stage, all the objects around us can help the voice. This is very interesting.

LTR: All the early Russian work we have been talking about is so inspiring, so… practical! Why isn't this training everywhere? Why can't we see actors using these skills on stage everywhere?

LM and EK: (sadly) This work was lost. So much was lost. But we are finding it again.

(All four of us nodded.)

* * *

CONCLUSION

Reading this account in the West, it may be tempting to compare the general levels and qualities of our vocal work with those in this other part of the world: whose training is more successful, demanding, liberating, classical or innovative? But my own train of thought does not travel in the direction of such comparisons. Substantial parts of my work have unfolded abroad, particularly in Asia, and I see that so much makes sense inside the context of a country or culture that often makes very little sense outside of it. A comparison of two nation's vocal abilities in the theatre accomplishes less than a comparison of the proverbial apples and oranges; it is more like the Surrealist encounter of the sewing machine and the umbrella with the operating table: juxtapositions informed by factors unseen; being or seeming arbitrary.

Instead, my thoughts venture towards a different kind of encounter—that is, the encounter of countries with one another. There, the theme surfaces without fail: the cultural arts can heal where there is political rift. It was the same on this trip last September. In the national theatres of Sweden, Latvia and Estonia, we heard repeatedly: the arts allow us to remember war without remembering the hatred; the arts give us all a common language; through the arts, we overcome cultural isolation. For the 20th anniversary of the prestigious Baltic House Theatre Festival in St. Petersburg, Russia, the promotional image was of a butterfly alighted on the toe of a combat boot: the arts mitigate our culture of violence.

In terms of making a contribution to cultural diplomacy, music, dance and painting have the advantage over the theatre because they rely on languages that need no translation. During the Cold War, for example, it is said that every diplomatic visit to the Soviet Union included a trip to the ballet, not to the theatre, precisely because the dance was accessible for the guests without interpreters. If the language-based theatre is going to participate in today's world culture, theatre students around the world need expanded vocal skills. It is true that in America, where we have no Ministry of Culture and no National Theatre to articulate our sensibilities and priorities, our teachers have a special obligation—and a special opportunity—to foster the intellectual and creative lives of America's voice and theatre students. But more importantly, in our globalized era, the language theatre everywhere needs the music of Speech Melody.

Notes

1. The countries covered in this essay are part of "Eastern Europe" only by some definitions. Other definitions may call Finland and Sweden "Nordic countries" or "Northern Europe," separate from both Eastern Europe and the Baltic States; others group the Baltic States with Northern Europe. Each of these designations is a construct that shifts with the context, whether cultural, economic, historical or geographical.

2. From a speech given in Tokyo, Nov. 2010. Kim is President of IATC.

3. Our delegation consisted of IATC critics representing Finland, South Korea, Mexico, Portugal, Romania and Russia; I represented the U.S. The Russian group we traveled with had about twenty members, a third of whom were prominent media journalists, and two-thirds of whom had titles with the word Head or Director in them, followed by the name of an incomparably illustrious Russian cultural institution.

4. In the *New York Times*, available online at http://theater.nytimes.com/2007/12/05/theater/reviews/05august.html.

5. The review, entitled "The Second Latvian Homer," can be found at www.criticalstates.org, in Issue no. 2 (2010), in the archive.

6. See http://www.toneelhuis.be/productie.jsp?id=71&p=persrecensie&prid=660.

7. Told in *Bennett Cerf's Vest Pocket Book of Jokes for All Occasions* (New York: Random House) 1956, p. 117.

8. The website for this production is at http://www.linnateater.ee/en/repertory/maarmastasinsakslast.html.

9. Only my colleague Ludmila Patlanjoglu of Romania and I represented IATC in St. Petersburg, where we saw tour members of the Russian group operating on their home turf, and spent time with those who run the Baltic House Festival as well as with actors and directors of the shows in the festival.

10. Roman Gromadsky has been a permanent member of Leningrad's vital Baltic House Theatre since 1966, the year he also made his film debut. He won the coveted Stanislavsky State Prize for a film role in 1980, and received the highest honor, the People's Artist of Russia designation, in 1983. Warmly admired, he has partnered many of Russia's most notable actors. He has served as Dean and Advisor to the Rector at his university and as a Leningrad City Councilmember.

11. Platunov is a major mastermind of the Baltic House Festival's International Department, along with Alexandra Efimova, who also facilitated the conversation.

12. I wrote on the subject of Shakespeare without Shakespeare's language in my 2010 review of *Chinese Shakespeares*, by Alexander Huang, in *Gramma Journal of Theory and Criticism*, ed. Savas Patsalidis (Thessaloniki, Greece: Aristotle University Press). The review was reprinted in Issue no. 2 of *Critical Stages* (2010) and can be read online at: www.criticalstages.org.

13. I wrote on the subject of festival culture that discourages use of language in *The Politics of American Actor Training*. Ellen Margolis and Lissa Tyler Renaud, eds. (New York and London: Routledge), Routledge Advances in Theatre and Performance Studies series. September 2009 (paperback 2011). See my essay, "The Wild, Wild East: Report on the Politics of American Actor Training Overseas."

14. Online, there is a brief clip of the Russian film, *The Italian* (2005), that includes just enough of his lines to hear him speak in a lower part of his voice: http://www.answers.com/topic/the-italian-2005-film.

15. Some glimpses of this act are online at http://www.youtube.com/watch?v=Qv81YoppPoM&NR=1, and include a taste of the vocal sound texture of the play.

16. Ludmila Patlanjoglu, PhD is a theatre critic, historian and Head of the Theatre Science Department at Romania's I. L. Caragiale National University of Drama and Film Arts. She was Director of the 2002 and 2003 National Theatre Festival. She has held a myriad of pivotal IATC positions since 1999, including President of the Romanian Section, Member of the Executive Committee and Organizer of the 21st Congress in Bucharest.

Essay *by Paul Ricciardi*

"I Want To Do That!" A paper exploring the value of mentorship between early career and established voice professionals

Photo by Manon Haliburton

Paul is an Assistant Professor of Theatre at Siena College. Prior to Siena, he spent three years on the theatre faculty at UAlbany. As an actor and award winning solo performer, Paul has worked extensively throughout NYC and regionally. He is a Designated Linklater Teacher Trainee and he is an active member of VASTA. Paul is Vice Chair for Region I of the Kennedy Center American College Theatre Festival. In 2009 he was awarded the Kennedy Center National Teaching Artist Grant. Paul earned his MFA in Acting from Trinity Repertory Company.

"I think, by being willing to share their experiences and take the time to really be a mentor.." She then reframed her thought, "I don't know if you'll find that willingness and openness everywhere."

-Melissa Baroni, Designated Linklater Teacher Trainee, Boston, MA

The goal of this paper is to explore what lies within the foundation of each voice professional's career: the unique relationship between the early career voice professional and his or her master teacher, advisor or mentor(s). Currently I am in my second year of a tenure track position at Siena College, a small liberal arts college in upstate NY. I am studying with Master Linklater Teacher, Andrea Haring, as I work towards my Linklater Teacher Designation. It is this relationship, coupled with the training that I received at Trinity Repertory Company that inspires me to explore the idea that as early career voice professionals, we are often taken under a wing, we seek out a master teacher, we are perhaps sought after by a master teacher; we are mentored.

Utilizing material taken from live interviews with five voice professionals, what follows is a road map or a collection of tenets for early career voice practitioners. All interviewees affirm a very similar set of professional principles in regard to teaching and mentoring. It should be acknowledged that the field of research is small; five subjects are not enough do declare a universal truth about teaching voice. However, this article submits that the likeness of each interviewee's philosophies of teaching voice and speech coupled with the fact that each interviewee expresses deep satisfaction in his or her work points to the great benefit of the mentor/mentee relationship.

Five careers are examined in this paper: two interviewees are early career, and three are well into their practice. These artists were chosen to be interviewed for this article as they represent a wide spectrum of experience and technique. The interviewees are:

- Melissa Baroni, a Designated Linklater Teacher Trainee, who is currently working towards a self-designed Master's degree from Lesley University in Voice Embodiment Studies. In August of 2010, she started going through the first half of her Linklater Teacher Designation at the Central School in London.
- Patsy Culbert is a teacher and actor who earned her MFA from Boston University and studied with Kristin Linklater in the early 90's in Boston. Patsy is a Senior Artist in Residence in the Theatre Program at Union College, Schenectady, NY. She is also a founding member of the Saratoga Shakespeare Company.
- Ginger Eckert, a New York City based editor, actor and voice teacher, earned her MFA from the Brown/Trinity Rep Consortium. She is currently an assistant teacher in the NYU/Playwrights Horizons Voice and Speech program.
- Andrea Haring is a New York City based Master Linklater Teacher, vocal coach and associate director of the Linklater Center; she is on the faculty at Circle in the Square, Fordham and Columbia Universities. She has also taught at Yale University and Dartmouth College. Andrea is a founding member of Shakespeare and Company where she also taught voice. Ms. Haring has been working as a teacher and coach for nearly thirty years. She was recently profiled in "The New York Times" for her work as a coach with attendees at the World Economic Forum.
- Thom Jones is a vocal coach, dialect coach and teacher; he is the director of Voice and Speech in the MFA program at The Brown/Trinity Rep. Consortium. He is also the resident vocal coach for Trinity Rep. He was the Director of Voice

"I Want To Do That!" A paper exploring the value of mentorship between early career and established voice professionals by Paul Ricciardi

- and Speech at Purchase College. He has worked with regional theatres across the country and in New York City. He also works regularly as a coach for film.

The interviewees were asked the following questions:

1. Describe your career.
2. How did you come to this work?
3. How have you moved forward in your career?
4. Are there individuals who you feel mentored you along the way?

   It should be noted that both the early career and the established voice professionals were asked this question.

5. How has your professional relationship changed with this mentor over time?
6. How does being a mentor/mentee inform your work?
7. Where do you perceive the mentee is most benefiting in the relationship? In the classroom? During one on one sessions?

   For the junior professionals, the question was rephrased to fit their perspective: "where do you think you get the most benefit from your mentor/mentee relationship?"

8. What kind of effect do you feel you are having on your mentee? Or, what kind of effect is your mentor having on you?

   The answers for this question were all very similar. Furthermore, the established professionals spent as much time talking about their role models and mentors as they did about the early career professionals they currently mentor.

9. How does a voice professional move forward in her career?

In recording the accounts of these mentor/mentee relationships, fine details about the art of teaching voice emerge. These discoveries are what frame this paper. In addition to sharing participant's responses to the questions outlined above, this paper reveals several truths or tenets for the voice teacher's practice. These truths are highlighted below.

1. Generosity.

Each of the five voice professionals questioned for this article discuss how generosity is part of the nature of their work. Through each interview, a pattern of voice professionals freely giving of themselves emerges: giving of their time, of their expertise, of their spirit. For example, Andrea Haring, the first subject interviewed for this paper, was in the middle of multiple projects when she was reached for her interview. Haring was met on the campus of Bard College where she was working at the Summer Playwriting

Retreat with the LAByrinth Theatre Company. Despite the fact that she was also in between trips to Germany, Italy and the UK, and a major teaching engagement at the World Economic Forum, she found time for this project. Not only did Ms. Haring spend over two hours answering questions for this article, but she was also very candid about her experiences.

There are other ways in which generosity shows itself as a common trait among these artists. Each interviewee describes how information, time and talent are freely shared in the mentor/mentee relationship. For example, Thom Jones says, in regard to the knowledge and passion he shares with his students, "I just keep giving it away and I want my students to keep giving it away […] if you don't you'll start to become small." Ginger Eckert, a former student of Thom Jones' says, "he [Thom Jones] and other really great teachers have that thing where they're like, 'I'm gonna work with you until you move forward. Whatever that is for you. It doesn't mean you have to move to the end, but you have to move forward.'" Furthermore, Melissa Baroni describes her experiences with seasoned voice professionals who have been giving of time and information: "The mentors I've had" and then she pauses to organize her thoughts; "there's no secrecy. There's no keeping the cards close to the chest." Baroni continues and describes her experience at Emerson College observing Master Linklater Teacher, Amelia Broome: "She made me more into a teaching assistant. She has been a wonderful mentor because she didn't have to do any of this. She even sometimes would let me teach her classes and she would watch and offer feedback."

As the interviews continue, it becomes clear that, "giving it away" as Thom Jones says, is, indeed, a consistent habit of each of these five artists. Ginger Eckert shares something that supports this idea of generosity being a tenet to the work we do; she quotes, "Somebody once said to me 'you don't pick your mentors, your mentors pick you.'"

2. Initiative.

In short, it seems that if you display initiative, people respond. Ginger Eckert shares this anecdote about Thom Jones: "I had turned in a score and Thom said to me, 'you're really kind of a super star at this.' He recognized that I had done a good job. I said, 'well, you know, this is what I want to do.' And he said, 'OH, WELL, then we've got a lot to talk about.'" Through Thom's generosity AND through Ginger's initiative, by the time Ginger finished at Trinity Rep, she had assisted Thom on the shooting for the pilot of the TV show "The Brotherhood." Andrea Haring puts it another way; she explains how when a person contacts her and expresses a desire to become a Designated Linklater Teacher, she always welcomes that person and says, "great, just show up." Andrea explains how it's the students who exhibit the most initiative that grab her attention and ultimately get her time and move forward.

In his interview, Thom Jones discusses how he got his start in the field. He explains how, when he was at Purchase College, the faculty had caught wind of how he had freely taken on tutoring the first year acting students. Because of this display of dedication and initiative, by the time Thom was in his final year at Purchase, he was leading warm-ups and assisting teachers. When Thom was 23 years old, Chuck Jones, a widely noted voice practitioner and Thom's mentor and teacher at Purchase, hired Thom to teach voice and speech at Playwrights Horizons/NYU.

3. Growth and discovery in the classroom: an appreciation of the personal connection.

The questions, "what keeps you in this business?" or "why do you do what you do?" are not included in the questioning for this paper. But at one point or another, each interviewee discusses their appreciation and respect for the deep personal connection that is possible in the classroom or studio; and although no interviewee expressly says, 'I am teaching solely for this personal connection' it is evident from the tone, demeanor, and passion expressed by each participant, that this personal connection is a major factor. Vocal training is very intimate as it deals with the retraining of the student and his or her relationship with a most personal form of expression: the voice. In the same way a massage therapy session might cause a release of toxins from the body, a vocal coaching session might release an undiscovered feeling or emotion. When this happens, the student is in a most vulnerable place, and the voice teacher is there to support and be present for the event. Ginger Eckert defines this personal connection. She says, "The really great teachers are the ones who not only have the knowledge, the expertise, the precision, in their discipline, but who are there in the room in the moment with you connecting with you. That is the kind of teacher I want to be. Then you're alive!" Thom Jones takes this notion of the personal connection in the classroom a step further. He says, "This work is very deeply related to affirming what it is to be alive and that's very close to what it is to give and take energy, what it is to love."

Andrea Haring spent time discussing how students might become emotional as a result of vocally relaxing and releasing. Haring quotes, "You have to be a larger vessel than the event that's happening in the room." Her point reveals how the voice teacher must have the ability to create space for a student's emotional moment while also pushing through and following up on responsibilities as a teacher and coach. Melissa Baroni clearly articulates this point when she says of her own experiences as a student where she may have

cried as a result of a vocal exercise. She says, "I have to think that it is a product of the nature of this work; it is so much about connecting and communication on a human level."

The major catalyst for the personal connection between teacher and student or mentor and mentee is the reality that the voice student is experiencing intense personal discovery. Because of this, the voice teacher becomes a witness to the student's personal and creative growth. Each interviewee spends time talking about how valuable these discoveries are for their development. What is more, although the seasoned professionals have accounts coming from both sides of the mentee/mentor equation, their personal stories of growth are notable. Of his mentors at Purchase, Thom Jones explains, "These were the teachers, more than any of the others, who really made me come through about who I really am in the world." In discussing her days studying voice at Skidmore College, Melissa Baroni explains, "It felt like I was getting in touch with an expanded sense of myself that I didn't know existed in me [...] I remember being very surprised by the sensation of my voice. It was really thrilling to sense a fullness in my voice." She finishes by stating, "for me, it was a whole burst of self knowledge." Andrea Haring describes her personal growth most pointedly when she talks about the early days of her career and getting a position teaching voice at Dartmouth following a family tragedy: "Teaching the Linklater work saved my life. It became a quest to figure out 'who the hell am I?'"

4. Vocation/diligence/ ongoing learning.

A common trait each interviewee shares is a strong commitment towards developing and maintaining a life-long vocal practice. At one point, Andrea Haring states, "You really want to train teachers because they want to do the work. It's a vocation."

Patsy Culbert speaks of how when she lived in Boston, she would train with Kristin Linklater in the midst of working full-time at the Huntington Theatre and working as an actor. Melissa Baroni discusses observing Amelia Broome in classes for two solid years at Emerson College. Ginger Eckert shares her current efforts working with NYU/Playwrights Horizons voice teacher, Francine Zerfas. Ginger is an assistant instructor to Zerfas, and to do her job well, to fully understand Ms. Zerfas' approach, Eckert has spent hours on end each day for over a year mastering Francine Zerfas' technique. Thom Jones shares how he was "down in the studios for three hours a night" during his four years at Purchase. Finally, to cap these examples of dedication, for a year, Andrea Haring drove from New York City to the Berkshires and back, all in the same day, every week (arriving in Lenox, Massachusetts by 9am)—spending nine hours each visit studying intensively with Kristin Linklater.

"I Want To Do That!" A paper exploring the value of mentorship between early career and established voice professionals by Paul Ricciardi

Melissa Baroni shares, "I love acting, but I almost feel that my bigger contribution will be in teaching [...] In deciding to teach this work, I did have the conscious thought, 'what better thing to make my life's work be about than something that's so personally challenging where I know there will be so much growth. It's such a fulfilling concept for me." Baroni's quote speaks to Andrea Haring's assertion, that the voice professional's work is a vocation, or a life's work; it is a contribution made to the world.

Evidenced in each interview is the fact that all subjects state that they believe that as voice professionals we must always be open to new information. Patsy Culbert, Andrea Haring and Thom Jones, the three interviewees who are currently mentors and well into their careers, each point to ways in which they are always open to new information within their own practice. A few examples: Andrea Haring explains, "You have to continually re-interest yourself in the work, otherwise you're going to get spiritually and mentally burned out." Haring goes on to say "I feel like I'm constantly shifting and adapting." Thom Jones puts it another way: "The more I learn, the more I feel like I have to learn." He also makes reference to his singing practice: "I continue to study singing and that is probably something I will continue to do until I drop dead." These teachers choose to continue to study voice, not because there is some sort of professional requirement or financial gain as there is in other professions. Culbert, Haring and Jones reveal the idea that as voice teachers, we must be dedicated to ongoing creative and technical growth, and that by doing this, we expand what we have to offer our students.

5. Value placed on maintaining a personal practice, often through performance.

Related to the last idea of vocation, dedication and diligence is this notion of "walking the talk." Melissa Baroni, Patsy Culbert, Ginger Eckert, Andrea Haring and Thom Jones all discuss the need for voice practitioners to be doing the work personally. Andrea Haring proves this point. Aside from the fact that during her interview, she is in the midst of working as an actor with the LAByrinth Summer Play Institute, she practices the work as she is teaching it. She says, "I actually have to do the work [while teaching]. I actually have to be relaxing and releasing." Melissa Baroni echoes this when she says, "It's so important to have the experience in your own body." She goes on, "It's the only way I can teach from an authentic place [...] I've experienced what it really means to release the back of my tongue." Patsy Culbert sums it up: "I am a better actor because I teach."

6. Honesty and directness: challenging the mentee.

In talking to each interviewee about their experience as a

mentor/mentee, it becomes clear that each subject places value on "not letting a student off the hook." In all interviews, there is an emphasis placed on not permitting a student to check out during a rough patch. Thom Jones' comment regarding his mentor, Chuck Jones, gets to the heart of this idea. He says of Chuck Jones, "he wouldn't let me make nice with my voice." Ginger Eckert supports this by saying of Thom, "Nobody is handled with kid gloves. He is strong and direct and sensitive without coddling." She goes on to say, "Bottom line with voice teachers and acting teachers in general, [...] is that the ones who push you, the ones who call on you and say 'you're right, that wasn't it' and point you closer in the direction and tell you to go further are the great teachers." This idea of being honest and direct shows up in other ways in each interview. For example, Andrea Haring discusses how she might manage her class or coaching session on a day that isn't going so well. She explains, "You bring your humanity to the work. [...] It's the ability to say 'this is where I am at and let's work [...] If you don't start with the basic 'this is who I am right now' then it's bullshit."

7. The utilization of a combination of approaches within the work.

The concept of voice practitioners utilizing several different approaches or techniques is nothing new. However, in hearing all of these interviewees clearly state the value of this idea and explain how this manifests itself into their own work is compelling. In her interview, Patsy Culbert talks about how she uses Kristin Linklater's work along with the Alexander Technique and yoga. Ginger Eckert discusses how, at Playwrights Horizons, Francine Zerfas utilizes a combination of Chuck Jones and Catherine Fitzmaurice. Ginger explains, "I think all of these phenomenal approaches to voice work are really valid [...] I ultimately believe you need to have all of these things, and I think that's part of what I learned from Thom." Andrea Haring echoes this idea of the value of looking at various approaches. You see this example supported in the preparation of a Linklater Teacher Trainee as each trainee must also be well versed in another complimentary vocal approach such as the Alexander Technique or Feldenkrais. Patsy Culbert, discusses how she supports each of her students in embracing the idea of utilizing a combination of approaches. Culbert explains, "I would say [to her students], 'you have to develop your own program.'"

8. A conclusion and final tenet: We are all mentored or "brought up" by someone.

In a presentation of this paper at the 2010 VASTA Conference in Mexico City, I made a joke that this paper might be called "the three degrees of Iris Warren" as each of the interviewees for this article brought up the late great voice practitioner, Iris Warren, as an example of remarkable mentorship. The reference to Iris Warren is a reminder that mentorship is deep; it spans generations. Andrea Haring affirms this depth in her interview: in discussing how Linklater Teacher Trainees are coached, she says, "it's great to be back to the old style of apprenticeship." Haring's notion of an apprentice evokes something ancient: a sense that a specialized skill is handed down through the years. The voice mentor/mentee relationship is a valuable, unique, age old tradition that ultimately paves the way for, as Andrea Haring calls it, a vocation. Patsy Culbert frames this concept perfectly when discussing Melissa Baroni, her former student: "She's one of the prime examples of that [mentoring]: Being mentored into her work through somebody who was mentored by somebody who was mentored by somebody who taught me in this way."

Writing this paper has had a profound effect on my development as an early career professor and voice practitioner. These collected stories that formed these eight principles are an inspiration and a model of the kind of voice professional I would like to become: generous, energetic and full of initiative, appreciative of the personal connection, and dedicated; one who walks the talk, who is honest and direct with students, open to approaches offered by fellow colleagues, and always mindful of those who have paved the way for us.

Bibliography

Baroni, Melissa. Telephone interview. 27 July, 2010.

Culbert, Patricia. Telephone interview. 31 July, 2010.

Eckert, Ginger. Telephone interview. 29 July, 2010.

Haring, Andrea. Personal interview. 15 July, 2010.

Jones, Thom. Telephone interview. 28 July, 2010

The Search for Irish Keening in the 21st Century

Anne Schilling, Assistant Professor, Voice and Speech, Southern Methodist University. Previously taught at California State University-Long Beach, Cincinnati's College-Conservatory of Music, Ohio University, and in the UK at Guildford School of Acting. Voice, text, and dialect coach for numerous professional productions, in addition to private coaching. Graduated with Distinction in Voice Studies, Central School of Speech and Drama and a certified Associate Teacher of Fitzmaurice Voicework®. Currently serving on the VASTA Board of Directors. Publications include "An Introduction to Coaching Ritualized Lamentation" for VSR 2007 and "Bringing Lamentation to the Stage" for VSR 2009.

The Quest

In *The Aran Islands*, Irish writer J.M. Synge describes a lamenting ritual he witnessed, stating: "This grief of the keen is no personal complaint for the death of one woman over eighty years, but seems to contain the whole passionate rage that lurks somewhere in every native of the island" (1907, 52).

I have been researching vocalized lamentation rituals since graduate school, with a particular interest in the keening traditions of Ireland. However, the knowledge I have gathered over the years was extracted from books and articles, or gleaned from discussions and workshops with other vocal practitioners, or learned from practicing various techniques and theories in my own coaching and work sessions. I wanted to go to the source. See the country. Listen to the stories. Talk with the people.

So in the summer of 2009, armed with a grant from California State-Long Beach and a host of questions, I set off for a month in Ireland. My hope was to gather information on keening and then distribute it to coaches and actors through writing, coaching and teaching. With the wealth of Irish drama on our stages and in our libraries, the oral tradition of keening is an important resource for directors, actors, and playwrights alike. Even after years of studying the keen, I had many questions I wanted answered by primary sources: What exactly does keening sound like? When did it take place? Who were the keeners? Where did it occur? Why did it come into existence? Why has it almost completely disappeared? And might I find someone in Ireland who practiced keening, and who would be willing to provide answers for all my questions?

But it was in the search for these answers that I became aware of how great a challenge I face. Became aware, too, of the most pressing question I needed to answer: How does one study an oral tradition that is slipping into oblivion? Synge was writing from the remote island of *Inis Meáin* off the west coast of Ireland where he spent his summers in the first few years of the 1900s. More than a century later I found myself sitting before the very fireplace that he had sat before, complete with a traditional turf fire, seeking for myself the Ireland he found so many years ago and wondering if the years that have separated our two lives provide too great a challenge to the answers I seek.

What is Keening?

The English word "keen" derives from the Irish/Scots Gaelic term *caoin*, pronounced /ki:n/ and the stem of *caoinim* which in Irish means "I wail" (Oxford English Dictionary 1989). In her article "Caoineadh os Cionn Coirp: The Lament for the Dead in Ireland," Patricia Lysaght explains, "In Ireland the art of improvised poetic lamentation by women was highly developed and persisted well into the twentieth century. As a poetic and song genre, it is part of the Irish language tradition and is termed *caoineadh*" (1997, 65). "Keen" can be used in the form of a verb, as in "to keen" meaning the act of wailing and lamenting, or of a noun, as in "the keen" meaning the text or song used when lamenting. Traditionally, "keening" refers to a ritualistic practice of vocally mourning the dead, though there appears to be some disagreement on what the English term implies precisely. Some scholars have stated that "keening" usually signifies the repetitive, inarticulate wailing that accompanies a textual lament, or caoineadh (Bourke 1988, 287). However, others have referred to keening as the vocal music—chanting and singing—that occurs during the ritual of lamenting the dead (Ó Madagáin 2005, 81). In the translation from Irish to English, it is possible that both definitions are correct, or perhaps the evolution and variations in keening over the years explains the discrepancy. Regardless, all agree that wailing, chanting and/or singing collectively tend to be present in a keening ritual. The *act* of keening was, and continues to be, practiced in a variety of cultures throughout the world. However, the *term* "keening" tends to be connected specifically to Ireland and Irish literature (though the word can be found in non-Irish contexts, often signifying the sounds or cries accompanying heightened states of grief).

Breandán Ó Madagáin, in his book *Keening and other Old Irish Musics*, explains how keening originally served a supernatural purpose in that it functioned to "transfer the spirit of the deceased from this world to that of the spirits" (81). He further describes how its function evolved into an emphasis on emotional release for the living combined with "echoes of the older supernatural function" (83). Anne Ridge, author of *Death Customs in Rural Ireland*, refers to a traditional belief held by many in the Irish Midlands that the corpse was in a complex transitional state immediately following death (2009, 91). The spirit did not immediately die with the body, and this intermediary state between life and death was considered an undefined and dangerous period for both the deceased and the living (91). The spirit of the deceased needed to pass from this world to the next, and those living needed to vocally help the spirit get there. The main phases of keening "occurred during the wake and funeral—that critical period during which the deceased remains among the living" in order to encourage the spirit's safe passing (Lysaght, 74). The ritual offered structure, definition and protection during this confusing and frightening stage, and acted as a guide through the separation of death (Ridge, 26). And whether for the living or the dead, for centuries the ritual was an integral part of traditional Irish culture.

But as important as keening was in funerary rites, a number of documents indicate that people also ritualistically keened for reasons other than a person's death. In such cases, keening happened for specific events. For example, the emigration of millions of Irish men and women to America in the 19th century created a custom often referred to as "The American Wake." Frequently, families treated these departures as they would a typical Irish wake, complete with ritualistic keening and sometimes refreshments and entertainment, since it was like experiencing a death in the family. At that time travel was expensive, dangerous, and often permanent, and the likelihood of family members seeing their relatives again was doubtful (Ó Madagáin 1981, 317 and V.B. 1996). Another 19th century example involves keening in reaction to the potato blight. There is evidence that women keened the loss of their crops as if it was a familial death (Ó Madagáin 2005, 8). It makes sense, considering that for many Irish families survival depended upon the crop yield.

When did Keening Originate in Ireland?

No one knows for certain when people began ritualistically keening in Ireland. It remains a mystery. Thus far, the earliest written documentation on ritualized lamentation is found in Greek texts, dating back to Homer and Aristotle, though the practice in both Greece and Ireland is believed to pre-date those references (Ridge, 56 and Homer 1996, xi-xiii). Irish records give evidence of its existence in the twelfth century, though publication of laments transcribed from the oral tradition does not appear to occur until the nineteenth century (Lysaght, 65 and Ó Súilleabháin 1997, 144). In *The Sacred Isle*, Irish Folklore scholar, Dáithí Ó hÓgáin claims, "The major difficulty with the early literature of Ireland is that it first came into being when Christianity had already—at least officially—replaced the earlier beliefs" (1999, vii). He argues that though Irish society is indebted to the wealth of information Christian authors recorded about Ireland, the fact is, "the ancient lore belonged to a belief-system which they felt obliged to eradicate" (vii). It leaves us wondering what information was left out of Ireland's written history, offering us only glimpses into Ireland's past as it is understood today.

Is Keening in Ireland Still Practiced?

The traditional presence of "professional keeners" constitutes an important component of the lamenting ritual. These were usually women with no connection to the family of the deceased, who were "recognized for their art" in keening (Lysaght 1986, 49). Families would often hire these women to lead the ritual and would pay them in some combination of food, drink and cash (49-50). It was a pivotal role, as these individuals were responsible for guiding the entire grieving community into public expression of their sorrow. However, some felt it was also a chance for the wealthy to flaunt status by promoting highly elaborate and especially noisy keening sessions led by these professionals. There is evidence that the Catholic Church viewed this act of paying professional keeners for their services as particularly condemnable. There are documented regulations created by Church representatives that delineate attempts to abolish the practice, particularly in the seventeenth and eighteenth centuries (Ó Súilleabháin 1997, 138-40). Church aversion to and action against keening is often cited as a significant reason it has now all but disappeared.

However, other factors appear to have played a role in its decline. For a ritual that was common practice and for centuries considered crucial for the transference of the spirit from the living to the dead, there are few written details. Information on keening and how to keen was passed down orally rather than through printed instruction manuals. Scholar Patricia Lysaght warns, "the nature of the lament as an oral product must be borne in mind" (1997, 69). The textual laments performed when keening, "may have been perceived as being of, and for, the moment, rather than for posterity" (69). For that matter, the entire keening ritual appears to have served a similar "in the moment" purpose, with apparently little reason or need to be documented for the archives. There was instead a dependency on oral transference of information and an ability to do impromptu keening and extempore lament composition. Yet the oral tradition faced many obstacles when reading, writing and printing became more commonplace for the average individual. The oral culture was further infringed upon with the advent of technologies such as radio and television. With this vast and direct connection into the rest of the world, people were forced to "question their old values and beliefs" (Lysaght 1986, 235). There were theories that, in particular, the assimilation of the English lifestyle and verbal preferences into the Irish way of life contributed to the decline, as exemplified by William Beauford in 1791 who wrote, "At present the Caoinan is much neglected, being only practiced in remote parts, so that this ancient custom will soon finally cease, English manners and the English language supplanting those of the aboriginal natives" (45).

Furthermore, while keening was already in decline by the early 19th century, the events of the middle of that century would deal the custom another devastating blow. The "Great Famine" and the mass emigration that came in its wake decimated the Irish population. The numbers are telling: "the census of 1845 counted the population of Ireland between eight and nine million. Six years later it was six and a half million, and by 1881 the number had dipped to five million. Three million people had died or emigrated in thirty-five years; one third of the native population was gone"(McCourt 2004, 198). Beyond the population loss, there were other impacts, not the least of which support Mr. Beauford's opinion that language alterations played a role in the decline of traditional customs. Mr. McCourt observes, "the Irish language, for example, all but vanished. Those that spoke Irish—the poor and the marginalized—for the most part had emigrated or died, save in a few pockets in the country" (198). How many ties to a past and its oral traditions are lost during such a period?

Yet even in light of all the changes, keening was of such importance to many Irish communities that people felt a need to preserve the ancient ritual for centuries (well into the twentieth century). This speaks to its deep-rooted role in Ireland's funerary rituals and Ireland's deep-rooted respect for its own history. And though the practice currently has all but died out, during my time in Ireland there was still mention of those professional keeners—some of whom are thought to be alive—and of the possibility that actual keening rituals still occur in remote, rural Irish villages.

A Community that Practiced Keening

In search of one such rural area of Ireland, I traveled to *Inis Meáin* (in English, "Inishmaan"), the middle of the three Aran Islands where Synge's turf fire lay in wait, hoping to find more details and possibly some answers about traditional Irish keening. As I stepped off the sleek, fiberglass ferryboat onto *Inis Meáin's* new concrete, EU-funded pier and looked out over the island, I was struck by the scarcity of buildings and people, and the predominance of stones stacked in a seemingly endless web of walls. I could almost feel the island straining between its history and the pull of modernity. I headed straight for *Teach Synge* (Irish for "Synge's house") and there had the opportunity to talk with Treasa Ní Fhátharta, Curator and caretaker of the house. The house had remained in her family for generations, even prior to Synge's arrival. In complete contrast to the concrete and steel of the pier, the house's wattle-and-daub walls and thatched roof looked a bit like something that had grown out of the land itself. Her great uncle Mairtin ("Michael" in *The Aran Islands*) taught Synge to speak and write in Irish, acted as his guide, and established a close friendship with him. The two maintained a written correspondence long past Synge's departure from the island, and interestingly, all letters were written in Synge's second language—Irish.

Ms. Ní Fhátharta answered a number of questions I had about keening and its presence in Synge's play, *Riders to the Sea*. She informed me that Maurya's last speech in the play (often believed to be a nod to Sophocles) actually has its source in a letter sent to Synge by Mairtin mourning the death of his wife. And the red skirts the keening women wear in the final scene were apparently the fashion of that time. They wore the heavy skirts over their heads sometimes for warmth. Days later, I visited the Museum of Country Life, National Museum of Ireland, where I also learned from the Curator, Clodagh Doyle, that red was a color that signified protection. It was made from madder, the plant source for red dye, and was considered to have curative properties.

Not only did Ms. Ní Fhátharta talk at length about Synge, she excelled at playing the role of the storyteller, dynamically recounting the history of the island. I was particularly struck by how Ms. Ní Fhátharta talked about the sea—a mysterious character unto itself in *Riders to the Sea*. On the Aran Islands, apparently parents told their children not to go near the sea. She recited the words of the parents: "Be afeard of the sea for drownen. Those who are afeared of the sea, only some of them get drownded. Those not afeard of the sea would go out in any weather and more times come back drownded." She added that many men were keened having been taken by the sea. Ms. Ní Fhátharta did not learn to swim until she was in her thirties and living on the mainland (Ní Fhátharta 2009).

When Ms. Ní Fhátharta first mentioned her swimming experience, I wondered how a person could live on a small island surrounded by water and not learn to swim. However, the ability to live within a combination of beliefs that may seem contradictory was a recurring theme I encountered in my exchanges with various Irish individuals. In discussions I had with different people about keening, many clearly stated the practice as currently nonexistent and then within the same conversation mentioned hearing of professional keeners still living in various rural villages who were known to perform the ritual at times. On two separate occasions, I heard claimed that no one knows what keening truly sounds like, just before the same individuals affirmed the current existence of professional mourners. I thought, "Wouldn't the professional mourners know what it sounded like?" Yet the contradictory nature of these statements did not seem to bother those I talked to. There appeared to be a sense of ease about living with elements of antithesis and mystery—a sense of being "in the moment" not unlike the requirements ritualized keening demands. I felt my need for answers was often met with a compassionate, albeit knowing smile. For me, a linear-thinking American, it was necessary to redirect my approach and my questions, ease up, accept some of the mystery, and go deeper into the roots of the ritual.

Roots of the Ritual

I met with Professor Breandán Ó Madagáin at his home in Kilcolgen, Co. Galway. In addition to his aforementioned book and other publications on language and song in Ireland, Professor Ó Madagáin has published two impressive articles—*Irish Vocal Music of Lament and Syllabic Verse* and *Functions of Irish Song*—reflecting his years of in-depth, solid research on Irish song and lament. Since my research has focused mostly on the history, wailing, physicality, and text of ritualized lamenting, the element of song is of particular interest to me. Professor Ó Madagáin suggested I listen to traditional Irish singing to get an idea of the type of singing heard in lamentation. In our conversation he returned again and again to the role of music and its importance, saying, "Music was at the heart of the Irish people. It was their life" (Ó Madagáin 2009). Professor Ó Madagáin's conviction is substantiated by William Beauford, who wrote, "the Irish then musically expressed their griefs, that is, they applied the musical art, in which they excelled all others, to the orderly celebration of funeral obsequies" (43).

Music is still very much "at the heart of the Irish people," as a visit to a pub often confirms. As the tin whistles, fiddles, and *bodhráns* fill the room with their traditional jigs and reels, the pub is a noisy blend of music, conversation, and drinking. But then "shhh's" are passed from the players outward and through the crowd until the pub is quiet so a ballad may be sung. Not a word is uttered, and the room—just moments ago filled with voices of many—is now filled with the voice of one. The ballads are most often sung *a capella*, though sometimes supported by a fiddle. Many are hauntingly beautiful tales of loss, mourning, and grief. In

juxtaposition to the upbeat jigs and reels, they perhaps provide a glimpse into what Synge described as, "the whole passionate rage that lurks somewhere in every native of the island" (52). Once the ballad concludes, applause is given and then the room seems to explode back to its previous self as the players start up another jig. I observed this custom on several occasions and believe it suggests the reverence many people still seem to hold for the sung word.

I attended the 2009 Willie Clancy Irish music festival in Miltown Malbay, Co. Clare at the invitation of Dr. Lillis Ó Laoire, a professor in the Irish Department of the National University of Ireland at Galway and a professional traditional singer. I learned of Dr. Ó Laoire's interest in the musicality of Irish lamentation through our email correspondence and like Professor Ó Madagáin, he affirmed I would hear the roots of the lament in traditional Irish singing. The performance consisted of many different variations of traditional Irish singing, but what struck me in particular were two *a capella* solos, both by young women. After hearing this type of unaccompanied, solo singing, I understood what both Dr. Ó Laoire and Professor Ó Madagáin were suggesting. In my notes about the performance I wrote, "It sounds like tiny note shifts—not vibrato [and not ululations, but left me with the impression of both]. Slight resemblance to a delicate yodel, but not fully. There is a haunting quality. I couldn't understand the meaning of most of the songs, as they were predominantly in Irish. However, each song seemed to hold a wealth of memory, belief, and deep felt passion for Ireland and its history, as was apparent in the murmurs of consent and praise from the listeners at the end of every piece."

The National Folklore Collection at University College Dublin holds a wealth of Ireland's oral history and ethnological material. The country proudly boasts of it being one of the largest collections of its kind in the world—further evidence of the attention and focus Ireland places on its oral tradition and history. I went to hear authentic recordings of chanting and singing of the *caoineadh*. One must make an appointment to hear the limited sound recordings available of men and women lamenting (solo, unaccompanied performances), and I could only listen to them on-site since making copies of these recordings was not permitted. I listened to the five they had available, all in Irish and all from the mid 1900s. Dr. Ó Laoire and Professor Ó Madagáin's advice was confirmed. I could discern what sounded like elements of traditional Irish singing in the lamenting: long extended phrases, lots of rhythmic, pitch and tonal shifting, repetition, vocal "slides," etc. I also noticed differences. More repetition of phrases in the lamenting pieces, as well as more chanting, more seemingly extempore sounds, and less adornment in the singing. I was aware that though similar, traditional Irish singing and keening serve different purposes. In the comparison, I also had to acknowledge them as two "traditional" (historical) modes of vocal expression at disparate stages in current societal acceptance. One appeared to be upheld as a vital part of Irish history, continuing to be practiced as an art and performed before audiences, while the other to be withheld as a part of Irish history that may no longer have a place. Nevertheless, the links between traditional singing and keening seem too strong to be ignored, and I believe that by tracing Irish music backward I will take another step forward in my research.

Keening for the Stage

In any production, an actor is responsible for creating an authentic and intelligible performance. The obligation to achieve committed, genuine and understandable implementation of keening onstage does not necessarily require a historical reenactment of the ritual, unless specified in the text. However, it does demand an actor identify and embody what the text wishes him/her to communicate through the lament. By understanding the elements observed and practiced in the keening ritual, an actor will be better equipped to develop a well-informed, comprehensive onstage performance of it.

Andrea Ainsworth has coached productions that involve keening for the Abbey Theatre in Dublin. Even living in Ireland as Voice Director for the Abbey, she agreed that gathering specific information on keening was difficult, mostly because factual documentation is scarce and aural examples are extremely rare. I asked what she did to help actors create committed, engaging, and authentic keening performances onstage. She emphasized, above all, the importance of encouraging actors to understand and embody how keening was intended to "pass through the keener" as if the keener was a medium through that transitional period between life and death. She added, "It's about taking space, isn't it? About giving in—giving space—not self-expression or self-emoting" (Ainsworth 2009). The channeling process is important so the actor avoids creating a performance based entirely in personal emotional expression and instead invites the audience into "participating" in the onstage ritual.

In *The Right to Speak*, Patsy Rodenburg states, "Theatre is obviously a remnant of rituals that once purged audiences and now it just entertains them. But when it does occasionally touch its ritual roots actors will speak of the audience as 'being at one' with them sharing the same breath" (1992, 92-3). Ms. Rodenburg mentions keening in particular, and explains how rituals practiced in groups provide "safety and support to the expression" (92). She highlights the Irish wake as a ritual preserved by the society due to this important service it offers people. Both Ms. Ainsworth and Ms. Rodenburg's comments took me back to Synge's descrip-

tion: "This grief of the keen is no personal complaint for the death of one woman over eighty years…" (Synge, 52). Ms. Ainsworth pointed out that contemporary Irish citizens seem to be moving further away from understanding the full, open throated, emoting nature of keening that was intended to encourage participation from the entire community. She, too, is interested in how to preserve some of the valuable lessons keening offers, and in what we, as voice teachers and coaches, can learn from the ritual and bring onto our stages.

These observations provide key concepts for my continued research and practice. If current Irish society is abandoning the act of communal expression offered through keening, as Ms. Ainsworth suggested, how can an American audience be expected to connect to the ritual? When faced with other similar antiquated rituals and customs, many directors choose to simply omit them from their productions. But I think Ainsworth, Rodenburg and Synge all tap into the reason a playwright chooses to include such rituals within the slice of life experienced through a play. They highlight what many argue is a basic human need—the need for communion. And that need is fundamental to the theatrical experience. So as I continue to grapple with researching the roots of keening, I find I am unearthing elements of the very roots, essence, and purpose of live theatre. The actors and audience "sharing the same breath" through the keening ritual models the importance of the communal ritual practiced in the theatre—be it Irish or American. For me, as researcher, coach, and practitioner, it is a strong reminder to emphasize the importance of including the audience as a member of the ritual, rather than solely as a witness.

Reflections on Keening

As my flight left Shannon bound for America, I reflected on my month in Ireland. What had I come to Ireland to find? Perhaps a bit naively I was looking for what Synge had found more than a century ago: the keeners, the culture, the Ireland itself. I didn't find it. And to my disappointment, I didn't find *her*: the mourner from ages past who would fulfill this part of my "quest" and answer my questions about keening. What I found instead in my search for the proverbial "lost keener of Ireland" was her shadow, her footsteps, her echo. And if that is all that remains, my investigation doesn't end—it just changes.

An article in the *Dublin Penny Journal* from 1833 describes how keening as a custom had "fallen greatly into disuse, and is now of the rare occurrence, except in some very few old families, and among the peasantry, and with them it has now generally degenerated into a mere cry of an extremely wild and mournful character" (O'G). This observation, made three-quarters of a century before Synge, certainly confirms the diminishing role of traditional keening in

Ireland, but it also highlights the nature of oral traditions to evolve and change. Perhaps keening never really vanished, but rather transformed itself by adapting to cultural developments and alterations. The mournful wailing and wild cries that depict keening even to this day seem to bear little resemblance to an older form of keening that Beauford described as predominantly musical, and that the *Penny Journal* reported as highly poetical with a specific metrical cadence. *The Penny Journal* went on to explain that "on the decline of the Irish bards these [metrical] feet w[e]re gradually neglected, and they fell into a kind of slip-shod metre among the women, who have entirely engrossed the office of *keeners* or [professional] mourners" (O'G). How did these transitions take place? What were their causes? How might keening differ between various timeframes? Exploring this transformation may be the next step to discovering and subsequently documenting the voice of the "lost keener." Additionally, it may provide the vocal coach not only with the means to teach and assist in onstage keening, but may supply the coach with a variety of ways keening could differ from one play to the next.

So while Synge's turf fire may not have shed enough light to reveal all the answers I sought, it did expose an Ireland I had not known through the books and articles and workshops. In meeting the people, listening to the music, and traversing the landscape, I left with a much stronger understanding of how the practice of keening was, and continues to be, revered as a defining ritual in Irish history. Even if it is on the brink of vanishing, keening's roots are so long and deep they continue to appear in contemporary Ireland through song, writing, traditions, and—it is my hope—the rare occasion of the performance of the ritual.

But the country, isolated by politics and geography for much of its history, is entering the twenty-first century along with its increasingly interconnected European neighbors. Ireland is in transition. With the thatched roofs and stone walls are urban landscapes with high-rise apartments and modern shopping centers. As with any nation, it is clear that this move toward modernity endangers the Irish cultural traditions, keening among them. This adds a sense of urgency to the research. I look forward to returning to Ireland and digging deeper, to pursue the answers that have eluded me and to discover the questions yet unknown.

Bibliography

Andrea Ainsworth, personal interview with author, July 13, 2009.

Beauford, William. "Caoinan: or Some Account of the Antient Irish Lamentations," *The Transactions of the Royal Irish Academy*, Vol. 4, Dublin (1791): 41-54 in the *Antiquities* section.

Bourke, Angela. "The Irish Traditional Lament and the Grieving Process," *Women's Studies International Forum*, Vol. 11, Issue 4 (1988): 287-91.

Breandán Ó Madagáin, personal interview with author, July 22, 2009.

Cahill, Thomas. *How the Irish Saved Civilization*, New York, Anchor Books, 1995.

Homer. *The Odyssey*, R. Fagles (Translator), London, Penguin Books, 1996.

Lysaght, Patricia. *The Banshee: The Irish Death Messenger*, Boulder, Roberts Rinehart Publishers, 1986.

Lysaght, Patricia. "Caoineadh os Cionn Coirp: The Lament for the Dead in Ireland," *Folklore* 108 (1997): 65-82.

McCourt, Malachy. *Malachy McCourt's History of Ireland*, Philadelphia, Running Press, 2004.

O'G. "The Irish Funeral Cry (the Ullaloo, Keeners and Keening at Irish Funerals)," *The Dublin Penny Journal*, Vol. 1, Number 31, (1833).

Ó hÓgáin, Dáithí. *The Sacred Isle: Belief and Religion in Pre-Christian Ireland*, Doughcloyne, The Collins Press, 1999.

Ó Madagáin, Breandán. *Caointe Agus Seancheolta Eile: Keening and Other Old Irish Musics*, Indreabhán, Conamara, Cló Iar-Chonnachta, 2005.

Ó Madagáin, Breandán. "Irish Vocal Music of Lament and Syllabic Verse," in *The Celtic Consciousness*, Vol. 1, Colin Smythe Ltd. (1981): 311-332.

Ó Súilleabháin, Seán. *Irish Wake Amusements*, Dublin, Mercier Press, 1997.

Oxford English Dictionary, 2nd Edition, 1989.

Ridge, Anne. *Death Customs in Rural Ireland: Traditional Funerary Rites in the Irish Midlands*, Galway, Arlen House, 2005.

Rodenburg, Patsy. *The Right to Speak*, London, Methuen Drama, 1992.

Synge, J.M. *Riders to the Sea*, London, Elkin Mathews, 1905.

Synge, J.M. *The Aran Islands*, Dublin, Maunsel and Co., Ltd., 1907.

Treasa Ní Fhátharta, personal interview with author, July 21, 2009.

V.B. "The American Wake," in *Ireland's Own*, collected by News Extracts Company, June 7th, 1996.

Acknowledgements

The author would like to thank Andrea Ainsworth, Clodagh Doyle, Treasa Ní Fhátharta, Lillis Ó Laoire, and Breandán Ó Madagáin for their time and willingness to contribute to my research and this article.

Voice and Movement Studies, *Dana McConnell, Associate Editor*

Photo By Theresa Smerud.

Dana McConnell, a director, performer and educator, is an Assistant Professor of Theatre and Music Theatre at Viterbo University. Her directing work includes regional premieres of *Metamorphoses* and *Crave, Company, The 25th Annual Putnam County Spelling Bee, Assassins* and *Cosi fan Tutte*. With Black Earth Collaborative Arts, she created original works including *Ball's Out* and *Sky*. The education director for two national tours with the American Shakespeare Center, Dana has also taught as a guest artist at RADA, the University of Bathurst in Australia, and on the faculty of the Interlochen Center for the Arts. Dana received an MFA in Directing from OU and has undertaken additional studies in Bartenieff Fundamentals.

The international focus of this issue of the VSR raises questions of connectivity for the theatre practitioner – how do we, using the body and the voice, forge connections between people of differing languages, ethnicities and experiences? How does the work that we do as individuals both define and expand the spaces that we share?

For as much as we have in common as humans, the differences revealed in our attempts to generate a common vocabulary are profound. I recall my surprise when, after disembarking from a plane in Sydney, Australia after a 16-hour flight, I tried to order a cup of coffee with cream to go. The woman at the counter looked at me blankly and did not reach for a disposable cup, pour coffee in it and add cream. A long, confused silence passed between us as I had my first in what would turn out to be a long series of lessons about the limits of shared language in different cultural and geographical contexts. In an impromptu dumb show, I acted out my request and learned that what I *actually* wanted was coffee, light, and take-away. Though the barista and I were both speaking English, we were clearly not speaking the same language. This pattern recurred throughout the teaching and production work with

Australian students: I felt continually like a mime sliding my hands along the contours of a real but invisible wall; there were boundaries where I'd expected none. But the boundaries invariably revealed new possibilities, new ways of thinking and speaking about familiar topics that opened them to a more expansive consideration and resulted in a deeper and more fully shared context for everyone involved.

Each of the authors who contributed to this section of the VSR is working at the nexus of body, voice and culture. Erica Tobolski's experience teaching and coaching in Malaysia reveals essential questions about Voice in a personal, cultural and theatrical sense. In the experiences about which she writes, we see her as both master teacher and curious learner. Tobolski's honesty, skill, sensitivity and perseverance allow her to shift what she is teaching and how she is working to best address what is happening in the moment with her Malaysian collaborators in ways that have had an on-going impact on her own work.

The focus of Ruth Rootberg's article is on the conundrum of what Alexander called "End-gaining"—the concern for "getting it right" that can result in achieving an end at the expense or to the exclusion of attention to the means. Through the example of her work with a student for whom effort and inefficiency are simultaneously familiar and damaging, Rootberg's work reminds me of the chaos we all feel when we venture away from the familiar, the known, and into the realm of the possible. When working free of habitual tension feels "like nothing," as it did for her student, Rootberg suggests alternatives to restore ease and clarity to speaking and moving, a re-union of body and voice that creates the field for our common engagement as artists and humans.

"End-gaining" and the "Means-Whereby": Discovering the best process to achieve goals of vocal training and pedagogy using the Alexander Technique

Photo by Clive J. Mealey

Ruth Rootberg, M.AmSAT, Designated Linklater Voice Teacher, Laban/Bartenieff Movement Analyst. Ruth has presented voice and movement workshops at the Voice Foundation, regional and national Alexander organizations, ATHE, SAPVAME (South Africa), and has been a guest of music, dance, and theatre departments around the country. She taught voice on the faculty at Yale School of Drama and Theatre School of DePaul. Ruth is editor of *Teaching Breathing: Results of a Survey*. A regular writer for *Voice and Speech Review*, she also contributed to *The Complete Voice & Speech Workout*. Ruth teaches *Moving Voices with Quiet Hands*, Alexander workshops for voice specialists.

"It is essential, in the necessary re-education of the subject through conscious guidance and control, that in every case the 'means whereby' rather than the 'end' should be held in mind." –F.M. Alexander[1]

Introduction

In a previous article for VSR (Rootberg, 164-170), I have written of the mechanical advantages accrued to the vocalist when the head is poised "forward and up" as taught through the Alexander Technique.[2] This principle of the relation of the head to the neck and the head and neck to the rest of the body, known as Primary Control,[3] and that of learning how to manage performance anxiety and release habitual tensions, may be the most prominent of conceptions people have about what the Alexander Technique is and why it is important for vocalists to learn it.

Between the intention to improve coordination and the accomplishment, lie our habits. It is a given, is it not, that we retain habitual tensions that must be addressed before a full vocal training can progress; that in the face of increasing stimuli it is harder to keep those tensions at bay? The Alexander Technique is a wonderful way to decrease tension. Beyond providing a means to reduce habitual muscular tension, the Alexander Technique addresses a different sort of habit, which is often related to tension, but bears independent consideration. It is pernicious, pervasive, and will thwart the very best-intentioned people: it is called End-gaining. In my earlier article, I did not include End-gaining and its counterpart, Means-Whereby in my list of principles (Rootberg, 164-165). This article will remedy my omission by describing this particular aspect of the Alexander Technique, offering and analyzing a case study and other examples, and encouraging the reader to pay attention to diminishing not only habits of misuse, but also to avoiding the habit of End-gaining by using the Means-Whereby to improve vocal performance and pedagogy.

What does it mean?

The term End-gaining was briefly defined in Connie DeVeer's article (*VSR* 2009, 32).[4] When one "End-gains," one wants to "get it right" and focuses on attaining the goal in the most direct means possible; it assumes the process of achieving that end is undergone without regard of consequences, or without reasoning first what the best steps would be to ensure success.[5] The opposite of End-gaining is to set a goal, but to consider the Means-Whereby as an important part of achieving the goal. So the "success" of the "end-gainer" might mean not forgetting one's lines; having enough breath; receiving a good review. Successful employment of the Means-Whereby to achieve the goal would mean "remembering one's lines without having to frown in search of words; phrasing well in a meaningful way without tightening the vocal or breathing mechanisms just to squeeze out the last bit of breath while staying in contact with other actors; knowing how one connected to the role and the audience to make the character memorable to the critic. Although the very existence of these oppositional styles means one can achieve a goal without regard to the Means-Whereby, paying attention to it will sometimes be the only road to achieving a goal, or making a lasting change.[6]

These concepts would be learned best through experience,[7] but as we are communicating via the printed word, I will provide context through an analysis of a case study.

Case Study

A student, whom I will call Talia, wanted to improve her speaking and singing; it had been several years since her last voice lessons with another teacher. I told her that some students coming for voice expect only to work on breath, voice, and a bit of posture; and I could use the principles of the Alexander Technique through that direct application, but that through my teaching experience I've learned that those who took the time to learn the principles first and then apply them to voice were—in the long run—happier with the outcome and stuck with the lessons longer so they could deepen their skills sufficiently to become more independent and confident in working on themselves.[8] Talia said she was willing to start with learning the Alexander Technique principles.

During her first lessons, I taught her the basics of Primary Control, Inhibition and Direction[9] and how to rest her back by lying with her knees bent and her head on books (semi-supine). She spent most of the lesson on a table ("table turn") while I put my hands on her in the manner I had been trained in during my Alexander Technique Teacher training course. The quality of touch is very light, and there is no massage or manipulation of tissue. Talia learned the principles through my explanations, my suggestions for sending herself mental messages, and the experience of my hands. Then Talia rose from the table and then received what is called a "chair turn." where I guided her in and out of the chair. During this part of the lesson, Talia applied what she was learning during table turns as she coordinated shifting her weight between standing and sitting. She learned to first recognize, and then curtail, her tendency to pull her head back and shorten her spine as she moved in and out of the chair. This ceasing of a habit is called Inhibition. She also learned to organize herself around her awareness of space—internal and external—and the spatial pathway her head took during movement. This spatial thinking, and the mental messaging one does to organize one's self, is called Direction. After several lessons, we were both pleased with the changes in her ability to send herself messages—simply put, her ability to think—, as well as with her lengthening spine as she moved in and out of the chair, and her ensuing ease of movement and decreased anxiety during her lessons and daily life. With an improving head/neck/back relationship and new skills of Inhibition and Direction in her toolbox, we agreed to focus the next lesson on voice.

Talia's voice was quite tentative and breathy when she spoke, and the sound had only occasionally changed when her Primary Control improved at the same moment she happened to say something aloud.[10] Talia sat in a chair while I put my hands on her head and neck. Her breath moved in and out quietly and easily, while she continued to Inhibit and Direct. There was a very slight backward pull of her head during each in-breath. Although her habitual exaggerated pull as she came to standing had decreased considerably over the course of several lessons, there was at this moment a small rhythmic pull that I associated with interference in her breathing. I asked Talia to not pull her

head back but to keep thinking "forward and up" as the breath moved in and out of her. As she Directed forward and up, she noticed the pull, inhibited, and reduced it during a few cycles of respiration.

Then I asked her to sigh out on an "ah." She immediately held her breath; the backward pull of her head increased as she inhaled with some force, braced her ribs, and then sighed.[11] She began with a slight glottal attack, and a harsh tone diminished to breathiness. I then asked her to return to quiet breathing, and to Inhibit and Direct. The pull in her neck muscles decreased again. I told her to not react to my instructions, but to just listen to them and continue to Inhibit and Direct. Then I said: "In a moment, after I stop speaking, would you sigh out your vibrations on an 'ah.'" Talia started to take a breath on a forceful inhale, but then remembered she didn't have to do anything, released, and continued breathing. "Don't do anything now. If you want me to repeat the instructions, ask." I waited, and as there was no response, I continued. "You've heard what the plan is; keep Inhibiting and Directing, and then give yourself this idea that you will sigh out, *but only do so when you can continue to Inhibit and Direct at the same time as you sigh out.*[12] See if you can just allow the thought of expressing yourself guide the breath. Don't take the breath. Don't inhale. I'm going to stop talking now. Keep Inhibiting and Directing until the sound does itself."

Talia continued to let the breath move in and out. Her head pulled back as she started sucking the breath in and I said "No. That's your habit. Wait." She kept Inhibiting and Directing. Then, without any interference in her Primary Control, a lovely, free, full-voiced sigh of relief with easy onset sprang forth.

> *"The new 'means-whereby' are unfamiliar, and any attempt on his part to carry them out will be associated with experiences which feel wrong…."*
> – F. M. Alexander

Talia was happy because the sound seemed better to her, and her throat hadn't bothered her. In fact, she said producing the sound "felt like nothing." I supported her report, acknowledging it was a free and resonant sound, and then asked her what she did to produce that change. She said she just kept Inhibiting and Directing, thinking forward and up. Then it just happened.

Talia was also a bit taken aback, because—although she knew the sound was what she wanted—it was not "her." She wasn't used to the sensation—or in her case, reduced sensation—because producing the sound "felt like nothing." It also brought up childhood memories of being told she was too loud. We talked about how many of our habits come from strategies of self-comfort and protection. When she was young, she would be scolded less often if her voice didn't carry as much. She had avoided insults and reprimands by making her voice breathy and weak. Now she was at the cusp of a new choice. She could use her tools of Inhibition and Direction to create a new voice full of resonance and nuance. Or she could react to the fear and discomfort of the unfamiliar sensation of nothingness,[13] or to the memories of old stories, and continue producing her old sound. I asked her whether she wanted to continue with voice work in the coming lessons. She was quiet for awhile and then replied she would like to continue table turns and spend the last part of the lesson doing vocal work rather than chair turns.

During the following lessons, I broke down elements of vocal production so that Talia had time to apply the Means-Whereby to all aspects of vocal production, and then re-integrate her learning into the whole. In this way she learned to have a consistent ease in breathing whether she intended to speak or breathe, an easy onset of vibrations, an ability to increase the vibrations as she practiced various humming exercises, a release of her jaw and tongue and toning of her soft palate. She began to say she felt more connected to herself when she spoke.[14] As we progressed, there was a moment where she would fall back into her End-gaining ways, but then as she Inhibited and Directed, she would integrate the new material.[15] As time went on, Talia could apply the Means-Whereby more rapidly and consistently. She learned how to continue applying the techniques of Inhibition and Direction even as she practiced speaking more rapidly, singing with a greater range, or expressing more deeply felt emotions. If she continues, I imagine she will still want to End-gain when faced with a new or stressful situation, but the choice to Inhibit that impulse and reason out her Means-Whereby will be available to her more and more frequently.

Analysis of End-gaining and Means-Whereby

Talia's stated goal was to improve her voice. My goal was to give her an experience that satisfied her so she would return for more lessons and have respect for my skills. My End-gaining tendency would be to jump right into voice work, because that's probably what she expected, and even if I couldn't teach her the best way I knew, she might be more inclined to continue if it seemed like a "regular" voice lesson, which would include scales, *arpeggios*, articulation drills, etc. I knew from experience that the students who first learned the Alexandrian skills of Inhibition and Direction had more consistent improvement in their posture, and an easier time correcting vocal habits and building the voice. So I chose my Means-Whereby to offer her a choice, with a recommendation based on my experience.

Inhibition and Direction became the Means-Whereby for Talia's vocal change. By learning how to Inhibit, Talia learned to literally stop and rest by lying down in the middle of her day, to pause before initiating an action, and to wait while she organized her thoughts to improve her use as she prepared to take an action (e.g., speak or sing), and as she executed the action. She learned to send messages to herself to cease unnecessary tension. As she learned to Direct, Talia awakened her spatial thinking to support expansion rather than contraction, lengthening and widening rather than shortening and narrowing.

When I noticed Talia's habitual breathing pattern, my Means-Whereby to work was to ask her to think more specifically of applying her Alexander skills to her head and neck in relation to her breathing. But when I asked her to create sound, she forgot her Means-Whereby and began to End-gain. She was stimulated by the request to perform a more complex activity, and probably triggered into a habitual physical action that included tensions associated with her hopes and fears surrounding her goals and memories of past experience, and it all converged on her. She lost her calm attitude and global perspective of herself, and focused on just getting the sound out. In doing so, she reverted to multiple old habits of misuse.

"I must continue this process…for a considerable time before actually attempting to employ the new 'means-whereby' for the purpose of speaking."

– **F. M. Alexander**

I needed to Inhibit a habit of rushing into a critique of her sound. I also needed to Inhibit my fear that my approach wasn't working. By giving myself time, I could call upon the principles: I asked her to return to her Means-Whereby. While I spoke for awhile, I gave Talia plenty of time to re-organize. Without any necessity to do anything but just listen, her system could calm down from the event of misuse, and she could use her mind to organize and plan for the next initiation of sound. She had the one false start; not every moment of Inhibition produces an exact and wonderful change: it requires rehearsal.[16] She was doing the best she could, applying her Means-Whereby, and I as teacher suggested she just take more time and do it again. By taking more time, she was able to more fully Inhibit her habits. The outcome was a distinct improvement in vocal use which ensured an easier onset and fuller resonance.

Then Talia focused on the outcome; the result. Of course she should be pleased with herself; she attained her goal of improving her voice, even if for just this moment. I next steered her to her Means-Whereby. If she remained focused on the results, she would probably approach the next vocalization by End-gaining, trying to just copy the

"End-gaining" and the "Means-Whereby": Discovering the best process to achieve goals of vocal training and pedagogy using the Alexander Technique by Ruth Rootberg

sound she made, trying to remember the feeling of nothingness and trying to make that happen again.[17] I wanted her to attend to her *thinking process* so she would reinforce using the Means-Whereby, because it was that thinking she could learn to recreate.

After Talia and I discussed her emotional reactivity to the change in her vocal use, she took some time to reason out what she wanted. Later Talia told me this is what she thought: She had already learned tools that were helping her in her daily life. She recognized that applying those tools to producing sound had resulted in a positive change. She worried there would be a repetition of disturbing memories, and didn't know how to deal with that in the lessons. If she stopped lessons, she wouldn't attain her vocal goal. She reasoned out her Means-Whereby; she would proceed slowly, at a pace where she could have time to process the change of reclaiming her right to express herself freely and fully, and would also follow her process through journaling.

As lessons continued, we both noticed a "two steps forward, one step backward" progress. Even when one has learned the tools that help make change, it is often difficult to consistently commit to conscious use of the tools. Habits are often formed so that the organism can perform an action with less attention. Until a new habit is well established, it is quite easy to revert to the old, because it's difficult to continue to work: one gets tired, loses inspiration, gets distracted, etc. This is where I as teacher need to commit to re-inspiring my student. The pull to do what the teacher wants can be very strong,[18] and it was a good reminder to me that I needed to remind Talia to use her tools each time we moved into new territory.

Time to get it right

When I work privately with students who do not have a time-sensitive goal, there is room for meticulous practice of the Means-Whereby to make the subtle changes Talia experienced. We do not wallow in process, but rather each step becomes a goal in itself. Taking time literally converts to creating physical and mental space; when my students are not rushed, they take the time to learn how to expand in their body and expression. As they gain confidence that their skills begin to consistently produce similar outcomes, they become more committed to finding the Means-Whereby to achieve their goals. That is, they do until the number of stimuli occurring—or the intensity of the stimuli—increases to the point where they are thrown back into habit. I have come to expect that when I teach a new movement or vocal exercise, students will first need to understand the actions themselves, and once they have learned the actions, they will be more willing to apply a reasonable Means-Whereby of Inhibition and Direction to attain their goal, namely, executing the movement or vocalization. If

> *"...man's craze is for speed and for the short view...he is a confirmed end-gainer."*
>
> – F. M. Alexander

the student arrives more harassed than usual, or is coming down with a cold or getting over one, there are fewer resources to even want to find their Means-Whereby. If my student is over-excited or in a rush, s/he forgets there is a Means-Whereby.[19] It continues to fascinate me how we use the lesson to restore poise, in the sense that the person becomes more calm, quietly alert, physically balanced and freed of unnecessary tensions—while the neck frees, the head goes forward and up, and the back lengthens and widens—and then the ability to use a Means-Whereby is once again possible. It's as if, without the Primary Control improving, it won't occur to a student that it (the Primary Control) *can* improve, even after having taken lessons.[20] The Alexander Technique is effective in a powerful, deepening way, but only as it is consciously applied. The power of habit must be contended with repeatedly; it takes courage and temperance to stick to the principles. But I have never seen the principles fail; I have only seen myself and others come to a state where we choose not to apply them, or forget that we can.

For those readers who teach within the structure of the university where you can't always choose your student-teacher ratio, the duration of a class period, the number of classes per week, the number of weeks in the semester, or the number of semesters the students take voice, I can imagine you throwing up your hands while you exclaim: "Sure, if I had more time, I could make miracles. I wouldn't even need the Alexander Technique; my system works fine when there is enough time to teach everyone." Or "I love the Alexander Technique, but it takes so much time to learn; I want to find a shortcut."[21] I commiserate. Things go better with time. But just as Talia was able to speed up her process, so can your students, once you take time to lay the groundwork. Speeding up the process is different from rushing. Please, avoid rushing through your curriculum. Whatever technique you are teaching, take time in the beginning to set up your principles, your Means-Whereby, so your students can learn to rely on them.[22]

Other Examples of End-gaining and an alternative Means-Whereby

Now that you have a basic understanding of End-gaining and the Means-Whereby, I'm going to offer a broader range of examples. F. M. Alexander often meant that one should take into consideration the Primary Control and use his techniques of Inhibition (stopping, pausing, ceasing unwanted tension) and Direction (giving guiding orders to organize oneself in space) as a Means-Whereby.[23] But I think it is useful to remember we can broaden the spectrum of stopping and considering, so these next examples represent both using Alexander's principles, and also a bit of common sense and planning. I will present the situation, and then postulate on two possible outcomes, depending on whether one End-gains or uses a Means-Whereby.

• Situation: You ask your students to take hold of the jaw with both hands and gently move it up and down.[24]

End-gaining: The student manages the distance between head and hands in part by pulling his neck forward, thus moving his head closer to his hands, rather than by freeing his shoulders sufficiently to allow the hands to come all the way up to the jaw. The jaw is shaken, but the neck has become tense, as has the jaw, because of the misalignment of the head and neck.

Means-Whereby: The student stops a moment, remembers that the head/neck relation is important to maintain while moving the arms, Inhibits and Directs, asks for freedom in the shoulders while moving the hands to the jaw, and shakes a jaw that already seems free.

• Situation: Your students are to report to class with a sonnet memorized.

End-gaining: One student waits until the last minute and does a speed memorization as he arrives. When you ask to work with him on the same sonnet the following week, he can't remember it.

Means-Whereby: The student prepares the sonnet in multiple ways so that the meaning deepens as he learns it. Three years later he is asked last-minute to recite a sonnet at his sister's wedding, and the words flow out.

• Situation: You begin giving detailed instructions to a student for a new exercise.

End-gaining: The student begins before you have finished explaining the task.

Means-Whereby: The student waits until you have finished your instructions, thinks about what she needs to do to follow them, and then essays the task.

• Situation: You teach the students a new tongue twister.

End-gaining: The students are enjoying the challenge, but they are slumping in their chairs and crossing their legs.

Means-Whereby: The students are paying attention to the whole self, sitting on the sit-bones, soles of feet on the floor, Inhibiting and Directing as they work.

• Situation: Your agent phones, the last task before going on vacation, and gives you information about a casting call.

End-gaining: You excitedly scribble the details and slam down the phone. But your handwriting is illegible and when you're on your way to the audition, you realize can't

read your directions. Your agent is in flight; the office is closed. You miss your chance.

Means-Whereby: Before hanging up, you read the message back to the agent, and notice you realize you can't read your handwriting. You ask for information again, and this time, you write more slowly, reading everything back out loud to be sure you have it all correct. You get to the audition, cool, calm and collected.

• Situation: You must fit into that costume by opening night!

End-gaining: You go on a crash diet, and your energy wanes at rehearsals. You get frustrated and eat candy bars during tech week. You're two pounds up by opening night.

Means-Whereby: You start the slow process of eating nutritious foods and cutting back on the sugars and fats; you'll have to ask the costume department for an alteration, but you're feeling good, have lots of energy, and know by the end of this long run, they'll be taking in the costume again.

These examples point to the need to stop, look, and listen; plan ahead; remain open to new experience. In some ways, using the Means-Whereby follows old adages like "look before you leap;" "a stitch in time saves nine," and "an ounce of prevention is worth a pound of cure." We actually have been taught a lot about considering the right Means-Whereby; we also live in a society where this value is diminishing.

This is especially true when we consider vocal use in relation to Primary Control. During Alexander Technique lessons, one learns the significance of improving the head/ neck relationship. One learns to talk to oneself so as to stop the old habit. One learns to turn on spatial orientation, to guide the head forward and up. But faced with new stimuli, the old habits will return. Faced with pressures of wanting to be right, do well, get the job done, one may trigger tensions and a rushed approach in a flash. If one becomes conscious of the misuse, there is an opportunity to change. For me, this opportunity brings fresh choices,[25] and is well worth the time taken to learn this Technique that is now over one hundred years old.

Conclusion

The Alexander Technique is known as a method to manage performance anxiety and release habitual tensions. The relation of the head to the neck and the head and neck to the rest of the body, known as Primary Control, is a key element to improving vocal use. The habit of End-gaining will thwart any serious attempt to improve Primary Control, which can better be served by learning how to attain goals using the indirect Means-Whereby of Inhibition and Direction.

Voice Related Movement Studies

"End-gaining" and the "Means-Whereby": Discovering the best process to achieve goals of vocal training and pedagogy using the Alexander Technique by Ruth Rootberg

Notes

1. Alexander, *MSI*, 117.

2. The Alexander Technique was developed by Frederick Matthias Alexander (1869-1955), an aspiring actor, who suffered from respiratory ailments and recurrent hoarseness. He "cured" himself, and as he did so, discovered principles of human movement and behavior that he relied on to develop a technique using words and hands-on to teach people to consciously address habits of reactivity that interfere with coordination. For more detailed biographical information of F.M. Alexander and discussion of the Alexander Technique, please see Rootberg, op. cit., the references in this article, and the numerous websites on the subject via the Internet, starting with amsatonline.org.

3. This definition arises from an unpublished letter written by F. M. Alexander to Frank Pierce Jones, December 1945.

4. "...hyper-focus on the achievement of a goal at the expense of noticing *the means whereby* we achieve it."

5. "... man tends to become more and more a confirmed end-gainer, one who too often insists on gaining his end by any means, even at the risk of disaster, rather than take time to consider means whereby the end can be gained so as to ensure the best possible result." Alexander, *UCL*, 90.

6. "The situation is one that no teacher, be he ever so expert, can deal with satisfactorily, one from which the pupil cannot possibly be extricated, until he stops trying to get things right—stops, that is, working blindly for his *ends*, and gives thought instead to the new *means* given to him by his teacher, *whereby* his ends can be attained." Alexander, *CCC*, 88.

7. "It is also necessary to remember, when considering methods for the changing of thought and action and selecting the means whereby this change can be put into practice, that no one can be said to have really accepted a new idea or approved of the "means whereby" of putting it into practice, until he has actually had the experience himself of employing the procedures necessary for doing this." Alexander, *UCL*, 94.

8. "That in order to secure the results desired, it is essential to teach the pupil to rehearse the dictated orders, not to do exercises, i.e. to devote his attention to apprehending the instructions of his teacher—those means whereby he is to gain what he requires, and not, as he will be apt to do, to concentrate his thoughts upon the end sought." Alexander, "Re-Education of the Kinæsthetic Systems" (1908), *AL*, 83-84.

9. Inhibition and Direction, along with Conscious Awareness, are the primary tools of the Alexander Technique. Be assured that Inhibition, in this technique, refers to stopping unnecessary habits, pausing before doing, and releasing unwanted tension. It by no means refers to an emotional or bodily constriction of expression or behavior. Direction has dual meanings of giving oneself mental instructions, and awaking one's spatial thinking to organize in space.

10 . "The marvellous efficiency of the respiratory machine, when properly employed, becomes apparent when we realize that we have only to continue to employ the same *means whereby* we secure the increase (expansion) to secure the decrease (contraction) of the intra-thoracic capacity...." Alexander, *CCC*, 132-133.

11. "This pupil also is so intent on his 'end' (singing) that he finds it irksome to wait to take breath properly." Alexander, *CCC*, 108.

12. "...and gain my original end, in which case *I would continue to project the directions for maintaining the new use* to speak the sentence." Alexander, *UoS*, 46.

13. "The new 'means-whereby' are unfamiliar, and any attempt on his part to carry them out will be associated with experiences which feel wrong...." Alexander, *UCL*, 93.

14. "It constitutes the 'means whereby' of free and full expression...." Alexander, *MSI*, 86.

15. "To this end, the person concerned must learn to say 'No' to every stimulus to psycho-physical activity until he has taken time to consider what are the reasonable *means whereby* the end he desires can be achieved...." Alexander, *CCC*, 181.

16. "...I must continue this process in my practice for a considerable time before actually attempting to employ the new 'means-whereby' for the purpose of speaking." Alexander, *UoS*, 42.

17. The role of sensation as information, guiding force, and learning tool is a topic in itself, which I hope to address in a future essay. For the time being, I ask the reader to accept the premise that, while changing sensation may inform us of an improving situation, (just as it informs us through pain of a situation needing remedy) trying to recreate the same sensation may thwart continued learning and improvement.

18. "The pupil, thinking only of what his teacher asks him (the 'end') and desiring to do it right...at the cost of undue strain and disadvantage in the use of the organism." Alexander, *CCC*, 87.

19. "To begin with, the methods of training and education in which he is versed have developed in him a habit of end-gaining through a too quick and unthinking response to stimuli...." Alexander, *UCL*, 80.

20. "...it is difficult for anyone to grasp its [sic, principles and procedures of the Alexander Technique] full force without having actual demonstration of the principle in operation." Alexander, *CCC*, quote from John Dewey's Introduction, xxv.

21. "...that in most fields of activity man's craze is for speed and for the short view, because he has become possessed by the non-stop attitude and outlook: he is a confirmed end-gainer. ..." Alexander, *UCL*, 181.

22. "...*when a person has reached a given stage of unsatisfactory use and functioning, his habit of 'end-gaining' will prove to be the impeding factor in all his attempts to profit by any teaching method whatsoever.* Ordinary teaching methods, in whatever sphere, cannot deal with this impeding factor, indeed, they tend actually to encourage 'end-gaining.'" Alexander, *UoS*, 66-67.

23. "These means included the inhibition of the habitual use of the mechanisms of the organism, and the conscious projection of new directions necessary to the performance of the different acts involved in a new and more satisfactory use of these mechanisms." Alexander, *UoS*, footnote, 41.

Notes (continud)

24. Jaw work attributed to Kristin Linklater.

25. "It is conscious inhibition that creates the moment of choice for the actor in rehearsal and performance." Dowling, *The Stage*.

Bibliography

Alexander F.M. "Re-Education of the Kinæsthetic Systems" (1908). *Articles and Lectures*. London: Mouritz, 1995.

Alexander, F.M. *Constructive Conscious Control of the Individual (CCC)*. Mouritz, 2004.

Alexander, F.M. *Man's Supreme Inheritance (MSI)*. London: Mouritz, 1996.

Alexander, F. M. *The Universal Constant in Living (UCL)*. London: Mouritz, 2000.

Alexander, F.M. *The Use of the Self (UoS)*. London: Methuen, 1932.

DeVeer, Connie . "The Alexander Technique: Rehearsal Tools for Releasing the Actor's Voice," *The Moving Voice: Integration of Voice and Movement Studies* presented by the Voice and Speech Review, 2009.

Dowling, Niamh, "A different take on technique," *The Stage*, August 17, 2010, accessed October 4, 2010 from: http://www.thestage.co.uk/features/letters/feature.php/29283/a-different-take-on-technique.

Rootberg, Ruth. "The Relation of Head Balance to Vocal Use: An Alexander Technique Point of View," *Voice and Gender and other contemporary issues in voice and speech training*, presented by the Voice and Speech Review, 2007.

Cultural Crossover: Teaching from a Western Perspective in an Islamic Environment

Erica Tobolski is an Associate Professor at the University of South Carolina. She has coached voice, text and dialects for the Tony Award-winning Utah Shakespeare Festival (3 seasons), Charlotte Repertory Theatre, The Lost Colony, Clarence Brown Theatre, Istana Budaya (Malaysia) among others, and for the film *The Wise Kids*. Her work is published in T*he Complete Voice and Speech Workout* and in *The Voice and Speech Review* (2003, 2007, 2009). She was named a Teaching Fellow for the Center for Teaching Excellence at USC for Spring 2011. In 2008-09 she taught at Universiti Teknologi in Malaysia as Distinguished Visiting Professor.

Introduction

"Shall I compare thee to a summer's day?
Thou art more lovely and more temperate:
Rough winds do shake the darling buds of May,
And summer's lease hath all too short a date;"[1]

Imagine trying to explain "summer" to those who live at the equator. Barely have you finished that when you encounter "temperate", "buds of May", and why summer has "all too short a date." This is where I found myself–in a culture and place that was as far from my imagining as was "summer" to my students. Welcome to Malaysia.

On sabbatical from the University of South Carolina in 2008-2009, I accepted a one-year contract with Universiti Teknologi MARA as Distinguished Visiting Professor. There I taught several levels of Voice, Speech and Acting and coached *Mimpi*, an Indonesian/Malay translation of *A Midsummer Night's Dream*, at the National Theatre in Malaysia's capitol of Kuala Lumpur.

This year-long adventure was more than a cultural exchange; it was a cultural *blending*. I moved from foreign to familiar and the students had a similar experience. By the end we were able to meet in the middle and create a theatrical event that synthesized aspects of our individual cultures. In hindsight, what I expected from the experience and what came to be were radically different. Now, a year since my return, I have resumed my previous life but with profound changes in my perspectives on teaching and learning. This article will focus on three areas of fundamental cultural differences: 1. the role of religion; 2. language barriers; and 3. teaching and learning styles. In conclusion, I will focus on how these experiences have impacted my teaching since my return to the United States.

Shifting Cultures

Thirteen years ago, in 1997, I moved from the Midwest to the South and experienced a cultural shift within my own country. Religiosity and conservatism is more pronounced in South Carolina than in Indiana, even in the relatively "liberal" university setting of the University of South Carolina. My single prior visit to South Carolina in no way prepared me for the cultural differences I would encounter and later come to understand. Social interaction is highly valued, and from their early years, children are taught how to facilitate conversation. Honor, to family and country, is highly prized. A paternalistic viewpoint prevails, evidenced in the fact that South Carolina ranks last in the nation in the number of women who hold statewide office.[2] In addition to regional allegiance, religious values influence and guide behavior. The sheer number of churches is indicative of the prevalence of religious practice. I was constantly asked what church I belonged to, students regularly requested to replace "offensive" language in their scenes and monologues, and Sunday Blue Laws restricted store openings and even sale of certain items. When in the first week I was asked, rhetorically, "You're not from around here, are you?" I recalled that I had learned about "Yankees," "Carpetbaggers" and the Civil War from a Northern viewpoint. My understanding of the South had been colored by an early reading of *Gone with the Wind*. Only after spending time in the South did I sheepishly admit my earlier assumption of an all-encompassing "Southern Dialect." It took time to recognize the many nuanced regional and cultural differences that mark speakers state-by-state and even county-by-county. I stumbled more than a few times in negotiating social and professional interactions as I learned to interpret customs, mores and linguistic usage that were different from those I had learned in the Midwest. A common language, the prevalence of Christian-based religions and a shared nationality led me to expect more commonality between U.S. regions, not less. In the ensuing years I have come to understand the extent to which pride, identification with home region, and cultural mores define a society.

These lessons revealed the wide scope of the work of encountering and adapting to a different community. Knowing that a 1,000-mile move within one country necessitated learning a new culture, I thought I realized the extent of preparation needed to live and work halfway around the world. In order to prepare for this experience, I researched the country I was about to enter. I read about the culture, the history and religion and tried to learn *Bahasa Malayu* (Malaysian Language). Malaysia is considered "moderate" in practice and custom among Islamic countries, particularly as compared to Islamic countries of the Middle East, such as Saudi Arabia and Afghanistan. While Islam is the official religion practiced by the vast majority of the country's citizens, other religions, notably, Buddhism, Hinduism and Catholicism, are also freely practiced.

Two excellent sources to consult before visiting any country are the *Culture Shock* series by Marshall Cavendish Editions and *The Art of Crossing Cultures* by Craig Storti. *Culture Shock! Malaysia* provides an overview for people who plan to spend an extended amount of time in that country beyond that of the typical tourist. It details customs for greeting, eating, dressing and more. In contrast with how casual American dress and customs have become, the sheer number of rules and guidelines for Malaysia were more than a little daunting. *The Art of Crossing Cultures* is written for the expatriate in any country and explains why adapting to another culture is so difficult and how to decrease that difficulty. Knowing intellectually that there will be some necessary psychological adjustment is not the same as negotiating the actual encounter with the new culture. It was helpful to learn that nearly everyone finds herself or himself going through a similarly disorienting process as "the foreigner." The feeling of frustration brought about by not being in control and losing all that is familiar is an experience common to travelers and was part of my experience teaching in Malaysia.

Negotiating the New

The university at which I taught was restricted to Muslim Malays and Bumiputra, the Malay word to describe the indigenous peoples.[3] In the context of my democratic sensibilities, I was shocked to find out that only Muslim students could attend the government-run universities free of charge (or nearly so); Chinese-Malays and Indian-Malays were required to pay for their education, and at much costlier private schools. This was one of many constitutional policies created by the Muslim-dominated government in order to ensure that Muslim-Malays maintain their rights and privileges in a multi-cultural country. These policies ensure preferential treatment for Muslim-Malays by providing more opportunities in employment, education and in reduced costs for housing.[4] Muslims themselves call it "reverse discrimination."

My efforts to gather information about the specific requirements of teaching at the University, including the type and number of classes, were not fruitful. In fact, I didn't know my class assignments until halfway through the first week of classes. Planning ahead and receiving information far in advance, I discovered, is a particularly Western practice. Given that my contract was not finalized until the month before classes began and plane tickets only arrived the week before departure this lack of organization should have been less surprising to me. My Malaysian colleagues probably wondered why this American was so obsessed with confirming every little detail of her appointment. I made a guess that I would teach some levels of acting, voice and speech and packed books and teaching materials accordingly. I tried in vain to find out what level the students were at in their studies: Had they had a previous voice class? What levels and/or styles of acting had they taken? The answers to these questions would soon become secondary to the more fundamental question, "Do they understand enough English to follow what I'm teaching?"

To an outsider, Malaysia is a land of contradictions. I had read that touching is taboo, and so was surprised to discover that students line up at the beginning and end of class to take your hand and touch it to their foreheads while saying "Good morning, Prof," and "Thank you, Prof." I found this behavior uncomfortably self-deprecating, but their intention was to show honor and respect. I initially perceived as disrespectful the students' chronic lateness but I discovered that, as a rule, punctuality doesn't carry the same significance as in Western culture. Malays regard time as flexible and beyond one's control; to rush or hurry is to lack grace (Abdullah and Pedersen, 2003, 81-83).

In my first month of teaching I encountered chronic lateness and accidentally stumbled upon the reason. Classes were scheduled back-to-back with no time for transition. Additionally, students asked to be released from class to work on extra-curricular projects. I explained that if we lost class time we would have to make it up; the entire three-hour class was necessary to accomplish certain goals. We agreed to begin class 10 minutes later in order to accommodate their schedule and the situation served to introduce to the students that time could be viewed as a commodity. Eventually the students grew to understand my expectations concerning focus and attendance and were more fully present in the class. By contrast, I came to understand the students' expectations of me in my role as their teacher.

Malaysian society is hierarchical and relationship-oriented rather than task-oriented. Malaysian professors are held in high esteem and interaction between students and teachers tends to be more formal than that found in American universities. I found this difference initially disorienting,

Cultural Crossover: Teaching from a Western Perspective in an Islamic Environment
by Erica Tobolski

but after several weeks, I learned to balance the role of authority figure with the more casual manner I conveyed in the U.S. This was accomplished by being more direct with feedback, but taking time to discuss differences between eastern and western cultures and theatre practices and answer their questions about American students, universities and ways of life.

Religion

After thirteen years in the American South I thought I had adjusted to the degree to which conservatism and religion influence life in that region. However, I was unprepared for the level of fundamentalism that permeated the Malaysian culture, despite its multi-ethnicity and religious tolerance. Islam permeates daily life, influencing what you hear, see and encounter. Lest you don't have a watch, the *azan*, or call to prayer, is broadcast on speakers loud enough to be heard indoors or out. The limited availability of foods considered *haram*, or non-halal, is further emphasized by their placement in the store. Forbidden items containing pork or alcohol are sequestered in a far corner with their own register as to avoid offending Muslim clerks who may have to handle these items. Religious sensibilities ensure that all religious based holidays be officially observed, including Muslim, Hindu, Buddhist and Christian celebrations. Islam, derived from the Arabic word meaning "peace" and "submission," in particular provides its followers with a guide for every aspect of their lives.[5] This is very different from a secular society like the United States, which separates church from state. Further, Western thought subscribes to a belief in reason and science, giving rise to questions and ambiguity.

As mentioned above, the students I taught were primarily of the Islamic religion. Of the 70 students I taught over two semesters, three were Catholic and belonged to one of several indigenous tribes on the island of Borneo. Animism predates both Islam and Catholicism, the undercurrents of which still guide certain beliefs and superstitions. A particularly revealing example was relayed by a student in the Stage Management program: at his birth, his grandmother asked his mother what profession she would prefer for her son; when his mother replied "lawyer" the grandmother buried a dictionary and an old laptop computer with the placenta. This folk belief prevailed even within an orthodox Muslim family in which the father has two wives (up to four wives are permitted based on Muhammad's practice).

The university at which I taught was a state-run school and as such religion influenced everything from scheduling to pedagogical approaches. Prayer times directly affect the scheduling of classes and rehearsals. One requirement of Islam is prayer five times a day, the first roughly an hour before sunrise, the last approximately an hour after sun-

set, signaled by the ever-present *azan*. Mosques or prayer rooms are everywhere, including on campus, in restaurants and at rest stops along the highways. If classes or rehearsals are scheduled during the afternoon prayer time, it is understood that students may excuse themselves to pray. At the time, I found this disruptive as it interfered with my need to stay focused on the task at hand. In hindsight, taking a break to focus on something other than work has its merits. Understanding that the day revolves around enforced breaks also helps explain to the Westerner the Malaysian concept of time being fluid and not always in one's control.

The Islamic calendar has a major influence during the religious observance of Ramadan, or the Fasting Month. Based on the Islamic lunar calendar, Ramadan changes from month to month each year. In 2008, it fell in September. Here is an account from that time:

> During the month of Ramadan, Muslims fast from the first call to prayer at about 5:30 AM, until sundown, roughly 12 hours. I meet my Voice/Speech class at 4 PM. They drag themselves in, weary and bleary-eyed. I usually remind students to constantly drink water to keep their bodies and vocal folds hydrated but even that is forbidden during fasting. I continue with enthusiasm, simultaneously encouraging and challenging. As Arthur Lessac would say "*Now* we're cooking with gas" (Tobolski, 2008).

Fasting is a real sacrifice. Despite the difficulty, or maybe because of it, there is a bonding, much like what happens when people are thrown into an emergency. From this, I understood a bit more about Islam and the solidarity it engenders. Several students and even one colleague asked if I was going to fast with them. At the time I was confused by their question; because they knew I wasn't a Muslim I took it as proselytizing. I later saw it as an invitation to join them in a special event, and view it as evidence that I was accepted despite my Western and Christian upbringing.

Islam also guides self-presentation, with modesty expected in both manners and dress. At the university, a dress code was enforced that required students to adhere to traditional Muslim mores. Both men and women are to dress modestly, showing less skin than their Western counterparts and avoiding form-fitting clothing. In Malaysia women can choose whether or not to wear the *tudung*, or headscarf, though all but two faculty members always covered their hair. The traditional *baju kurung*, or "cage dress" is a loose-fitting tunic with long sleeves that is worn over an ankle-length skirt. Among the students, Western-style dress is widely worn. In studio classes, theatre students of both sexes wear t-shirts and long stretch pants and women rarely wear *tudung*. One morning I began class and a student was late. Apparently he was avoiding the campus guards, posted to hand out fine-carrying tickets for not adhering to the even more restrictive dress code on "professional dress" days. Another dress code incident came about at the end of one of my classes. A female student was last to leave and pulled out of her bag what looked to be small leg warmers and proceeded to draw them over her arms. Stupefied, I asked her if she was cold (in itself a silly question as it is 95° F and 85% humidity every day). "No," she replied, "we are not allowed to show our bare arms on campus." Unaware of this, I had been wearing short-sleeved t-shirts for weeks. "I think it is OK for foreign lecturers," she assured me. Having received no reproach for my style of dress, I concluded that I was permitted a certain level of tolerance in my attire. Less obvious was sorting out the level of communication in my classes.

Language Barrier

Prior to arrival, I was told that the students knew English and that all classes were taught in English.[6] This was a relief, as I knew I would not have an interpreter and my attempts to learn the Malaysian language resulted in minimal acquisition. What I didn't know was the students' level of fluency and how this would impact communication.

Without an interpreter, students who had a better grasp of English and a larger vocabulary acted as unofficial translators for the others. This led me to simplify and edit my vocabulary. I used more gestures, listened more closely, avoided shorthand phrases or jargon and instead focused on the fundamental meaning behind key concepts. I made a note to remember this lesson when I returned to the American classroom: Just because we share a language doesn't automatically insure that the concept is clear.

The following is writing I did during the first semester:

Training students in Malaysia, where English is the second language (and a distant second for many) has been challenging. Concepts must be simplified and nothing can be taken for granted. I am a more careful listener than I was with students in the U.S, both because their English is accented and to judge whether or not they understand my words and instructions. Lacking a translator, I am more aware of the words I choose. Phrases such as "connect to the thoughts," "stay in the moment," and "work on telling the story" are simply words that do not translate beyond their literal, dictionary meaning. Watching the students react to these comments and listening to their response—what they think the phrase means—is humbling and I have begun to ask myself, "What do I really mean?"

Some of my students are in the last semester of their three-year Diploma (loosely equivalent to an undergraduate degree) program. We work on poems, which I chose based on their length, but the greater challenge is obvious now: How do I, with my limited knowledge of *Bahasa Malayu*, explain the nuance of heightened language when my students struggle with English? So, off we go into conceits and uncommon words, chosen by the poet for their sound and specificity. I question whether or not metaphor is cross-cultural. Understanding "noble maladies" or "holy dread," starts with defining "noble" and "dread." Explaining irony and antithesis is complicated; the word "opposites" doesn't quite capture it, so I say, "They are two words that you don't usually find together-- they push up against each other (demonstrating with my fists). It's like the Durian[7]: It's the most wonderful tasting fruit with the most terrible smell."

I've found a new love of my language with its countless words, each with its own shade of meaning. I want the students find the essence of a line, but they struggle with translating the words, let alone understanding the illuminated image...when the students "get it" we celebrate, although I'm not exactly sure what it is that they are getting. However, I have no doubt that this sharpening of my listening and evaluative skills will be helpful when I return to teaching in the United States.

The students have an inherent understanding of rhythm, however, no doubt due to early exposure to the gamelan orchestra...(the) Lessac Consonant Orchestra makes sense to them and they join the scat band with abandon!

For their final project I take a chance, altering the original assignment to perform the assigned poems in English. After all, I didn't want the primary lesson to be about English articulation. I have them translate their poems into Malay and then incorporate the (Lessac) Body Energies into a full physical and vocal performance. Their creativity and enthusiasm in this project assures me that it was a chance well taken. They are more comfortable in their native Malay and can therefore fully embody the meaning of the poems (Tobolski, 2009).

"Work within the context" was the most important lesson I learned from this experience. Not knowing what I would find in terms of the students' level of English, or their understanding of my Western methodologies of vocal production or text interpretation, I plunged in with what I knew. Along the way, I determined to the best of my ability what the students understood and adjusted my expectations and methods of delivery accordingly. What surprised me were the differences in sensibility to language. The Malaysian students in general were more comfortable with sound, rhythm and music. It was not uncommon to hear people walking down the hallway or street singing a tune. When given freedom to incorporate musical instruments, song and movement that drew on their traditional performance techniques they worked in a scale and style much larger than their American counterparts.

Here is another incident concerning language, this one from a class of the more advanced Degree students:

> In my acting class one day, I went on about the richness and inherent challenge of Shakespeare...Su, a quick, attentive student jumps in at the name recognition, reciting, "Shall I compare thee to a summer's day? Thou art more lovely and more temperate..." I finish the next few lines, "Rough winds do shake the darling buds of May, and summer's lease hath all too short a date." She says she performed the poem in English but wasn't quite sure how to convey the meaning of the lines. I launch into an explanation, realizing that the lack of seasons in Malaysia, which is 3° north of the equator, must hinder her understanding. "Shakespeare came from England," I say, "where for much of the year, the earth is brown and barren. But then spring arrives with a riot of color—much like you have here all year round with the flowers and orchids. Summer only lasts a few months and then it all dies, leaving it brown and barren again." I see them trying to picture it, but given my own experience could I imagine Malaysia before I arrived? I saw pictures, but that doesn't do justice to the feel of moisture on your skin, the hundred shades of green, the call to prayer emanating from the mosque five times a day or the smells of curry alongside burning trash. How do we understand that which we have not experienced? This is the question that arises when we cross cultures in theatre training (Tobolski, 2008).

It is an understatement that language difficulties and conceptual references proved a formidable challenge in teaching abroad. As an acting teacher with a specialization in voice and speech, words are both my work and my passion. Those that teach skills of encountering and illuminating words wrestle for deep communication. I discovered, however, that language is but one element in the cultural landscape. Less obvious, but perhaps more influential, are the underlying values and assumptions that guide and shape people's behavior. The vastly different value systems between North America and Southeast Asia made for a steep learning curve on my part.

Teaching/Learning Styles

In Malaysia, hierarchy is all-important. Superiors and elders are respected and not questioned. If a Muslim has made the pilgrimage to Mecca, they include *Haji* (male) or *Hajah* (female) as one of their titles. Other honors or inherited positions are similarly noted. Teachers, or *gurus* are more highly valued in Malaysian society than in the United States and this creates a teacher-student relationship where status is rigidly enforced. Students are instructed to call their "lecturers" with a title such as Mr., Mrs. or Prof. and automatically confer respect. This explains the bowing to the hand gesture described earlier. Even lower-ranking lecturers find it necessary to address older or more advanced faculty with a title (such as Professor) rather than by name only. Compare this with a growing trend in American universities to treat students as "the customer" who pays an enormous sum for their education and you get a sense of the nearly insurmountable contrast between these two cultures.

Although the respect and appreciation is a welcome element, the downside is the Malaysian student's reluctance to speak out for fear of appearing defiant or giving the wrong answer. A U.S. colleague who had recently taught in Japan remarked that offering one's opinion was a risky prospect on the part of the student and that she had to wait three times as long for a response. Individualism is neither encouraged nor practiced to the extent that it is the West. American teaching philosophy in particular has encouraged individualism and independent thinking. In many Asian cultures, the group is more important than the individual, in order to engender harmony and solidarity (Abdullah and Pedersen, 2003, 67-71). In an early email to a colleague I wrote of the differences in teaching styles. Having observed three separate classes in traditional dance performance, I understood the model to be that of master/apprentice. The master demonstrates and the student copies each move. This approach would likely explain why students were uncomfortable with my inquiry-based teaching.

In the U.S., I have found that students are much more apt to offer their opinion and contribute to discussion in the classroom. Teachers tend to encourage personal feedback, in part to gauge the efficacy of a particular exercise and also to encourage reflection and thought processes on the part of the student. Contrast this with the Malaysian concept of "saving face" or avoiding embarrassment and you can imagine the silence I encountered the first time I asked, "What did you discover after that vocal exploration?" The Malay students also had little experience with the Socratic method of teaching. By the second semester they were much more comfortable with my approach and were finding their voice in the creative process.

Traditionally, much of Malaysian schooling is based on rote learning: listening to instruction and taking tests. Assessment is largely based on marks received. In a conversation with one of my fellow lecturers, he explained that the university was trying to teach students to think for themselves, to develop and execute original ideas. It was difficult, he said, because this was not the method employed in primary and secondary school. From his explanation, I discovered that the first formal learning experience of Muslim children is reciting the Qu'ran. The process is this: around the age of four or five you go to the house of the teacher, usually someone who lives in the neighborhood; you listen to the sounds and repeat the prayers and verses. However, the words are in Arabic, so learning is at this point a memorization of sounds without specific meaning. Only when you begin formal schooling do you begin to learn Arabic and thus gain greater understanding of the meaning behind what you've been saying.

Islamic based values helped explain experiences I encountered in the classroom, including the status of the teacher and the role of the student. It was a combination of differing values and performance traditions that led to the difficulty of introducing a Stanislavsky-based acting style in an acting class. The students in the advanced class worked on monologues from contemporary plays, including *The Cherry Orchard*. Questions from the students initially revolved around external manifestations such as the character's gestures, facial expressions and tone of voice. They had no system for determining psychological motivation based on text and given circumstances. A student working on the role of Lyubov started the session describing the character as overly emotional and a bit "crazy." Walking her through the character's experiences, I introduced the concepts of "what if" and personalization. The student seemed quite affected by this new understanding and decided that Lyubov wasn't so easily defined. Lyubov wasn't a good or a bad character who deserved judgment, but was more human, ambiguous.

The traditional performing arts of Malaysia center around folk tales and legends, many based on stories from the *Mahabharata* and *Ramayana* (Yousof, 2004, 78) as expressed in the dance performance of *Mak Yong* and *Menora* and the *Wayang Kulit* (Shadow Puppets).

Historically these per-

Wayang Kulit characters: Seri Rama and Hanouman

formance styles were not based in 20th and 21st century realism; characters, until recently, behave because they are "good" or "bad" rather than for psychologically motivated reasons. Students in Malaysia are exposed to film, one of the biggest exports of the Western Hemisphere, and have been influenced by English drama and dramatic literature since the English rule from the 1890s to 1957. However, psychological realism as a basis for acting is not a familiar concept in Malaysia. Regardless of the acting style or styles Western trainers employ, part of our (Western) cultural understanding includes an awareness of the work of psychologist Sigmund Freud and subsequent theories on psychological motivation.

In the advanced class I concluded the semester with scenes from *The Glass Menagerie*. I was reminded once again of the difficulty in speaking a second language, let alone acting in it. I discovered that the students' command of English did not allow them to think spontaneously in English so that they were most likely thinking in Malay but saying the lines in English. This was not the sort of task I had set out to teach. Fortunately, I had a second semester in which to learn from my beginner's mistakes. Differences in language, learning/teaching styles and religious custom were not obstacles to overcome but provided context from which to learn. I came to the realization that acquiring skill sets was important but not more so than learning about, and from, each other.

A Second Semester, A Second Chance

Shifting one's viewpoint is a chance to re-evaluate and reconsider what one already knows, whether or not one goes abroad. I hoped that the students I taught learned something about acting and voice, but more importantly, I wanted them to take ownership for their work and think for themselves.

With the advanced students I introduced mask work and improvisation. This provided an opportunity to rely on impulse and active play with a partner. The spontaneity required for this work is counter to the kind of mimicry I observed in some of the traditional performance classes. It taught them the kind of problem-solving and creative thinking that I believe is the hallmark of advanced education. Discussion and analysis became easier as they became more comfortable expressing themselves in English and they trusted

Voice Related Movement Studies
Cultural Crossover: Teaching from a Western Perspective in an Islamic Environment
by Erica Tobolski

that I would respond to their comments without judgment. Initially I avoided any sort of touching in the classroom, save for the students' respectful "handshake." Instead of my usual hands-on assistance with breathing or alignment I had students feel their ribs for themselves. In the second semester, I gradually returned to using more hands-on instruction, primarily with the advanced students and always with permission first (as I do in the U.S.). No one seemed uncomfortable and I was able to assist them in finding more freedom with their body and voice.

With the help of a colleague, I located plays that had both Malay and English translations. These ranged from contemporary plays by Malaysian playwrights to Euripides' *Medea*. This proved to be much more valuable for the students who could then focus on putting acting skills into practice as opposed to struggling with language translation.

During this second semester, I also served as voice and acting coach for a student production of *A Midsummer Night's Dream* that had been translated into Indonesian, a language nearly identical to Malaysian.

The author coaching Mimpi

Directed by Jim O'Connor, another Distinguished Professor from the U.S. who was a member of the faculty that year, the production was presented at the National Theatre in Kuala Lumpur. We endeavored to introduce the element of psychological motivation into the playing of *A Midsummer Night's Dream* while at the same time drawing from traditional Malaysian performance styles. It was a challenge for both the actors and us as we were initially bound by our respective approaches to theatre.

As discussed above, the realistic acting style that is so familiar in American universities is a bit of a mystery in Asia. The students in Malaysia are certainly influenced by films from all countries, many of which are performed in a realistic style. However, the primary methodology in the traditional Malaysian performing arts is to imitate rather than create. More than one student asked me what film to study in order to play their role. For example, after two weeks of working on the meaning of her lines, the student playing Puck asked me if she should watch *Snow White and the Seven Dwarves* in order to learn how to play her role. I was mystified as to why she thought this would be a good choice, but maybe dwarves were close enough to Titania's band of faeries? The director and I discovered after the fact that nearly all the students had watched the 1999 film version of *A Midsummer Night's Dream*. After initially lamenting their action, we decided that it was in fact useful as it clarified the narrative for them. We could then move on to teaching the more interesting concepts of playing actions vs. emotions and character vs. caricature.

Coaching sessions focused on finding text-based choices and translating written words into physical action. Shakespeare was a challenge for the students even though the play had been translated into Indonesian/Malay. "These words are so difficult, " exclaimed one student, "can't we change them into something more modern?" I laughed, explaining that my American students experienced a similar struggle, despite the fact that English was their first language. This reassured them that the difficulty was not based on a deficiency with English and gave them confidence to continue. A particularly enlightening session came about when I had the students perform their scenes in gibberish. They knew what the scene was about but it was not revealed by their behavior. Gibberish illuminated relationship and action immediately. Afterward, one of the students put it succinctly when he said "Oh, in acting you want us to be honest!"

Mimpi rehearsal: characters of Titania and Bottom

There are strict Islamic rules governing gender roles. One is required to dress and behave according to the social expectations for men and women. Given that homosexuality is strictly prohibited in the Islamic religion we wondered if this would necessitate a change in Shakespeare's cross-dressing character of Flute/Thisbe in the play-within-the-play. However, having seen *Mak Yong*, a traditional Malaysian dance performance, invariably there is a male dancer playing a female role to hilarious laughter. The strict social roles might in fact account for the audience's enjoyment of cross-dressing characters; it is an acceptable outlet. Given the precedence for this type of character on the stage we kept the scene intact. The actor portraying Thisbe played it very broadly but with complete commitment. It was very funny but also very touching. The production as a whole sought to blend Eastern and Western elements and this was reflected by using traditional Malaysian costumes for the court, traditional and contemporary dance pieces and a score that was played with a band of live musicians, blending gamelan instruments with electric guitar and keyboard. Judging from the audience reaction, Shakespeare successfully transcended both time and culture.

Mimpi characters Hippolyta and Theseus in traditional Malaysian costume

Perhaps the most rewarding moments were at the closing performance. I dared, some nine months after arriving in Malaysia, to wear my comparatively revealing knee-length dress for the first time. I figured that the students and faculty knew me well enough to not judge me as a loose *orang puteh*, or white person. They did they tease me, to my surprise, with calls of "ooh, sexy, Prof!" but later were much more serious when they asked, "Prof, can I hug you?" The impact of how we had affected one another was apparent; we had moved from a formal handshake to an embrace. And when the students said, "I'm going to miss you, Prof," I replied without hesitation, "I'm going to miss you, too." Even more surprising was the next statement from the students: "I love you, Prof." It was at this point that I moved

from being an outsider to being part of the family. This cultural exchange was far deeper than either group expected or thought possible. In the end, my Malaysian students surprised me with their ability to move beyond their own cultural restraints: they learned to be bold, industrious and demonstrative. I learned to be more flexible with time and expectations and discovered that relationship need not be separated from leadership.

Effects on Current Teaching

Now that I have returned to the United States, I see how my teaching has shifted after spending a year abroad. In Malaysia I found myself to be an unofficial ambassador of the United States and Western culture; in return, I now take the opportunity to introduce American students to the wider world. The students in my class know how to say "Selamat pagi," or "Good Morning" in Malay, and have added Malay tongue twisters[8] to their warm-up. They are introduced to the traditional Malay performing arts such as *Wayang Kulit* or Shadow Puppet play in order to expose them to the virtuosity of the *Dalang*, or Shadow Puppet Master, who performs the multiple facets of the production, alternately or simultaneously singing, voicing 15-20 characters, handling the puppets and conducting the gamelan orchestra. The classroom tenor is now more universal, less apt to focus solely on the voice, speech or acting lesson of the day but includes current events and people in order to broaden the context.

In Malaysia, I learned to share more about my background and myself and found that this engendered the students' trust. In the past I had perhaps focused more on the work to avoid a preponderance of "war stories." Students want to know about their professors' professional work and outside experiences; such dialogue has a necessary place in education.

Operating successfully in a foreign culture requires expert listening skills and the classroom is no different. Assessing what is being conveyed verbally and non-verbally provides an opportunity to understand the situation and shape the outcome. Since my return to the U.S. I am more attuned to the students' level of comprehension, which has led to greater flexibility on my part. Following an intuitive decision to alter a final project in my first semester at Universiti Teknologi MARAproved to be a good choice. If an approach doesn't work, change it. Improvisation is a life-skill as much as an acting skill.

Malaysian teachers are revered in status, if not in monetary awards. This was a pleasant surprise and reminded me of the power to affect students' lives, despite the increasingly ambiguous attitudes and practices toward education in the United States. In the American classroom, this has translated into stronger leadership on my part. I am more willing to assume a leadership role rather than that of "knowledgeable guide." Guiding and encouraging will always be a primary teaching style, though now it is accompanied by a renewed sense of authority.

Today, I do not take understanding for granted. The students in the United States may have heard or encountered words such as "temperate" and "darling" in Shakespeare's sonnet but understanding is not automatic. I have learned to take more time in teaching students how to access meaning. I am more direct in my explanations, looking to simplify without reducing a concept. I encourage students even more to resist the desire to gratify instantly, to check it off the list, to "get it right," and instead to process the work, consider the possibilities and to honor the difficulty and joy of expressing oneself in language.

Upon returning to the United States, I was struck by the dichotomy in physical and emotional transparency between each culture. Malaysian students dressed modestly and revealed little skin in direct proportion to their emotional openness and comparative naiveté. They lack the outward sophistication and often accompanying cynicism displayed in the U.S. Conversely, American students tend to mask their insecurities and are reluctant to express their emotional lives, yet are quite willing to wear revealing clothing. The increasing lack of interpersonal communication I see in the U.S. has strengthened my goal of teaching students greater vocal and verbal expression, both in the context of theatre and in their lives.

On a personal level (but not exclusive of the academy) was an unexpected realization: that being in control and self-determinism is a two-way street. It sets up an expectation that you can be successful and accomplish goals. It can also lead to a false sense of control. I learned from my Malaysian experiences that one is not always, or maybe even rarely, in control, particularly when outside your own culture. What was once frustrating and puzzling became an opportunity to "let go." "It will be what it will be," was my mantra. Initially this was hard to practice. I willingly took the responsibility that came with making choices. Giving up control felt like giving up responsibility. Today, I continue to practice this balance between willfulness and flexibility. The sense of "family" and relationship are part of who I am in the classroom, not separate from it. I will continue to encounter difficulties but I have learned from my time in Malaysia to listen more closely, look beyond the surface and suspend judgment. Some answers are revealed in their own time and not according to our egocentric schedule.

Afterword
In addition to the wide range of teaching and production experiences, I have forged collaborative projects with several of my Malaysian colleagues on traditional Malay theatrical forms of dance performance styles of Mak Yong and Menora and on Wayang Kulit, or Shadow Puppet theatre. Currently I am working with Maszalida Hamzah, faculty member in film studies at the Universiti Teknologi MARA, on the vocal dynamics of the Dalang, or Puppet Master of Wayang Kulit. The article "The Voice" was presented at a conference in Rome, Italy in December 2009, the first of many anticipated articles exploring the Dalang's vocal dynamics and how prosody and paralinguistics intersect with character and audience. Future projects include blending of east and west performance training techniques and faculty/student exchange.

Bibliography

Print Media
Abdullah, Asma and Paul B. Pederson, *Understanding Multicultural Malaysia*. Selangor, Malaysia: Prentice Hall, 2003.

Brooks, Geraldine, *Nine Parts of Desire: the Hidden World of Islamic Women*. New York: Anchor Books, 1994.

Chekov, Anton, trans. Curt Columbus, *Chekov: The Four Major Plays*. Chicago: Ivan R. Dee: 2005.

Hodge, Alison, Ed., *Twentieth Century Actor Training*. London & New York: Routledge, 2000.

Jamal, Datuk Syed Ahmad, Ed., *The Encyclopedia of Malaysia, Volume 14: Crafts and the Visual Arts*. Singapore: Archipelago Press, 2007.

Munan, Heidi, *Culture Shock! Malaysia*. Singapore: Marshall Cavendish International (Asia) Pte Ltd, 2005.

Richmond, Simon, Damian Harper, Tom Parkinson, Charles Rawlings-Way and Richard Watkins, *Malaysia, Singapore and Brunei*. Oakland, CA: Lonely Planet Publications Pty Ltd: 2007.

Shakespeare, William, *A Midsummer Night's Dream*. London: Thompson Learning, 2006.

Storti, Craig, *The Art of Crossing Cultures*. Yarmouth, ME: Intercultural Press, 1989.

Yousof, Prof. Dr. Ghulam-Sarwar, Ed., *The Encyclopedia of Malaysia, Volume 8: Performing Arts*. Singapore: Archipelago Press, 2004.

Vendler, Helen, *The Art of Shakespeare's Sonnets*. Cambridge, MA: The Belknap Press of Harvard University Press, 1997.

Williams, Tennessee, *The Glass Menagerie*. New York: Dramatists Play Service, 1975.

Electronic Media
20th Century Fox. *A Midsummer Night's Dream*,1999.

http://islam.about.com/

http://www.carolinalive.com/news/story.aspx?id=566558

http://chronicle.augusta.com/stories/2009/07/06/met_529981.shtml

http://www.lessacinstitute.com/

http://en.wikipedia.org/wiki/Politics_of_Malaysia

Tobolski, Erica, "Finding Voice in Southeast Asia." *Lessac Buzz Newsletter*, Vol. 6, issue 1, Spring 2009.

Tobolski, Erica, "Twelve Hours and Half a World Away." *URTA Update Newsletter*, Fall 2008.

Pronunciation, Phonetics, Linguistics, Dialect/Accent Studies

Erik Singer, Associate Editor

Erik Singer teaches and coaches voice, speech and accents. He has taught speech, phonetics and accents at the Mason Gross School of the Arts at Rutgers University, and voice, speech and accents at HB Studio in New York. Erik has also provided the voice for numerous television and radio commercials, documentaries, animated shows, and best-selling audiobooks. He is the Associate Editor for the "Pronunciation, Phonetics, Linguistics, Dialect/Accent Studies" section of the *Voice and Speech Review*. He is a graduate of the Webber Douglas Academy of Dramatic Art in London and of Yale University.

The wonderfully unwieldy name of this section (known within *VSR* as PPLD/AS [ˈpəpələˌdɑs]) is quite a breadbasket. Each of the titular areas of inquiry could fill a journal in its own right, and some do—there are more than a few journals devoted to phonetics and linguistics, certainly. And so any given edition of PPLD/AS can never hope to do more than gesture towards the infinite universe of possible investigations. This section is particularly well-suited, however, to the theme of the current issue. "A World of Voice" lends itself, for example, to examinations of language variation across cultural, linguistic, socioeconomic, and ethnic groups. Three of the articles in this issue may fairly be said to engage with this subject, albeit in very different ways. Rebekah Maggor's "International Speakers" describes a novel alternative to traditional "accent reduction," based on her experience working with non-native English speaking professors at Harvard University on improving their English-language communication and presentation skills. Sociolinguist Jaclyn Ocumpaugh's "Regional Variation and Mexican American English," reviews and summarizes the literature regarding accent variation within Mexican American English, examines the evidence for regional

variation within these populations, and asks how these regional patterns interact with the prevailing local "White" accents. And Louis Colaianni's "Bearing the Standard" bravely tackles some of the thornier issues surrounding accent variation in American primary and secondary education, politics and all.

A different type of accent variation—what linguists call diachronic variation, change over time, as opposed to synchronic variation, variety across or between populations at a given moment in time—is the subject of Paul Meier's two-part interview with linguist David Crystal. Crystal, who has painstakingly reconstructed the phonology of Elizabethan English, collaborated with Meier on a 2010 University of Kansas production of *A Midsummer Night's Dream*—the first US production to be presented in "Original Pronunciation."

The final article in the current issue is concerned not with accent variation, but rather with the reverse: accent standardization. Eleven years ago, the very first *VSR* was titled *Standard Speech*. The centerpiece of the issue was a debate between Dudley Knight (the current Editor-in-Chief), and several disciples and partisans of the late Edith Skinner. To vastly simplify the debate, Knight proposed to do away with the prevailing pedagogy and philosophy of speech training for actors, even going so far as to suggest abandoning altogether the teaching of *any* "standard" speech pattern. The others disagreed, standing by the models and methods of Skinner and her "Good American Speech." Both sides were passionate in their advocacy. Now, ten years on from that original issue of VSR, as Michael Barnes explains in his article "Standard Speech Practices and Pedagogy: a Snapshot of the Moment," the time seems ripe to revisit the subject. How many teachers have been persuaded by Knight and other proponents of newer, less prescriptive pedagogies? How many still base their teaching on Skinner? (The percentage ten or fifteen years ago was probably close to 100%.) How many view themselves as occupying territory somewhere in between these two poles? The answers to these questions have important implications for actor training and for American theatre. To some extent, they reflect, and perhaps even influence, the culture as a whole. Though the survey's methodology, and therefore the results, were not scientific, Barnes offers a valuable sense of where the field stands today. I would be remiss if I did not mention that special thanks is due to all those speech teachers who took the time to provide thorough and thoughtful answers to Barnes' survey.

In an ideal world, this issue of *VSR* would also include pieces describing the history and current state of "standard speech" issues in other countries, both Anglophone and otherwise. It is my hope that future issues will include such articles.

Finally, I should mention that one of the enduring goals of this section is to build bridges to other fields and disciplines whose areas of inquiry overlap with those of voice and speech professionals. And once again, "A World of Voice" provides the cue, and the injunction, to continue the work of building these bridges. The subdiscipline of linguistics known as *sociolinguistics*, which takes as its special subject language and accent variation across social and ethnic boundaries, has an enormous amount to offer. Many theatre and film accent coaches already avail themselves of the rich insights of sociolinguistics. As a rigourous academic discipline, however, it can sometimes seem innaccessible, recondite, or jargon-filled. Our sociolinguistic contributor, Jaclyn Ocumpaugh, in her article on Mexican American accent variation, has taken great care to explain many of the terms and conventions of her field. So in addition to being a valuable and fasinating article in its own right, it may also serve as something of a primer to the discipline, equipping the reader to approach and benefit from other sociolinguistic research.

Empowering International Speakers: An Approach to Clear and Dynamic Communication in English

Rebekah Maggor teaches dramatic texts in performance in the Department of English at Vanderbilt University. She taught rhetoric and public speaking at Harvard College and was founding director of the Program in Speaking and Learning at Harvard's Derek Bok Center. She has coached voice, speech and dialects on Broadway, in regional theater, film and television, and consulted for PBS and NPR. She is an Associate Teacher of Fitzmaurice Voicework and an Associate Editor of the International Dialects of English Archive. She holds an M.F.A. from the American Repertory Theatre and B.A. from Columbia

In this article I propose an approach to help non-native speakers of English improve their oral communication skills. I developed this approach as a research fellow and then director of the Program in Speaking and Learning at Harvard University's Derek Bok Center for Teaching and Learning. While I initially created these methods for academics, I find them equally effective when working with international speakers such as business executives, politicians, lawyers, religious leaders, doctors, and other public figures. This article does *not* deal with teaching English as a second language (ESL). The international speakers discussed here have a broad vocabulary, proficient grammar and good reading, writing, and oral comprehension. Their main challenge is to more effectively engage their audience. They aim to improve the overall intelligibility and dynamism of their speech.

* * *

Kirill got tenure at an age when many scholars are still in graduate school. He has published several highly influential books and articles, and co-authored a textbook. When he came to Harvard several years ago he was considered a hot-shot new faculty acquisition. One afternoon Kirill dropped by my office at the Teaching and Learning Center. "My students look bored," he said. His voice was relaxed and resonant. "It's my accent. I think." His Russian accent was strong, but his speech was intelligible. "Maybe they can't understand me." His pacing was unhurried and his tone was resilient and confident. "Is that what they say in the course evaluations?" I asked, and he nodded. "In general, my public speaking is…I don't know. I feel like I'm not the same person when I'm lecturing. I am not reaching my audience." Kirill casually mentioned that he had a new book coming out in the spring. He considered it a crossover book, aimed at both a scholarly and a popular audience. He would need to give a series of high-profile public talks and numerous radio and television interviews. He felt an acute pressure to address his long-term concerns about public speaking.

The next morning I observed Kirill's political science lecture. There were eighty undergraduates sprinkled around the 200-seat lecture hall. Kirill, behind the podium, looked different from the eloquent, compelling person I had met in my office the day before. His delivery was hesitant, almost apologetic. He spoke at a rapid pace. His accent was heavy and his articulation indistinct. Even with a microphone, his voice sounded smaller, tenser, and higher-pitched than it had the previous day. He offered a sophisticated approach to the topic, and the content was fascinating. The vividness of the material, however, was largely lost on the students as he repeatedly stared down and read from his lecture notes or gazed up at his PowerPoint slides. The clarity, calm and resonance had vanished.

Kirill is a typical case. After seven years of working with professors in thirty departments throughout Harvard's Faculty of Arts and Sciences, I had seen many academics in the same boat. In one-on-one casual conversation, they are brilliant, self-possessed, engaging, and lucid scholars. But place them behind a lectern or hook them up to a microphone and much of the charisma and clarity dissipates.

The challenges these non-native speakers face are in some ways no different from those of native English speakers. Even in their mother tongue, all speakers are prone to getting nervous, losing their train of thought, or having a hard time deciphering a question from the audience. Non-native speakers, however, face these challenges in more intensified ways. They lack the ease and fluency of their native language. Whereas a native speaker can wiggle his way out of a tough moment, an international speaker is frequently hard pressed to get back on track. Additionally, international speakers confront a set of unique challenges. Speaking in a second language often adds a distracting level of self-consciousness. They worry that their audience hears only their accent and grammatical errors rather than the content of their talk. Furthermore, they face a strong audience bias.

Audience members who have difficulty grasping the content of a presentation tend to incorrectly attribute that difficulty to language barriers. As a result, international speakers' presentation skills have to meet higher standards than those of their native-speaking peers.

The approach I describe here is different from many traditional pedagogical methods of teaching oral communication to non-native speakers of English, which focus primarily on pronunciation. Hundreds of books and courses offer "accent reduction" or "accent elimination." They promise to make the speaker sound like an American by teaching him a "standard" or "general" American accent. As one book explains, learning the "Standard American Speech model" will "give you clear and professional sounding speech" (Peterson 2008, 1). But a non-native speaker need not adopt this hypothetical standard American accent to communicate cogently and effectively. International speakers bring different perspectives and ways of thinking to the academic community. Much of this is reflected in the way they communicate. When the speaker asks himself "how can I engage this audience with my ideas?" the answer is rarely, if ever, to eliminate his accent and adopt a different speaking style. Using my methods, instead of aiming to sound American, non-native speakers build on their existing skills while working to improve overall intelligibility and flexibility.

Many elements in my approach are inspired by the voice and speech training of actors. My colleagues Dudley Knight and Philip Thompson developed an innovative training method called "Speechwork: Experiencing Speech and Experiencing Accents." (Knight-Thompson 2010). Theirs is a "physical-based approach" that focuses on experiencing and analyzing all the actions of speech. Rather than teaching their students a single accent pattern—the canonical "Good American Speech" or "Standard American"—Knight and Thompson emphasize pluralism and plasticity. Through a physical exploration of the actions of speech, their students gain the flexibility to assume any dialect appropriate for a specific role or occasion. They shift away from the almost exclusive focus on proper pronunciation to the "Detail Model of American Speech," which teaches students to add or take away linguistic detail depending on the character they portray, their audience, and the space in which they perform. In his article "In the Cause of Freer Speech," Mike Boehm gives a pithy description of Knight-Thompson Speechwork: "Master the physicality of sound, acquire a body-memory of the possibilities of speech, and you are ready to jump into whatever accent, whatever mode of talking, may be required" (*Los Angeles Times*, December 3, 2000).

Another central Knight-Thompson innovation is a greater emphasis on voice pedagogy. They recognize the indissoluble connection between speech actions and vocal production. They integrate voice training approaches, such as Fitzmaurice Voicework, to help actors develop powerful and supple voices capable of great variation in pitch and volume. Rather than defining a normative euphonic sound, their students gain skills to develop a range of tones and timbres effective for different characters and occasions. Their method ultimately improves clear communication—intelligibility—while allowing for a greater diversity of speaking styles. My own approach builds on their theoretical and practical foundation. As non-native speakers let go of the preoccupation with sounding American, they shift their attention to enhancing voice and speech techniques. This ultimately helps them to more effectively communicate with their audience, while encouraging them to develop their unique style of speaking in English.

Inspired by Knight and Thompson's approach, I have developed seven strategies that consistently help international speakers achieve clear and dynamic communication in any setting, from large public lectures to more intimate interviews. The strategies break down into two overarching categories—mindset and practice. The speaker simultaneously reconsiders his thinking about his audience and what constitutes effective speaking while practicing exercises that, over time, allow him to form new speaking habits. Rather than trying to eliminate his accent, he instead focuses on speaking clearly *with* an accent. As long as his speech is intelligible, his accent can make a powerful contribution to his ethos as a speaker. With this outlook, he develops effortlessly coherent speech through work on the combined areas of pronunciation, articulation, pacing, and voice. At the same time, it is important not to discard the many good speaking habits the speaker brings from his native language. These older practices provide a foundation that he can build on while speaking English. They are vital to developing a unique and vibrant public speaking persona. Throughout this process, he develops the skill of focusing his attention on his audience, so he can adjust and adapt to every speaking situation.

1. Speaking Clearly with an Accent

Many international speakers assume that the root of all their speaking ills is their foreign accent. They request coaching in "accent reduction." My experience has shown that a foreign accent in itself is rarely a genuine obstacle to effective public speaking. As long as the non-native speaker is intelligible, his accent can in fact be an advantage. The speaker's native linguistic identity is an essential part of his temperament. It adds gravitas, validity, and even magnetism to presentations or lectures. The emphasis on eliminating a foreign accent in these cases is not only counterproductive but also distracts from viable and far more critical goals. Rather than eliminate their accents, it is better for international speakers to focus their efforts on the goal of speaking clearly with an accent.

Certain altered pronunciations by non-native speakers do not stand in the way of intelligibility, and there is little reason to invest extensive time and effort trying to adjust or change them. For example, Kirill tapped or trilled his intervocalic /r/ (used [ɾ] or [r] in place of [ɹ] or [ɚ].) This altered pronunciation did not hurt his intelligibility. On the other hand, his occasional tendency to realize /h/ as [g] made entire sentences incomprehensible for his academic audience.

It is helpful for the international speaker to hear a recording of excellent orators speaking in accented English, particularly when the orator originates from his home country (or the same linguistic background). For Kirill I played a recording of the legendary head of the Moscow Art Theatre School, Anatoly Smeliansky. Professor Smeliansky speaks with a thick Russian accent. He trills his /r/ with flair, his /h/ crackles forth as a resounding fricative [x]; he sits deep into his vowels, turning diphthongs into triphthongs and triphthongs into quadraphthongs. His numerous mispronunciations and erroneous emphases reveal him as a bookworm who has never actually heard many of the words in his extensive English vocabulary spoken aloud by a native speaker. Despite these inaccuracies, his lectures are not only intelligible, they are spellbinding. His knowledge of Russian drama is unparalleled. He lays out a powerful argument and supports it with the detailed narrative evidence of a master storyteller. His delivery is self-assured and unselfconscious. Even when he mispronounces a word, the audience understands him because his pacing is slow, his articulation muscular, and his pitch variation dynamic. If Professor Smelianksy were to suddenly eliminate that rich, rolling Russian accent he would ruin the unique character, melody, and rhythm of his lectures. Hearing this recording empowered Kirill to relish aspects of his own accent. He could savor the sounds which add richness and color to his speech and alter the handful of pronunciations that actually obstruct his intelligibility.

2. Exploring the Mechanics of Speech

Some international speakers, like Kirill, start out with a fairly intelligible accent, while other international speakers have heavier accents that impede intelligibility. These speakers need more time to identify and alter the sounds obstructing the clarity of their speech. Rather than "reducing" an accent, it is more useful to think of the process as improving intelligibility. Again, the goal is not to eliminate the accent, but to bring the speaker to a level of comprehensibility that allows him to be effortlessly understood. The speaker focuses on making the necessary pronunciation changes rather than perfecting an accent.

While this focused approach is less daunting, it nonetheless remains an intimidating challenge for many speakers to alter any aspect of their pronunciation. Speakers commonly assume that even the smallest shift demands an inherent gift for language. They will say things like "I just don't have a good ear." A "good ear," however, is not necessary for changing pronunciation. Instead of trying to *hear* the nuances of phonetic sounds, it is more effective for the speaker to *feel* the physical actions, or mechanics, of speech. By gaining practical knowledge of the mechanics of speech almost any speaker at any age can quickly and dramatically increase the clarity of his speech. When the speaker understands the range and combination of movements in the tongue, lips, soft palate, and jaw, he can make almost any sound. As he learns to control and isolate these muscles, he is better able to alter his pronunciation as well as add varying level of detail to his speech. For example, if a Chinese speaker does not hear the difference between *sung* [sʌŋ] and *sun* [sʌn], hearing someone repeatedly model the word with the correct pronunciation is more irritating than helpful. When he discovers how to move the tip of his tongue to the alveolar ridge, rather than lifting the middle of the tongue to the soft palate, he can *feel* the difference and alter his pronunciation. Once he can physically distinguish between the speech actions, he can typically hear the difference as well.

Focusing on the physical actions of speech is an approach I adapted directly from Knight-Thompson Speechwork. Their training begins with an exploration of anatomy and the physical mechanics of articulation before attaching sounds to letters or symbols. When a speaker sees a familiar symbol or letter, he associates a habitual action with it, which may or may not be phonetically accurate for the target sound or language. In other cases, he has long ago deemed himself incapable of pronouncing certain sounds and consciously relies on a substitute sound that is easier for him to pronounce. He can gain awareness of these false associations and begin to master new articulations by freely exploring the actions of speech. Later, symbols and letters can be reintroduced, and attached to the newfound awareness of the physical actions involved. In short, he feels the sound first before he tries to see it or hear it.

Fahad, a doctoral candidate in anthropology from Qatar realized /p/ as [b]. There is no /p/ in Arabic and he had given up on correcting this sound. Without making reference to letters or symbols, I told him to bring both lips together, build up a pocket of air behind the closed lips, and let the air explode. He made a [p] sound. Next I told him repeat the same action, but add voice at the time of explosion. He made a [b] sound. Through this simple exercise he gained a physical memory for the difference between voiced and unvoiced bilabial plosives. Before breaking down the mechanics he did not have conscious control over the muscles involved in making these sounds, nor did he understand the concept of voiced/unvoiced pairs. With some practice he integrated the new sound into his speech.

There are two approaches to exploring the mechanics of speech, depending on the amount of time the speaker can devote to this training. When the speaker is pressed for time it is possible to identify sounds that need changing and practice the mechanics of those sounds alone. This method is highly effective in instantly raising the speaker's level of intelligibility. However, I have found that exploring all the actions of speech methodically, by going through a blank chart of the International Phonetic Alphabet (IPA), is the best approach for a more profound and permanent improvement of intelligibility. It may seem like a contradiction to suggest that the international speaker alter only the sounds that obfuscate his intelligibility and then also advocate a systematic exploration of all the actions of speech. Yet exploring all the actions of these sounds will, as Thompson writes, expand the speaker's "range of linguistic possibility" (Thompson 2007, 349-58). It gives the speaker an understanding of how to not only alter specific areas of pronunciation, but also sharpen his overall articulation. He can adapt his level of detail, depending on a specific speaking situation. When he is in a large lecture hall he can hit certain consonants and draw out certain vowels, while in an intimate meeting he can speak more casually, by leaving out some linguistic detail. Exploring all the mechanics of speech also empowers him to understand the proximity between sounds in his own language and sounds which are difficult for him to pronounce in English. He becomes adept at creating and perfecting new sounds by building on familiar actions. The goal of a complete exploration of the mechanics of speech is not accent elimination; such an exploration is a highly effective approach to improving intelligibility and empowering the speaker to adapt nimbly to various speaking situations.

3. Muscular Articulation and Pacing

Articulation, Pacing, and the Accent Bias
After observing hundreds of lectures and seminars and reading the correlating student evaluations, I have noticed a common bias: audiences tend to hold international speakers to higher standards of clarity than native speakers of English. When students have a hard time understanding an international speaker of English, they are quick to lay blame on accent and tune out. When I observed the lectures of faculty or teaching assistants who received complaints from students about their accents I found, not surprisingly, that accent was only a part of the picture. In some cases a speaker's accent was indeed unintelligible, but in other cases a speaker's pronunciation was more than satisfactory. There were usually several elements contributing to the instructor's lack of clarity. The first area involved content. The

instructor's lectures may have been poorly organized or pitched above the heads of the undergraduates. Even when a lecture is superbly organized, quantum physics or high modernism is complicated. In some cases a student was unprepared for an advanced level course and blamed his difficulties on the instructor's "really heavy accent." In the area of delivery, many instructors spoke rapidly and with a low level of linguistic detail. In other words, they rushed and did not articulate well. Rather than pinpointing these specific elements of delivery, the students wrote general comments like "his accent makes him hard to understand."

Whatever the actual causes of a student's frustration, it is apparent that an accent bias exists. Recent neurological research may provide evidence of such a bias. A 2010 study of non-native accent perception, conducted by the Voice Neural Cognition Laboratory at the University of Glasgow in Scotland, found that an area of the brain called the temporal voice area (TVA) "tuned out a bit" when volunteers were asked to process information spoken in accents different from their own. When the same volunteers heard information spoken in versions of their own accent "the TVA actually perked up a lot." While the researchers do not yet know why this reaction occurs they hope that this kind of research "may eventually give us new insights into the prejudice and snobbery that often accompany reactions to other people's accents" (University of Glasgow 2010). The Glasgow study does not mention how the listening samples of different accents vary in terms of linguistic detail, pacing, and voice. It would be interesting to find out whether these same volunteers reacted differently to variations of these elements by the same speaker. How would the TVA react, for example, to an accented speaker who significantly increases his intelligibility through muscular articulation and a slower pace?

From practical experience in the classroom, I would venture to theorize that at least part of the bias against accents is due to perceived level of effort on the part of the listener. When the listener hears a foreign accent or a dialect of English different from his own, he might hastily assume that following this speaker's lecture demands a higher level of concentration and tune out. One way for a speaker to dispel this assumption is to strive for effortlessly intelligible speech. The goal should be this: within the first thirty seconds of a talk, the international speaker expresses himself with such deliberate clarity that he obliterates any need for increased effort by the listeners. His muscular articulation and excellent pace allow them to forget accent and focus on content. Student evaluations show that international instructors with exceptional intelligibility receive significantly fewer comments on their accent and more specific comments on content, organization and pedagogy.

Pronunciation, Phonetics, Linguistics, Dialect/Accent Studies

Empowering International Speakers: An Approach to Clear and Dynamic Communication in English by Rebekah Maggor

There are a few interesting challenges for international speakers in attaining this high level of intelligibility. Many speakers equate speed with fluency and worry that if they take their time, they will sound as if they have poor English language skills. To avoid drawing attention to their accent or possible grammatical errors, some international speakers, whether knowingly or unknowingly, speed up and mumble certain words. When the international speaker is of the mindset that clarity of content and connecting with the audience outweigh avoiding or covering up the occasional error, speaking with outstanding articulation and pacing becomes an achievable goal.

Approaching Articulation
Before making some basic suggestions for specific exercises to improve articulation and pacing, I would like to include a few observations on how best to introduce speech and voice work to academics or other public speakers without a background in acting. Almost none of the international speakers I encounter in academia have acting or voice and speech training. Unlike actors, who are accustomed to stretching and making funny faces during a voice and speech warm-up, many international speakers find such exercises strange, silly or intimidating. There are three ways I encourage participation. First, I add a brief explanation before each exercise. Understanding the reasoning and desired result behind each exercise builds trust and encourages risk taking. Second, I lead exercises with full commitment. By taking the lead with unapologetic confidence, I assure the participants that each exercise is serious and practical. Third, I eliminate on-lookers. Those present can either participate or leave the room. When every person participates—even people who may have only come to observe—everybody feels more comfortable and willing to experiment with these new exercises. The preceding suggestions may appear obvious to the voice and speech coach, but for those without time or access to serious long-term voice and speech training, a few simple exercises can make an enormous difference.

Each speaker builds an individual speech warm-up that addresses his specific challenges. He begins with an articulation warm-up that stretches the jaw, tongue, lips, and palette. The warm-up might include a combination of slapping and massaging the articulator muscles, stretching, gurning and tongue twisters. (An extensive list of specific articulation exercises can be found in the Knight-Thompson workbook "Experiencing Speech." In addition, Patsy Rodenburg, in her excellent book *The Right to Speak: Working with the Voice*, suggests many useful speech exercises for non-actors.) For the last part of the warm-up the speaker practices with material from an actual lecture. He focuses on hitting final consonants and elongating emphasized syllables of operative words. During the warm-up exercises, the speaker attempts to exaggerate his articulation, or

over-articulate. He then adjusts it for an actual presentation. The challenge here is that usually the speaker feels he is over-articulating when he may have changed very little about his speech. Having the speaker listen to a recording of himself will help build an accurate perception of his speech. Through exercises that compel him to step out of his comfort zone (such as attempting an exercise in a non-traditional space), the speaker can make significant change. When the speaker stands on the edge of a huge field and yells across to a colleague at the other side he immediately opens his mouth wide, hits consonants with force and elongates vowels. Alternatively, the speaker can stand on one end of a large room and attempt to communicate with a colleague on the other end, speaking in a whisper, or using no voice at all. When the speaker depends entirely on the friction, shape and movement of vowels and consonants, without voice, he gains a physical experience of increased articulation. The physical memory of this experience helps him adjust the level of linguistic detail in his habitual public speaking.

Pacing Transformation through Discrete Sentences and Active Pauses
Hitting consonants with force and elongating vowels slows down the general pace of speech. Pausing between sentences further transforms the speed of one's speech. What does it mean to pause? When told "you need to pause more" many speakers stop awkwardly between sentences and hold their breath. They presume that a pause is a moment devoid of speech or action. This inactive type of pause constricts the general flow and pace of the speech, builds tension, and causes shortness of breath. An active pause is an intake of breath. A pause as an intake of breath between sentences relaxes and grounds a speaker. In this instance the intake of breath is intimately connected with the thought process. As Catherine Fitzmaurice explains in her essay "Breathing is Meaning," "'inspiration' denotes both the physical act of breathing in, and the mental act of creating a thought" (Fitzmaurice 1997, 247-55). When I first suggest the technique of breathing between sentences some speakers take luxurious inhalations and exhalations of breath, as if they are in a yoga class. Obviously breathing in this manner between every sentence is ungainly and time-consuming. By breathing between sentences I mean that the speaker takes one efficient intake of breath—the ribs expand quickly, the belly releases, and a nice volume of air rushes into the lungs. The speaker feels replenished, energized and, without holding his breath, immediately continues his speech.

Active pausing goes hand in hand with discrete sentences. In order to control the breathing between sentences, the speaker shortens his sentences and ends them with purpose. If we were to transcribe our own impromptu speech, many of us (both international and native speakers) would discover that our habit is to speak in lengthy run-on sentences. Phrases follow one after the other, trailing superfluous conjunctions, adverbs, and fillers. In a native speaker this habit can make speech hard to follow; for an international speaker, already dealing with accent bias, it provides the perfect excuse for his audience to tune out. An example of this common speech pattern comes from Lucy, a captivating doctoral candidate in sociology from Mexico. Students praised the passion she conveyed for the material, but complained that her accent was hard to understand. A video of her section revealed that while her pronunciation and articulation were excellent, she spoke remarkably quickly, in long run-on sentences with few pauses. On average, each sentence was the length of a paragraph. Here is an example from her section, in which she spoke from notes:

So, we can see here on this slide that, uh, uh, uh, in South Los Angeles around forty-five percent of the food options are fast food, versus only sixteen percent of restaurants in the higher-income West Los Angeles and, uh, uh, to actually give you an example of the reality on the ground , uh, uh, you see, uh, in some neighborhoods, as one resident said, you can't buy a salad within twenty minutes of this neighborhood and so, uh, uh, for communities trying to make healthy choices and to, uh, uh, in some way, change their eating habits, it's very hard, or, uh, in other words almost impossible to, uh, to make any kind of practical and sustainable change.

I asked Lucy to shorten her sentences, and take an active pause in between each sentence. Specifically, I instructed her to make her sentences "comically short." After several attempts she spoke the following:

Take a look at this slide. In South Los Angeles around forty-five percent of the food options are fast food versus only sixteen percent of restaurants in the higher-income West Los Angeles. The reality on the ground is bleak. In many neighborhoods you'd have to drive twenty minutes to buy a salad. There are no healthy options. That makes it next to impossible for communities to make any kind of healthy and sustainable changes to their diet.

As with most exercises, when the speaker feels she is exaggerating to an extreme, she usually hits the mark. Lucy was convinced that this speech pattern slowed her pacing down to a crawl. When she heard the recording of herself she changed her mind. "It's much clearer. Better organized. I sound like I really know what I'm talking about. And I quit saying 'um' all the time." She also mentioned the other powerful effect of distinct sentences and active pauses. "Pausing—breathing—in between sentences gives me time to think about what I'm saying. It helps me stay calm and think on my feet." This speech pattern also gives the audience more time to absorb the speaker's ideas. In addition, practicing aloud with this technique refines not only the delivery, but also the content and organization of lectures.

4. Voice

Let us return to Kirill, our political science professor from the beginning of the article. I mentioned that his voice sounded "smaller, tenser, and higher pitched" when he lectured. He said he felt "like a different person" in public speaking situations. The change in his voice and his discomfort stemmed from a high level of tension. For Kirill the tension was most evident in the neck, upper chest and shoulders. Perspicacious speakers like Kirill regularly have an unconscious notion that there exists a direct path from the brain to the mouth. They may not have thought about the fact that producing voice demands, as Fitzmaurice points out, the involvement of many physical structures from "the diaphragm, intercostal, abdominal and back muscles; larynx; articulators; body form and cavities." The speaker who combines muscular articulation and excellent pacing with a flexible and resonant voice creates not only an intelligible, but also a compelling delivery. Creating this level of captivating delivery takes a willingness to explore and develop the physical connection between voice and body.

International speakers face the usual intense pressures of speaking in public, along with the added stress of expressing themselves in a foreign language. As a result of this added burden, they frequently feel an immense increase in physical tension. Many of them are acutely aware of this new and taxing tension. Because of this keen awareness, international speakers can be relatively open-minded and enthusiastic about trying physical exercises aimed at releasing tension and developing the voice. As with any voice student, the international speaker studies the two basic components of voice work: tension release and isolated vocal support. I approach this process in different ways depending on the background of the speaker and the amount of time I have to work with him. The most difficult challenge is to balance voice work with other demands. For Kirill the physical tension was at the core of the challenges he faced as a speaker. For other speakers, whose level of intelligibility is not as strong, articulation exercises will dominate the warm-up and subsequent exercises.

With Kirill, I started out with some simple stretches to open his intercostal muscles and release tension in the neck and torso. During the second session I added some floor exercises and a few Fitzmaurice tremors for relaxation and breath-flow. A crucial element in the tension release was finding what Fitzmaurice calls the "fluffy" voice, or the released voice, on the unstructured outbreath. Just hearing and feeling this resonant sound made Kirill aware of how much pressure he normally exerted on his vocal chords. For building support we first located the most internal abdominal muscle (the transversus abdominis). One of several helpful exercises was leaning forward with straight back, hands on knees and breathing out with swift "fff, fff, fff." Next we focused on recreating the released rich sound with structure and intention. For Kirill the trick was vocalizing without tensing his neck. Rolling the head gently while humming was a useful start. Another beneficial exercise was counting in increments and taking an efficient and relaxed breath between each increment: "One. (Breath). One, two. (Breath). One, two, three. (Breath)." Etc. This exercise revealed Kirill's tendency to tense his shoulders and neck on the inhalation and breathe "up." Two exercises that helped restructure his in-breath were placing the hands on the back ribs and imagining that, for each inhalation, he was sending the breath into his palms. Next, with his hands hanging comfortably at his sides, he imagined sending the breath down through the tailbone. Following relaxation and support exercises we did a number of exercises to broaden his pitch range, such as sirens and scales. After several sessions of warm-ups and voice exercises Kirill began to feel a noticeable difference in his undergraduate lectures. "I feel more in control." He added, "Sometimes it's actually fun to add a bit of color to a word with more volume or a pitch change. I didn't know how to consciously do that before."

Physical voice work of this kind can be a revelation for the speaker. But Kirill expressed a concern common to many of the speakers I've worked with in this way. In higher-stakes situations, like large conference presentations or television interviews, Kirill feared that attempting to concentrate simultaneously on wording, organization, articulation, breathing, pausing, volume, and pitch variation would render him speechless. In these instances he felt he needed to concentrate fully on explaining content logically to his audience. I think this attitude is correct. The best way to make substantial and long-term change is to practice new techniques in low-stakes situations over an extended period of time. For example, Kirill would choose one or possibly two things to work on during his small graduate seminar or even during lunch with a colleague. One afternoon he might choose to focus on releasing his neck muscles while talking and not raising his shoulders when taking an in-breath. Another day he might focus on hitting final consonants and adding more pitch variation. After a time these once-new techniques, which demanded a conscious effort to sustain, turn into habit and become an unconscious element of his public speaking.

5. Building on Good Habits

Many international speakers have certain highly effective communication skills in their native language which they do not use in English. They may talk more slowly, loudly, and articulate more deliberately in their mother tongue. Mastery of their own language allows them to speak less self-consciously and focus on content. If the international speaker can identify his good habits in his native tongue he can, with practice, integrate them into his English speaking. An excellent way to uncover these good native language habits is to ask the speaker to present a short two-minute talk in English, immediately followed by a short talk in his native tongue. Through this juxtaposition he may identify glaring differences between his pacing, volume and muscularity of articulation in the two languages. Realizing these differences is the first step to integrating these good habits to his public speaking in English. The speaker also discovers habits that affect matters beyond basic intelligibility, and which impact his ability to engage his audience.

Eva, a professor of Islamic Art History from Austria and a world-renowned expert on medieval manuscripts, was in the midst of preparing for a keynote address at a major conference, when she received a few student comments about her accent. I watched a video of a recent lecture. She stood stiffly behind the podium and read her lecture verbatim from a printed page. She spoke with little pitch variation and her voice sunk frequently into glottal fry. Her accent was light, but she barely opened her mouth, which had the effect of making her articulation wispy and full of delicate, but undifferentiated consonants. I asked her to give the first few moments of this same lecture in German. She leaned her elbows slightly on the podium and filled her lungs with air. Her voice was not creaky, but warm and full. Her consonants were distinct and she elongated her vowels beautifully with elegant pitch variation. She opened her mouth to let the sound out. After a few minutes I asked her to stop and reflect on the experience. She noticed the differences in stance, and volume. I asked her to give the same lecture again in English, but emulate the stance and volume she used in German. She relaxed her stance behind the podium and concentrated on infusing more volume. Her clarity improved slightly, but it was still not effortlessly intelligible. I asked her to focus on opening her mouth and hitting her final consonants, as she had in German. This was a key change for her. She had developed a habit of tensing her lips and jaw when speaking in English. Defusing this tension encouraged her to breathe, allowed her to articulate more muscularly, and eliminated the glottal fry, which instantly infused her speech with greater pitch variation.

Eva's case also demonstrates the extraordinary effect that reading verbatim has on a speaker's delivery. Some international speakers prefer reading aloud from a text because they can avoid fishing for the right word choice and phrasing. Reading aloud, however, demands a different skill set from speaking more extemporaneously. Unless the speaker has considerable experience and practice reading aloud in English, this form of delivery intensifies the speaker's accent and hurts her ability to connect with the audience. Speaking from notes, instead of a full text, is helpful in a myriad of ways. When Eva lectured in German, she spoke more extemporaneously. She briefly glanced at her paper to remind herself of major points and made direct eye contact with the audience. Her phrasing was more conversational and easier to follow. She also revealed an unexpected charisma when she was able to directly engage with the audience. She was surprised by how much of the content she remembered without looking down at the paper. After this experience, Eva committed to delivering her lectures in English from a detailed outline, rather than reading a complete text. This change drastically improved both her intelligibility and her ability to engage her audience.

To create a public persona the speaker draws not only from good habits in her native language, but also from speaking habits she may have used in other areas of her life. All speakers do some form of code-switching, or speaking in different ways to different people in different situations. The speaker can transfer speaking habits from one life situation to another. As an example of how powerful this simple technique can be, consider the case of Liu, a young professor in applied mathematics from Shanghai. At the same time that his cutting-edge research was breaking boundaries in his field, his undergraduate students claimed that he was hard to understand and could not teach the basic material of his introductory course. I observed one of Liu's classes together with a colleague from his department. My colleague assured me that Liu explained the material quite capably. Liu's accent was rather heavy, but fairly intelligible. His soft, half-muttered speech was hard to hear. He spoke quickly, routinely fixing his gaze on the chalkboard. The hesitant nature of his delivery gave the impression that he did not know what he was talking about.

In one-on-one speaking Liu was more relaxed. He spoke more intelligibly and at a slower pace, but was still extremely quiet. His manner was not significantly different when I asked him to speak in Chinese. He used slightly more volume, but continued to rush. I asked if he had ever spoken in public outside of academia. He mentioned that he had worked as a tutor for grade school children in China. I asked him to demonstrate, in Chinese, how he taught these children. He found this exercise strange, but played along. He stood up at the front of the room and elongated his spine. He seemed to grow three inches. He raised his eyes from the floor and in a deep and resonant voice addressed his imaginary students. I told Liu that all he needed to do was use this strong voice with his undergraduate students. He cringed; he saw no connection between grade school children and Harvard undergraduates. He was afraid he would insult his students. I explained that he could create a powerful public speaking persona by combining his observant and insightful academic side with the volume and confidence of his grade school tutor persona. I asked him to explain a mathematical concept to me in English, while

pretending to be a grade school teacher. As I had expected, the combination was delightful. His volume and enunciation were effortlessly clear. He appeared assertive, but modest, and in no way condescending. When he finished I asked him to describe his performance. He was certain that he had sounded patronizing and unpleasant. When we listened to the recording together he laughed and said the person on the recording sounded like the kind of confident lecturer he had always wanted to be.

6. Creation of a Public Persona

Not all speakers harbor an inspiring and half-forgotten past like Liu. If a speaker cannot mine his own experience for different modes of expression, he can draw inspiration from other speakers, particularly great orators. By studying the delivery of these orators, the international speaker adds range and dynamism to his speech. The speaker does not aim to imitate these orators, but to extract specific elements of their delivery to combine with his own. In order to help the speaker analyze and experience these elements he finds a recording of a speech or poem and memorizes a one-minute section. The orator he chooses should have a style that suits his temperament. As the speaker prepares to recite the selection, he focuses on the dynamics which he most wishes to infuse in his own speech.

Tomoko, a visiting professor of comparative literature, and an internationally-cited expert on Japanese popular culture, felt her voice sounded "small" and "hurried" in English. For American audiences, she wanted to combine a more direct and confident tone with her modest and soft-spoken style. She had recently seen a video of Maya Angelou reciting a poem. She was struck by Angelou's rich voice and her use of meaningful pauses. As she memorized a section of the poem she marked Angelou's breaths. She noticed that Angelou appeared physically calm, which reminded Tomoko to work on relaxing her neck and shoulders when she spoke. Her recitation was astounding; she seemed to have transformed her speaking habits entirely. Her voice dropped comfortably into a lower base tone. Her pauses consisted of a calm intake of breath. This revised pacing gave her words a gravity of a sort that only silence can provide. Tomoko then tried to transfer this same placement of voice, easy breathing, and calm, lingering pauses into her own words. At first she feared that modeling her lecture style after a poetry recitation would sound ridiculous. When she heard the recording of herself speaking she changed her mind. "I thought I was exaggerating much more. It doesn't sound like a recitation; it just sounds like I have something important to say." She later commented that putting on her "poet" persona allowed her to feel completely in control. The calm, regular breaths, combined with the overall slower pace, enabled her to think on the spot.

7. Focus on the Audience

As a number of these examples show, a speaker's internal concept of intelligibility and dynamism is often very different from that of the listener. What the speaker perceives as exaggerated enunciation and volume and an excessively slow pace is often appropriately clear and expressive to the audience. The speaker can adjust his perception of his own delivery by listening to recordings or watching videos of himself. But it is also essential to build the skill of reading and reacting to the audience in the moment, or while in the midst of delivering a talk. Rather than fixating on his own speech, he directs his attention outwards and concentrates on reaching his audience. Based on the cues he receives, he adjusts his presentation style and content. He makes eye contact, not for the sake of making eye contact, but to confirm that his listeners understand him. Based on their responses, he knows to adjust his volume, increase the detail or vigorousness of his articulation, or add an additional example to clarify a point.

A powerful metaphor for the desired connection between speaker and audience is the simple act of playing catch with a ball. As Nancy Houfek points out in her video *The Act of Teaching*, the speaker focuses his attention not on himself, but on "landing his message" with the audience (Houfek 2007). Every form of public speaking—from large lecture to intimate seminar— is a game of catch, a dialogue rather than a monologue. When playing catch, one goes through three motions: making eye contact, throwing the ball, and checking to see if the other person caught it. This physical exercise corresponds to the actions of an engaged speaker. Making eye contact is a way for the speaker to both check in with the audience and prepare them. He asks with his eyes, "Are you ready?" He then throws out an idea, just as he would throw a ball. As he tosses out ideas he checks to see if they are landing with the audience. Through eye contact or through direct questioning he asks "Did you get it?" This cycle repeats throughout a presentation. Are you ready? – Throw out an idea. – Did you catch it? Taking the attention off himself and placing it on the audience not only helps the speaker improve his technical delivery, it also liberates him from a great deal of onerous self-consciousness.

* * *

There are quite a few similarities between the approach I suggest here and the older systems of teaching a standard American accent. Both aim to give a diverse group of people access to a playing field where they can communicate freely. Since the late nineteenth century, versions of a so-called standard American accent, such as Good American Speech or World English, have been taught as elocution in the United States. In his article "Standard Speech: The On-Going Debate," Dudley Knight points out that Good American Speech is an artificial creation; "no Americans actually spoke it unless educated to do so." Theoretically, anyone with the gumption to adopt a new dialect could acquire Good American Speech. International speakers as well as native English speakers from different circumstances and regions of the country studied this dialect. Learning a uniform manner of expression was one instrument that promised to provide all speakers, no matter their background, access to the same forums and resources. On the other hand, labeling one dialect as superior to another by calling it "good" or "standard" is to deem all other regional, social, and ethnic dialects inferior. As Knight writes, the distinctly Anglo-Saxon inspired Good American Speech was "mired in a self-serving and archaic notion of Euphony, and in a model of class, ethnic, and racial hierarchy" (Knight 2000, 177).

In academia today, as in so many other fields, globalization has radically expanded the geographical reach of our institutions. Professors and students come from increasingly diverse ethnic, racial, religious, and linguistic backgrounds. It is no longer desirable or even tenable to expect such a heterogonous population to speak in the same way. For better and for worse, we have abandoned the project of creating a common American accent. In light of these new challenges, my method aims to accommodate pluralism even while enhancing communication in a diverse community. One distinct advantage of expanding the accepted forms of communication in English is the unique perspectives international speakers contribute to the academic community. Embracing a rigorous level of intelligibility while building on, rather than discarding, certain native linguistic habits and modes of expression empowers international speakers to express themselves with distinctiveness, clarity, and purpose.

Notes

1. A sample of best-selling book titles on Amazon.com include: *Accent Reduction 101, Lose Your Accent in 28 Days, Accent Reduction Made Easy, Accent Reduction Made Easy: Learn in Your Car, The American Accent Made Easy, American Accent Training, The American Accent Guide, American English Pronunciation, Improve Your American English Accent.*

Bibliography

University of Glasgow Institute of Neuroscience and Psychology. "Neural Correlates of Non-native Accent Perception." Patricia D. Bestelmeyer, Robert Ladd, and Pascal Belin. Last modified December 8, 2010. http://vnl.psy.gla.ac.uk/NCNNAP.php .

Boehm, Mike. "In the Cause of Freer Speech." *Los Angeles Times*, 12 December 2000, Calendar, 1.

Fitzmaurice, Catherine. "Breathing is Meaning." In *The Vocal Vision*, edited by Marian Hampton. New York: Applause Books, 1997.

Houfek, Nancy. *The Act of Teaching with Nancy Houfek*. Cambridge: Harvard University, Derek Bok Center for Teaching and Learning, 2007.

Knight, Dudley. *Speaking with Skill* (working title). Forthcoming, 2011.

Knight, Dudley. "Standard Speech: The Ongoing Debate." *The Voice and Speech Review: Standard Speech* (2000): 155-83.

Knight-Thompson Speechwork. "Speechwork: Experiencing Speech: An Intensive Workshop in the Skills of Articulation." Last modified 2010. http://www.ktspeechwork.com .

Peterson, Elizabeth. *Accent Reduction 101*. Denver: Speech and Voice Enterprises, 2008.

Thompson, Phillip. "The Deep Case for Phonetics Training." *The Voice and Speech Review: Voice and Gender* (2007): 349-358.

Regional Variation and Mexican American English

Jaclyn Ocumpaugh (Old Dominion University) specializes in sociophonetics and in the ethnography of language. For her MA (North Carolina State University), she developed new acoustic methods for studying /r/ variation in the American South. Her dissertation (Michigan State University) examines the sociolinguistic situation of L1 and L2 Mexican Americans in Benton Harbor, Michigan. She was recognized as Presidential Honorary Member (2007-2010) of the American Dialect Society for her innovative research and her outstanding contributions to the field.

Despite many strong beliefs in our culture about the normalization power of media outlets (e.g. television, radio, etc.), sociolinguistic research has shown that regional pronunciation patterns are diverging in this country. However, this research (e.g. Labov, Ash, and Boberg 2000) has largely centered around White populations. Studies of ethnic minorities have focused largely on their divergence from mainstream/White populations, usually with minimal consideration of their relationship to these regionalisms. In fact, in the mid-1990s William Labov went so far as to suggest that ethnic minorities do not participate in mainstream sound changes at all (Labov 1994), a claim which he no longer appears to endorse (Labov, Ash, and Boberg 2000, 297). The current study will summarize evidence from available acoustic studies of Mexican Americans to illustrate ways in which Mexican Americans exhibit regional and ethnic variation in their production of vowels; this small body of research will be supplemented with information from second language acquisition, which will help to demonstrate possible Spanish transfer effects, and with information from studies of regional variation among White populations to determine which vowels may evidence accommodation to known patterns of regional variation.

The goal is to educate the readership on the range of known vowel variation found among Mexican Americans, but to do so with the most precise research available—that which has been conducted using acoustic phonetic technology. These criteria limit the geographic range of this study considerably; most of the published acoustic research on Mexican American English vowels has been limited to the Inland North and California, although some research has been conducted in Texas and North Carolina. To a lesser extent, relevant regional variation among White speakers will be also be discussed, but only as it pertains to variation among Mexican Americans.

The organization of this article is as follows. The first section addresses the phonetic labeling system used in this article. The second discusses established models for phonetic acquisition processes, demonstrating the predictions that second language acquisition models make for Spanish transfer effects on English. This section illustrates why regional variation should be considered in these models and serves as a baseline for understanding stereotypical representations that readers may associate with Mexican Americans. Finally, the third section summarizes the patterns found among Mexican Americans for each area of the vowel space. The primary focus for this section is to highlight acoustic research on the F1 and F2 vowel space, since that is probably the most reliable and scientific data in the literature, but impressionistic data is also reported when strong stereotypes of this speech seem contrary to evidence being presented. In particular, this paper highlights distinctive patterns which might be influenced by Spanish or by accommodation processes to regional norms. However, in some cases, both of these influences might condition similar effects. In others, language internal processes (those used to create maximal distinction, for example) might be at work.

1. Phonetic Labeling Systems:

Many sociophonetic researchers continue to use the phonetic symbols that are associated with mainstream pronunciations of a word even though the International Phonetic Alphabet (IPA) was designed to describe these sounds uniquely. For example, it's not uncommon for researchers to refer to the vowel in *bat* as /æ/ even in conditions where it might have a pronunciation that is closer to a high, front vowel. However, a growing number of researchers, including Erik Thomas, who is now one of the leading researchers in vowel variation in the United States (see for example Thomas 2001), recognize the problems associated with this practice. This paper will follow the conventions that Thomas and Yeaeger-Dror outline in their recent investigation of African American vowel systems (Thomas and Yaeger-Dror 2010), where they modify Ladefoged's (2005) system of referring to sounds by historical word classes. In their system, which will be adopted in this paper, vowels are given in a B_T paradigm, as shown in Table 1. IPA symbols will be used only as reference points to describe differences in their pronunciations.

Table 1: Keywords Used to Represent Vowel Classes2

IPA	Keyword
/i/	beet
/ɪ/	bit
/e/	bait
/ɛ/	bet
/æ/	bat
/ɑ/	bot
/ɔ/	bought
/o/	boat
/ʌ/	but
/ʊ/	book
/u/	boot
/aɪ/	bite

2. Language Acquisition Processes and Their Probable Effects on the English Dialect Development of Mexican Americans

Early research on Mexican American dialects had the formidable task of establishing them as English dialects, rather than interlanguage, or Second Language Acquisition (SLA) phenomena. This is no longer a debate among sociolinguistic scholars who study Latino varieties of English. Despite the recent influx of new immigrants, evidence suggests that many Mexican Americans—even those with ethnically distinct accents—are monolingual English speakers. The 2000 Census shows that 20% of Latinos speak only English at home, and that another 35-40% speak English at home in addition to another language. Carmen Fought points out that many students who were classified as Limited English Proficiency (LEP) by the public school she was working with in California were actually monolingual English speakers (Fought, personal communication). Thus, many of the features of this dialect which "sound Spanish" may be substrate effects learned from previous generations and instantiated into this ethnically marked dialect, rather than the transfer effects of a particular speaker.[3] Identifying with a Mexican American community appears to motivate such patterns. Among residents in Benton Harbor, Michigan, the speaker whose vowel patterns most closely matched transfer effect patterns had no memory of having to learn English, while the one whose vowels most closely matched regional patterns found among White speakers was the child of immigrants who were monolingual Spanish speakers. Evidence like this proves that the "Spanish sounds" of this language variety are not simply SLA phenomena.

Spanish clearly played a role in the development of Mexican

American English Varieties which are ethnically marked, and since it may continue to do so indirectly with the monolingual English speakers, those who are interested in the development of Mexican American English Varieties (MAEV) should have a working knowledge of the acquisition processes involved in its development. Understanding both L1 (first language) acquisition and L2 (second language) acquisition (or SLA) helps researchers to understand the perceptual strategies that might induce differences between those who acquire different dialects of the same language. Two leading theorists in the L1 and L2 acquisition of vowels are Patricia Kuhl and James Flege, whose common beliefs about the primacy of the F1/F2 vowel space (the acoustic correlates of vowels that are commonly described as the height and front/backness dimensions)[4] have led to the development of highly compatible theories (for example, Kuhl 1991, Kuhl 1992, Kuhl 1993, Kuhl and Iverson 1995, Flege 1995, Flege 2004, Flege, MacKay & Meador 1999, Flege, Munro & MacKay 1995, Flege, Schirru, & MacKay 2003).

Kuhl's model suggests that as children are exposed to their first language, they develop prototypes that warp the perceptual differences in the F1/F2 vowel space. Two sounds that are very close to a prototype will be very difficult to discriminate from one another because they are treated as an example of the same vowel, but two sounds that are the same distance from one another in another part of the F1/F2 space (one that is not "sufficiently" close to a prototype) are easier to discriminate from one another because there is not a category label causing interference. There are some problems with this approach, particularly the fact that F1 and F2 are given equal weighting while other factors (like duration, for example) are excluded, but there appears to be enough truth to this theory to make it worth considering, especially in relationship to SLA processes.

Flege's model, like Kuhls, suggests that speakers acquire prototypes in their first language, but since he is interested in L2 acquisition, his theory must also address transfer effects. He believes that L2 phonemes that are sufficiently distinct from those in the L1 system are, in some ways, easier to acquire since the speaker does not have to divide an already existing category, thus avoiding transference effects. By this logic, acquiring the vowel in bat is easier for an L1 Spanish Speaker than acquiring the vowel in *bit* because the *bat* vowel is sufficiently distinct from any other Spanish phoneme, but the *bit* vowel is too close to the vowel in *beet*, which Spanish has, to easily maintain a distinct perceptual category.

One critical flaw with much of the SLA research on this subject is that it fails to take into account the massive diversity in vowel pronunciations in North American English. In the Inland North,[5] for example, where White[6] people in large urban centers are undergoing a vowel change known as the Northern Cities Shift, we are seeing dramatic changes, including:

(1) fronting and raising of the vowel in *bat* so dramatically that it may sound like *bit* or *beet* in isolation: /æ/→ [ɪ] or [i]

(2) fronting of the vowel in *bot* so that it starts to sound like *bat*: /ɑ/→[æ]

(3) fronting and lowering of the vowel in *bought* so that it starts to sound like *bot*: /ɔ/→[ɑ]

(4) lowering and backing of the vowel in *bit* so that it starts to sound like *bet*:/ɪ/→[ɛ]

(5) lowering and backing of the vowel in *bet* so that it starts to sound like *bat* or the backing of it so that it starts to sound like *but*: /ɛ/→[æ] or /ɛ/→[ʌ]

(6) lowering and backing of the vowel in *but* so that it starts to sound like *bought*:/ʌ/→[ɔ]

Figure 1 illustrates the difference between the more conservative vowel system that researchers typically use as a baseline for American English (the shaded rings) [7] and the NCS system (indicated with arrows originating from the more conservative location of the relevant vowels); the Spanish five-vowel system is overlaid for comparison.

Figure 1: Conservative Estimation of American English compared to a divergent NCS system and a Spanish five vowel system

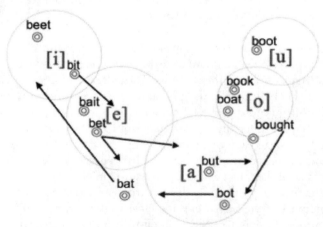

Contrast the possible NCS effects on the acquisition process with the potential effects of the shifts happening in the South (Figure 2) and in California (Figure 3). If phonetic details are important, as Flege's model suggests, L2 English speakers who are acquiring English in an environment where they are in frequent contact with NCS speakers would have a very different set of confusion patterns than those in other regions of the country.

Figure 2: Conservative Estimation of American English compared to a divergent Southern system and a Spanish five-vowel system

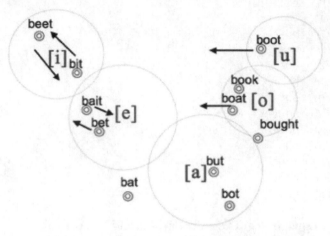

Figure 3: Conservative Estimation of American English compared to a divergent California system and a Spanish five-vowel system

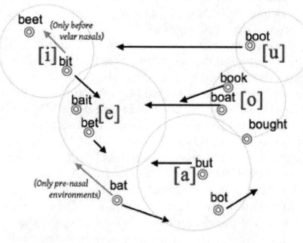

Finally, we should remember that even when Spanish impacts English, it doesn't always do so in straightforward ways. For example, English speakers rely very heavily on F1 and F2, the acoustic measurements that correspond roughly to the height and backness of the tongue position, but Spanish speakers, who have only five vowels in their phonemic inventory, may be far less reliant on F2 (the front/back dimension) as an acoustic cue.[8] So when Spanish language transference happens, it may have as much to do with the relative importance of the acoustic cues as with their actual qualities.

3. Regional and Ethnic Variation in the Vowel Space 3.1 The vowels in *beet* and *bit*:

L2 English speakers often have difficulty with vowel pairs like /i/ and /ɪ/, especially when they come from a five vowel system like Spanish that only has /i/. However, contrary to what is sometimes reported in the SLA literature, L2 learners do not just have difficulty with the new vowel (*bit*); they also have different boundaries for the *beet* vowel. For example, one Michigan informant reported that she was terrified to ask for a "*sheet*" of paper after an awkward incident where she accidentally produced a swear word. Still, the actual incidences of this overlap among native English speakers may be overreported.

Acoustic studies of Mexican Americans who are fluent English speakers have not shown widespread overlap of these two vowels that would indicate that Spanish transference dominates this dialect,[9] even among bilingual speakers in California (Godinez and Maddieson 1985). Other cues (e.g. duration, surrounding consonant variation, etc.) may condition perceptual similarities between *beet* and *bit*, but acoustic research on the F1/F2 vowel space suggests that most native English speakers are maintaining distinct productions (Godinez and Maddieson 1985, Ocumpaugh 2010, Ocumpaugh and Roeder 2007, Roeder 2006, Konopka and Pierrehumbert 2008).

Separation of these two vowels appears to be even more dramatic among Mexican Americans who are in contact with the lowered, backed *bit* vowel of the Northern Cities Shift. For example, in Benton Harbor, Michigan, only one of twenty speakers[10] showed conflation or reversal of the *beet* and *bit* vowels, results which are consistent with studies in the neighboring cities of Chicago and Lansing, which are also in the NCS region (Konopka and Pierrehumber 2008, Roeder 2006). In fact, this research indicates that Mexican Americans in the Inland North appear to be participating (at least minimally) with the lowering and backing of the *bit* vowel that is typical of the NCS.

To the extent that the separation of *bit* and *beet* is due to accommodation to regional variation in the Inland North (or even in California), it's possible that other regions of the country might induce overlap. The Southern Vowel Shift, most typical among rural Whites, is characterized by the reversal of these two vowels. It's possible that contact with this variety has caused overlap among some Mexican American varieties, though tense racial relationships between Whites and Mexican Americans in some parts of this country would probably inhibit accommodation between the two groups.

3.2 The vowels in *bait* and *bet*:

The Spanish vowel system has a sound that is very similar to the /e/ in *bait*, so this is not usually a vowel that language learners struggle with. However, the Spanish vowel is shorter and more monopthongal. This sometimes results in an ethnically marked pronunciation of the English *bait* vowel, both among second language learners and among native English speakers.

Spanish /e/ also overlaps English /ɛ/ in the F1/F2 vowel space, but the *bet* vowel, which is more monopthongal than the bait vowel, may be more difficult for L2 learners to acquire when they are in contact with more conservative varieties of English. Research shows that accommodation to regional variation can mitigate this effect in areas like the Inland North, where the bet vowel may start to sound like /æ/. (See discussion below in "The vowel in *bat*" section.)

Although the *bet* vowel is lowering among Whites in both the Inland North and California, it is somewhat raised in certain phonetic environments in parts of the South. The so-called *pin/pen* merger is a result of the blurring of pronunciations between the *bit* vowel and the *bet* vowel in prenasal environments. Mexican Americans in Pearsall, Texas (close to San Antonio), have been shown to participate in this merger, indicating accommodation to the regional White norm.

3.3 The vowel in *bat*:

There is no vowel in Spanish that is close enough to /æ/ (the vowel in *bat*) to cause perceptual confusion for L2 speakers, but we still find interesting patterns of variation in its production—both among those whose speech is considered ethnically marked (e.g. Mexican Americans) and among those whose speech is considered mainstream (e.g. conservative White speakers). In fact, there is tremendous variation in the bat vowel in the U.S., sometimes even within a single speaker. In large part, this is caused by phonological markedness. Put more simply, most languages don't have a vowel in this part of the vowel space because it is just a strange place to have a vowel. Given this crosslinguistic effect, it is no surprise that we see variation within the Mexican American community.

In Texas and other parts of the South, Mexican American speakers are known for their lower, backer productions of the *bat* vowel, so that *cat* might sound like *cot*. One study from North Carolina suggests that this backed production of the *bat* vowel has become such a salient identity marker that speakers who want to linguistically demonstrate their ethnicity actively manipulate this variable (Carter 2007). This pattern appears robust, but it may be geographically restricted.

In other parts of the country, Mexican Americans may be more likely to raise the *bat* vowel. In California, this variation appears to be somewhat restricted either in frequency or by phonetic context. Fought reports that Mexican Americans in California occasionally have a raised the *bat* vowel so that *bad* sounds more like *bed*, but that "they nonetheless maintain a contrast between [æ] and [ɛ]" (Fought 2003, 81-82). Other studies in California have reported overlap between the bat and *bet* vowels, but only pre-laterally (as in *elevator* or L.A.). Regardless, these instances do not appear to be an example of accommodation to regional variation since in California, Whites only raise the *bat* vowel in pre-nasal environments.

In the Inland North (Chicago, Benton Harbor, and Lansing), Mexican Americans have been found to show considerably greater overlap between the *bat* and *bet* vowels, a result that is highly compatible with the NCS. For example, many NCS speakers (who are usually urban, middle-class, White people) are beginning to show a complete reversal of these two vowels so that *laughed* sounds like *left* and vice versa. However, the overlap between these two vowels among Mexican Americans in the Inland North appears in a different part of the vowel space than in California. In California, Fought's research suggests that the *bat* vowel raises to meet the *bet* vowel, while evidence from the speakers in Benton Harbor, MI, suggests that the *bet* vowel is lowering far more than the *bat* vowel is raising. So, while Mexican Americans in both California and the Inland North are showing considerable overlap between *bat* and *bet*, the Californians are doing so at a height that is comparable to [e] or [ʌ] (and only pre-laterally), while the Northerners are doing so at a height that is comparable to [ɑ] (regardless of the phonetic environment).

In addition to establishing a regional distinction between Mexican Americans in the Inland North and California, this pattern (the lowering of the *bet* vowel with minimal raising of the *bat* vowel) also means that the Benton Harbor speakers are distinguishing themselves from other ethnicities within their own region. Recall that local Whites who participate in the NCS typically raise the *bat* vowel so much that it encroaches on the territory of /e/ or even /i/. By lowering the *bet* vowel, Mexican Americans in Benton Harbor, MI are showing accommodation to the regional norm, but they resist the raising of the *bat* vowel. The resulting overlap of *bat* and *bet* is similar to that of more mainstream speakers, but it is generally lower in the vowel space. The research on Mexican Americans in Lansing supports this conclusion, showing similar patterns of substantial convergence low in the F1/F2 vowel space (Roeder 2006). It has also yielded information about the differences in the relative importance of various acoustic cues. Instead of relying on the cues that most other English speakers favor (F1 and F2), the Mexican Americans in Lansing may be distinguishing between *bat* and *bet* with durational differences or by processes of dipthongization (Roeder 2006, Konopka 2011, Roeder 2010).

3.4 The vowels in *bot* and *bought*:

The vowels in *bot* and *bought* have been undergoing a change for the last several decades that has been quite interesting for those of us who study sociolinguistic variation, in part because it is one of the first documented sound changes that we have seen spread from the West coast to the East coast of the United States. However, it is also interesting because this is a case of a merger of two phonemes /ɑ/ and /ɔ/, and mergers are relatively rare in terms of sound changes.

Within the field of sociolinguistics, there are a number of debates raging about the nature of this merger, which is generally referred to as the *cot/caught* merger.[11] Not everybody believes it is a complete merger, though some who acquired it natively (myself included) are so merged that we often do better following this debate on paper than in person. Some believe that production differences are being maintained, if not in the F1/F2 space, then in other acoustic cues. Others are interested in how close the two vowels can get within the speech of a single speaker before that person is no longer able to hear the difference. Interestingly, though, this near-amputation from the vowel system does not attract much attention from the general public. As a native speaker of this change, no one but fellow linguists ever laughs at me for my missing vowel, and only a former professor has ever accused me of being "phonemically deformed." Instead, it is generally accepted as a mainstream pronunciation of Standard English.

For Mexican Americans who show substrate Spanish influence, the cot/caught merger is easy to accommodate to. Not only is it compatible with the Spanish system, which does not have two vowels in this space, it is so unobtrusive that there are no stereotypes to avoid with it. In fact, in parts of the country, Mexican Americans may be better producers of this merger than the White speakers who seem to have originated the change. Cynthia Bernstein (1993) demonstrates that in places like Texas, we see a tri-ethnic distribution pattern where Mexican Americans are most likely to be merged, African Americans are least likely to be merged, and White people fall somewhere in between.

However, the *cot/caught* merger is not found among White speakers in places like the Inland North, where the Northern Cities Shift is having a very different effect on these two vowels. Here, the situation is more complicated. In the NCS, the *bot* vowel fronts so that *cot* sounds like *cat*, and the *bought* vowel fronts and lowers so that *caught* sounds like *cot*. The NCS's fronter production of the *bot* (*cot*) vowel is compatible with Spanish phonetic patterns and appears to be easy to accommodate to. The low, front *bought* (*caught*) vowel of the NCS should also be easy to accommodate to if Spanish phonology is causing it to be produced like *bot* anyway. What we still don't understand is how, precisely, the NCS interacts with those who are L2 learners and how it interacts with those from regions of the country where the *caught/cot* merger is the norm. Evidence from native speakers in the studies conducted in Chicago, Lansing, and Benton Harbor suggests that Mexican Americans in the Inland North usually have distinct productions of these vowels, but some may still show some overlap or confusion if they are second language learners. We also find Mexican Americans in that area who are native English Speakers from Texas, where they might have acquired the *caught/cot* merger, and this complicates their acquisition of the NCS.

3.5 The vowel in *but*:

Like the vowels in *bought* and *bat*, the vowel in *but* is not part of the Spanish inventory. For that reason, we expect to see some assimilation of it to /ɑ/, at least among non-native speakers. Among Mexican Americans who are native English speakers complete overlap seems less common, but not unheard of. In some parts of the country, a lowered pronunciation of the vowel in *but* may be a marker of ethnic identity even if the vowels are still remaining distinct.

Regionally, though, we do find variation that is tied to mainstream sound changes. Mexican American speakers in the Inland North are backing the vowel in *but* so that *cut* sounds more like *caught* than it might in other parts of the country. Remember, however, that this accommodation to the NCS is not likely to cause overlap in the pronunciations of these two vowels since the vowel in *bought* is also lowering and fronting among these speakers.

3.6 The vowel in <u>bite</u>:

The English vowel /aɪ/, as in *bite*, is a dipthong that usually begins very low in the mid-front[12] part of the mouth (near [a]) and raises towards [ɪ]. Southern varieties of English (and, for historical reasons, African American varieties of English) tend to show monopthongization of this vowel that is often socially stigmatized, but those who study dialects have found considerably more variation, much of which is probably not noticeable even to those who use monopthongal pronunciations of the *bite* vowel to stereotype Southerners and African Americans.

Within the South, there is substantial variation. There are areas in the South that do not typically monophthongize at all. For example, the Tidewater regions of Virginia and North Carolina tend to pronounce these with [əɪ]. Among those who do monophthongize, there are differences in

the phonetic environment that conditions it. In most of the South, speakers monopthonigize only in (1) syllable final positions and in (2) pre-voiced conditions (when the following, tautosyllabic consonant[13] is voiced, rather than voiceless). This means that you would find a pronunciation of [a] for [aɪ] in (1) *lie* and (2) *lied*, but not in (3) *light*. There are pockets in the South that do monopthongize in all three conditions, such as the Appalachians and parts of Texas, but this is less common.

It might seem strange that Southerners differentiate between a pre-voiced and a pre-voiceless condition, but acoustic research in other parts of the country have found variation even among those whose diphthongal pronunciations are considered standard. Thomas has shown that in front of voiceless consonants (like /t/), you find a steep transition from [a] ending in a near-steady-state acoustic pattern for [ɪ]. Meanwhile, in front of voiced consonants, (like /d/), you find a steady-state formant pattern for [a] followed by a steep transition towards [ɪ] (Thomas 2000).[14] Among Mexican Americans, we tend to find very different patterns. Thomas's (2000) study shows that Mexican Americans in Laredo, TX tend to have two steady-state formants with a very short, steep transition between them. He suggests, based on Manrique's research on Spanish dipthongs, that this is a case of Spanish transference (Borzone de Manrque 1979). (Spanish diphthongs tend to always have two steady states and it is unlikely that the White population in Texas would have such pronunciations.) It is possible that this became a linguistic marker of ethnicity in many parts of the country, but we also find accommodation to regional norms.

Figure 4: Some spectral differences in the pronunciation of the *bite* vowel. The first drawing approximates the F1/F2 pattern of the word *tide*, as spoken by one of Thomas' speakers from Ohio. The second approximates the formant pattern of the word *tight*, as spoken by the same speaker. The third approximates the Mexican American pattern.

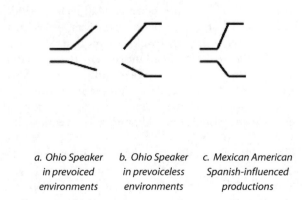

a. Ohio Speaker in prevoiced environments *b. Ohio Speaker in prevoiceless environments* *c. Mexican American Spanish-influenced productions*

Pronunciation, Phonetics, Linguistics, Dialect/Accent Studies
Regional Variation and Mexican American English by Jaclyn Ocumpaugh

Research among Mexican Americans in Siler City, North Carolina finds that the Spanish-sounding pronunciation of /aɪ/ appears to be preferred but raises interesting questions about the development of Mexican American English regionally. Spectral analysis finds large disparities in the pronunciation of the *bite* vowel, even among individual speakers who are producing it as a diphthong. Some appear to be accommodating to the local pattern of monopthongization in open syllables and in pre-voiced conditions, but there is not evidence of widespread, wholesale accommodation to this local norm even though these speakers are L2 English speakers who have acquired their English locally. Given the particularly hateful anti-immigrant sentiment that greeted many in this town,[15] it is no surprise to linguists that these speakers might hesitate to accommodate even to the most pervasive local norms. However, if race relations improve locally, we may find that the fledgling pattern of monopthongization becomes more widespread.[16/17]

3.7 The vowel in *boat*:

The English vowel /o/ (as in *boat*) is very similar to the Spanish vowel, though the English version is longer, less rounded, and usually more dipthongal. For this reason, second language learners sometimes have a marked pronunciation of /o/, but it is rarely confused with other sounds. Among some Mexican American Native English speakers, the shorter, rounder pronunciation appears to have become a marker of ethnic identity. However, since duration is rarely studied in sociophonetic studies, very little can be said about the acoustics of this phenomenon.

3.8 The vowel in *boot*:

The /u/ in English words like *boot* is very similar to the Spanish vowel in most dialects of American English. However, White speakers in California show some variation in the pronunciation of this vowel, namely fronting, and two different acoustic studies of Mexican Americans in California suggest that they are also participating in this change. The first, published by Godinez and Maddison in 1985 showed instances of /u/ that were as far forward as these speakers' tokens of the *bot* vowel (Godinez and Maddieson 1985). The second, conducted more than 10 years later, showed tokens of /u/ that were beginning to overlap with /i/(Fought 1999, Fought 2003). Cumulatively, this research suggests that Mexican Americans are becoming more advanced in this regional sound change as the years go by.

4.0 The roles of social networks and identity:

As discussed earlier in this paper, sociolinguists spent a considerable amount of time trying to persuade people that the language varieties of Mexican Americans and other Latino groups are legitimate linguistic systems and not just imperfectly learned English. Though this is now a well-established fact in our literature, socially-stigmatizing stereotypes still exist, so it would be irresponsible to report these variables in the vowel system without discussing the ways in which social networks and identity also play a role in establishing these dialects. Sociolinguists would never suggest, for example, that these are genetically inherited language traits or that deviation from what is considered "Standard English" is in anyway indicative of anything other than one's social network or the identity one is trying to project.

The research that is drawn upon for this article is based mainly on aggregate data from a number of different acoustic studies (Godinez and Maddieson 1985, Carter 2007, Fought 1999, Fought 2003, Konopka and Pierrehumbert 2008, Ocumpaugh 2010, Ocumpaugh and Roeder 2007, Roeder 2006, Roeder 2009, Roeder 2010), but individuals do not always pattern like the aggregate. In fact, sociolinguists typically find variation based on a variety of social variables, including the following:

(1) region, including urban vs. rural distinctions
(2) race/ethnicity
(3) sex/gender
(4) socioeconomic status
(5) age/generation
(6) religion
(7) and any other grouping that is important to the community we are studying

In many cases, analysis of these factors provides a sufficient understanding of the mechanisms involved in sound change. For example, we know that young, White, urban women are leading the change in the NCS (Eckert 1989, Roeder 2010).

In other research paradigms, we rely on studies of social network structures to understand how a change might be spreading through the community. For example, Leslie Milroy has designed a survey that many researchers duplicate in order to understand the strength of different network ties in a community, and we have learned that those communities where people have dense, multiplex ties (e.g. your neighbor is also a family member or a coworker), language variables tend to remain more stable. Conversely, in communities where those territorial ties are weaker, language change can spread rapidly. In fact, the research on Mexican Americans in Benton Harbor, Michigan seems to confirm the hypotheses of the network paradigm. This loose-knit community, composed largely of former migrant workers, has only been in the region for a generation, but is already beginning to show partial accommodation to the Northern Cities Shift.

Mere proximity is not always enough for one group of people to begin to sound like another, however, and while network ties can certainly help to explain some differences, they cannot explain all of them. Clearly, language variation is sometimes exploited as a performance of identity, and this may be especially true for some Mexican Americans since, some might argue, a wider range of variance is available to them than to some other ethnic groups. Duran, for example, has shown in her study of prosody and pronunciation shifts that the English of Mexican Americans may vary widely even among generational cohorts in a closely-knit family (Duran 2001). Duran's study, which demonstrates that Spanish pronunciations are used symbolically by speakers who might otherwise pass as part of the mainstream, highlights the ideological involvement in the development of linguistic patterns, but the motivations for these changes are sometimes not carefully studied within sociolinguistics.

Speakers who want to show linguistic allegiance to the Mexican American community may actively work to develop networks that foster similar linguistic patterns, while others may choose to pursue linguistic contacts with those in less ethnically-marked linguistic communities. Ideology probably plays a role both in the initial development of these networks and in the (often) subconscious decisions people make about whether or not to accommodate linguistically to those with whom they interact.

Those who are in the profession of voice coaching should take these factors into consideration as they help speakers to find their own voice or the voice of the character they are portraying. Many of the changes that we see regionally are likely a result of language-internal reorganization processes caused by conflicts between ease of production and ease of perception. (Put more simply, languages change even when their speakers are not in contact with significantly different systems because the needs of the tongue and the needs of the ear do not always perfectly align.) Groups like Mexican Americans, who have contact with second language influences (directly or indirectly), may have an additional set of language-internal influences, but this is a largely quantitative difference more than a qualitative one. Most people, regardless of their ethnicity, have a range of linguistic options that they can exploit. It's important to remember that even though people ascribe social hierarchy to the linguistic differences that they notice, linguistically, they aren't really any different from any other changes that are occurring in the American English landscape.

Notes

1. Gratitude for help with this work is owed to a great number of people. My research in Benton Harbor was supported by a grant from the National Science Foundation (BCS-0444349). A number of people helped me with my initial fieldwork in Benton Harbor, including many anonymous subjects and Drs. Rebecca Roeder and Tara Sanchez. Dr. Dennis Preston and the other members of my dissertation committee have provided valuable insights that have helped me to better understand my own data and the literature reviewed here, and I have benefited greatly from the suggestions of Erik Singer and two anonymous reviewers who commented on an earlier version of this article. Any mistakes are, of course, my own.

2. Note that while the dipthongal quality of /e/ and /o/ is often represented as /ei/ and /oʊ/ in phonetics textbooks, sociolinguists do not always follow this convention. Some do measure the off-glides on these vowels, but since their changes are far less dramatic than /aɪ/ (for example), many simply measure the onset.

3 Substrate Spanish effects are probably used symbolically by members of this community to distinguish themselves from other ethnic groups, and in some cases, may be considered stereotypical features of Mexican American speech. Unfortunately, both acoustics and perception are desperately understudied within sociolinguistics. For example, few studies have investigated what acoustic cues people are relying upon when they categorize someone as "sounding Standard," though perceptual dialectology research by Dennis Preston suggests that these judgments would vary regionally. Similarly, research on which acoustic qualities cause someone's speech to be categorized as "sounding Mexican" is also needed, so the reader will have to tolerate some educated guesses about the stereotypes surrounding these varieties.

4. The vocal folds produce a fundamental (repeating) frequency, which is then filtered by the vocal tract. In vowels, this results in bands of energy, which are referred to as formants. When wideband spectrographs are used, the first one is labeled F1, then F2, then F3 and so on. The first two bands of energy correlate closely with tongue position. F1 inversely correlates with tongue height so that the higher the tongue, the lower the F1 value. F2 correlates with frontness so that the higher F2 is the closer the tongue is to the lips. F3 correlates with lip rounding. These are not perfect correlations, but it is relatively uncontroversial to conflate the acoustics with the articulation in sociolinguistic circles, since, while the use of F1 and F2 is somewhat lacking in precision when it comes to describing tongue position, these acoustic cues are far more precise than the impressionistic estimations of where the tongue is that were traditionally given in dialectology. Most sociolinguistic research relies solely on F1 and F2, with a tacit understanding that these acoustic cues often interact with each other and with cues like duration, pitch, etc. Some try to capture this interaction by augmenting these measurements. For example, they might adjust F2 based on F3 (or F1 based on F2), since, when these formants are close together, the brain doesn't necessarily process them as separate entities. Methods discussions continue among members of the field, but the use of F1 and F2 is still the primary vehicle for exploring sociophonetic variation in American vowels.

5. The Inland North dialect region borders the southern shores of the Great Lakes, including western New York state, Northern Ohio and Indiana, most of the lower Peninsula of Michigan, Chicago and

its surrounding suburbs in northern Illinois, and eastern Wisconsin. The Northern Cities Shift affects this region, though it is generally thought to skip over western Pennsylvania, due in large part to the unique dialect situation in Pittsburgh, PA.

6. Although many researchers have conventionally referred to "White" people using lower case letters, there are a few social scientists who are beginning to capitalize this term. This is largely due to the fact that there is not a good parallel for the term African Americans. The term Anglo Americans denotes White people who descended from the Anglo Saxons peoples of England. While Anglo Americans have substantially shaped American culture, the term excludes many White people, including others who descend from the British Isles. The term Caucasion has similar problems, denoting people who are from the Caucus regions (near Turkey and Russia), and the term European American excludes Whites who descended from other parts of the world (e.g. Russia or former British colonies).

7. The use of Peterson and Barney's (1952) vowels to represent a conservative American English vowel system is traditional in sociolinguistic research, but it is not without controversy. Peterson and Barney averaged the systems of 76 men, women and children, and little is known about the background of these speakers. The field would probably benefit from the use of a controlled sample from a single, known dialect area, but so far we continue to rely on this early study.

8. Note, for example, that Escudero and Boersma (2001) have shown that Scottish English speakers rely more on duration than on F2. Given the extreme differences in F2 in a five-vowel system, it seems likely that Spanish speakers would be far less sensitive to this.

9. Further research is needed, but it is not uncommon to find some overlap in the vowel space even among speakers who are not speaking English varieties that have been influenced by a foreign language. Nothing in the literature or in my own research indicates that these two vowels show the kinds of overlap you might expect based on transfer effects among most speakers of this dialect.

10. The twenty speakers in this sample represented a large range of language backgrounds. Most acquired English before the age of 10, but more
concrete acquisition details were difficult to confirm. Most of them were bilingual. The speaker who showed reversal was a man in his 70s who had
acquired English in the Valley region of South Texas, but who had lived in Michigan for several decades. He had no memory of learning English, suggesting he had learned it at a very young age.

11. See Chapter 2 of Bowie's (2000) dissertation for a thorough review of
the literature on vowel mergers.

12. Note that while /aɪ/ is classified phonologically as a mid-front vowel, it exhibits considerable regional variation. Thomas (2001, 34-38) discusses this variation at length, and his subsequent vowel plots of speakers from across North America show extreme variation in its phonetic realizations.

13. A consonant in the coda of the same syllable, as opposed to a consonant in the onset of the following syllable.

14. This appears to be a difference in the timing of the articulation, rather
than a difference in tongue gestures. In the first, the transition between the [a] and the [ɪ] takes up the first half of pronunciation of this diphthong; in the second, the transition is delayed.

15. See Moriello's discussion of this situation in her 2003 MA thesis, which documents a David Duke KKK rally that occurred in Siler City in response to the rapid increase of first generation immigrants from Mexico.

16. I have recently spoken with Moriello, and she was uncomfortable speculating on whether or not racial tensions have cooled since this research first came out. Her MA thesis documents anti-immigrant rallies, including one led by David Duke, and to our knowledge, there have not been any recent repeats of this situation. On the other hand, anti- immigrant sentiments appear to be on the rise in this country, and there's no reason to believe that Siler City would be immune to this hostility.

17. It is generally accepted within the field of linguistics that, if all other factors are equal, speakers are more likely to accommodate to someone that they like than they are to someone that they dislike. Accommodation Theory, as this is known has, is often associated with researchers like Giles (e.g., Giles, Coupland, & Coupland 1991).

Bibliography

Bernstein, Cynthia. 1993. Social Causes of Phonological Variation. *American Speech*. 63 (3): 227-240.

Borzone de Manrique, Ana Maria. 1977. On the recognition of isolated Spanish vowels. *Current issues in phonetic sciences: proceedings of the IPS-77 Congress, Miami Beach Florida*. 677-682.

Bowie, David. 2000. The Effect of Geographic Mobility on the Retention of a Local Dialect. PhD diss., University of Pennsylvania.

Carter, Phillip M. 2007. Phonetic Variation and Speaker Agency: Mexicana Identity in a North Carolina Middle School. *University of Pennsylvania Working Papers in Linguistics*. 13 (2): 1-13.

Duran, Amanda R. 2001. Language Use and Identity in a Bilingual Community: Re-Examining the English of Mexican Americans. PhD diss., University of Texas.

Eckert, Penelope. 1989. The Whole Woman: Sex and Gender Differences in Variation. *Language Variation and Change*. 1:245-67.

Escudero, Paola and Paul Boersma. 2001. Modeling the Perceptual Development of Phonological Contrasts with Optimality Theory and the Gradual Learning Algorithm. *Proceedings of the 25th Penn Linguistics Colloquium. Penn Working Papers in Linguistics*.

Flege, James Emil. 1995. "Second Language Speech Learning Theory, Findings, and Problems," in *Speech Perception and Linguistic Experience: Issues in Cross-Language Research*. Baltimore: York Press, 233-277.

Flege, James Emil and Ian R. A. MacKay. 2004. Perceiving Vowels in a Second Language. *Studies in Second Language Acquisition*, 26 (1): 1-34.

Flege, James Emil, Ian R. A. MacKay and Diane Meador. 1999. Native Italian speakers' perception and production of English vowels. *Journal of the Acoustical Society of America*, 106 (5): 2973-2987.

Flege, James Emil, Murray J. Munro and Ian R.A. MacKay. 1995. Factors affecting strength of perceived foreign accent in a second language. *Journal of the Acoustical Society of America*. 97 (5): 3125-3134.

Flege, James Emil, Carol Schirru, and Ian R. A. MacKay. 2003. Interaction between the native and second language phonetic subsystems. *Speech Communication*. 40:467-491.

Fought, Carmen. 2003. *Chicano English in Context*. Palgrave: New York, New York.

Fought, Carmen. 1999. A majority sound change in a minority community: /u/-fronting in Chicano English. *Journal of Sociolinguistics*. 3 (1):5-23.

Giles, Howard, Nikolas Coupland, & Justine Coupland. 1991. Accommodation Theory: Communication, Context, and Consequence. In *Contexts of Accommodation. Developments in Applied Linguistics*, edited by Howard Giles, Nikolas Coupland and Justine Coupland. Cambridge: Cambridge University Press.

Godinez, Manual Jr. and Ian Maddieson. 1985. Vowel differences between Chicano and General California English. *International Journal of Society and Language*. 43-58 Gordon E. Peterson and Harold L Barney. 1952. Control Methods Used in the Study of Vowels. The Journal of the Acoustical Society of America. 24(2):175-184.

Konopka, Kenneth and Janet Pierrehumbert. 2008. Vowels in contact: Mexican Heritage English in Chicago. Texas Linguistic Forum *Proceedings of the Sixteenth Annual Symposium About Language and Society* – Austin [SALSA]) 52:94-103.

Konopka, Kenneth. 2011. Community Consensus and the vowels of Mexican heritage English. Paper presented at the annual meeting of the *Linguistics Society of America*. Pittsburgh,PA.

Kuhl, Patricia K. 1991. Human adults and human infants show a Perceptual magnet effect" for the prototypes of speech categories, monkeys do not. *Perceptual Psychophysics*. 50:93-107.

Kuhl, Patricia K. 1992. "Psychoacoustics and Speech Perception: Internal Standards, Perceptual Anchors, and Prototypes," in *Developmental Psychoacoustics*, ed. L. Werner and E. Rubell. American Psychological Association, Hyattsville, MD.

Kuhl, Patricia K. 1993. Early linguistic experience and phonetic perception: implications for theories of developmental speech perception. *Journal of Phonetics.* 21:125-139.

Kuhl, Patricia K. and Paul Iverson. 1995. Chapter 4: Linguistic Experience and the "Perceptual Magnet Effect," in *Speech perception and Linguistic experience: Issues in Cross-Language Research.* Ed. Winfred Strange. York Press, Baltimore, 121- 154.

Labov, William. Sharon Ash and Charles Boberg. 2000. *The Atlas of North American English: Phonetics, Phonology, and Sound Change.* Berlin: Mouton de Gruyter.

Labov, William. 1994. *Principles of Linguistic Change. Volume 1: Internal Factors.* Oxford: Basil Blackwell, 1994.

Ladefoged, Peter. 2005. *Vowels and Consonants: An Introduction to the Sounds of Languages.* 2nd ed. Malden, Mass.: Blackwell.

Moriello, Rebecca. 2003. 'I'm feeksin' to move . . . ': Hispanic English in Siler City, North Carolina. MA thesis, North Carolina State University.

Moriello, Rebecca, and Walt Wolfram. 2003. New Dialect Formation in the Rural South: Emerging Hispanic English Varieties in the Mid-Atlantic. *Penn Working Papers in Linguistics.* 9 (2): 135-147.

Ocumpaugh, Jaclyn, 2010. Regional Variation in Chicano English: Incipient Dialect Formation among L1 and L2 Speakers in Benton Harbor, Michigan. PhD Diss, Michigan State University.

Ocumpaugh, Jaclyn and Rebecca V. Roeder. 2007. Mexican American English in Context: Accommodation to Other Available Norms in Lower Michigan. *Linguistica Atlanatica,* 27:71-75.

Roeder, Rebecca V. 2009. The Effects of Phonetic Environment on English /æ/ Among Speakers of Mexican Heritage in Michigan. *Toronto Working Papers in Linguistics* 31.

Roeder, Rebecca V. 2006. Ethnicity and Sound Change: Mexican American Accommodation to the Northern Cities Shift in Michigan, PhD diss., Michigan State University, 2006.

Roeder, Rebecca V. 2010. Northern Cities Mexican American English: Vowel production and perception. *American Speech.* 85 (2): 163-184.

Thomas, Erik and Malch Yaeger-Dror, 2010. *African American English Speakers and Their Participation in Local Sound Changes: A Comparative Study.* Publication of the American Dialect Society 94. Durham, NC: Duke University Press

Thomas, Erik, 2001. *An Acoustic Analysis of Vowel Variation in New World English.* Publication of the American Dialect Society 85. Durham, NC: Duke University Press.

Thomas, Erik, 2000. Spectral differences in /ai/ offsets conditioned by voicing of the following consonant. *Journal of Phonetics* 28:1–25.

Wolfram, Walt, Phillip Carter, and Beckie Moriello. 2004. Emerging Hispanic English: New dialect formations in the American South. *Journal of Sociolinguistics.* 8 (3): 339-358.

Essay *by Louis Colaianni*

Bearing the Standard: Issues of Speech in Education

Photo credit: Larry F. Levenson

Louis Colaianni a former editor of The Voice and Speech Review, is the author of *The Joy of Phonetics and Accents; Bringing Speech to Life; How to Speak Shakespeare: and Shakespeare's Names: A New Pronouncing Dictionary*. His innovative approach to phonetics and stage accents is used in dozens of Universities and training programs. Recently, he was Vocal Coach for Will Ferrell's Broadway and HBO productions of *You're Welcome, America*, Dialect Coach for the Off-Broadway revival of *Bram Stoker's Dracula*, and Dialect Coach for the feature film *Little Red Wagon* (2012). He teaches Speech and Acting Classics in The Actors Studio MFA program at Pace University. He has taught at universities from coast to coast and given workshops internationally.

In April, 2010, many in the voice and speech community were alarmed to learn of a recommendation from the Arizona Department of Education that certain "heavily accented" teachers of English be reassigned to other duties (Jordan 2010). At that time, amidst a small flurry of emails, some of us contemplated writing an official VASTA position. But the University of Arizona Department of Linguistics' cogent response to Arizona Governor, Jan Brewer, below, addressed the issue so thoroughly that further comment was unnecessary:

1) 'Heavily accented' speech is not the same as 'unintelligible' or 'ungrammatical' speech.
2) Speakers with strong foreign accents may nevertheless have mastered grammar and idioms of English as well as native speakers.
3) Teachers whose first language is Spanish may be able to teach English to Spanish-speaking students better than teachers who don't speak Spanish.
4) Exposure to many different speech styles, dialects and accents helps (and does not harm) the acquisition of a language.
5) It is helpful for all students (English language learners as well as native speakers) to be exposed to foreign-accented speech as a part of their education.
6) There are many different 'accents' within English that can affect intelligibility, but the policy targets foreign accents and not dialects of English.
7) Communicating to students that foreign accented speech is 'bad' or 'harmful' is counterproductive to learning, and affirms pre-existing patterns of linguistic bias and harmful 'linguistic profiling'.
8) There is no such thing as 'unaccented' speech, and so policies aimed at eliminating accented speech from the classroom are paradoxical.
 (Nilep 2010)

At a time of division over immigration policy and border control, "heavily accented" teachers whose first language is Spanish are particularly vulnerable to linguistic bias. Yet as the response indicates, there are many varieties of accented English, including native varieties, which may be subject to bias as well. As with the accents of foreigners, heavy accents of native speakers may also be intelligible and grammatical. Communicating to students that "standard speech" is the only type of "good speech" and that regional or ethnic native accents are "bad" or "harmful" is also counterproductive to learning. Yet educators and others may consider these accents unsuitable academically, in the workplace, and on the national scene, and appropriate only for use in the home and in insular communities.

In my career in theatre and education, having taught speech to students from around the world, I have come to regard "standard speech" as an oppressive, bland and archaic tool for speech improvement. In its place, I find that the only fair and reliable indicator of "good speech" is intelligible eloquence. Irrespective of the listener's judgment of a speaker's accent, or the connotations of culture, status, mores or standards which the listener may infer, if the language is clearly understood and the content is compelling, good speech has been achieved. I have partially learned this lesson from my work in the theatre, where I often coach actors to recreate national, regional and class-based speech when dramatic literature requires it. Yet for plays that do not require specific stage accents, I often encourage actors to speak in their own language patterns, rather than any sort of stage standard. I find, for instance, Shakespeare usually sounds better in an actor's native accent than it does with any other accent imposed. When working outside of the theatre, with individuals, often foreign, who are seeking personal improvement, I have learned to value their accents as witnesses to life's adventure and proud proclaimers of origin and heritage. I have learned through the courage and persistence of my students that intelligible eloquence is a hard-earned right and that one of the major obstacles in

Pronunciation, Phonetics, Linguistics, Dialect/Accent Studies
Bearing the Standard: Issues of Speech in Education by Louis Colaianni

their quest for it is the disapproval of others. Having spent my career in higher education, I can only imagine how these issues compound in public schools where administrative edicts, educational trends and, perhaps, negative perceptions harbored by teachers and peers, might conspire to devalue a child's way of speaking.

Issues of linguistic bias in education set the stage for Anne H. Charity Hudley and Christine Mallinson's book *Understanding English Language Variation in U.S. Schools.* The authors' particular focus is language variation among African American and Southern American students, K-12. They address how students with identifiably Southern and African American language patterns can adjust to the school environment and meet its requirements. They examine the confusions that arise because of language difference and describe in some detail Southern and African American language patterns in contrast to standard American English. The authors state four main goals: teaching standardized English (including standardized accents) to students with Southern American and African American dialects; sensitizing teachers not to interpret students' use of these dialects as linguistic errors; improving student performance on standardized tests (which are often biased against these dialects); and appreciating the students' dialects as significant, both individually and culturally. In defining these goals the authors confront the susceptibility of these dialects to ridicule, judgment and exclusion and the unfairness that this is so. They note: "Non-standardized varieties of English are as rule-governed, patterned and predictable in their linguistic structures as standard varieties are" (Charity Hudley and Mallinson, 2).

In describing the authors' goals, I use the word *dialect* to encompass an individual's entire language style: grammar, vocabulary, idiom, accent and intonation. In this context, the authors actually avoid the term dialect, using "non-standardized" American English in its place (Charity Hudley and Mallinson, xvii). Citing "register," the linguistic term for levels of formality, the authors condone written and spoken "home" language varieties for casual, social situations. But they warn that students whose dialects identify them as Southern or African American may experience disadvantages in the pursuit of housing and employment, as well as in interaction with authority figures. As a voice and speech specialist, and for the purposes of this article, I am primarily concerned with how the authors address the way their students talk.

In fairness, the authors are grappling with the difficult, heretofore unsolved problem of linguistic equality in education, but at times I find this book difficult to embrace. The authors attempt to coalesce traditional language standards and multicultural ideology into a unified pedagogy. Their promise of multiculturalism—"mainstream cultural as-

similation is not achievable, required, or desirable for a harmonious society"—and their hard-line prescriptivism— "educators know that students who do not sound Southern... are more likely to succeed in their educational and job experiences,"—do not easily coexist (Charity Hudley and Mallinson 49). The authors' efforts to reconcile these polar opposites result in a dense web of perspectives, definitions and jargon from which their point of view is hard for me to discern. Of particular concern are the corrective measures they suggest for students' accents. Aware that Southern and African American accents are subject to negative attitudes in educational and professional settings, they choose to accommodate these attitudes rather than dispel them.

> There is often a stigma attached to Southern English, expressed in the media, by outsiders, and sometimes by Southerners themselves.... Educators know that students who do not sound Southern are more likely to...succeed in their educational and job experiences and less likely to be told that they sound country, redneck, ignorant, or uneducated. (Charity Hudley and Mallinson, 49)

It may be advisable to adhere to certain standards of written English on job applications and the like. But, the authors justify suppression of "non-standardized" *speaking* patterns on the same basis as "non-standardized" written *grammar*. This defies the sociolinguistic premise recognizing a far greater level of tolerance for variation in spoken forms than written forms. Spoken and written forms are not subject to a comparable standard. Writing, by its nature, is held to a far more stringent standard than speaking. Rosina Lippi-Green illuminates this in her book *English with an Accent: Language, Ideology and Discrimination in the United States:*

> Spoken language is an innate human capacity... written language is not universal and must be rigorously taught...
> Spoken language draws heavily on paralinguistic features... tone of voice, body language... written language cannot rely on these resources and must use punctuation, [and] additional constructions when written letters do not suffice...
> Spoken language is primarily a social activity... between two or more persons... written language is... a solitary pursuit with an audience removed in space and time...
> Spoken language allows confusion and ambiguity to be resolved directly by repair and confirmation procedures... written language does not allow confusion and ambiguity to be immediately resolved...
> Spoken language is used in a social, temporal context... written language is contextless and thus more prone to ambiguity...

Spoken language can be planned or spontaneous...
written language is by nature planned...
Spoken language is ephemeral... written language is
permanent...
Spoken language is inherently variable... written language actively suppresses and discourages variation.
(Lippi-Green 1997, 20)

Despite the sociolinguistic principles expressed in their
goals, Charity Hudley and Mallinson emphasize the
need for students to suppress their Southern and African
American accents, albeit on a situational basis, in order to
"sound educated" (Charity Hudley and Mallinson, 6). Yet
to sound educated is to say educated things, not to acquire
a speaking style intended to create the impression of saying
educated things. Sounding educated is nothing if it lacks
the authenticity of being educated and education is not
fertilized by any particular accent. A preoccupation with
the external effect of "educated speech" may hinder the
student from the deeper developmental practice of speaking eloquently, voicing learned perspectives in persuasive,
intuitive and expressive ways.

The authors reject the term "standard English," because
it implies "some sort of single standard variety of English
exists, irrespective of social norms, registers or situational
contexts.... Different situations often yield different standardized forms of talk." (Charity Hudley and Mallinson,
12) They use, instead, the term "standardized." They offer
an analogy between "standardized English" and standardized tests. Specific types of language are valued in education "just as specific types of knowledge are valued on standardized tests." (Charity Hudley and Mallinson, 11) Many
such tests include spoken, as well as written, components
and one of the authors' goals is to raise the test scores of
their "non-standardized speaking" students. This is offset
by their acknowledgement of the long-standing cultural
biases for which standardized tests are notorious. In the era
of the federal initiative "No Child Left Behind," (NCLB)—
which emphasizes the raising of scores on standardized
tests and commensurate rewards for teachers, schools and
districts—I almost can't blame the authors for focusing on
external outcomes rather than the rich internal processes of
language development.

One criticism made by detractors of NCLB is that it
forces teachers to "teach to the test" (Scrag 2000), fostering regurgitative, rather than experiential learning. In the
sensitive environment of language skill development, where
the authority and eloquence of individual students must be
nurtured and supported, it seems inappropriate to impose
the stringent standards of heavily biased tests. The authors
spend a great deal of time offering practical strategies for
coaching students in the written and oral tasks required
of standardized tests. Owing to test bias, students from

"non-standardized" backgrounds are sometimes taught to
interpret the emotions associated with facial expressions
depicted in standardized test illustrations, i.e. Test illustration: Smiling face; answer: Happy. Test illustration: frown-
ing face; Answer: Sad (Charity Hudley and Mallinson, 127).
Teaching emotion as a testing strategy is a bleak proposition for teachers of the living, expressive subjects of English
and Language Arts.

From page one the authors use the term "standardized
English" in intentional contrast to "standard English" and
in Chapter Two they greatly expand on their reasons for
doing this. Even then, they do not offer a concise definition of the term, but parcel out the definition in pieces
at various points. By consolidating the threads of their
definition, I gather that "standardized English" refers to a
multiple set of language standards, gauged for situational
use, encompassing the "rules, norms, conventions, patterns and features" of American English, with the caveat
that identifiable traits of Southern and African American
English are only tolerated to a limited extent. The authors
also name "standardized English" as "the variety of privilege and prestige" spoken by "powerful decision makers." I
find myself confused by their varying definitions of "standardized English" as multiple patterns and a single variety,
but, eventually, the multiple, situational definition prevails.
"Standardized English" might be thought of as a situational
slide rule for all activities, not just school-related ones.
While the authors might consider it "non-standardized" to
converse with friends in what they call the "home variety,"
all situations beyond the most casual register would call for
some degree of "standardized English." In order to achieve
"standardized English," as the authors conceive it, students
must learn to calibrate the appropriate level of "standard"
grammar and accent for situations of every register.

Charity Hudley and Mallinson identify their approach as
multicultural and pro-diversity. They seek to "honor the
students' linguistic and cultural backgrounds" while also
teaching "standardized English that students need to succeed in school life." This is somewhat persuasive if the authors are referring to written English. But they consistently
use the single term, "standardized English," to refer to two
very different attributes of language, the written standard
and the sound of their students' speech:
"Educators know that students who are comfortable with
using standardized English... are probably more likely to
get ahead in their educational and academic pursuits and
less likely to face discrimination based on the sound of their
voices" (Charity Hudley and Mallinson, 77-78). Words such
as "likely," "probably," "perhaps," and "may" are ubiquitous
in the authors' quest to reinforce their speculative arguments for student success. Yet I do not believe the multicultural classroom can afford such speculation. The only
acceptable standard in the multicultural classroom is

an aggregate one, inclusive of immutable difference in skin color, birthplace, accent, etc. Multicultural teachers are not charged with holding or teaching the values of the majority culture. Rather, they facilitate equitable learning for students with various cultural styles, beliefs and heritages. If the subject is English, the multicultural teacher need not teach the group to "sound American" or to "sound educated" by arbitrary standards, especially if those standards pay deference to bigotry or xenophobia. It is unfair to predict or debate a student's future success on the hypothetical basis that his accent will be negatively perceived at some point in the future.

Charity Hudley, assistant professor of English and Linguistics, College of William and Mary, an "upper class African American," and Mallinson, assistant professor in the Language, Literacy and Culture program, University of Maryland, Baltimore County, a Southern "middle class" white (Charity Hudley and Mallinson, 7), include their own profession in the list of powerful decision makers influential in creating standards for language: "dictionary writers, educators, and politicians." It seems paradoxical for them to support the subordinators of Southern and African American Speech. As teachers, they have the power to do more than reflect the norms of society and aid their students to adapt to them. Responsible teachers also have a hand in changing the world. If legitimate language varieties are subordinated in the classroom they will certainly be subordinated in the world beyond. The classroom is not only a place to have compassion and understanding for linguistic difference, it is a place to endorse it. Those with negative judgments of Southern and African American speech may claim these language patterns are unintelligible when they actually mean that they disapprove of them. It is vital that teachers not correct or modify intelligible speech patterns in their students. The correction of intelligible speech is without basis.

Bob Scheiffer, moderator of "Face The Nation," credited David Brinkley with "making the world safe for regional accents" and said that he would not have been able to speak with credibility in his own Texas accent on national television had Brinkley not paved the way. ("Face the Nation," June 15, 2003) In fact, the authors actually support the credibility of Southern Accents in national culture, citing the accents of "Jimmy Carter, Bill Clinton and George W Bush" and "the sermons of famous ministers including Billy Graham, Jesse Jackson and Martin Luther King, Jr." (Charity Hudley and Mallinson, 37) These examples would seem to contradict the need for standardization of speech.

Studies have shown that in many cases, an unseen African American or Caucasian Southern speaker is not racially identifiable by the sound of their accent. (Wells 554) In their dual examination of Southern and African American

language patterns, Charity Hudley and Mallinson illuminate overlapping characteristics. But, in the case of African American English, language discrimination is but one factor in the larger issue of racism. The authors acknowledge the dilemma of "sounding white," faced by African American teachers and students alike (Charity Hudley and Mallinson, 76). Yet the authors' conclusion appears to be that if speaking in a standardized accent means being perceived as "sounding white," it may be necessary for the attainment of "privileged" status. (Charity Hudley and Mallinson, 35-36) Again, this is persuasive to a point. Students who do not read and write standard grammar prior to entering school may feel less prepared than those who do. But, here, as throughout the book, the authors imply a conflation of grammar and accent. They define Southern and African American accents as non-standardized and therefore, non-privileged. At this point, they create yet another permutation of standard English: "In this section, we focus specifically on one kind of standardized English: *School English*, or the kind of standardized English specifically called for when students are at school." (Charity Hudley and Mallinson, 21)

The authors never provide a concise definition of "school English." As a "situated" standard, we are told that "school English" will vary from school to school and region to region. It would seem to be an amalgam of standardized features, some named and others left unnamed, which are intended for writing and speaking in formal registers. What they imply in the term "school English" is that if students know and practice the more rigorous and rule-driven forms of spoken and written language, they will eventually gain an ease with maneuvering to the appropriate formal or informal tone necessary for the situation. The authors call this concept "navigation," referring to students as "multicultural navigators." The navigational chart demands that in progressively more formal situations, students steer clear not only of "non-standardized" grammar, but of their regional and ethnic accents.

The authors delineate seven points of "privilege" possessed by students whose "standardized speaking" backgrounds have prepared them for "school English." My responses follow, in italics:

1. Standardized English-speaking students can usually be assured that the newspapers, magazines, books, and other media they encounter in school will be in the type of English they are already familiar with.
2. Standardized English-speaking students can usually be assured that they will not be mocked or teased for how they pronounce their words.

Rather than denouncing the bigots and bullies who tease and belittle, the authors imply the solution to the problem is to conform to "standardization" and thus, by rejecting or concealing identity, to avoid mockery and gain privilege.

3. Standardized English-speaking students can usually be assured that they will not be thought of as less intelligent because of how they talk.

The emphasis here, as elsewhere in the book, is on the external effect of "sounding educated," rather than the true issue of language education, which is to become confident in discourse and expression, and to exude authoritative command of language, which transcends negative dialect connotations.

4. Standardized English-speaking students can usually be assured that standardized test instructions and materials will be written in the English they are already familiar with.

This assurance is owing to the bias of standardized tests, which the authors document at various points throughout the book. Their solution to bias is to conform to "standardization" and suppress the language forms that standardized tests do not tolerate.

5. Standardized English-speaking students can usually be assured that most of their educators will communicate with them in the type of English the students are already familiar with.

If this is so, can this "privileged" group of "standardized-speaking students," actually insist that their educators speak in a standardized accent? If so, "heavily accented" teachers, as the Arizona Department of Education suggests, could find themselves reassigned to other duties.

6. Standardized English-speaking students can generally be assured that the way they talk will not be the subject of jokes and belittling in mainstream TV shows or movies.

The authors imply that in the attainment of privilege, "non-standardized" English-speaking students would do well to suppress language patterns ridiculed in popular culture. This is another example of self-subordination through conformity.

7. Standardized English-speaking students can generally be assured that their pronunciation, intonation and sentence structure will not interfere with their ability to be assessed accurately, to interact with authority figures, or later in life, to obtain housing or be hired for a job. (Charity Hudley and Mallinson, 22)

There are some heavy assumptions here. I know of no proof which holds that "standardized speech" is more appropriate for interacting with, or growing up to become, an authority figure. Further, how can the authors predict the climate in which students will

attain jobs and housing ten or more years from now, when the shrinking white majority will give way to a majority of color?

The authors note that the South, where a quarter of the teachers are non-white, is already more diverse than the rest of the country. 20% of Southern teachers are African American, compared with 6% nationally (Charity Hudley and Mallinson, 46).
Balanced with this optimistic data, the authors invoke the ever-persuasive bottom line argument, that if Southern-sounding students don't change their accents, they will not be competitive in the job market. (Charity Hudley and Mallinson, 45) They back this up by citing research: "[Jeffrey] Grogger found that speakers who sound Southern earn salaries that are lower than workers with comparable skills who do not sound Southern, even if these speakers live in the South" (Charity Hudley and Mallinson, 42). If this is so, it cannot be proven through Grogger's data. I have learned from Mr. Grogger himself that the statistic referring to Southern-sounding people earning less than those who did not sound Southern "was in a preliminary version of the paper, but that result went away when new wage data became available" (Grogger, personal communication, December 2010).

The authors acknowledge the lack of funding for schools in the South, and the dire circumstances of a high rate of poverty, unemployment and population growth in which low-income children constitute 54% of the student body. Yet beyond references to "lower educational expectations" for "non-standardized speaking" Southern and African American students, they don't connect these economic factors directly to their educational concerns. Their core solution is to standardize school English, making it less identifiable with language patterns of the South and of African Americans. "Sounding educated," is, in my opinion, a band-aid approach to an economic crisis.

The authors make the point that if a student's Southern pronunciation of a word is at variance with its spelling it will be difficult for that student to learn how to spell and read such words. Pronunciation and spelling may seem to disagree when the word get is pronounced "git," or when spellings that denote diphthongal pronunciations in other accents such as "high" and "toy" are pronounced in Southern accents as "ha" and "taw." While these difficulties exist, they are also factors for students with non-Southern accents. The rules of English spelling are not uniform or reliable. All students must face irregularities of spelling and reconcile them with variance in pronunciation. Here are myriad representations of the spelling of words commonly pronounced with the "long e" vowel: *Receive, shield, tea, seek, people, Phoenix, Caesar, trampoline, quay, debris.* Although there may be specific challenges of spelling and pronunciation that arise for students with a given accent, changing pronunciation to conform to spelling is not a reliable solution. In today's schools, the promising "Balanced Literacy" pedagogy is an effort to merge two approaches: Phonics, in which words are sounded-out, and whole-word recognition, popularized in the 1980s as Whole-Language. But, short of spelling reform, complications and misunderstanding in spelling and pronunciation are a fact of life in the English language.

Above and beyond grammar and pronunciation, the authors prescribe certain word choices as more "literary" and in-keeping with school English:

> School English, both written and spoken, tends to use vocabulary items that are more literary than colloquial, such as entrance, rather than door, employ, rather than use, beginning, rather than start, collaborate, rather than work together, acquire, rather than get. (Charity Hudley and Mallinson, 26)

This sort of concern with the external effect of language, rather than with content, continues a theme of superficial remedies to complex problems. Even the most formal literature, devoid of colloquialism, will contain such words as "door," and "get," when precision of language calls for them. To suggest, out of hand, that there is an advantage to choosing larger, less common words is pretentious, rather than literary. The authors recommend that students cultivate "a large academic vocabulary." But, they never clearly define a substantive difference between a merely large vocabulary and a large academic one. (Charity Hudley and Mallinson, 30)

The authors do not stop at prescriptions for word choice, they actually attempt to curricularize "tone of voice" and other expressive attributes of language:
> Teaching about tone is often overlooked in education. Intonation patterns in standardized English are closely tied to politeness and emotion, but students who are less familiar with standardized patterns of intonation may inadvertently express boredom, disinterest, or displeasure. (Charity Hudley and Mallinson, 31)

Their intention here is twofold: to sensitize teachers to variable cultural styles of students, including intonation patterns, in order to avoid misinterpretations, and to suppress certain cultural styles in the "school English" environment as well as in crucial situations in the world beyond.

The authors have crossed into a very subjective area. I don't think that someone's tone can be standardized as part of learning the subject of English. The authors seem to impose their personal mores in the name of "school English." I believe students should be encouraged to express themselves in their cultural style, accurately, consciously

and meaningfully. If misunderstanding arises, owing to language difference, spoken language allows for what Lippi-Green calls "repair and confirmation strategies." Granted, in promoting a standardized intonation pattern to which students should aspire, the authors advise that teachers must be careful not to chastise students for using intonations which the teacher perceives negatively. They advise that intonation should be standardized, but with understanding:

> A student who is perceived to be saying "My name is Jenny? And I'm in the sixth grade?" rather than, "my name is Jenny and I'm in the sixth grade" may be thought of by adults as uncertain, approval-seeking, silly, nervous, air-headed, or unintelligent, rather than simply speaking with an intonation pattern that has become very widespread among her peer group. (Charity Hudley and Mallinson, 31)

I will go further: Jenny is, perhaps, exhibiting a generational speech pattern, which will remain prevalent in her peer-group throughout her personal and professional life. It is, perhaps, an innovation in language, an evolutionary occurrence in American English. In my opinion, it is not a factor to be corrected as a point of standardized speech.

The authors cite several "typical conventions" of school English:

> Educators may actively discourage such behaviors as yelling, whining, and speaking in a high pitch. Some students may also be chided for speaking too slowly or too quickly, too loudly or too softly. Typically, the conventions of School English suggest that speech should be delivered at a moderate volume. (Charity Hudley and Mallinson, 32)

These behaviors may be part of a teacher's classroom discipline, but naming them features of "school English," or calling them "standardized" is misleading.

The authors overstep a boundary between standardized English and personal expression in describing "non-standardized" story-telling, in which students' stories "may not be presented in a linear way with a clear beginning, middle and end. This style differs from the more directly linear, single topic narrative style that is considered normative in standardized English" (Charity Hudley and Mallinson, 102).

The authors, aware of student resistance to their precepts, offer this:

> There are many cultural and social reasons why students may want to sound distinctly different

from educators. The general lack of male educators may pose an impossible linguistic situation for male students who do not want to sound like their female educators, yet do not have many male educator role models. Some boys may resist the word choices, pronunciations, speech rate, volume, pitch, and tempo that are being advocated by their female educators. (Charity Hudley and Mallinson, 35)

Very true. Some boys may prefer their fathers and brothers, or mothers, for that matter, as role models over their teachers. Some girls may also resist for reasons of their own.

The authors articulate attitudes toward Southern speaking tempo:

> Speech rate may be a particularly challenging issue for students who speak Southern English... as Southern speakers have been found to speak at a slightly slower rate than students from other regions. Educators (and students themselves) may hold negative stereotypes that Southerners who are slower talkers are slower, less intelligent thinkers; it is critical to dispel this harmful misconception. (Charity Hudley and Mallinson, 32)

Their remedy is to be understanding, and then to get Southerners to talk faster. It is indeed a slippery slope to make a generalization that the tempo of 140 million Americans is too slow for credibility and to educationally mandate that they speed up. A dictated pace for speaking and an encouraged intonation pattern are not reliable as enhancements of language content. Pace and intonation come from the nuances of thought and the expressiveness of feeling. To foster these dynamics, it behooves teachers to encourage students in a deep involvement in what they are reading and a commitment to what they are saying. To quantify tempos in measurable, testable ways in the name of fulfilling standardized English is an inappropriately external method of addressing an internal language function.

The authors target "mumbling," another feature which they call "non-standardized." They define the "concept" of being articulate and not mumbling, as "the clear production of all sounds of a word and pronouncing them in phonetically standardized ways," and they sensibly encourage teachers to address this issue using specific instructions, rather than "don't mumble" (Charity Hudley and Mallinson, 23). They give examples of pronunciation features that may be perceived as mumbling. One example is reduction of the consonant cluster *sk* in the phrase "Put my Halloween *mask* down." But the issue of mumbling requires more information and detail than they provide. There are many ways in which segments of words are reduced in order to facilitate

the flow of connected speech and are not perceived as mumbling. For example, reducing, but not quite eliminating the final "d" in the phrase "di(d) too." These forms exist in all types of connected speech, in all registers. I find these forms appropriate for "oratorical" and "slow, deliberate speech," and there is no necessity for correcting such forms in formal registers. As a subjective, popular term, mumbling stands in for a series of objectively measurable linguistic phenomena, occurring in all types of speech. These include:

Deletion
The linguistic term for the omission of a sound from the pronunciation of a word or phrase, such as "enter" being pronounced "enner."

Dissimilation
The linguistic term used when a repeated sounds within a word is reduced or deleted as in "surprise" being pronounced "suprise."

Assimilation
The linguistic term for the alteration of a sound within a word or phrase to be closer in formation to an adjacent sound, such as "don't believe" being pronounced "dom'p believe"

Relaxed pronunciation
The phonological term for the alteration of sounds within words or phrases for easier articulation, or greater flow, such as "going to" being pronounced "gonna."

Characterizing "mumbling" as non-standardized seems off the point. Any individual is capable of mumbling in their own accent. Mumbling can be done in "standard English," as well as other varieties. Calling "mumbling" non-standardized may open up misunderstandings in which intelligible "non-standardized" speech could be referred to within the "concept" of mumbling. But in cases of unintelligibility, or when a student's speech is not compelling or persuasive, the student can be coached into more expressive and energetic use of speech sounds, while continuing to reduce consonants to facilitate the flow of connected speech in the ways indicated above. Improving unintelligible speech requires precise instructions for adjusting formations of the lips, tongue and soft palate. As the authors point out, it is clearer to address these adjustments in terms of how to articulate, rather than how *not* to mumble. The positive instruction to articulate implies the joining of sounds into words, whereas the instruction to not mumble may imply separating words and sounds into discrete units. But their suggestion that educators adhere to standardized conventions of speech presupposes that educators are not, in the words of the Arizona Department of Education, "heavily accented." In a multi-cultural milieu, "heavily accented" teachers are a reality. To say that "educators typically are supposed to" speak in "standardized ways" (Charity Hudley and Mallinson, 23) is neither fair nor realistic.

In the name of standardized English, the authors address certain social behaviors:

> Students may not know that certain linguistic features such as the use of the fillers *like* and um are not received favorably by educators at school (despite the fact that, at home, or outside of school settings, educators themselves may frequently use these same language variants). (Charity Hudley and Mallinson, 32)

The authors use the terms "home variety," "home accent," "the language they bring with them from home," interchangeably with "non-standardized" (Charity Hudley and Mallinson, 330). "Home variety" is not a term I am comfortable with. Non-school English has a far wider application than home use. What the authors refer to as a home accent may be the accent that students' parents use at work, when conferring with teachers and other authority figures, and in a great variety of other situations. Nor, by any means, does "home variety" encompass a student's entire experience of language outside of "school English."

In the final chapters, the authors delineate the spoken and written traits first of Southern English and then of African American English. For Southern speech, they give several examples of word pronunciations that they fear will meet with disapproval in the presence of "authority figures," landlords, employers, and those who do not share their linguistic background. Here is a sampling:

• "r-absence" or the "dropped r" in words like far and farm.

• "ing and in alternation" which is to say, variably pronouncing words like "talkin(g)" with "ing" and "in." I often hear authority figures, and eloquent ones at that, say "in" rather than "ing"; the president of the United states being a prime example.

The authors list such African American pronunciations as "axe" for the word "ask." One of the book's highlights is a brief account of the 1,000 year history of "axe" and "ask" as homophones dating back to Old English. (Charity Hudley and Mallinson, 79-83) They continue with consonant pronunciation examples such as "skraight" and "brootiful" for the words straight and beautiful and consonant cluster reductions, as, "des" for the word "desk." In an earlier chapter, the authors point out that most "standardized" speakers also reduce consonant clusters, particularly at the ends of words.

The authors provide descriptions of Southern and African

American speech patterns to facilitate teaching "standardized" speech. As earlier, they are clear in pointing out that "non-standardized" speakers may retain their own accents for casual and home use, but should appropriately switch to standardized speech for the purposes of school and the world beyond.

By recommending that students alternate between personal and standard accents for different situations, teachers may employ euphemisms for right and wrong such as, "standardized" and "non-standardized" "larger world-use" and "home-use" "appropriate" and "inappropriate." Accent modification of this sort may create an educationally-induced schism, increasing conflict and distance between the private language of the home-self, and the "success"-minded language of the standardized self.

The authors' research, in sheer numbers of books, studies and papers cited, is impressive. Yet limited fact-checking revealed obsolete and misinterpreted conclusions. In addition to the inaccuracy in quoting Grogger (above), the authors err in citing the research of their own mentor, William Labov. They describe a child in one of his studies who pronounces the word "played" as "play," and inaccurately identify this as an example of final consonant cluster reduction. (Charity Hudley and Mallinson, 88) In actuality, the word "played" does not contain a final consonant cluster, but the single consonant "d." The book's level of phonemic detail, desire to illuminate multiple points of view, style of catch-up terminology (standard, standard-*ized*, *school* English) have layered the authors' primary goals, making it difficult for me to "meet" the authors on paper. Perhaps the workshops they offer to teachers illuminate their work in a way which is more immediate and accessible. The book leaves many questions unresolved, such as the ethical implications of grading students' attitudes and aptitudes toward standardized speech; whether second-language student populations, such as much-marginalized Mexican immigrants, would benefit from this approach; and the implications of this book for foreign-accented and non-standardized-accented teachers.

While I don't often teach the age groups to which this book is addressed, I believe that pride and confidence in an individual's speech must be developed from an early age and students should be taught to bring their native accents, without apology, to all situations. Below are some details and insights that I have found useful for teaching speech skills in a multi-cultural environment. My comments are intended to support the premise of this article: intelligible eloquence without accent "standardization" is a viable road to success:.

Endorse students' accents: Teach that there is a greater tolerance for idiomatic and dialect forms in spoken language than in written language, and that what might be considered incorrect when written down may be totally acceptable when speaking. Teach that all accents of English are correct and acceptable in all spoken registers, and that intelligibility is a key criterion of speaking well. Except in cases of non-intelligibility, do not intervene with "accent modification" or "standard pronunciation." In early learning, teach the phonics principles of long and short vowels, diphthongs and voiced and voiceless consonants, to expose students to all aesthetic possibilities for spoken English. In later grades, teach speech skills, which improve intelligibility in all accents. Skills taught might include consonant links, *onsets* and *rimes*, sound symbolism, and using unconnected speech for clarification. Each of these is defined below.

Consonant links: rather than teach that "standardized English" pronunciation always includes final consonants, give situational examples of when to sound final consonants, or, for maximum fluency and intelligibility in connected speech, when to hold them. For example, the plosive final consonant "d," in the word "did," may be sounded in the phrase "did it." But, it is a very common feature of speech, by any standard, to form a final consonant, hold the position of it for a short pulse without sounding it, and then to sound the beginning consonant of the next word, as in the phrase "did the." If this form is not taught, confusion will arise regarding the directive to sound all final consonants for articulate speech.

Dental consonants: It is often observed that in certain accents the consonant "th" is pronounced as "d" for words like "the" and "t" for words like "think." However, this is not the only variation used in accents. The consonant "th," which in standard English is formed with the tip of the tongue protruding slightly forward under the top front teeth, is formed in certain dialects and accents by touching the tip of the tongue behind the top front teeth. This formation, when voiced, will indeed sound somewhat like a "d," and, when voiceless, sound somewhat like a "t," but it will be confusing if it is referred to as an actual "t" or "d." Telling a student the TH sound is not formed the same way as a d or t will not give the student accurate information about how they are forming the sound, nor will it give a clear direction about how to change the formation.

Onsets and *rimes* (this concept comes from the "Whole-Language" movement of the 1980s): Each syllable can be broken down into two potential pieces, the "onset," which is the consonant or consonant cluster which may appear at the beginning, such as, the "br" cluster at the beginning of the word "brick," and the "rime," the vowel and consonant ending which might appear in completion of the syllable, such as the "ick" in the word "brick." A word beginning with a vowel, such as the word "am" has no onset. All

words have rimes, which are their matching endings, or "rhymes" with other words. The words "brick" and "bright" have the same onset, "brick" and "tick," the same rime. Onsets and rimes are helpful in teaching pronunciation, as they combine phonemes into larger sound units, which begin or end words or syllables. Their use in speech education creates a context much more specific and situational than "make sure to sound all your consonants in standardized English." In relatively rare incidents where pronunciation affects intelligibility, it is possible to dialogue about onsets: "Your onset in the word "thread," sounded like the onset for the word "Fred" It is equally possible to dialogue about rimes: "Your rime in the word "girl" sounded like the rime of the word "sir."

Foster students' self-sufficiency in learning pronunciation: Teach students to use the dictionary for learning pronunciations as well as definitions. Teach students how to pronounce unfamiliar words, whenever possible, by analogy to words which they already know. This will help them to pronounce new words in an aesthetic consistent with their own accent. Pronunciation keys in dictionaries are designed to be used in this way.

One accent for all levels of formality: Formal situations require unambiguous language because opportunities for dialogue and clarification may be limited. Coach students to anticipate the need for unambiguous language for formal settings. Emphasize that clear thinking reflected in precise wording is possible in any accent. Remind students that unconnected speech can be a helpful form of clarification if a word or phrase is not understood. Take care not to identify "standardized" accents as more polite or professional than native accents. Eloquent content is expressed equally well in all accents.

Speak in unconnected speech for clarification: In all accents of English, portions of words are often omitted to achieve an easy flow in connected speech, as with "held" consonants in Consonant Links, above. But if connected flow obscures meaning, as in the sentence "I can'(t) take it," the speaker can, in order to clarify, remove the word from connected speech and repeat "I— CAN'T— take it." It is not a language error to hold a final "t" in connected speech and it is a tool of language to say a word unconnected from the other words in a phrase for clarification or emphasis. Therefore a direction such as "always say all the sounds in a word," or, "use your final consonants," is often confusing or misleading. This can be a useful tool for teaching registers; whereby students can learn to anticipate sounds which, in one-on-one communication may be understood, or easily clarified, but which could be misunderstood in more formal, group settings.

Sound symbolism: There is a linguistic principle that the

sounds of words are not rooted in the meanings of words, but are arbitrary. But it is often helpful when developing articulation skills, to use the individual sounds of words to boost the expression of meaning. For example, the forward flung "k" sounds of "kick" and the explosive "p" sounds of "pop" echo the meanings of these words. The formation of the tongue for the "L" in the word "delicious" can remind us of the act of tasting something. The "sh" in the word "shine" can call to mind a ray of light. It is possible to dialogue with students about using all of the sounds necessary for intelligibility on this basis. "Use the "t" in the word "point" to make the word sound like what it means."

As the Arizona Department of Linguistics wrote to Governor Brewer, "there is no such thing as unaccented speech." The recommendations above are meant not as accent "correction," but as ways to aid in creating true diversity in multi-accented, multi-cultural classrooms.

In closing, I quote, again, from Lippi-Green's English With an Accent:

> We do not, cannot under our law, ask people to change the color of their skin, their religion, their gender, but we regularly demand of people that they suppress or deny the most effective way they have of situating themselves socially in the world.
> *You may have dark skin we tell them, but you must not sound black.*
> *You can wear a yarmulke if it is important to you as a Jew, but lose the accent.*
> *Maybe you come from the Ukraine, but can't you speak real English?*
> *If you just didn't sound so corn-pone, people would take you seriously.*
> *You're the best salesperson we've got but must you sound gay on the phone?*
> Accent serves as the first point of gate-keeping because we are forbidden, by law and social custom, and perhaps by a prevailing sense of what is morally and ethically right, from using race, ethnicity, homeland, or economics more directly. We have no such compunctions about language, however. Thus, accent becomes a litmus test for exclusion, an excuse to turn away, to refuse to recognize the other. [Charles] Taylor describes the opposite of recognition as *misrecognition*:

> our identity is partly shaped by recognition or its absence, often by *mis*recognition of others, and so a person or group of people can suffer real damage, real distortion, if the people or society around them mirror back to them a confining or demeaning or contemptible picture of themselves. (1994: 25) (Lippi-Green 1997, 63-64)

Historically, it has taken the general public many swings of the pendulum to catch up with the wisdom of linguistics. Dialectologists, by virtue of their analysis of African American speech, were among the early advocates of racial equality in America. (Baugh, 9) In this current time of cultural and linguistic flux, with growing minority and second-language populations, standard speech is a myth to some and an edict to others. Fervent "English only" rhetoric and desperate efforts to revive literacy in failing schools find some educators opting for stringent language standards, even in the name of multiculturalism. Teaching students to navigate away from their native accents for life's crucial interactions is not the solution. Such survival techniques look to the past rather than the future. The language that makes us human also serves to dehumanize when the primacy of one group's accent negates the value of the accents of other groups. We cannot reliably predict the attitudes toward speech our students will confront in their futures. But we can fortify our students to face negative bias with eloquence, intelligibility and the pride of their own accents. Rather than to navigate and standardize, we might teach them of the power to negotiate. So they might speak with the sound of who they are, seeking common ground and mutual advantage with those who speak in other ways. In the language of negotiation, dialogue is vital, eloquence transcends standards, accents are not hidden and difference is the norm.

Bibliography

Baugh, John. *Black Street Speech*. Austin: University of Texas Press, 1983.

Charity Hudley, Anne H. and Christine Mallinson. 2010. *Understanding English Language Variation in U.S. Schools*. Teachers College Press.

Lippi-Green, Rosina. *English with An Accent*. London and New York: Routledge, 1997.

Wells, J. C. *Accents of English*. Cambridge University Press, 1982.

Schrag, Peter. "High Stakes Are for Tomatoes." *Atlantic Monthly* CCLXXXVI
 no 2 (August 2000): 00-00.

Jordan, Miriam. "Arizona Grades Teachers On Fluency." *Wall Street Journal* (April 30, 2010): 00-00.

Nilep, Chad. "University of Arizona Department of Linguistics Letter to Lawmakers." SLA Blog (Official Blog of the Society for Linguistics Anthropology) (June 3 2010).

Essay *by Paul Meier*

A Midsummer Night's Dream: An Original Pronunciation Production

PAUL MEIER is a professor in the Theatre Department at the University of Kansas. He is the Founder and Director of IDEA (International Dialects of English Archive) at http://web.ku.edu/~idea/. He is the author of *Accents and Dialects for Stage and Screen*, and *Voicing Shakespeare*, available from Paul Meier Dialect Services at www.paulmeier.com. His "show-specific" dialect CDs are leased world-wide, while he has coached more than a dozen feature films, including Ang Lee's *Ride With The Devil*, and Paul Cox's *Molokai: The Story of Father Damien*.

Part One: Before

David Crystal, author of *Pronouncing Shakespeare, Shakespeare's Words*, and over 100 other titles, is the foremost champion of the use of Early Modern English, or Original Pronunciation (OP), as he calls it, in the production of Shakespeare's plays.

When Meier was planning his month-long masterclass at the Shakespeare Centre in Stratford-upon-Avon in June 2007, David Crystal was the first guest speaker he invited. Meier had recently read Crystal's Pronouncing Shakespeare, the account of the groundbreaking experiment with an Original Pronunciation Romeo and Juliet at Shakespeare's Globe in 2004 under David's guidance and design. Meier had been instantly intrigued: He says, "David's book set me on fire! He was the hit of the class, and I was determined to someday direct or coach a Shakespeare production in OP myself, with David's collaboration, if possible."

After further conversation with Crystal, Meier chose Early Modern English and Shakespeare's Original Pronunciation as the research topic for his 2009 sabbatical leave. This was in preparation for a production of A Midsummer Night's Dream, which

Meier would direct in the fall of 2010. Crystal would provide pre-production advice and be in residence with the company in Kansas for a short time in the first days of rehearsal.

The interview published here, the "before" of a before-and-after pair of interviews, took place over twelve days in December 2009 as the two planned their collaboration on A Midsummer Night's Dream and Meier was deepening his own understanding of the way English was spoken in Shakespeare's lifetime. The interview was conducted by e-mail, later edited by Paul and subsequently recorded in a conversation via Skype.

To help readers, the recording may be heard at: http://www.paulmeier.com/Crystal_Interview1.mp3, which is especially important when Crystal is demonstrating OP.

The production script, containing a phonetic transcription and embedded recordings of Crystal reading the text in OP, may be freely downloaded from http://paulmeier.com/DREAM/ script.pdf, *while other documents and production details are available at* http://paulmeier.com/shakespeare.html.

MEIER: David, you are a rare treasure, an academic linguist with a deep interest in and a long history of involvement in the theatre. How did those two strands get entwined in your career?

CRYSTAL: I can't remember a time when I wasn't fascinated by theatre. My mum used to produce plays for a repertory company in Holyhead [Wales, where Crystal grew up], and I'd be brought along to rehearsals. That was before I even went to school. Then as a teenager she took me to Stratford, and I saw my first Shakespeare play—I still have vivid memories of Paul Robeson's Othello, in his flowing white robes, with Sam Wanamaker darting about as Iago. I've kept up the theatre connection since. I did some acting and playwriting at university, I've had dozens of roles in various reps, from panto villains to Shylock, and I've toured a couple of solo shows. I've done a little bit of directing too—a production of *Under Milk Wood* a few years ago—and written a play about endangered languages. So there's definitely a theatre gene somewhere—which has been passed on, as a matter of fact, for son Ben is an actor who's also done some directing and producing; and keeping up with what he's doing has added a fresh dimension to the theatrical side of my life.

My fascination with language has run in parallel to all this. I can trace it back to growing up in a bilingual community in Wales, and then being exposed to several languages in school. It came to the boil when I went to university, where there were courses on the history of English, comparative philology, phonetics, and all sorts of other goodies. I was reading English, and the beauty of that course—which was at University College London—was the nicely balanced language and literature syllabus. So, it was Shakespeare in the morning, linguistics in the afternoon, sort of thing, for three years. I had great teachers on both sides—Hilda Hulme on Shakespeare, Randolph Quirk on language—and learned from them my basic principle, that language and literature are two sides of a single coin; they inform each other so marvelously. When I started teaching linguistics myself, much of my early work was on stylistics, and that's been a major theme in my writing ever since.

Photo by Luke Jordan for The University Theatre

Sam Voelker as Robin Starveling

Shakespeare has always been the great unifying factor for me, so I suppose it was only a matter of time before I started researching and writing about his language myself. But this didn't happen until the 1990s. Three things happened then to bring him into center-stage, as it were. A new repertory company was formed in Holyhead, and I found myself acting in several of his plays, along with Hilary [David's wife and business partner] and Ben. Then Ben decided to go into the theatre professionally, and eventually we collaborated on various projects, such as *Shakespeare's Words* and *The Shakespeare Miscellany*. And then, thirdly, the editor of the magazine at Shakespeare's Globe asked me to write regular pieces on Shakespeare's use of language for *Around the Globe*. And I found myself being sucked in to the professional Shakespeare world, adding a linguistic perspective to various projects, such as the Wells and Taylor edition of the collected works [*The Oxford Shakespeare*: *The Complete Works*]. Once Shakespeare gets hold of you, he doesn't let you go, it seems.

The links with the Globe grew. I went to see most of their productions and gave various talks for their education department. I was their Sam Wanamaker Fellow in 2003. So when the Globe called with a new idea, in 2004, I was well primed!

MEIER: The story of that "new idea" is thrillingly told in *Pronouncing Shakespeare*, of course, which I picked up at the little bookstore across from the Shakespeare birthplace in Stratford in 2005. I couldn't put it down. Devoured it in a single sitting. I won't ask you to tell that whole story again here, but I would love to hear you talk about the different relationship that Elizabethans had with language from the relationship we have with it today. Spelling closer to pronunciation, no standard prestige dialect yet, or was there? They certainly seemed in the throes of actually creating language, something we are scared to do. Were the poets deliberately trying to elevate English to stand alongside the classical languages of Greek and Latin?

CRYSTAL: Not just the poets (to take your last question first). Scholars too were anxious to show that English had "come of age." There's a splendid statement from William Camden in 1605—he was Ben Jonson's tutor. "Our English tongue," he says, "is (I will not say as sacred as the Hebrew, or as learned as the Greek) but as fluent as the Latin, as courteous as the Spanish, as courtlike as the French, and as sonorous as the Italian." Nobody would have been able to write this a century before, but during the 16th century a huge amount of linguistic development took place, with tens of thousands of new words of classical origin entering the language, offering fresh opportunities for stylistic expression. The rapid pace of development worried some, of course. Poets wondered if their words would be understood by later generations: "We write in sand," said one, sadly. And it was this sense of unchecked progress, chaos even, which led to later writers wanting to fix the language—[Jonathan] Swift with his notion of an Academy, [Samuel] Johnson with his Dictionary, and so on.

Actually creating language? Certainly. I've said in several places that the main linguistic lesson we can learn from Shakespeare (and others of the time) is how to be daring with language. There was an instinct to be creative, and no institutional mindset to counter it, no dictionaries yet. (The first, Cawdrey's alphabetical table of hard words, didn't get published until 1604.) And there were no influential grammars and only the first primitive attempts at fixing spelling, such as Richard Mulcaster's spelling lists. Now Mulcaster is one of the pedants who may have been the model for Holofernes in *Love's Labour's Lost*. And it's interesting to see, in the way Holofernes treats spelling, the beginnings of a prestige usage. You're right: there was no standard pronunciation yet (Received Pronunciation didn't develop in Britain until the end of the 18th century), but there was an emerging sense of the special status of the written language. You should pronounce <u>debt</u> as d-e-b-t, says Holofernes, and he's horrified to hear Don Armado leave out the "b." This privileging of writing over speech we still have today (e.g., pronouncing the "t" in <u>often</u> because it's there in the spelling). It was the only way educated people in Elizabethan England could show in their pronunciation that they were educated. There was no expectation that an upper-class person on stage would have a "posh" non-regional accent, for there was no such accent at that time. Regional accents weren't a barrier to social advancement, as they would be later. Raleigh and Drake had strong Devonshire accents. And after 1603 the sound of the court was strongly Scottish.

Spelling was indeed closer to pronunciation, and this is an important source of evidence for OP. When Mercutio talks about Queen Mab's whip having a lash of film, and both Folio and Quarto spell film as philome, we can deduce a two-syllable pronunciation. It's natural enough, as we know from Modern Irish English, where we hear exactly that: fillum. Or, to take another example: In Sonnet 67, we find live at the end of line 1 and achieve at the end of line 3. Is there evidence to justify that rhyme? Yes, because there are spellings elsewhere in Shakespeare of achieve as a-t-c-h-i-v-e. This sort of thing is gold dust when we start focusing on the detail of OP.

"The fairy kingdom buys not the child of me." Titania (Leslie Bennett), Oberon (John Staniunas), Puck (J.T. Nagle), and Fairies (Mary McNulty, Sara Kennedy, Hailey Lapin), Musical Director/ Composer (Ryan McCall)

Photo by Luke Jordan for The University Theatre

MEIER: Perhaps we should spend a little time on the evidence question—always the biggest question, right? You told me you had some new thoughts about the evidence for OP that you didn't write about in *Pronouncing Shakespeare*. Are you going to break new ground here?

CRYSTAL: It's certainly the question that leaps into the mind of an audience whenever they hear OP. "How do you know?" It's not so much that I've had new thoughts about the process, just a wider range of examples. As I say in the book, there are three kinds of evidence. The spelling evidence we've just mentioned. The second kind is what we can deduce from the puns and rhymes which don't work in Modern English. Each new transcription of a play

or poem into OP brings to light fresh examples—and I expect the process to continue for quite some time, as so far only two plays have been done in their entirety, *Romeo and Troilus* (three, of course, when your *Dream* is produced), and the Sonnets. But the most important kind of evidence comes from the comments of contemporaries—especially the orthoepists, writing about the spelling system and telling us, often in considerable phonetic detail, how words were pronounced, where the main stress was, whether they rhymed, and so on. I've read more of these sources than when I worked on *Romeo*, and the evidence for particular OP decisions has built up as a result. For example, the Sonnets rhyme love with such words as prove and move several times. Which way should the rhyme go? Should we lengthen the vowel of love to make it like move or shorten the vowel of move to make it like love? Ben Jonson, in his *English Grammar*, gives us the answer. This is what he says about letter O. "It naturally soundeth ... in the short time more flat, and akin to 'u'; as cosen, dosen, mother, brother, love, prove." And in another section, he brings together love, glove, and move. This doesn't exclude the possibility that in other accents there might have been a long-vowel version of love, of course, but it does provide clear support for the choice I made in my transcription.

MEIER: When I told you I wanted to direct an OP Shakespeare, I asked you if there was one that deserved this treatment or begged for it. Your immediate answer was *A Midsummer Night's Dream*. And that's the one you and I are working on together. Why *Dream*?

CRYSTAL: Chiefly because it's got lots of rhyming couplets, many of which don't work in Modern English. One of the big things about OP is that it makes the rhymes work. Here are a couple of examples from Dream. One and alone don't rhyme today in this couplet from Puck, but they do in OP:

Then will two at one woo one–
[ðɛn wɪɫ tuː at ɒns wuː oːn]
That must needs be sport alone
[ðat mʏs neːdz bɪ spoˑt əloːn]

And here's an example from Oberon, where in Modern English there's a phonaesthetic clash between the ee endings of archery, gloriously, and remedy and the eye endings of die, eye, sky, and by. In OP, the repeated /əi/ endings produce a dreamy hypnotic effect, highly appropriate to what he's doing at this point, to my mind:

Flower of this purple dye,
[floˠ əv ðɪs pɚˑpɫ dəi]
Hit with Cupid's archery,
[ɪt wɪð kjəpɪdz aˑt͡ʃəɹəi]
Sink in apple of his eye.

[sɪnk ɪn apł əv ɪz əɪ]
When his love he doth espy,
[ʍɛn ɪz lʏv ɪ dɣθ ɪspəɪ]
Let her shine as gloriously
[lɛt ə ʃəin əz gloɹɪəsləɪ]
As the Venus of the sky.
[az ðə veːnəs ɑv ðə skəɪ]
When thou wak'st, if she be by,
[ʍɛn ðəʊ weːkst ɪf ʃeː bɪ bəɪ]
Beg of her for remedy.
[ɪɹbɛwaɹ ɛʃ ə fə ɹɛmədəɪ]

But making the rhymes work isn't the only reason. I'm also expecting OP to reveal some interesting puns. I can't say what these are right now—they'll become apparent only as the transcription proceeds. But to take an example from *Romeo*, I had no idea (nor, it would seem from editors' notes, had anyone else) that there was a possible wordplay in the Prologue:

From forth the fatal loins of these two foes
[fɹəm fo θ ðə feːtəl ləinz əv ðeːz tuː foːz]

In OP, <u>loins</u> and <u>lines</u> would sound the same. There are bound to be examples like this in *Dream*.

And finally, there's the novel auditory experience that arises simply from hearing this kind of pronunciation for the first time—an accent that hasn't been heard on stage for 400 years. People generally find it exhilarating, especially when (as routinely happened in the Globe productions) the OP made the actors reinterpret their relationship with their characters. I recall the actor playing Mercutio saying that he found his Queen Mab speech much more meaningful in the "earthy" tones of OP than in the "posh" tones of RP [Received Pronunciation, Standard British English]. So I'm expecting to hear some interesting effects when the *Dream* fairies and mechanicals start to use it. The tongue-tripping rate of OP also affects the actors' movement, and that too is likely to be important in this play.

MEIER: I'm glad you brought up "earthy" and "posh." Modern Shakespeare productions, certainly British ones, have a ready-made device in today's accents for revealing

"I am your spaniel!" Helena (Lynsey Becher), Lysander (Austin Robinson), Oberon (John Staniunas)

Photo by Luke Jordan for The University Theatre

the social status of the characters. As a dialect coach, I gravitate toward the use of accents and dialects as a way to sharpen the narrative and reveal character differences. I worry rather that with everyone speaking OP in *Dream*, I won't have the same scope. The mechanicals, obviously, beg for OP, but what about the fairy kingdom and the courtly characters? Will you be recommending dramatically different shades of OP for our production?

CRYSTAL: Indeed, though the decision as to what counts as "dramatic" is yours (as director), not mine. One has first to appreciate the difference between phonetics (the study of human-produced sound) and phonology (the study of the sound system of a language). OP is (my attempt to establish) the phonological system of Early Modern English, and it allows the same kind of phonetic variations as happen in Modern English. No two people have exactly the same accent, because of their voice-quality differences. And people from different parts of the English-speaking world have more or less the same phonological system, despite their many regional differences. (One has to say "more or less" because some accents are more different than others.) It would have been the same in Early Modern English. London would have contained dozens of accents, with its multicultural population, and a huge inward movement of people from the Midlands and East Anglia. We know which parts of the country many of the actors on the Globe stage came from, and they would have ended up with an accent that was a mix of their home region and London. So there would never have been phonetic uniformity on the Globe stage, and we would have heard many shades of OP. It's perfectly possible to rhyme <u>one</u> and <u>alone</u>, for example, in a Norfolk way, or a Cockney way, or a Scots way, and so on. Or again: Everyone in the 1580s would have pronounced <u>musician</u> as mu-zi-see-an, and this would have been pronounced in various regional ways. Also, OP has nothing to say about regional variations in intonation and tone of voice, which can be as varied as people want. So it's a mistake to think of OP as if it were a single accent.

When we did *Romeo* and *Troilus*, we maintained this principle. The actors were told not to lose their natural accents, but to speak the OP speech as trippingly as they could in their natural voices. So, we had a Juliet who sounded Scottish, a Nurse from the East End of London, a Peter from Northern Ireland, as well as some RP speakers. But they all modified their accents to rhyme <u>one</u> with <u>alone</u>, and so on. Some of these accents were closer to OP than others, of course. Those who already had a postvocalic /-r/ in their accents found OP easier to acquire than those who didn't. And there were different phonetic qualities of postvocalic /-r/, from a fricative to a trill. At least some speakers in Jacobean England trilled their /-r/, for Ben Jonson tells us that the sound hurreth (that is, vibrates).

It's important to appreciate that none of these accents had a ready-made association with poshness. That kind of association came in much later, in the late 1700s, with the emergence of Received Pronunciation. There were, of course, accents associated with the court—notably, the Scots accents would have been everywhere after 1603. But there was no "upper-class accent." Drake and Raleigh, as I've already mentioned, are famous examples of people who kept their strong Devonshire accents. If one wanted to show one was really educated, then one might pronounce words as they were spelled—as satirized in Holofernes— but this was a new trend, which is presumably why Shakespeare homed in on it in this way. My *Romeo* actors were at first a bit nonplussed by this information. "How are we to show poshness (e.g., in the Prince) if there's no RP?" they asked. The director, Tim Carroll, had an answer for them: "Act," he said. And indeed, through their posture, clothing, facial expressions, movement, and so on, they had no trouble.

Having said that, there are some variations which can help to suggest character differences, and any director has some choices to make. The fact of the matter is that OP was changing throughout the period Shakespeare was writing. "Mu-si-see-an" in 1580 was becoming "mu-zi-shee-an." <u>Gone</u> was pronounced sometimes to rhyme with <u>John</u> and sometimes with <u>Joan</u>. It's no different today, of course; many words have alternative pronunciations. But a director can make use of these variations in interesting ways. So, for example, in *Romeo*, we gave the more conservative pronunciations (like "mu-zi-see-an") to the older characters, and the trendier ones to the young bloods. It was the director who decided who said what (who would Juliet identify with?). Tim generally felt that, as the audience was coming to the play to hear OP, they should get their money's worth, as it were; so whenever there was a choice, he would go for the older variants. Another example of this choice was the use of initial /h-/, which could be present or dropped (again, without any suggestion of lack of education or carelessness). Since the 18th century, h-dropping has had a bad image, so it's possible for an OP director to capitalize on this, by having some characters keep their h's and some not. It wouldn't be doing harm to OP to have the courtly characters in *Dream* keep their h's and the mechanicals

not. It would of course be reading in some modern values into OP, but I doubt if it's possible to avoid that completely anyway, given that our audience experience can never be an authentic duplication of the Elizabethan setting.

MEIER: That distinction between the phonological and the phonetic is tremendously helpful, David. In the notes to accompany your transcription of *Troilus and Cressida* for Shakespeare's Globe in 2005, you wrote:

The pronunciation represented is (my interpretation of) an underlying system for Early Modern English. Its aim is to show the major differences between then and now. It is not an attempt to show the phonetic detail of each sound. Any one of the sounds shown could have been articulated in a variety of subtly different ways—just as today, the sound in, say, <u>two</u> can be said with slightly more or slightly less lip rounding, slightly higher or slightly lower in the mouth, and so on. Doubtless, at the time, the actors (who came from different parts of the country) brought their individual accents to their parts. The same can happen with this production. There should be no effort made to make everyone sound exactly the same.

"**Let me come to her!**" Hermia (Hannah Roark), Lysander (Austin Robinson), Demetrius (Ben Sullivan)

Photo by Luke Jordan for The University Theatre

213

Pronunciation, Phonetics, Linguistics, Dialect/Accent Studies
A Midsummer Night's Dream: An Original Pronunciation Production by Paul Meier

But in the absence of a standard, prestige pronunciation system, and given that there were differences between regional pronunciations as noticeable as today's, what led you to advocate mouth [əʊ], price [əi], strut [ɤ], and trap [a] with those specific phonetic values when offering your interpretation of OP? I can't help wondering if the Lancashire and Sussex sounds of 1600 were as different from each other as they are today. After all, today's strut [ʊ] and strut [ʌ] are not just shades of the same vowel but live in rather different regions of the vowel space.

CRYSTAL: There certainly were regional differences comparable to those we hear today. We know this because occasionally orthoepists remark on it or sometimes make an unusual recommendation that could reflect the part of the country they come from (e.g., the writer John Hart came from Devon, and he permits long vowels in such words as above). And the dramatists sometimes help, e.g., Shakespeare's use of /z/ in the representation of rural speech in *King Lear*. But these observations are rare. We know next to nothing really about Early Modern English regional-accent variation.

I've done nothing original in choosing phonetic values for the various vowels. A huge amount of research into the phonology of the period (by such scholars as Dobson and Kökeritz) has led to conclusions about which areas of the vowel space are involved in the articulation of each phoneme, and I've stood on their shoulders and made my own decisions when they disagree. This isn't the place to explain how historical phonology works, but it should be obvious that deductions about the values of the Elizabethan period have to mesh with deductions about Old, Middle, and Modern English. We have a system in continuous development from the days when the English alphabet was first devised down to the present day. We know the end-point, which is how we speak now. And we assume system in the beginning-point: If a vowel sound is represented by one letter, we assume it was a pure vowel; if with two identical letters, a long vowel; if with two dif-

"**Churl! On thy eyes I throw/All the power this charm doth owe.**"
Puck (J.T. Nagle) , Lysander (Austin Robinson)

Photo by Luke Jordan for The University Theatre

ferent letters, a diphthong, with the letters representing sounds similar to the vowels as shown in isolation; and so on. The evidence of rhymes and orthoepist descriptions helps to sharpen the analysis for the Early Modern period. The results are that, for some vowels, we can be quite precise about the area of vowel space involved - /u:/, for instance; for others, such as the strut vowel, there is less certainty. You have to make a judgment, and this is where other linguists might—almost certainly, would—reach different conclusions from mine. The best one can say is that my version is plausible—one of several possible plausible versions.

One also reflects one's upbringing, in such matters. No one is an intellectual island. I learned my historical phonology from A. C. Gimson—see, for instance, the representation of Early Modern English in his *Introduction to the Pronunciation of English*—and I remain influenced by that. When I was preparing for my encounter with *Romeo*, I went to see John Barton at his London flat to compare our two versions—for John had supervised an OP production of *Julius Caesar* in Cambridge many years before and had retained his interest in it. He did some; I did some. The two versions were almost identical. But then I reflected: Who had taught him his OP? It was Daniel Jones. And Daniel Jones was Gimson's teacher too. So there was an inevitable family resemblance.

What this means in production, of course, is that there are no grounds for being phonetically pedantic about actors' versions of these sounds. When I worked at the Globe, if someone tried to do a strut vowel and didn't get it exactly like mine—say, by fronting it a bit more or rounding it slightly—I wouldn't bother to correct them. On the other hand, if they went too far away from it, so that there was a danger of confusion with another sound, or of missing a rhyme or a pun, then I would. Actors are actors, not phoneticians. But they do have to be reasonably competent phonologists.

MEIER: This is sharpening my vision of our production immensely! Also my enthusiasm for it. Incidentally, as an actor who got deeply into phonetics, my heritage is also through Gimson, who came to Rose Bruford's [Rose Bruford College of Speech of Drama], where I trained, to administer the IPA proficiency test. We'd practiced for it listening to the old 78rpm Daniel Jones cardinal vowel LPs! I haven't gone into historical phonology, though, other than briefly in Gimson's book, and *Accents of English* by J.C. Wells, who took over the phonetics chair at University College, right? I must come to grips with Kökeritz. But switching topic a little, other than your productions at the Globe, and John Barton's at Cambridge, have there been other professional OP productions you know about? Other "academic" theatre productions? You must be approached all the time by people like me whom you've inspired. And how would you sum up audience reactions to OP productions? They're scared enough that they won't understand, so why on earth am I trying to intimidate them further, I ask myself? Even my own department had misgivings when I proposed the production.

"Oh Wall. Oh sweet, oh lovely Wall." Bottom (Scott Cox) and company

CRYSTAL: To take your last point first: I'm not surprised. There's a huge ignorance about OP out there—which the Globe had too. That was the main reason they hadn't done this before. They'd done "original" everything else—movement, costumes, music... but not pronunciation. And that was because they thought like this: "We're open only half of the year. We don't get a government subsidy of any kind. So to survive, we have to fill the place for every performance. If we put on an OP production, people won't understand it, the news will get around, and audiences will drop. We can't take the risk." Tim Carroll managed to

persuade them that they should have a go by using a clever stratagem. He said, "If you don't do it first, Stratford will!" So the Globe management agreed—but cautiously, because the *Romeo* production was only to be for a weekend in the middle of a season in Modern English.

Of course, it only takes a few moments to realize that the belief that "people won't understand it" is absolute nonsense. All you have to do is listen to it. But of course, at the time, there were no easily available recordings to get rid of the panic. There are now. There are downloadable files from my own site, www.pronouncingshakespeare.com. The Globe has produced a CD of words and music, called *This World's Globe*, which has some dialogue in OP. And I'm sure more audio material will become available as more productions take place. Unfortunately, the Globe has never gone in for marketing its productions in the way that the RSC [Royal Shakespeare Company] has. Every production at the Globe is filmed, and both of my OP productions are there in the archive, accessible upon request, but they're not on sale at all, which is a shame. So I hope your production, Paul, will be made available in some way.

The fact of the matter is that OP is no more different from the accents we hear on the BBC or NPR than most other regional accents in the UK, USA, or anywhere else. In fact, some regional accents in Modern English are much more difficult! I went around the audiences in both the *Romeo* and *Troilus* productions and asked people how they were finding it. Most said they were quite used to the accent by the end of Act 1, Scene 1! None said they had difficulty with it. All claimed to recognize it—in the sense that they heard echoes of their own regional background (if they had one) in OP. And this isn't surprising, as this accent was one that traveled. It interacted with other accents in the British Isles, and crossed the Atlantic in the Mayflower. This might be the point to hear a longer piece of OP, and listeners really then need to ask themselves the question: Was there any of that which I *didn't* understand? Here's Oberon's speech from *Dream*. It well illustrates the way in which the accent expresses a rural theme. And of course the rhymes now work, which didn't before.

I know a bank where the wild thyme blows,
[əɪ noː ə baŋk mɛ̝ː ðə wəiɫd̩ təɪm bloːz]
Where oxlips and the nodding violet grows,
[mɛ̝ ɑkslɪps an ðə nɑdɪn vəɪələt gɹoːz]

Photo by Luke Jordan for The University Theatre

Pronunciation, Phonetics, Linguistics, Dialect/Accent Studies
A Midsummer Night's Dream: An Original Pronunciation Production by Paul Meier

Quite overcanopied with luscious woodbine,
[kʍəit o:vɚ kanəpəid wɪ lʏsɪəs wʊdbəin]
With sweet muskroses and with eglantine.
[wɪð swe:t mʏskɹo:zɪz an wɪð ɛgləntəin]
There sleeps Titania sometime of the night,
[ðɛ: sle:ps tɪtanjə sʏmtəim ɑv ðə nəit]
Lulled in these flowers with dances and delight.
[lʏɫd ɪn ðe:z flo˞:z wɪð dansɪz an dɪləit]
And there the snake throws her enamelled skin,
[an ðɛ: ðə sne:k θɹo:z ɚ ɪnamɫd skɪn]
Weed wide enough to wrap a fairy in.
[we:d wəid ɪnʊf tə ɹap ə fɛɹəi ɪn]
And with the juice of this I'll streak her eyes
[an wɪ ðə d͡ʒəis ə ðɪs əiɫ stɹe:k ɚ əiz]
And make her full of hateful fantasies.
[ən me:k ɚ fʊl əv ɛ:tfɫ fantəsəiz]
Take thou some of it, and seek through this grove.
[tɛ:k ðəu sʏm əv ɪt ən se:k θɹu: ðɪs gɹʏv]
A sweet Athenian lady is in love
[ə swe:t əte:njən lɛ:dəi ɪz ɪn lʏv]
With a disdainful youth—anoint his eyes;
[wɪð ə dɪsdɛ:nfɫ ju:θ ənəint ɪz əiz]
But do it when the next thing he espies
[bət ˌdu: ɪt ʍɛn ðə nɛks θɪŋ i: ɪspəiz]
May be the lady. Thou shalt know the man
[mɛ: bɪ ðə lɛ:dəi ðəu ʃaɫt no: ðə man]
By the Athenian garments he hath on
[bəi ðɪ əte:njən ga˞mənts i: əθ ɑn]
Effect it with some care, that he may prove
[ɪfɛkt ɪt wɪð sʏm kɛ: ðət i: mɛ: pɹʏv]
More fond on her than she upon her love.
[mo˞ fɑnd ɑn ɚ ðən ʃe: əpɑn ɚ lʏv]

"Now you and I are new in amity" Oberon (John Staniunas), Titania (Leslie Bennett)

Now when I say that such a speech is understandable, what I mean, of course, is that it's just as understandable as it would be if it were spoken in a modern accent. I'm not saying that OP makes all Shakespeare immediately understandable! If you don't know what eglantine is, for example, then that's a problem for you, but it's a totally different issue, nothing to do with OP at all. All I'm saying is that anyone who knows what [eglantine] is will know what [e:gləntəin] is. The accent won't stop them.

I'm not sure how you get rid of the imagined fear of OP in advance. One has to form a climate, I suppose, and this takes time. Maybe in the advance marketing for a production one should illustrate the accent in some way. That's so much easier now, with iPhone downloads and such-like. There haven't been many attempts at it, though, and that's part of the problem. The Globe hasn't repeated the experience since 2005, mainly because it had a change in artistic direction the following year. The RSC showed interest; indeed, at one point I went over and talked to the company, but then a couple of minor things got in the way, such as rebuilding their theatre! Maybe they'll take up the

idea again one day. I know of a couple of theatrical productions of fragments in OP. Mary Key, who visited the Globe during the *Romeo* production, did something in connection with the Blackfriars project in Virginia. And Alex Torra put on an evening of OP in 2007 called *As I Pronounced It To You* in New York. This was his account to me by e-mail of how the evening went:

We presented thirteen scenes from eleven different plays performed by seven actors. The event happened at a tavern in Times Square called The Playwright, and right outside the window there was a giant billboard that read "Speechless." It was perfect. We invited folks to come and have some food and drinks, and about sixty people came and we had some great responses. The most popular responses of the evening were: how the sound changes allowed the language to move faster and how incredibly enjoyable that was; how the OP actually clarifies rhetoric and word play; how many particularly enjoyed the comedies. (We had a very successful scene from *Taming of the Shrew*, when Petruchio and Katherine meet for the first time...the scene had absolutely no physical life [they were sitting at music stands], and it was as enjoyable as ever.) At the end of the evening, I kept being asked what the next step is. It's encouraging to know that others know that this exploration does not stop here.

That sums up the audience-reaction question very well. I got exactly the same reactions at the Globe in 2004 and 2005. And you will too, Paul.

MEIER: I am looking forward so much to working on the production with you. There is great excitement as well as trepidation about it here. And I look forward to our publishing a second conversation, after *A Midsummer Night's Dream* closes. Many thanks indeed, David.

Shakespeare in OP

This is an extract from Meier's eBook,
The Original Pronunciation of Shakespeare's English,
a free download from
http://paulmeier.com/shakespeare.html.

Edmund, *King Lear*, **Act 1, Scene 2**
Go to http://www.paulmeier.com/OPtrack5.mp3
to listen to Meier speak this speech in Original Pronunciation as you read along.

Thou, nature, art my goddess; to thy law
ðəʊ nɛːtʰə aˑt mɪ gadɛs   tʰə ðəɪ lɑː

My services are bound. Wherefore should I
mɪ sɐˑvɪsɪz ə bəʊnd ʍɛˑfɔˑ   ʃʊd əɪ

Stand in the plague of custom, and permit
stand ɪ ðə pʰlɛːg ə kʰʏstəm an pʰɐˑmɪtʰ

The curiosity of nations to deprive me,
ðə kʰjuˑɹɪasɪtʰəɪ ə nɛːsjənz tʰə dɪpʰɹəɪv mɪ

For that I am some twelve or fourteen moon-shines
fə ðatʰ əɪ am sʏm tʰʍɛɫv ə foˑ tʰeːn mʉnʃəɪnz

Lag of a brother? Why bastard? wherefore base?
lag əv ə bɹɤðə   ʍəɪ bastəˑd   ʍɛˑfɔˑ   bɛːs

When my dimensions are as well compact,
ʍɛn məɪ dəmɛnsjənz a əz wɛɫ kʰəmpʰaktʰ

My mind as generous, and my shape as true,
mɪ məɪnd əz d͡ʒɛnɹəs and mɪ ʃɛːp əz tɹuː

As honest madam's issue? Why brand they us
az anɪst madəmz ɪsjə   məɪ bɹand ðə ɤs

With base? with baseness? bastardy? base, base?
wɪ bɛːs   wɪ bɛːsnəs bastʰɐˑdəɪ bɛːs bɛːs

Part Two: After

This interview, the "after" of a before-and-after pair of interviews, took place in December 2010, after David Crystal's September residence in Kansas at the beginning of rehearsals, and after *Dream* had closed in late November. The interview was conducted by e-mail, later edited by Meier, and subsequently recorded in a conversation via Skype.

To help readers, the recording may be heard at http://www.paulmeier.com/Crystal_Interview2.mp3, especially important when the two discuss the dialect.

The production script of the University of Kansas production, as cut by Meier, and containing a phonetic transcription and Crystal's embedded recordings, is available freely online from http://paulmeier.com/shakespeare.html, where details of the DVD of one of the performances are also available, along with airdates for the radio drama production, the OP dialect instruction eBook, and Meier's eBook, *Voicing Shakespeare*. Details of David Crystal's book, *Pronouncing Shakespeare*, plus extensive recordings of Crystal reading Shakespeare in OP are to be found at his Website: http://www.pronouncingshakespeare.com/

MEIER: David, your visit was a triumph. The production was extremely well received (glowing reviews), with the public's evident curiosity about OP reflected in box office receipts—triple what was projected! So the University of Kansas is very grateful to you. As we recall our work from early September to the present (December 2010), I should begin by asking for your recollections of your residency, particularly your work with the cast.

CRYSTAL: I think a good first move was to get the whole cast to come to a general talk on OP, before we began rehearsals. In it I was able to explain the background to OP, to illustrate it in detail, to answer the inevitable question "How do you know?" and to present some of the issues we discussed in the first part of this interview. It was an open lecture, so the cast found themselves sitting in an audience of other academics, theatre people, and the general public. The audience response, you'll recall, was very enthusiastic, and I think this would have been sensed by the cast, some of whom may well have been feeling a bit tentative about this experiment. Certainly everyone was very upbeat in the reception which followed, and I got the impression that they couldn't wait to get started. And when we did, the next day, the fact that I could rely on this background saved a lot of time, as otherwise much of the first rehearsal would have been devoted to general issues. In that first hour, we were able to get them talking in fragments of OP, individually and in unison, and even joking in it a bit (saying good night with a centralized diphthong, for instance). From that moment, I had no doubts that they would be on target by the time of the production.

What was really good was to see the production moving in parallel with the OP learning. The play's the thing, after all. And it was important that they started to develop some of their blocking and characterization while still getting to grips with the accent. This is certainly what I would recommend, for future productions. Otherwise what happens is that a cast learns their OP while sitting down calmly, and then, when they have to add emotion and pace, they lose the plot, and revert to their native accents. This happened a bit in any case, but it would have been a far greater problem if you hadn't got them moving around from the very beginning.

I haven't yet heard the recording of the final production (I did so miss not being there!), so I can't yet give the OP a grade, as it were. But based on what they had achieved by the time I left, after only an hour a day with the group as a whole, plus a session with each of them individually, I think I will need to have a marking scale that goes higher than A. Certainly the reviews suggested a performance of real excellence. Part of their rapid progress, I suspect, must be put down to the preparation they put in before I arrived, using my audio recording and the parallel transcription. I don't think any of them expected that they would be so fluent after only a dozen hours of rehearsal. A couple of them did find the accent more of a problem, but that's normal—it happened with my Globe casts too. And there were a few sounds that seemed to present more of a difficulty than I think you were expecting. But what was so rewarding was to see how, despite the initial glitches, they were so quickly able to assimilate the OP and make it part of their character.

MEIER: You're right. Any lingering fears among the cast about the dialect vanished rapidly during your ten days with them, to be replaced only by enthusiasm. All your predictions were spot on: The cast quickly fell in love with the dialect's swiftness, its earthiness, its lower point of resonance in the body, its way of guiding us in metrical considerations, its restoration of rhymes and puns. And audiences

"Here comes my messenger" Oberon (John Staniunas), Puck (J.T. Nagle)

Photo by Luke Jordan for The University Theatre

were genuinely intrigued too. So many expressed delight with how the dialect enriched their listening experience and surprise at its clarity. You will see the DVD shortly; that and the radio-drama production we made of the show will allow you to give us an OP grade in due course.

And you're right about the couple of surprises too. You had wanted us to phonetically transcribe THOUGHT words, indicating [ɑ]; I had insisted that because [ɑ] is the dominant Midwestern American sound, we could safely leave the cast to their default vowel (not possible with your Globe casts who might have defaulted to [ɔ] if they were RP speakers). But you were right; fall, thought, daughter, etc., should have been indicated in our transcription, as many of my rehearsal notes were reminders of this lexical set. I think they left their Midwestern English tendencies behind when moving into OP, and THOUGHT words were a casualty of this tendency. That's my theory, anyhow.

I was also surprised by the tight jaw that the dialect seemed to induce at first, when actors were trying to correctly seat PRICE and CHOICE vowels and achieve the prescribed [əi] sound for these two sets. I think the extra close onset for this diphthong is the culprit. And some actors experienced a strong urge to render MOUTH words Irish style [ɛʊ] instead of [əʊ]. That needed reining in.

CRYSTAL: Yes, that effect was notable—and natural, as they left behind their familiar [a] onset, aimed for the [ə] and overshot. There was an Irish-style lip-rounding sometimes on [əi] too, resulting in the characteristic moi for my sound in that accent. I think it's the closeness of these OP diphthongs to Irish which givespeople an initial impression that OP is Irish (a theme of an online forum recently). "Enriching the listener experience," you say. That's critical. With *Dream*, the primary surprise must be to hear all the rhymes working. There are so many that fail in modern English, such as stars and wars, or one and alone. To hear them all fall into place was, for me, one of the most striking effects, especially when associated with a magical moment in the play, such as Oberon's juice-inducing lines.

And you say, "surprise at its clarity." Yes, but I recall we had to work hard at that. A very useful strategy was the focus on the last content word in a line. Get that clear and a speech immediately becomes intelligible. Indeed, it was fascinating to see how you can often summarize the content of a speech by following the last word of each line. But there were some difficult phrases sometimes, weren't there, and I remember you had to get the actors to think very hard about what they were saying rather than how they were saying it, to get the meaning across—tell the story with their faces and bodies.

MEIER: Yes. One of my constant tasks in my rehearsal notes was to remind the actors of possible ambiguity and to ask them to take extra care to inflect the line so as to reveal the desired meaning. Since CHOICE and PRICE words share the same vowel in OP, [əɪ], voice could be misheard as vice. Voice occurs a dozen times in this play, and several instances are particularly tricky:

> But in this kind, wanting your father's voice, The other must be held the worthier. (Theseus)

> Yea and the best person too; and he is a very paramour for a sweet voice. (Quince)

Of course, actors have to anticipate possible confusion constantly in Modern English too (night/knight, due/Jew, do/dew, etc), but as the audience's sound palette is not attuned to the unfamiliar homonyms thrown up by OP, I knew the actors had to be more than usually vigilant.

Some actors feared that h-dropping would fatally wound a line—[ɐ˞kleːz] for Hercules, for example. And in working on Hamlet's speech to the players in OP recently, I myself wondered whether I would be able to make a line like "it out- Herods Herod" actually work without h's. But after you explained that h-dropping was highly variable in OP, the cast felt they had the tools they needed for clarity. I did have to constantly remind my actors not replace a dropped "h" with a glottal stop; this North American actors' tendency makes for extra difficulty. When an elided "h" is smoothly replaced by a legato treatment of the adjacent sounds, however, everything works much better.

The realization that consonants carry the chief burden of intelligibility, and that they haven't significantly changed in English since 1600 (unlike the vowels), is very reassuring.

In our first interview, you anticipated that OP would reveal puns in *Dream* hitherto unremarked by editors, as it had

in *Romeo and Juliet* and *Troilus and Cressida*. Did you find some?

CRYSTAL: There were three instances, and you've just mentioned one of them. But before I answer your question, I think it's important to appreciate what makes a pun. It isn't just a play on words: It's a play on words motivated by context. For example, in Modern English, bear and bare are homophones, so there could in principle always be a pun when one or the other is used. But when someone talks about "the sun harming their bare arms" or "I visited a bear park," the other meaning doesn't even arise. You have to set up a pun. The context has to allow both meanings. And it must be a context that the listener is going to understand. So, the pun works in "Why do the Grenadier Guards always get sunburnt? Because they have bearskins" because the notions of bear and bare are both applicable to these soldiers—but to be effective, you have to know who the Grenadier Guards are and what a bearskin is.

The same principle applies in Early Modern English. There's always a potential pun between voice and vice (both pronounced [vəis] in OP, or whore and hour (both pronounced [oˑː] in OP), but to activate it, we need to have a relevant context in which both words could operate. The

John Staniunas as Oberon

Photo by Luke Jordan for The University Theatre

Theseus quotation doesn't provide it, nor do most of the other uses of <u>voice</u>, but the Quince one certainly does, as <u>paramour</u> sets it up. The pun works because paramours have both voices and vices, but to be effective you have to know what a paramour is.

The other two I noticed were Lysander's "And all my powers, address your love and might" in 2.2, where <u>powers</u> and <u>pores</u> would be a possibility (both pronounced [pɔˑːz]), and Demetrius' "No die, but an <u>ace</u>, for him; for he is but one" in 5.1, where the OP makes ace a homophone of <u>ass</u> ([no dəi bət ən as fɚ hɪm fɚ hi ɪz bət oːn]). I haven't looked at all the editions, but the note to this line in Arden, for example, tries to explain it solely in terms of the number of spots on a die, which is only part of the pun.

However, as I said before, I think in *Dream* the main novelty was to hear the rhymes working so well, rather than the discovery of new readings. And I'm sure in the final production some parts of the play would have been thrilling to hear, as a result. Which bits of the play do you think were most affected?

MEIER: My favorite example is the one you quoted in our first interview–the antidote spell Oberon casts on Demetrius:

> Flower of this purple dye,
> Hit with Cupid's archery,
> Sink in apple of his eye.
> When his love he doth espy,
> Let her shine as gloriously
> As the Venus of the sky.
> When thou wak'st, if she be by,
> Beg of her for remedy.

In Modern English, the fact that <u>dye/archery, gloriously/sky</u>, and <u>by/remedy</u> all fail as rhymes fatally wounds the speech, casting the actor into nebulous blank-verse territory. Clearly Shakespeare intended the drivingly insistent eight-fold [əi] rhyme (<u>eye-rhyme</u> if you will permit the pun) to heighten the magic.

Since all the play's rhymes are restored by the use of OP, the various uses or effects conjured up by rhyme become impossible to ignore, and so the switch from blank verse to prose, from couplets to alternating rhyme scheme, from pentameter to tetrameter, challenges us more directly to confront rhyme as an important part of the play. Some modern actors are faintly embarrassed by rhyme anyway and do their best to evade it, but they are doomed to failure if they attempt this in an OP *Dream*. The duelling wit of the lovers, the incantations of the fairy spells, the sly mischief of Puck—all are aided by rhymes, and the play is infinitely richer when they are restored. And to make the rhymes potent, the actor must crescendo toward the line-final word, always, as you have pointed out, a wonderfully clarifying tactic in itself.

CRYSTAL: One of the interesting things about *Dream* is that some of the actors need to adopt different voices— Puck mimicking Lysander and Demetrius, and of course the mechanicals in the Pyramus play. I tried to reflect this in my transcription, having Puck (who, like all the fairies, normally drops his h's) put them in, and giving the mechanicals a more careful style of speech (reflecting the spelling, Holofernes-like). Did this work or did you/they change it?

MEIER: Puck did mimic Lysander and Demetrius' more courtly diction, yes, as you will hear in due course. And the mechanicals, particularly Bottom, of course, used a more histrionic speaking style, restoring normally dropped h's and so forth. Your transcription and recording were very helpful in prompting that kind of work. I must mention something that Scott Cox (Bottom) reported. His skill with RP gave him an immediate strategy when playing Pyramus: just heighten the dialect. But, deprived of RP, he had to employ other strategies. Scott couldn't parody early 20th century British stage speech: "Curs'd be thy stones for thus deceiving me" had to be [khɚst beː ðəi stoːnz fɚ ðɚs dɪseːvɪn meː] instead of [khɜʂ t bɪ ðai stɛʊnz fɔ ðʌs dɪsiːvɪŋ mɪ], which is what he might have done in another production; but did very well instead by hilariously mouthing his diction like Hamlet's town crier.

Since OP has such rich rewards to confer, clearly pleasing audiences; and since our Kansas production attracted so much attention internationally, I remain puzzled by the fact that this experiment has been attempted only four or five times in living memory. Some of my VASTA [Voice and Speech Trainers Association] colleagues are now itching to give it a go, they tell me. What's your sense of the future of this fascinating but almost completely neglected aspect of Shakespeare performance research?

CRYSTAL: I think the reasons for the neglect are clear. Fear of the unknown, chiefly. That was the reason the Globe didn't do it: They were scared that audiences wouldn't understand it. Once they realized how intelligible and enticing it was, they went for it. And I imagine you had colleagues who felt the same way at first.

The second reason is that it needs linguistic expertise, to provide advice, and this is rare. When the Globe approached me in 2004, my first thought was: Go find someone who's already done this. And, after digging around, I realized that nobody had—at least, not for fifty years (because both John Barton in the UK and Helge Kökeritz in the US had had a go in the 1950s)—and a great deal of linguistic research had taken place since then anyway, helping us develop a sharper sense of what Early Modern English phonology was like. So I had to become an expert myself, and this meant reading up on the linguistics of the period and thinking about how to apply it and teach it, in a way I hadn't had to do before. What I hope, more than anything else, is that other specialists will contribute to this emerging field of applied historical linguistics, as—apart from anything else—I'm well aware that there is room for difference of opinion. You'll recall that there were several occasions when you asked me how a word should be pronounced and my answer was, "We don't know for sure" or "There are alternatives." Proper names are a good example. How exactly was Theseus pronounced: with a "th" sound or with a "t"? We know that classical words like apothecary had a medial "t" [əˈpɒthəkhɹeɪ] (from the many cases where such words are spelled in that way), but would Theseus have had a "t" (as in Modern Irish [ˈtheːsɪəs])? I kept it as [θ], but someone else might reach a different conclusion.

Anyway, in the last five years or so, expertise has become available, and is increasing in quantity (through your good self, for example). And as a result, more information about OP is readily accessible. The biggest problem hitherto has been *How do we get to hear it*? That was a real battle, which for a while I repeatedly lost. I wanted Cambridge University Press to issue a CD along with my book *Pronouncing Shakespeare*, but they wouldn't. I wanted the Globe to release the videos of the two productions we made, but they wouldn't. I asked for an audio recording of the actors, and eventually they let me make just a 20-minute CD using three of the *Troilus* cast, but a restricted number of copies for educational distribution only (I still have a few of these left, by the way) and not for general release. Well, better than nothing! It's so important to illustrate the accent with a variety of speakers, not just me, to get across the point that it is a phonology we are talking about. One of the commonest misconceptions is that *everyone in OP will speak the same*. On the contrary: On top of Early Modern English phonology, we hear the regional resonance of the speakers—the OP you hear from me is audibly slightly Welsh/Liverpudlian, reflecting my regional background, and your OP reflects features of your accent and voice quality.

All this is rapidly changing. My Website (http://www.pronouncingshakespeare.com) now has several downloadable recordings. You've put a tutorial up on your Paul Meier Dialect Services site (http://www.paulmeier.com/OP.pdf). And thanks to your production, we will have a good-quality video and audio recording of the *Dream* event, which will be enormously useful in showing people what can be achieved. A full transcription of the play (including the lines you cut) will be available in due course, along with my recording. And given enough notice, I am very happy to repeat our recent experience and make an initial transcription and recording of a play, in collaboration with a director. Depending on what you recognize as Shakespeare, there are 39 plays in the canon. *Romeo*, *Troilus*, and *Dream* have been done, along with a few fragments from other plays. So that leaves 36 still to do. The first-time excitement you have experienced is there for anyone who wants to have it. OP is always waiting, beckoning, in the wings.

MEIER: Working with you on this project was a glorious experience. Thank you, David.

Shakespeare in OP

This is an extract from Meier's eBook, *The Original Pronunciation of Shakespeare's English*, a free download from http://paulmeier.com/shakespeare.html.

SIGNATURE SOUNDS

1. Use of /r/. What surprises many is that Early Modern English (EME) was a *rhotic* dialect, with heavy *r-coloration* of vowels that are followed by /r/. The silent /r/ of today's Received Pronunciation (Standard British English) is a more recent development.

EXAMPLES: nurse, start, north, force, letter, air, flower, Orsino, Ferdinand

2. The *mouth* lexical set. This diphthong had a centered onset and started with the schwa, or neutral vowel,[ə], resulting in [əʊ].

EXAMPLES: out, loud, noun, count, crowd, bough

3. The *price* and *choice* lexical sets. This *diphthong*, too, had a centered onset and started with the *schwa*, or neutral vowel,[ə], resulting in [əɪ].

EXAMPLES: price, tribe, time, Friday, isle, eider, fight, Viola; AND choice, point, boil, toy, ahoy, royal

4. The *goat*, *near*, *square*, *face*, and *cure* sets. These vowels, diphthongs (two-stage vowels) in RP and GenAm, were more *monophthongal* in EME. We would

have heard [goːt, fɪɾ, skʌɛɾ, fɛːs, kçuːɾ].

EXAMPLES: goat, home, near, beer, square, bare, bear, face, stay, fatal, cure, tour, poor

5. The happY lexical set. Crystal tells us that this unstressed syllable also had a neutral onset, like *price*, *choice*, and *mouth*. The result: [əɪ]

EXAMPLES: happy, lovely, city, baby, money, Feste, valley

6. The *strut* lexical set. Crystal suggests that the close-mid, back, unrounded vowel [ɤ] captures the likely quality of this vowel.

EXAMPLES: cup, rub, butter, love, monk, blood, hum, summer

7. The *trap* lexical set. Crystal suggests a more open, front vowel than today's [æ], similar to the [a] vowel we hear in the dialects of Northern England. He includes any and many in this, although they fall into the RP *dress* set today. *Any* and *many* are still pronounced today in much Irish English as they were in OP.

EXAMPLES: trap, ham, scalp, arrow, Capulet, Malvolio, Andrew, battery, action

8. Since the *lot* and *thought* lexical sets were pronounced without the lip-rounding of today's RP, Crystal directs us to the less rounded version spoken in mainstream American English. [ɑ] is the vowel he suggests.

EXAMPLES: lot, stop, rob, profit, honest, swan, knowledge, want, watch AND daughter, awkward, ought, call, stalk

9. Crystal cautions us to retain the lip-rounding of conservative RP [ʉ] in the goose lexical set, though he lists several words like *fool*, *conclude*, *tooth*, *proof* (today part of the *goose* set) for which he recommends [ʊ], which allows puns such as that in *thou full dish of fool* [ðəʊ fʊɫ dɪʃ əv fʊɫ]. This creates some difficulty over words like *blood* and other double-o words that are today part of *strut*. Confusion with words in the *foot* set (like *put*, *full*, *cuckoo*, *good*, *woman*, *could*) is also possible. Proceed with caution! It is probable that both pronunciations would have been current in Shakespeare's time.

EXAMPLES: loop, mood, dupe, Juliet, funeral, duty, fruit, beauty

10. Crystal addresses the *bath* and *start* sets together, telling us that [a] is the target (though r-colored [ɑ˞] in the case of start words, of course). Interestingly, words like *warm*, *war*, *quarter*, and *warn* – today members of the *north/force* set – were pronounced in EME identically to *start* words, which are all spelled with the letter /a/. He also lists *daughter* (now a *thought*-set word, and suggests [dɑːtə˞].

EXAMPLES: staff, path, brass, blast, ask, master, basket, AND start, heart, barn, sergeant

11. Although we covered the heavy r-coloration of this dialect in signature sound #1, Crystal additionally asks for a slightly different vowel shape for the *nurse* set – slightly more open. [ɚ] is his suggested target.

EXAMPLES: usurp, turn, mercy, shirt, assert, earth, worst, scourge

12. The *fleece* lexical set (whose spelling nearly always involves the letter /e/) calls for the slightly more open vowel [e] or one even closer [ẹ].

EXAMPLES: see, field, be, people, breathe, complete, Caesar, Phoenix
Additional Features

a. Crystal encourages us to be more casual in our diction than is the fashion in today's British stage speech, using lots of *elision*, *weak forms*, etc. For examples, the following words in unstressed positions should involve the weakest form possible (as indicated): *and* [ən], *as* [əz], *being* [bɪn, bən], *for* [fə˞], *he* [ə], *I* [a], *my* [mɪ], *mine* [mɪn], *thine* [ðɪn], *must* [məs], *of* [ə], *or* [ə], *them* [əm], *thou* [ðə], *thee* [ðɪ], *thy* [ðɪ], *to* [tə]. The speech is generally rapid – "trippingly upon the tongue," as Hamlet counsels.

b. Initial /h/ on *he*, *he's*, *him*, *his*, *him*, *her*, *her's*, in unstressed positions will be dropped. Hence: *what's his name* [wɑts ɪz neːm], *who's her best friend* [huz ə˞ bɛs fɪɛn]. Crystal recommends /h/ dropping on more substantial words too, on occasion. He tells us that /h/ was very variable: It would be dropped by lower-class speakers generally, but upper-class speakers might drop it too without being penalized; everything would depend on the extent to which they had learned to pronounce following the spelling, as Holofernes[1] recommends.

c. Medial /v/ and voiced /th/ [ð] consonants in some common words will be *elided*. Hence: *heaven* [hɛ˘ən], *even* [i˘ən], *seven* [sɛ˘əm], *eleven* [əlɛ˘əm], *devil* [di:ɚɫ], *hither* [hiɚ], *thither* [ðiɚ].

d. Abundant *elision* of vowels. Crystal cites the following examples: the *unworthiest* [ðʌnwɚˀðjəst], *delivery* [dəlɪvɹəi], *leavening* [lɛvnɪn], *venomous* [vɛnməs], *everybody* [ɛvɹibdi]. Often scansion of the verse line will alert you to a likely elision.

e. *-ing* suffixes should be reduced to [ɪn]. No connotation of reduced social status attaches to this, as is often the case today. Hence: *calling* [kɑlɪn], *singing* [sɪŋɪn], *praying* [pɹɛ:ɪn].

f. /wh/ should be aspirated in words like *which* [ʍɪt͡ʃ], *when* [ʍɛn], *why* [ʍəɪ], *whither* [ʍɪðɚ], *whence* [ʍɛns], etc., where today's dominant pronunciation is [w]. (*Who* [hu], *whom* [hum], *whole* [hoɫ], etc., today pronounced with [h] do not get this treatment, of course.)

g. Many polysyllabic words have a different stress pattern today than in EME. Particularly when these words are part of a verse line, the OP rhythm becomes important. Consider the three examples Crystal cites: can**on**ize, ad**ver**tize, gall**an**try. There's a very full list of such polysyllabic words in *Shakespeare's Pronunciation*[2].

h. Fuller soundings of *-sion* and *-tion* spellings [sɪən] instead of [ʃən].

Notes

1. Holofernes is the pedantic schoolmaster that Shakespeare satirizes so cleverly in Love's Labour's Lost.

2. Shakespeare's Pronunciation is the seminal work by Helge Kökeritz.

Bibliography

Crystal, David. Various magazine articles. *Around the Globe* 3-37, 39-46 (1997-2010).

Crystal, David. *Pronouncing Shakespeare*. Cambridge: Cambridge University Press, 2005.

Crystal, David. *The Shakespeare Miscellany*. London: Penguin, 2005.

Crystal, David. *Shakespeare's Words*. London: Penguin, 2002.

Gimson, A.C. *Introduction to the Pronunciation of English*. London: Hodder & Stoughton Educational, 1962.

Johnson, Samuel. *A Dictionary of the English Language*. London: 1755.

Meier, Paul. *Accents and Dialects for Stage and Screen*. Lawrence, Kansas: Paul Meier Dialect Services, 2001.

Meier, Paul. *Voicing Shakespeare*. Lawrence, Kansas: Paul Meier Dialect Services, 2009.

Shakespeare, William. *The Oxford Shakespeare: The Complete Works*, eds., Stanley Wells, Gary Taylor, John Jowett and William Montgomery. Oxford: Oxford University Press, 2005.

Shakespeare, William. *King Lear*. London: 1606.

Shakespeare, William. *Love's Labour's Lost*. London: 1598.

Shakespeare, William. *A Midsummer Night's Dream*. London: 1595.

Shakespeare, William. *Romeo and Juliet*. London: 1597.

Shakespeare, William. *The Taming of the Shrew*. London: 1590-1594.

Shakespeare, William. *Troilus and Cressida*. London: 1602.

Thomas, Dylan. *Under Milk Wood*. New York: New Directions Publishing Company, 1954.

Wells, John Christopher. *Accents of English*. New York: Cambridge University Press, 1982.

Essay *by Michael Barnes*

Standard Speech Practices and Pedagogy: A Snapshot of the Moment

Michael J. Barnes is the Voice & Speech Specialist at Wayne State University and its Hilberry Theatre Company. Previously, he taught at University of Miami and Temple University. Training includes an MFA from The National Theatre Conservatory, a BFA from the University of Oklahoma, Cambridge University, and as a Certified Associate Teacher of Fitzmaurice VoiceWork. He has coached regionally and off-Broadway. Theatres include the Utah Shakespearean Festival, Shakespeare Santa Cruz, Arena Stage, Wilma Theatre, Studio Theatre (DC), Rep Stage Company, Pearl Theatre, People's Light and Theatre, Venture Theatre, Denver Center Theatre Company, and Colorado Shakespeare Festival. Films coached include: *Convicted* (Aiden Quinn, Kelly Preston and Tim Daily, directed by Bille August) and *Broken Bridges* (Kelly Preston, Toby Keith, Burt Reynolds, Tess Harper; directed by Steven Goldman), and *Master Class*. (Starring & directed by Faye Dunaway). He is also on the Board of Directors for VASTA.

"Standard Speech." These two words can often spark a heated debate amongst voice and speech trainers. While training for my MFA in Voice & Speech Coaching, I can still remember being told a story—that may simply be our own speech trainers' urban myth—about Kristin Linklater heatedly walking out of a workshop at ATHE/ATA where they were speaking of training people in Edith Skinner's Good Speech for the American Stage. I would guess that stories of those strong feelings are exactly the reason why Rocco Dal Vera chose to make it the topic of the first issue of the Voice and Speech Review ten years ago.

In that first issue, there was a hearty debate that seemed to be centered on an article entitled, "Standard Speech: The Ongoing Debate" that Dudley Knight had originally written for *The Vocal Vision*—an anthology that had been put to-gether by Marion Hampton and Barbara Acker for VASTA in 1997. This debate focused on the idea of whether one should teach a Standard American accent, as had been set forth by Edith Skinner in her book *Speak With Distinction*. Though some of the various articles argued the pluses and minuses of teaching a standard speech pattern, much of this debate seemed to center more on Edith, herself, rather than her teachings.

Nevertheless, that first issue of the VSR illustrated that there were differences of opinion when it comes to training actors. The debate seemed to point to a dividing line between teachers who believed in training actors in a form of standard speech, mostly based on Edith Skinner's "Good American Speech," and those who believed in a less pre-scriptive manner of teaching.

Now, a decade later, it seems an ideal time examine the views of contemporary voice & speech trainers toward a standard speech pattern. How exactly are they viewing this same subject when teaching their acting students? How prevalent is the teaching of Edith Skinner's "Good American Speech?" Are teachers employing a different methodology for teaching speech to acting students? I set up a questionnaire/survey to ask speech trainers across the country to answer these questions. I sent it to approximately seventy teachers teaching in a number of settings. Thirty-eight people answered the questionnaire and survey questions.

In order to better understand current practices in speech training, I felt that a survey/questionnaire would be the best method. Whom to ask? After a lot of deliberation, I really felt that it was best to get a good cross section of people training in a variety of situations. Thus, I ended up sending invitations to participate to trainers who worked in university settings—in MFA programs, BFA programs, and BA programs; in private practice; and in well-known acting studios. Knowing it would be difficult to speak one-on-one with this many people, I chose to create an online survey using the SurveyMonkey website, even though I knew it could lead to discrepancies (individual questions could be skipped). Knowing the best way to glean information was to allow individuals to write about their processes, I wanted mostly open-ended questions where individuals could explain teaching practices. However, I felt that some questions that could give statistics would be helpful. Thus, I came up with a structure that included yes/no questions that would lead to further questions requesting more detail. These open-ended questions asked the speech trainers about how they taught their students, how they were taught, whether they used any type of transcription method, and other points. Though all of the trainers supplied amazing answers that—taken together—provide some interesting insights into current trends in speech training in North America, in no way can I assert that the results yielded scientific conclusions. Rather, the results give an impressionistic snapshot of current speech-training practices. All answers from all the respondents are available online at http://vasta.org/publications/voice_and_speech_review/2011/standardspeechsurvey.pdf.

The survey began with the question "Do you train actors to speak any variety of 'standard' speech?" I was somewhat surprised by the answers. Having had many discussions with teaching colleagues, observed many professional theatres' movement toward color-blind/culture-blind casting in productions, and followed conversations on VASTAvox, it seemed to me that there was a trend toward actors retaining elements of their personal idiolects. I had expected to find something of a balanced split, but 76% of respondents answered "Yes." This led me to be extremely interested in the answers to the questions that followed:

- What do you call it?
- How would you describe it?
- What, in your view, are the advantages for your students of mastering the "standard" speech pat-tern you teach them?
- Do you expect your students to adopt this speech pattern as their personal everyday speech? *Yes/No Answer*

  Yes Answer:
  - To the best of your knowledge, how well do the students comply with the expec-tation of adopting this "standard" speech pattern, both during and after their training?
  - What sort of reactions do you observe in your students when they are asked to change their normal speaking patterns? Do they change over time?

  No Answer:
  - Under what circumstances are the students expected to use the "standard" speech pattern?

In terms of using this survey to better understand teachers' ideas of standard speech, much of the most interesting information came in response to the first two questions. The surveyed teachers' names for this standard speech pattern varied. Some of these included: Standard Speech, Elevated American Speech, Standard Stage Speech, General American, Neutral American, and Non-regional American. As one would expect, the description of the pattern itself held as much variety. One might expect to have thirty varying descriptions of the teacher's desired speech pattern, since every teacher has his or her own way of presenting information. I was, however, able to create groupings based on the similarities of the teachers' descriptions. I labeled the major groupings as follows: Skinner Standard, Modified Skinner Standard, "Detail Model" (a term coined by Dudley Knight, and used in the Knight-Thompson Speechwork taught by

Knight and Philip Thompson), and General American. There were a few individuals whose surveys did not land them entirely in these groupings, but could be described as follows: Lessac Speech, Detailed General American (K-T/GenAm Hybrid), and one I deemed Detailed Skinner (it used the Skinner sound patterns and transcription, but viewed the patterns as choices that could be added and subtracted).

I should briefly address the use of the term "Detail Model," as several respondents wrote that they teach a standard speech pattern which they call "the Detail Model." Dudley Knight, a survey respondent himself (and the Editor-in-Chief of this issue of *Voice and Speech Review*), stated in his response that he, himself, does not teach a standard speech pattern. This is consistent with his previously published work on the subject. Unlike the other pedagogies mentioned by the teachers in the survey, however, Knight's teaching has not been extensively described in published form. Knight states,

> The Detail Model is an attempt to provide more vo-cal variety and consonant muscularity than is found in most regional accents. So our jaws will stay relaxed and our tongues and lips active. We will sound iden-tifiably American; we will also sound fully engaged in the physical act of speech. We will use our language to reveal ourselves and our imaginative creations, not hide ourselves from the world. (Knight, 99)

In the Knight-Thompson approach, students spend a large amount of time physically exploring the production of all sound possibilities. They then learn to classify the sound possibilities using the International Phonetic Alphabet. The Detail Model is the part of the methodology that then outlines phoneme usages that can aid in clarity of linguistic understanding. However, Knight does not see this as being a specific pattern that creates a standard accent, as the speaker can choose to add or subtract the outlined pho-nemes depending on the speaking situation (and there is, furthermore, considerable latitude afforded in the realiza-tion of many of the individual phonemes).

> For many speech interactions, in life or onstage, too much detail would be as much a hindrance to precise communication as too little. Virtually everything in The Detail Model is negotiable, given the particular demands of any speech task. Because it provides us with access to a lot more speech detail than most of us are in the habit of using, The Detail Model opens new worlds of expression to us. But it is never a rigid pattern of 'good speech.' It is a model of useful physi-cal actions" (Knight, 99)

Recognizing that the Detail Model could be misapplied as a

kind of standard speech pattern, Knight's most recent revision of his manuscript (working title: *Speaking with Skill*) has abandoned the Detail Model entirely. (Knight, personal communication, February 2011)

By compiling and examining the groupings of like descriptions, I was able to gain the impression that there has been a general shift in attitude as to what defined the "standard" over the past decade. A plurality (40%) of the survey respondents fell into what I described as the "General American" group. Another word about the terminology: General American was not necessarily the term used by many of the individual respondents, but seemed to fit. I gave this name to those who were describing a rhotic, non-regional sounding American speech without those added phonemes that could be deemed "Mid-Atlantic." (I am thinking primarily of /a/ and /ɒ/). These individuals want students to find a fairly non-regional sound, but did not want it to have the sense of elevation that was perceived in Skinner's methodology.

Some of the specific descriptions:

I define American Non-Regional Dialect as 'a pattern of spoken English that identifies someone as a native-speaking American, but does not give the average listener clues about the speaker's geographical or ethnic roots within the country.' This is not to say that there is one, inflexible, 'correct' non-regional pattern. Even among those whose speech is widely perceived as non-regional, certain pronunciations may vary. (Stern, survey response)

General, neutral or regionless American speech. (Goldes, survey response)

A dialect of American English that is not readily definable as being from anywhere in particular. (Devore, survey response)

Non-regional American dialect. (Houfek, survey response)

A basically "neutral" American accent with flexibility to make it more and more formal as necessary. I acknowledge that "neutral" is very misleading and actually implies straight, white, educated, Christian, Midwestern, upper-middle-class—which is not "neutral" at all. (Johnson, survey response)

Of the respondents stating that they teach a standard speech pattern, 13% of the answers fell into what I would describe as a "Modified Skinner" speech pattern. This pattern still follows many/most of the principles in *Speak with Distinction*, but has allowed an evolution of some of the sounds to sound less British and more familiar to the average American listener. Artemis Preeshl, of Loyola University-New Orleans, described it as "A regional [sic] Mid-Atlantic dialect as put forth by Edith Skinner tempered with contemporary American news reporting today." Other descriptions were:

A rhotic version of Skinner's work, and without her use of intermediate [a]. (Julian, survey response)

A 'made-up' dialect of English. It is a dialect that allows one to be understood by most English speakers world wide. I teach a modified version of it. 'Modified' is a code for 'modern' or 21st Century. (Adrian, survey response)

I describe the SASD (Standard American Stage Dialect) as a school of phonology, taught only as a dialect, that seeks to neutralize, not neuter, strong regionalisms for the sake of making the speakers (when they desire) seem as if they are of one kind, similar in nature, and linguistically indistinguishable in terms of geographic origin. It is the grandchild of what was once known as 'mid-Atlantic,' and the child of what Edith Skinner called, 'Good Speech for the American Stage.' It has undergone significant generational changes that have occurred in response to modern American proclivities, and in the industry is usually deemed to be the least regional using pronunciations that are thought to resonate most broadly through the mainstream of American society. The SASD is regarded as neutral or universal, a productive bridge across the boundaries of social class structure and indigenous speech patterns, since the indigenous dialects it seeks to bridge are influenced by major geographical contours, population densities, and various social strata, including ethnicity, education, and even the differences between generations. I do not describe the SASD as 'proper' or 'correct' speech, and I do not describe the various idiolects and regionalisms used by students as 'substandard' or 'incorrect.' (Logan, survey response)

Ten percent of the respondents teach a speech pattern that varies little from that described in *Speak with Distinction*. This group also included a protégé of Alice Hermes (Alice Hermes was a student of William Tilley, alongside both Edith Skinner and Margaret Prendergast Mclean, who was Skinner's teacher at the Leland Powers School). This pattern represents what many describe have described as a "Mid-Atlantic" accent. This was described as:

Little or no r-coloring, use of liquid "u", use of weakened penultimate syllable in words like 'Secretary' or 'Dictionary' (tuh-ri instead of tear-y), use of 'wh', use of 'will' sound in prefixes and suffixes, the 'ask' list, use of pure vowel, 'o' in 'obey' words. (Shane , survey response)

Standard English is used in America and also internationally but it is not British speech! At one time only Standard English was used on the stage and in movies whether the character was a Baron or a newspaper reporter but that changed to accommodate a more realistic truth of the background of characters in stage plays (starting in the Group Theater) and film scripts. This more closely reflected the background of the person in the audience watching the film as opposed to going to the movies to be taken out of your ordinary life. (Harris , survey response)

Of the teachers that teach a standard speech pattern, three of them spoke of teaching several levels of standard speech. The commonly–described levels were "General American" and a level referred to as "Standard American," "Standard Stage Speech," or "Elevated American." They noted the requirements of a play may point toward either a non-regional speech or a non-regional pattern where the characters might have a sense of "elevation" to their speech. Rocco Dal Vera, from the University of Cincinnati, pointed me towards the descriptions that he used in his book:

1.   General American Stage Speech: neutral, non-regional, yet clearly American speech, also called Broadcast Standard.
2.   Elevated Speech, Stage Standard Speech: an accommodation between British and American speech designed to be internationally neutral. Also called Mid-Atlantic, Elevated Stage, Classical, and Trans-Atlantic Speech.

Finally, two of the instructors who spoke of teaching a standard speech pattern stated that they instructed their students in the Detail Model. This is an aspect of the speech training pedagogy developed by Dudley Knight and taught in the Knight-Thompson Speech workshops. This is particularly interesting since Mr. Knight was one of the respondents in the survey and stated that he teaches no standard speech pattern. The two explanations were:

A flexible model of speech that allows students to increase the amount of variety and proficiency in their speech based on the demands of the character. (Lush, survey response)

A collection of prescribed sounds, along a continuum, some of which may be called for in auditions and production. (Nevell, survey response)

The reasons offered for training students in a standard

speech pattern did not vary too greatly. Though things were worded differently, several answers cropped up repeatedly. There seemed to be an overall opinion that (1) a standard accent gives actors a baseline from which to learn other accents, (2) a non-regional accent is frequently desired for stage and media work, and (3) such training develops listening and muscular skills essential to actors' abilities to connect with and deploy language. Some specific responses:

When I teach at a school that asks me to teach a standard, I tell the students that a standard is a dialect and that learning any dialect is an occasion for exploring how we make vowel and consonant sounds and for developing the physical skills required for acquiring dialects of all kinds. (Robinson, survey response)

An awareness of many versions of speech compared with their own current speech, an ability to speak in many different sorts of styles for formality vs. informality, for different eras, for different aesthetic choices. Also they can become skilled and "at home in" many sorts of phonetic choices for many sorts of reasons. The ability to hear and make these different sounds prepares them for accents and dialects, and makes them employable for different directors, agents and projects. They can also feel the many ways the tongue and its parts relate to the hard and soft palate, the teeth, and gum ridge. They can feel and hear how tone placement can be effected by articulator shapes. (Gist, survey response)

With Lessac Kinesensic training in place, the student is ready to adopt and adapt to any regional or social mode of pronunciation and enunciation, yet retain his/her own individuality. Our criteria for a desirable standard emphasizes: a pleasant, warm voice quality, an energetic and vibrant vocal 'life,' complete intelligibility, a voice capable of having power without pain, strength without strain, healthy posture, breathing, and awareness of optimal body functioning, the ability to incorporate this high-quality voice and speech into everyday life --both professional and personal. (Krebs, survey response)

It would seem that there has been a shift away from expecting students to adopt a "standard" accent as their own. Of all the teachers who asked that students learn a standard speech pattern (76%), only four (13%) expected their students to adopt the pattern in their everyday speech, whereas the rest (87%) spoke of it as being a dialect to be used almost exclusively for chosen texts. Though I know of no prior survey comparable to this one, I would suspect that this has eased over the past ten years. In past conversations with friends from VASTA, many speak of having been encouraged to personally adopt a standardized pattern during their own training. The four respondents who expect this of their students fell into several of my categories: two were Skinner Standard, one was Lessac, and one was "Detail Model." It seems that the best explanations of their reasoning came in response to the question: "To the best of your knowledge, how well do the students comply with the expectation of adopting this "standard" speech pattern, both during and after their training?" The responses:

Students are very receptive to the Detail Model. There is no right or wrong that isn't driven by context, so it can adapt to whatever they need. (Lush)

It varies. I speak to them at all times in Standard, in and out of class, and tell them first day that their grade will be affected by whether I hear them trying to apply it outside of class. As much as possible the students are encouraged by their acting teachers to employ it as well, insofar as it is appropriate for their work. Some of the students eagerly embrace the challenge. Many are skeptical, especially those who have a strong sense of truthfulness in their work and who may feel that it separates them from their impulses. We do stress that they need to work on it consistently in order to master it, and that they cannot be thinking about it in their rehearsals, performances, etc. Many of the students really start to use it more comfortably in the second year of training, especially when they begin to apply it as a starting place for dialect work. They also seem to love being able to catch regionalisms and idiolectical elements in friends, family, other professionals. (Beck, survey response)

I try to respectfully accept and embrace all students, believing that they want to become an actor in the most serious way and the same for non-actors that want to improve their speech for self-confidence in other careers. Even those that are timid, lazy or skeptical, I continue to give them the information and skills. I love my profession and worked too seriously and care about being an actor too much to teach any student with an attitude of hopelessness. Sometimes I feel like I am a motivational coach and I say so jokingly because an artist/teacher is not a therapist. But sometimes with teaching Speech you have to show them the relevance through some sort of inspiration. Many students have no idea of the discipline and practice and years of study that go into developing a craft and technique. It's understandable....it's the "behind the scenes" work....especially Speech. Sometimes for the American student studying speech there is a stigma when they hear "speech class" compared to "acting class" which is where they really want to be! In his initial interview with the actor, Paul Mann

would ask "what kind of actor do you want to be"? "What roles do you want to play"? I think if the actor can answer those questions, the path to doing the necessary work becomes very clear. (Harris)

I believe that most students after a few years (or even weeks) of this training on a regular basis, incorporate this euphonic standard in their own lives--simply because their awareness of the positive benefits grows to the point where they recognize when something positive is missing or present and take steps to maintain or correct the situation. They enjoy the work during the training period so much--that they begin to notice in themselves the effects of using this training in their profesional and personal lives. (Krebs)

Given that 87% of the teachers did not expect their students to speak in a standard speech all the time, I was curious to know the contexts in which they required a standard speech pattern to be used. Of course the reasoning behind this varied greatly from person to person, but there was some similarity to responses. There was generally a feeling that this "standard" speech pattern would be used in texts that did not specify an accent, especially classic texts and particularly those translated from another language.

In various projects. I begin by using "translation" monologues, such as Chekov and Ibsen. Then I also utilize Shaw's "Arms and the Man" and Shakespeare as well as other texts of their choosing. (Johnson)

When in a play that requires a neutral dialect, for example, a Shakespeare play, a Greek play, Chekov, other translations, or other situations where the director wishes to keep the speech patterns not identifiably connect to a particular region of the U.S. (Houfek)

They can use or not use it as they see fit, though they do have to apply it to a piece of Shakespeare text we happen to be working on at that point. I make it clear that the accent is no more appropriate than any other for Shakespeare; this just happens to be the text we have handy. (Armstrong)

I leave it to them. Some people want to use it in their everyday life. (In fact, most of my foreign students do.) Others only want to use it when they work on scenes or monologues that would require a General American accent. (Quaid, Survey response)

It is one of the criteria for passing Voice and Speech for the Actor. Additionally, after two-semesters of Voice/Speech study, it is a requirement in Acting III that they employ this dialect on Chekhov, Ibsen, and Strindberg texts. This is only to give them more practice with the dialect not because Standard Stage is THE ONLY way to speak these texts. The next section after Cheknov, Ibsen, Strindberg is Shaw and Wilde so Standard Stage is a good precursor for tackling RP. At my college which is in NYC, we have guest directors and faculty directors who have requested (depending on the material) that the cast speak in Standard Stage. The director may not call it that, but it becomes evident when he/she speaks to the cast and coach about what they want the show to sound like that the desire is for some form of Standard Stage. This kind of request probably happens about every other year, or once out of every six shows we mount on our main stage. (Adrian, survey response)

For those people who responded that they do not teach any form of standard speech pattern, it seemed important to know what occurs in their classroom. Overall, the responses pointed toward the students exploring sounds, the muscularity of sounds, and possibilities. When asked what they taught, some responses from these teachers were:

The training of articulation skills. The opening to the actor of all the sounds in the world's languages and the mastery of the specific skills needed for formal and informal speech in the English language. (Knight, survey response)

IPA sounds for a base line: to train their muscular strength and precision for clarity onstage, for listening skills, to open up resonance possibilities, to anticipate dialect work for deviations from their own pronunciations. (Moulton, survey response)

Awareness of the kinesthetic feeing of vowels and consonants and imagining of sounds moving through the body. introduction to Lessac symbols. Introduction to IPA symbols. Use of the IPA to describe idiolect. Use of the IPA to learn dialects. (Anderson, survey response)

I do not teach them "standard speech patterns". The benefit of mastering the making any sound is the ability to transform one's speaking to match the needs of the play and character. Sometimes the demands of the play may call for little change. However, other plays may demand greater change o r diversity from the way we "normally" express ourselves. Mastery gives one choice. Mastery opens up possibilities. (Burke, survey response)

To better understand the teachers, I thought it would be helpful to know some facts about their backgrounds. Knowing how they were trained, how long they had been teach-

ing, and if there had been any shifts in their views since their training could lead to further insights. Of all the respondents, 79% had been teaching ten years or more, with 22% having taught less than ten years. Of all the teachers, 79% had been trained in some form of standard speech. When asked if they, personally, had been asked to adopt a standard speech pattern during their training, only twenty-nine of the thirty-eight respondents answered the question, but of those, 62% answered "yes." Finally, when I asked whether they felt that their speech had modified since their training, 75% said that their own speech patterns had shifted. For those that felt that there had been modification, the survey asked when, why, and how the modifications occurred; whether the changes were conscious; and if the changes were gradual or abrupt? The answers were some of the most interesting of the entire survey:

I became more relaxed with my own speech, too, though it has been gradual. I don't think I sound like the stereotypical speech teacher, which I consider a positive. (Julian, survey response)

I am sure my speech has modified since I first learned this dialect, which was in the late '70s. I am sure those changes in speech patterns, (the ones that "stick," came on gradually and mostly unconsciously. After all, we are talking about 30 years of living and teaching and studying and (hopefully) growing! I would have to hear a recording of myself from various stages over the 30 years to really know what changes took place. As to "why?" Well, life happens. (Adrian, survey response)

Unconsciously it became more in line with General American, but I would still consider it to be closer to "Standard" than most people's "regular" speech. But to me it feels like quite a shift. (Shane, survey response)

I started out performing a lot Shakespeare as a new Equity actor right out of grad school, and I used the Edith Skinner good American Speech I learned for this through the 80s and 90s. Only consciously adopted it for my own everyday speech during grad school, pretty much stopped doing that immediately after. Stopped doing a lot of Shakespeare, did more contemporary work, in late 90s and early 00s, and stopped paying attention to using any "standard" sound. Learned in workshop 2-3 years ago that students aren't taught the same "standard" sound I was taught, and it surprised me! I haven't been asked to use a specific "standard" sound in any professional production, although I suppose for Shakespeare I assumed it and did it. Now that I am a new/returning speech teacher, I have been asked to teach "General

American" at one school and been given leeway at an-other. Given leeway, I choose Dudley Knight's Detail Model. (Robinson, survey response)

The changes were conscious and mainly had to do with terminal "r's". Edith's method and expectations didn't fit with my experience in regional repertory theatre, mainly west of the Mississippi, including Kansas City, Denver, and San Francisco. I opted to strengthen the rhotic nature of those sounds. (Logan)

As a working actor, I felt that Edith Skinner's Stan-dard Speech for the Stage was too formal a speech pattern for the contemporary stage. I consciously had to modify my learned speech behaviors. (Houfek)

I was trained in Skinner, and I started out teaching Skinner, and teaching "standard" mid-Atlantic speech and calling it "good" speech. But ultimately, I real-ized that what I wanted to help my clients achieve was flexibility, and I saw the limitations in Skinner. So I began altering it. I would have clients do Skinner exercises as written, then have them do the exact op-posite and explain why that might be the best choice for a particular kind of character. Nevertheless, I did continue to use the word "standard," as in, "quote-un-quote standard English, there is a difference between the words *caught* and *cot*, but if you're playing some-one who's a young American and you want a more casual sound, you can make them the same." So now, I use the term "standard" with a caveat, and frequently to present a contrast to what I'm actually suggesting the student do. (Quaid)

In examining the responses, it also seemed important to better understand those who come from a background where their training did not ask them to speak in any particular standard speech pattern. What was of particular interest is that, though these eight respondents were not trained in any form of standard speech, 50% of them state that they teach a standard pattern. To gain a basic under-standing of their thoughts on their own training, I asked if they understood why their teachers did not train them in any form of standard speech:

In Canada, [there is] not as much focus on this issue. Dialects across the country are not as pronounced as in US or UK so not seen as a need to 'standard-ize'. That said, good size in the vowel sounds and full pronunciation of words like 'your, I'll, just, to' was encouraged in texts that weren't modern colloquial speaking. (Moulton)

My teacher taught Skinner, as a Classical Stage Standard. There was no focus on standard speech for

contemporary. But she might have pointed out our regionalisms. (DeVore)

We had a voice teacher who was not interested in teaching speech. As an MFA class, we requested that she teach us the IPA, and she responded by giving us some tools. (Anderson)

My actor-training program was of very poor quality. My formal training in speech was not designed to create either performers or voice & speech trainers. (Stern)

My teacher, Dudley Knight, was already in the pro-cess of interrogating Edith Skinner's approach, and while I was taught quite a bit about that approach, I wouldn't say I was trained in it. (Thompson)

To further understand their training, they went on to ex-plain what they adopted for their everyday speech:

I had a teacher who simply went to the dictionary for pronunciations. (Ufema)

More sounding of consonants for clarity and allowing varied lengths in vowels and overall word duration. (Moulton)

My personal speech pattern, a slight New York accent that is close enough to "standard" that most people don't recognize it as New York, has changed relatively little over the years. I code-switch readily, depending on personal and professional context, and have since I was a very small child. (Stoller)

My own accent, modified by my sensitive, musical ear. (Anderson)

Only after I became a voice and speech trainer did I become aware that my own speech still retained some NYC regionalisms. Having discovered that, I used my own method to refine my ability to live my life through non-regional speech--a skill that can still be interfered with by a glass of wine. (Stern)

I did make changes in my everyday speech growing out of my curiosity about the sounds I was learn-ing about. I probably adopted some of my teacher's accent through an only partly conscious emulation. (Thompson)

The last part of the survey asked how people treated transcription of speech and its relation to speech training. A resounding 95% stated that they taught some form of phonetic transcription. All but Nancy Krebs, who has her

Masters Certificate in Lessac training, use the International Phonetics Alphabet (IPA), though two others state that they give reference to Lessac's transcription system alongside the IPA. Of all the people using the IPA, 21% stated that they used the unconnected script that was promoted in Edith Skinner's *Speak with Distinction*, while 73% stated that they teach the printed symbols. One person teaches both styles.

To better understand how people used phonetics, I wanted to know whether people were using the IPA to teach a "correct" sound for each symbol in order to create a base for their "standard" speech pattern. In response to the question, "Do you use phonetics as a tool toward teaching a "standard" speech pattern?" 71% answered "yes." This "yes" answer led to the question, "Do you use the phonetic transcription to teach a correct sound for each symbol? Can you explain how?" whereas a "no" answer led to the question, "If you do not use phonetics as a tool to teach standard speech, why not?" Little did I know the confusion I would cause with the first yes/no question. Many of the trainers responded positively that they do use the IPA to teach a standard, but then went on to say that, though they do teach a sound-to-symbol relation, it does not mean that any sound is more "correct" than the other. Though the question did not work exactly as intended, it did yield interesting responses:

Yes. We investigate and tune each vowel and diphthong, sound by sound. I list the phonetic transcription for each sound on the blackboard. Beside each sound I write a word for reference. I also use phonetic transcriptions to contrast and compare the sounds of the students' accents to the sounds of standard speech. Phonetic transcriptions are also used on the balls that I use for Speech Sound ball play. (Murphy)

I teach a specific muscular action and mouth posture for the articulators for each symbol. (Adrian)

Yes. I follow Skinner's directions how to produce the sound and my own speech to model that production. (Shane)

I use phonetics with relatively narrow diacritics in order to try to record exactly what a speaker is physically doing. In this way, it can be helpful to identify, visually and kinesthetically, the subtle differences between one phoneme and another. (Nevell)

Your previous question is worded in a way that makes it a "yes and no" if I had such a button. I am not teaching a "standard speech pattern". I use phonetics to teach all the sounds of spoken English and to relate the sounds we hear to something written. I don't talk about them as correct or incorrect. There are sounds

we need in particular situations based on the play. I use phonetics as a way to help my students identify what those sounds might be in a written form, as a tool. I spend much more time in the making of (an enormous variety) of sound than in the writing of it. (Burke)

I teach sound to symbol connection. I do use mnemonic words but have to do ear training to teach the "cardinal" sounds. I use the web to provide audio so they aren't just learning that their sound is the sound of a symbol. (Armstrong)

My position is that there is a one-to-one relationship between a given symbol and a given sound. That does not mean, however, that any given sound is "correct" or "incorrect" within a specific dialect. For example, [æ] does represent a specific, "pure" sound. Non-regional American speakers usually use that "pure" [æ] in the words "cat" "attach" and "map." The same non-regional speakers would usually move slightly toward the "diphthongization" of that vowel in the words "branch" "jazz" and "laugh." The modification of that "pure" vowel does not regionalize their speech. The "non-pure" vowel is, in fact, a characteristic of the non-regional dialect. Substituting the "pure [æ] in those words would sound "heightened" or "elevated" or, in some cases, "affected." All that being said, [æ] is still the symbol that represents the non-regional sound in "cat," and the diphthong symbol is the one that represents the non-regional sound in "man." (Stern)

I describe the symbols by saying there are ranges of speaking, around each symbol, that evoke the impression of that sound. And I demonstrate how some vowels are symbolized the same even though Americans might speak them differently than British speakers do. I have them listen to each other on the different sound/symbols to hear the range of ways they can still be perceived as that vowel, diphthong, consonant. I ask them to hear, see, and feel their own articulation and other people's articulation for each symbol. I show them how Skinner used diacritic marks to further describe each sound thus calling it "narrow" transcription. (Gist)

Though the question did not work as expected, the "no" answers did yield answers that were in line of my original intention—using the the IPA symbols to teach a prescribed "correct" sound. The respondents who answered "no" to the question about using phonetics as a tool toward teaching speech were unified in their belief that one sound cannot be described as being more "correct" than another.

I use phonetics as a tool to prepare actors to adjust their speech patterns to suit any required set of phonetics and phonology in any given artistic project. I do not think of "standard" speech as an end goal of any kind. (Timberlake)

If you mean a way of speaking that is the same as a prescribed standard, I do not teach that concept as 'a general way of speaking they must learn/use'. The sounds are completely dependent on the style of the play being performed, so there is no 'standard' sound the actors are asked to adopt as a complete way of speaking in their in and out of class lives. Specific speech sounds that are lacking in their own dialects are worked on so that they can use them in whatever style requires them, and whatever clarity in a theatre space requires them. I believe I use phonetics to notate a fully sounded, resonant sound that can carry full meaning in context. So in this way, they are a tool to teach that kind of speaking. (Moulton)

I use some form of a standard to teach phonetics. Here is the 'standard' for the 'I' as in the lexical set 'kit'. (Bailey)

I don't believe a standard is necessary to teach transformation, characterization, sensitivity and awareness. (Anderson)

When I began putting the questions together for this survey, I could only speculate about exactly what I might find. Given the format in which the survey was administered, any conclusions we might draw from it may lack a certain scientific rigor. I can say, however, that—after multiple readings of the respondents' surveys—I feel I can make some meaningful deductions about the direction in which speech training has been moving since the "Standard Speech" issue of the Voice and Speech Review.

1. There seems to be a relaxation of what was considered "standard" ten years ago. It seems to be shifting more toward what was termed as "General American" when I went through my training in the late 80s and early 90s, without as much need for "elevated" speech.
2. There is less need to point toward what is correct—even for classical plays. We, the teachers, seem to be embracing more of the gray and looking less and less for black and white.
3. We, the teachers, seem to be celebrating the diversity of sounds we hear and are far more interested and accepting of the various ideolects that we find in our students. We do, however, want to hold them to standards of clarity, articulation, and good communication.

4. There is a general acceptance that the given circumstances of the play dictate the way in which the characters, and thus the actors, should speak.
5. Though a good number of people still feel strongly about teaching a "standard," the majority recognize it as a dialect, not a prescription for correctness.
6. There is still a good percentage of trainers (26%) who are basing their work on Edith Skinner's *Speak with Distinction*, but there has been a "modernization" to the method.

Interestingly, much of the evidence for these conclusions came not from the answers to the more specific questions in the survey, but from the final question: "Any last thoughts you would like to add?" As I have come to expect from my colleagues in VASTA, some very thoughtful and intelligent responses were given. I would encourage you to continue to the online resource to read more of the responses to the entire survey. Here are some of those final thoughts:

I'm very clear with my students that the Non-regional American Dialect is a useful DIALECT to learn. It is simply a baseline for the rest of our dialect study. I want them to be transformational artists, using speech patterns as an inroad into a character or a play. I stress that all dialects are valuable and useful and viable, and the more specific they can be about accurate dialect choices for each production, the more specific they will be about the world they will inhabit. (Houfek)

I know it is not fashionable to say there is a correct way of speaking. I understand that what I am teaching is a particular aesthetic that is linked to my own tastes. Also, because I am hired to teach Skinner technique, I do my best to maintain that. However, even within that I have made my own judgments when I think something is just too dated. Edith taught that language evolved and I believe I have enough experience now to make some decisions. I always tell my students that a choice is how Edith taught it and that I believe this change has occurred. For example, I don't think "constable" uses the "cup" vowel in any current standard or general American speech. But I do think there are three distinct final back vowels. (All, Honest and Fathers). I know some find this aesthetic pompous and pedantic. I don't. Some speak it that way, but well-spoken it doesn't call attention to itself, but allows for a graceful expression of text. Not appropriate for many texts to be sure, but for some. In the same way that not all texts use good grammar. But we don't dismiss all of grammar as old-fashioned. (Shane)

Personally, I am saddened when these questions are discussed as right vs. wrong; old and useless vs new and popular, or in any other sorts of limited ways that judge rather than consider. I want all of us to consider the range of values, reasons and possibilities for all ways of speaking. I want my students to be skilled and comfortable with all sorts of ways of speaking, and to hear what is being expressed and why and how. I want my students to value the way they speak as modeled on their families and their own identities. And I want them to be able to be clear, precise, and at ease in "standard," "general" and any selection of sounds they could select to create those impressions. I do ask them to say "question" with "s" then "ch" so it sounds like "kwes-chuhn" rather than "kwesh-n", in class. This topic of "standard speech" is complex and ever shifting, and even as I typed in my answers to these questions, I thought of many different nuances of possible answers. (Gist)

Standard Speech can be a useful tool and I have seen some powerful actor transformation through its use by a student in training. That's not the goal per se, but, like mask work, some actors are better able to reveal themselves and their art when they can be 'other' than their everyday. It's a surprising benefit and not a primary goal but sometimes it really makes it worth it. I am considering another strategy in the future but haven't yet figured out all the steps necessary. (Armstrong)

There have been so many changes to the study/teaching of speech over the last 20 years. It is a marvelous and evolving thing. The study of speech has been controversial as long as I have been teaching. Most teachers I encounter feel the same and work in a similar manner. The controversy really arose around a small group of teachers who were the exception rather than the norm. Each year this number dwindles. I think it's time to let the politics rest and just do our work. (Burke)

It is an ever interesting subject and one I don't think will be easily pinned down. We are talking about esthetic taste in sound, rather than what is proper or correct by everyone's standards. I believe the best thing voice and speech coaches and teachers can do, is to awaken training actors to the dramatic values of sound and give them lots of practice in using sound to make meaning happen in context. (Moulton)

Thank you for investigating this. I was horrified when I went to the ATHE conference this year and heard speech teachers use the words correct and incorrect—this is an ever changing field where every sound is useful—our students need to be clear that every character is going to sound different than they do in some way we help build the tools and flexibility to achieve that. (Loree)

Obviously, the diversity in styles of speech training in North America is still vast. I do not believe that chasm will ever entirely disappear. It seems that many teachers believe that as we see growing populations of minorities in this country, it will become more necessary for audiences to not only see actors with whom they can relate but also to *hear* actors with whom they can relate. Prominent theatres are embracing color-blind casting, media is showing far more racial diversity, and we come across more cultural diversity in our daily lives. The USA, as a "melting pot," has an ever-increasing span of cultures. Can we avoid the political implications that come along with judgments or analysis of a person's speech? I doubt it. A simple examination of the current political climate in the USA, as well as attitudes of our government's international relations, shows that reactions to difference can sometimes be volatile. It would seem that we, at a minimum, need to prepare actors not only to embrace the cultural differences of speech but also give them flexibility to move to other choices. With that, as time marches forward and training styles evolve, I believe that the most important goals of speech training will be clarity, understanding, and versatility, and that concerns about the "correctness" of particular speech sounds will continue to fade into the background, or may disappear altogether. As "correctness" gains translucence, it seems that the controversy surrounding it will also fade away.

Bibliography

Barnes, Michael. "Standard Speech Survey." Survey. September-October 2010.

Dalvera, Rocco, ed. *Voice & Speech Review: Standard Speech, and Other Contemporary Issues in Voice and Speech Training* 1 (2001). Print.

Dalvera, Rocco and Robert Barton. *Voice: Onstage and Off.* Fort Worth: Harcourt Brace College Publishers, 1995.

Knight, Dudley. *Experiencing Speech.* Pre-publication manuscript. 2007.

-----. Personal Correspondence. February 2010.

Pronunciation, Phonetics, Linguistics, Dialect/Accent Studies

Standard Speech Practices and Pedagogy: A Snapshot of the Moment by Michael Barnes

Survey Respondents

Adrian, Barbara–Marymount Manhattan College
Anderson, Claudia–DePaul University
Armstrong, Eric–York University
Bailey, Erika–University of Missouri, Kansas City
Beck, Brenda–American Academy of Dramatic Art-Los Angeles
Burke, Deena–University of Delaware
Christian-McNair, Robin–HB Conservatory Program, New York city
Dal Vera, Rocco–University of Cincinnati/Cincinnati Conservatory
        of Music
Devore, Kate–Total Voice, Inc., Chicago
Foh, Julie–Webster University
Gist, Jan–University of San Diego/Old Globe
Goldes, Joel–Freelance, Los Angeles
Hale, Debra–Florida State University
Harris, Lenore–HB Studio and The Speaking Image, NYC
Houfek, Nancy–American Repertory Theatre
Johnson, Jim–University of Houston
Julien, Melanie–Temple University
Knight, Dudley–University of California-Irvine (Emeritus)
Krebs, Nancy–Baltimore School for the Arts
Logan, Gary– Shakespeare Theatre Company's Academy for Classical
        Acting at The George Washington University
Loree, Kristen–University of New Mexico
Lush, Gregory–Freelance, Dallas
McGuire, Beth–Yale School of Drama
Moulton, Betty–University of Alberta
Murphy, Gayle–University of British Columbia
Nelson, Kathryn–Intercall, Alabama
Nevell, David–California State University-Fullerton
Preeshl, Artemis–Loyola University-New Orleans
Quaid, Amanda–HB Studio, New York City
Robinson, Diane–Columbia College, Chicago
Shahn, Judith–University of Washington
Shane, Lester– Freelance AADA, NYFA, Pace University, Marymount
        Manhattan
Stern, David Allan–University of Connecticut
Stoller, Amy–Stoller System, New York City
Thompson, Phil–University of California-Irvine
Timberlake, Phil–DePaul University
Ufema, Kate–University of Minnesota, Duluth
Young, Courtney–Freelance

Private Studio Practice, *Ginny Kopf, Associate Editor*

Ginny Kopf, in private practice for over 25 years in Orlando, gives private lessons to actors, singers, business and media clients, teaches at two colleges, and has done extensive dialect coaching for Disney and Universal Studios. She does corporate training, studio training in voiceover, and dialect coaches theatre, film, and television in Central Florida. She holds a Masters Degree in theatre voice, and an MFA in vocal science. Author of *The Dialect Handbook, Accent Reduction Workshop (CD set)*, S Drills, and numerous journal articles, including for the first three issues of the *Voice and Speech Review*.

Making a comfortable living solely in private practice is a challenging but rewarding adventure. The jobs, though they come and go, are so satisfying that it is worth the risk of putting ourselves in such a tenuous position, year after year.

We proud but few are a hugely diverse population. Our backgrounds, training, scope of experience and methods can range from self-taught to having multiple degrees. Some of us got our expertise over the years in the trenches, similar to the "speech therapist" in the film, *The King's Speech*, who makes no claim to having a doctorate, but rather learned his craft literally under fire. Our résumés are strange, to say the least. The work we've done does not easily fit on one page, nor can it adequately summarize exactly what we did for that individual or group. What *do* we do? A little of this, a lot of that. Like those of you who are tenured university teachers, or in salaried positions with theatre companies, we help people to find their voice. We work with actors, singers, broadcasters, voiceover artists, media personalities, public speakers, business executives, or as Fonta Hadley calls them: "everyday people." Though it may seem a cliché, no job is too big or

too small. We design programs to fit a company's budget and time constraints, and are constantly reinventing ways to train and inspire our clients. We're constantly learning. It's a huge part of the joy and satisfaction of being a private practitioner. Some of us keep up with the latest technology, such as Skype and video conferencing, and the newest ways to record and send a file of a private session to our client. Others prefer to go "old school"—face to face and low-tech. Our "World of Voice" employs diverse methods, diverse backgrounds, diverse personalities.

We private practitioners are keenly aware of the pros and cons of our choice to be independent contractors. The downsides to not having a full-time (or tenured) position at a school, academy, or through one company are:
--less security (not just financially, but emotionally and mentally)
--no employer-provided health benefits (we have to arrange our own)
--ongoing expenses for advertising and business development (licenses, copyrights, etc.)
--running all over town—or the state, or the globe—chasing the jobs. (There are many days that I go to three or four locations.)

The practical realities of our work contribute to a fair amount of stress, even when things are going well in our careers. True, there is some measure of security and pride in building up a strong client base and an excellent reputation. However, we never know when the phone will ring to offer us a job, or when we may lose a job. We have to negotiate our own fees, aware we'll most likely be underpaid for one job and paid richly for the next. We must continually promote ourselves, coming up with creative and current ways to make people want to hire us. And we don't necessarily reap where we've sown. Advertising is costly, and is often the least fun part of our job. Word of mouth (or trusting people will "Google" our services) can be our most powerful advertiser. One phone call can send us into bliss and a notion of security—at least for a season. Then we become reconciled to the idea that the next phone call could inform us that our services will not be needed. It is seldom (I want to believe never) because we aren't good enough. We lose a job for a myriad of reasons, from a shift in the client's budget, or because they found someone who is cheaper (who, of course, is not going to do nearly as good a job as you!) or my favorite reason: "We've decided to go in another direction." We in the private sector learn how to toughen up and cope with the disappointments. We learn how to not "count our chickens before they hatch." We juggle and budget our time and money throughout the year as best we can. And we learn how to constantly and consistently improve not only our teaching and coaching methods, but also our marketing, to make us more desirable and indispensible. Most of all, we love everything we do with a passionate enthusiasm that keeps us going, year in, year out.

It is difficult to describe what we do in a private or group sessions with clients, because…well, frankly, you weren't there. But this is exactly what the authors on the following pages have graciously tried to do. We use a tremendous amount of insight and instinct once we are in front of a student. We may have a plan going into it, but we must always call upon our instincts to serve the student in front of us at that moment. Corporate clients, in particular, want to know, "What exactly are you going to do when we meet this Friday?" They want a full breakdown of everything you will cover in the hour, or the eight-weeks. They also want you to confirm in writing the specific *results* of your training. As experienced teachers, we know we are incredibly effective, and we want our client to simply trust we know what we're doing; but we have to give them an answer because they are not satisfied with, "Let me meet them first, and we'll go from there." So we provide them with outlines, course descriptions, and even a chart of probable outcomes to every step of our training. Although it seems difficult to describe in words what we do in our coaching sessions, what we've done in the past, what we will do in future sessions, five expert voice and speech trainers have put pen to paper for your benefit.

In the five articles that follow, you will have the privilege of peeking behind the closed doors of these private practitioners' sessions. They describe their methods in rich detail, and offer tips and techniques you may find useful for working with your own students. They reveal the joys and challenges of their tasks, and even how they rebounded from trial and error to become better teachers, better motivators. Hilary Blair's article explains the importance of code switching when working with the business client. Fonta Hadley's article shares how she meets the challenges of teaching voice and speech to everyday people, using verbal and nonverbal communication. Bonnie Engel Lee leads us through her work with clients seeking accent reduction, all the way from intake to intervention. Rebecca Root shares her work with transsexual and transgender voice modification. And Cheryl Moore Brinkley's article offers her observations on teaching voice with multicultural awareness. As our work as voice and speech trainers spreads across the globe, the diversity of perspectives from around the world helps to expand our field. Our passion continues to be 'to help others find their voice.'

Whether you are a voice and speech trainer in private practice or in a salaried teaching/coaching job (or have a foot in both worlds), these five articles offer you eyes and ears into the private studios of these five brave and wondrous teachers.

Teaching Communication

Photo by Evan Sornstein.

Fonta is a voice and speech instructor who teaches verbal and non-verbal communication in her San Francisco based private practice. Using perceptual and behavioral tools she teaches a rich mix of logical and emotional communication for personal and professional development. Fonta teaches rhetoric and oration for the San Francisco Bar Association's Continuing Legal Education, is a voice, speech and text teacher at the American Conservatory Theater's Training Congress and conducts leadership trainings for Bay Area Fortune 500 companies including Goldman Sachs, Apple, American Express and Google. Fonta holds an MA in vocal pedagogy (spoken) from the Central School of Speech and Drama in London.

Introduction

In my San Francisco-based practice I teach verbal and nonverbal communication or in more practical language, I teach what you say and how you say it. Because of my training as a voice and speech teacher my practice offers particular emphasis on the latter. Like most private practices I have an open door policy, which means that anyone is welcome to come and train regardless of their profession, cultural background or any previous experience with this type of work. Communication is by its very nature complex, encompassing all manner of variables in intention, expression and interpretation. I have grappled with its complexity and with the challenges of teaching it to anyone who walks in the door by developing what can only be called an "in progress" methodology. The biggest challenge that I found early on was to quantify communication in a way that would create some guidelines from which to teach. The pedagogical structure needed to be flexible enough to honor the endless variables of the subject but I also needed to have some clear guidelines based on quantifiable elements.

It has been my observation that communication is a highly habitual process. In my work over the years I've started noticing patterns of behavior that attract other patterns of behavior. It is from these observations that the logical communicator and the emotional communicator are derived. These two types of communicators are referred to, for lack of a better word, as archetypes and they are the embodiment of habitual communicative response systems that follow a pattern. The two archetypes are representatives of opposing ends of the communication spectrum and are radically different from one another. While the archetypes make up the ends of the spectrum, there is a fertile middle ground between them. This middle ground, referred to as the "mid-spectrum worktable" is where communication training happens. Mid-spectrum training draws upon "opposite spectrum tools" as well as "same spectrum tools" from each of the archetypes, combining them to create live, responsive and authentic "mid-spectrum communication."

In addition to examining this pedagogical framework, this article also looks at the challenges of teaching communication to everyday people. The archetypes are examined in relation to various professions and learning types. Two case studies are offered giving examples of how to utilize opposite spectrum tools to create mid-spectrum communication and results are demonstrated and explained. This pedagogical framework offers teachers guidelines for grappling with the open door policy of their private practice.

Fundamentally, this methodology is based on the observation that communication is a highly habitual practice so the goal in teaching mid-spectrum communication is to shift that person's communication into a more conscious realm. In simplistic terms, utilizing opposite spectrum tools offers clients options that may not have occurred, or come naturally to them. Providing them with new tools updates their communication and gets them listening and responding instead of reacting or deploying auto-pilot responses. The methodology is offered not as a rigid formula but a framework upon which to build and improvise.

Communicator Archetypes

You can break down communicators into two types: logical communicators and emotional communicators.

Logical communicators are results-driven communicators. Their goal is to establish truth (versus the perception of truth) and to be right. Discerning right from wrong is achieved though comparisons of data, so logical communicators are information-driven, or in pedagogical terms, content-driven communicators. Word choice and phraseology are fundamental tools for a logical communicator and are selected and deployed with great care. In addition to word content, other favored tools of the logical communicator are reason, debate, fact, word stress and volume. These tools are excellent instruments for achieving the perception of intelligence, a highly prized quality for the logical communicator.

Emotional communicators are process driven communicators. Their goal is to be understood, and therefore, *how* information is exchanged (versus imparted) is vitally important. Since the emphasis for any emotional communicator lies in the delivery of content, expressive tools such as pitch and inflection, warm and cool tones, facial expression and gesture are important tools. The underlying goal for emotional communicators is to understand, so using these tools to create interest and accessibility is vitally important.

The logical communicator and the emotional communicator represent very different ways of communicating. Whether we're talking about what they hope to achieve by the communication, the tools they use for expressing that intention, or the interpretation of other people's responses, they are stark opposites. This makes it quite interesting to observe when they come in contact with one another. A misunderstanding between a logical and an emotional communicator might go something like this.

LOGICAL: "Are you ready to go?"

EMOTIONAL: "Why do you say it like that?"

LOGICAL: "Like what? I said 'ARE-YOU-READY-TO-GO?'"

EMOTIONAL: "But the way that you said it made it sound like I am making us late! And I *always* make us late.'"

LOGICAL: "That's not what I said."

EMOTIONAL: "It is what you *meant*."

LOGICAL: "Where are you getting this? All I said was, 'Are you ready to go?' And you suddenly flew off the handle and now you are accusing me of something I didn't say. And I hate to point this out, but this conversation *is* making us late."

The emotional communicator is responding to how the content was said and the logical communicator keeps referring to what was said. The emotional communicator wants to establish the full meaning of what was communicated, while the logical communicator is attempting to gain a fair and legitimate outcome based on the facts. In simple terms, the debate between the two archetypes comes down to what (logical) versus how (emotional), or in pedagogical terms: content versus delivery.

Archetypically, emotional communicators are more adept at subtle communication cues. These are important skills for achieving their goal of understanding and being understood. Not only do they use these skills to express themselves but they also use them when listening and observing. This is not because emotional communicators are able to perceive more cues than the logical communicator but because they give more credence to those cues. A logical communicator often dismisses subtle communication because it is more difficult to quantify as fact. Subtle is not considered direct by a logical communicator and directness most efficiently achieves the logical communicator's goal of a just and fair outcome. Though logical and emotional communicators have equal capacity to perceive multi leveled communication, it is the emotional communicators that archetypically validate the subtle or subconscious cues.

Both archetypes have important and powerful skills with positive and negative traits. By outlining the traits of the archetypes you can clearly see the strengths and weaknesses of each. So this is not a debate about which one is better. "Good" communication is "effective" communication that enables the communicator to accurately express his or her intention and achieve the desired result. Usually this requires a combination of both logical and emotional communication skills in amalgamations determined by the needs of that precise moment.

It has been my observation that clients will have varied communicative abilities, but their habits will consistently default to either logical or emotional communication. I believe this is because communicating is such habitual behavior. Think about how many times you respond automatically without thinking using the same verbiage and the exact same inflection. To demonstrate, try and eliminate habitual usage of vagaries such as "like," "kind of," or "sort of" from your vernacular for a day. It is amazing how much more conscious you have to be in your communication to accomplish this. These habitual vagaries are rampant in every day speech and are used automatically without consideration or purpose. Trying to eliminate them is incredibly difficult and demonstrates not only how automatic communication can be, but also how difficult it is to shift those habits. It takes incredible focus and dedication to change communication habits. So the archetypes represent our habitual communication default, not our conscious communication.

Communication training is a reboot of the current behavior; it is not a break down and rebuilding process. Training meets the client's existing ability and makes it more conscious by integrating new tools. These tools are sourced, mixed and assimilated using the mid-spectrum pedagogical framework. The logical/emotional archetypes represent the opposite ends of the framework and their main purpose

Teaching Communication by Fonta Hadley

is to offer guidelines for identifying the client's habitual communication default and to offer opposite and same spectrum tools to mix and match with their current repertoire of tools. The fertile middle ground between these two archetypes, called the "worktable" is the primary focus of training and is where updated communication is built. There are many opposite spectrum tools but an archetypal example would be to teach a logical communicator to read and respond to more subtle communication cues or help an emotional communicator with solution-oriented content-framing to help them get to the point.

It is also important to note that though the emphasis of mid-spectrum communication is primarily focused on the integration of opposite spectrum tools, there is also frequently a need to integrate same spectrum tools as well. Just because someone is an emotional communicator does not mean that they are adept at using all the tools that fall in the emotional communication roster, as is demonstrated in the second case study. Opposite as well as same spectrum tools are combined in the mid-spectrum worktable to create amalgamations appropriate for the development of good communication skills. The pedagogical goal is to update behavior by using tools outside of the habitual default, regardless of which spectrum they fall in. This process will update that person's communicative ability and help them to express themselves more accurately and with greater awareness.

Integrating Opposite Spectrum Tools: Logical Communicator Case Study

The challenge in working with logical communicators is to help them feel comfortable using opposite spectrum tools. Expressive tools such as hand gestures, pitch and inflection usage, and facial expression are all very common opposite spectrum tools for a logical communicator to get used to using. But many of these tools are unfamiliar for a logical communicator and often come with a stigma that these are performance tools and will look inauthentic in every day use.

Take Barbara for example. Barbara is a trial lawyer, which means that if the case goes to court she is the one that will stand in front of the judge and jury and argue the case. Barbara was originally interested in communication training to hone her persuasion skills. She was confident in her ability to represent her client, but wanted to have more sway with the jury. Her reasonable concern in studying communication was that she didn't want her communication to come off as studied or melodramatic in the courtroom.

Barbara is an extremely intelligent person and her manner of communicating follows a classic logical communicator

pattern. You understand everything that she says and her communication is clear, succinct and direct. She has great physical focus, which is demonstrated through her use of eye contact and a lack of any fidgety or distracting physical mannerisms. Her body posture and stance carry authority and dignity, which assist with the focus, and her use of gesture is clear. Vocally, she uses a lot of word stress instead of pitch variety, and her voice is placed low in her range and stays relatively contained in that lower range.

The targeted areas of training for Barbara were to increase her physical ease and integrate a wider use of pitch and inflection into her delivery. Physical ease and physical focus are separate categories but pack a punch when combined. Physical ease is traditionally more of an emotional communicator's tool and physical focus is more of a logical communication tool. Physical ease directly relates to confidence. The more confident you are, the less tension you have in your body and the more freely it will move, allowing full body communication. The face will move responsively and expressively, as will the hands and arms, for example. The body stance will be grounded and centered and will have fluid easy movement that is connected to other body parts. So for example if one were to gestures to the left, the hands and arm will join the eyes and head in a leftward movement. Additionally the thoracic cavity will participate by moving slightly forward and pivot on that mid body access bringing the right shoulder slightly forward and around to the left. If the gesture is made with strong intention, then the knees will soften allowing the hips to also be included in making it a full body gesture.

In pedagogical terms, teaching physical ease means teaching the student to release tension in the joints. If a person does not have physical ease, certain joints will not move, while others move around them. So, if the gesture goes to the left, the hand may participate but the elbows inhibit full arm movement preferring to stay glued to the sides of the body. Or, the eyes move to the left but the head does not rotate. So, increasing Barbara's physical ease entailed working with small joint movements, helping her gain a sensory as well as rational understanding of the most efficient level of joint tension and how the joints moved freely in relation to one another. She found this odd and unfamiliar, and said that it felt unbalanced when the joints started to move together. The work proceeded from that point in front of a mirror so that she could get instant visual confirmation. The mirror helped her understand that though it felt different, making it an odd sensation, it did not look preposterous or contrived.

Continuing the work with the ease, hand gestures were also examined. Barbara used gestures largely for literal back up, instead of figurative, and they were primarily informational instead of invitational. Literal gestures are risky choices since they often come off as condescending. If the hands duplicate the verbal communication exactly (putting up two fingers and then putting them to your ear while saying that you tried twice to call them), then the listener is getting the same message in duplicate. This is needless and comes off as treating the listener as if they are stupid. Gestures are better used to communicate the emotional content. They support how you would like the listener to feel about what you are saying. These are called figurative gestures. The general rule of thumb is to use literal gestures sparingly and figurative gestures liberally but specifically (not vaguely).

The majority of Barbara's gestures were informational and existed on a horizontal plane from left to right and right to left. She was asked to integrate invitational gestures that extend forward inviting listener focus and participation. These forward gestures are called invitational gestures. Barbara was much more adept at the left to right gestures because she was used to laying out facts or sequences of information but she found the invitational gestures extremely useful, especially when asking the jury to consider a point or a different perspective. She referred to them as the "you and I know' gestures as they suggested camaraderie without verbally committing to that intention on the court transcript.

Vocally, Barbara liberally used word stress as a communication tool. This is a common logical communication trait. Logical communicators default to using word stress and emotional communicators default to using pitch and inflection. These tools accomplish different things. Word stress is a directional tool that gives guidance for navigating the content of what is said, while pitch and inflection give emotional orientation for what is said. The following italicized words are used as examples of word stress.

The cat sat *where*?

The cat sat on the **mat**.

Who sat on the **mat**?

The *cat* sat on the **mat**.

If you read just the italicized words aloud by themselves you will see how they work to clarify the content. They are not stressed to clarify emotional information. The bolded words are where inflection would be needed in order to clarify the emotional information. Additional pitch and inflection could be used as the speaker saw fit, but the bolded words require some movement of pitch in order to clarify a question versus a statement.

Barbara was clear in her use of inflection with questions and statements but she didn't habitually employ a wide expres-

sive pitch range in her everyday speech and when she was under pressure her vocal modulation became even narrower. Her inflection (the amount of pitch used per word) didn't have much variance so her speaking style came off as monotone and lacking commitment. Barbara was asked to do her opening statement as if she was doing it to engage elementary school children and then asked to do it without any personal commitment to what she was saying. There was a significant difference between the two. Barbara described the first as melodramatic and the second as boring. We found that getting Barbara to use more specific, committed gestures helped to keep the voice buoyant and the pitch moving. The more she used her body to communicate the wider and more expressive her pitch and inflection became and the more committed and convincing her communication came across.

Over time Barbara successfully integrated a number of opposite spectrum tools. She liked them because of their nonverbal nature. Barbara's opposing counsel will contest the words, phraseology, sequence or facts but could not make an objection based on her body language or pitch usage. Using nonverbal communication enhanced her emotional connection with the jury and it couldn't be noted by the court recorder, or contested by opposing counsel. This gave her an edge that she continues to build.

Integrating Opposite and Same Spectrum Tools: Emotional Communicator Case Study

As a result of their ability to emotionally engage and connect with others, emotional communicators are often good at "people skills" since their strength often lies in their interpersonal abilities. Diplomacy training is a less obvious opposite spectrum tool for an emotional communicator, since one would assume that people skills translated to good leadership skills. But this is not always the case, as this study will demonstrate.

Determining the relevance of one's personal feelings and determining if/how to communicate them is tricky no matter what kind of a communicator you are. In a business setting, knowing when your personal emotions are relevant and when they are not is a challenging area of communication training, particularly for emotional communicators.

Alexander was an up and coming manager who always met the bottom line and was consistently able to deliver no matter what the odds. But his supervisor insisted that he receive communication training because she didn't trust him in executive meetings. Alexander was described as a "live wire." He would energetically and sometimes explosively disagree with managers who significantly outranked him. He offended members of his staff with what was described as "bluntness," and some of his peers described him as "passive aggressive." The end result was that his superiors didn't trust him, so he couldn't be promoted.

Alexander described his own communication as "honest" because he said what he thought or felt no matter what the context or situation. But he was frustrated that this honesty wasn't yielding the desired results. He described himself as a good manager because he always delivered on his projects, but he wanted help with his leadership skills because people sometimes responded to him the "wrong way."

Helping Alexander gain diplomacy tools was the primary focus for his training. This was executed using a three-part process. The first was to help him decipher when to communicate his personal feelings and when to refrain from expressing them. The second was to put a positive spin on his content. And the third was to help him deliver highly charged information in a calm and focused manner.

The first task was addressed by assigning Alexander to use a logical communication tool called "big picture framing." Big picture framing is a content focusing tool. It helps the speaker get to the point using the bigger picture goal as a navigation tool. In Alexander's case, big picture framing meant that he would learn to refocus his communication by examining the relevance of his personal feelings in relation to attaining the big picture goal. Alexander was given the challenge of evaluating whether expressing his personal feelings helped or hindered (attaining) the big picture goals. The answer to the challenge became the red or green light for expressing them. Big picture framing was difficult for Alexander because he said it was difficult to remember to implement. His habitual response mechanism was so ingrained that he didn't even know he was doing it. He said it was easier to use big picture framing in conjunction with the second part of training, called "Positive Framing," because the structure of positive framing gave him a really clear formula to apply, no matter what the situation or context.

Positive framing applies to all dialogue, whether written or spoken, in person or via technology. The formula is simple, circular in nature, and has three components: big picture, problem, solution, and then relating those back to attaining the big picture.

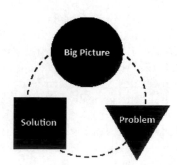

You begin by touching on what the current situation is and how it relates to the big picture goals (where you want the project to go and the current situation); you then move on to the current problems or challenges; you offer a solution(s); and then you link how these solutions would help to attain the big picture.

Alexander used both of these tools successfully in his staff meeting that week. It was particularly relevant on that week because Alexander found out right before the meeting that the delivery date of their product was set back due to a mistake made by a member of his team. Alexander said that he was furious about the delay and wanted to make an example of the team member by berating him in the staff meeting. But he took the time to outline the project goals using the basic premise of big picture framing and he realized that the fastest way to get the project back on track was to focus the meeting time on brainstorming solutions. He used positive framing to execute the goal.

In Alexander's case, berating a team member for making a mistake is only accomplishing one aspect of positive framing. He is only working with the problem without contextualizing why it is a problem or offering any solutions for solving it. So the example that he is setting up for his team is that problems will become escalated problems, so in order to achieve his goals of becoming a better leader he agreed to include solutions and link both the problems and the solutions to the big picture in order to positively motivate the team to make up for lost time. Alexander liked this tool a lot and used it very successfully. The meeting was constructive and solutions were found to make up for the delays.

Positive framing is not just a tool for oral communication. Alexander was also asked to apply it to all aspects of his communication in the coming weeks. He made significant progress very quickly and described his process over the next few weeks:

> "I have two stickies on my computer that say "big picture" and "solutions" and in the beginning it was really hard for me to always include a solution every time I sent an email or picked up the phone. Sometimes my emails would take twice as long because I sat there and couldn't think of a solution. But it's gotten easier because now I have a really good idea of where this project needs to go. Solutions are hard if you aren't sure where you are headed."

In addition to using logical communication tools to focus what Alexander said, it was also necessary for diplomacy tools to be integrated into his delivery to address, among other things, the "explosive outbursts." Archetypically, delivery techniques, especially the nonverbal variety, fall in the emotional communicator's habitual spectrum of tools. But there is frequent need to teach same spectrum tools as well as opposite spectrum tools as is demonstrated here.

The focus in the delivery work was to help Alexander stay calm under pressure. By utilizing big picture framing, it was clear to him that not all of his personal feelings were relevant all the time. It was also important to integrate focusing delivery techniques that would support his content focus. Alexander did not utilize any calming tools in practice at the outset of his training, so getting him familiar with muscle relaxation and breath work were important fundamentals to address with him.

When a person is under pressure he or she experiences a variety of physical responses, but a fairly universal symptom is that the level of tension in the body dramatically increases. Most of the time this creates uncomfortable sensations such as stiff or tight jaws, shoulders, gestures etc. It can also create a lack of sensation in certain areas of the body and can cause difficulty breathing. We addressed this tension by using progressive muscle release techniques such repetitive tighten and releasing of particular part of his body. When he got really angry, Alexander said that he clenched his fists, his mouth got tight and he often felt light headed. So we worked on clenching and releasing the hands, tightening and releasing the arms and shoulders, head rolls and spinal rolls. Repetitively tightening and releasing a muscle eventually reduces the level of tension in that muscle and gives the speaker a reference point for what an appropriate level of tension feels like as well as a practical tool for achieving it. To address the tight mouth, we also included relaxing the muscles of the face by utilizing yoga techniques such as "the Lion" which requires the speaker to theatrically widen eyes, raise brows, open mouth, stick out tongue and audibly exhale. We also tried more energetic approaches such as full body stomping – which requires the speaker to stand in place and energetically stomp for 30 seconds. This gets the body breathing, the energy redistributed, the circulatory system moving and helps to reduce numbness. These preparation techniques help Alexander get grounded, focused and present for the challenges ahead.

In addition to preparations done before speaking we also worked on calming and focusing techniques to be used while listening or speaking. Mindful muscle release and breathing techniques are unobtrusive and effective calming tools. *Remembering* to breathe is one of the most effective calming tools. Under stress people often hold their breath, which compounds the level of tension in the body, so simply remembering to breathe and using the breath consciously as a tool for calming and focusing the mind and body is a significant step toward creating a more composed speaking presence.

Habitually, Alexander breathed quite high in the body with much of the emphasis on the upper thoracic cavity and shoulders. The derivative was a narrow, short breath cycle, which primarily focused on inhalation. To lower this placement, Alexander was asked to lie on the floor and observe his breath. After identifying sensations in that position, he was asked to stand, release his stomach, and turn his focus to the lower ribs allowing a similar movement to what he felt on the floor. Using the analogy of an upside down umbrella, he was asked to observe how the breath flowed down the handle (trachea), into the bowl (diaphragm) and out to the tips (diaphragm attachment to the side ribs). In addition to lowering the placement of the breath so that it flowed effortlessly into and out of a more central region of the body, Alexander was also encouraged to focus on his exhalation. Using negative practice as a teaching tool he was asked to suck in air for inhalation and to push air out for exhalation. He said this was a familiar sensation and was surprised that the goal was not to control the breath but to allow and encourage inhalation and exhalation to happen on their own, paying particular attention to the exhale to avoid light headedness.

Building on the progressive muscle release preparation work, Alexander was also asked to use anger management tools such as mindfully flexing and releasing parts of the body that became uncomfortable, tight or shaky. Alexander liked these best and found them to be the most helpful because "it gave him something to do" when he started to get frustrated or angry during a meeting. Like the breath work, mindful muscle release can be done fairly unobtrusively during a meeting. For instance, Alex was encouraged to flex and release his hands under the table or to flex and release his toes. Another option was be to arch his heels up so that only his toes made contact with the floor and then release them back down or clench and release his stomach. Alexander said that the most helpful were the hands and the stomach. He said that sometimes he would get so angry that his stomach would ache and that tightening and releasing of his stomach helped him feel "more in control" in stressful situations. These techniques gave Alexander constructive tools for focusing and calming energy in the body, enabling him to stay composed.

Alexander's communication needs were best met by using a combination of opposite spectrum and same spectrum tools. Logical tools such as big picture framing and positive framing combined with emotional tools such as focusing delivery techniques offered Alexander the appropriate combination to keep his communication constructive. It helped him to integrate a positive approach to all his communication, calmly express that approach, offer solution-based management and develop a leadership style that was motivated by the big picture. A "lack of diplomacy" often translates to a lack of a positive approach and an inability to stay connected to the wider context. Solution oriented leadership is inherently positive and by simply adding solutions to every aspect of his communication Alexander began to be perceived as more diplomatic and trustworthy. Keeping his motivations linked to the big picture helped him evaluate elements of his communication that were inefficient, including if and when to express his own feelings. Integrating logical communication tools helped Alexander build some mid-spectrum communication, which constructively assisted him toward being the type of leader he wanted to become.

Pedagogical Process for the Archetypes

I realized almost immediately after opening my practice that teaching logical communicators was really different than teaching emotional communicators. It required a very different skill set, which my training had not prepared me for. Since I am trained as a voice and speech teacher, all of my student teaching was in drama schools. I was used to working with that free-form, intuitive process. I remember the first workshop that I taught at the Bar Association very clearly because I had a room full of litigators who were extremely uncomfortable doing the interactive, exploratory exercises that I was asking them to do. I have found that drop-kicking a logical communicator into a kinesthetic learning process is not usually the most efficient or constructive entry point for training.

Kinesthetic or creative learning processes are often unfamiliar to a logical communicator and, therefore, uncomfortable. Often their only reference point for kinesthetic training is in relation to exercise or learning a sport, so this is an excellent point of reference for them and there are a lot of parallels that can be drawn as part of the pedagogical practice. Communication training, like athletic training, is primarily a body training process. It incorporates a brain process, but the point is that you have to *do* it. I have found that most logical communicators are impatient with the "doing" part of training. For them, communication concepts are easy to understand so they are often satisfied with stopping at understanding. Understanding alone will only take you so far. It is the process of *doing* that takes your ability and skill to the next level. Just as you would practice to become a better golfer, you have to practice to become a better communicator. Understanding alone will not change the behavior. But this assumption makes sense given their brain training education. Keep in mind that most educational institutions evaluate students by their ability to memorize and apply memorized information.

So I have found that giving a logical communicator's brain something to chew on, such as an explanation of what to expect from the exercise, buys me some modicum of patience when we then move on to the body training. This is different from working with emotional communicators where giving "the answer" ahead of time would undermine the whole process and heavily influence the outcome. Logical communicators are used to receiving an explanation at the outset and are more willing to try (do it) if the exercise is set up with the information (or even an explanation of a reasonable outcome) ahead of time. Telling a logical communicator what to expect is not cheating them out of a personal exploration process the way it would be for an emotional communicator. Rather, it offers them the opportunity to work more comfortably while acclimating to the process of self-discovery. If they respond well to more process oriented exercises, the training obviously continues along those lines. Either way, the point is that I get them to do it.

I have found that this process does not work as well for emotional communicators. Personal expression is a big part of the emotional communicator's process so they will seek out professional guidance to help them discover and create. Unlike the logical communicator, emotional communicators are process driven. They want to discover the answers themselves and they respond well to kinesthetic training, such as sense awareness, and imaginative tools like imagery. Most emotional communicators are interested in enhancing their creative process and frequently use communication as a means for doing so. Generally speaking, working with emotional communicators is a free-form, intuitive process. The pedagogy is based on the needs of the moment. Structures are flexible and responsive, and the process is not formulaic. The process determines the results and the goal of training is to attain personal understanding.

I have discovered that what I teach has to be as flexible as how I teach it. Originally I had thought that the emotional communicator's process would be the ideal for everyone because it had so much appeal to me personally. Plus it was the way that I was taught to teach everyone. But I have found the sooner I can meet the client at their learning ability, and facilitate learning in a way that is comfortable for them, the quicker I can get results.

Professions That Attract the Archetypes

The most logical of logical communicators can be found in number-driven professions such as the technical or financial fields. They are attracted to professions with clearly defined rules and structure where the truth is based on fact (content) versus interpretation or perception of fact. Accounting, programming, engineering and investment managing are all examples of fields that attract logical communicators.

Creative fields attract emotional communicators with professions such as entrepreneurs, speakers, sales staff, artists and teachers. These fields support an emotional communicator's love of process and they utilize the emotional communicator's interactive and interpersonal abilities. Entertainers, such as actors and singers, tend to attract the most emotional of emotional communicators, since these professions require real ability in the expressive arts.

The sciences, legal and political professions are a mix of logical and emotional communicators as mandated by the needs of their professions. Researchers in these fields tend to be more logical communicators while practitioners typically have a more integrated approach. In order to excel in their field, a pediatrician for example, would have more need for emotional communication or "people" skills than, say, a research biologist.

In my private practice I work with, and market to, all of the above. I find that emotional communicator clients are a shoo-in. They understand the value of training, enjoy the process and will seek out assistance for personal as well as professional reasons. If your practice is marketed to business clientele, then the logical/emotional mix category in particular will seek you out to enhance their interpersonal skills. These professions recognize the power of opposite spectrum tools even if they don't know much about it. Their education primarily prepares them for the logical aspects of their career, though some educational institutions offer some interpersonal skill enhancement training. For example, bedside manner in medical school or moot court's oral argument in law school incorporate elements of emotional communication. But basic common sense and/or experience have taught logical communicators the value of enhancing their emotional communication. It has been my experience that the most logical of logical communicator clientele seek communication training for work instead of personal reasons. Usually their boss has suggested training or it has come up in their review. They also come around the time that they are seeking promotion.

Boosting Your Credentials

After graduating from school with my new credentials as a voice and speech teacher, I honestly thought that having a master's degree in my subject would provide me with all the credentials I needed to attract the masses to my private practice. This erroneous assumption was quickly disproved. In fact, there are several other things that helped me boost my credentials in different professional areas. I found that the key to marketing myself to a particular profession was to gain some credentials that they understood and respected. Presenting at a conference in their field, such as lecturing at a medical conference, helped to increase my perceived credibility within the medical field. I found the same to be true of becoming part of or teaching for

professional associations. For example, I was interested in working with lawyers so I began teaching for the Bar Association. Working for an association carries a lot of weight with that particular professional group. It means that they don't have to do the research themselves to see if you are qualified. They trust that the association has already done that. In addition to enhancing the momentum of your private practice, working for an association also starts the ball rolling for lecturing or conducting workshops at companies within that field, such as law firms or law schools.

Conclusion

Though the challenges are great while grappling with such a complex and elusive topic as communication, the attraction is clear. There is a lot of room for growth on the subject. Watching any reality TV show or sitting through a holiday dinner at someone else's family table or staying married for more than five minutes will all reinforce the theory that there is a need for communication training.

The methodology that I work with is specifically designed to honor this complex subject by offering some quantifiable elements and some flexible elements and making them pedagogically accessible. It is built from my experience as a teacher and is intended as a pedagogical resource, not a formula for success. The archetypes give practitioners quantifiable information that provides an anchor for navigating the complexities of the subject. The archetypes offer habitual behavioral patterns that can be used as a reference for analyzing and identifying a client's communication. They are intended to be combined and used to create mid-spectrum communication. The mid-spectrum framework is set up as a worktable for creating combinations of opposite and same spectrum tools in amalgamations that develop good communication skills. Through this structure, pedagogical guidelines are offered to help private practitioners grapple with the formidable challenge of working with all professional types, different kinds of communicators and various styles of learning.

There is no right way to communicate, so pedagogically the goal becomes to update behavior by bringing conscious awareness to a habitual process. This is accomplished by introducing new communication tools to supplement the habitual ones and by guiding students to blend them productively in combinations that produce authentic and responsive communication. This process achieves not just a broadening of understanding and ability, but most importantly, it takes that person's communication out of the auto-pilot response and into choice driven communication. Making conscious choices is the most powerful communication tool of them all, and if communication training is able to accomplish this then we are on to something.

Essay *by Bonnie Engel Lee*

Accent Reduction: From Intake to Intervention

Bonnie Engel Lee, Ph. D., is currently a public school Speech/Language Pathologist, where she works with children ages three to nine. In her private practice, she works directly or via Skype addressing clients' accent reduction and communicative needs. In conjunction with her training as a voice actor, she maintains a home recording studio. She produces a podcast called "Talking Kidz: What Parents Want to Know" as a means to reach parents who need information and support. She also blogs about topics pertinent to professional speakers and voice actors. Additional information is available at: BonnieEngelLee.com

The purpose of this article is to share some of the procedures used in my private practice while working with clients whose first language is not English. These clients are often referred to as English Language Learners (ELLs). Their goal is to improve their speech intelligibility by improving their pronunciation of English. Improved speech intelligibility results from changes in clients' sound systems, as well as the stress and intonation patterns they use. These changes are often sought to improve a client's ability to obtain employment and/or for job advancement. While the major focus of this article is on ELLs, several of the procedures can be used with people who speak professionally, such as actors, voice actors and public speakers.

My approach to working with clients has been shaped by more than thirty years of training and experience as a speech/language pathologist, and also by courses taken from Daniel P. Dato, author of *Psycholinguistic Aspects of Foreign Accents*, and the work of Arthur J. Compton, Director of the Institute of Language and Phonology. The article addresses various phases of the process from intake/evaluation and analysis through interventions with clients.

Evaluation

The evaluation usually takes more than an hour and consists of several probes. The intake process includes an interview with the client to obtain the following information: the client's purpose for seeking services, information about languages spoken, relevant medical history, prior training, length of time in the U.S., length of exposure to English, client's attitude about modifying or losing an accent, and the client's expectations of outcome of accent reduction coaching. The interview is typically recorded and analyzed as a sample of the client's spontaneous speech. An attitude rating scale, developed by Daniel Dato, is used to assess the client's attitude toward changing his/her accent. Items are rated in terms of the frequency (often, sometimes, and rarely) with which an item applies to the client. An example of one such item is: "I avoid situations where I have to speak English."

While there are many standardized assessments of articulation available, I prefer to use Dato's *Pronunciation in Words and Sentences* probe, which contains sounds produced at various places within the mouth: bilabials (lips), alveolars (alveolar ridge), velars (near velum), labio-dentals (lips and teeth), interdentals (between the teeth), alveolo-palatals (mid palate) and final sound clusters. Clients read the words and then make up sentences using each word. A reading sample is also obtained from the client using *The Rainbow Passage*, a phonetically balanced passage, which is also recorded and analyzed. It's interesting to compare a client's speech pattern during spontaneous speech to their reading sample. At times, because the speaker has to not only think of what to say while speaking, but also how to pronounce the words, there may be differences between reading and spontaneous speech samples, so both are analyzed. The last part of the assessment examines a client's ability to detect differences in stress and intonation patterns (Dato, 1996). The client listens to pairs of words or sentences and is asked to judge if word or sentence pairs sound the same or different. For example, the verb "permit" is produced with primary stress on the second syllable, as in the sentence, "They will permit only two people to go to the conference." Then in contrast, the same word is used as a noun with primary stress on the first syllable as in, "The permit was approved." Since some languages express meaning in different ways, such as with tonal differences, clients may not be aware of the differences conveyed by stress and/or intonational changes.

One technological change that has dramatically impacted my clinical practice is the ability to record and store digital files of clients for analysis and pre/interim/post intervention assessments of performance. Audacity is a free audio recording program that is readily available on the internet for voice recording. Also, there are many tutorials available to assist the new user. In my practice, I use GarageBand, a program which came with my MacBook, for this purpose. Recording with either program is easy and allows the user to create a file which can also be re-played for clients to listen to their own speech, to make them aware of what you would like to address, and also to inform them of the changes you've noted over time. I also record my sessions with clients and send them home with a CD that I burn for them at the end of each session. When working with clients who are voice actors and who are comfortable with and often have home recording studios, I ask clients to send me mp3 files of their auditions, practice sessions and/or jobs to assess their speech and progress toward goals.

Accent reduction coaches might find that it is beneficial to listen to the speech patterns of speakers of a variety of languages to make them aware of the differences. The *Speech Accent Archive*, available at http://accent.gmu.edu/browse_maps/samerica.php is a collection of 248 speakers of different languages, reading the same paragraph. While the speakers may or may not be representative of the speech of the region, the resource is helpful in developing one's listening and identification skills.

Analysis

The speech sample is analyzed phonetically and at the same time for inappropriate stress and intonation patterns that not only distract the listener but may also affect the speaker's message. Unique speech patterns are often associated with each of the world languages. I typically consult a resource manual, *Foreign Accent Norms of American English for 47 Languages*, written by Arthur J. Compton, Ph.D., to research a client's first language to identify the typical phonetic patterns of the language. The manual reports on the various pronunciation patterns observed when the speaker of a given language produces English phonemes. For each language, speech patterns are organized by manner of production: stops, fricatives, affricates, nasals, liquids, consonant clusters, vowels and diphthongs, with data pertaining to the percentage of speakers who display a particular pattern. This information is used to determine if a particular sound substitution, an /s/ for a /z/ for example, is typically observed in a particular language. As noted previously, each client's speech samples and test results are summarized in terms of the phonemes (both vowels and consonants) to be addressed, with an explanation of how the client typically produces them. The summary also identifies the stress and intonation patterns that do not follow typical English conventions. Segments of the client's assessment are replayed to illustrate the areas identified for intervention and to enable the client to better understand the assessment results.

Just as there are differences in terms of how ELLs produce English consonants based upon the sound system of the speaker's first language, the same is true for vowels. It is interesting to note the importance of the accuracy of vowel production because of the important role vowels play in conveying the meaning of a word, phrase or sentence. Therefore, analysis of the vowels used by the speaker is critical.

When working with a professional speaker who wishes to acquire a particular dialect or to lose a dialect to improve his/her marketability, attention to vowel differences is of the utmost importance. Use of the International Phonetic Alphabet (IPA) symbols is helpful in this process.

Intervention: Speech Patterns

Clients can be seen individually or in small groups. While I prefer to work individually with clients on their sound system, group classes can be successful if clients' needs are similar. When a client's speech pattern has improved to the point where he/she is ready to work on intonation and stress patterns (if needed), group sessions are often helpful, as clients can learn from each other, and the English stress patterns that are modeled are applicable to many of the clients.

Direct instruction begins by educating clients on how speech sounds are produced and how they sound when they are correctly articulated. Beginning with sound system, the client and I systematically work through the sounds identified in the client's evaluation. It is important to understand how a particular client pronounces a given English phoneme in order to help the student improve. When addressing vowel differences, it is helpful to introduce a client to the vowel diagram for English vowels. The following link helps clients understand how the tongue moves when producing vowels (http://lizsandler.co.uk/articulation/articulation_homepage.html). The diagram visually conveys to clients that vowel differences relate to the height of the tongue (high, middle or low) and to whether the tongue is positioned in the front, middle or back of the oral cavity. In English, some of the vowels are produced with more tension than others and the duration of the vowel sound may play a role in dialectal differences. For example, a voice actor with whom I worked wanted to lose his southern accent. He produced the diphthong /aɪ/ as in words such as "high" or "my" by lengthening the duration of the first vowel and omitting the second vowel. After identifying that he correctly pronounces the /ɪ/ vowel (as in words such as "hit" or "sit") he was taught to pronounce the diphthong using the *minimal pair* approach. Using this approach, a client practices saying a word such as "my" two different ways, first with only one vowel as /ma/ where the /a/ is lengthened and second as /maɪ/ with the diphthong.

Here is an example that relates to consonants. One of my

clients produced all initial /l/ sounds as an /n/ so the word, "light" was pronounced as "night." By asking the client to occlude his nostrils and knowing that the /l/ and/ /n/ are both produced with the tongue tip on the alveolar ridge (gum ridge behind the top teeth), the client was able to quickly understand and learn how to say the /l/ sound correctly in structured speech. When an English sound is not included in a client's first language, sounds that are similar to the sound are used to teach the sound. For example, if a client's first language does not include the /ʃ/ sound in the word, "shoe" but does include the /s/ sound, then the client's production of the /s/ sound is modified by teaching the client to use a more posterior tongue placement and to use a rounder lip position.

There are a variety of techniques that clients find helpful in the learning process. I often begin with a general overview of the production of English speech sounds and then focus specifically on the sounds identified in the assessment. The features of voicing as well as place and manner of phoneme production are explained to the client. Thanks to University of Iowa Flash Animations Project (http://www.uiowa.edu/~acadtech/phonetics), students can select a particular vowel or consonant and become acquainted with how the specific sound is produced by watching an animated diagram of the mouth. At the same time, they are able to simultaneously listen to the words pronounced by the speakers.

After educating the client about speech sound production, I focus on listening. This phase of the coaching process, which might also be referred to as "ear training" or auditory discrimination training, enables the client to hear sounds produced correctly in various contexts and to compare how he/she produces the same sounds. After a client has become familiar with how a particular sound is produced, it is important for a client to be able to differentiate between correct and incorrect productions of a particular sound. Through the use of *minimal pairs*, as mentioned previously, a client is presented with pairs of words that contrast the sound the client is learning to produce. It is also helpful to include sounds that the client is currently using as a replacement for the target sound. For example, a client who is working on the /ɹ/ sound might hear a list of words such as "run" and "won" or "red" and "wed," which help him/her appreciate the auditory differences between the target sound and the client's own productions. Minimal pairs can also be used in the production phase, where clients practice saying minimal pairs of words and making them sound different from each other. An accent reduction coach can develop a list of words that contrast the client's speech pattern with the targeted English phoneme or use the online minimal pair resource compiled by John Higgins, which can be found at: http://myweb.tiscali.co.uk/wordscape/wordlist. After identifying the two vowel or consonant

sounds which you wish to contrast, you click on the number which indicates how many minimal pairs have been collected for your contrast and you will see a list of pairs of words that are contrasted on the two sounds selected.

After a client understands how a particular sound is produced and is able to discriminate between correct and incorrect productions of a targeted sound, the client begins to practice saying the sound. If a facilitating context is identified during the assessment, then practice begins with that specific context. For example, if a client tends to produce the /j/ sound as in "yes" instead of an /l/ sound, but is able to produce an /l/ when followed by the vowel /i/ then practice would be expanded to include words that contain the same vowel such as "leek" and "leave," "lean," etc. Next, production is attempted with other vowels produced near the front of the mouth such as the vowel /ɪ/ in the word, "pick" or the vowel /ɛ/ in the word, "bed." After practicing with the front vowels, central vowels such as the schwa /ə/ or /ʌ/ as in the words, "vanilla" or "cut" would be used in practice materials. The general pattern of increasing from syllables, to words, phrases and sentences is typically followed. It is important for a client to be engaged in self-evaluation early on in the process and to continue to do so throughout the intervention phrase. An easy to use method is to have clients extend their thumb upward if they rate a particular production as successful, while a horizontal thumb position might mean the production is "fair" and a downward thumb position might mean that the production is not a good approximation of the target sound. By attending to your client's speech, you might notice other facilitating contexts. I recently noticed that one of my current clients is able to say the /l/ sound when it is followed by a /d/. Therefore, we practiced words such as "hold," "cold," "called," "held," etc.

Non-native speakers of English can often be identified as such, not only because of the speaker's speech pattern, but also because the speaker does not use the reduced forms that native speakers use. Specifically, in conversational speech, native speakers of English tend to omit or change sounds, which enable them to speak more rapidly, and the absence of these patterns is easy to identify. For example, where a non-native speaker might say, "I have to go," a native speaker might express the same idea by saying, "I hafta go." One can argue the value of teaching non-native speakers to use reduced forms. However, clients may have difficulty understanding reduced forms if they are not familiar with these patterns. Of course, it is also important to acknowledge that there is a time and place for different speech patterns and one would not use reduced forms when giving a formal presentation.

For more extensive examples of reduced forms, refer to my July 10, 2008 post, ***Want to Speak Naturally? Use Reduced Forms***, which can be found at http://speechdoc.blogspot.com.

Intervention: Intonation Patterns

Intonation patterns can be conveyed to clients using the numbers one through four. The number two is used for the client's consistent or habitual pitch level, the one he/she would use if speaking in a monotone. The number one is used when the client's pitch drops below number two, and numbers three and four are used for pitch levels that are successively higher than the client's habitual pitch. Practice materials beginning with two syllable words and then extending to phrases and sentences can be used with numbers written over each syllable to convey to the client when his/her pitch level should be increased or decreased. There is a common misconception that the pitch rises at the end of all questions and drops at the end of a statement. While statements tend to having a falling pitch level at the end of the statement, certain questions tend to have a falling intonation pattern, such as questions that begin with words such as "who," "what," or "where," while questions to which the reply is typically a "yes" or "no," tend to have intonation patterns that rise toward the end of the question. The meaning or intent of the speaker can account for intonation patterns that do not follow these general rules. Modeling intonation patterns for clients and enabling them to hear your model in comparison to their speech is often helpful. Sometimes, tapping one's hand on a table can help clients become aware of the rhythm and intonation patterns of English. You can find examples of how numbers are used to convey intonation patterns in my August 2, 2008 post, ***The Golden Rule of Intonation***, which can be found at http://speechdoc.blogspot.com

Intervention: Stress Patterns

While there are some rules about stress patterns that can be taught to clients, there are probably as many exceptions as there are rules. Some of the rules relate to the part of speech of the word. As mentioned previously, if a word is a verb, the primary stress tends to be on the second syllable while the same word used as a noun tends to have primary stress on the first syllable. Using a stress marker, prior to and above the syllable with primary stress can be a helpful visual cue for clients. A very helpful resource for clients who want to hear someone pronounce a word is the online site, ***Howjsay***, which pronounces words that a client can type into a box and can be accessed at: http://www.howjsay.com

Summary

An accent reduction coach brings a variety of skills to the coaching arena, whether the client is an English Language Learner or a professional speaker. These skills include: a knowledge base about speech and voice production, the ability to translate the information in a way that is meaningful to the client, a good ear for listening to clients' voice and speech patterns, a comfort level with technology for recording and analyzing speech samples, and a significant amount of creativity, which is the part of the process I thoroughly enjoy. Also, since clients tend to be highly motivated and successful, the coaching process is very rewarding.

Business Culture – Code Switching

Photo by Linda Russell

Hilary Blair is a professional voice-over artist and actor with over 30 years experience teaching and coaching. She specializes in voice, public speaking, and voice-over with the Denver Center for the Performing Arts, National Theatre Conservatory, and HB Voice/ARTiculate and is vocal coach for shows with the Denver Center Theatre Company. She works across the U.S. providing presentation coaching for entrepreneurs with MakeMineAMillion. org. She holds an MFA from the National Theatre Conservatory and a BA from Yale University. She is an active Toastmaster, teacher for Colorado Speakers Assoc. and currently Director of Membership for VASTA.

"Code switching" has become a commonly used term, referring to our human capacity to adjust our communication depending on our setting and our audience. Code switching fascinates me. When I hear this term, I am delighted to begin a process to decode a message. As a presentation coach, it has become an effective way to open discussion with my clients about vocal choices which shape their message.

For the purposes of this essay, we are referring to code switching as defined by Chad Nilep as "the practice of selecting or altering linguistic elements so as to contextualize talk in interaction." (Nilep, 1) And in her new book, *Code Switching: How to Talk So Men Will Listen*, Claire Damken Brown defines it "as the ability to use your knowledge of two or more cultures or languages and switch between them, depending on the situation, to best communicate your message." (Brown, 3)

Code switching can be observed in the different voices we use in a variety of situations. We make subtle, and sometimes not so subtle, adjustments in tone, pitch, inflection, loudness, word choice, etc., depending on our audience. I

speak quite differently to my dog than I do to my boss. If I did not, there could be problems, and I say this in earnest. To state the obvious, when communicating, we need to make adjustments for our audience in order for information to be transferred clearly and with the least resistance. My dog responds to a certain voice, and my boss responds to a different voice, and I make those vocal choices innately.

But what happens when our instinct for code switching may be guiding us to make the wrong choice, or at least not the most effective choice? I'm fairly certain a lesson with Cesar Millan, the "Dog Whisperer," may point out to me that the voice I've instinctively been using with my dog is not the best choice for the behavioral response I want. And it did turn out that the voice with which I was addressing my boss was not effective for the results I was wanting. In this essay, I am addressing those miscued instincts, and I am specifically exploring this topic as it pertains to the business/professional voice.

As with most presentation and voice coaches, my client base is varied—attorneys, doctors, business owners, ministers, sales people, storytellers, entrepreneurs, radio hosts, rock band singers, bankers, CEOs, CFOs, teachers. It is understood in the world of voice specialists that there are multiple influences that affect vocal choices. Age, gender, class, culture, socio-economic standing, as well as numerous other factors determine these influences. But regardless of professional standing, most clients introduce themselves to me in one voice, transition into a variation on that voice as we talk and later switch to a different voice when they present—whether it is delivering a speech, a power point slide show, a song introduction, or a meeting report. They are code switching.

One can clearly see this distinction by looking closer at a presentation scenario. The voice often used in presentations by a business professional can be described as lacking color and variety. It is commonly thought that, although the percentages shift slightly depending on studies and sources, information is conveyed 10% by the words, 30% through prosody and 60% non-verbally. It seems that with the business voice there is undue reliance upon the words alone, and without the prosody to back it up, key information is being lost or information is being conveyed that the speaker may not realize.

This business vocal choice is often pitched lower, using less inflection, phrasing and rhythm with a tendency toward monotone or lack of internal inflection. In both men and women, there is a tendency to lower the pitch to the extent that they often end up in what is termed "vocal fry" or "pulse phonation" and is at the lowest vocal register. There is often a rather fast rate of speech, shallow or clavicular breathing, and a complete neglect of the vowels; therefore most of the cues used for clear communication are eliminated. Basically, from a vocal point of view, the business or professional voice is decidedly uninteresting and conveys less information. What is this trend? I started questioning: Is this voice, devoid of specific information, exactly what the professional world expects in order to create a fact-filled climate devoid of more emotion or opinion? Is emotion in a business setting avoided? Incorrect? Is there a fear of appearing too enthusiastic? Too invested? Too revealing? Would it be professionally incorrect to use more inflection or intonation? Is more vocal information simply sharing too much opinion? These are questions that race through my mind, and I discuss them openly with my clients, both in groups and in one-on-one training sessions.

When I introduce the idea of code switching to the business professionals, they immediately note examples from their lives. It seems to both fascinate and relax them, and allows them to observe the vocal choices they are making with new insight. These clients share their surprise at discovering that they have assumed that their vocal choices were expected and necessary. They readily admit that this vocal production sounds flat and may contribute to a boring presentation style. Also, they realize that they have been limiting what information is conveyed. When asked, they have no idea where they learned to adopt this communication style, nor when they first started. They have given a great deal of energy to detailed choices around what suit to wear, which power point slides to use and the correct wording to select, but little attention has been given to the actual voice being used. It just is what it is.

What are the origins of this presentation style? Where did they learn this? In my research, I have not found any reference to a monotone voice being suggested as a communication style. Quite to the contrary, most public speaking texts suggest vocal variation to be important to clarifying a message and to ensure its impact. The prevalence of this presentation voice does suggest that we learn by example. Habits, perhaps masquerading as suggested protocol, are passed from person to person without a real understanding of their etiology.

In coaching and training sessions, we often make audio or video recordings of our clients. In playback, vocal choices are noted and speakers are amazed at how different they appear and sound. This recorded presentation is often in stark contrast to the internalized image clients have of themselves. When it is suggested that a more animated or colorful voice may be warranted, many clients will admit they hold a certain belief that the flat, monotone choice is both necessary and expected in their professional settings. They are wary of giving it up. It is assumed that it carries more authority and more power. Replacing it has never even crossed their minds. One client dubbed it "business

neutral" and "serious and necessary." Of course settings may vary, but in general when we give a presentation of a simple report at a weekly meeting or a full presentation in a formal board meeting, those situations tend to suggest use of the monotone, business voice.

When I ask business people to observe other professionals with whom they work and interact, they recognize that not everyone communicates in this monotone manner. Students quickly notice that the speakers who hold their attention and are thought of as good presenters or communicators do not use a monotone or flat voice, or one with excessive glottal "fry." Students had assumed it was the information being conveyed, the position the speaker held, or any number of other traits and techniques that held their interest. But through a more informed lens of observation, they begin to equate the use of intonation and vocal variation with a more interesting delivery. In addition, they note that the use of vocal placement carries with it varying perceptions of authority. They already have an instinctual awareness of which voices are more effective, but through training they can learn to identify and utilize the vocal choices that make that so.

Many clients come to work with me on familiar public speaking topics such as wording, use of gesture, volume, posture, and so on. They are very successful and accomplished. They know what they want in coaching and request to focus on specific issues in their presentations. When it does become apparent that the voice is a key to unlocking their communication, the challenge then becomes how to address vocal production issues. Clients can have an initial hesitation to attempt new things regarding the sound and use of their voice. Voice is a very personal and emotionally charged element in how we identify ourselves. The hesitation to venture into changing their voice is reinforced when their first attempts into this totally new vocal realm may sound fake and forced. They react negatively quite quickly, saying it is the "actor voice." Most business people, unfamiliar with the acting world, usually associate the "actor voice" with an overly loud and overly emotional presentation that they correctly read as unauthentic or untruthful. I then have to describe how actors train many hours to be more truthful and connected to their words. With a clarification of the difference between a trained, connected actor voice and a fake, disconnected actor voice—along with a reassurance that I, too, respond as they do to untruthful communication—clients become curious and more open to exploration. These business professionals also embrace the idea that they are unlearning a habitual way of speaking and it may take a bit of trial-and-error and time to learn to make new choices.

Once the distinction between the voices is understood, we begin to work on how they can apply that distinction to their own presentation. I reassure them that if they trust the instinct about what they believe or buy into in someone else's presentation, they will be able to take that same instinct and apply it to their own work. It is often a well honed skill they already have, they're just not aware of it. We work on reconnecting them with their own instincts.

The video and audio recording is very helpful to point out at which moments in the presentation the speaker sounds disconnected. Each time I highlight a seeming disconnect, they share that a series of thoughts went through their heads at the time and may have undermined their authenticity. They are amazed that their communication can be betrayed by their voices. The detailed feedback helps them rethink their message and their objectives. When I pointed out to one client that he seemed to truly dislike what he was talking about, he was completely startled. He let me know that he was not even aware of how much he disliked the topic and yet there it was coming through in his vocal choices. By shifting his objective as to why he was sharing the particular information (which was necessary due to his job), he was able to adjust his whole presentation style, and his voice became more engaged and engaging.

Another client became aware that her presentation style had shifted soon after becoming a partner in a law firm. With her promotion, expectations were higher. One partner had suggested she needed more presence. The interpretation of her partner's comment was that she needed to alter her young female sound. Her vocal manipulation eventually sent her voice into her lower register and created a consistently monotone, vocal fry.

Her newly gained awareness of the constant monotone production, informed by her viewing of her own video, surprised and informed her of what her vocal production had become. In addition she pointed out that she had added a variety of gestures to compensate for the lack of vocal variation. The gestures were much more energetic than her voice, and appeared very odd and distracting. She interpreted her own addition of gestures as an ineffective attempt to clarify her message. Interestingly, after establishing better vocal placement and more inflectional variety, her gestures became more connected and efficient, enhancing her message and not overshadowing it.

A male client discovered that he had compensated for appearing too loud and inappropriately enthusiastic by adopting a monotone, vocal fry. He was very wary of increasing vocal variety. Through a series of Shakespearean text exercises, where he was able to play with his voice, he discovered a balanced and connected vocal choice that conveyed a business sense with enough variety to communicate clearly and interestingly.

Many of my female clients deal on a daily basis with a need to be assertive in the business world without being labeled a "pushy broad." They struggle with the how-to of expressing power and self-assurance in a culture that seems to ask them to mimic the authority of a masculine voice. Some women, fearful of the societal repercussions of using the upper register, have manipulated their voices down into their lower register, thus creating the vocal fry. By avoiding the higher register's sounds, their presentations have become dull and monotonous. In these cases, assumptions about business culture's expectations have influenced vocal choices related to code switching.

Once clients are aware of code switching, and that they have control of the production of their voices, they can find their vocal authenticity through a series of basic vocal exercises focusing on breath, resonance and placement. It was freeing for many of my clients, both men and women, to realize that opening up the resonance of their voices allowed them to have more depth to their sound, more vocal variety, and more efficient resonant placement. Consequently, when they experienced the variety and freedom of this new vocal production, they felt they had more authority and power. One client felt she was finding her own voice for the first time. When I asked her to explain further, she said she had always felt she had more sound available to her but her own explorations had led her into a tight voice. As she comes to understand her own vocal instrument, her code switching is now more informed by her own choices, versus simply an instinctual reaction.

The traditional training program for actors involves an intensive vocal journey, often over a period of 4–6 years. Few of the business professionals who come for training possess that level of commitment to their instrument, nor can they invest the same amount of time that is required of an actor. However, the business professionals do recognize the need for the results. They respond to the ROI—return on investment—in both time and money, and I personally enjoy the challenge of adapting the training for this specific audience. My challenge as a trainer is to tailor the time and vocabulary to address the needed presentation skills. Then I start incorporating more vocal work with simple explanations and shortened versions of exercises that can speed their adoption of a theatrical process in a non-theatrical context.

With awareness and training, the business presentation voice is no longer the habitual voice used without consideration of other choices. It is now a voice expressing specific information resulting from a conscious awareness of the message and the appropriate audience. That last mention of "appropriate" is very important. Sometimes, it may be the correct choice to use a voice that has less prosodic information, but with training, the vocal choices become part of the design of the presentation as much as what to wear and the layout of the power point slides. Sometimes the black suit and blue shirt is what is necessary and expected, but sometimes that is not the most informed choice. Knowledge of the conscience use of code switching enhances the ROI, return on investment, for the business professionals with whom we work, and therefore for us as well. With awareness of code switching, clients are better prepared to understand and capitalize upon the power of their own voices.

Bibliography

Brown, Claire Damken, and Nelson Audrey. *Code Switching*. New York: Alpha, 2009.

Nilep, Chad. "Code Switching in Sociocultural Linguistics." *Colorado Research in Linguistics*. University of Colorado. Vol. 19. (June 2006): 1-2.

Essay *by Rebecca Root*

Stepping Off the Stone: Transsexual and Transgender Voice Modification and Presentation. A Practical Resource from a Personal Perspective

Photo © 2006 Steve Lawton

Rebecca Root is the recipient of the 2010 Clyde Vinson Memorial Scholarship bestowed by VASTA and holds MA Voice Studies (MAVS) from Central School of Speech and Drama. Her workshop on transgender voice, upon which this article is based, was presented at the 2010 VASTA/Ceuvoz Conference in Mexico City; her earlier paper *There and Back Again: Adventures in Genderland* is published in *The Moving Voice* (VASTA 2009). Ms Root is a guest lecturer on MAVS; is Professional Consultant for the International Centre for Voice; and is principal voice instructor at Performers College, Essex. Ms Root continues her performance career.

In this essay I discuss and review some of the methods applied in helping transsexual and transgender people find a vocal quality they feel to be more appropriate to their identified gender. This work underpins my private studio, and is the primary source material for anticipated further research at Ph.D. level.

The paper is based on the workshop I ran at the VASTA/CEU-VOZ Conference "Muchas Lenguas, Una Voz/Many Languages, One Voice" in Mexico City in August 2010. The workshop was interactive and participants learnt a variety of tools for working with transsexual people. Transsexual myself, I used this opportunity to relate some of the experiences I encountered as I made the vocal journey from male to female. Although much of this article relates to vocal adaptation for the trans-female, the exercises are also pertinent for the trans-man.

Invitation: Destination: The Other Side of the Fence

This is an invitation to take a journey of the imagination.

I invite you to close your eyes. Empty your mind of the distractions of the day, the sounds of the office, or street beyond your window; empty yourself of your preoccupations, and imagine yourself on a journey. You have dreamed of this journey for a long time. You've planned it thoroughly, studied it on maps, atlases, have downloaded the most accurate GPS data. This journey takes you to the Other Side of the Fence.

The Other Side of the Fence is a place uniquely yours. It is the expression of your most precious desires. The Other Side of the Fence is your promotion. It is your exam success. It is your dream house, the move to the country, the retreat from the Rat-Race. It is the birth of your child. It is your wedding day. Your divorce. The Other Side of the Fence is the place, the thing, the state of being you yearn for. It is everything you have ever wanted. I invite you to stop, to close your eyes, and imagine your journey to this place.

I invite you now to contemplate the possible pitfalls of this journey. Is the path smooth or rough? Are there obstacles in your way? What must you do in order to reach your destination? How much energy–emotional and physical– must you expend in order to realize your ambition? Who gives you permission to try? Who suggests you may fail? What is the risk of failure, the price of success?

And how do you know when you are there, at the Other Side of the Fence? Consider your breath as you picture this journey. Pause in the moment; enjoy your liberty.

Open your eyes, notice your surroundings. I invite you to remember the Other Side of the Fence.

We all have our individual Other Side of the Fence. This is something like the experience of being transsexual or transgender[1] ("TS" and "TG" respectively). Gender identity, like the promotion, wedding, divorce and house move, is simply a different Other Side of the Fence, longed for and day-dreamed of by unknown thousands the world over. And like the fulfilment of any ambition, it takes a certain amount of determination to attain.

The purpose of this paper is to impart some of my professional knowledge and personal experience to my peers; that they may better understand the perspective of the TS/TG individual, and more effectively respond to the psychophysical requirements of this client population.

Introduction: A Brief History of Rebecca Root, 1969-present

I was born in southern England, just before the first Moon landing. My family is middle-class. I have two sisters;

I'm in the middle. My childhood was fairly normal. I did reasonably well at school, I enjoyed acting, I had the usual interests of most boys in the 1970s. Except I always felt something was not quite right with me. My body felt wrong, my head felt wrong; I wanted most ardently to be a girl.

I suppressed this feeling, not without some trauma, throughout my childhood and adolescence. I trained and worked as an actor, generally cast as leading man material: a romantic knight, a shell-shocked soldier, a proselytizing evangelist. My voice, a bass baritone, was integral to this life: I worked in voiceovers and television, playing urbane doctors and consultants. I was a jobbing actor; living the life.

But the greatest and most exhausting acting role I undertook required complete immersion and psychological commitment, and after a lifetime of it I needed out. For me, being male was like an impossibly arduous performance. Imagine playing a character in an interminable soap and never being offered a get-out clause. After 34 years it was time to make a stand, time to change. It didn't matter that I might not work as an actor again: I just needed to be true to me. I needed to make that journey to the Other Side of the Fence–and stay there.

In 2003 I changed my name to Rebecca and began living full-time in female role. My family and friends supported me. Almost immediately I found acting work, but I was soon to discover that the roles available for a TS performer were limited. Nevertheless I was far happier than I had ever been: here on the Other Side of the Fence the grass was, and still is, very much greener.

Yet the journey was not all plain-sailing. My voice remained a significant issue for me. Despite extensive speech therapy I was still not happy with it, as it felt too "male" for my new persona. A surgical procedure known as cricothyroid approximation helped[2] me to an extent, but I only really developed the voice I now comfortably use after the year of intensive practise and study on the MA Voice Studies ("MAVS") course at Central School of Speech and Drama, University of London ("CSSD"). My final thesis[3] investigated the nature of voice and speech differences between the genders, and how those differences may be negotiated by the TS/TG person wishing to find a voice more appropriate to their identified gender.

Digression: "Male" and "Female" Voice types

What makes a voice sound "male" or "female"?[4] In the course of researching and writing my thesis, I made an extensive review of the voice literature.[5] I further sought opinions of voice teachers, actors and directors, as well as people from non-theatre backgrounds, as to what they felt identified a person as speaking with a specific gender voice. Some of the people who shared their views with me were TS/TG.

I determined that many factors contribute to the perception of gender voice. Intonation, speech rate, language/vocabulary pattern, vocal onset[6] and articulation all play a part in denoting one's gender. The principal differences, however, between male and female voices are generally regarded to be *pitch* and *resonance*.

Shewell defines pitch as "a psychological word that describes our impression of the highness or lowness of a sound" (Shewell 2009: 185). Pitch is related to the frequency of vocal fold vibration per second and is measured in Hertz (Hz); the higher the frequency, the higher the note, and vice versa. Variation in pitch is caused by altering the shape and length of the vocal folds. Since male vocal folds are generally thicker and longer than female vocal folds they tend to vibrate more slowly, and the resulting sound is therefore deeper[7] (see also Shewell 2009, 185).

Higher notes are created by stretching and tensing the vocal folds; so pitch perceived as female may be simulated by constantly elongating them. Many people (both males and females) "do" a stereotypical female voice by going into a falsetto range (think of Terry Jones' screeching portrayal of Brian's mother in the Monty Python film *Life of Brian* (1979): ("He's not the Messiah, he's a very naughty boy!"). This falsetto is achieved by lengthening and thinning the vocal folds. Yet this is not necessarily what constitutes "female quality" (it is also inefficient breath usage, particularly over extended periods (Kayes 2004, 161)).

Resonance – the amplification of sound in an air-filled space – is equally significant to the perception of gender. Resonance differences may be affected by the dimensions of the individual speaker's vocal tract; since the average female pharynx is smaller than the male, the resonation is higher.[8] We tend to think of a female sound as resonating more in the head space, while the male sound is felt to be lower down, more in the chest area. The perception of resonance in these areas is largely attributed to the body picking up on the secondary vibrations of the initiated sound. Because of these vibrations, the perception of resonance and pitch is sometimes blurred. Nevertheless, it can be a broad (and useful) rule of thumb to recognize female voices as containing predominantly upper resonances and pitch, and males the opposite.

Discussion: Traditional Speech Therapy for the TS/TG population; first steps, 2004-05

When I transitioned to the female role in 2003, I knew

Private Studio Practice
Stepping Off the Stone: Transsexual and Transgender Voice Modification and Presentation
A Practical Resource from a Personal Perspective by Rebecca Root

that I would need assistance in modifying my voice to my new gender identity. (This was four years before studying at Central.) As previously noted, my voice was deep and "chocolatey", and entirely unsuitable, I felt, for the life I was now living. The more female in appearance I became, the more incongruous was the male-sounding voice. This desire to match the voice with the identified gender is not uncommon amongst the TS/TG population; it is one of the first things my clients ask me to help with.

In 2004 I was referred to Christella Antoni, Senior Speech and Language Therapist at Charing Cross Hospital in west London. The hospital is a major centre of treatment[9] for TS/TG people in the UK. I worked with Antoni for over a year, meeting initially every fortnight; subsequently less frequently. The exercises Antoni used were designed to raise the pitch of my voice at the same time as developing a more appropriate (to me) female-sounding "head" resonance.

In keeping with many speech and language therapy (SLT) sessions, the work was conducted in a seated position. Despite my theatre background this did not strike me as odd, since I saw the work to be more *scientific* than *creative*, and I connected the voice not with the whole body but solely with the larynx; at least insofar as the development of my TS voice was concerned.

I practised rigorously. By humming on an extended /m::/ the sound would be encouraged "out of the chest and into the face" (Antoni, 2004). This was followed by opening the sound into /mi:/, /mɑ:/, /meɪ/. (Later, during my time on the MAVS course, I would recognize the similarity to Kristin Linklater's resonance exercise, "Mee-May-Mah" (Linklater 2006, 269). This is an exercise I now employ in my private studio practice, as it specifically addresses the forward placement locations of nose, cheekbones and mouth.)

The vowels became words, elongating the initial /m/ before adding the rest of the word: "mmmany", "mmmmany mm-mmen", "mmmmagic mmmmountains" (Antoni, 2004) and so on.

In order better to perceive pitch differentials, Antoni asked me to recite a sequence of vowels, words, short phrases, and finally numbers, on a three-part rising scale. It's designed to reiterate the "natural" or habitual male pitch (i.e., low), and contrast it with subsequently higher pitches, ending on the target "female" pitch.

The first sound was low, imagined in the belly. The pitch increased and the sound was felt more in the chest. Finally, the uppermost notes were felt in the head.

LOW PITCH/BELLY:	a-e-i-o-u[10]
MIDDLE PITCH/CHEST:	a-e-i-o-u
HIGH PITCH/HEAD:	a-e-i-o-u

The sequence continued with the words "any-every-inside-only-oozing"; the phrases "any day, every way, inside out, only you"; finally counting the numbers 80-89 (Antoni, 2004).

Sirening or scale-gliding on /ŋ/, an act which flexes the velum and thus helps increase oropharyngeal resonance, also encouraged awareness of upper pitch and range, although this did not always translate to common usage.

After a year of speech therapy, still not entirely content with results, I opted for the surgery mentioned earlier (CTA). It is noteworthy that this procedure does not in itself raise the pitch of the voice; rather, it "deletes" the lower notes from the range, thereby removing the possibility of unexpectedly sounding "male", for example when sneezing, coughing, or in other moments of involuntary speech. The principal drawback is a likely loss of range, but this is largely outweighed by the expectation of vocally passing, particularly on the telephone.

The surgery was successful and my bass notes disappeared. One aspect the operation could not explicitly address was my use of range and intonation. Monotone and lack of range are noted "male" traits (Vicary, 2007). When living in the male role, my effective range was approximately 2.5 octaves. A limited range might indicate a lack of confidence; using a range in which one is most comfortable is psychologically convenient, and certainly from my personal experience I felt at times very safe "hiding down there" in the regions of C below Middle C (approximately 130Hz).

Digression: MA Voice Studies (MAVS); progress, 2007-2008

The MA Voice Studies course at Central School of Speech and Drama is one of the most established practical and academic courses for voice and speech training in the world. Rather than confine its scope to any single practitioner, MAVS draws on the work of an eclectic range of teachers, from Berry to Bunch Dayme, Linklater to Lessac, Rodenburg to McCallion. The course's aim is to produce voice practitioners who can teach creatively and multifariously; who can generate their own line of pedagogical enquiry and praxis.[11]

Undertaking this course in 2007-08, I used my experiences as a TS performer and pedagogue to form the springboard of my own practice. During the course of my studies, I continued to develop my own "female" voice, and refine my future pedagogy.

I wanted especially to work on increasing my pitch; stretching my range; and developing intonation. I continued sirening and humming, using arpeggios and scales. I found one exercise in particular wonderfully helpful: singing a five note scale counted on numbers, then rising or falling by a semi-tone at the end of each phrase. This final note becomes the first note of the next scale, and so on. I am indebted to my colleague Dr. Johanna Wood for introducing me to this exercise.

Start on Middle C, or your habitual centre note:

1-2-3-4-5-5-4-3-2-1 [∿] or [↗]
1-2-3-4-5-5-4-3-2-1 [∿] or [↗]
1-2-3-4-5-5-4-3-2-1 [∿] or [↗]

In the above diagram, the symbol [∿] indicates a downward semi-tone while the symbol [↗] indicates the opposite.

An issue that became apparent to me was the male tendency to conflate pitch and volume. It has been observed that where a female speaker may use pitch as emphasis, a male speaker might habitually employ *volume* (see Mordaunt in Adler et al 2006, 182). A deceptively simple exercise that helps the TS/TG client discern and play with pitch versus volume is described by Michelle Mordaunt in Adler et al (2006, 181). With the phrase "I want that hat" Mordaunt illustrates the four permutations of meaning within it:

The emboldened word in each line is uttered with a change of pitch or volume
1. **I** want that hat
2. I **want** that hat
3. I want **that** hat
4. I want that **hat**

Although the exercise chiefly illustrates variation of meaning through variation of pitch, the same sentence may be utilized as a comparative sample for male and female speech patterns. Thus, the sentence may logically be expressed in at least twelve different ways: four variations with volume, four with pitch, and four with both.

The exercise invites an exploration of these levels through a clearly defined progression, and is remarkably effective.

Discussion: Contemporary Voice Work for the TS population, in development by Rebecca Root

I am not a speech therapist and certainly not a speech scientist and I do not claim to possess an in-depth anatomical knowledge of the nature of the TS/TG voice. Yet my background as an actor, and my ongoing research and practise in this field has given me an insight to the work that I now wish to share with my peers, as well as my clients.

Although I remain grateful for the exposure to Christella Antoni's work, it was rather too sedentary for my liking.[12] My experience of her exercises was fundamentally different to the creative arts vocal practice I learnt on MAVS. Borrowing elements of the traditional (scientific) model, I use material that represents a synthesis of the two modes of voice work; in other words a marriage of art and science.[13]

As in the creative arts, I approach the work through physicality, believing that a healthy and effective TS/TG voice cannot come from the head alone. Open almost any book on voice and speech and one of the earliest chapters will most likely be on posture and alignment.[14] I encourage my clients to think about their breath and body work, and spend time on "everyday" voice exercises[15] in addition to those designed more specifically for TS/TG clients.[16]

Presently, I am exploring two voice systems from the creative arts world with my TS/TG clients. These are the Laban *Efforts*[17] and *Archetypes*.[18]

I. Rudolf Laban's "Efforts"

Many readers will be familiar with the work of Rudolf Laban (1879-1958). Laban was a dancer, choreographer and dance/movement theoretician. He conceived eight "Efforts" as a means to express what he regarded as the fundamental components of human movement and energies. Simply put, the Efforts describe elements of body-voice articulation. Widely used by voice teachers[19] and performers, the Efforts can be a useful tool when you are probing access to a different voice or physicality, especially in relation to genders.

Relating to DIRECTION, PRESSURE and SPEED the Efforts may be, respectively:
- **Direct** or **Flexible**/multi-directional
- **Light** or **Strong**/heavy
- **Sudden** or **Sustained**/slow

Each Effort has its own image designed to stimulate an emotional and physical connection to the work. The table on the next page lists some examples; you may find your own.

Private Studio Practice

Stepping Off the Stone: Transsexual and Transgender Voice Modification and Presentation
A Practical Resource from a Personal Perspective by Rebecca Root

THE LABAN EFFORTS	
Gliding Direct, Sustained, Light <u>Image</u>: Ice Skating	**Flicking** Flexible, Sudden, Light <u>Image</u>: Flicking away a fly
Pressing Direct, Sustained, Strong <u>Image</u>: Pushing a heavy object	**Slashing** Flexible, Sudden, Strong <u>Image</u>: Swashbuckling swords
Dabbing Direct, Sudden, Light <u>Image</u>: Painting a picture a la Seurat	**Floating** Flexible, Sustained, Light <u>Image</u>: Floating parachute descent
Punching Direct, Sudden, Strong <u>Image</u>: Hitting a punching bag	**Wringing** Flexible, Sustained, Strong <u>Image</u>: Wringing out a wet towel

When commencing work with the Efforts, I use a sentence like "I want that hat" (see above), which is by now familiar to the client, although any short phrase will do. The client is invited to practise the phrase using different Efforts. The experiment may influence the voice and physicality in relation to the individual's identified gender.

While I regularly employ the Laban material in this field, I take care not to prescribe any one Effort for any one particular gender identity. Rather, I encourage clients to use the Efforts more as a means to an end, to help find a way towards expressing more freely their felt gender.

II. *Archetypes.*

I combine the Laban Efforts with work grounded in the realm of archetypes. These are "universal essences that we all recognize" (Rodgers and Armstrong 2009, xiii). They are drawn from mythology and folk tales and were initially considered in the work of psychologist Carl Jung (op cit, xiv). They can be significantly instrumental in voice work since they encourage the client to examine psychophysical elements of their vocal personality they might previously have struggled with. As Rodgers and Armstrong remind us, "A stereotype is a stricture where an archetype is an enabler" (Hall in Rodgers and Armstrong 2009, xiv). The archetype paves the way for the TS/TG client to investigate on a profound level the voice of his or her psychophysical gender identity.[20]

Influenced by the work of Margaret Pikes and Laurann Brown, who separately introduced me to the fundamentals of Roy Hart Theatre, I have slightly adapted the archetypes. In much the way that Antoni suggested a contrastive low-medium-high pitch voice, I employ a tri-character pattern to compare differences within TS/TG voice. These are the *Bloated Bear*, the *Confident Commander* and the *Wailing Woman*.

a. Bloated Bear

"Oooh, I'm cross, someone's woken me up," Bear grumbles. Bear had been dozing after supper, but now lumbers about moodily in a post-prandial strop. The extended /uː/ vowel of the word "Oooh" reaches deep into the belly area; the Bear's physicality utilizes the client's own weight, combined with lower pitch and resonances. Clients usually have fun with this character as it involves an element of light-hearted play.

b. Confident Commander

The Commander's voice is based confidently within the chest resonance area; he is open and assured; he fears nothing. He has a mantra, "I am the master of all I survey." The long open /ɑː/ vowel of "master" helps to open the pharyngeal channel, encouraging the speaker to explore his or her lower chest resonances. I used this archetype in a recent workshop. It had a strong effect on a female actor who was playing a drag king[21] in a short film. She reported that she was able to move and speak with much more confidence in the male role having experimented with the Commander voice.

c. Wailing Woman

The Wailing Woman holds her hands aloft, beseeching the world "Why, Why, Why?" Although she is described as wailing, the emotional quality of this character should never be forced or become distraught. The intention is to focus the client towards the upper resonances; an increase in pitch is an additional desired consequence. The /aɪ/ diphthong of "why" aids lifting the tone into the head resonances.

For additional text, as with the Efforts, I use the ubiquitous "I want that hat", or an anonymous poem, "This is the Key" (see below). This is effective since it is a "list poem", and offers in its structure a variety of short phrases which may be explored in increasingly contrasting manners.

Maya Angelou's "Still I Rise" is also useful. Many clients respond to its rhythmic, easy style, and find it life-affirming and confidence-boosting.

This is the key
This is the key of the Kingdom:
In that Kingdom there is a city.
In that city there is a town.
In that town there is a street.
In that street there is a lane.
In that lane there is a yard.
In that yard there is a house.
In that house there is a room.
In that room there is a bed.
On that bed there is a basket.
In that basket there are some flowers.
Flowers in a basket.
Basket on the bed.
Bed in the room.
Room in the house.
House in the yard.
Yard in the lane.
Lane in the street.
Street in the town.
Town in the city.
City in the Kingdom.
Of the Kingdom this is the key.

Envoi: **conclusions; travel safely forwards**

Using Laban's Efforts and the Archetypes in my work this way has so far produced interesting results. Clients attest to feeling more energized in their identified gender, with increased confidence and commitment to the sound. I work both with actors playing cross gender roles and TS/TG people who are coming to terms with the vocal demands of their new life. The suggestion that they might more easily inhabit a new and different vocal gender identity through their physicality is, I believe, an innovative approach to this field.

Where I continue to employ exercises from the SLT arena, I ask clients to devise their own phrases and sentences. This gives them ownership of the work and reinforces their muscle memory.

Central to my practise, however, is the fact that I am from the same population as my clients: I am TS, and clients respond to my ability to draw on my own experiences in developing my own re-gendered voice. This is not to say that my non-TS peers are not qualified to instruct TS clients: anyone who participated in the imaginative journey with which I opened this paper will have more than a modicum of empathy they can share with this client group. But when a TS client describes the distress of being "read"

(the failure to pass as non-TS which is so important to so many individuals), I can truly say, "I know what that's like", because it has happened to me. I believe this is what makes my practise unique, certainly in the UK where I am the only known TS voice practitioner.[22]

At the 2010 VASTA/CEUVOZ conference in Mexico City, several delegates told me they had been previously approached by TS/TG people seeking assistance in vocal re-gendering, but that they didn't know how best to support them. It is my sincere hope therefore that this essay has met a certain demand for practical information from a personal perspective. Of course, it is not exhaustive, and cannot provide solutions for every pedagogue and her client. Yet by sharing some of my experiences, I trust more of my peers will now feel better enabled to assist people like myself. I wish that when I was growing up I had had access to someone like me. I believe it would have made my journey less stressful.

I close with a story and an *envoi*. Recalling my earlier invitation I ask you now to consider your own individual journey; the steps you have taken on your road so far, the avenue that stretches away to the horizon before you. To regard this road is to understand a little of what it's like to be transsexual. "Changing sex" or fulfilling your gender identity is really no different to moving house, getting married, starting a job. It's just a little more permanent…

In the summer of 2003, just after I changed my name and began living as Rebecca, I took a holiday, alone, in the Greek Islands. I chose the remotest, most barren islands I could find as I went about the Aegean. My new life had brought happiness but not without some uncertainty and stress, and I needed space, light and warmth.

On my final day, just before catching the ferry back to Piraeus, I found myself on an outcrop of rock on the emptiest coast of the island of Schinoussa. I stood at the edge of the flat stone, the turquoise water just inches from my toes. The sea floor was visible thirty feet or more below. I reflected on my gendered journey thus far; and welcomed the tears of relief that now blurred my vision. I considered the journey ahead of me: the facial hair removal; the gender surgery; all the voice work I needed to undertake in order to fulfill the potential of my new identity. I took a breath and stepped off the rock. And I swam.

I invite you to relish your journey, wherever it may take you, whatever fence you may be crossing, whatever rocky shelf you may be balancing upon.

Open your eyes. Take a breath, and step forwards.

Private Studio Practice
Stepping Off the Stone: Transsexual and Transgender Voice Modification and Presentation
A Practical Resource from a Personal Perspective by Rebecca Root

Notes

1. Gender identity terms are fluid and there is variance amongst the population as to which descriptor is most appropriate for which client. For the purposes of this paper I define Transsexual (TS) as a person who has in some way surgically altered his or her body in order to match another (self-perceived) gender identity. I define Transgender (TG) as someone who identifies with, and possibly lives as a member of another gender, but who does not seek to undergo surgery to achieve this goal. Both TS and TG people may be described as male-to-female (MtF) or female-to-male (FtM) in their ultimate designation.

2. *Cricothyroid approximation surgery*, or CTA, repositions the cricoid and thyroid cartilages so they maintain vocal fold tension. This limits range, rather than changes the voice per se; effectively, CTA "deletes" the lower notes of the range.

3. Later published (2009) as "There and Back Again: Adventures in Genderland," in *The Moving Voice* (edited by Rena Cook), Cincinnati, VASTA.

4. Inverted commas indicate the notion that gender identity may be subjective as well as objective.

5. The 2007 edition of *Voice and Speech Review* (edited by Mandy Rees), entitled Voice and Gender, was informative reading. Especially useful were articles by Jane Vicary ("Cross-Gender Vocal Transformation," 236-245), Tara McAllister-Viel ("Casting Perceptions: the Performance of Gender as a Career Strategy," 216-223), Terri Power ("Sonic Trans-dressing: Somewhere in Between," 246-259), John Tucker ("Breaching the Ultimate Cultural Divide – Voice Work as the Key to Changing Gender," 148-154) and Richard Adler ("Voice and Communication Therapy for Transsexual/Transgender Clients," 293-299). Adler subsequently steers the reader to *Voice and Communication Therapy for the Transsexual/Transgender Client–A Comprehensive Clinical Guide* by Adler, Hirsch and Mordaunt (eds.) (San Diego: Plural, 2006). This book's references lead to additional background reading, e.g.: Gorham-Rowan, M. and R. Morris, "Aerodynamic Analysis of Male-to-Female Transgender Voice," *Journal of Voice*, vol. 20, no. 2, (2006): 251-262; and King, J.B., D.E. Lindstedt, M. Jensen, and M. Law. "Transgendered Voice: Considerations in Case History Management," LPV 24 (1999): 14-18. For further comment on the literature, see Root 2009: 146-147.

6. Breathy onset, where the vocal folds do not adduct completely during phonation, has long been regarded as the archetypical female sound. Marilyn Monroe's onset is generally regarded as an example of breathiness as sexiness.

7. Average male fundamental frequency (f0) is 120Hz (+/- 20Hz) (Andrews in Adler et al 2006: 172). The shorter female folds vibrate more quickly and have an average f0 of some 220Hz (+/- 20Hz).

8. A smaller space resonates to a higher pitch than a larger space.

9. Patients may be seen privately or under the auspices of the NHS (National Health Service).

10. Phonetically: [eɪ-iː-aɪ-əʊ-juː]

11. See Central's website at http://www.cssd.ac.uk/node/768 (accessed 29-09-10)

12. Interestingly, Antoni herself now indicates the usefulness of working with the body. "A Voice Specialist's input may feature around issues such as communication skills, communicative intent, non-verbal communication, e.g., use of gesture, and confidence. These issues, although more indirect, are no less important than the sound of a person's voice and can help aid in the client's overall passability as female." (Antoni, 2010)

13. Christina Shewell (2009) provides an extensive discussion on the overlap and disparity of voice and speech work models (Shewell 2009: 6-18).

14. See Barrows and Pierce 1933: 17-25, Colson 1982: 18-26, McCallion 1998: 3-35 to name but three.

15. By this I mean: aligned posture, supported breath, clear articulation and effective prosody.

16. In 2009 I ran a workshop for a group of UK NHS Speech and Language Therapists who had a professional interest in voice work for the TS/TG client. Many of the participants had never before experienced the sort of voice-body practice that I shared with them that day; much of the post-workshop feedback expressed delight at the novelty of the physical nature of the exercises.

Bibliography

Articles
Adler, Richard K. "Voice and Communication Therapy for Transsexual/Transgender Clients." In *Voice and Speech Review (VSR)*: Voice and Gender, edited by M. Rees. Cincinnati: VASTA. (2007): 293-299.

Antoni, Christella. "Working With Transsexuals." British Voice Association website: http://www.british-voice-association.com/articles_working-with-transexuals_antoni.htm (accessed 27-09-10)

McAllister-Viel, Tara. "Casting Perceptions: the Performance of Gender as a Career Strategy." In *VSR: Voice and Gender*. (2007): 216-223.

Power, Terri. "Sonic Trans-dressing: Somewhere in Between." In *VSR: Voice and Gender*. (2007): 246-259.

Root, Rebecca. "There and Back Again: Adventures in Genderland" In *VSR: The Moving Voice*, edited by R. Cook. Cincinnati: VASTA. (2009): 144-155.

Tucker, John. "Breaching the Ultimate Cultural Divide – Voice Work as the Key to Changing Gender." In *VSR: Voice and Gender*. (2007): 148-154.

Vicary, Jane. "Cross-Gender Vocal Transformation." In *VSR: Voice and Gender* (2007): 236-245.

Books

Adler, Richard K., Sandy Hirsch, and Michelle Mordaunt, eds. *Voice and Communication Therapy for the Transgender/Transsexual Client – A Comprehensive Clinical Guide*. San Diego and Abingdon: Plural Publishing Inc., 2006.

Barrows, Sarah T. and Anne E. Pierce. *The Voice: How to Use It*. Boston: Expression Company, 1933.

Colson, Greta. *Voice Production and Speech*. London: Pitman, 1963, third edition 1982.

Houseman, Barbara. *Tackling Text [and Subtext]*. London: Nick Hern Books Ltd., 2008.

Kayes, Gillyanne. *Singing and the Actor*. London: A&C Black Publishers Ltd., 2000, second edition 2004, reprinted 2007.

Linklater, Kristin. *Freeing the Natural Voice: Imagery and Art in the Practice of Voice and Language*. London: Nick Hern Books Ltd., 1976, revised and expanded edition 2006.

Newlove, Jean and John Dalby. *Laban For All*. London: Nick Hern Books Ltd., 2004.

McCallion, Michael. *The Voice Book: For Everyone Who Wants to Make the Most of Their Voice*. London: Faber and Faber Ltd., 1988, reissued with new material 1998.

Rodgers, Janet B. and Frankie Armstrong. *Acting and Singing With Archetypes*. Milwaukee: Limelight Editions, 2009.

Sharpe, Edda and Jan Haydn Rowles. *How to Do Accents*. London: Oberon Books Ltd., 2007.

Shewell, Christina. *Voice Work: Art and Science in Changing Voices*. Chichester: Wiley-Blackwell, 2009.

Film

Handmade Films and Python (Monty) Pictures. *Life of Brian*. 1979.

Journals

Cook, Rena, ed. *Voice and Speech Review: The Moving Voice*. Cincinnati: VASTA, 2009.

Rees, Mandy, ed. *Voice and Speech Review: Voice and Gender*. Cincinnati: VASTA, 2007.

Poem

Angelou, Maya. *Still I Rise*. http://www.poemhunter.com/poem/still-i-rise/ (accessed 28-09-10)

Workshop/Practical

Antoni, Christella. Speech therapy sessions with author and practice notes. London: Charing Cross Hospital, 2004-5.

Pikes, Margaret. Introduction to Roy Hart Theatre. London: Central School of Speech and Drama, 2008.

Essay *by Cheryl Moore Brinkley*

Observations on Teaching Voice & Speech with Multicultural Awareness

Photo by Amber Johnson

Cheryl Moore Brinkley, AEA, SAG, AFTRA, VASTA, holds a BFA in Acting/Directing from Ithaca College, NY, where she received a strong foundation in Lessac. A professional actor and director, she teaches Acting and Voice & Speech in the theatre dept. of Macalester College, St. Paul MN, and is owner of B. VOCAL, www.bvocal.net , offering communications skills (including accent modification) training for business professionals. In 2010, Cheryl was voted "Favorite Speech Communications Coach" in the MN Womens' Press What Women Want survey.

When the artistic director of a Kathak dance theatre (northern India) introduced me to her assembled company as guest artist and voice coach, she held her arm toward me, out from her body at a 45 angle, palm facing down, and moved her fingers in a gentle grasping motion. I saw this as the gesture many Westerners do when we want a small child to come take our hand. I thought it odd, but very sweet, so I went up to her and took her (I thought) proffered hand. We stood there, holding hands throughout the introduction and my opening remarks. Later I learned, to my dismay, that her gesture was a simple beckon, used in many areas in Asia, and similar to what I might have done with raised arm, upward-facing palm and cupped fingers waved toward myself. She was kind enough to go with my blunder. Indeed, as Michele Obama is reported to have learned on her recent trip to India, it's perfectly acceptable for women to hold hands in public there. Fortunately for me, the hand I held was a woman's, but what if the situation had been a corporate training workshop and the hand I took had been a man's? I shudder to think.

Since my topic is multicultural awareness, I feel compelled to tell you something about myself, so you'll know through what cultural lenses these observations have been filtered. I identify as: woman, at least 6th generation American, Caucasian of Northern European descent, Boomer, middle class East Coast Protestant upbringing, currently living and teaching in Minnesota. Please reserve all judgment. Formal training in multicultural awareness and leadership? Except for public school world cultures and history classes in the 1960s; zero, zip, *nada*. I learned the embarrassing way, and share these tips from my experiences working with a diverse array of students and clients representing 33 countries, in hopes you'll be spared.

Advance Prep: Do some research! If you are about to present to a diverse group, find out whatever you can about the various cultures that might be represented in that group. Sometimes a list of the names of the participants is enough of a clue to aid your research. For business workshops, I'll find out whatever I can from HR or the manager who hired me. Fortunately, at Macalester College, where I serve as adjunct in the theatre department, when a student registers for a class, home contact information and photo are available to faculty. Familiarization and close approximation of pronunciation of names are appreciated and communicate to your clients and students that they matter, are respected as individuals and that you cared enough to make the effort (more on names a bit later). I always spend some time on the Internet, informing myself with basic info., such as history, religions, current politics, customs and, most importantly, communication gestures.

Case in point: Two years ago, I was hired to help start a dramatic arts curriculum at an inner city high school in Minneapolis. I asked about demographics and was told that the school population included a high percentage of Somalis – a culture about which I was ignorant. I hopped online and found out that the ubiquitous "thumbs-up" gesture Americans use for "good job!" or some other form of approbation (especially for kids), is a highly obscene gesture in Somalia – so obscene that the website declined to define. Disaster averted! I shared this tidbit with a grateful school principal. By the way, thumbs-up is also obscene in Australia.

Other gestures I've had to train myself to amend include never using my index finger to point to or beckon another person. In many countries in Asia, Africa and the Middle East, being pointed at is insulting to humans, essentially relegating them to the status of a dog. Beckoning with one finger is how one calls a prostitute. A fairly safe gesture to use when referring to someone is to extend a flat, open, upward-facing palm. Clapping of the hands has to be prolonged somewhat to mean applause, for often a quick clap or two might be used to drive out evil spirits, or as a reprimand. I learned that from a Liberian couple who physically flinched and looked worried every time I responded to their positive progress with a short, sharp clap of my hands. Fortunately, they took my actual meaning from my big smile and cry of, "Good!" I sincerely hope you know to never, ever touch a Hmong child on the top of the head, to point to anything with your feet in a Buddhist culture, or to touch the feet of a Hindu unless you know them intimately or wish to show great respect.

Another tidbit I like to know in advance is what major religious observances might be concurrent with my teaching. In North America, publicly acknowledged holidays are Christian-based while all others go largely unacknowledged. You will connect better with your audience if, for example, you know that you happen to be teaching on a major Jewish holiday on which it's very important that they be home by sunset, so you can adjust your timeframe to accommodate. Or, during Ramadan, Muslims among your audience might be struggling with thirst and hunger, and might feel weak or tired because they must fast in the daytime. Everyone likes to be wished a "Happy, (*insert THEIR holiday here*)!" You get extra points if you can wish someone a traditional holiday salutation in their own language, i.e. *Habari Gani* at Kwanzaa, *Saehae Bok Mani Baduseyo* for Korean lunar New Year. There is much to learn and plenty of online resources. Don't feel pressured to become globally savvy all at once; you can learn one client, or one class, at a time as part of your content prep. Here's one link to get you started: http://soc302.tripod.com/soc_302rocks/id6.html

Dress for success. Generally, modest professional attire aids in establishing a positive respectful relationship. Why risk offending your audience before you begin speaking? Men have fewer constraints about attire and can easily pass muster anywhere with trousers, a tucked-in, pressed shirt and a tie (no jeans or polo shirts for first impression). Most tips apply to women, because women are more restricted in many cultures. I'm not talking about going so far as to costume oneself in the traditional garb of another culture or country, as that would read as inauthentic and patronizing. For instance, though I actually own and wear salwar suits (in my opinion the most comfortable and flattering women's clothing on earth!), I would not wear one to teach people from India or Pakistan until they knew me better. At the other end of the spectrum, I am not Muslim and would never wear a *hijab* or cover my head indoors, but I do own and wear decorative scarves. I also own long-sleeved blouses and long pants. So, my typical, safe, first-impression garb, from my normal wardrobe, would be a pantsuit or 3-pieced, high-necked (no cleavage!), long-sleeved ensemble with a scarf draped around my neck or shoulders. Wearing that, I'm not compromising who I am; I'm simply choosing what would be least potentially offensive to a diverse group of strangers. The quick take on this is: cover up.

I received validation about this in a conversation with my neighbor, a retired US Navy nurse and world traveler. She told me that before visiting a sacred shrine to see the Jade Buddha in Bangkok in 1975, she read the guidebook's fine print note that suggested "women should wear dress or skirt." She and her group complied with simple long skirts and "peasant dresses" that were popular at the time and which they already owned. They were warmly welcomed and hosted. A guide came out, selected them and led them into the temple past the waiting lines of bewildered and disgruntled American and European tourists who were wearing shorts and miniskirts. When questioned about why they had been preferentially treated, their guide smiled and replied that they had shown respect for the shrine by dressing appropriately.

Teaching tips: Though it's a mouthful, always refer to what you teach as American English, or Standard American English, or North American English, but not simply English. I once had a student from Mumbai politely inform me that his first language WAS English, but not American-accented English. He grew up speaking only English in his home. Though I knew that many Indians speak English because it is the language of higher education and urban schools there, and that most Indians speak several Indian languages as well, I had not done my homework, and assumed incorrectly that he had learned English secondarily.

Make every effort to speak without idiom or colloquialism. If you are asked, "What?" your first response should be to simply repeat exactly what you just said, a bit more clearly and slowly, because sometimes your student or client simply needs a chance to hear your words again to gain comprehension. If, however, you realize you had slipped into idiomatic speech, correct the idiom with an explanation or a literal translation. Generational note: if you have a younger group who has been privileged to grow up with the Internet and learned American culture through film and TV, there are many pop culture references you can make that most will understand. As Deborah Rodriguez wrote in *Kabul Beauty School*, everyone there knew the movie, *Titanic*, by heart. And, like it or not, since the 1990s, Disney is global.

It's vital to create an atmosphere in which students feel free to speak up and question you if they don't understand a word, reference or example you might use. North Americans will speak their needs more often than those from many other cultures, especially those who are taught that one does not question authority (teachers, elders) because that would be very rude. Even if you check in by asking, "Do you understand?" many are too polite or embarrassed to answer you with, "No," if they don't. A method I discovered that works well is to ask each participant to "teach" me how to pronounce her/his name right at the top of the class or presentation. This makes me a learner in the situation, too, and shows that I'm not a know-it-all, that I'm willing to try, to be vulnerable, and make mistakes in the interest of change. In short, I model how to be a speech student, and struggle good-naturedly with new and difficult phonemes (my most challenging thus far has been a Mongolian name). Often, your students will quickly realize that, beyond re-peating the sounds, they have no idea how to tell you how to make specific sounds and they gain an instant awareness of the skill and experience it takes to teach this material. With a momentarily even playing field (a sports metaphor I would avoid in an ESL group), trust, humor and acceptance come more easily into the teacher/student relationship.

Finally, consider that you will rarely know the sexual preference or gender identification of everyone in your audience. Please don't assume that everyone is attracted to or partnered with someone of the opposite gender. Think through the anecdotes and examples you regularly use in teaching and adjust your language to be LGBT aware and inclusive.

My students and clients have taught me so much and I hope that my personal offerings help you to better connect to your students and clients, and also pique your interest and excitement to explore more about the diverse cultures of our shared planet.

Voice and Speech Science, Vocal Health, *Dr. Ron Scherer, Associate Editor*

Dr. Ron Scherer, Professor in the Department of Communication Sciences and Disorders, Bowling Green State University, teaches voice disorders and speech science courses. His research interests include the physiology and mechanics of basic, abnormal, and performance voice production and intervention, and the methodologies involved in such research. He was Senior Scientist at the Denver Center for the Performing Arts and taught in the DCPA's voice and speech trainers program. He received his Ph.D. from the University of Iowa, a master's degree from Indiana University in speech-language pathology, and also spent two years as a music major at Indiana University.

The theme for this issue of the Voice and Speech Review, "A World of Voice," is approached in this section in a variety of ways. The essay by Katherine Meizel explores the topic of "vocality", which is a special feature of deep interest for us. It is a scholarly and practical ethnological approach to central issues of voice training. The term vocality is a very broad term dealing with the widest possible conceptualization of the voice. In Katherine's words,

> This concept [vocality] goes beyond qualities like timbre and practice, and encourages us to consider *everything* that is being vocalized—sounded and heard as vocal—and offers a way to talk about a voice beyond simply the words it imparts or its color or production techniques. Instead it encapsulates the entire experience of the speaker or singer and of the listener, all of the physiological, psychoacoustic, and sociopolitical dynamics that impact our perception of ourselves and each other.

Many or our readers will feel very much at home with this piece. The essay will help illuminate many broad notions in the bigger picture of voice.

The research essay by Catherine Madill fits our issue's theme in that she offers an "Australian perspective" on voice training. The goal is to

> consider the Australian evidence that exists for the effectiveness of vocal training across different approaches, theoretical paradigms and research contexts. It will also describe the new wave of research into training vocal skill currently underway in Australia.

"Interpretive research paradigms," which are quite qualitative and deal with overall effects of voice training on the individual, are contrasted with "empirico-analytical research paradigms," which are more quantitative and stress "specific vocal characteristics" and "vocal skill acquisition [rather] than transformation of the individual overall". There is a nod to the Estill work, which is a fitting inclusion with the tribute to her presented separately in this issue. Cate Madill also emphasizes the use of principles of motor learning in future training schemes, an important inclusion into all theories of pedagogy.

Joe Stemple and Maria Dietrich offer an erudite essay on the aging voice and how the changes with age can have negative consequences for the professional voice user. They offer suggestions for body and vocal fitness of importance to all voice and speech trainers as well as the older actor. The information certainly has no geographical boundaries and is thus quite relevant for "A World of Voice".

Ron Scherer and Melissa Maas present an essay on research on public speaking, and report the surprising finding that there is extremely little research directly related to voice and speech training for public speakers. They offer a research structure to encourage voice and speech trainers to collaborate with scientists to rectify the problem of little solid research specifically for the public speaker, of which there are of course millions around the world.

We hope that you will enjoy these selections and allow them to add to your understanding, pedagogy, and health within "A World of Voice."

Essay *by Katherine Meizel*

A Powerful Voice: Investigating Vocality and Identity

Katherine Meizel is a Visiting Professor of Ethnomusicology at Oberlin Conservatory. Though she earned her Ph.D. in ethnomusicology at the University of California, Santa Barbara, she also holds doctoral, master's and bachelor's degrees in vocal performance, and has taught singing for many years. Her book *Idolized: Music, Media, and Identity in American Idol* was released by Indiana University Press in early 2011. Other publications include a recurring blog feature for the magazine *Slate*, chapters for Ashgate Press and America University in Cairo Press, and articles in the *Journal for the Scientific Study of Religion, Popular Music and Society*, the *Pacific Review of Ethnomusicology*, and *eHumanista: Journal for Iberian Studies*.

The singing voice is an embodied instrument—inseparable from the musician, and therefore just as resonant in the broader contexts of human communication, social relationships, and the construction of identity as it is in a theater or concert hall. Voices inform how song and singer are heard, serving as perceptual markers for deeply intertwined ideas about music and identity. Music studies within the humanities and social sciences, today focusing heavily on the place of music in human life, show increasing interest in exploring the difficult implications of these ideas. But it can be a daunting task to address the multiplicity of linguistic, acoustic, cognitive-perceptual, and cultural factors that shape how we produce and hear human voices. One step with which researchers have approached the problem is a broadly applicable but meaning-specific notion: *vocality*. This concept goes beyond qualities like timbre and practice, and encourages us to consider *everything* that is being vocalized—sounded and heard as vocal—and offers a way to talk about a voice beyond simply the words it imparts or its color or production techniques. Instead it encapsulates the entire experience of the speaker or singer and of the listener, all of the physiological, psychoacoustic, and socio-political dynamics that impact our perception of ourselves and each other.

Though the word has been naturalized to the point that writers rarely offer a working definition, a reexamination of its interrelated uses across studies of cognitive science and acoustics, language, literary criticism, and music reveals its layered significance as a site where the making of sounds and the making of identity intersect. Each approach looks for different meaning, investigating the voice as a vehicle for the variety of communicative, expressive, and ideological processes at the heart of speech and song. This essay surveys the idea of vocality as it has developed across history and disciplines, proposes a holistic model for its study in the context of music, and begins to unpack the heavy sociocultural baggage that accompanies it. It is my hope that these efforts may be of use to voice and speech professionals as they seek to tap the fullest potential of the voice in performance, and to grasp the entirety of *what* a voice carries, when it carries across a theater or podium—not only lexical meanings and emotion, but also vital information about culture, identity, and the dynamics of power that suffuses human communication.

Toward a Holistic Definition of Vocality

While the term *vocality* has gained currency in music scholarship in recent years, it is not a neologism. In the 1910s and 20s, psychoacoustic researchers (e.g. Modell and Rich 1915, Weiss 1920) discussed its application to a newly suggested acoustic relationship between tuning fork tones and vowels, a perceived vocality—a vowel-ness, a human sound—in the "pure tone" of the fork's sinusoidal wave. When a group of music scholars (Bairstow et al.) broached the idea of vocality in 1929, they were curious as to how one might (and who should) determine the suitability of a piece of music to the voice, or the capability of a voice to perform music. This group of authors were responding to a *Music and Letters* editor's query about what exactly made a piece of music "vocal" or "unvocal," and British musicologist Edward J. Dent raised the issue of social context as an important dynamic in such judgments. Taking up the proposed question of why folksong seemed "vocal enough but difficult to sing well" (235)—an inquiry regarding the potential vocality or unvocality of folksong—Dent, rather than implicate any inherent quality in the structure or aesthetics of the music, instead pointed to class relations and the nationalistic impulse that fueled many collections of European folk songs in the late nineteenth and early 20th centuries:

> People may possibly have come by now to accept folksongs as national possessions, but for a long time it was as much a matter of pretence as Marie Antoinette's dairymaiding. Cultivated singers had by dint

of technical skill to acquire a style which suggested the manner of the imaginary peasants who ought to have sung folksongs all day by natural instinct, and at the same time to sing their songs sufficiently well (judged by ordinary artistic standards) to make them a success in the concert-room…The difficulty of singing folksongs is mainly a matter of self-consciousness, vanity and snobbery. (240-241)

For Dent, the appropriateness of folk songs to the voice was never itself in question, and the difficulty classically trained ("cultivated") singers felt in performing them was due to an unavoidable unawareness of lost stylistic practices and a hyperawareness of class distinctions. Though he did not define vocality explicitly, Dent's acerbic remarks suggested a sense that "folk" and "concert-room" singing might involve irreconcilable aesthetics, techniques, and, most critically, *social perspectives*.

It was several decades later before vocality was more directly associated with social context. In 1987, scholar of medieval poetry Paul Zumthor proposed vocality (*vocalité*) as a concept that could circumvent the habitual but problematic binary opposition of orality and literacy, and allow for the possibility of their intersection. He employed the word to critique a neglect of the human voice in the study of poetics, and was followed by Ursula Schaefer (1992, 1993), for whom *Vokalität* also added a third field to the oral and the literate, a way to acknowledge the continued significance of the (oral) voice in the presence of literacy. Vocality entered the picture, she wrote, in "a cultural situation that very much depended and relied on the voice for mediation of verbal communication even though writing had already been well established" (1993: 205). If we return to Edward Dent's assessment of folk song in the hands (or throats) of classically trained singers, this updated definition is especially appropriate. "Folksong," since Johann Gottfried Herder coined the phrase in 1778, has been understood as a kind of people's song (*Volkslied*) that expresses the essence of a group or nation, and contributes to the creation of a "sense of place" (Bohlman 1988: 52). It was, to Herder, rural, orally transmitted, and an antidote to the artificiality he found in Enlightenment thinking (Filene 2000: 10).

The interconnection between oral and written culture has long been a theme of both historical musicology and ethnomusicology, two closely related disciplines with overlapping but diverging histories—while the first tended through the 20th century (though by no means exclusively) to emphasize the historical study of Western classical tradition, the other developed with a view toward the practices, discourses, and structures of music in human life around the globe. For some time in these areas, folk song remained a category considered as purely oral, or aural, tradition, but in the mid-20th century, some (e.g., Seeger 1950) began to suggest

that the aural and the written were unavoidably entangled together. Dent's scenario perfectly illustrates this entwinement: the English folk songs collected in the early twentieth century (for example, by Cecil Sharp) were transcribed, written down by enthusiasts and scholars from the performances of singers who had learned them by ear. When published in the new transcriptions, they became part of written tradition, but at the same time never stopped being part of aural/oral tradition. The oral/written binary is also complicated by the role of transmission when music becomes a commodity. As far back as the 17th and 18th century, British ballad broadsides—the commercial music industry of early modern Europe—offered printed lyrics to accompany preexisting tunes that might be learned either by ear from a ballad-seller, from attending the theater, or from peers, or that could be learned from published books of dance music. In the 20th century, recordings, as materials of music culture, certainly contributed to the transmission of tradition, but they cannot be corralled easily into either the aural/oral or literate category. They are in many ways fixed texts (though perhaps not fixed indefinitely), but reproduce the processes of aural/oral transmission, ear to mouth. So when classically trained singers today perform celebrated ballads like "Barbara Allen" or "Greensleeves," they are participating in a long historical interplay between the aural/oral and the literate—including folk tradition and broadsides and 20th or 21st century recordings—and highlighting Zumthor's and Schaefer's interpretation of vocality.

In their seminal work *Embodied Voices: Representing Female Vocality in Western Culture* (1994), musicologists Leslie C. Dunn and Nancy A. Jones borrowed from Zumthor, defining vocality as dependent on context, the meaning of voices past indecipherable without the reconstruction of their historical hearing. The move from *voice* to *vocality*, wrote Dunn and Jones, "implies a shift from a concern with the phenomenological roots of voice to a conception of vocality as a cultural construct" (Dunn and Jones 1994: 2). Drawing on French poststructuralist thinking, they described vocality as "all of the voice's manifestations"—speaking, singing, crying, laughing—including and beyond linguistic content. This vocality encompasses both the *pheno-song* and *geno-song* that Roland Barthes expounded (after Julia Kristeva's pheno- and geno-texts): the verbal, linguistic text juxtaposed with the non-verbal, embodied meanings that he famously heard as the "grain of the voice" (Barthes 1977).

Barthes, in *Image, Music, Text*, was also exploring the ties between different forms of human communication, and found in his "grain" something like the middle ground between orality and literacy that Zumthor would locate in vocality ("The sung writing of language," Barthes expounded (185)). Barthes' grain, though, linked the aural and the written not simply with the voice, but explicitly with the *body*. "The 'grain' is the body in the voice as it sings" for Barthes, "the hand as it writes, the limb as it performs" (188). And, significantly, the burden of embodiment does not fall only on the singer; it is borne by the listener as well. "If I perceive the 'grain'…" Barthes continued, "I am determined to listen to *my relation* with the body of the man or woman singing…" (188, my emphasis). That relationship between the singer and the listener is another key theme in the study of vocality. In an application of linguistic anthropology to music, Steven Feld, Aaron A. Fox, Thomas Porcello and David Samuels map vocality as a site where music and language meet, serving "among the body's first mechanisms of difference"— where we learn to hear distinct individualities, to aurally separate our own voices from others'. Vocality in this view is "a social practice that is everywhere locally understood as an implicit index of authority, evidence, and experiential truth" (Feld et al. 2004: 341).

Given these precedents, vocality helps to shape the self- and other-knowledge of the body. It is metaphor and meaning, style and content, idea and performance. To arrive at a comprehensive model for its study, I turn to ethnomusicologist Cornelia Fales' three-part schema for research in musical timbre, or sound color. She recommends a broad view, taking into account three domains of sound: the productive, acoustic, and perceptual . The productive domain has to do with the source of the sound, the ways in which the physical vibrations are produced. The acoustic domain comprises the way the sound is structured and transmitted, and the perceptual domain involves the sensations produced by sound (Fales 2005: 157). I propose the explicit supplementation of these areas with a sub-domain of perception that is already implicit in her ethnomusicological work—an attention to sociocultural context that profoundly informs the making of sonic meaning. I understand *vocality* as encompassing the act of vocalization and the entirety of that which is being vocalized—it is a set of vocal sounds, practices, techniques, and meanings that factor in the making of culture and the negotiation of identity. Vocality, then, is part and parcel of how we interact with the world around us, of who we think we are.

Vocality and history

The study of vocality as a symbol of identity is intimately tied up in a set of difficult, painful, and interlaced histories—of European modernity and colonialism, of ideas about race and nation, and of the study of humanity as an academic discipline. Documents from the early years of European expansion provide a glimpse into how vocality attracted the Western gaze (or ear) even at the beginning of the colonial project.

Calvinist missionary Jean de Léry's 16th century reports of his time in Brazilian Tupi territory, *History of a Voyage to the Land of Brazil*, are illuminating, though not easy to read. The voice in the body became the locus for de Léry's understanding of difference, as he watched Tupinamba dancing and singing, their voices shifting during "rites and ceremonies" from "tuneable" and "pleasing" to "muttering," "trembling," and "howl[ing]," signaling to de Léry what he believed must be possession by the Devil (de Léry 1578)—an embodied difference, essentially, of the soul.

Later, during the Enlightenment, as the seeds were planted for the ascendance of the modern nation-state, Jean-Jacques Rousseau found proto-national identity in the voice. He suggested in his *Dictionnaire* that differences between spoken French and Italian led to different ways of singing. It is an idea that Sally Sanford returned to in 1995, in the service of historical performance practice, to propose that the two languages involve different patterns of airflow, leading to distinct "schools of breathing" and disparate French and Italian singing techniques in the 17th century (Sanford 1995).

In the late 19th century, around the same time that the British Empire began to expand its hold on the Middle East and the African continent, and Queen Victoria became empress of India (1876), anthropology began to flourish as a scientific pursuit, and scholars debated the existence and meaning of physiological differences among the world's peoples. Concepts of nation and race were both conflated and reified separately, but to some the racialized body, and voice, were indicative of national character. In 1869, "London's foremost laryngologist" (Laurenson 1997) Sir G. Duncan Gibb delivered an unusual paper to the Anthropological Society of London on "The Character of the Voice in the Nations of Asia and Africa, Contrasted with that of the Nations of Europe" (published 1870). The Society, founded in 1863, was not yet representative of an independent academic field, but was established by supporters of polygenesis theory—followers of surgeon Robert Knox, who imagined that anatomical comparisons of various racial groups could show that they were actually different species (Lorimer 1988). Though their literature may inspire incredulity today, at the time it provided fuel for the justification of imperialist work. On the voice, Gibb spoke his position plainly:

> Europe is the cradle of song, although a large cradle, if you like, but it points to superiority of voice in strength, power, compass, and sound…the character of the voice is superior in the European to the Asiatic and African. He, perhaps, cannot *bellow* as loud as the Negro, nor can he screech as loud as the Tartar; nevertheless, his vocal character is superior to both. (Gibb 1870: 258)

Gibb systematically discussed what he believed to be a number of distinctions among African, East Asian, Central

Asian, South Asian, and European (he included German, French, Russian, Italian, and English voices in this category) voices; strikingly, he deemed some to be *powerful*—German and Tartar (Tatar)[1] voices—and some to be *weak*—Chinese, Japanese, and also the colonized Indian voices. He guessed that the cause of such weakness might lie in the structure of the larynx, which he believed differed among peoples in the "pendency" of the epiglottis and the length of the vocal folds. In India, for example, he had learned from a secondary source that men were never basses or baritones (aural purveyors of masculinity), but always sang falsetto. This he attributed to a "pendant" and "curled under" epiglottis he supposed to cause a "loss, or rather absence, of physical power and strength in the entire inhabitants of the plains" (253). Non-European voices were characterized by unpleasant sounds he named "twang" or "whining"—notably, the hearing of "twang" as vocality has carried on and crossed the Atlantic, today often used as a race- and class-associated descriptor of American country music, an adjective that in five letters implies race, place, and status (whiteness, ruralness, and working-class). In Chinese and Japanese voices, the twang Gibb heard was "metallic," but he could not be certain whether it was due to linguistic peculiarities or "a shallow formation of the larynx, approaching to that in the female sex" (245).

Here, Gibb's Victorian attitudes about the embodied voice extend not only to racialized and geographical thinking but also the perception of gendered sounds. The superiority of European voices, for Gibb, depended in part upon a "good length of vibrating vocal cords" (258). We are aware today that adult fold length varies among individuals, and that it contributes to the cultural engendering of sound as male and female—the longer associated in Western discourse with male voices, and range depth associated with masculinity. And the conjunction of race and gender in Gibb's description of Indian, Chinese and Japanese voices is not coincidental; the desexualization or feminization of the Asian male body in the Western imagination is today a well-theorized phenomenon (e.g. Sinha 1995, Cheng 1999, Espiritu 2008). Conversely, the Tatar voice, which he admired as powerful, is to him just as potent in women—he quoted renowned traveler Évariste R. Huc, echoing his assertion that rather than the "soft languishing physiognomy of the Chinese women, the Tartar woman presents in her bearing and manners a power and force well in accordance with her active life and nomad habits, and her attire augments the effect of her masculine, haughty mien" (quoted in Gibb 1870: 249[2]). Gibb's views, derived from diverse sources including personal observations, the travelogues and communications of other authors, and his own study of the epiglottal characteristics of Englishmen, seem untenable today (and he acknowledged himself that he was opening the door to potential criticism), and his contemporaries did cast doubt on his methods in a response summary. They also critiqued

his theory: one disapproved of his failure to distinguish Germans from German Jews, who he believed "were distinct in the shape of the head, as well as in the character of their voice" (Gibb et al. 1869: lxiii). A Dr. Rowdon thought that there might be other anatomical differences outside of the larynx—"the nasal organs, for instance" (lxiv)—and a Mr. McGrigor Allan wished Gibb had praised further "the Negro, who had a most musical voice,--so musical, in deed, that a Negro could almost be distinguished by his voice alone" (lxiv).

In the postcolonial 21st century, we understand race as a construct, and we know that there is no scientific evidence of any morphological laryngeal or skeletal characteristics indicative of it. In her 2008 dissertation *Voice as a Technology of Selfhood: Towards an Analysis of Racialized Timbre and Vocal Performance*, musicologist Nina Eidsheim discusses the continuing association of race and voice in classical music discourse, particularly in a multiculturalist United States, and provides an overview of scientific research that finds against the existence of any collective structural distinctions among the world's voices (Eidsheim 2008: 32-33, see also Miller 2004: 220, Wilbur J. Gould in Rubinstein 1980). Eidsheim posits that, instead, the differences listeners hear in timbre are "based on the flexibility and possibility of the instrument, and the choices made" as to the vocal qualities emphasized (33). In other words, like race, vocality is perhaps best considered as a social construct. Nevertheless, a substantial body of scholarship and ethnographic work demonstrates the very real discursive persistence of vocality as a marker of identity and difference, among singers and listeners across identity groups.

Vocality and Identity

While marking difference often carries negative implications and effects, it is important to note that the idea of a sound with identity-specific meanings can serve as a source of pride, too. Country musician George Strait's 2009 hit "Twang" went gold, and Tim McGraw's manifesto of regional vocality "Southern Voice" started 2010 with a jump to first place on *Billboard's* Hot Country Songs chart. In the sphere of opera—a genre with its own discursive associations of race and class—singers of color have walked a notoriously uphill road to the stage, accompanied along the way by the notion that their voices are racially distinct. Though this imagined[iii] vocality often blocked the way, the meaning it has for black singers varies. In a 1991 interview in the NAACP's magazine *The Crisis*, baritone Simon Estes and tenor George Shirley, both African American, affirmed their belief in the existence of a "special black timbre." Author Carla Maria Verdino-Sullwold recounted that Shirley told her, "There is such a thing as a black voice, and it is a compliment to recognize it because black voices are generally warm and round—dusky in color." (Verdino-Sullwold

1991: 14) In 2009, an interview I conducted with Marion Caffey, creator of the hit revues *Three Mo' Tenors* and *3 Mo' Divas*[4], underlined for me the power of such ideas. I asked him if he thought there was such a thing as a "black voice." "Yes. Of course," he said, without hesitation, though he was less certain whether the source of difference was located in physiology or practice. But, he continued, reiterating his concerns about the underemployment of black opera singers, "I don't see how it [the sound] becomes 'right' or 'wrong'" (Interview, 4 November 2009).

In Western opera, the concept of a "black voice" is a loaded one that has followed African American, and to a degree other black singers, for decades, if not centuries. Nina Eidsheim pinpoints the idea's inception at the moment of Marian Anderson's 1955 debut at the Metropolitan Opera, and though descriptions of African American classical singers had tended to racialize their voices long before—consider Sissieretta Jones, called the "Black Patti" in contrast to the European-American opera star Adelina Patti—1955 is indeed a watershed time in the ideation of the "black voice." It is nearly the precise moment when the nationalized commercial vocality in the U.S. began to shift from the operatically-tinged crooner to a sound overtly and explicitly informed by the vocal practices of gospel and the then-infant genre to be known as soul—it was at that time that Ray Charles transformed Harry Dixon Loes' "This Little Light of Mine" into the secular hit "This Little Girl of Mine," in one of his earliest endeavors to bring the musical energy of the church to the secular charts. As America's old racialized culture of appropriation grew into the new and powerful business of rock 'n' roll, voices like Charles' became a fulcrum upon which the possibility of a cross-racial market balanced. The vocality that he and his contemporaries helped to fix in the music industry's consciousness—characterized by acoustically noisy (rough) timbres, extramusical shouts, and melisma—is pervasively evident and drawn upon across popular genres today.

Vocality can also figure significantly in the negotiation of national cultural identity. As I have discussed elsewhere (Meizel 2011), the omnipresence of melismatic singing in U.S. popular music highlights the centrality of the "black voice" in the construction of 21st century American culture. It is not for nothing that Barthes includes "the coded form of the melisma" as a part of his pheno-song (Barthes: 182)—it holds a multitude of meanings, a multivocality, for those who sing and hear it. It is for some an embodied spirituality, a heightened mode of expression, even a symbol of black history. John Burdick recounts that a gospel singer he interviewed in Brazil heard the effects of American slavery in melisma, believing that it had developed as a way for slaves to exercise rhythmic skills when they were forbidden to play drums (Burdick 2009: 34).

Late 20th century and early 21st century performances of the U.S. national anthem have underlined the nationalized cultural weight placed on melismatic practices. While José Feliciano shocked the nation with his unorthodox and somewhat melismatic arrangement at the World Series in 1968, the trend began in earnest with a revolutionary soul-influenced rendition Marvin Gaye performed at the 1983 NBA All-Star game. For Mark Anthony Neal, Gaye's "Star Spangled Banner" was a performance that "suggested that African-Americans had a right to 'African-Americanize' the composition, because of the price they paid for American democracy, while highlighting African-American music's hegemony within American popular music and perhaps American popular culture" (Neal 1998:72).

The United States is not the only case in which vocality has factored in nation-building. In the last decades of the Ottoman Empire and the first of the Turkish Republic, for example, music was caught up in the complicated business of balancing a long, rich history of Ottoman culture and a fraught near-century of Westernizing reforms. Musical aesthetics and technique, vocabulary, historical perspective, and presentation all became contested sites in the early 20th century, and vocal style, John Morgan O'Connell has argued, "provided a locus for debating larger social and political issues" (O'Connell 2002: 781). Music was discursively divided into *alaturka*—representative of the Eastern in Turkish music—and *alafranga*—aesthetically European style—with an increasing preference for the latter. Along the road to the 1923 establishment of the Republic, the debate led to a synthesized national style, *millî musiki*, that reimagined Turkish culture within the parameters of Western conventions. *Alaturka* was at times considered a foreign influence, due to its historical relationship with Arab music, and vocality was disparaged for its Eastern qualities, such as "chest register, guttural nasality, sobbing character, and amplitude," as well as for its "intense melismas." Even the lifestyle of *alaturka* singers was criticized as an unfortunate remainder (and reminder) of "Ottoman disorder" (782-3). As the new Republican government pushed music education and vocal instruction toward the adoption of Western conservatory methods, singers developed new ways of voicing Turkish culture. The celebrated Münir Nurettin Selçuk (ca. 1900-1981), for example, composed and performed music categorized as *alaturka* using *alafranga* vocality, applying Western techniques, timbre, breath management, enunciation, and a certain amount (though O'Connell does not mention it) of vibrato, but keeping, to a restrained degree, the melisma and ornamentation associated with the Turkish musical system called *makam*. In his famous "Kalamış," one of Selçuk's many songs paying homage to a Turkish place (see Stokes 1997), his special blend of vocalities is especially apparent in acoustic terms.

In the spectrographic representation (using Praat) in

Voice and Speech Science, Vocal Health

A Powerful Voice: Investigating Vocality and Identity by Katherine Meizel

Ex. 1 below, a moment from Selçuk's 1945 recording of "Kalamış," we can see some aesthetic characteristics of Western classical vocality, and some that more typically correspond to Turkish vocal *makam* practice. The passage comes on the last syllable of the phrase "eski zamanlar" ("bygone times," literally "old times"). It is in a *makam*—a Turkish melodic mode with a set of characteristic practices—called *Nihavend*[5], on the tonic D, and I've chosen this particular segment because in a monophonic performance by voice and instruments, it is a pause in which only the voice is heard. On the spectrogram, the thin, upper line traces the fundamental frequencies (F0s) sung, describing a 5.5-second passage entered through a slightly-portamentoed ascending octave leap; then the top F0 (the pitch A) is held for approximately 1.5 seconds with an even vibrato that measures 5.579 cycles per second—within the range of preferred rates in Western classical singing (Titze suggests that this range includes a qualified 4.5-6.5 Hz, and acknowledges that what is considered acceptable varies situationally and over time—in the first half of the 20th century, he writes, faster vibratos between 6.0 and 7.0 were common (Titze 2000: 325)). Then follows a brief shake or trill succeeded by an ornamented, mostly stepwise descent to G (the fourth degree of the *makam*). The spectrogram also highlights the formant areas, and it is plain that Selçuk employs the singer's formant (here outlined, at left, in the area of 2860 Hz.) so valued among vocalists trained in Western classical technique.

Through his carefully constructed Republican vocality, and his performances in recital format and Western concert dress, Selçuk both adapted and contributed to the establishment of a new national culture.

Concluding Thoughts

Its far-reaching significance in the formation of personal and cultural identity makes vocality a complex and often fraught idea. The notion of vocality as vowel quality broaches issues of language and difference; the position scholars have granted it between orality and literacy ties it to the processes of industrialization and ideas about class and race; the role of vocality in human relations raises questions about the voice and power. And thinking about vocalities in terms of nation, race, ethnicity, and gender brings up the very troubling danger of essentializing *the singer or speaker. Patsy Rodenburg, in The Right To Speak* (1992), argued against what she astutely called "vocal imperialism," and cautioned voice users about the risks of believing in "the sound of one right voice" (105). The discursive history we've seen in this essay highlights the very real connections between political and cultural imperialism and thinking about the voice, and at a historical moment when political scandals still arise over the perceived blackness of a presidential candidate's speech patterns[6], it is clear that the voice remains an important site for the negotiation of power. When we investigate vocality, then, attention to cultural meaning is more urgent than ever, so that we hear the voice as integrated with the body, and the embodied voice as a crucial component in how we listen and speak to the world around us, to each other, and to ourselves.

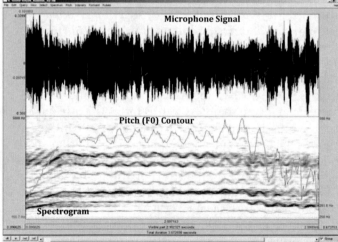

Ex. 1. Passage from Münir Nurettin Selçuk's "Kalamış." The top of the figure shows the microphone signal. The bottom figure shows a narrow band spectrum (black and grey lines) from 0 to 5,000 Hz (left vertical axis) and the fundamental frequency (F0) contour whose referent axis is the right vertical axis (with a range of 250 to 500 Hz). The F0 contour indicates an ascending portamento followed by vibrato on approximately A440, with a subsequent short trill and descent to approximately F4.

Notes

1. Turkic peoples then largely inhabiting a swath of central and northern Asia, including today's Russia and neighboring states, and Manchuria in China. (While sometimes European sources conflate the Turkic and Mongol peoples of the region, Gibb does separate them in his assessment.) It is worth noting, also, that Gibb was praising the power of German voices on the eve of German unification (1871) and the establishment of the German empire.

2. It is unclear which edition of *Souvenirs d'un voyage dans la Tartarie, le Thibet, et la Chine pendant les années* 1844, 1845 et 1846 Gibb was citing.

3. To be clear, I use "imagined" here not to mean "*imaginary*," but in a manner after Benedict Anderson's *Imagined Communities* (1982) in the sense that it is invisible, intangible, and created through thinking.

4. *Three Mo' Tenors* has been performed by exclusively black casts; Caffey says that *3 Mo' Divas* has included other singers of color on occasion (Interview, 4 November 2009).

5. Many thanks to fellow ethnomusicologist Eric Ederer for his assistance in identifying *Nihavend*, and for explaining the nuances of the Turkish text.

6. In early 2010, U.S. Senate Majority Leader Harry Reid came under fire for a comment recounted in the newly released book *Game Change: Obama and the Clintons, McCain and Palin, and the Race of a Lifetime* (by John Helemann and Mark Halperin). Reid had told the authors two years before, as the nation followed perhaps the most racially fraught campaign in its history, that the public was "ready to embrace a black presidential candidate, especially one such as Obama – a 'light-skinned' African American 'with no Negro dialect, unless he wanted to have one.' " Though some called for his resignation, Reid made apologetic phone calls to President Obama, to African American congressmen, and civil rights leaders, and the president declared, "the book is closed" (Cillizza 2010). Reid's faux-pas was heavily criticized for its focus on (shade-specific) skin color, for its unwelcome resuscitation of the loaded term "Negro," and for reinforcing the long-controversial idea of an identifiable and universal African American form of English.

Bibliography

Anderson, Benedict. 1982. *Imagined Communities: Reflections on the Origin and Spread of Nationalism*. London: Verson.

Bairstow, Edward G., Edward J. Dent, Ernest Walker, Steuart Wilson, Paul England, H. Gregory Hast, and Owen Colyer. 1929. "Vocal and Unvocal." *Music & Letters 10* (3): 235-255.

Barthes, Roland. 1977. *Image, Music, Text*. Trans. Stephen Heath. New York: Hill and Wang.

Bohlman, Philip Vilas. 1988. *The Study of Folk Music in the Modern World*. Indianapolis: Indiana University Press.

Burdick, John. 2009. "The Singing Voice and Racial Politics on the Brazilian Evangelical Music Scene." *Latin American Music Review* 30 (1): 25-55.

Cheng, Cliff. 1999. "Marginalized Masculinities and Hegemonic Masculinity: An Introduction." *Journal of Men's Studies* 7 (3): 295-315.

de Léry, Jean. 1578. Excerpt from *History of a Voyage to the Land of Brazil*. In *Norton Anthology of English Literature, Norton Topics Online*. <http://www.wwnorton.com/college/english/nael/16century/topic_2/delery.htm> (2 September 2010).

Dunn, Lesley and Nancy Jones. 1994. "Introduction." *Embodied Voices: Representing Female Vocality in Western Culture*. 1-13.
Eidsheim, Nina. 2008. *Voice as a Technology of Selfhood: Towards an Analysis of Racialized Timbre and Vocal Performance*. Ph.D. Dissertation, University of California at San Diego.

Espiritu, Yen Le. 2008. *Asian American Women and Men: Labor, Laws, and Love*. Lanham, Maryland: Rowman & Littlefield Publishers, Inc.

Fales, Cornelia. 2005. "Short-Circuiting Perceptual Systems: Timbre in Ambient and Techno Music." *Wired for Sound: Engineering and Technologies in Sonic cultures*. Paul D. Green and Thomas Porcello, editors. Middletown, CT: Wesleyan University Press. 156-180.

Feld, Steven, Aaron A. Fox, Thomas Porcello, and David Samuels. 2004. "Vocal Anthropology: From the Music of Language to the Language of Song." *A Companion to Linguistic Anthropology* (Alessandro Duranti, editor). Malden and Oxford: Blackwell Publishing. 321-346.

Filene, Benjamin. 2000. *Romancing the Folk: Public Memory and American Roots Music*. Chapel Hill: University of North Carolina Press.

G. Duncan Gibb. "The Character of the Voice in the Nations of Asia and Africa, Contrasted with that of the Nations of Europe," *Memoirs Read before the Anthropological Society of London*, vol. 3 1867-8-9. London: Longmans, Green, and Co., 1870. pp. 244–259.

Gibb, Duncan G. et al. "Comments on 'On the Character of the Voice in the Nations of Asia and Africa, Contrasted with That in the Nations of Europe.'" *Journal of the Anthropological Society of London* Vol. 7. 1869. pp. lxii-lxvi.

Laurenson, R.D. 1997. "George Duncan Gibb (1821-1876): London'd Foremost Laryngologist." *Journal of Medican Biography* 5 (4): 205-209.

Lorimer, Douglas. 1988. "Theoretical Racism in Late-Victorian Anthropology, 1870-1900." *Victorian Studies* 31 (3): 405-430.

Meizel, Katherine. 2011. *Idolized: Music, Media, and Identity in American Idol*. Bloomington: Indiana University Press.

Miller, Richard. 2004. *Solutions for Singers: Tools for Performers and Teachers*. Oxford and New York: Oxford University Press.

Modell, J.D. and G.J. Rich. 1915. "A Preliminary Study of Vowel Qualities." *The American Journal of Psychology* 26(3): 453-456.

Neal, Mark Anthony. 1998. *What the Music Said: Black Popular Music and Black Public Culture*. New York: Routledge.

O'Connell, John Morgan. 2002. From Empire to Republic: Vocal Style in Twentieth Century Turkey. *In The Garland Encyclopedia of World Music VI: The Middle East*. (Virginia Danielson, Scott Marcus, and D. Reynolds, editors). New York: Routledge. 781-787.

Rodenburg, Patsy. 1992. *The Right to Speak*. New York: Routledge.

Rubinstein, Leslie. 1980. "Oriental Musicians Come of Age." *New York Times*, November 23. Page SM8. Accessed at nytimes.com (2 September 2010).

Sanford, Sally. "A Comparison of French and Italian Singing in the Seventeenth Century." Journal of Seventeenth-Century Music. 1:1 (1995) <http://sscm-jscm.press.uiuc.edu/jscm/v1/no1/sanford.html>

Schaefer, Ursula. 1993. "Alterities: On Methodology in Medieval Literary Studies." Oral Tradition 8 (1): 187-214.

---------------------. 1992. Vokalität: Altenglische Dichtung zwischen Mundlichkeit und Schriftlichkeit. Tubingen: Gunter Narr Verlag.

Seeger, Charles. 1950. "Oral Tradition in Music." *Funk and Wagnalll's Standard Dictionary of Folklore and Mythology* 2 (Maria Leach, editor). 825-829.

Sinha, Mrinalini. 1995. *Colonial Masculinity: the 'Manly Englishman' and the 'Effeminate Bengali' in the Late Nineteenth Century*. Manchester: Manchester University Press.

Stokes, Martin. 1997. "Voices and Places: History, Repetition and the Musical Imagination." *The Journal of the Royal Anthropological Institute* 3 (4): 673-691.

Titze, Ingo. 2000. *Principles of Voice Production* (Second Edition). Iowa City: National Center for Voice and Speech.

Verdino-Sullwold, Carla Maria. 1991. "No Such Word as 'Can't': The Uphill Struggle of the Black Classical Singer." *The Crisis* 98 (2): 10-16, 47.

Weiss, A.P. 1920. "The Vowel Character of Fork Tones." *The American Journal of Psychology* 31(2): 166-193.

Zumthor, Paul. 1987. *La Lettre et la Voix: de la "Littérature" Médiévale*. Paris: Editions du Seuil.

Essay *by Cate Madill*
Spoken voice training research – an Australian perspective

Cate is a lecturer / researcher at the University of Sydney, Australia. Her research focuses on the processes and efficacy of voice training for professional voice users and people with functional voice disorders. This includes the effect of voice quality on listener perceptions of the speaker and the efficacy of voice training for professional voice users, specifically actors and radio broadcasters. She is a certified practicing speech pathologist specializing in voice disorders. She has studied and worked as a professional actor, singer, voice coach and lecturer in voice in the performance department of the University of Wollongong and the Australian Film, Television and Radio School, Sydney, Australia.

There are many documented approaches to training the speaking voice around the globe. They range from the theatre voice traditions of Linklater (1976), Berry (1973), Lessac (1997) and Rodenburg (2000), which focus on the experiential and holistic nature of vocal production to more recent programs of Estill Voice Training Systems (1997) and Christine Shewell (2009), which have a functional focus and concentrate on the individual mechanics or areas of vocal production. Whilst different approaches to voice training will inevitably be based on different theories of vocal control and focus of attention in the learning of vocal skills, it is unquestionable that the basic anatomy of the vocalist is predominantly the same. The necessity of learning to control these anatomical structures (either consciously or unconsciously) is also common across approaches. This paper will consider the Australian evidence that exists for the effectiveness of vocal training across different approaches, theoretical paradigms and research contexts. It will also describe the new wave of research into training vocal skill currently underway in Australia.

Effectiveness of holistic theatre voice training approaches

Theatre performers have specific demands made of their voice. Vocal projection, the ability to vocally convey emotional expression, and vocal stamina are essential skills of a competent and successful actor (Acker, 1987; Pinczower and Oates, 2005; Roy, Ryker and Bless, 2000). Holistic approaches to theatre voice training consider the act of vocal production as a complex phenomenon involving not only muscle activation, awareness and skill, but an act that is influenced by societal and cultural factors, internal perceptions of self, emotional expressiveness, habitual behaviours, and specific intentions of the communicative act (Linklater, 1976). Thus, the act of voice training is considered a transformative process, addressing all aspects of the individual, not just vocal skill.

To date, only a limited amount is known about the effectiveness of holistic theatre voice training approaches as the efficacy of training has not been thoroughly investigated. Australian researchers have begun to explore both holistic and more physiologically-based voice training approaches in research conducted over the last 10 years. Recognising that methodological issues in this research are many, with the issue of establishing a valid and reliable measure of the outcome of voice training predominating, different approaches to research have resulted in different solutions.

An interpretative research paradigm has been used to analyse the meaning of paradigms and reported outcomes of the process of holistic theatre voice training approaches (Peart-Reid, 2003). A hermeneutical analysis was conducted on the training process undertaken by participants during two 10 week voice training courses taught by a master Linklater teacher. The research was based on observations and in-depth interviews of 9 participants from the 2 courses. The research approach acknowledged the multiple complex factors that influence the process of vocal change in a training environment. These include society and culture, the theatre voice teacher, other participants, personal influences, frames of reference, and motivations and directions of the individual. From analysis of participant observations and interviews, Peart-Reid proposed that there were 5 dimensions of experience and transformation that were impacted by the vocal training process; the individual's sense of self, knowledge of skills and understanding, emotions and feelings (emotional expressiveness), sensorimotor perceptions, and behaviours and intentions.

In contrast, empirico-analytical research paradigms have also been utilised to investigate the outcomes of the holistic theatre voice training approaches. In this type of research, measuring specific vocal characteristics is the focus of the research, rather than the overall effect of the voice training process on the individual. Vocal features can be measured using various methods, including auditory-perceptual judgments, acoustic analysis, and visualisation of the larynx during phonation. Whilst auditory-perceptual impressions of the voice are considered the 'gold standard' due to high ecological validity (i.e., that is how the voice is experienced in the world by others), there are well documented problems with reliability of auditory-perceptual judgements (Oates, 2009). Also, to date, there is no standardised or commonly accepted auditory-perceptual schema for evaluating the theatre actor's voice.

Many researchers have turned to acoustic analysis of the voice as an objective measure, often attempting to correlate acoustic measures with auditory-perceptual judgements. For example, projected resonant voice has been evaluated using sound spectra (Feudo, Harvey and Aronson,1992), clear voice using perturbation measures (Roy et al., 2000; Timmermans, De Bodt, Wuyts and Van de Heyning, 2004; Laukkenan, Syrja, Laitala and Leino, 2004), and flexible voice using measures of frequency range and mean frequency (Roy et al., 2000; Feudo et al., 1992; Laukkenan et al., 2004). Thus, previous research has typically examined vocal components that either relate to the source characteristics of vocal production or to filter characteristics (Fant, 1960). Positive improvements in actor voice quality have been observed over periods of nine to eighteen months (Feudo et al., 1992; Timmermans et al., 2004; Walzak, Mc-Cabe, Madill and Sheard, 2008); however, a description of the training was not presented in all the studies and longer-term outcomes were not assessed.

Australian research has attempted to add to this knowledge by evaluating the effects of a holistic theatre voice training approach on a range of acoustic parameters over a 3 year period, explicitly using the source-filter model of voice production (Fant, 1960) to interpret the results. The outcomes of actor voice training using an eclectic voice training approach based on the work of Linklater and Rodenburg, was evaluated in two studies (Walzak et al., 2008; Walzack, McCabe, Madill and Sheard, 2010). Selected vocal measures were used to investigate whether a holistic approach to voice training had an effect on both source and filter components of the voice. Eighteen students (9 male and 9 female) in a tertiary 3-year acting program were assessed at the beginning of their acting course, and then again at 12 months, 2 years, and completion of their course (3 years). Questionnaire and interview information, reading, spontaneous speaking, sustained phonation tasks, and a pitch range task were all assessed. Maximum phonation time (MPT), fundamental frequency across tasks, pitch range for speaking and reading, singing pitch range, noise-to-harmonic ratio (NHR), shimmer, jitter, long-term average spectra (LTAS), and the dysphonia severity index (DSI) were all analysed from acoustic recordings.

This research provided insight into the value of long-term research projects when assessing the outcomes of training as outcomes were different at different stages of the course. After 12 months of training, shimmer significantly increased for both male and female participants, suggesting more instability in the voice on a prolonged vowel task. Pitch range increased significantly and mean frequency of the lowest pitch was lowered significantly for female participants (Walzak et al., 2008). Analysis of subsequent recordings of 14 (6 males and 8 females) out of the original 24 students, later in their course and at completion, revealed an improvement in some resonance measures such as alpha ratio and peak differences in LTAS measures, but an increase in other measures such as the DSI (Walzak et al., 2010). These results provide evidence that the training was effective in developing skills to change the resonant characteristics of the sound (i.e., manipulate the filter or vocal tract), but was not as effective in controlling the source of the sound, as evidenced by a an increase in dysphonia severity, that is a deterioration in the voice quality (Walzak et al., 2010).

Whilst this research provides some insight into the outcomes of holistic voice training in the context of actor training, its value is limited by its observational design and lack of control over variables that may contaminate the results. These methodological problems have been addressed more specifically in the experimental investigations into more recent, functional voice training approaches.

Effectiveness of functional parameterised approaches to voice training.

The more recent approaches to voice training that have emerged over the last 20-30 years have suggested a different approach to how individuals may access control of the voice. Technological advances in voice science and voice measurement have lead to more empirico-analytical research which focuses on physiological control and manipulation on the vocal instrument, with greater emphasis placed on vocal skill acquisition than transformation of the individual overall. The work of Estill (1997) for both speaking and singing, and that of Bagnall (1998) and Shewell (2009) all use an analytical approach in which perceptual and/or muscular parameters of voice are identified as being able to be manipulated separately from other parameters. In all three cases, these authors contextualise this approach as being a foundation for the performance context of voice, which is unquestionably holistic in nature. The notion that parameters of the vocal apparatus can be manipulated separately from others is, however, a controversial one.

The concept of differentiated vocal tract control (DVTC) is currently described in two models of vocal training:

Estill Voice Training Systems™. (EVTS, Santa Rosa, CA) (Estill, 1997) and Voicecraft™ (Adelaide, SA) (Bagnall, 1997). Both EVTS and Voicecraft™ propose that specific muscular and biomechanical structures within the larynx and vocal tract can be consciously and voluntarily manipulated following voice training. Both approaches claim to be based upon the results from observational physiological studies conducted in the 1980s and 1990's (Citardi, Yanagisawa and Estill, 1996; Kmucha, Yanagisawa and Estill,1990; Yanagisawa, Estill, Mambrino and Talkin ,1991; Honda, Hirai, Estill and Tohkura,1995). The question of whether individuals can actually learn to manipulate different muscular parameters of the voice has not been tested using an experimental methodology until recently.

Using experimentally designed research, Madill, Sheard and Heard (2010) investigated whether trained speakers were successful in manipulating a range of vocal parameters identified in clinical and voice training literature, following voice training. Twelve vocally trained unimpaired speakers received 3 -12 hours of further training time to learn to differentially manipulate three groups of laryngeal muscles in four conditions: false vocal fold activity (constricted or retracted), true vocal fold mass (thicker or thinner), true vocal fold closure on phonation (closed vs open), and larynx height (lowered vs neutral). The speakers were asked to produce the movements in all possible combinations to produce eight specific vocal qualities each. The speakers were asked to perform the vocal manoeuvres in a reading task while undertaking video-nasendoscopy visualisation and recording of their larynx. The video footage was then rated by three experienced voice clinicians. Results indicated that the judges agreed on 71.6–94.8% of occasions on the direction of change in the functioning of the vocal parameters but did not agree on the amount of change in direction. At least two of the three judges agreed on the direction of rating that matched the voice target on 323 of 384 judgments. This suggests quite strongly that the speakers were trained successfully to manipulate and change individual biomechanical aspects of their laryngeal function on the majority of occasions, as judged by two of three expert voice clinicians.

Further evidence for the effectiveness of training control of specific parameters of vocal function can be found in the study by Bagnall and McCullough (2004). This study describes the training process and evaluated the outcomes of training using acoustic analysis, perceptual voice analysis, and speaker ratings of comfort, ease and exertion. Whilst the results are not explicit in the detail provided in the published report, the authors claim that there was an improvement in the participant's vocal control, as demonstrated by a self- reported increase in ease and comfort during phonation and improvements in perceptual voice quality and acoustic measures.

All of these findings provide evidence that conscious training in the manipulations of specific muscle groups can be effective in learning to control the vocal mechanism in the majority of speakers. Whilst not definitive or absolute, these studies provide valuable knowledge from which further investigations can follow to further clarify and test the efficacy of physiologically-based voice training approaches in more naturalistic contexts.

The future of voice training research – Principles of Motor Learning

Current Australian research in voice training has begun to focus on the application of principles of motor learning (PML) to performance and learning of vocal skills. These principles form a schema that provides insight into the variables that affect the acquisition and retention of a motor skill (Wulf and Shea, 2002). Vocal training involves learning a motor skill in which the muscles of respiration, the larynx and the vocal tract are manipulated to produce sounds in specific ways. As such, PML can and should be applied to vocal training. PML identifies two distinct phases of intervention: pre-practice and practice. To date, little research has addressed the application of PML to voice modification and no research has addressed the pre-practice phase of voice training. The pre-practice phase is the process by which the learner acquires knowledge of the movement goal (also known as internal reference-of-correctness) and can perform the task under optimal conditions (Maas et al., 2008). These conditions are required for the learner to then begin practice.

Research currently taking place is focusing on the variables that affect the acquisition of a voice motor task, that is, what processes may be useful or essential in the pre-practice phase of learning a new vocal task. McIlwaine, Madill and McCabe (2010a) have recently conducted a review of the motor learning literature and developed a schema summarising all of the variables that influence the pre-practice phase. A number of key variables are theoretically essential elements in the pre-practice phase: motivation, instruction, modelling, perceptual training, and feedback (McIlwaine, Madill and McCabe, 2010b). There are a range of additional variables that influence the acquisition of a target movement including learner and teacher characteristics, task complexity, prior knowledge, beliefs, skills, and attitudes and interactions between the learner and teacher (Magill, 2007).

To test the validity and reliability of the schema, McIlwaine et al. (2010) undertook to use the schema in the analysis of 3 commercially available voice training videos that demonstrate instruction in different voice therapy techniques; Lessac Madsen Resonant Voice Therapy (LMRVT) (Verdolini Abbott, 2008), Yell Well (Bagnall, 1995), and Vocal

Function Exercises (VFE) (Stemple, 2002). Nine final year speech-language pathology students participated in a pilot study whereby they categorized clinicians' behaviors in voice therapy training videos according to general and specific pre-practice variables within the PML Pre-practice Schema. The students demonstrated good intra-rater reliability, but inter-rater reliability was not consistent across the pre-practice variables and training approaches. In general, there was relatively high agreement for *modelling* and *verbal information* and lower agreement for *motivation* and *feedback*. Investigation of the sources of reduced reliability in rating *instructions*, *explanations* and *perceptual training* showed there were consistent patterns in disagreement, indicating that ratings were not random. The study demonstrates that the pre-practice variables identified in the PML literature can be identified across different voice training contexts. The PML Pre-practice Schema may therefore be a useful tool for analysing and improving the process of vocal training and as a means of understanding the process of learning a vocal task in more detail. It is currently being used to investigate whether there are observable, clearly identifiable differences in pre-practice behaviours between graduating speech pathologists versus experienced clinicians when teaching vocal tasks (Lawrie, Madill, McCabe, McIlwaine and Heard, 2010). The PML Pre-practice Schema provides a new approach and a new language to further analyse and understand the process of learning vocal skill, and adds to the holistic and physiologically-based approaches discussed above.

Conclusions

Research into the mechanisms, processes and outcomes of holistic and physiologically-based vocal training approaches in theatre voice is still emerging. Whilst there is evidence that different training approaches have different outcomes, the challenge of distilling clear effects of holistic voice training approaches remains and the clear outcomes of experiments in physiologically-based training have yet to be tested in real-world contexts. The key issue in both of these dilemmas appears to be that of selecting the most appropriate vocal measure in each individual context. New information, analyses, theoretical paradigms, and observational and experimental research have shown that there are many ways to measure and analyse voice training and its outcomes. To conduct meaningful research, we must ask what aspect of the voice training process does a particular approach address and what is the best way to measure it?" For example, there is no point measuring the external acoustic characteristics of the actor's voice if a training approach focuses on the actor's internal process of relating their voice to text.

Meaningful research of a training approach also requires a clear statement of purpose of each training approach, and a 'gold standard' to which the training aspires. Without

these, research findings become observations of a specific situation and training becomes an undefined, directionless process, the outcomes of which can never be assessed or predicted across different situations, teachers and students. Defining the processes and goals of our training approaches more clearly and asking ourselves how we will measure our success in the training process may therefore provide a way forward to more informative research findings and better training outcomes. It is therefore essential that further exploration for the voice training process be informed by dialogue and collaboration between voice teachers and voice scientists so that a common understanding can be established and research questions pursued in a way that can be implemented into practice.

Research will hopefully continue to challenge all those who train, teach and work with vocalists to reconsider what we have previously thought of as irrefutable fact. New research approaches provide opportunities to understand not only the voice but learning processes that give us greater transparency and common understanding, and more effective training outcomes across theatre voice, public speaking, and speech pathology contexts alike.

Bibliography

Acker, B.F. (1987). Vocal tract adjustments for the projected voice. *Journal of Voice.*;1:77-82.

Bagnall, A. (1995). Yell Well. North Adelaide, S. Aust: AB Voice International. [videorecording]

Bagnall A.D. (1997) Voicecraft™ Workshop Manual. Adelaide, SA: Voicecraft International

Bagnall A.D and McCulloch, K. (2005) The impact of specific exertion on the efficiency and ease of the voice: a pilot study. *Journal of Voice.* 19:384-390.

Berry, C. *Voice and the actor*. New York: Wiley Publishing Incorporated; 1973.

Estill J. (1997) Compulsory Figures for Voice—Level One, Primer of Compulsory Figures. Rev. ed.). Santa Rosa, CA: Estill Voice Training Systems™.

Citardi M.J., Yanagisawa E. and Estill J.(1996) Videoendoscopic analysis of laryngeal function during laughter. *Annals of Otolology, Rhinology and Laryngology.*;105:545-549.

Fant, G. *Acoustic theory of speech production*. The Hague, Paris. Mouton & Co. Printers; 1970.

Honda K., Hirai H., Estill J. and Tohkura Y. (1995) Contributions of vocal tract shape to voice quality: MRI data and articulatory modelling. In: Fujimura O, Hirano M, eds. *Vocal Fold Physiology: Voice Quality Control.* San Diego: Singular; 22-38.

Kmucha S., Yanagisawa E. and Estill J. (1990) Endolaryngeal changes during high intensity phonation: videolaryngoscopic observations. *Journal of Voice.* 4:346-354.

Lawrie, Madill, McCabe, McIlwaine and Heard, 2010. The use of pre-practice phase variables by graduating and experienced speech pathologists in voice therapy. Unpublished Honours Thesis: The University of Sydney.

Linklater, K. *Freeing the natural voice* (1st Ed.). New York: Drama Book Publishers; 1976.

Lessac, A. (1997) The use and training of the human voice (3rd ed.) Mountain View: Mayfield.

Maas, E., Robin, D. A., Austermann Hula, S. N., Freedman, S. E., Wulf, G., Ballard, K. J., et al. (2008). Principles of motor learning in treatment of motor speech disorders. *American Journal of Speech-Language Pathology*, 17, 277-298.

Madill, C., Sheard, C., & Heard, R. (2010). Differentiated vocal tract control and the reliability of interpretations of nasendoscopic assessment. *Journal of Voice*, 24, 337-345.

Magill, R. A. (2007). *Motor learning and control : concepts and applications* (8th ed.). Boston: McGraw-Hill.

McIlwaine, A. Madill, C. and McCabe, P. (2010a) The Principles of Motor Learning Pre-practice Schema: A Pilot Study (Unpublished thesis, University of Sydney)

McIlwaine, A. Madill, C.and McCabe, P. (2010b). Voice Therapy Pre-practice and the Principles of Motor Learning. *ACQuiring Knowledge in Speech*, Language and Hearing.12.

Oates J. (2009) Auditory-perceptual evaluation of disordered voice quality: pros, cons and future directions. Folia Phoniatrica et Logopedica. 61(1):49-56, 2009.

Peart-Reid, K.L. (2003). An investigation of theatre voice training (based on the Linklater method). Unpublished PhD thesis, University of Sydney.

Pinczower R., & Oates, J. (2005) Vocal projection in actors: the long-term average spectral features that distinguish comfortable acting voice from voicing with maximal projection in male actors. *Journal of Voice.*;19, 440-453.

Roy, N., Ryker, K., & Bless, D. (2000) Vocal violence in actors: an investigation into its acoustic consequences and the effects of hygienic laryngeal release training. *Journal of Voice.*;14, 215-230.

Rodenburg, P. *The actor voice and the performer speaks*. United States: St Martin's Press; 2000.

Shewell, C. (2009) Voicework; Art and science in changing voices. West Sussex: Wiley-Blackwell.

Stemple, J. C. (2002). Vocal function exercises [videorecording]. Gainesville, Fla: Communicare Publishing.

Verdolini Abbott, K. (2008). Lessac-Madsen Resonant Voice Therapy Overview [videorecording]. San Diego, Calif: Plural Pub.

Walzak, P. McCabe, P., Madill, C., & Sheard, C. (2008). Acoustic changes in student actors' voices after 12 months of training. *Journal of Voice*, 22, 300-313.

Walzak, P. McCabe, P., Madill, C., & Sheard, C. (2010). Acoustic changes in student actors' voices following 3 years of training. (*submitted*)

Wulf, G., & Shea, C. (2002). Principles derived from the study of simple skills do not generalize to complex skill learning. *Psychonomic Bulletin & Review*, 9, 185-211.

Yanagisawa, E., Estill, J., Mambrino, L. and Talkin D. (1991) Supraglottic contributions to pitch raising—videoendoscopic study with spectro-analysis. *Annals of Otolology, Rhinology and Laryngology.*;100:19-30.

For Your Vocal Health: Keeping the Mature Voice Healthy

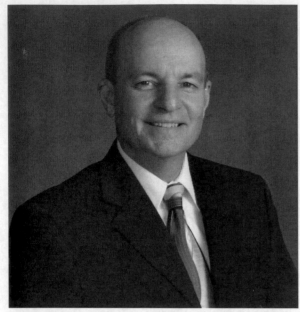

Joe Stemple is a Professor of Communication Sciences and Disorders, College of Health Sciences, University of Kentucky. He is the author of the texts *Voice Therapy: Clinical Studies* (3rd ed.) and *Clinical Voice Pathology: Theory and Management* (Plural Publishing, 4th ed.) as well as research articles and text chapters related to clinical voice disorders. His current research involves a translational study of various aspects of the aging voice including epidemiology, treatment outcomes, and the biology of aging laryngeal muscles as well as central neural control of normal and disordered voice production. He is a Fellow of the American Speech-Language-Hearing Association.

Maria Dietrich is a Post-Doctoral Scholar in the Division of Communication Sciences and Disorders, Department of Rehabilitation Sciences, University of Kentucky. Dr. Dietrich completed her Ph.D. in Communication Science and Disorders in 2009 at the University of Pittsburgh. Leading up to her Ph.D., she received a M.A. degree in Speech Language Pathology in 2003 from Kent State University, OH, and a degree in Diplom-Heilpädagogik in 2001 from Universität zu Köln in Germany. Dr. Dietrich has completed her Clinical Fellowship Year at the University of Pittsburgh Voice Center and holds the ASHA Certificate of Clinical Competence in Speech-Language Pathology since 2004. Dr. Dietrich studies the neurobiological and psychobiological processes involved in modulating vocal functioning.

The successful actor is dependent upon a voice that is healthy, flexible, and dependable. Considering vocal demands of the profession, maintaining the healthy voice can be a challenge. Lifestyles, survival jobs, medical illnesses, psychological stressors, character voice demands, and so on, all place challenges on the vocal mechanism to remain healthy. Another challenge is one that with luck, all of us will need to face; that is the challenge of the aging voice. This article will discuss some of the changes in the voice producing mechanisms that occur as the voice ages with suggestions for keeping the mature voice healthy.

At present there are 36 million older adults (65+ years) in the United States, and the majority is non-institutionalized (approximately 32 million). It is projected that the number of older adults will double by the year 2030 and represent 20% of the U.S. population (Census, 2001). This rapid older population growth is driven by two factors, first, greater longevity and second, baby boomers reaching

retirement age. Seniors are healthier and wealthier than the previous generation, but this population is far from being homogeneous (NIA, 2009). Apart from gender, age group, income levels, racial and ethnic differences, two opposite subgroups are the (1) sedentary and medically compromised versus (2) active and healthy older adults. According to national statistics, 76.9% of adults 65-74 years are not considered sedentary and 64.1% of adults 75 years or older are not considered inactive (CDC, 2009). The currently active and healthy aging population is fueled by baby boomers entering their senior years. This subgroup already maintains a far healthier and active lifestyle than any previous generation and strives to continue to do so (AssociatedPress, 2005; Mortland, 2006; UMHS, 2008).

Communication is an important part of maintaining an active and healthy lifestyle whether that lifestyle involves maintaining employment or for social and volunteer activities. Effective communication is dependent upon normal voice production (phonation). While the aging vocal process (termed presbyphonia) is clearly not a voice disorder per se (Verdolini, Rosen, & Branski, 2005), age-related changes in voice production mechanisms can contribute to the perception of a voice disorder. A voice disorder may be perceived due to a change in voice quality, loudness, and a noticeable decrease in vocal endurance (Verdolini, et al., 2005). Such changes can contribute to increased effort to talk, difficulty projecting voice, significant discomfort and fatigue during voice production. Ultimately, changes in voice decrease overall communication effectiveness and thus, alter daily function and quality of life (Benninger, Ahuja, Gardner, & Grywalski, 1998; Krischke et al., 2005; Murry, Medrado, Hogikyan, & Aviv, 2004; Smith et al., 1996; Verdolini & Ramig, 2001; Verdonck-de Leeuw & Mahieu, 2004; Wilson, Deary, Millar, & Mackenzie, 2002). The negative consequences of voice disorders are well-established and cut across domains, impacting social interaction, general, and emotional health, and psychological well-being (Benninger, et al., 1998; Krischke, et al., 2005; Smith, et al., 1996; Verdonck-de Leeuw & Mahieu, 2004; Wilson, et al., 2002). The functional impact of dysphonia even has been shown to meet or exceed that of chronic conditions such as sinusitis, angina, and sciatica (Benninger, et al., 1998).

One can readily see how the impact of the aging voice could have negative consequences for professional voice users. In the general non-elderly population, there is ample evidence that voice disorders (1) substantially limit or render many individuals unable to perform tasks in their current occupation, (2) contribute to high rates of voice-related absenteeism, and (3) cause many individuals to change their occupation (Roy, Merrill, Thibeault, Gray, & Smith, 2004). Moreover, it is well-established that behavioral risk factors for voice disorders include voice use patterns and employment in occupations that require heavy voice use such as teaching and acting (Coyle, Weinrich, & Stemple, 2001; Herrington-Hall, Lee, Stemple, Niemi, & McHone, 1988; Miller & Verdolini, 1995; Roy, Merrill, Thibeault, Gray, et al., 2004; Roy et al., 2004; Schneider & Bigenzahn, 2005; Smith, Gray, Dove, Kirchner, & Heras, 1997; Smith, Kirchner, Taylor, Hoffman, & Lemke, 1998; Smith, Lemke, Taylor, Kirchner, & Hoffman, 1998; Thibeault, Hirschi, & Gray, 2003; Thibeault, Merrill, Roy, Gray, & Smith, 2004; Verdolini & Ramig, 2001; Williams, 2003). This is relevant for the aging population to the extent that active, older adults are choosing to continue to be active professionally and socially or feel pressured to do so in light of economic reasons. As a common consequence, any older adult in a vocally demanding occupation or social activity may sooner or later experience that the aging phonatory system may not be able to fulfill the ongoing demands placed upon it. Finally, there is mounting evidence that seniors appear to suffer greater quality of life consequences from dysphonia

than other age groups (Smith, et al., 1996). The ability to communicate through effective voice production across the lifespan is vital to maintaining independence, social interaction, and psychological well-being, and ultimately ensuring quality of life.

Epidemiology of the Aging Voice

Recently, research has increased efforts to qualitatively and quantitatively describe voice problems specific to the aging population. Among non-treatment seeking individuals ages 65 years and older who live independently, 20% report experiencing difficulties with voice (Golub, Chen, Otto, Hapner, & Johns, 2006) and 29% indicate that they currently have a voice disorder (Roy, Stemple, Merrill, & Thomas, 2007). Moreover, those seniors with current voice problems as opposed to seniors without voice problems reported significantly more voice-related effects, primarily "getting anxious or frustrated because of your voice" and "having to repeat yourself to be understood" (Roy, et al., 2007). The combined results confirm that a substantial segment of the older population is currently experiencing a voice disorder with a significant impact on quality of life. Further, studies that included visualization of the vocal folds of treatment and non-treatment seeking elderly adults provided support that the occurrence of presbylarynx (typically thin or bowed vocal fold appearance) was a valid problem for a subset of the aging population apart from voice problems secondary to multi-system changes during aging (Casper & Colton, 2000; Coyle, et al., 2001; Hagen & Lyons, 1996; Kandogan, Olgun, & Gultekin, 2003; Lundy, Silva, Casiano, Lu, & Xue, 1998; Reulbach, Belafsky, Blalock, Koukman, & Postma, 2001; Woo, Casper, Colton, & Brewer, 1992).

Characteristics of the Aging Voice

Optimal vocal functioning depends on the integrity and efficient interplay of three major subsystems: respiration, phonation, and resonance. We will describe each briefly and include changes that occur with aging.

Respiration is the power source for voice. Age-related changes in the structure (e.g., calcification of costal cartilages, alteration of thorax and lung size, infiltration of respiratory skeletal muscle by connective tissue and fat) and mechanics (e.g., decrease in chest wall compliance, decrease in lung elastic recoil) of the respiratory system have been documented (Hoit & Hixon, 1987). Associated changes in lung volumes (e.g., decrease in vital capacity, increase in residual volume) have also been observed (Hoit & Hixon, 1987; Hoit, Hixon, Altman, & Morgan, 1989). As a result of these changes, speech breathing in older adults is altered, characterized by: reduced number of syllables per breath, increased amount of lung volume expended per syllable,

Voice and Speech Science, Vocal Health
For Your Vocal Health: Keeping the Mature Voice Healthy
by Joseph C. Stemple and Maria Dietrich

and larger lung volume and rib cage excursions during normal speech (Hoit & Hixon, 1987).

Phonation is the vibratory source of voice production. As part of the communication system, the larynx undergoes a number of structural and functional changes with aging (Bach, Lederer, & Dinolt, 1941; Hirano, Kurita, & Sakaguchi, 1989; Honjo & Isshiki, 1980; Leslie, Drinnan, Ford, & Wilson, 2005; Mueller, Sweeney, & Baribeau, 1984, 1985; Robbins, Hamilton, Lof, & Kempster, 1992; Sato, Hirano, & Nakashima, 2002; Segre, 1971). Phonation is produced by the vibration of a multi-layered vocal fold complex (Hirano, 1981). The importance and contribution of each layer to phonation is well established (Gray, Hirano, & Sato, 1993; Hirano, 1981; Hirano & Kakita, 1985; Kahane, 1988; Titze, 1994; Zemlin, 1988). Numerous age-related changes have been documented for each individual vocal fold layer that can be summarized as stiffening of the lamina propria of the vocal fold (tissue that connects the vocal fold mucosa with the vocal fold muscle) along with muscle atrophy of the thyroarytenoid and vocalis muscles, contributing to age-associated voice change (Hollien & Shipp, 1972; Mysak & Hanley, 1959). Perceptual features of vocal aging vary across individuals but generally include: altered pitch, hoarseness, breathiness, strain, vocal tremor, and slowed speech rate (Hartman, 1979; Ptacek & Sander, 1966; W. J. Ryan & Burk, 1974). Perceptual changes are noticed by listeners (Hartman, 1979; Hartman & Danahuer, 1976; Linville & Fisher, 1985; Ptacek & Sander, 1966; W. J. Ryan & Burk, 1974; Shipp & Hollien, 1969) and may be sufficient to negatively affect the listener's attitude toward the aged speaker (E. B. Ryan & Capadano, 1978). Overall, a number of factors – metabolic, hormonal, neurological, and behavioral – likely contribute to the changes in laryngeal structure (e.g., mucosal thinning, muscle atrophy) and function (e.g., inadequate glottic closure due to vocal fold bowing, altered frequency of vocal fold vibration) which underlie the age-related changes in voice production (Thomas, Harrison, & Stemple, 2008).

Resonance of the voice signal occurs in the supraglottic vocal tract, made up of the pharynx, velopharynx, and oral cavity. Vocal tract changes with age include: continued craniofacial growth, increased endocranial dimensions, increased facial dimensions along both bony and soft aspects, tongue atrophy, pharyngeal muscle atrophy and weakening, and a lowering laryngeal position in the neck (Israel, 1968, 1973; Kahane, 1981; Lasker, 1953; Sonies, 1992). Changes in vocal tract size and configuration contribute to alterations in the tract's response to the laryngeal tone, thus altering the vocal quality. These changes in combination with phonatory and respiratory changes contribute to voice quality that is identified by listeners as being characteristic of advanced age (Linville & Fisher, 1985).

Managing the Mature Voice

Maintaining a healthy voice at any age is dependent upon sound principles of vocal hygiene which are well known such as adequate hydration, no smoking, limited caffeine and alcohol, minimal use of phonotraumatic behaviors, and so on. Management options for the aging voice have been proposed by voice specialists including behavioral approaches such as overall fitness exercises and more directed voice therapy. In addition, surgical options are becoming more refined and available for the mature voice as well.

Overall Body Fitness

Biever Lowery and Bless (1993) demonstrated that a whole body fitness program can enhance the overall voice quality of seniors. Maintaining excellent overall body fitness will help keep the voice healthy. Aerobic exercise combined with light weights, Tai Chi, yoga, and Pilates have all been demonstrated to help maintain overall body fitness in both younger and older populations. Physically active individuals also tend to be more socially active and will therefore use the voice more on a daily basis helping to maintain the vocal fitness as well.

Guided Vocal Fitness Program (Voice Therapy)

Seniors might also want to consider a vocal fitness program under the guidance of a speech-language pathologist. Vocal fitness programs can make a difference in voice production characteristics such as reduced breathiness, improved projection, and more vocal stamina in populations over the age of 65 (Berg, Hapner, Klein, & Johns, 2008; Gorman, Weinrich, Lee, & Stemple, 2008). We would suggest that even the normal voice of all ages can be enhanced through directed voice production exercises such as Lessac-Madsen Resonant Voice Therapy (Verdolini Abbott, 2008), Vocal Function Exercises (Stemple, 2006), and the Accent Method of Voice Therapy (Kotby, El-Sady, Basiouny, Abou-Rass, & Hegazi, 1991), among others. Common to these programs is the goal to increase vocal efficiency by balancing the three subsystems respiration, phonation, and resonance; in other words, to optimize vocal function to produce the best possible voice with the least amount of effort. A regular vocal maintenance program may be a key for a lasting functional voice. The numbers of people who present with presbyphonia in our clinical voice centers is increasing and treatment is often covered by insurance. When seeking treatment, a laryngologist (ear, nose, and throat doctor) should be seen first, differential diagnoses cleared, and then a speech-language pathologist who is certified by the American Speech-Language-Hearing Association and specializes in rehabilitation of voice disorders should be consulted.

Surgical Treatments

Finally, some people may be candidates for surgical treatments to improve the steadiness, strength, or endurance of the voice. Such surgery offers individuals with vocal atrophy or vocal bowing the option to "plump up" their vocal folds with injectables for better vocal results (Caton, Thibeault, Klemuk, & Smith, 2007; Rosen et al., 2009), a procedure that is repeated periodically. Results are generally positive, but vary depending on the injection material used, the individual case, and the experience of the surgeon. See your otolaryngologist for further information regarding these procedures.

Summary

Demographics leave us with predictions for a growing number of active older adults who want to stay *vocally* active in the future, be it professionally or socially. A major goal should be to meet the long-term voice-related needs of this rapidly expanding population with efforts to educate this population about age-related voice changes and development of affordable behavioral as well as minimally invasive management options (Casper & Colton, 2000; Golub, et al., 2006; Roy, et al., 2007). The impetus to offer active seniors voice treatments that enhance quality of life is three-fold: (1) the presence of a proactive aging population that chooses to address vocal aging, (2) healthy aging through a physical and psychosocially active lifestyle as public health priority (CDC, 2009; PRB, 2007), and (3) refined treatments that have potential for meeting these demands. The aging voice should not signal the end of an active professional career as both preventative and treatment options are now available.

Bibliography

AssociatedPress. (2005). Active seniors demanding surgery Retrieved 03/03/2009, from http://www.msnbc.msn.com/id/7789139/

Bach, A. C., Lederer, F. L., & Dinolt, R. (1941). Senile changes in the laryngeal musculature. *Archives of Otolaryngology*, 34, 47-56.

Benninger, M. S., Ahuja, A. S., Gardner, G., & Grywalski, C. (1998). Assessing outcomes for dysphonic patients. *J Voice*, 12(4), 540-550.

Berg, E. E., Hapner, E., Klein, A., & Johns, M. M., 3rd. (2008). Voice therapy improves quality of life in age-related dysphonia: a case-control study. *J Voice*, 22(1), 70-74.

Biever Lowery, D. (1993). *Aerobic exercise effects on the post-menopausal voice*. Ph.D., University of Wisconsin-Madison, Madison, WI.

Casper, J. K., & Colton, R. H. (2000). Current understanding and treatment of phonatory disorders in geriatric populations. *Current Opinion in Otolaryngology & Head and Neck Surgery*, 8, 158-164.

Caton, T., Thibeault, S. L., Klemuk, S., & Smith, M. E. (2007). Viscoelasticity of Hyaluronan and Nonhyaluronan Based Vocal Fold Injectables: Implications for Mucosal Versus Muscle Use. *The Laryngoscope*, 117(3), 516-521.

CDC. (2009). *Promoting active lifestyles among older adults*. US Department of Health and Human Services Centers for Disease Control and Prevention Retrieved from http://www.cdc.gov/nccdphp/dnpa/physical/pdf/lifestyles.pdf.

Voice and Speech Science, Vocal Health
For Your Vocal Health: Keeping the Mature Voice Healthy
by Joseph C. Stemple and Maria Dietrich

Census. (2001). *Census 2000 Summary File 1 - United States.* Washington, D.C.: U.S. Census Bureau.

Coyle, S. M., Weinrich, B. D., & Stemple, J. C. (2001). Shifts in relative prevalence of laryngeal pathology in a treatment-seeking population. *Journal of Voice*, 15(3), 424-440.

Golub, J. S., Chen, P.-H., Otto, K. J., Hapner, E., & Johns, M. M. (2006). Prevalence of Perceived Dysphonia in a Geriatric Population. *Journal of the American Geriatrics Society*, 54(11), 1736-1739.

Gorman, S., Weinrich, B., Lee, L., & Stemple, J. C. (2008). Aerodynamic changes as a result of vocal function exercises in elderly men. *Laryngoscope*, 118(10), 1900-1903.

Gray, S. D., Hirano, M., & Sato, K. (1993). Molecular and cellular structure of vocal fold tissue. In I. R. Titze (Ed.), *Vocal Fold Physiology: Frontiers in Basic Science* (pp. 1-35). San Diego: Singular Publishing

Hagen, P., & Lyons, G. D. (1996). Dysphonia in the elderly: Diagnosis and management of age-related voice changes. *Southern Medical Journal*, 89(2), 204-207.

Hartman, D. E. (1979). The perceptual identity and characteristics of aging in normal male adult speakers. *J Commun Disord*, 12(1), 53-61.

Hartman, D. E., & Danahuer, J. L. (1976). Perceptual features of speech for males in four perceived age decades. *J Acoust Soc Am*, 59(3), 713-715.

Herrington-Hall, B. L., Lee, L., Stemple, J. C., Niemi, K. R., & McHone, M. M. (1988). Description of laryngeal pathologies by age, sex, and occupation in a treatment-seeking sample. *J Speech Hear Disord*, 53(1), 57-64.

Hirano, M. (1981). *Clinical Examination of Voice.* New York: Springer Verlag.

Hirano, M., & Kakita, Y. (1985). Cover-body theory of vocal fold vibration. In R. G. Daniloff (Ed.), *Speech Science: Recent Advances* (pp. 1-46). San Diego: College-Hill Press.

Hirano, M., Kurita, S., & Sakaguchi, S. (1989). Ageing of the vibratory tissue of human vocal folds. *Acta Otolaryngol*, 107(5-6), 428-433.

Hoit, J. D., & Hixon, T. J. (1987). Age and speech breathing. *J Speech Hear Res*, 30(3), 351-366.

Hoit, J. D., Hixon, T. J., Altman, M. E., & Morgan, W. J. (1989). Speech breathing in women. *J Speech Hear Res*, 32(2), 353-365.

Hollien, H., & Shipp, T. (1972). Speaking fundamental frequency and chronologic age in males. *J Speech Hear Res*, 15(1), 155-159.

Honjo, I., & Isshiki, N. (1980). Laryngoscopic and voice characteristics of aged persons. *Arch Otolaryngol*, 106(3), 149-150.

Israel, H. (1968). Continuing growth in the human cranial skeleton. *Arch Oral Biol*, 13(1), 133-137.

Israel, H. (1973). Age factor and the pattern of change in craniofacial structures. *Am J Phys Anthropol*, 39(1), 111-128.

Kahane, J. C. (1981). Anatomic and physiologic changes in the aging peripheral speech mechanism. In D. S. Beasley & G. A. Davis (Eds.), *Aging: Communication Processes and Disorders* (pp. 21-45). New York: Grune and Stratton.

Kahane, J. C. (1988). Histologic structure and properties of the human vocal folds. *Ear Nose Throat J*, 67(5), 322, 324-325, 329-330.

Kandogan, T., Olgun, L., & Gultekin, G. (2003). Causes of dysphonia in patients above 60 years of age. *Kulak Burun Bogaz Ihtis Derg*, 11(5), 139-143.

Kotby, M. N., El-Sady, S. R., Basiouny, S. E., Abou-Rass, Y. A., & Hegazi, M. A. (1991). Efficacy of the accent method of voice therapy. *Journal of Voice*, 5, 316-320.

Krischke, S., Weigelt, S., Hoppe, U., Kollner, V., Klotz, M., Eysholdt, U., & Rosanowski, F. (2005). Quality of life in dysphonic patients. *J Voice*, 19(1), 132-137.

Lasker, G. W. (1953). The age factor in bodily measurements of adult male and female Mexicans. *Hum Biol*, 25(1), 50-63.

Leslie, P., Drinnan, M. J., Ford, G. A., & Wilson, J. A. (2005). Swallow respiratory patterns and aging: presbyphagia or dysphagia? *J Gerontol A Biol Sci Med Sci*, 60(3), 391-395.

Linville, S. E., & Fisher, H. B. (1985). Acoustic characteristics of perceived versus actual vocal age in controlled phonation by adult females. *J Acoust Soc Am, 78*(1 Pt 1), 40-48.

Lundy, D. S., Silva, C., Casiano, R., Lu, F. L., & Xue, J. W. (1998). Cause of hoarseness in elderly patients. *Otolaryngology - Head and Neck Surgery, 118*(4), 481-485.

Miller, M. K., & Verdolini, K. (1995). Frequency and risk factors for voice problems in teachers of singing and control subjects. *J Voice, 9*(4), 348-362.

Mortland, S. (2006). Orthopedic boom continues; More active lifestyle in aging population, improved surgical techniques lead to local hospitals beefing up their operations in order to keep pace. (St. Vincent Charity Hospital)(University Hospitals Geauga Medical Center)(Cleveland Clinic)." Retrieved 03/03/2009, from http://www.highbeam.com/doc/1G1-154155728.html

Mueller, P. B., Sweeney, R. J., & Baribeau, L. J. (1984). Acoustic and morphologic study of the senescent voice. *Ear Nose Throat J, 63*(6), 292-295.

Mueller, P. B., Sweeney, R. J., & Baribeau, L. J. (1985). Senescence of the voice: morphology of excised male larynges. *Folia Phoniatr (Basel), 37*(3-4), 134-138.

Murry, T., Medrado, R., Hogikyan, N. D., & Aviv, J. E. (2004). The relationship between ratings of voice quality and quality of life measures. *J Voice, 18*(2), 183-192.

Mysak, E. D., & Hanley, T. D. (1959). Vocal aging. *Geriatrics, 14*, 652-656.

NIA. (2009). *Americans living longer, enjoying greater health and prosperity, but important disparities remain, says Federal Report.* National Institute on Aging Retrieved from http://www.nia.nih.gov/NewsAndEvents/PressReleases/PR20080327OlderAmericans.htm.

PRB. (2007). *Healthy aging.* Population Reference Bureau Retrieved from http://www.prb.org/pdf07/TodaysResearchAging1.pdf.

Ptacek, P. H., & Sander, E. K. (1966). Age recognition from voice. *J Speech Hear Res, 9*(2), 273-277.

Reulbach, T. R., Belafsky, P. C., Blalock, P. D., Koukman, J. A., & Postma, G. N. (2001). Occult laryngeal pathology in a community-based cohort. *Otolaryngology - Head and Neck Surgery, 124*(4), 448-450.

Robbins, J., Hamilton, J. W., Lof, G. L., & Kempster, G. B. (1992). Oropharyngeal swallowing in normal adults of different ages. *Gastroenterology, 103*(3), 823-829.

Rosen, C. A., Gartner-Schmidt, J., Casiano, R., Anderson, T. D., Johnson, F., Remacle, M., . . . Zraick, R. I. (2009). Vocal fold augmentation with calcium hydroxylapatite: twelve-month report. *Laryngoscope, 119*(5), 1033-1041.

Roy, N., Merrill, R. M., Thibeault, S., Gray, S. D., & Smith, E. M. (2004). Voice disorders in teachers and the general population: effects on work performance, attendance, and future career choices. *J Speech Lang Hear Res, 47*(3), 542-551.

Roy, N., Merrill, R. M., Thibeault, S., Parsa, R. A., Gray, S. D., & Smith, E. M. (2004). Prevalence of voice disorders in teachers and the general population. *J Speech Lang Hear Res, 47*(2), 281-293.

Roy, N., Stemple, J., Merrill, R. M., & Thomas, L. (2007). Epidemiology of voice disorders in the elderly: preliminary findings. *Laryngoscope, 117*(4), 628-633.

Ryan, E. B., & Capadano, H. L., 3rd. (1978). Age perceptions and evaluative reactions toward adult speakers. *J Gerontol, 33*(1), 98-102.

Ryan, W. J., & Burk, K. W. (1974). Perceptual and acoustic correlates of aging in the speech of males. *J Commun Disord, 7*(2), 181-192.

Sato, K., Hirano, M., & Nakashima, T. (2002). Age-related changes of collagenous fibers in the human vocal fold mucosa. *Ann Otol Rhinol Laryngol, 111*(1), 15-20.

Schneider, B., & Bigenzahn, W. (2005). Vocal risk factors for occupational voice disorders in female teaching students. *Eur Arch Otorhinolaryngol, 262*(4), 272-276.

Segre, R. (1971). Senescence of the voice. *Eye Ear Nose Throat Mon, 50*(6), 223-227.

Shipp, T., & Hollien, H. (1969). Perception of the aging male voice. *J Speech Hear Res, 12*(4), 703-710.

Smith, E., Gray, S. D., Dove, H., Kirchner, L., & Heras, H. (1997). Frequency and effects of teachers' voice problems. *J Voice*, 11(1), 81-87.

Smith, E., Kirchner, H. L., Taylor, M., Hoffman, H., & Lemke, J. H. (1998). Voice problems among teachers: differences by gender and teaching characteristics. *J Voice*, 12(3), 328-334.

Smith, E., Lemke, J., Taylor, M., Kirchner, H. L., & Hoffman, H. (1998). Frequency of voice problems among teachers and other occupations. *J Voice*, 12(4), 480-488.

Smith, E., Verdolini, K., Gray, S., Nichols, S., Lemke, J., Barkmeier, J., . . . Hoffman, H. (1996). Effect of voice disorders on quality of life. *Journal of Medical Speech-Language Pathology*, 4(4), 223-244.

Sonies, B. C. (1992). Oropharyngeal dysphagia in the elderly. *Clin Geriatr Med*, 8(3), 569-577.

Stemple, J. (2006). *Vocal Function Exercises*. San Diego: Plural Publishing.

Thibeault, S. L., Hirschi, S. D., & Gray, S. D. (2003). DNA microarray gene expression analysis of a vocal fold polyp and granuloma. *J Speech Lang Hear Res, 46*(2), 491-502.
Thibeault, S. L., Merrill, R. M., Roy, N., Gray, S. D., & Smith, E. M. (2004). Occupational risk factors associated with voice disorders among teachers. *Ann Epidemiol*, 14(10), 786-792.

Thomas, L. B., Harrison, A. L., & Stemple, J. C. (2008). Aging thyroarytenoid and limb skeletal muscle: lessons in contrast. *J Voice*, 22(4), 430-450.

Titze, I. R. (1994). *Principles of Voice Production*. Englewood Cliffs, NJ: Prentice-Hall.

UMHS. (2008). Big boom in boomer knee replacement surgeries at earlier age Retrieved 03/03/2009, from http://www2.med.umich.edu/prmc/media/newsroom/details.cfm?ID=333

Verdolini Abbott, K. (2008). *Lessac-Madsen Resonant Voice Therapy*. San Diego: Plural Publishing.

Verdolini, K., & Ramig, L. O. (2001). Review: occupational risks for voice problems. *Logoped Phoniatr Vocol*, 26(1), 37-46.

Verdolini, K., Rosen, C. A., & Branski, R. C. (Eds.). (2005). *Classification Manual for Voice Disorders* - 1. Mahwah, NJ: Erlbaum.

Verdonck-de Leeuw, I. M., & Mahieu, H. F. (2004). Vocal aging and the impact on daily life: a longitudinal study. *J Voice, 18*(2), 193-202.

Williams, N. R. (2003). Occupational groups at risk of voice disorders: a review of the literature. *Occup Med (Lond), 53*(7), 456-460.

Wilson, J. A., Deary, I. J., Millar, A., & Mackenzie, K. (2002). The quality of life impact of dysphonia. *Clin Otolaryngol Allied Sci, 27*(3), 179-182.

Woo, P., Casper, J., Colton, R., & Brewer, D. (1992). Dysphonia in the aging: physiology versus disease. *Laryngoscope, 102*(2), 139-144.

Zemlin, W. (1988). *Speech and hearing science: Anatomy and physiology* (3rd ed.). Englewood Cliffs, NJ: Prentice-Hall.

Essay *by Ronald C. Scherer and Melissa Volk*
Research on Public Speaking

Melissa Volk (Maas) received her bachelor's degree in Communication Disorders from Bowling Green State University in 2008 and her master's degree in Speech Language Pathology from Bowling Green State University in 2010. Melissa is currently employed as a Speech Pathologist at MetroHealth's Skilled Nursing Facility in Cleveland, Ohio. Special interests include neurological rehabilitation, voice, fluency, and bridging the gap for clinical application between the daily variance of the swallow function and what is shown on dysphagia evaluations.

Dr. Ron Scherer: *See Editorial Column*

Introduction

To address the importance of public speaking training and skills, the Voice Foundation Symposium in 2009 included a session entitled "The Speaking Voice: What You Need to Know About Speaking in Public" organized by Nancy Pearl Solomon. It featured Diane DiResta, Deborah Rosen, and Susan Miller[FN1], whose professions deal with public speaking training and concerns, and panelists Donna Snow, John Rubin[FN2], and myself (RS). I was asked to present the final short talk to emphasize what research there was on public speaking and suggest directions for the future. One of our master's students interested in voice research, Melissa Volk, the co-author here, was currently a teaching assistant in a section of our university's public speaking course, a requirement of most students at BGSU, so I invited her to join me in this task. It was obvious to me that we would find research on many topics about how to give good speeches and be a proficient public speaker, including, of course, appropriate voice and speech production, *per se*. How wrong I was about the latter!

Research Topics in Public Speaking

We scoured research data bases for journals (see Appendix A) and articles and found that most of the research on public speaking centered around anxiety (anxiety, social phobia, apprehension, stage fright, performance anxiety), followed by topics such as nonverbal aspects (gestures, facial expression, eye contact), preparation, feedback, instruction methods, attitude change, arousal styles, visual aids, gender and competence, and 21 other topics (see Appendix B).

Conspicuously *missing* were topics on voice and speech production characteristics, respiration, acoustics, aerodynamics, perception, etc., as well as training of voice and speech characteristics for public speaking. This seemed rather odd, given that effective public speaking would appear to require highly audible, intelligible, and interpretational voice and speech production. Obviously members of VASTA who work with public speaking and other non-members train individuals to be highly proficient in these regards; it is just that there is scant published research.

However, there are numerous areas of research that indirectly address aspects of effective public speaking from a voice and speech production point of view. These include studies in "clear speech", where research articles have been published dealing with speaking rate, speaking mode, intelligibility, coarticulation, perception, phonetic invariance, articulation and vowels, etc., usually with an acoustic methodology. Furthermore, there is a wealth of studies that do not address public speaking *per se*, but have given us much basic information pertinent to the voice and speech mechanism, especially relative to voice quality, speakers' and actors' formants, vocal expression of emotion and depression, the voice source, expressive speech, voice disorders, technology, and 28 other primary topics in recent years (see Appendix C).

Funding Sources Related to Public Speaking

Perhaps the lack of research in voice and speech production in public speaking is due to funding difficulties so that researchers are not attracted. We therefore attempted to determine all of the (primarily American) funding agencies that potentially might fund such research. We came up with the Axe-Houghton Foundation, the American Society for Theatre Research, the National Humanities Alliance – NEH, the Voice Foundation, the American Council of Learned Societies, the National Speaker's Association, and 18 other viable sources (see Appendix D). If you are interested in being funded in such research, you might consider looking into these.

Voice and Speech Science, Vocal Health
Research on Public Speaking by Ronald C. Scherer and Melissa Volk

Dealing with Production Research in Public Speaking

Public speaking is a complex field. Relative to potential research into voice and speech production, as well as training, public speaking is or should be highly influenced by four specific areas, namely, the maintenance of high levels of health and the science of voice and speech production pathologies, the borrowing of research designs and goals from the science of clear speech as well as normal speech, and the pedagogy of performance voice and speech for the stage (see Figure 1). Strategies to study effective public speaking from a sound production point of view need to include methodologies from the research in these four areas, for public speaking appears to be an integration of them all that results in a unique identity.

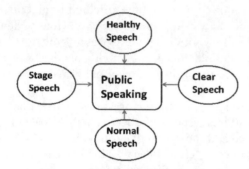

Figure 1. Connections to Public Speaking

An Integrative Structure For Public Speaking Research

Both the speaker and the audience member come to a "public speaking talk" with needs, expectations, and goals relative to the talk (see Figure 2). The speaker has the need to communicate a particular message, and may be motivated by numerous influences, especially and typically the need to satisfy some perceived audience desire. The speaker's goal will be to inform, persuade, and/or entertain. The audience member also comes to the talk with his or her own special needs, expectations for the potential gain from the talk, anticipations from the experience of being at the talk, and in general has the goals of learning, growing, being entertained, and other personal or professional gains.

SPEAKER (Producer)	AUDIENCE (Perceiver)
Needs	Needs
Motivations	Expectations
Satisfy Audience Needs	Anticipations
Goals: Inform, Persuade, Entertain	Goals: Learn, Grow, Be entertained, etc.

Figure 2. Speaker and audience member

Voice and Speech Production

It is within this broad context that we now should consider a research structure into which studies of voice and speech production can be imbedded. What would constitute a useful research orientation? The simplest and quite effective approach would be to determine an important characteristic the audience member requires and a corresponding plausible production variable of the speaker, and link them in a study. For example, take a variable such as audibility. We might recognize that audibility on the audience member's part should be highly related to the loudness of the speaker. So the research design would have the speaker give a portion or all of his or her speech, and alter the loudness three times so that it was directly altered by technology or perhaps even by the speaker, so that three different audiences (of reasonable size) each would hear a different loudness with all other characteristics of the production (delivery) held as constant as possible. Here, then, loudness is the variable that is *parameterized* (three different values) and audibility is a *dependent variable* (in that the audibility rating depends on what the audience member hears). The audience member would be asked to rate how easy it was to hear the speaker (audibility). But they might be asked to rate other factors in addition to audibility such as speaker credibility, how well the message was understood, how well they accepted the speaker and the message, etc. In this way, the research would be on a production variable (loudness) and the effect of intentionally changing loudness would give rise to audience reactions relative to basic perception (audibility) as well as aspects important to the general public speaking situation (speaker credibility and acceptance, message understanding, etc.). Thus, this is a general and effective research approach: choose important *production variables*, *parameterize them* into different levels, *present each level* to the same or different groups of people, and *obtain reactions* (usually ratings of some sort) by the audience members. These reactions can be relative to a wide assortment of important speaker-audience factors.

Another speaker production variable of interest, for example, is the speaker's voice quality. This can be parameterized in steps (varied in logical and reasonable ways) for the listener's rating of pleasantness, distraction, etc. The speaker's articulation can be parameterized (less specific to more specific) for the listener's judgment of intelligibility. The speaker's use of prosodics (pitch contour, loudness contour, use of durations and pauses) can be altered in many ways for the listener's judgment of interest, naturalness, etc. (Figure 3)

Other Categories of Interest

This same approach can be used with the more typical categories of known interest in public speaking.

For example, one could vary (parameterize) the speaker's message content in specific ways for the listener's rating of understanding. Indications of the speaker's expertise (credentials, knowledge, competence, warmth, honesty, enthusiasm, appearance, confidence) could be parameterized in specific (logical) steps for the listener's rating of credibility (trustworthiness, believability, acceptance) (Figure 3).

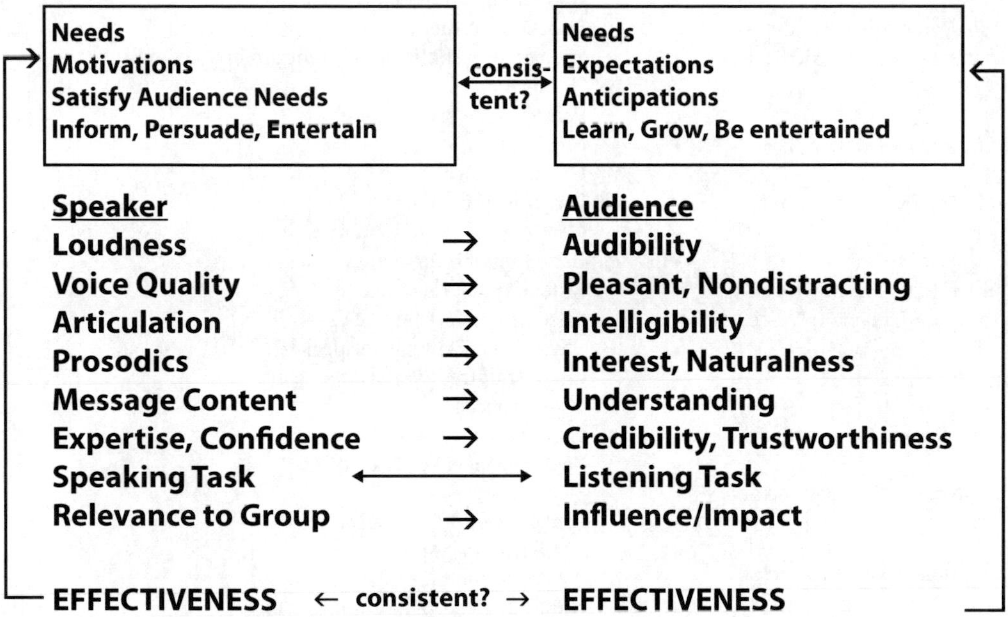

could be altered and presented to different groups, and then each group rate characteristics such as influence and impact (behavioral, attitudinal, emotional, skill-based, knowledge-based, and importance).

The overall judgment of a good public talk is the general effectiveness of the talk (Figure 3). The effectiveness for the speaker relates to all of the factors that go into the talk (preparation, delivery) relative to the speaker's original notions of needs, motivation, audience satisfaction, and the desire to inform, persuade, and entertain. Likewise, the general effectiveness for the listener is whether or not the talk was effective in matching the listener's original needs, expectations, anticipations, and desire to learn, grow, or be entertained. The goal in all good public speaking is to match, or exceed, the effectiveness of the speaker relative to the effectiveness for the listener so everyone goes away from the talk highly satisfied.

Needs Motivations Satisfy Audience Needs Inform, Persuade, Entertain	consis- tent?	Needs Expectations Anticipations Learn, Grow, Be entertained

Speaker		**Audience**
Loudness	→	Audibility
Voice Quality	→	Pleasant, Nondistracting
Articulation	→	Intelligibility
Prosodics	→	Interest, Naturalness
Message Content	→	Understanding
Expertise, Confidence	→	Credibility, Trustworthiness
Speaking Task	←——→	Listening Task
Relevance to Group	→	Influence/Impact

EFFECTIVENESS ← consistent? → **EFFECTIVENESS**

Figure 3. General research design. The speaker variables on the left would be parameterized, and the audience reactions on the right would be ratings or judgements.

There is an additional speaker-audience connection that deserves research attention. This could be called the speaker task associated with the listener task. The speaker's task is to prepare and organize material for the talk (find supporting sources, prepare strategies for clarity and interest and remembering), apply learning principles, choose the best words and word structures, deal with performance anxiety and related physiological responses, prepare visual and auditory aids, deal with audience interaction strategies, prepare nonverbal behaviors, and plan the desired speaking style and delivery methods, as well as (and quite importantly) determine the level of emotional display that would seem appropriate and the level of ethical concern in dealing with the message. These could all be parameterized in meaningful ways. The listener's task would be to judge the obvious presentation elements in the speaker's list (supportive information, choice of how the information is conveyed, the speaker's apparent memory, appropriateness or distractibility of the use of nonverbal gestures, effect of perceived level of anxiety, etc.) as being appropriate for the talk.

Another primary area of concern that could be parameterized for the speaker and rated by the listener is the relevance of the talk to the audience. The potential relevance

Conclusion

There is a dearth of research in voice and speech production for public speaking. This is surprising given the economic and cultural importance of professional public speaking around the world. This short essay highlights a simple research structure and approach that relates voice and speech production for public speaking to a variety of listener response categories. The structure encourages choosing relevant variables that can be parameterized for the speaker and evaluated by the listener for levels and types of effects and influence. It presupposes that inadequate voice and speech production elements are detrimental to the impact and effectiveness of a talk, and that the study of these factors will bring about better pedagogies for public speaking training and more satisfying, effective, and healthy professional and avocational communication experiences for both the speaker and the audience.

It is recommended that voice and speech trainers and coaches collaborate with those in the communication sciences and with voice and speech scientists to carry out viable and useful research projects that enhance the science and the art of public speaking.

Voice and Speech Science, Vocal Health
Research on Public Speaking by Ronald C. Scherer and Melissa Volk

Acknowledgements

The authors would like to thank Lucille Rubin for a generous early communication on this topic and Nancy Solomon for helpful suggestions on the manuscript.

Footnotes

FN1:

a. Nancy Pearl Solomon, Ph.D., CCC-SLP, Research Speech Pathologist, Army Audiology & Speech Center, Walter Reed Army Medical Center, Washington, DC

b. Diane DiResta, founder of DiResta Communications, Inc., NYC

c. Deborah Rosen, Ph.D., Director of Healthcare Outreach, Temple University Health Care System

d. Susan Miller, Ph.D., founder of Voicetrainer, LLC, Washington, DC, and Clinical Associate for the George Washington University Voice Treatment Center, Washington, DC

FN2:

a. Donna Snow, M.F.A., Theatre Department, Temple University

b. John Rubin, M.D., Royal National Throat, Nose & Ear Hospital and University College, London

APPENDIX A: List of journals that publish public speaking articles:

- Journal of Voice
- Journal of the Acoustical Society of America
- Journal of Speech, Language, Hearing Research
- Speech Communication
- Cognition & Emotion
- Voice and Speech Review (VASTA)
- Communication Education
- Communication Quarterly
- Communication Research Reports
- System
- Journal of Language & Social Psychology
- Folia Phoniatrica et Logopaedica
- Logopedics Phoniatrics Vocology
- The Volta Review
- Sprache-Stimme-Gehor
- American Journal of Speech Language Pathology
- Language and Speech
- Journal of Phonetics
- Journal of Medical Speech Language Pathology
- Acta Acustica united with Acustica

APPENDIX B. List of topics in public speaking research:

- Anxiety/apprehension/stage fright/ performance anxiety
- Anxiety and/ competence, preparation, type of speech, habituation (changes in anxiety),
- Anticipatory, assumed, audience acceptability (perceptions), audience perception,
- Anxiety reduction, self perceived competence, audience, treatment
- Nonverbals/Gestures/Facial expression/eye contact

APPENDIX B (continued)

- Preparation
- Feedback
- Instructional methods
- Attitude change
- Arousal styles
- Visual aids
- Gender and competence
- Impact on audience
- Presentation skills for different professions
- "Eloquence"
- Performance visualization
- Media use
- Use of humor
- Persuasive speaking
- Confidence
- Retention of information
- Listener rate preference
- Effects of dialects and accents
- Physiological change in speaker
- Linguistic stress/variety
- Group speech
- Content & Delivery
- Posture & Speaker Credibility
- Stereotypes
- Pedagogy on Public Speaking
- Audience attention
- Audience characteristics
- Cultural effects on speaking style

APPENDIX C: Research topics related to speech and voice that do not address public speaking:

- Clear speech
  –speaking rate; speaking mode; intelligibility; visual; coarticulation; perception; phonetic; invariance; in noise; bilingual; articulation & vowels; language & timing
- Voice Quality
  –sarcasm; adduction and trained subjects; emotion/mood/attitude
- Speaker's Formant/Actor's Formant
- Technology
- Resonant Voice & therapy
- Vocal expression of emotion & depression
- Voice source
- Expressive speech
- Voice disorders
- Vocal hygiene
- Effects of voice training
- Pulmonary function
- Production & perception
- Vocal warm up
- Different professions' voices: broadcasters; radio professionals; voice-over; physicians; nurses; aerobic instructor; actors
- Teachers & voice; various measures & conditions; vocal health; voice training
- Perceived voice robustness
- Effect of humming
- Speech & stress conditions
- Speaking style
- Speech melody

APPENDIX C (continued):

- Speaker's ring
- Voice range profile
- Prosody & training for successful communication
- Vocal fatigue/ endurance
- Voice therapy
- Perception of talker characteristics
- Speaker size related to voice
- Therapy outcomes for professional voice users
- Influence of room acoustics
- Vocal loading/ Dosimetry
- Phonatory effort
- Phonation threshold pressure
- Occupational voice
- Stress & anxiety
- Medical Problems
- Dehydration

APPENDIX D: Agencies that may be appropriate funding sources for public speaking:

- Axe-Houghton Foundation
- American Society for Theatre Research
- National Humanities Alliance-NEH funding
- Voice Foundation
- American Council of Learned Societies
- National Speaker's Association
- Dispute Resolution Research Center Postdoctoral Fellowship
- Kellogg Team and Group Research Center Postdoctoral Fellowship
- Metcalf Institute Diversity Fellowships in Environmental Reporting
- Multi-Arts Production Fund Grants
- White House Fellows Leadership & Public Service Fellowship
- Educational Foundation of America Grants
- Freedom of Expression Foundation (Institusjonen Fritt Ord) Grants
- Arthur W. Page Center at Penn State College of Communications Page and Johnson
- Legacy Scholar Grants
- Corporation for Public Broadcasting Greenhouse Fund Grants
- Council for Advancement and Support of Education Alice L. Beeman Research Awards
- Academy of Television Arts & Sciences Fred Rogers Memorial Scholarships
- National Science Foundation Perception, Action and Cognition Grants
- National Science Foundation Linguistic Grants
- National Education Association Foundation Learning and Leadership Grants
- National Institutes of Health/ National Institute on Aging- Archiving and Development of
- Socialbehavioral Datasets in Aging Related Studies
- New York Community Trust Grants
- Stanford University John S. Knight Fellowships

Singing, *Joan Melton, Associate Editor*

Joan Melton is a pioneer in the integration of Singing Techniques and Voice/Movement Training for the Actor. The author of *Singing in Musical Theatre: The Training of Singers and Actors* **(Allworth 2007), and with Kenneth Tom, PhD, of** *One Voice: Integrating Singing Technique and Theatre Voice Training* **(Heinemann 2003), she trained at the Central School of Speech and Drama, London, holds a PhD from UNC, Chapel Hill, and has taught at leading drama and music centers in the US, UK, Ireland, Australia, and New Zealand. She currently heads groundbreaking research projects in the US and Australia.**

Contributing authors for this section come from widely different parts of the globe: Singapore to Sydney, New York to Boca Raton, Los Angeles to Brisbane. And their essays and articles span the world of singing from Gregorian chant to crossover techniques in the twenty-first century.

One particularly intriguing discovery highlighted in my own research over the past few years is that what we do as performers is not simple. Nor is it formulaic, as in "one size fits all." Hence, I am delighted by the first two pieces, which exemplify that discovery magnificently.

Amanda Colliver is a remarkable performer and teacher who spent 20 years as a leading member of opera companies in Australia. She now heads Paper Kite Studios in Singapore, writes and sings her own material, and is the author of a new book, *Can Anybody Sing?* Her unique view is expressed succinctly in "Sound is a Symbol."

Pat Wilson is a consummate artist, writer, teacher and researcher who, with her husband, director Adrian Barnes, run Springboards Performing Arts, in Sydney. Always speaking from the inside out, Pat takes us to the leading

edge of current research on performance training in her article, "Act, Sing, Speak: Voice in the World of Theatre."

The next two essays address specific pedagogical concerns and suggest creative answers for studio and classroom application, respectively.

Neil Semer is an extraordinary teacher of singing. Based in NYC, he teaches internationally and works with singers from a wide range of performance genres. "The Three Word Diet" is a prescription for singers who have difficulty getting "out of their heads."

Laura Wayth is a gifted young actor/teacher who integrates singing into her theatre voice classes at Florida Atlantic University. In "Reinvesting in Language: The Use of Singing in Verse Text Exploration," she offers exercises to help the actor find "a visceral connection to both the qualities and the structure of language."

The final two pieces were written quite independently by authors on two different continents. Yet they seem distinctly related, as the essay takes up where the article leaves off.

Heather Lyle is a working singer—with an eight-piece band—as well as a teacher in the Los Angeles area. Her fascinating article, "A Historical Look at Breathing Methods for Singing," helps to clarify some of the diversity we all encounter in approaches to breath management. Heather takes us on a journey through Italian treatises, pedagogical disagreements, and finally to the advent of research into vocal styles outside the classical milieu.

Also an active performer, Sean Andrews is a crossover artist much in demand, both in opera and in musical theatre. In his essay, "The World of Vocal Crossover," he writes with insight and honesty about the vocal challenges facing singers who can and do work in more than one genre.

Interacting with each of these authors has been an honor and privilege.

Essay *by Amanda Colliver*

Sound is a Symptom

Amanda Colliver began her career as a songwriter/recording artist in commercials and film. She was a Young Artist for the Victoria State Opera in 1989, and boasts a twenty year career as a soloist with all of the major opera companies and orchestras in Australia. Amanda is a top vocal trainer in theatre today, preparing such stars as Hugh Jackman, Nicole Kidman and Ewan McGregor for *Beauty and the Beast* and *Moulin Rouge*, respectively. Now a freelance artist heading Paper Kite Studios, she is writing her first book, *Can Anybody Sing?* and recording her second original album.

There are many schools of thought on how to achieve great singing, and although most will generally agree on what wonderful vocal results are, the methodologies used to achieve them are diverse and arguable. Although sound manifests as an external experience for the listener, it is an internal and often intangible or nebulous experience for the singer. Many try to create sound through external means, but in fact the vocal mechanism is housed within the body and therefore it can only be created from the inside out. What then will guide us to the right answers when sound is invisible and coming from within? The simple answer is by the sensation of the required result, but the complex answer lies in understanding what the required result is in the first place. All action begins with a concept, but unless the action or outcome is understood, it will remain just that, a concept. Equally, for one to consciously manipulate muscles is to misunderstand how they organize and coordinate themselves. Instead, a fascinating and complex process of autosuggestion is at play, where thought is converted to sound and sound is converted to experience. Under analysis this can become confusing and overly complicated, as transferring experience into the limitations of language is, in my opinion, a teacher's greatest challenge.

The desire to sing is the pull to return to who we truly are.

Some things are universal. Music heals, nourishes and has the power to transcend separation. For some, singing has been a cultural expression for centuries, but for others, an empty space waiting to be filled. Pure, unadulterated potential, your voice waits to be invited to the party of your imagination, happy to rise and fall with your sorrow and joy, or randomly laugh and play for no reason at all. Your voice will reveal you, leaving you naked and unsure, but in that vulnerability, you will find a freedom unlike any other experience. To fear your voice is to fear yourself and in my opinion, that simply cannot be justified. Best of all, your voice belongs only to you.

What is largely overlooked in our quest to sing is why we make sound in the first place.

In the beginning there was sound, and in that sound was life. From the time we were created until the time we cease to be, we will express ourselves through a myriad of vocal pitches and dynamics for a multitude of reasons, and at one time or another we will scream, weep, yell, grunt, groan, moan, whine, whisper, sob, sigh and laugh. The primary reason we are given a vocal mechanism is to communicate, which at the most primal level secures our chances for survival. Why then do we question our ability to breathe, support, project, pitch, animate, articulate and resonate, when these are the technical components integral to the coordination and manifestation of sound? Perhaps one of the reasons is the way in which we learn language and the lack of conscious awareness needed to do it. For example, when a baby screams it doesn't think about how to project the sound, but rather, the desire for attention instructs the body to form the necessary vocal energy to meet his or her needs. When the baby progresses from raw sound to the specific articulation needed to form words, it will mimic what it hears without the need to understand how it is achieving it.

It is the desire behind the intention that creates the physical coordination necessary for communication, making sound a symptom of that desire.

The difficulties many singers experience today are due to the failure to understand that singing is an extension of speech, just as running is an extension of walking. Unfortunately this allows us to form false conclusions that lead to unnecessary actions. The motivation behind speaking and singing is fundamentally the same, and they are simply *variations* on a theme. One misunderstanding amongst singers is that there is one generic shape for each vowel sound. If we look at speech patterns we will find that when at a lower dynamic in the lower range the mouth shapes become smaller, and when at a higher dynamic in the higher range more space is required. Breath, support, placement, range, tone, volume and projection are all organized by

295

Sound is a Symptom by Amanda Colliver

the requirements of the result. It is simply not possible to measure this intellectually, so they must be allowed to organize and coordinate themselves. If we look at the order in which we do things, we will find that sound begins with the *thought* of what I want to say which organizes the *space* needed to voice it, followed by the *shape* and *sound* of the language. Even with physiological knowledge, it's impossible to see our own vocal process at work, so any attempt to measure or manipulate shapes or placement out of context interrupts the delicate inner process of communication.

Learning to sing is the unlearning of the barriers that prevent free flowing sound.

By and large we are conditioned by what we see externally in the form of shapes, color, texture and distance. The analytical mind processes it until it believes it knows what it is and what it means and this perception creates our experiences. For example, when we see a keyboard or manuscript with notation, we see distance, or what we call intervals. This is merely a structure created for reading music and not at all indicative of the real distance between notes. Sound is a continuum as are water and air, and as their very nature is *flow*, they cannot be broken or lost, but they can be interrupted and blocked. As we generally experience the world in a finite and external way, the conscious mind finds this hard to comprehend, and a struggle begins between the analytical mind and organic action. It is not enough to be told that distance is an illusion and cannot be measured, so we need to understand that if a vocal result is unstable, the execution of that action cannot have been correct. Although each individual will describe it differently, there are definite sensations connected to a sound that is well placed and flowing freely, just as there are definite emotions connected to upper and lower frequencies. Higher notes are informed by extreme emotions like passion, joy, laughter and rage, and lower notes by more intimate and speech-like intentions. The nature of these emotions helps to create the correct degree of muscular activity, which moves the emphasis from intellectual analysis to a more intuitive approach.

Freedom is grounded in all things positive, constriction is grounded in fear.

If sound is a symptom of the human condition and we are largely unaware of what we do and how we do it, the challenge is to become more conscious of our thoughts and actions. The job of a teacher is to act as a *bridge* while we learn to become the master of our own instruments. However, teachers cannot do it for us, so personal responsibility becomes a non-negotiable element. This effectively places singing in the metaphysical arena of Personal Development and Inner Alignment. Every thought we have about ourselves manifests into energy. Fear creates negativity, which compromises the body and therefore the freedom of the voice. Although none of us consciously decides to

be negative about our voices, we are often complacent when it comes to working on behavioral patterns that don't serve us in positive ways. There isn't anyone who knows everything just as there isn't anyone who knows nothing at all. Therefore it is essential to validate your achievements before moving towards improving your knowledge and skills. Integration cannot occur without validation. Although singing is, in fact, a physical skill, it is motivated by the mind. If the mind is unfocused and fearful, it clouds the messages to the body and your voice becomes a victim of this negative frame of mind. Fear is not always easy to pinpoint or resolve, and in this current era of superficiality and limitation, we have almost come to accept fear as being normal. Spontaneity, creativity, imagination and joy live in the realm of intuition as intuition encourages freedom without judgment. Children live in this place until parental, religious, cultural or educational conditioning teaches them to mistrust it and turn to things of a more *tangible* nature. Intuition is not only about imagination and play, but is the deep, inner voice that encourages us to aspire to levels of greatness despite our conditioning.

In the silence lie the subtleties and in the subtleties lie the answers.

Some of us choose to live simply in peaceful surroundings that imbue harmony and healing, but most live and work in crowded cities amongst nonstop stimulus and abrasive vibrations. Many love the energy and excitement of these conditions, but in a world that is becoming increasingly externally fixated, peaceful environments are becoming increasingly difficult to find. It is now completely acceptable to be hooked up to some computerized gadget, or phone 24/7, and extraneous noise has become societies' *security blanket*. This is not necessarily a bad thing in itself, but the absence of silence and contemplation can prevent the development of self-awareness and intuition. Every day I observe students struggling with their breathing without understanding that what they're doing is completely unnatural. As breathing is an automatic reflex action, it is not necessary to pay attention to it to stay alive. However, stress and anxiety result in muscular constriction and compromise the natural flow of breath. By tuning into the way we breathe, we begin to see the order in which things occur. The way we think creates an emotional impulse, which dictates the state of the breath, which is then converted into sound. Therefore we must understand the importance of turning inward to the elements that motivate and support the outward action of singing. This cannot be experienced or understood without an environment conducive to contemplation and silence.

No one is ordinary and uninspiring; we simply learn to be that way.

I have often heard it said, "You either have it or you don't." What exactly it is that one does or doesn't have is the subject of endless debate. We are all on the merry-go-round of life, but each of us is at a different stage of development. Our reality is experienced through our perception of the world and how we move in it, so it is not hard to understand that sound becomes a symptom of the way we perceive ourselves. No matter what level of skill we have achieved, it is still part of the human condition to seek encouragement and support. To tell a sapling that it will never become a tree is to risk stunting its growth. To tell students that they do not have the capacity to express themselves is to deny them the creative potential that belongs to us all. Apart from the inherent differences of every individual, fear is the only limitation there is. Those who communicate fearlessly are authentic and aligned with who they truly are, making them powerful and charismatic communicators. Those who don't, are simply unable to see that they too possess light, they too have the right to be heard, and they too have the ability to shine.

Act, Sing, Speak: Voice in the World of Theatre

Pat Wilson is a singing teacher who specializes in music theatre and lives in Sydney, Australia. Initially trained in classical singing and piano, she also works as a singer, actor, composer, musical director and voice researcher. Currently teaching at the Australian International Conservatorium of Music and Springboards Performing Arts, as well as in her own studio, she is the author of *The Singing Voice: An Owner's Manual* and *How to Sing and See: Singing Pedagogy in the Digital Era*, co-authored with Dr. Jean Callaghan. Visit her websites at www.patwilson.com.au and www.spans.net.au.

"The act of speaking literally turns you inside-out. Your voice travels from the deepest center on its way towards the outer world and carries with it the qualities of your inner world." Robert L. Benedetti (1939 -), American actor, director and teacher

"Words are beautiful but restricted. They're very masculine, with a compact frame. But voice is over the dark, the place where there's nothing to hang on: it comes from a part of yourself that simply knows, expresses itself, and is." Jeff Buckley (1966 – 1997), American singer-songwriter and guitarist

Introduction

The defining sound of theatre is vocal. With the exception of mime, human phonation lies at the heart of all theatre art-forms, where the stories of our many tribes are recounted in spoken or sung sounds—mostly organized into intelligible language. The expertise of professional voice practitioners is demanded in a number of specialist areas within the world of theatre. From the initial training of performers' voices through to coaching for auditions or coaching as part of the rehearsal process in productions of live theatre (as well as radio, television and film), and on

to specialist training for the acquisition of accents, dialects and languages other than the performer's native tongue, the work of professional voice practitioners in theatre is diverse and demanding. An additional (and vital) area of work is that of vocal rehabilitation, where interdisciplinary teams of otolaryngologist, speech-language pathologist and voice practitioner(s) (singing teacher or speaking-voice coach or both) collaborate in the treatment and remediation of vocal problems. In all of these roles, the voice expert engaged in this practical work has an added responsibility which is unique to the world of theatre. As has been implied by the title of this paper, acting is the primordial element—the research for which needs to happen *before* any performer speaks or sings; voice professionals who work with theatre performers ignore this precept at their peril.

The Work

Although the range of tasks undertaken by voice professionals in theatre is broad, this paper is principally concerned with the practical psychomotor training aspects of voice work. In tertiary training institutions (universities, colleges, conservatories), it is the physically-based developmental training that sets practical performance courses apart from the mainly academic-learning approach of the majority of subject areas. Singing teachers and theatre voice teachers in tertiary institutions will readily recognize that this uniqueness can sometimes be more curse than blessing.

So, then, what do voice teachers do? "Singing is really a form of sport, within which neuromuscular training, aesthetic education, and exposure to the history and literature of the genre, and an understanding of current performance philosophies are just some of the tasks a good teacher undertakes with a student" (Callaghan and Wilson 2002, 112). This summary of a singing teacher's responsibilities holds equally true for the work of voice coaches and spoken-voice teachers. And, again: "Performers are athletes, from whom their director and producer demand high-energy, meticulously accurate, consistent and emotionally honest performances eight times a week" (Wilson 2010, 296). Although written in a music theatre context, this precept holds true for all theatre performers.

If, then, speaking and/or singing at professional performance level can be considered a form of sport, then the principles behind our work differ little from those that underlie sports training. Funding levels for sport science continue to be consistently higher than those for scientific investigations into arts-related activities. The silver lining of this cloud is that many of the findings of sport science in the areas of neuromuscular skills acquisition are readily translated into practical information which enhances the effectiveness of performance training. In particular, sport science continues to offer useful training and performance enhancement protocols which relate directly to the singing and speaking voice needs of theatre performers in training, rehearsal, performance or rehabilitation.

It is vital that performers are carefully and thoroughly prepared to use their voices at professional level, where demands on stamina and skill are high. Investigations into the vocal fatigue of actors post-performance by Novak et al. (1991) indicate the need for pre-performance voice preparation and appropriate vocal warm-downs. The findings of Roy *et al.* include a clear indication that "…vocal training defends the laryngeal system from unwanted changes related to vocally violent maneuvers" (Roy 2000, 226).

When voice students or professional theatre performers sustain vocal damage, or are in danger of losing the full facility of their voices, there is urgent need for a vocal health team to be set up to deal with the presenting problem. Voice in theatre is an extreme of vocal usage (Rodenburg 1997, viii), and performers have need of specialist assistance when things go wrong, in much the same way as an elite athlete would seek medical assistance from a sports medicine practitioner rather than a mainstream medico. On voice specialists consulting with injured professional performers, Jeannette LoVetri says "…this performer is the vocal equivalent of an Olympic athlete who needs to be treated accordingly" (2006, 211). Singers' and actors' bodies are shaped both by their training and the ongoing practice of their chosen profession. Their torso musculature will be vastly different from that of people of comparable age and gender who do not use their voice professionally. Furthermore, the neuroanatomy of performers differs from that of non-performers as a direct result of the neuromuscular training (including voice training) that they receive (Mithen and Parsons 2008).

Where Theatre Performers Work

It is all too easy for singing teachers and voice coaches to overlook the work and life contexts of the performers with whom they work. This oversight can be perilous. It is likely that tertiary-level students are working at a part-time job (at least one) to help them survive. Theatre performers who can live comfortably on their performance income alone are the exception to the rule. Professional actors and singers usually need to do one or more other jobs to maintain themselves. It is very important for the voice professional who works with these people to know exactly what work they do, and under what circumstances.

Jobs commonly undertaken by tertiary-level students in order to pay their way through college can inflict vocal damage. One simple example suffices. Call centres love employing actors—they have good voices, excellent people skills, and are trained to manage and defuse emotionally challenging responses. Regular six-hour shifts on the phones as a telemarketer or call centre worker can impair vocal health, while continuing call-centre work over a lengthy period leads to structure/function vocal damage (Titze et al. 1997, 256; Jones 2002). Because telemarketers also operate computer keyboards simultaneously during calls, the fascinating correlation between keyboard operation, RSI (repetitive strain injury) and vocal dysfunction (Verdolini and Ramig 2001, 41-43) should also be noted.

A useful rule-of-thumb to remember is that, in modern western-style economies, about one-third of the workforce relies on voice as the primary tool with which they do their job (Vilkman 2000). The vocational list includes teachers, trade unionists, auctioneers, counsellors (psychologists, psychiatrists, social workers), checkout staff, clergy, waiters, bar staff, lawyers (especially barristers), sales assistants and health care workers. Although a healthy and functional voice is required for all of these professions, some jobs are disproportionately represented in an otolaryngologist's waiting room. A warning flag should be mentally hoisted if a performer or student performer with whom you are working tells you that his or her part-time job is as a teacher, an aerobics instructor, a dance teacher, a telemarketer, a waiter or a bar attendant (Fritzell 1996; Titze et al. 1997; Verdolini and Ramig 2001).

Even if performers' part-time jobs present no likelihood of damage to their voices, dangers lurk when they come to do their *real* job. Pyrotechnics offer fire hazards, theatrical makeup can cause a range of skin irritations and allergies, stage lighting and wiring present the continuing possibility of electrical accidents, rigging can fail, and some costumes in the more fanciful areas of theatre, opera, and music theatre are windfalls for local physiotherapists. (Music theatre pieces beloved of health practitioners for their kinky costuming include *The Lion King* and *Beauty and the Beast*.)

In addition, "life upon the wicked stage" presents a huge range of potential vocal stressors. Prudent theatre voice teachers and singing teachers will not only alert their performers-in-training to these likely pitfalls, but also teach them to be proactive and alert to occupational health and safety issues which may in some way impinge upon their vocal health and strength. Sound levels in the modern rock musical can be set at rock-concert levels in order to please their audience members. Pity the actor/singer attempting to pitch accurately and maintain functional vocal health in extreme noise levels eight times a week; there will inevitably be vocal repercussions for long-term exposure to dangerous noise. The patrons enjoy two or three hours of it. The performers work for 24 hours a week within it. Should the sturdy performer survive all this, there are still a number of vocal hazards in the theatre (Richter et al. 2002),

Act, Sing, Speak: Voice in the World of Theatre by Pat H. Wilson

chief of which is dust. Performers "…frequently complain of dry and dusty air at rehearsals and performances." (Richter et al. 2000, 80). The findings of Richter et al. validated performers' protests; they regularly found that, in theatres without compensatory humidification, the conditions were usually far too hot and dry for healthy vocal work. (Richter et al. 2000, 80). Extremes of vocal sound (screaming, yelling, sobbing) may be required of the performer. Some scripts demand cigarette, cigar or pipe smoking. Theatres are no longer allowed to use tobacco products on-stage in many locations now, but herbal stage cigarettes are by no means vocally safe. Investigators have found that they produce a level of carbon monoxide at least as high as that produced by tobacco cigarettes (Groman et al., 1999). Stage combat, and its concomitant physical and vocal effects, places a very specific range of demands upon the performer (Raphael, 1991). Added to these hazards is the frequent use of smoke and fog effects, some of which may cause respiratory irritation.

Richard Miller's acute observation holds as true for actors as it does for singers: "It is difficult to determine where the instrument of the singer leaves off and where the instrument case begins. In any event, the singing instrument is dependent upon the condition of its carrying case" (Miller 1996, 218). Thus, the duty of care for all theatre voice teachers, vocal coaches and singing teachers should be not only to the *instrument* of the theatre performer, but also to the functional health of each instrument's carrying case.

Chickens and Eggs

In a chicken-and-egg manner, theorists have long debated which came first—speaking or singing? The British composer Ralph Vaughan Williams believed that singing began as a natural outcome of emotional, impassioned speech. In support of his assertion, he musically notated a loud and passionate political speech, observing that its intonation pattern resembled the melodic structure of a folk song (Vaughan Williams 1955). However, the recent research of anthropologist Steven Mithen proposes that musicality has far more ancient evolutionary roots than spoken language (Mithen 2005). In this, Mithen confirms the earlier speculations of philologist Otto Jespersen, who proposed that, in human evolution, the capacity to sing preceded the capacity to speak (Jespersen 1922), and Charles Darwin, who hypothesized, "Primeval man, or rather some early progenitor of man, probably first used his voice in producing true musical cadences, that is in singing" (Darwin 1871, 133).

"Singing and speaking are accomplished by the same instrument; we can move easily from one activity to the other in the same breath; and speaking and singing onstage have similar technical requirements" (Melton and Tom, 2003, 135). "We have one voice, not two… Speaking and singing are two ways we coordinate our one voice to express ourselves. There is more similarity in the two co-ordinations than there are differences" (Thurman and Welch, 2000, xx). Cultures in which singing is as commonplace as speaking often lack a formal division between these two vocal functions. However, traditional Western cultures familiar to most readers of this paper will tend to break up human vocal performances into spoken or sung modes. The ways in which theatre voice skills and singing skills are currently taught often reflect this unspoken perceptual divide. Because it is commonplace for peoples of Western cultures to use their speaking voices every day in both private and public contexts, the importance of acquiring spoken-voice skills can tend to be downgraded by the less-aware would-be theatre performer.

An awareness of the interdependence of both phonatory activities can only assist any voice professional. The work of Jeffries et al. (2003) has given great insight into the ways in which the brain manages both spoken words and sung words. Their PET (positron emission tomography) study (which employed intravenous $H2150$ as a radiotracer) asked trained singers to sing a song which was very familiar to them, and then speak the lyrics of that same song at a natural, conversational rate. Scans of the subjects' brains taken during the performance of these tasks revealed, amongst other data, that speaking results in relative increases in activity in the left hemisphere of the brain, whilst singing the same text produces roughly three major focal areas of activity in the right side of the brain, with none of the left-brain activity noted during the speech tasks. The training of actors and singers can only benefit from this insight into the central processing functions of the brain during speech and song. Since the right-hemisphere and left-hemisphere activities are not mirror-imaged, it is advisable for vocal coaches to employ singing as a part of their theatre voice training work, and equally as sensible for singing teachers to use spoken-voice work as part of their singing training, in order to gain as wide a range of brain activity as possible in the learning process.

The findings of this investigation also validate a process used by those singing teachers who insist upon students being able to speak the lyrics of their songs in natural (non-rhythmic) prosody. This practice ensures that the singers have functional data for the song stored in a range of different places within both hemispheres of the brain. Teachers generally devise and formalize their preferred process for this. As a recent example, Gerald Seminatore's (2010) paper "Teaching poetry through song: A modest proposal," details the processes for speaking, analyzing and paraphrasing song lyrics by which he instructs singers to speak the text they intend to sing well before they attempt to sing it in performance. Seminatore's stated goal is "…to teach students not only how to sing notes and phrases, but also to *speak* words and ideas in songs as if they were the student's own" (Seminatore 2010, 515). It is telling that this material appears in the *Journal of Singing*. Most acting teachers would regard Seminatore's work as worthy but hardly groundbreaking.

Patsy Rodenburg, in her fine book, *The Actor Speaks*, says, "Many singers are frightened of speaking. Many speakers are frightened of singing. The two voices rarely meet and overlap with ease. There is often a grinding of vocal gears as a singer moves into speaking or a speaker into singing. Energy ceases to flow naturally and the voice can make alarming jumps in terms of placing and pitch" (Rodenburg 1997, 137). Linda Gates (1998) suggests that the reason that there appears to be much more scientific research undertaken into the singing voice, as opposed to the speaking voice, is because the singing voice "…is easier to measure, as it deals with exact, not approximate pitches" (Gates 1998, 6). Gates interviewed a number of voice professionals regarding the development of "…a shared pedagogy that recognizes the demands of both the singing and the speaking voice" (Gates 1998, 6). One of Gates' interviewees, Sunny Joy Langton (opera singer and voice teacher at the School of Music, Northwestern University) said, "There is seldom training of the speaking voice when training the singing voice"; and added, "There is need for an integrated approach to professional voice for actor/singer that is team taught" (Gates 1998, 8). Gates herself concludes, "Training institutions should implement joint training of both the speaking and the singing voice, with full communication between teachers of speaking and singing" (Gates 1998, 9).

Joan Melton, well-known for working across both singing and theatre voice, offers the following observation about the current lack of interdisciplinary thinking in voice training courses for actors and singers. "Actor training programs frequently include techniques for every possible use of the voice except singing, and training curricula for singers seldom include theatre voice. Acting for Singers is becoming a regularly required course for many opera majors but is seldom supported by the prerequisites of theatre voice and movement. Likewise, singing is often available as a peripheral and/or optional course in acting training but is seldom supported by appropriate connecting links to the rest of the actor's work" (Melton and Tom 2003, 135). My anecdotal experience is that it is rare to find an undergraduate opera course or B. Mus. singing-major course which offers spoken-voice training as an integral part of its curriculum, and not just as one of a group of electives. This would seem to be a gap in any well-structured tertiary singing voice curriculum, in the light of Callaghan's advice, "misuse of the speaking voice, or use of a tired speaking voice, has direct and indirect effects on the singing voice" (Callaghan 2000, 105). Some of the actor training programs I have either observed or worked within have done a little better integrat-

ing singing voice training into their full-time undergraduate drama courses. Unfortunately, Melton's observations still hold largely true.

I once worked as Head of Voice in a university where the Department for the Arts was divided into two major areas – Visual Arts and Performing Arts. Funding for our department was allocated as a single amount. The mandarins of the university, in their wisdom, asked the departmental Joint Committee (a bunch of dancers, painters, actors, sculptors and singers) to divide this amount into equitable portions with proper regard for the needs of the department as a whole. Committee meetings were lengthy and bloody; politics ruled. I would like to think that the theatre voice teacher, the singing teacher and the acting teacher could invent new ways of working together which would enrich and empower the performers whom they train. The multidisciplinary approach favoured by some professional voice associations (British Voice Association and Australian Voice Association are just two of which I am aware) forms a useful model for collaborative enterprise in the voice world.

The Consolations of Neuroanatomy

The work of spoken-voice teachers and singing teachers is, in essence, practical psychomotor training (Callaghan and Wilson 2002, Nisbet 2003). It should be an encouragement to all these training professionals that the work they do effects profound changes within the performers with whom they work. It is common knowledge that training changes both behaviours and bodies. However, recent research quantifies the nature and amount of structural and functional changes to the brains of participants in any neuromuscular skill acquisition tasks.

Mithen and Parsons' (2008) paper, "The Brain as Cultural Artefact," argues that our brains are a direct product of the society and culture within which we exist, and offers direct correlational evidence of this cause-and-effect relationship. Their research investigates adult learning and "… the extent to which the anatomy and function of the brain can be deliberately manipulated in much the same manner that one can mould a piece of clay…" (Mithen and Parsons 2008, 417). The measured outcomes of Mithen's self-experiment of learning to sing as an adult (Mithen, 2008; Mithen and Parsons 2008) serve as a real encouragement to voice teachers. Prior to undertaking any formal singing training, Mithen's brain activity was monitored via a functional MRI (fMRI) brain scan, whilst he sang a range of technical exercises and two songs. A year later, during which Mithen attended regular one-on-one lessons with a singing teacher, he repeated the same exercises and songs that he had performed previously, again whilst being monitored by fMRI. Significant increases in brain activity were noted in the second set of fMRI data, when compared with

Act, Sing, Speak: Voice in the World of Theatre by Pat H. Wilson

that of the initial brain scan of a year before. Much of the enhanced activity was in the right hemisphere (c.f. Jeffries et al. 2003). Mithen and Parsons observe that the results are "…consistent with the hypothesis that changes in processing music and singing occur in the right hemisphere early in the development of skills, with higher levels of skill development associated with bilateral brain mechanisms" (Mithen and Parsons 2008, 420).

The research work of Maguire (2000) using London taxi-drivers found that the posterior hippocampus (the region of the brain which facilitates spatial memory, i.e., navigation tasks) in London taxi-drivers was consistently larger than that of comparable non-taxi-drivers. Investigations by Draganski et al. (2004) used a sample of adults who could not juggle. These participants were taught to juggle over a three-month period. Brain structures of the jugglers were compared before and after their acquisition of a new neuromuscular skill, and also compared with a group matched for age and sex who did not learn juggling. The study reports a significant expansion in the jugglers' brains, specifically in those brain areas which manage visual-motion information. A strong positive correlation was noted between juggling performance and the amount of additional grey matter in subjects' brains. In a fascinating addition to the study, the investigators asked the participants to do no juggling for the next three months, after which time, participants' brains displayed a marked decrease in those areas of grey matter which had increased during the juggling.

It can be drawn from these experiments that we who train adults to acquire new sets of neuromuscular skills are, in reality, helping our students to build new structures and pathways in their brains. That frequent injunction to "keep practicing" (voice exercises, singing exercises) is clearly advice designed to help students retain the new brain structures that their training has sculpted.

In 1986, Dr Candace Pert, pharmacologist and research neuroscientist, wrote in a discussion of her research into molecular transmitters, biochemical receptors, and their role in communications between the nervous, endocrine and immune systems of the body, "I believe that neuropeptides and their receptors are a key to understanding how mind and body are interconnected, and how emotions can be manifested through the body. Indeed, the more we know about neuropeptides, the harder it is to think in the traditional terms of a mind and a body. It makes more and more sense to speak of a single integrated entity, a 'body-mind'" (Pert 1986). Fourteen years later, Thurman and Welch entitled their fine three-volume monograph of vocal pedagogy and all things voice, *Bodymind and Voice: Foundations of Voice Education*, observing that they sought to use "…a single term that reflects the unity of psychophysical processes" (Thurman and Welch 2000, xiv).

A further extrapolation of Pert's thought is found in neuropsychologist Antonio Damasio's book, *Descartes' Error: Emotion, Reason, and the Human Brain*: "It is not only the separation between the mind and brain that is mythical: the separation between mind and body is probably just as fictional. The mind is embodied, in the full sense of the term, not just embrained" (Damasio 1994, 118). It is with this fully embodied mind that any theatre performer must work; in fact, Pert's comment (above) contains a fine definition of every actor's challenge: "…how emotions can be manifested through the body." Thus, acting, the *sine qua non* of all theatre performers, can be seen to be somatic—a body-based task which engages the actor from cell level upward throughout the whole body organism. It is this overriding principle which should serve as guide and inspiration to all singing teachers, voice coaches and teachers of theatre voice.

Conclusion

Is it utopian to dream of a collegial cohort of interdisciplinary acting/singing/speaking experts who train theatre performers? Can a future for theatre training be seen where experts have been cajoled out of their safe old pigeon holes (labelled "singing teacher," "acting coach," or "spoken-voice teacher") and all work under the banner of "vocal/emotional theatre specialists"? While wholeheartedly agreeing with Linda Gates' (1998) call for a shared pedagogy between theatre voice and singing, I think that performers would derive even more benefit from theatre training which moves seamlessly among the crafts of acting, singing and speaking, whilst maintaining sensitivity towards the spirit of integrated emotional truth behind it all. After all, acting is *conditio sine qua non*. It is the ur-component which provides the voice with that precious vector of intention, from which flows catharsis, empowering utterances with the Aristotelian theatrical ideal.

Two authorities on performance should share the epilogue to this discussion about the training of performers in speaking and singing for the passionate arts of theatre:

> "At the start of their training few young actors realize how fundamentally important their voices will be for them throughout their careers…They have yet to think of their bodies and their voices as instruments which they must learn to 'play' properly…" (Rodenburg 1997, 4).

> *"Master your instrument, master the music, and then forget all that shit and just play."* Charlie 'Bird' Parker (1920 – 1955), American virtuoso jazz saxophonist and composer

Bibliography

Callaghan, J. *Singing and Voice Science*. San Diego: Singular Publishing Group/Thomson Learning, 2000.

Callaghan, J, and P.H. Wilson. "Sing and See," *Voice: The Cutting Edge. 6th Voice Symposium of Australia*. Adelaide: Australian Voice Association, 112-113, 2002.

Damasio, A.R. *Descartes' Error: Emotion, Reason, and the Human Brain*. New York: Avon Books, 1994.

Darwin, C. *The Descent of Man, and Selection in Relation to Sex*. London: John Murray, 1871.

Draganski, B., C. Gaser, V. Busch, G. Schuierer, U. Bogdahn and A. May. "Changes in Grey Matter Induced by Training," *Nature* 427: 311-312, 2004.

Fritzell, B. "Voice Disorders and Occupations," *Journal of Logopedics, Phoniatrics, and Vocology* 21: 7-12, 1996.

Gates, L. "The Need for a Shared Pedagogy for the Successful Use of the Singing/Speaking Voice in Theatre Voice Training," *Journal of Logopedics, Phoniatrics and Vocology* 23 (Suppl. 1): 6-9, 1998.

Groman, E, G. Bernhard, D. Blauensteiner, and U. Kunze. "A Harmful Aid to Stopping Smoking," *The Lancet* 353(9151), 6th February: 466-467, 1999.

Jeffries, K.J., J.B. Fritz, and A.R. Braun. "Words in Melody: an H215O PET Study of Brain Activation during Singing and Speaking," *NeuroReport* 14(15) April: 749-754, 2003.

Jespersen, O. *Language: Its Nature, Development and Origin*. London: George Allen and Unwin, 1922.

Jones, K, J. Sigmon, L. Hock, E. Nelson, M. Sullivan and F. Ogren. "Prevalence and Risk Factors for Voice Problems among Telemarketers," *Arch. Otolaryngol. Head Neck Surgery* 128, May: 571-577, 2002.

LoVetri, J. L. "Treatment of Injured Singers and Professional Speakers: The Singer/Actor, Singer/Dancer, and Singer/Musician," *The Performer's Voice*, ed. Michael S. Benninger and Thomas Murry, 209-218. San Diego: Plural Publishing, 2002.

Maguire, E.A., D.G. Gadian, I.S. Johnsrude, et al. "Navigation-related Structural Change in the Hippocampi of Taxi Drivers," *Proceedings of the National Academy of Sciences of the USA*, 97: 4398-403, 2002.

Melton, J. and K. Tom. *One Voice: Integrating Singing Technique and Theatre Voice Training*. Portsmouth, NH: Heinemann, 2003.

Miller, R. *The Structure of Singing: System and Art in Vocal Technique*. New York: Schirmer Books, 1996.

Mithen, S. J. *The Singing Neanderthals: The Origins of Music, Language, Mind and Body*. Cambridge, MA: Harvard University Press, 2005.

Mithen, S. "The Diva Within," *New Scientist* #2644, 23rd February: 38-39, 2008.

Mithen, S, and L. Parsons. "The Brain as a Cultural Artefact," *Cambridge Archaeological Journal* 18(3): 415-22, 2008.

Nisbet, A. "Singing Teachers Talk Too Much," In *Reimagining Practice: Researching Change*, Vol. 3, ed. Brendan Bartlett, Fiona Bryer and Dick Roebuck, 8-17. Nathan, Queensland, Australia: Griffith University, School of Cognition, Language and Special Education, 2003.

Novak, A., O. Dlouha, B. Capkova, and M. Vohradnik. "Voice Fatigue after Theatre Performance in Actors," *Folia Phoniatrica et Logopaedica* 43: 74-78, 1991.

Pert, C. B. "The Wisdom of the Receptors: Neuropeptides, the Emotions and Bodymind," *Advances: The Journal of Mind-Body Health* 3(3): 8-16, 1986.

Raphael, B.N. "The Sounds of Violence: Vocal Training in Stage Combat," *Theatre Topics* 1(1), March: 73-86, 1991.

Richter, B., E. Löhle, W. Maier, B. Kliemann, and K. Verdolini. "Working Conditions on Stage: Climatic Considerations," *Journal of Logopedics, Phoniatrics and Vocology* 25: 80-86, 2000.

Richter, B., E. Löhle, B. Knapp, M. Weikert, J. Schlömicher-Thier, and K. Verdolini. "Harmful Substances on the Opera Stage: Possible Negative Effects on Singers' Respiratory Tracts," *Journal of Voice* 16(1): 72-80, 2002.

Rodenburg, P. *The Actor Speaks*. London: Methuen Drama, 1997.

Roy, N., K. S. Ryker, and D. M. Bless. "Vocal Violence in Actors: An Investigation into its Acoustic Consequences and the Effects of Hygienic Laryngeal Release Training," *Journal of Voice* 14(2): 215-230, 2000.

Seminatore, G. "Teaching Poetry through Song: A Modest Proposal," *Journal of Singing* 66(5), May/June: 515-525, 2010.

Thurman, L., and G. Welch (Eds.). *Bodymind and Voice: Foundations of Voice Education* (Rev. Ed., Vols. 1-3). Collegeville, MN: The VoiceCare Network, National Center for Voice and Speech, Fairview Voice Center, 2000.

Titze, I., J. Lemke and D. Montequin. "Populations in the U.S. Workforce Who Rely on Voice as a Primary Tool of Trade: A Preliminary Report," *Journal of Voice* 11(3): 254-259, 1997.

Vaughan Williams, R. *The Making of Music*. Westport, CT: Greenwood Press, 1955.

Verdolini , K. and L. O. Ramig. Review: "Occupational Risks for Voice Problems," *Journal of Logopedics, Phoniatrics and Vocology*, 26: 37-46, 2001.

Vilkman, E. "Voice Problems at Work: A Challenge for Occupational Health and Safety Arrangement," *Folia Phoniatrica et Logopaedica* 52: 120-125, 2000.

Wilson, P.H. "Showtime! - Teaching Music Theatre and Cabaret Singing." In *Perspectives on Teaching Singing: Australian Vocal Pedagogues Sing Their Stories*, ed. S.D. Harrison, 293-305. Brisbane: Australian Academic Press, 2010.

The Three Word Diet

Neil Semer teaches voice and gives workshops internationally. His main studio is in New York. He also teaches regularly in Toronto, throughout Europe and Australia, and in summer 2011, will lead his 15th annual Neil Semer Vocal Institute in Germany. His students sing leading roles in the world's most important opera houses and star in Broadway productions. His teaching combines the old Italian School of Bel Canto with scientific understanding of vocal function. The focus is coordination of the heart, mind and body. He welcomes correspondence at neilsemer@aol.com; his website is www.neilsemer.com.

Diet—what an unpleasant word! The associations with it tend to be that of denial of the pleasurable, sensuous experience of food and drink. However, in my twenty five or more years of teaching singing I have found a teaching tool I call the *three word diet*, that actually puts professional singers and aspiring singers more, rather than less, in contact with their sensuous selves.

As a singer's technician, I believe it is my job to acquaint students with a large body of physical information meant to illuminate and optimize the processes of the body in creating beautiful, healthy, efficient and expressive song.

It is normal in our world to have unresolved control issues and to presume that it is through clear analytical thinking and judgment that we will solve all of our problems and gain control over our environment. Unfortunately, however, true control is often counter-intuitive. For example, it is the counter-intuitive, scary act of putting one's weight on the downhill part of a ski (making one immediately accelerate) that gives one control while skiing. It is the counter-intuitive act of trusting the buoyancy of water by flipping onto one's back that is the beginning of real control while swimming. It is the counter-intuitive act of surrendering to the realities of the present moment that allows us to chart a clear course to where we wish to go in our lives. And giving over to increased breath flow (for the hyper-adductor) or intensifying sub-glottic pressure (for the hypo-adductor) is almost always counter-intuitive. If it were not, the singer would be doing it already.

I often tell new students that I proudly teach *singing for dumb people*. What I mean, humor aside, is that singing, when done at an elite level, is an extremely sensuous activity, involving fine motor coordination and an acutely attuned ear. Intellect can play only a supporting role. Those people who are strongly identified with their intellect and have loud, judgmental chatter obliterating their proprioception are at a distinct disadvantage when learning to sing. This is where the *three word diet* comes in.

I pose the question, "How does that feel?" dozens of times in a lesson. Often I am met with a response that goes something like "Well, it's not as good as it could be," or "When I hit the high note, I felt something tighten," or "It sounds weird," or "I need to get more slender in the passaggio." The singer is completely unaware that he or she has failed to hear or respond to the actual question. I then say again, "But how did it *feel*?" If I am met with an intensification of the need to judge, condemn, praise, figure out what is perceived to be the problem or the creation of a plan of attack for the next exercise with ever longer verbiage, I will put that artist on the *three word diet*. I'm ruthless on this, since it is my sad experience that when it comes to singing matters, the more people talk, the less they say—so ruthless that, truth be told, the singer is really on a *one* word diet, as it is I who provide the first two words. They are, "I felt…" and the singer is allowed to add only one word. It still surprises me how often people who have just said paragraphs diagnosing their own problems or judging their actions are unable to say one simple word that accurately describes a piece of their experience from seconds ago.

I prompt with words describing physical experience such as: pleasurable? uncomfortable? tight? loose? vibrant? released? whole? disconnected? spacious? high? low? tiring? energized? If any of these words prompts a response of, "Yes," I may further inquire, "Where?" so that the perception of the experience is deepened. I also prompt with words such as: fun? sad? painful? silly? enraged? anxious? emotional? However, these words are only provided as an initial guide to developing a vocabulary of sensuous and emotional words with which to identify experiences. The singer is strongly encouraged to develop her or his own ever-lengthening list.

I may also recommend spiritual reading (non-religious) to students, as the need for mental control frequently has its deepest roots in the great spiritual issues that confront us all, such as mortality and abandonment anxiety. Held breath and tight musculature are often cues to spiritual and emotional issues that need to be gently, sensitively addressed. Another indication of the need for this sort of work may be that a gifted student does something well quickly, and thereafter does it less well or not at all. While the skill was a *circus trick* it was quickly mastered; then it began to take on emotional meaning, triggering fears buried in the unconscious. Where there was previously ease, there is now tension and lack of intuitive coordination. Trying has replaced doing. The student, unknowingly, is more comfortable with struggle than with success, if that success is tied to uncomfortable emotional issues.

Obviously, any instructor who wishes to do this sort of work with a pupil needs to do exhaustive, life-long work on his or her own emotional and spiritual consciousness, so as to be truly available to the student without projecting her or his own issues onto the matter at hand.

It is the naming and sorting through of experiences, rather than intellectual postulations that create the environment in which a physically coordinated, artistically attuned technique can be developed. Generally, as the singer notes the simple clarity of physical sensations and emotions, and as evidence mounts that sifting through them, both alone and with a teacher, yields greater results than years of attempted mental domination of the instrument, the artist gains confidence and begins to value the evidence of his or her body and heart.

Ah, a diet that embraces the body and heart, and frees the spirit to soar in song!

Reinvesting in Language: The Use of Singing in Verse Text Exploration

Laura Wayth received her MFA from the American Repertory Theatre Institute for Advanced Theatre Training at Harvard University, and the Moscow Art Theatre School Institute in Russia. Ms. Wayth has taught and coached voice and acting at Tufts University, the College of the Holycross, the University of Miami, and the University of Wisconsin Eau-Claire. She was a 2002/03 Fulbright Fellow to Moscow. In addition to her teaching and training in Russia, she has worked internationally as a teacher and coach in Italy, Morocco, China and London. She is currently the Master Acting Teacher at Florida Atlantic University.

We are becoming an increasingly visually dependent culture. As our dependence on visual images to transmit meaning increases, our awareness of and reverence for language slowly and steadily declines. We can see the shift in the primacy of language everywhere around us: in media, in daily speech and in the fragmented cyber-language which has overtaken and transformed traditional forms of communication.

As a result of this, young actors, largely unacquainted with the power of words, tend to throw away language. They may be bright, aware, inquisitive and imaginative, and yet, to most, language has become something murky and unspecific. Words all seem to carry the same weight, lacking distinction and vibrancy. Language is not viscerally connected to the body or intellect; it is something separate, pragmatic and taken for granted. In short, the joy of making sound, particularly sound which transmits both meaning and emotion, is missing.

This phenomenon is troublesome in all areas of actor training, but is particularly problematic in navigating the multiple challenges of heightened and classical voice and text work. The casualness of today's culture, the vocal and emotional flattening of language, and the lack of commitment to energetic and varied speech make it difficult for students to truly elevate and heighten verse texts. The intimacy of film has caused many of these actors to equate truth with a kind of settled smallness. Fearing falseness, the actor under-energizes heightened text, resisting not only its size, but its natural musicality. The result is a classical text that sounds strangely and anachronistically contemporary.

How, then, do we as educators and trainers re-ignite the voice as an instrument of nuanced communication in order to truly communicate the richness, beauty and power of classical texts? How do we guide students to discover a heightened sense of line—the flowing, forward-moving, lyric and elevated quality of language— in verse texts?

One day in my undergraduate voice and text class, both the urgent need for action and the beginnings of a solution became clear:

> Foul devil, for God's sake hence, and trouble us not,
> For thou hast made the happy earth thy hell,
> Fill'd it with cursing cries and deep exclaims.
> If thou delight to view thy heinous deeds,
> Behold this pattern of thy butcheries.

Richard III (Lady Anne I, ii, 53-57)

My young actor began to work on this monologue from *Richard III*. In introducing and discussing her work, it was evident that she had a clear understanding of the play, not only of her given circumstances, but of Anne's complexity as a strong woman in powerless circumstances. Yet, when she began to speak her text, one word blurred into another; each word steadily and squarely spoken in the same rhythm and pitch, one idea indistinguishable from the next. When asked to paraphrase the language, she did an admirable job of reconstructing the meaning of the text. Understanding the content did not appear to be the issue. Yet, despite her intellectual command of the material, she communicated little understanding or specificity in her work.

I asked her to sing the first five lines of her text, singing on a single pitch that was comfortable in her vocal range. I asked her to concentrate on the length of the words; did she instinctively want to lengthen and elongate each word or shorten it? How, I asked her, did the words flow together? She discovered that the language was not *square*, as she had originally spoken it, but that some words naturally lengthened and elongated while other words were quick and clipped.

Next, I asked her to identify the antitheses in the first lines of the text. She identified the opposition of the phrase *foul devil* with the word *God*, and the phrase *happy earth* with the word *hell*. I asked her to sing the *malevolent* words; first the

307

phrase *foul devil*, and then the word *hell*. I then asked her to sing the *benevolent* words; first the word *God* and then the phrase *happy earth*. I suggested that both she and the class notice the difference in the vocal qualities that she instinctively chose. She identified that the first words that she sang were heavy and lower in pitch with a staccato quality, and that the second set of words was higher in pitch, light, lyric and lengthened.

I then asked her to sing the lines again, feeling free to lengthen and shorten words on impulse, being mindful not only of oppositions, but of the qualities of *all* of the words that she sang. I suggested that she expand her pitch range, moving up and down her registers on impulse. After she sang the first five lines, I had her sing the entire monologue. When the full text had been sung, I asked her to return to speaking, and to speak the full text.

The results not only surprised me, but greatly surprised the actor herself. This simple exploration opened up a reinvestment in the language of the piece, and ultimately resulted in a spoken monologue that was not only more understandable, but more passionate, connected and truthful. An investigation into the musicality of the language unlocked a new and varied use of the actor's vocal instrument. What had at first been monotonous and measured grew into a present, varied and powerful use of the voice and body. Additionally, the exploration engaged both her imagination and her spirit in a new way; she had not only unlocked the language of the piece but had somehow unlocked a part of herself.

In addition to the challenge of reconnecting actors to the power and specificity of words, another problem exists in the training of actors in verse text. Often there appears to be a huge disconnect and resulting chasm between intellectual understanding and visceral understanding. The rules of verse construction define and order the world of classical speech, just as the rules of music define and order the world of song. Therefore a full exploration of scansion, the mapping and utilization of the metrical underpinning of verse text, is clearly essential. Such analysis is the framework upon which heightened text rests and is the foundation for any exploration of verse. Though scansion is critical to the acting of verse texts, actors are often either resistant to the analysis or confused by it.

Some actors balk at the idea of poetic analysis, fearing that scansion *rules* will limit their freedom and individuality. They fear that it is somehow prescriptive, dictating terms and removing artistic choice. They express that the application of scansion makes them feel *boxed in* or *controlled* by the verse. Others are not resistant to the idea of verse analysis in theory but simply cannot navigate the transition from a thought on paper to a thought in action. For

these students, an intellectual understanding of what makes heightened text work does not necessarily translate into an inspired navigation of the language in performance. In both cases students have struggled terribly—they either do not know how to or are unwilling to marry analysis of the verse to the acting of the text. For these actors, again, the tool that I have found to best reveal the structure and musicality of heightened text is music itself.

I ask the students to begin to *sing* their scansion on two steady and distinct pitches that are clear and comfortable in their vocal range, using a lower pitch for unstressed beats and a slightly higher pitch for stressed beats. Though at first the strangeness of the request can generate reticence, discomfort quickly melts away as the actor becomes carried away by the natural flow of the language. After a few passes through the text on these two distinct pitches, I suggest the actors use multiple and varied pitches as they explore the text. As the actor begins to open up the vocal range, not only does the underlying framework of the text begin to truly reveal itself, but new colors begin to appear. Once the actors have investigated singing the scansion on pitches of their choosing, I gently return them to speaking. I have the actors remove the idea of fully *singing* the text and ask them to simply *speak*, engaging the vocal support and placement that they had experienced while singing—seeing what discoveries made during singing can be retained and expanded upon during speech.

These three distinct steps advance the actor from a kind of passionless technical exercise to an inspired performance rapidly and effectively. The transition from scansion analysis on a page to spoken text in the past has proven highly problematic; actors seem to either throw away the analysis work that they have done, or they wind up speaking in a stilted, almost robotic way. Through singing, however, the actor can successfully translate written poetic analysis to performance in a way that is far more integrative. The use of singing in scansion exploration seems not only to unite intellectual processes with visceral ones, but also to connect the breath and adjust vocal placement in a way that optimally serves and appropriately elevates heightened text.

Most importantly, the act of singing the text creates a sense of freedom for the actor. The poetic analysis and scansion of verse text, once seen as stifling to the actor, now reveals itself as an ordered framework from which to launch creativity and expression. Through singing—through its heightened use of body, emotion and intellect—the actor awakens the sleeping power of language. Once a visceral connection to both the qualities and the structure of language is ignited, the actor connects, not only with the power and nuances of the text, but with the power and nuances of his or her own instrument.

Bibliography

Blakemore Evans, G., Ed. *The Riverside Shakespeare*. Boston: Houghton Mifflin, 1997.

A Historical Look at Breathing Methods for Singing

Heather Lyle is a singing and Fitzmaurice teacher who operates a private studio in Los Angeles. She holds Bachelors and Masters degrees in vocal performance and completed a doctoral internship at Indiana University School of Music. Lyle has contributed to Emmy award-wining TV shows and received critical praise from Dramalogue for musical direction. She has sung on every type of stage, from world-class opera houses to the Great Pyramid in Egypt for a movie soundtrack. Lyle presently sings with her 8-piece jazz band and has performed at major music festivals alongside Herbie Hancock, Kenny G, and Dee Dee Bridgewater.

Natural breathing, abdominal breathing, rib-swing breathing, back breathing, the debate has gone on for centuries. Although we have made many advances in voice science, there is still a lack of agreement among voice teachers regarding the subject of breathing. A historical look at the evolution of breath management techniques and the ideas espoused on the subject may give the voice specialist an understanding of the reasons for the continuing debate.

Professional singing is known to have existed all the way back to the days of ancient Greece. The very first schools of singing in Italy were created to prepare choirs to sing the liturgical chants of the Roman Catholic Church. The earliest known school of singing for chant was founded in the fourth century by Pope Sylvester (314-336 AD). The employment of trained singers in the service of the church in its earliest centuries led to the institution, in 590 AD, of the famous *Schola Cantorum* of Pope Gregory (540-604 AD). As early as 535 AD, there is evidence of manuals of instruction used by teachers of chant. It is likely that the choristers had to develop breath control and unity of resonance in order to perform the chants in perfect unison. By the thirteenth, fourteenth, fifteenth and sixteenth centuries,

the leading musicians were not only composers of vocal music, but also singers, revealing that singing had evolved into a high art. There is a direct lineage of the art of vocal pedagogy descending from the schools of chant immediately preceding the birth of modern Italian opera. Many of the chants used in the liturgies of the Catholic Church have survived, but little is known of the vocal instruction, as most of it was passed down orally from master to singer. Nevertheless, it is evident that the techniques of the Italian choristers were incorporated in the advent of Italian opera. These were the techniques that most strongly influenced international singing pedagogy.

During the sixteenth century, the first major treatises appeared on singing and the first glimpse into vocal training by the Italian masters was revealed. Names of the "old masters" such as Porpora, Pacchiarotti, Crescentini, Veluti, and Rubini are sprinkled throughout these works. This was the beginning of the attempt by voice teachers to write down some of the techniques known as the Italian Method of singing. Each teacher in subsequent centuries attempted to shed light on what the teachings were but, in actuality, many of the techniques of the "old Italian method" are still a mystery as most were never entirely written down and have been subjected to both alteration and interpretation.

Most voice teachers believe that the study of breathing is paramount to good singing, but most of the references to breathing in the early singing manuals focused on when to take a breath, how to navigate musical passages and how not to interrupt a musical line. There was little mention of how specifically to use the body for breathing or breath control until the late sixteenth and early seventeenth centuries, when treatises on singing by Giovanni Battista Bovicelli and Guilio Caccini appeared.

Giovanni Battista Bovicelli (1550-1597), *Regole de Musica* (1594), was one of the first voice teachers to advocate silent breathing and to advise against forcing the breath. He wrote that the singer should always think about the breath and complained of singers who took breaths every few notes. He objected to the use of a half breath and remarked that singers whose inhalations are louder than their voices are very distasteful (Stark, 2003, 94).

Guilio Caccini (1551-1618), in his treatise *Nuove Musiche* (1602), was one of the first teachers to write down a breathing exercise thought to have originated in the *Schola Cantorum*. This exercise advocated practicing singing from a soft tone to a loud tone (crescendo) and from a loud tone to a soft tone (diminuendo) in order to control the breath. Caccini called this technique *crescere e scemare la voce* (to grow and diminish the voice). It became one of the main exercises for breathing and its use continues into the twentieth century. It was eventually called the *messa di voce* and required the singer to have impeccable command of the breath and the voice.

During the eighteenth century, the important treatises on the voice were written by well-known castrato singers. The first was by the castrato soprano Pier Francesco Tosi (1647-1732). *Osservazioni Sopra il Canto Figurato* was released in 1723. Tosi also advocated (like Caccini) the *crescere e scemare la voce*, which he renamed the *messa di voce*. Mastery of the breath was important to Tosi. He wrote that the master must train the scholar to "…manage his Respiration that he may always be provided with more Breath than is needful; and may avoid undertaking what, for want of it, he can not go through with" (1723, 16).

The *messa di voce* started as an exercise for the castrato singer and was then adapted for the un-castrated male and female singer. Tosi suggested to the teacher the method of attaining the *messa di voce*:

In the same Lessons, let him teach the Art to put forth the Voice, which consists in letting it swell by Degrees from the softest *Piano* to the loudest *Forte*, and from thence with the same Art return from the *Forte* to the *Piano*. A beautiful *Messa di Voce*, from a Singer that uses it sparingly, and only on the open Vowels, can never fail of having an exquisite Effect (1723, 10).

The voice in *messa di voce* needed to remain constant and full in both *piano* and *forte*, as well as during *crescendo* and *decrescendo*. The vibrato rate, intonation and resonance also had to remain as close to constant as possible. The *messa di voce* trained the singer to adjust breath support to the changes in volume and intensity. This exercise remains an important part of voice training today.

The main method of breath management during the eighteenth century was to fill the lungs with as much air as possible and keep the chest fully inflated to hold back or dam, as it was called, the breath so that the singer could control the expiration of the breath stream. The majority of pedagogues during this century believed that chest position would ensure good breathing.

The castrato soprano Giambattista Mancini (1714 -1800) was thought to be the chief authority of singing in the eighteenth century. Mancini published *Practical Reflections on Figured Singing* in 1774. Mancini recommended that the singer use an "elevated robust chest assisted by the graduation of breath" (1774, 154). Mancini was one of the first teachers to give specific exercises to achieve breath control. He recommended that the singer practice long, sustained notes (on a single pitch), or an extended row of notes that are gradually increased in length.

Mancini devoted a full chapter to the *messa di voce* and warned against its use before the student was ready. "The student should not presume to be able to execute the messa di voce before he has acquired the art to hold, reinforce, and take the breath back" (1774, 131).

Carlo Broschi, called Farinelli (1705-1782), was one of the last great castrati. He was famous for his amazing breath control. To increase breath control, he recommended that the singer "sip the breath slowly and steadily through the smallest possible opening of the lips; hold it a few counts, then exhale very slowly and steadily through the smallest possible opening of the lips" (Fillebrown, 2009, 54). This exercise became known as the Farinelli exercise and had been passed down orally to Farinelli by the great voice teacher, Nicola Antonio Porpora (1686-1768).

Ingo Titze, Executive Director of the National Center for Voice and Speech, advocates similar exercises (2010) using phonation into a straw or other "semi-occlusion at the mouth" to train "vocal fold adduction, registration and epi-larynx tube narrowing for the best acoustic power transfer from the glottis to the lips." Titze is quick to point out that this kind of exercise has a long tradition in vocal pedagogy.

The first attempt to study the voice scientifically was by a well-known French anatomist, Antoine Ferrein (1693-1769), who published a work on the vocal organs in 1741, titled *De la Formation de la Voix de l'Homme*. He coined the term *vocal cords*. This was the first scientific treatise to influence voice teachers of the era. Even so, there was little use of scientific knowledge in voice pedagogy until the middle of the nineteenth century.

By the nineteenth century, voice teachers had begun to create relationships with medical doctors resulting in the emergence of voice techniques based on the anatomy and physiology of the body. Voice teachers became very specific with regard to how they required students to use the body for singing. Teachers began to adopt the new scientific ideas, some in hopes of clarifying and strengthening the historic Italian Method, some as a new pedagogy.

Two clear schools of thought regarding breath control emerged in the nineteenth century, pioneered by two great educators of singing and their treatises, Manuel Garcia II and Francesco Lamperti. At this time, breathing methods were divided into three categories: clavicular, diaphragmatic and thoracic. The first category, clavicular breathing, was quickly ruled out for sound production. Scientists had studied the act of respiration for sound production and clavicular breathing was deemed ruinous to the voice and never to be practiced. Dr. Gordon Holmes in his book, *A Treatise on Vocal Physiology and Hygiene* (1879), stated that error and injury could be caused by the use of clavicular

Singing

A Historical Look at Breathing Methods for Singing by Heather Lyle

breathing. He wrote, "…no speaker or singer can practice it to any extent without showing a marked deficiency of his endurance if called on to use his voice for a lengthened period" (1879, 165). Devices were sometimes used to discourage clavicular breathing. Dr. Holmes recommended that the singer, while singing, stand with his back to the wall with two "projecting ledges" on top of the shoulders, to inhibit their rise on inhalation (1879, 165).

In the nineteenth century, most of the teachers of singing were in agreement that clavicular breathing was not adequate for singing; thus, breathing for singing became divided into two categories: thoracic (also called ribcage or lateral breathing) and diaphragmatic (also called abdominal breathing), propelled by their enthusiastic advocates, Manual Garcia II and Francesco Lamperti, respectively.

Manuel Garcia II (1805-1906) is regarded as the founder of voice science and is considered one of the greatest voice teachers of all time. Garcia inherited the historic Italian Method from his father, Manuel Garcia I.

Manuel Garcia I (1775-1832) was a celebrated tenor and voice teacher who wrote two treatises rooted in the Italian Method, *Exercises pour la Voix* (1820) and *Exercises and Method for Singing* (1824). Garcia I's teachings can be traced back to the teachings of the Italian master, Nicola Antonio Porpora. The role of Count Almaviva in Rossini's Il *Barbiere di Siviglia* (1816) was written specifically for Garcia I.

Garcia I advocated an erect standing posture for singing with the shoulders back and the hands crossed behind the lower back, with the palms facing outward. His son carried on the use of this posture. Garcia I claimed it would "open the chest and bring out the voice" (Coffin, 1989, 16). This posture became known as the Garcia posture and is still used today by some singers. Garcia I also recommended that the singer "always take the breath slowly and without noise and The Throat, Teeth and Lips, must be sufficiently open so that the voice may meet with no impediment" (Coffin, 1989, 16). Garcia I continued the tradition of using the *messa di voce* for breath management.

Manuel Garcia II began his vocal education in the Italian Method, but he also desired to have scientific knowledge of the voice. He created the first vocal pedagogy based on the physiological functions of the voice combined with the historic Italian Method. Garcia II worked in administration in French military hospitals where he studied the physiological aspects of the voice and later wrote three treatises: *Traité Complet de l'Art du Chant I and II* (1841, rev. ed. 1847), *Mémoire sur la Voix Humaine* (1841) and *Hints on Singing* (1894).

Mémoire sur la Voix Humaine was presented to the French Institute in 1840 and is considered to be the foundation of all subsequent investigations into the voice. In 1855, Garcia II invented the laryngoscope, an instrument that would revolutionize voice science. The laryngoscope is a small mirror with a long metal handle that can be inserted into the mouth for observation of the vocal cords. This instrument is still widely used today. The invention of the laryngoscope allowed the vocal cords to be observed in real time in a living subject. He published the results of his investigations in a paper that he presented to the Royal Society of London in 1855 and included the laryngoscope in his last book, *Hints on Singing*. Garcia II's books were some of the first to include anatomy illustrations and to rely on science as a basis for teaching voice.

In Garcia II's first book, he advocated the noble posture and the *messa di voce* of the Italian Method for breath management. In *Hints on Singing* (second edition) he added exercises specifically for breath control, recommending Dr. Roth's Chinese breathing exercises for "strengthening the chest and regulating its movement" (1982, 4).

Dr. Roth was a Hungarian who settled in London in 1848 after studying Chinese in Paris. He was an advocate and practitioner of Chinese Kung-fu and pioneered its health benefits in Great Britain. He believed in the use of Kung-fu breathing exercises to cure illness and alleviate pain. Dr. Roth published numerous works on the subject: *The Cure of Chronic Diseases by Movements, Handbook of the Movement Cure*, and others. His work was popular in the nineteenth century among scientists and health enthusiasts.

Garcia II also created his own breathing exercises to strengthen the lungs for singing. He said that since the lungs were independent of the vocal organs, breathing exercises would not create voice fatigue. In *Hints on Singing* (1982, 5), he suggested the following:

1. Draw a breath slowly through a very minute opening of the lips; then exhale freely.
2. Breathe freely and exhale slowly through the same small opening.
3. Breathe freely and retain the breath during ten seconds or more.

Garcia II's method of inspiration was one of both diaphragmatic lowering and ribcage expansion. He wrote of the act of respiration as being a two-part process, beginning with the diaphragm lowering and the stomach slightly protruding. He called this abdominal breathing and stated that this is only a partial breath.

During this partial inspiration…the ribs do not move, nor are they filled to their full capacity, to obtain

312

which the *diaphragm must and does contract completely*. Then and only then are the ribs raised, while the stomach is drawn in (1982, 4).

Garcia stated that a complete breath is not achieved until the ribcage fully expands. "This inspiration is complete and is called thoracic or intercostal" (1982, 4). When asked to choose between diaphragmatic or thoracic breathing, Garcia II's preference was for the latter:

This double procedure, on which I insist, enlarges the lungs, first at the base, then by the circumference, and allows the lungs to complete all their expansion and to receive all the air which they can contain. To advise abdominal breathing exclusively would be to voluntarily reduce by one half the element of strength most indispensable to the singer, the breath (Stark, 2003, 97).

In 1876, a famous physiologist in Paris, Dr. Louis Mandl (1812 - 1881), wrote a treatise on the voice, *Hygiéne de la Voix* that revolutionized the world of singing. Dr. Mandl advocated abdominal (diaphragmatic) breathing instead of chest breathing. *Hygiéne de la Voix* contained the first definite statement of the opposed-muscular-action theory of breath control that Mandl called *lutte vocale*. Mandl stated that the "*lutte vocale* is primarily the struggle between the abdominal muscles and the diaphragm, and that this struggle is reflected in the contractions of the larynx as well" (Stark, 2003, 100).

Francesco Lamperti (1813-92), a celebrated teacher of the Italian Method, became an advocate of the studies of Dr. Mandl. He and his son Giovanni Battista Lamperti (1839-1910) were instrumental in spreading Mandl's theories to the world. Lamperti began his book, *A Treatise on the Art of Singing*, lamenting the decline of good singing brought on by the new style of opera emerging in the nineteenth century. He chose to "avert the ruin of voices" by imparting some "practical and fundamental rules" of singing (1890, 4). In a section of the book, called "Note," he stated that he was in complete agreement with Dr. Mandl's theories on respiration and inserted a page and a half of passages from Mandl's book. Most notable is the description of the *lutte vocale*, which is still widely used by singing teachers today:

To sustain a given note the air should be expelled slowly; to attain this end, the respiratory muscles, by continuing their action, strive to retain the air in the lungs, and oppose their action to that of the expiratory muscles, which, at the same time, drive it out for the production of the note. There is thus established a balance of power between these two agents, which is called the *lutte vocale*, or vocal struggle. On the retention of this equilibrium depends the just emission of

the voice, and by means of it alone can true expression be given to the sound produced (1890, 21).

Lamperti believed that the best way to achieve breath control was through the use of *appoggio*. He is considered the first to introduce the concept of *appoggio* in pedagogical literature. "By singing *appoggiata* is meant that all notes, from the highest to the lowest, are produced over a column of air by which the singer has perfect command, by holding back the breath" (1890, 18). Like Mandl, Francesco Lamperti was an advocate of abdominal breathing. "Any effort about the chest-ribs in breathing must be absolutely and entirely avoided. It is here that the evil lies" (Stark 2003, 100).

To experience an abdominal breath, Lamperti instructed the singer to sit in a chair and cross the arms behind the back as high up as possible and then to take a breath. He believed that in this position, the shoulders and chest would be immovable, therefore the inspiration would be purely abdominal (1890, 20).

Giovanni Battista Lamperti (1839-1910), the son of Francesco, was a well-known teacher in his own right. In his treatise, *The Techniques of Bel Canto* (1905), he expanded his father's theories on *appoggio*, and advocated a more scientific, systematic method of vocal technique. G. B. Lamperti also believed that the sole method of inhalation to be used was abdominal: "It cannot be too strongly emphasized, that the diaphragm is the principal and essential breathing-muscle (if it should be crippled, breathing would cease and death ensue), and that Expiration is effected chiefly by the abdominal muscles" (1905, 7).

A marked difference between G. B. and his father was the mention of additional muscles in the body that may activate during sustained singing. "There are also so-called auxiliary breathing-muscles, those of the neck, back, and thorax, which may aid in sustaining an impaired breathing, but can never replace the regular function of the diaphragm" (1905, 7).

During the late nineteenth century, teachers of singing became divided into supporters of either the Garcia School (thoracic breathing) or the Lamperti/Mandl School (abdominal breathing). Both sides felt that theirs was the only true method for correct breathing. G.B. Lamperti addressed the ongoing debate and suggested that there was actually no need for argument. Since other muscles activated during exhalation, he believed that both ways of breathing were viable and actually interdependent: "This shows that a sharp distinction between chest and abdominal breathing, such as was formally generally accepted, cannot be maintained" (1905, 7).

Although G.B. Lamperti seemed to convince voice teachers

A Historical Look at Breathing Methods for Singing by Heather Lyle

that there was no need for debate between diaphragmatic and ribcage breathing, it is commonly thought that there was an actual rivalry between the Lamperti School and the Garcia School. G.B. Lamperti was quoted as professing his "dislike for voice doctors" who taught tricks, instead of sound vocal pedagogy (Brown, 1957, 21).

Another important teacher of the nineteenth century was Giovanni Sbriglia (1832-1916). He was a celebrated Neopolitan opera singer and teacher who is sometimes credited with the founding of the Paris School of singing. Sbriglia was the teacher of the famous and flamboyant opera singer Jean de Reszke.

It is thought that Sbriglia created his own technique, as he was not a student of Garcia or Lamperti. Sbriglia did not write a book on singing because he believed that "voices vary like faces and the treatments that might be useful for one voice will not be suitable for another" (1905, 1). Sbriglia stated that he taught the way the old Italian teachers did: "The foundation of my teaching is perfect breath control without tension . . . high chest held high without tension by developed abdominal and lower back muscles and a straight spine" (1905, 1).

Sbriglia was the inventor of the abdominal belt for singing. He had belts made that he would tie around the upper abdomens of his students after they took a breath. While singing, their upper abdomen, waist and base of ribcage would need to stay expanded to hold the belt in place, or the belt would fall down.

Sbriglia's method of breath control was to focus the breath, during exhalation, against what he called the *point d'appui*. The *point d'appui* was a focal point in the chest that, he said, was the major place of support:

> [As you sing] the air is slowly pushed out of the body through the small bronchial tubes, which merge into the big bronchial tube at the focal point in the chest . . . the *point d'appui* - the place of support, the place where everything rests . . . (Coffin, 1989, 99).

This method became very popular, and many opera singers sang with their hands clasped in front of their chest at the place of point d'appui. The famous opera singer Luisa Tetrazzini (1871-1940) liked to press her chest against her clasped hands, which she said increased the activity of support of the chest and ribcage.

During the middle of the nineteenth century, the florid, flexible vocal style of the Italian operas of the seventeenth and eighteenth centuries fell out of fashion and new types of singing emerged in several different geographical regions of Europe, leading to new national schools of singing.

In Germany, the composer Wilhelm Richard Wagner (1813 – 1883) designed and constructed the famous Bayreuth Festspielhaus for his music dramas and changed the configuration of the stage, orchestra and seating. Wagner wrote for the largest orchestra ever used in opera and invented the orchestra pit, as he felt the orchestra detracted from the drama onstage. Greater demands were also made on the singers. Wagner disliked the Italian style that had dominated opera up until the middle of the nineteenth century and deemed it inadequate for his works. He called for a German Method of singing and a more speech-like production of sound called *Sprechgesang*. In response, Friedrich Schmidt published *Grosse Gesangschule für Deutschland* in 1854, and in 1884-86, Schmidt's protégé Julius Hay wrote *Deutsche Gesangs-Unterricht*. Hay was also hired to help train singers under Wagner's watchful eye (Frisch, 2005, 53). Müller-Brunow and Lauritz Christian Törsleff continued to write on the German Method in the 1890s (Stark, 2003, 106).

With the new need for declamatory, sustained tones, singing became more athletic and required a more robust vocal production. The German teachers instructed their singers to take in a very large amount of breath and hold it back by a method of *appoggio* they called *Stauprinzip* (damming principle). *Stauprinzip* required a more muscular production than the Italian approach and often resulted in higher sub glottal pressures that produced a laryngeal sound similar to a primitive grunt called a *Stöhnlaut*.

One faction of the German School favored low abdominal breathing and another favored breathing in the lower back at the level of the lowest ribs. Breath support, known as *Atemstütze*, was achieved by retarding the movement of the diaphragm upward and the movement of the abdominal wall inward by muscularly pushing out on the belly. This technique was called *Bauchaussenstütze*, which means distended belly support (Miller, 2002, 21). The pushing out on the lower abdominal wall made it difficult for German singers to maintain an elevated chest, resulting in a relatively low chest posture. The German School also required the singer to firm the pelvis, squeeze the buttocks, and squeeze the anal sphincter to help engage the lower back muscles for additional breath support. The teachers of the Italian Method were appalled by these new techniques that were gaining popularity in Europe. Giovanni Sbriglia did not like what he called "the new pushing method of singing with the back of your neck, sunk in chest and muscularly pushed out diaphragm." He felt that it would rapidly ruin a voice (Coffin, 1989, 98).

In England, there was also a new school of singing emerging. William Shakespeare (not the playwright, 1841 – 1931) was a student of Francesco Lamperti and wrote two treatises, *The Art of Singing*, (1910) and *Plain Words on*

Singing (1924). Shakespeare felt that natural breathing was not adequate for singing. He believed that singing required "a considerable amplification of the ordinary breath-taking" (1910, 9). Shakespeare had an interesting view on breathing that became specific to the English School. He felt that breathing should be diaphragmatic, causing considerable abdominal expansion to be felt by the singer, but "for singing purposes diaphragmatic breathing must be combined with rib breathing" (1910, 13). "The singer must have recourse to the additional aid of yet another type of respiration" which he called rib spreading (1910, 11). He stated that the group of muscles "which join the ribs to the backbone and the shoulder blades is that on which the singer must chiefly rely in order to raise the ribs during inspiration" (1910, 12). This resulted in expansion of the back, little chest expansion and the abdomen to bulge up in the epigastric region. "Considerable pressure and expansion should be felt at the soft place under the breastbone, below this we should be slightly drawn in" (1901, 16).

Shakespeare advocated a special posture for singing to facilitate his breathing method:

> Balance the body on one foot and touch the ground behind with the other . . . Now extend both arms forward and outwards, keeping the elbows in, the palm of the hands upwards, as though in the act of imploring. This position slightly twists the muscles under the shoulder-blades, and shows us, while drawing in the breath, whether we are using the important back rib-raising muscles. We now raise the chest but very slightly, and the points of the shoulders not at all; nor can we breathe too deeply, for we have already raised the ribs with the back muscles and contracted the diaphragm (1910, 16).

Shakespeare also advocated the use of a special exercise to master his method of inspiration:

> Half fill the lungs through the mouth and then breathe in and out small amounts of air quickly and noiselessly until you feel yourself panting, yet doing nothing with the chest and without filling the lungs. Now extend this quick, noiseless panting or quivering until it is felt not only at the soft place but at the sides and near the shoulder-blades (1910, 16).

Shakespeare's posture and shoulder blade breathing method led to the back spreading techniques of the English choirs. The English choirs are famous for singing with their books held in front of them as they spread their backs on inhalation.

Another and different technique specific to the English School was a method aimed at stabilizing the diaphragm called "fixed diaphragm breathing." Fixed diaphragm breathing is a technique in which the singer thinks of inhaling into the epigastric region of the abdomen and then pulls the abdomen in quickly. At the same time as the inward pull of the abdomen, the singer raises the ribs upward and laterally. The Royal College of Music and Royal Academy of Music have within their teaching manuals the specific directions for taking a fixed diaphragmatic breath that they call "Correct Breathing."

> Take breath down, until there is a slight expansion of the *upper part of the abdomen* (viz., the soft part just below the breastbone), and follow this *immediately* by pulling in the abdomen, and raising and expanding the ribs…By means of this pulling in of the abdomen, the organs contained therein are pressed up into position, thus supporting, or as it is sometimes called, 'fixing' the diaphragm (Miller 2002, 36).

Vennard (1968, 28) states that "at one time it was thought that the action of the diaphragm pulled the ribs up," so that if the singer pulled in the abdomen tightly, holding the abdominal viscera upward, "the central tendon would then become a 'fulcrum' for the lifting of the ribs" (1968, 24).

The final national school of singing emerged in France. Regarding breathing, the French believed that we know how to breathe everyday for life, thus no special method of breathing was required for singing. Pierre Bonnier in his treatise, *La Voix Professionnelle* (1908), stated:

> The pupil since birth has breathed to breathe and hasn't managed badly; he learned instinctively to breathe for speaking; it remains up to him to learn *every bit as instinctively* to breathe for singing (Miller, 2002, 40).

The techniques of the Italian, German, French and English Schools of singing are still in use today. Of the four, the Italian School tends to be the most favored, although it is filled with inconsistencies. The treatises of Mancini, the Garcias, Lampertis and others are still available and sold in music stores around the world and many teachers use these books and their vocal exercises as the foundation of their teaching.

Regarding the debate between diaphragmatic and ribcage breathing, voice scientist Willard Zemlin in his book, *Speech and Hearing Science, Anatomy and Physiology* (1998), states that breathing for sound production is both diaphragmatic and intercostal. One does not operate independent of the other, thus both methods have validity. William Vennard in *Singing: the Mechanism and the Technic* (1968), states that the "most efficient breathing for singing" is a combination of rib and diaphragmatic (or abdominal breathing) (1968, 20),

A Historical Look at Breathing Methods for Singing by Heather Lyle

although, as a singer, he admits a preference for abdominal breathing: "Probably more breath can be inhaled in this manner than by the sideward expansion of the ribs, though the point is academic since both movements occur at once" (1968, 28).

The breath management system for classical singing most widely in use today is the Italian method of *appoggio*, or some variation thereof. However, singers of contemporary commercial styles (jazz, pop, rock, country, and even musical theatre), may employ a variety of other breathing strategies. To date, very little has been written describing those strategies in any detail.

Ingo Titze, in his book, *Principles of Voice Production* (1994), states that current research reveals that the best method for breath management may be more individualized than previously thought. He says that he withholds judgment regarding the best method for breath support but refers to two prevalent methods: the "up-and-in" and the "down-and-out method" and states that there is no guarantee that what is thought to happen physiologically actually happens (1994, 76). Body type (endomorph versus ectomorph) may play an important role in what might be the most suitable method for a given individual. When recently asked if his opinion had changed, he responded that it had not, but that the method of breath support may affect the resonance of the vocal tract:

> I have not changed my opinion much. The high ribcage breathing (up and in) does two things: 1. Most of the breathing work is done during inhalation (against the recoil force). 2. The overall airway length must become shorter, possibly producing a brighter sound due to higher formants. The lower ribcage position (with a down and out approach) puts more of the breathing work on the exhalation phase and the overall airway length may increase, allowing a darker sound (I. Titze, personal communication, Oct. 28, 2010).

As scientists continue to observe the details of contrasting techniques, a single "best method" may not be forthcoming. Recent studies focusing on muscle activation patterns in the chest and abdominal walls across a range of performance genres (Hodges, Melton 2010) noted considerable individuality and variation even within a single category, e.g., actors, classical singers, jazz singers. In addition, although voice research has tended to focus exclusively on classical singing, that is beginning to change. So the debate regarding breath management is likely to continue; however, by taking a historical look at its roots we may proceed with a broader and clearer view.

Bibliography

Brown, William Earl. *Vocal Wisdom: Maxims of Giovanni Battista Lamperti*. Whitefish, Montana: Kessinger Publishing LLC, 2008.

Caccini, Guilio. *Nuove Musiche*. 2nd Ed. Ed. Wiley K. Hitchcock. Middleton, Wisconsin: A-R Editions, 1979.

Coffin, Bernard. *Historical Vocal Pedagogy Classics*. Metuchen, NJ: Scarecrow Press, 1989.

Dudgeon, John. "Kung-Fu, or Tauist Medical Gymnastics," *Internet Sacred Texts Archive*, 1895. Web. 12 Oct. 2010. <http://www.sacred-texts.com/tao/index.htm>.

Frisch, Walter. *German Modernism: Music and the Arts*. Berkeley and Los Angeles: University of California Press, 2005.

Frisell, Anthony. *The Tenor Voice*. Boston: Brandon Publishing Co, 2003.

Garcia, Manuel. *A Complete Treatise on the Art of Singing*, 1st and 2nd ed. Translated by Donald V. Paschke. New York: De Capo Press, 1975.

_____. *Hints on Singing*. New York: Joseph Patelson Music House LTD., 1982.

Goldstein, M.D., Ed. "The Laryngoscope." *American Otological Society Journal Devoted to the Disease of the Ear-Throat-Neck*, Volume XII. St. Louis: Perrin and Smith Printing, 1902.

Henderson, William James. *Early History of Singing*. New York: Longman's Green and Co., 1921.

Hodges, Paul, Joan Melton. "Breath Management Strategies of Elite Vocal Performers across a Range of Performance Genres," Division of Physiotherapy, School of Health and Rehabilitation Sciences, University of Queensland, 2010.

Holmes, Gordon. *A Treatise on Vocal Physiology and Hygiene*. London, England: J & A Churchill, 1879.

Lamperti, Francesco. *The Art of Singing*. Translated by J.C. Griffith. Boca Raton, FL: Kalmus Classic Editions, 1928.

Lamperti, Giovanni Battista. *The Techniques of Bel Canto*. New York: G. Schirmer, 1905.

Mancini, Giambattista. (1774). *Practical Reflections on Figured Singing*. Translated by Pietro Buzzi. Boston: Oliver Ditson, 1907.

Miller, Richard. *National Schools of Singing*. Lanham, Maryland: The Scarecrow Express Inc., 1977.

_____. *Solutions for Singers*. New York: Oxford University, 2004.

Monahan, Brett Jeffrey. *The Art of Singing: a Compendium of Thoughts Published Between 1777 and 1927*. Metuchen, NJ: Scarecrow Press, 1978.

Bibliography (continued)

_____. *The Singer's Companion, a Guide to Improving Your Voice and Performance. Pompton Plains*, New Jersey: Limelight Editions, 2006.

Sbriglia, Giovanni. The "Old Italian Vocal Method" *Philharmonic Magazine*. Chicago: Philharmonic Company, 1905. Web. 12 Sept. 2010. http://www.ancientvocalmethod.blogspot.com>.

Shakespeare, William. *The Art of Singing*. Boston: Oliver Ditson Company, 1910.

_____. *Plain Words on Singing*. London, England: Putnum Sons, 1924.

Stark, James. *Bel Canto, A History of Vocal Pedagogy*. Toronto, Canada: University of Toronto Press, 2003.

Taylor, David C. *The Psychology of Singing, A Rational Method of Voice Culture based on a Scientific Analysis of All Systems, Ancient and Modern*. New York: The Macmillan Company, 1922.

Titze, Ingo. "Introducing a Video for Using Straw Phonation," Journal of Singing, May 2010.

_____. *Principles of Voice Production*. Englewood Cliffs, New Jersey: Prentice-Hall, 1994.

Tosi, Pier Francesco. *Observations on the Florid Song*. London, England: William Reeves, 1723.

Vennard, William. *Singing: The Mechanism and the Technic*. 5th ed. New York: Carl Fischer, 1968.

Zemlin, Willard R. *Speech and Hearing Science: Anatomy and Physiology*. Needham Heights, MA: Allen and Bacon Press, 1998.

The World of Vocal Crossover

Sean Andrews has performed, produced, musically directed, directed, and taught in opera and musical theatre since 1996. His performance credits are extensive and include a national tour of Pirates of Penzance, more than 30 operas with Opera Australia, Ensemble and Piangi cover for Phantom of the Opera throughout Asia and Australia, the role of Chauvalin in The Scarlet Pimpernel, and Mr. Andrews in Titanic in Australian Premier performances. He has produced and directed numerous Broadway Hits shows for his company called Musaeus and is a candidate for the Master of Music degree at Queensland Conservatorium, Griffith University, Brisbane.

Many performing artists now look to diversify their skills so as to become more employable as industry demands increase and potential employment seems to decrease. Singers are not immune to this diversification phenomenon, and even opera casts frequently include performers from both operatic and musical theatre backgrounds. Such was the case in Opera Australia's recent production of *Pirates of Penzance*, where in vocal rehearsals, we often heard, "Please no musical theatre sound in this section," or "We would like a full operatic sound here please."

Singing multiple styles, or vocal crossover, although not new, comes with great controversy and polarized opinion. Indeed, classically trained students are often banned from or "warned off" delving into other vocal genres because of the perception that it will harm and/or destroy their classical technique.

Classical singing itself includes a variety of styles and vocal colors, for example, opera, oratorio, Lieder and French melodies; likewise musical theatre encompasses a wide range of vocal styles. Therefore, what is so different about

changing the color of one's voice to suit another genre, from changing it to suit another style within a genre? And why are we so concerned about destroying our classical technique by singing commercial styles? Is it simply a matter of changing the color of the voice, or do we use totally different techniques?

In my opinion, some of the polarization on the subject of vocal crossover is due to the abundance of literature on classical vocal pedagogy and the almost non-existence of literature on commercial vocal styles.

As a crossover artist having been employed in both opera and musical theatre since 1996, I am here to tell you, it is very possible to sing different styles and not damage your technique. In fact, singing a variety of styles has positively informed and improved my technique and musicality across the board, and I am now doing an advanced degree in Crossover—yes, I am studying opera, musical theatre and jazz concurrently!

My introduction to crossover came while coaching in Sydney many years ago. While working a classical piece, the coach requested a decrescendo on a long held note at the end of a phrase. The coach was quick to suggest that I should think of the decrescendo as an increase in head voice rather than thinking I was taking something away from the sound. My understanding was to increase the head ratio on the decrescendo to give a lighter sound. At that moment, it occurred to me that this was a vocal quality that was present in my singing of musical theatre and of pop songs for weddings, a quality that I had always applied to the singing of these commercial forms. The notion of head voice was not new to me, but the concept of changing the ratio of the mix in that direction made me think about the negotiation through opera to musical theatre, and now to jazz, and how easily that negotiation can be achieved through muscular knowledge and the singer's kinesthetic understanding of the sensations of registration. From my teaching and personal performance, the comparison of singing opera to singing commercial music includes a feeling of withdrawing much of the perceived operatic tone.

The notion of vocal color is a strong element when crossing styles. For example, looking at Tom Rakewell's aria from Stravinsky's *The Rake's Progress* and "Maria" from *West Side Story*, are these two pieces of music really that different in color? How many times have I been in an opera chorus when the conductor has asked for really soft sounds and wondered how close the breath and registration are to crooning? Working on French Melodie of Reynold Hahn, I have wondered the same thing about registration and the use of breath.

So, is it more about having a *flexible* technique, than about having a totally new and foreign technique for some of these styles? Good healthy singing is good healthy singing, regardless of style. Technical faults like poor breath management, tongue root or jaw tension have no place in any style.

While classical audiences are often looking to experience the thrill of the *perfect sound*, musical theatre audiences want to be taken on a journey, and jazz audiences expect change and challenge. Therefore we might, roughly, categorize classical vocal music as an aesthetic experience, musical theatre as a dramatic experience and jazz as a musical experience. Obviously, each category includes elements of the other two; however, identifying a main focus helps to determine how we vocally and mentally approach them.

Distortion of rhythm and tempo, particularly in jazz, is a musicality issue in the crossover phenomenon. So there are not only vocal considerations, but also text interpretation and musicality to master.

Vocal Considerations

In my experience, there are at least three main areas of skill development (closely linked and intertwined) that are essential to successfully negotiating the cross between classical and commercial styles:

1. Registration
2. Breath management and support/control
3. Venue Acoustics and Amplification

Registration

Terminology in the area of registration tends to be varied and confusing, as "The action of registration is nowhere clearly explained and the exact causes remain undecided" (Fields 1970, in Miller 2002, 99). Nevertheless, looking at all sides of the subject can assist in understanding one's own kinesthetic, or singer sensations.

For classical singers to move successfully into musical theatre and jazz, they must embrace a much smaller *feeling* of their sound with an understanding that the use of amplification is imperative in these later styles. This can be especially difficult for opera singers to do, as *less voice* and lighter quality are not their known sensations.

Being a tenor, I have found the classical concept of *voix mixte* very helpful in understanding the sensations of registration in my own voice. Donald Miller explores *voix mixte* registration in the male voice as he compares the A4 (3 semitones below high C) sung by Pavarotti with that of Simoneau in Mozart's aria "Un'aura amorosa." Miller notes that the formants of Simoneau are close to speech values

and lighter in quality than those of Pavarotti (2008, 82-86). An interesting observation when one considers that a major stylistic factor of musical theatre and jazz is based on speech values and lighter quality registration.

In many ways, opera singers have an advantage in crossover because their singing musculature is so heavily developed. However, in my experience, this greater muscular athleticism brought to the styles of musical theatre and jazz from opera is often accompanied by a lack of understanding and ability to reregister the voice. This can be a major hurdle, as opera singers often feel they are not singing with tone when they are not singing operatically and, therefore, neglect to reregister the voice.

Accommodating changes of registration is closely linked to breath management and the ratio of volume of air to air pressure.

Breath Management and Support/Control

As singing is a heightened sound and usually needs more volume of air than everyday speech, in my mind, a heightened intake of air is required to accommodate this increase, regardless of style.

Scott McCoy cites four principal approaches to breath management:

> Almost all voice pedagogues agree that four principal methods of breath management can be described: clavicular (upper chest), thoracic (lower chest), abdominal (belly breathing) and a balanced breath, often now called appoggio, which is a combination of the latter two (2004, 93).

It is that combination of the latter two, the balanced breath or *appoggio* that I find most vital for crossover. There can be a strong temptation in contemporary styles for the singer to breathe in the upper chest due to the amplification of the voice and the need for less volume, as compared to opera. Less volume means less air is needed, therefore less intake, the temptation toward high, upper chest breathing and the danger of losing antagonistic control between the muscles of inhalation and exhalation. Hence, I strongly suggest that musical theatre and contemporary singers establish their breathing on a solid technique of balanced breath in order to maintain healthy and efficient control of their sound.

Opera singers, on the other hand, have a tendency to take larger breaths and need to relax their intake if they are to sing more contemporary material. However, the danger for opera singers as well, is that relaxing the breath can lead to clavicular breathing, which means losing the opportunity to establish antagonistic control, and that control can be even more important when singing amplified music.

What I am inferring is a close synchronization of breath management and breath *support*—a word that always stirs the pot of controversy in singing pedagogy. For me, support is the supply of air to the larynx and how the glottis uses that air.

As a crossover artist, I subscribe to the pull-in of the lower abdominals, as advocated by Janice Chapman and the lean out or *appoggio* technique described in the classic literature of Richard Miller. Chapman describes a "diamond" of support, the lowest point of which is "2 to 6 centimeters above the pubic bone" (2006, 44). And Miller says, "A sensation of transverse expansion across the entire body is experienced upon inhalation and is present throughout the sung phrase" (2002, 42-43). Regardless of the approach used, "the goal of breath support in singing is to provide a stable supply of air at the correct pressure for the desired pitch and loudness" (McCoy 2004, 96). Crossover is very much the interplay of volume versus support and airflow, and the techniques of both Chapman and Miller move the singer toward that ultimate antagonistic control, regardless of style.

Venue Acoustics and Amplification

The fact that many commercial styles use amplification and do not require high decibels of vocal sound to get over a large orchestra or fill a large hall, does not mean that when singing commercial styles the glottis has no air pressure. With softer sounds must come a control and support equal to, if not greater than, that for loud singing. If the voice is too thick, or TA (thyroarytenoid) dominant, then it is very difficult to sing with less air and less volume. As many classical pedagogues have suggested, soft singing can be difficult for a young singer to achieve because of the need to understand that volume of air is not directly related to the amount of lower abdominal activity, or *support*. I do believe the advantage that opera singers have, as mentioned before in the context of registration, is that their developed muscularity is better than their contemporary counterparts—an opinion that may not be received well in the contemporary voice community!

Techniques and Tools for Crossing among Styles

Speech Quality

Speech quality is no stranger either to classical or contemporary vocal techniques. The historic Italian tradition of voice training has a familiar adage, *si canta come si parla* (One sings as one speaks), which is based on the assumption that one speaks efficiently, as when using energized stage delivery (Spivey 2008, 483). *Sing as you speak*, however, is a phrase reserved for the very fortunate few whose voices seem to be naturally free (Spivey 2008, 485).

Norman Spivey goes a step further by stating that "Singing is not simply sustained speech spun out over wide-ranging pitch fluctuations, except in the most simplistic and technically limited vocal styles," and that "many problems singers encounter stem from a false conception that singing is nothing more than an extension of [ordinary] speech, and requires only the same degree of energy as speech" (2008, 485).

As a tenor, the notion of speech quality is not useful when I am singing a sustained top C (although one could certainly speak at that pitch), and if I am very honest it doesn't make a whole lot of sense when I am singing classical, musical theatre or jazz styles in my upper middle and top registers. However, it is very appropriate in much contemporary music. Speech quality, or a speech-like delivery, is a specific tool and color used to create the ambiance of style needed for musical theatre and jazz, where many of the vocal lines are in the middle to low range of the voice and use rhythms that are similar to speech.

> In musical theatre, singing is an acoustical and emotional extension of speech and, while something similar might be said of operatic singing, I would argue that opera seeks to transcend speaking. But musical theatre is a vernacular forum and owes its credibility to its ability to touch the prosaic. Therefore, it is important that singing in musical theatre, rather than transcend speaking, amplify and extend it without distorting or transfiguring it (Saunders-Barton 2001).

It follows then, that opera singers wanting to cross into musical theatre and particularly into jazz, need to embrace more speech-like air pressure and a freedom of rhythm that emulates spoken text.

Vowel Perception/Modification

Vowel perception and modification are integral to changes of colors from one style to another and are closely linked to speech quality. The subject of vowels is complicated and extensively discussed in vocal literature. Hence, for purposes of crossover, I will stay with the kinesthetic sensations of vowel production. So much of vowel production is affected by the pitch at which the vowel is sung and is closely linked to the shape of the vocal tract which, in turn, relates to vowel perception and modification. I use the word modification here in the context of discriminating vowels from one style to another, not for the use of passaggio attention. When I am singing classically the vowels seem to be rounder in the mouth, whereas when I am sing

ing musical theatre and jazz, the vowels feel much squarer in the mouth and, dare I say, wider in the throat.

Pharyngeal Space or Open Throat Technique

The kinesthetic sensation of pharyngeal space or throat opening is interesting in that what the singer feels and what is happening physiologically are often two very different things. In order to achieve the strong harmonic overtones that are required frequently in contemporary styles, I feel as though the pharynx widens and becomes squarer when, in fact, it has been suggested in vocal literature that it becomes slimmer. On the other hand, when singing opera, the pharyngeal space feels rounder in conjunction with the vowel production.

Interestingly enough, finding the squarer and wider *sensation* for musical theatre and particularly for Bublé style big band, has improved the pharyngeal space for my classical singing—one of many instances in which singing a variety of styles has improved the overall technique.

Low Larynx versus High Larynx

In contemporary literature, there is mixed opinion on laryngeal position, and much of the discussion is focused around *belt* and its permutations (e.g., Collyer 1997, Edwin 1998, 2004, Titze 2007, Urech 2006). Important as belting is, this seems a shame, as belt is only one of many vocal colors used by singers of contemporary music.

My own perception of low, high or neutral larynx is that laryngeal position is closely linked to vowel shape and the kinesthetic sensation of the vowel. I make no conscious attempt to lower or raise my larynx in any style. Rather, I suggest allowing the position of the larynx to be dictated by the stylistic change of vowel shape required to negotiate the change in sound.

Onset and Offset, Release or Decay

Three types of onset are explained in great detail in the literature of classical pedagogy: hard, soft and balanced, the latter being the most appropriate for classical and musical theatre singing. Jazz, on the other hand, uses a variety of onsets for color and style and to enhance the text. For example, in jazz, the beginning of a phrase can have a soft onset and/or the beginning pitch may be scooped. Ideally, it is a millisecond scoop and the appropriate pitch is eventually established; nonetheless, the pitch is not immediately established as it would be in classical singing. Dynamic muscle equilibrium occurs only when the correct pitch is established and before that, there is more airflow than adduction at the glottis.

The challenge for singers coming into jazz is first, to find the scooped pitch soft onset and second, not to withdraw all sense of air pressure relating to the onset. This specific onset does not lack breath support; it does, however, modify onset to the slightly lighter side of dynamic muscle equilibrium.

As with onset, decay/release/offset, or how you finish the sound, can also be used as a stylistic trait and may be hard, soft or balanced. Variation of the classical notion of equilibrium, or balanced decay or release, is not unique to jazz vocal styles. Many classical singers use noticeably hard offsets, particularly tenors, singing large Italianate opera styles. This requires a very forceful adduction of the glottis and is used for dramatic effect. It may also be employed in musical theatre for the same dramatic intent, but the ideal in both classical and musical theatre singing is to have breath flow stopping at the exact time of vocal fold abduction for a balanced release.

Jazz, however, uses soft release as one of the stylistic traits in its tool bag of colors. In jazz, the pitch of the last note is established and then air pressure is dropped and airflow increased, which coincides with a drop of pitch until the voice is in a type of speech modality. This can be a challenge for the classical singer who is used to singing to the end of the phrase with full vocal tone and air pressure.

Articulation of Text

My thinking about articulation was strongly influenced by the performance of a fantastic Australian baritone, John Bolton Wood, in Opera Australia's production of *Iolanthe*. Wood's articulation of the text was absolutely clear and crisp at any speed and without any loss of beauty in his voice.

Richard Miller suggests that "...consonants need not be considered unwelcome intruders that impede good vocalization. If each consonant is permitted to enjoy its brief but exact phonetic location and is allowed a clean departure when its stint is over, the singer's ideal of the 'pure' vowel will not be violated" (1996, 79).

Brief consonants, however, are not invariably the rule, even in classical singing. For example, the songs of Strauss and Schubert demand similar consonant attention to that of *Martin Guerre*. So, for purposes of crossover, there may be little difference in the articulation of text from German song to musical theatre.

There is a difference, though, between the articulation of the final consonant of a phrase from classical and musical theatre to jazz and contemporary. Because of the prominent emulations of speech, many of the final consonants in jazz and contemporary are not articulated or are very lightly articulated. This is different from classical and musical theatre, where final consonants are clear and on breath and breath pressure.

Vibrato

In an article for the *Journal of Singing* (2009), Virginia Sublett poses the question, "Vibrato or Non-Vibrato in Solo and Choral Singing: Is there Room for Both?" She concludes:

> When all is said and done, I firmly believe that the voice is a sturdy instrument, capable of a far greater range of sounds, timbres, and expressive devices than any other. Although as teachers we want to help our students make the best and most efficient use of their natural instruments, there doesn't seem to be much valid scientific reason to discourage non-vibrato singing, only an argument in favor of a particular aesthetic choice (2009, 543).

Both vibrato and non-vibrato singing are used in all styles of vocal music, from early music and Lieder to musical theatre and other contemporary styles, as a color or expressive value. Many of the great Lieder singers use non-vibrato singing, and music theatre singers use it most effectively and thrillingly on last notes of songs for dramatic suspension and tension.

Nevertheless, non-vibrato singing remains a contentious issue. My understanding, from vocal literature and from my own experience is that vibrato is a natural occurrence in the voice, and that by withdrawing it, one is adding tension. Richard Miller says, "The singer who first produces a straight-tone onset, followed by vibrato (a favorite device of some Wagnerian and certain Lieder singers), does not arrive at free (efficient) muscle synergism until that moment at which vibrato makes its appearance" (1986, 187).

I would suggest that tension in the vocal folds caused by non-vibrato singing can be minimized to a degree, thereby limiting vocal fatigue, by a continuous monitoring of tongue tension and increased awareness of air flow to counteract the increase in air pressure. It is a fine balance of airflow and subglottic pressure, regardless of style, but the balance of airflow becomes vitally important when singing contemporary styles and when using straight or non-vibratoed tones.

Finally, this interesting phenomenon is worth mentioning. When Dr. Scott McCoy made a recent visit to Australia, I had the privilege of working with him in an open seminar. While we were working he applied a narrowband spectrogram to me singing a note with vibrato, as in classical style, and then without vibrato, as in commercial styles. The straight tone or vibrato-less note was aurally perceived by the audience as straight, but the spectrogram told the story of a note that still maintained a small presence of vibrato.

Conclusion

These are some of the basic techniques and colors of vocal crossover. I have not dealt with musicality, the notion of dramatic intent, body awareness, stagecraft or physiology, all of which are crucial. In addition, an understanding of *style* is particularly important. Many opera singers have performed—live and recorded—non-classical material and have shown conscious or unconscious disregard for the bounds of stylistic truth. As with the respective styles of classical music such as Lieder, opera and French song, non-classical genres have stylistic traits that must be acknowledged. I would also strongly suggest that learning to sing these styles appropriately can positively inform artists musically, dramatically and vocally.

Exploration and research on crossover in Australia and world-wide is almost non-existent; yet the demand for singers to cross over is becoming more and more evident. Vocal crossover is happening in the professional world, so perhaps the time has come for positive debate and discussion on the vocal challenges. Robert Edwin writes:

> Competitive athletes are encouraged to participate in cross training activities that will exercise muscle groups differently from the way they are normally used in their specific sport. Just as cross training promotes optimal performa nce levels and mitigates against injury in athletes, cross training for the voice promotes similar results for "voice athletes" (2008, 73).

Bibliography

Chapman, J. L. *Singing and Teaching Singing: A Holistic Approach to Classical Voice*. Abington, Oxfordshire: Plural Publishing, 2006.

Collyer, S. "The Classical Teacher and Belting," *Australian Voice*, 3, 37 – 41, 1997.

Edwin, R. "Belting 101," *Journal of Singing*, 55 (1/2), 53 – 55, 61 – 62, 1998.

_____. "Belt Yourself," *Journal of Singing*, 60 (3) 285 – 288, 2004.

_____. "Cross Training for the Voice," *Journal of Singing*, 65 (1), 73-76, 2008.

McCoy, S. *Your Voice: An Inside View*. Princeton, NJ: Inside View Press, 2004.

Miller, D.G. *Resonance in Singing: Voice Building through Acoustic Feedback*. Princeton, NJ: Inside View Press, 2008.

Miller, R. *National Schools of Singing: English, French, German, and Italian Techniques of Singing Revisited*. Lanham, MD: Scarecrow Press, 1997, paperback 2002.

_____. *Solutions for Singers*. New York: Oxford University Press, 2004
.

_____. *The Structure of Singing: System and Art in Vocal Technique*. New York: Schirmer Books, 1986.

_____. "Voice Pedagogy: Registration," *Journal of Singing*, 62(5), 537-539, 2006.

Saunders-Barton, M. Position Paper, National Association of Teachers of Singing (NATS), 2001.

Spivey, N. "Music Theater Singing ... Let's Talk, Part 1: On the Relationship of Speech and Singing," *Journal of Singing*, 64(4), 483-489, 2008.

Sublett, V. "Vibrato or Non-Vibrato in Solo and Choral Singing: Is There Room for Both?" *Journal of Singing*, 65 (5), 539-544, 2009.

Titze, I R. "Belting and a High Larynx Position," *Journal of Singing*, 63 (5), 557-558, 2007.

Urech, C. "Belting for Contemporary Performance," *Voice of ANATS* (Australian National Association of Teachers of Singing), 4 – 8, July

Reviews and Sources, *Tara McAllister-Viel, Associate Editor*

Reviews and Sources, *Tara McAllister-Viel, Associate Editor*

Editorial Column *by Tara McAllister-Viel, Associate Editor*

Tara McAllister-Viel is a professional voice director, Equity actress, and voice-over specialist working In the US, Asia, Europe and the U.K. over the course of 18 years. She is resident voice director for London-based company, Unanimous Cohort and is Voice lecturer at Central School of Speech and Drama, University of London, England, leading the voice programme on The Collaborative and Devised Theatre specialty within the acting conservatoire. Previously, she was Visiting Professor-Voice at The Korean National University of Arts, School of Drama, Seoul, Korea. Publications include articles in *Modern Drama, Theatre Topics, Contemporary Theatre Review, Voice and Speech Review*, and a chapter in Boston and Cook's *Breath in Action*.

In this issue, *A World of Voice*, we celebrate the international and intercultural practices and pedagogies of the voice. This section brings you a unique collection of book reviews and sources articles authored by distinguished colleagues from different countries and cultural backgrounds. From colleagues in the U.K., Betsy Allen, Helen Ashton, and Claudette Williams, the issue theme is addressed through reviews and articles on practice set in different intercultural contexts. Betsy suggests resources for voice trainers moving to London on short or long-term stay. For those interested in incorporating Western and Asian modes of training, Helen explores the possibilities of interfacing praxis from different traditions and suggests a few texts for the voice teacher's bookshelf. Claudette's review of Phillip Zarrilli's *Psychophysical Actor Training* proposes that Eastern breath work, when integrated with Western actor training, can provide voice trainers with alternative ways of thinking, talking and training the voice.

From colleagues in the U.S., Karen Ryker contributes a

review of *Breath in Action*, which looks at breath work from a variety of different cultural and disciplinary perspectives. Julia Lenardon's review of *Zygmunt Molik's Voice and Body Work* considers the reflections of one of Jerzy Grotowski's original acting members and leading voice trainer of Teatr Laboratorium. *The Politics of American Actor Training*, reviewed by Elise Robinson, is an anthology of diverse essays that scrutinizes training programs not only in the United States but also "as they are transmitted to other countries and cultures outside of U.S. national borders." Scott Nice's review of Janet Rogers and Frankie Armstrong's *Acting and Singing with Archetypes* highlights one approach to vocal and physical engagement with mythological figures from a variety of different cultures.

Several reviews focus on a perennial favourite, Shakespeare. Erik Singer's review of *Filthy Shakespeare* looks at the bawdy bard's sexual puns and wordplay. Krista Scott examines The *Eloquent Shakespeare*, a pronouncing dictionary and valuable resource for voice and text coaches. *Thinking Shakespeare*, reviewed by Marlene Johnson, offers a concise method for embodying the text.

Reviews of books specifically targeting singers, but also useful to spoken voice practitioners, include *Get the Callback: The Art of Auditioning for Musical Theatre*, reviewed by Julio Matos and *What Every singer Needs to Know abut the Body*, reviewed by Debra Garvey.

In addition, this section presents reviews of voice and acting texts that voice professionals will find worthwhile. Anne Schilling's review of the second edition of Rocco Dal Vera and Robert Barton's *Voices Onstage and Off* points out a few of the revisions made to the original text. David Carey and Rebecca Clark Carey's newly released *Verbal Arts Workbook* is examined by Rena Cook and Christina Shewell's *Voice Work: Art and Science of Changing Voices* is reviewed by Erica Bailey. Rebecca Root looks at *The Thought Propels the Sound*, a guide for fostering a closer relationship between the theatre director and production voice coach.

Finally, this section offers master thesis abstracts from voice professionals recently graduated from voice training programs in Canada and the U.K. Dovetailing with the theme of this issue is Wing-Hong Li's abstract, entitled *Is the acquisition of the British RP accent necessary, desirable or achievable for Cantonese-speaking Hong Kong migrants entering the UK, speaking ESL?* [Birmingham School of Acting]. Thrasso Petras, from the University of Alberta, Department of Drama, Theatre Voice Pedagogy program, submits his abstract entitled *Developing a Responsive Relationship Between Sound, Motion, and Text*. Two graduates from Central School of Speech and Drama, University of London, MA-Voice Studies program, offer their abstracts: Christian David Fellner authors *Giving Autism a Voice* and Liz Flint submits *An Evaluation of the Effectiveness of using a Spoken Voice Workshop to Improve the Performance of a Song.*

In total, this section is a snapshot of the interests of voice professionals at this moment in time—what is being read, talked about and implemented in voice studios and rehearsal spaces. Hopefully, the reviews and sources articles here have introduced you to a few new ideas and resources for your praxis. Enjoy!

Moving to London

Betsy Allen was certified an Associate Fitzmaurice Voicework teacher in 2003. She holds an MA in Voice Pedagogy and Voice Performance from New York University, where she studied individually with Catherine Fitzmaurice and Jonathan Hart Makwaia. She has taught voice and speech for seven years, including such places as, The Actors Centre, Millennium Dance, Arts Educational Schools, Kingston College and London Metropolitan University and has performed as a singer and voice artist for over 15 years in LA, NYC and London. As a US native, she specializes in teaching American dialects. She is also a certified Pilates Mat instructor.

Moving to London? Going on sabbatical? A special visit to catch a few shows at The National Theatre or the BITE series at The Barbican? There are many attractions in the UK for a curious and ambitious tourist. But as a voice artist and tutor who's been living in London for five years, I've found a tremendous wealth of artistic avenues to explore. With a little investigation, you too will find that London is one of the greatest and diverse cities for the arts in the world.

Your success depends upon the length and type of your visa and where you will reside (try to connect with a Londoner who will swap homes with you, let you stay on their sofa, or give you solid advice on affordability of travel/living within the city and easy access neighborhoods, because London is HUGE). If you are able to take up residence, join the British Voice Association (www.british-voice-association.com) and VASTA (www.vasta.org). These groups will publicize the many seminars and special interest workshops offered to its members, which provide many opportunities to network with other voice professionals.

For example, I have been able to assist in Fitzmaurice Voice

(FV) workshops in London (www.fitzmauricevoice.com), attend the Breath conference held at RADA (www.rada.ac.uk), and study extended voice with Roy Hart Theatre artists at ALRA, (www.alra.co.uk). I was also a panelist at the Theatre Noise conference at Central School of Speech and Drama (www.cssd.ac.uk), and held my own FV workshops at The Actors Centre (www.actorscentre.co.uk), and at LAMDA (www.lamda.org.uk), all during which I met other voice professionals that have helped me get work and performance opportunities. Never underestimate the power of a good workshop!

If you are a performer, join Spotlight (www.spotlight.com), which is an essential casting tool used by industry professionals throughout the UK. If you are here for a extended period of time, become a member of The Actors Centre (www.actorscentre.co.uk). This has been an invaluable resource for me and many of other teaching artists. There is a studio both in the north of England, and in Covent Garden in London. In the realm of performance and in the spirit of keeping your own body moving and in "the work," check out what the experimental theatre company, Complicite, has on offer for workshops (www.complicite.org), and look to these two dance studios that are performance venues as well as places to train: The Place (www.theplace.org.uk) and Siobhan Davies Studios www.siobhandavies.com). There are ongoing classes, contact improvisation jams and school break workshops.

Two great studios one can drop into and become reacquainted with the most important muscle for vocalists, the transversus, are TriYoga (www.triyoga.co.uk) and Ten Pilates (www.tenpilates.com). Each with a few locations scattered around north, west and central London. The Southbank Centre (www.southbankcentre.co.uk), is colossal in artistic scope and size. There is film, art, music and theatre all in one stretch alongside south bank of the River Thames. There are free talks, seminars and concerts for all to join. They're especially great for those of us who might be pinching pennies. The Barbican, The Young Vic, Riverside Studios, Hampstead Theatre, The Lyric and Battersea Arts Centre are excellent venues for seeing new theatre work and all are great places to meet people as well.

London's vibrant arts community knows no bounds. With an indulgence in the kinds of activities that brought you to become a teaching artist in the first place, London will not disappoint.

Helen Ashton trained at The Central School of Speech and Drama, graduating with Distinction from the MA in Voice. She specialises in speech and accent work, which she teaches at Drama Centre London and The Central School of Speech and Drama. She has privately coached actors in many different accents for Stage and Screen, and is Southern England Associate Editor of the International Dialects of English Archive. Her work also includes training individuals in business and community settings. Helen also holds an MA with First Class Honours in History from The University of Edinburgh.

This article offers some ideas for building the beginnings of a bookshelf that looks towards the East for inspiration. There are huge spaces in this list waiting to be filled, just as there are huge spaces in our knowledge of how the distance between Eastern and Western voice practices could be reduced. Thanks to very accessible international travel, and the internet, we now have more access than ever before to knowledge and wisdom from other cultures. This article explores the rich interface between different spheres of knowledge, and the new practices and understandings that can be generated at the boundary.

My Perspective

Early in my career, I quickly discovered that Western Voicework (at least the small part of all the practice taking place that has been written down!) traditionally seldom drew explicitly on Yogic or Eastern principles. In fact, there was very often caution expressed, or distancing of the two schools of practice. "The breathing processes developed by… Yoga practitioners are of no use to the actor (Linklater, 2006, 43-44)." I was ready to accept that for the actor-in-training this might well be the case. But for

myself, as a practitioner involved in both worlds (I practice *Astanga Vintasa Yoga*), I was keen to understand the relationship between the two disciplines, and explore any areas where cross-cultural fertilisation might occur. Upon starting to do so, as part of my MA thesis, I quickly discovered that this is a flourishing area of emergent research.

My interest in India and in yoga has dictated the shape of this article. There are many other practitioners who are drawing on other non-Western principles to inform Western Actor training. For example, *Butoh, Suzuki, Noh* and *Kathakali* are all finding places internationally in drama conservatoires. However, these are not areas about which I am well-informed, and for that reason, this article will be confined to Indian Yogic principles.

If you are also interested in the ways that Yoga can inform our work as voice trainers, the list that follows may be useful. The works referred to here have all been helpful to me in my research. I have divided the list into various sections to make it easy for you to dip in depending on what you're looking for. In each paragraph, I give an explanation of the ways in which the works have helped me to develop my understanding.

The Master Sources

To fully understand the way that breathwork is used in yogic traditions, it is important to understand the context in which it is studied, and the reasons for which it is studied. The original Yogic texts, written between ca. 400 and 200 AD can provide this information. The Yoga-Sutra of Patanjali outlines the path of Yogic life, and offers good background on the way in which *pranayama* (breath exercises) fits into this. Many translations exist. I found this one very accessible: Hartranft, Chip, *The Yoga-Sutra of Patanjali, A New Translation with Commentary*, London 2003.

Patanjali's *Raja Yoga* is largely contemplative. The more physical practices and specific breath exercises (*pranayama*) and poses (*asana*), are outlined in the *Hatha Yoga Pradapika*. This was written in the fifteenth century by Yogi Swatmarama as a means to achieve the purification outlined by Patanjali. This is one of the three foundational texts of the Hatha yoga practiced all over the world today, and outlines clearly the details of *pranayama* practices. Modern breathwork exercises being taught in yoga studios have their roots in the techniques outlined here.

Outlines of Pranayama and breathwork

Saraswati, Swami Niranjanananda, *Prana, Pranayama, Pranavidya*, India, 2002.

There are numerous of texts explaining yogic breath and

pranayama for Western students. I particularly like this one because it is very thorough and includes everything you need to gain a well-rounded understanding of the subject. It begins with a detailed explanation of the theoretical foundations of *pranayama* practice, and concludes with details of advanced practice and the transcendental possibilities offered by working with *prana*. These properly contextualise the second section, which is the part of the work that I think is most useful to us as practitioners. This is a detailed guide to the many different *pranayama* techniques. It includes drawings, and thorough instruction in each of the exercises. Many of the exercises outlined are excellent as methods of deepening connection to and understanding of the anatomy and physiology of breathing.

Saraswati, Swami Ambikananda, *Principles of Breathwork*, London 1999

This is a very useful introductory text which explains the perspective taken on breathwork in the Yogic tradition. It is extremely accessible, and clearly outlines the unity of body and mind which is central to many practices arising from Eastern training traditions, and certainly to those arising from Yoga.

Farhi, Donna, *The Breathing Book*, New York 1996

This book on breath is written by internationally renowned yoga teacher Donna Farhi, and is a wonderful deep and thorough exploration of breathwork from a Yogic perspective. The book includes more detailed anatomic knowledge, and exploratory exercises to deepen awareness of the breath. These exercises could be taken from the early part of a breathwork book for actors. She then moves on to more explicitly yogic exercises- exploring the effect of different postures (*asanas*) on breath, and guiding the reader through *pranayama* exercises drawn from yogic texts.

Yoga and Voicework

Philip Zarilli's extensive published research is very interesting for exploring the interplay between East and West in Actor Training. Although he doesn't specifically narrow his focus to address voice training, he does include a lot of information on breathwork techniques. His work is nonetheless very useful for us, because he introduces the Eastern paradigm for understanding the relationship between mind and body in very clear terms. Whereas we in the West often separate the two, Eastern systems of knowledge frequently locate one within the other. "Yoga, the martial arts…. allow(s) for a shift in one's experience of the "body" and "mind" aspects from their gross separation, marked by the body's constant disappearance , to a much subtler, dialectical engagement of body-in-mind, and mind-in-body" (*Senses in Performance*, pp54-55).

Morgan, Michael, *Constructing the holistic actor: Fitzmaurice Voicework*

This recent book looks at the context in which Fitzmaurice voice work operates, exploring the various disciplines and practices which inform and relate to the system. It is made clear that yoga was not an influence in the development of the Fitzmaurice system, but rather that comparisons may be drawn. The book examines the interplay between meditation used in yoga, and Fitzmaurice destructuring work; *pranayama* techniques and theory of breath in Fitzmaurice voicework; and the asanas of yoga and the postures used by Fitzmaurice.

Garfinkle, David, '*Pranayama* Bandhas and Voice Training', in *The Moving Voice: The Integration of Voice and Movement Studies* presented by the Voice and Speech Review, 2009, p. 24-30.

Garfinkle's article in 'The Moving Voice' VSR explores the ways in which voicework and yoga can inform each other, particularly in relationship to *pranayama* and the *Bandhas*. He situates his work as follows: (Begin quote)"It is in the hara, the location where multiple systems come together in the ongoing flow of the breath, where the mind and body, the physical and mental realms, the subtle and physical energies where consciousness and being, breath and thought, tone and word, have the potential of integral transformation…when I become this dynamic unity and can skilfully work with my core, the metaphor of the hara becomes a real source for my voice and emotional expression." (p.30)
Tara McAllister-Viel

McAllister –Viel has devised a vocal warm-up based on Hatha Yoga postures that she uses with BA students at the Central School of Speech and Drama. She has not published this work, although full details of it can be found in her PhD thesis: *McAllister-Viel, Tara. Toward and Intercultural/Interdisciplinary Approach to Training Actors' Voices. Unpublished PhD: University of Exeter, 2006: pp.187-259 and Chapter 3 DVD*. This is an example of the innovative crosscultural practices going on in studios around the world, that aren't written down in books. If we aren't lucky enough to find ourselves with access to these studios, details of this sort of work can often be found in MA and PhD theses.

Beyond the breath

Until now, this article has focussed on the ways that non-western understandings of the body-mind relationship, and in particular the breath, can inform our practice as voice teachers.

Sources

The voice teacher's bookshelf: Incorporating Asian Principles and Practices with Western Voice Training
by Helen Ashton

My current teaching is mainly centred in Accent and Dialect work. And my major area of interest and research is the politics of coaching accents in postcolonial contexts, in particular the dynamic which exists between Britain and India.

The field of World Englishes is a fascinating area of study. Now that English operates as lingua franca in so many international locations, there is a need to re-frame our views of who speaks English with the 'correct' accent. When two syllable-timed speakers communicate with each other, does it matter if neither use British or American stress patterns? A good introductory reader which presents many of the major arguments in this field is: Jenkins, Jennifer, *World Englishes 2nd ed.*, New York 2009.

Another fascinating text on the politic of accent and its role in creating power-relations is Rosina Lipi-green, *English with an Accent*. This book situates itself in an American context, but the issues it raises are nonetheless relevant to those of us in the UK. The book examines the operation of accent stereotypes, and discrimination using examples from educational, judiciary, media and entertainment sectors. This work, in the context of growth of *Globish* (McCrum) and World Englishes is a fascinating and thought-provoking read.

The interplay between East and West continues to be an area of emergent scholarship as the ways that cultures and spheres of knowledge interact with each other change and shift. This is something that many of us are engaging with daily in some respect as we get approached by accent-modification clients from post-colonial cultures, or as we use yogic breathing systems at our local after-work class. As ever, there is much more diverse and interesting research practice taking place in studios around the world than sitting on my bookshelf, but I hope that this article has offered some starting points for anyone hoping to engage with the knowledge available in the field.

Book Review *by Claudette Williams*

Psychophysical Acting: An Intercultural Approach After Stanislavsky by Phillip Zarrilli

Claudette Williams trained as an actor at Guildhall School of Music and Drama and has worked extensively within theatre and television. She has been a member of the Royal Shakespeare Company and while there directed a devised theatre piece as part of Not the RSC production at the Almeida Theatre; she received an Arts Council Bursary to develop the production, which was performed at the Bloomsbury Theatre. As an actress she has worked with Adrian Noble, Roger Mitchell, Katie Mitchell and Phyllida Lloyd. Claudette joined Central in 1998, working on the BA (Hons) Acting course, with a specialism in Voice, Speech and Text. In 2006 and 2007 she led workshops for young people for the Tricycle and Talawa theatre companies, and the Moscow Arts Theatre as part of the ICV.

PSYCHOPHYSICAL ACTING
AN INTERCULTURAL APPROACH AFTER STANISLAVSKI

PHILLIP B. ZARRILLI

WITH A DVD-ROM BY PETER HULTON
FOREWORD BY EUGENIO BARBA

This groundbreaking book and DVD-ROM outlines a course of study that not only integrates theory and practise in an accessible form but also integrates it into a practical pedagogical process for actors. Each chapter is imbedded with liberating exercises that put breath at the forefront of the acting/embodied experience! Drawing on his extensive experience in Asian martial arts and yoga training, author Phillip Zarrilli has set about theorizing the performer's body and experience to create a methodical series of psychophysical exercises. Zarrilli's belief is that 'Martial arts training can take one to the "edge of a breath, the nuance of the space between in-and out-breath. Action is given birth on the cusp of an in /out breath from the space between" (90).

Peter Hulton's interactive DVD-ROM enlightens the practices throughout the book, offering exercises, reflection, production documentation and interviews.

Part one of the book reflects on the 'Work of the Actor.' Chapter one focuses on an historical overview of the psychophysical approach to acting from Stanislavski to the present by looking at Western psychological realism and its receptiveness to body mind duality. In chapter two, Zarrill begins with breath. He outlines the practical methodology of psychophysical training with theory/exercises in preparing the actor's body mind for performance. Zarrilli defines the concept of training using repetition within an Asian martial arts context as the constant "(re)discovery of the self." From re-discovery he then "(re)considers" acting and the actor in chapter three. This chapter is imperative for all voice teacher/specialists as it defines with great eloquence what we do daily in class with breath work as a discovery of self in the moment and the repetition of that self/moment discovery into voicing.

Zarilli investigates the paradoxical dilemma of body absenteeism within the performance experience. His methodology integrates his use of phenomenology within theatre research and his implementation of the philosophical inquiry of Merleau-Ponty's theory of perception and Drew Leder's theories of body absence. The chapter concludes by providing a phenomenological model of the actor's modes of embodied experience and discusses the implications of this view for actor training and process. The chapter also provides several breath activation exercises in developing practical strategies of engaging the body and mind to become one bodymind.

Part two, "Work on Oneself," provides an account of his approach to the psychophysical process of acting via Asian martial/meditation arts. Chapter four examines three practices that make-up his training references

Psychophysical Acting: An Intercultural Approach After Stanislavsky by Phillip Zarrilli

the underlying principles and philosophy of each practice and provides exercises within each form on how the breath is used in defying the various psychophysical states. Zarrilli states that training in traditional disciples cultivates and provides access to the artists 'inner world' which is "not actualised through psychology but rather by the circulation and shaping of energy." He argues that by mastering and embodying the various states of 'being' whilst engaged in the 'doing' the martial artist becomes one with the inner life of each movement/moment.

Chapter five deals with 'playing' as a methodology for the development and investigation of new modes of performance embodiment expected within post dramatic texts with its emphasis on multiple roles and personae. Using structured improvisation (the pre- formative training process of acquiring embodiment), Zarrilli begins with exercises on heightening concentration, attentiveness of the breath, exploration of active images, and activating phrases to open the actor's sensory awareness within rehearsal.

Part three presents several case studies which detail the application of Zarrilli's approach, highlighting abstract conceptualisation and dynamic experimentation within a varied range of non-naturalistic texts in which ambiguity is part of its structures.

This eminently readable book, backed up by prodigious research, adds its voice to other integrated approaches for contemporary actor training. Its focus on breath in action as a performance score may be of particular interest to voice trainers, "for in that breath the actor senses and experiences simultaneously (114)."

Routledge; Pap/Dvdr edition (November 28, 2008)

Book Review *by Karen Ryker*

Breath in Action: The Art of Breath in Vocal and Holistic Practice
edited by Jane Boston and Rena Cook with Foreword by Cicely Berry

Karen Ryker teaches voice and acting at the University of Connecticut. As a Fulbright Scholar she recently directed *The Magic Flute* in Dublin, Ireland. She regularly coaches for Connecticut Repertory Theatre and has worked with Berkshire Theatre Festival, Illinois Shakespeare Festival, American Players Theatre, Madison Repertory Theatre, and Shakespeare and Company. A member of Actors' Equity, she has performed in New England theaters and in a good variety of commercials, industrials, and voiceovers. She has served VASTA as a board member, as Associate Editor of the *Voice and Speech Review* and on the Endowment Grants and Awards Committee.

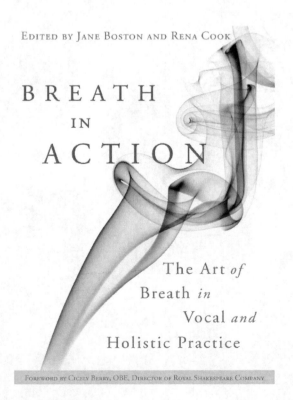

This work is shaped by the two editors' premise that breath, that most complex but repetitive activity—occurring nearly 26,000 times a day—cannot be taken for granted and plays a significant role in a broad spectrum of contemporary practices beyond the performing arts. Further, that advances in science, shifting social norms and contemporary aesthetics argue for a reexamination of the place of breath in these practices, and that a healthy interchange between the disciplines can lead to more effective teaching and learning.

The contributors to this collection represent divergent disciplines—medical scientists and practitioners and respected voice, movement and acting teachers. Although they are currently based in the UK and the USA, many describe practices influenced by a variety of cultures and various practices within the sciences. They merge eastern and western influences as they share their experience of breath and its place in their practices, offering some thoughtful intersections.

The organization of the seventeen essays flows with logic and grace, like the ebb and flow of breath itself. Section One: *Breath and the Body*, begins with a scientific (and eminently understandable) essay about the breathing organs and their functioning by Dr. Yolanda Heman-Ackah. Speech-Language Therapist Stephanie Martin describes how breath informs the health and well being of the individual. She differentiates between the voice we inherit and the voice we acquire. From the perspective of Alexander Technique practitioners, April Pierrot describes the effects of posture on breathing and voicing, and Jessica Wolf provides case studies of the effects of Alexander Technique on performers in distress. She includes an engaging and instructive log of adjustments for a young actress in vocal distress.

In ensuing sections the contributing practitioners sometimes work scientifically, sometimes intuitively or more often from a combination of the two.

In Section Two, *Breath and the Mind*, intuitions about breath moving the actor led Rebecca Cuthbertson-Lane to recent medical, chemical and neurological data which supports the notion that breath is integral to retention—and release—of trauma. Joanna Weir Ouston examines breath as an agent of change in relation to performance anxiety and peak performance. Kristin Linklater emphasizes that active consciousness of the breathing function will "enable the actor to become more available to the audience and thereby transport the audience to achieve new levels of imaginative connections" (70).

This reviewer found Section Three's *Breath and Holistic Practice* and its introductions into a variety of eastern

Breath in Action: The Art of Breath in Vocal and Holistic Practice
edited by Jane Boston and Rena Cook with Foreword by Cicely Berry

breathing practices to be particularly illuminating. Tara McAllister-Viel invites us to adopt a more holistic approach in which west can meet east. She leads the reader through the "Dahnejeon Breathing Exercise" to experience "how the architecture of the body shapes breath/sound production" (121). Marj McDaid shares the influence of Siberian shamanism on her breathing practices and describes exercises to develop twelve different ways of breathing that lead into different emotional energies. Michael Morgan explores the ways in which Chinese Qi Gong can be applied to western mindbody training. He then shares a well-illustrated exercise in Qi Gong self-massage with sound. Debbie Green describes a more personal journey for "seekers of authentic self" (161) as they integrate eastern and western movement and breath work. Rena Cook's review of contemporary literature of voice and healing arts practitioners reaffirms that attention to breath is essential to create authenticity and "access to the unconscious where the artistic, creative spirit resides" (178).

The final section, *Breath and Performance*, draws from the performance training traditions of the west in this past century and illuminates the differences in the application of breathing skills to performance and to arenas beyond performance. David Carey outlines foundational processes involving breath which have emerged from the British conservatory over the century. The premise is that deep breathing expands the actor, and the actor must develop a responsive psycho-physical breathing system. Jane Boston treats the use of breath in heightened verse. She provides inspiring examples of practical and metaphorical uses of breath to help students surrender to the poetic texts. Lisa Wilson explores the authentic breath as a source for integration of body, mind and voice and offers intriguing case studies of student issues and outcomes. Katya Bloom outlines her use of Laban Movement Analysis and Indonesian Amerta Movement work to encourage student actors to make choices beyond their ordinary patterns. And Judylee Vivier provides a personal account of her artistic and pedagogical journey involving the breath as intimately related to the experience of self. She describes her training as grounded in conscious awareness of breath and its psycho-physical connections, its key to release of tension and its transformative power for the actor.

Engaging case studies or personal experiences often support the points made by the authors. Many practitioners conclude their chapters with useful exercises. Illustrations, when included, are infinitely helpful in clarifying the descriptions. The collection as a whole provides evidence for what makes such intuitive sense—that free, efficient and deeply connected breathing can lead to health, authenticity and imagination in the performer and the human being. *Breath in Action* is inspiring, engaging and eminently useful. To conclude I offer comments made by Cicely Berry in the *Foreward* which summarize its value quite effectively:

I was delighted to be asked to write the forward to this book for I believe it to be extremely important in that it brings together the views and beliefs of so many voice, holistic, alternative health and movement practitioners, each of whom have their own very specific way of viewing the place of breath in their practice. This collection will dispel some of the mystery, which I think builds up once we start talking about 'methods'. From my own standpoint as a theatre voice practitioner, it has enabled me to catch up on the many new and different approaches in the way we think about breath –our perception of both its artistic and its technical values—its inspiration in other words (11)!

Jessica Kingsley Publishers, London and Philadelphia, 2009.

Book Review *by Julia Lenardon*
Zygmunt Molik's Voice and Body Work: The Legacy of Jerzy Grotowski
by Guiliano Campo

Julia holds a B.F.A Acting (University of Windsor), B.Ed. (Queen's University) and an M.F.A. Acting and Voice Teaching Diploma (York University). Voice/Speech teaching positions include: The National Theatre School of Canada in Montreal, The Prince Edward Island Conservatory, Michigan State University, guest teaching of text and dialects at The Institute for Higher Learning (MFA Program) at Harvard University and voice apprentices at The Denver Center Theatre Company and the Canadian National Voice Intensive. Julia coaches professionally full-time in theatre and film. Recent film projects include: *On the Road, Immortals, Voyez Comme Ils Dansent* and *Ubisoft's Assassin's Creed II* and *Brotherhood*.

Zygmunt Molik's *Voice and Body Work: The Legacy of Jerzy Grotowski*, is a collection of conversations between Zygmunt Molik (one of Jerzy Grotowski's original acting members and leading voice trainer of the Teatr Laboratorium), and the author, Guiliano Campo, (research associate for the British Grotowski Project). A DVD-ROM, attached to the book, contains video and film material of Molik's work as described in some of the conversations.

This book is neither a How To Manual of Grotowski's training nor a biography of his life. These conversations provide a special and very personal insight into Grotowski's work and productions via Molik's memories of his own work as acting company member and Master voice trainer. As a result, a familiar knowledge of Grotowski's work, productions and directorial style may be needed to fully grasp the many subtle and fleeting references to various people and events. I suggest, for those who wish more clarity of background knowledge before diving into the conversations, to perhaps begin with the *Appendix: Grotowski, Theatre and Beyond*, which provides an excellent thumbnail overview of Grotowski's background, work and training.

The nine chapters are divided into 'Days' and during each day new topics are broached and discussed. Campo, without question, has thoroughly researched his subject and feels passionately for the subject matter. He provides a battalion of questions, in a self-admittedly spontaneous and non-sequential manner. Molik's responses are refreshingly honest and range from blunt monosyllabic replies to detailed, colourful accounts. The revelatory moments that Molik describes as an "encounter with the unknown" exemplify the difficulty of translating memories of physical experience into words and the discussion of this theme, as well as the debate about balancing the relationship between practise and theory; these recur often throughout the book.

There are a host of other insightful topics, all of which I cannot list here but some of the highlights include: Molik's professional training background and theatrical work before joining Grotowski; Molik's work in the Paratheatre; the working difference between Gesture and Action; differences of training vision between Molik and Grotowski; the beginnings of, the training and integration of his Body Alphabet, including photographs that allow visual support to the discussion of this systematic training approach of the open connection between body and voice and the use of vocal resonators; and what could be meant as the "Life" in the work, which is at the centre of Molik's explorations and training.

The DVD-ROM contains exceptional support audio and video material including: THE BODY ALPHABET (2009) where Master Teacher Jorge Parente demonstrates each action and moves into physical and vocal improvisation;

Zygmunt Molik's Voice and Body Work: The Legacy of Jerzy Grotowski
by Guiliano Campo

ACTING THERAPY (1976), a film where we witness
Molik in action as coach in one-on-one vocal sessions; and
DYRYGENT (2006) where we witness a group training
session under Molik's direction.

These records of discussion—in both text and audio form—
of Grotowski's and Molik's unique theatrical expression are
definitely a worthwhile addition to one's collection of works
by and about ground-breaking theatre practitioners.

Routledge (May 2010)

Book Review *by Elise Robinson*

The Politics of American Actor Training
edited by Ellen Margolis and Lissa Tyler Renaud. Routledge, 2010.

Elise Robinson got her BA in theatre from the College of St. Benedict, her MA in theatre at the Ohio State University, and did doctoral work (ABD) at the University of California, Santa Barbara. An experienced performer, Ms. Robinson has participated in workshops with Patsy Rodenburg, Marcel Marceau, Diavolo Dance Company, and Aquila Theatre among others. To date, Ms. Robinson has also directed over 30 fully produced plays, including children's shows, classical & contemporary pieces, and several original works. Ms. Robinson currently teaches theatre and communication classes at McNally Smith College of Music in St. Paul, MN.

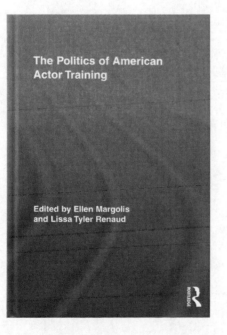

It is relatively easy to find books on the various methods, history and theory of actor training. These works typically aim to describe such training, compare differing methods, or analyze the training's effectiveness. Such approaches, while necessary and worthwhile, nevertheless leave a gaping hole in the profession's analysis of some of its most vital programs. Why are we not consistently applying the same critical eye to the politics of actor training that we have long applied to the study of dramatic texts or productions? Where is the examination of actor training programs in light of recent developments in gender, race, class and sexuality theory? Why haven't the discussions that have been happening in the hallways and meeting rooms of programs across the country been collected into a critical study that we can use to further the conversation? Such a volume is sorely needed and long overdue. Thank goodness, then, for Ellen Margolis and Lissa Tyler Renaud, who remedy this deficiency with their anthology of essays, *The Politics of American Actor Training*.

Embracing a diversity of experiences and perspectives, the anthology truly offers something for everyone. Looking to debunk classical training methods? Read Jonathan Chambers' nuanced chronicling of how he was led to reconsider his whole approach to teaching the "System" or Stanislavsky-based acting method. Or try Sharon Marie Carnicke's incisive study of the influence of Soviet propaganda on the mistranslation of Stanislavsky's acting texts in America. Her rehabilitation of Stanislavsky disciple Maria Knebel will be of particular interest to feminist theorists. Or, for those interested in more practical applications, Carnicke's summary of Stanislavsky's Active Analysis is detailed enough to allow readers to employ the technique in their own classrooms or rehearsal halls. Tired of acting and voice being seen as the non-intellectual side of theatre studies? You'll enjoy Lissa Tyler Renaud's persuasive call for the reinvigoration of American actor training as an intellectually rigorous, historically grounded practice, set firmly within a broad interdisciplinary tradition. If diversity is on your mind, Donna Aronson offers useful practical information in her account of diversifying her theatre program's curriculum and student body.

Part II offers a series of insights into little-explored facets of American theatre training, leading to persuasive calls for radical shifts in the status quo. Ellen Margolis' characterization of the student/teacher and actor/director relationship as fundamentally erotic is both challenging and insightful, and will surely resonate with many acting and voice teachers and students as a reflection of their own experience in the classroom. David Eulus Wiles makes the practical—and revolutionary—suggestion that we enlarge our definition of "success" for acting graduates to include the important work they do in *all* their diverse communities, both in and out of professional theatre settings. Di-

Book Review *by Elise Robinson*

The Politics of American Actor Training
edited by Ellen Margolis and Lissa Tyler Renaud. Routledge, 2010.

versity is a major theme, with provocative essays on gender, sexuality and race, and a fascinating look by Victoria Ann Lewis at the specific issues facing physically disabled students, and the (sadly few) programs that offer them a home. What is delightful—and, to me, unexpected—about both parts of the anthology is that the editors have taken seriously the politics of American actor training programs not only in the US proper, but also as they are transmitted to other countries and cultures outside US national borders. Lissa Tyler Renaud offers vivid reportage on the perception of American acting in Asia; renowned director Chandradasan's essay on Indian theatre, though bombastic in tone, nevertheless provides an important glimpse of the potentially negative effects of exporting American training to another culture; and Micha Espinosa and Antonio Ocampo-Guzman discuss strategies for Latino/a actors struggling with the limited opportunities offered them in American training programs. This multicultural perspective broadens the usefulness of the anthology as a whole, and offers an important check on discussions of actor training politics. The authors remind us that the question cannot only be "what do we owe our students and our country in the way of actor training" but also "how do we want to represent our national identity in the broader context of global theatre training practices?"

Acting and Singing with Archetypes
by Janet B. Rogers and Frankie Armstrong; foreword by Kristin Linklater

Scott Nice is an Assistant Professor of Voice & Movement at the University of North Carolina at Wilmington's Department of Theatre. He is a Certified Associate Fitzmaurice Voicework® Teacher and specializes in teaching the Loyd Williamson technique and the work of Rudolph Laban. Scott has worked with Gately/Poole Acting Conservatory as their resident voice and movement coach since 2002 and is owner operator of "Studio Nice," a body/voice training company, in Wilmington, NC. He coaches actors for both stage and camera in the Fitzmaurice Voicework®, voiceovers, stage combat, and dialects. He has been a member of VASTA since 2002.

In a journal celebrating voices from around the world, what better venue could there be for the review of *Acting and Singing with Archetypes* by Janet B. Rogers and Frankie Armstrong. In the Introduction, Rogers states; "Archetypes are figures and creatures that inhabit the pools of the world's mythology, folk tales, epics and ballads. There is great similarity between these figures and creatures across the cultures of the world, even between figures from cultures that have never had contact with one another." xiii

Janet Rogers, Professor of Voice and Head of Performance at Virginia Commonwealth University and Frankie Armstrong, an internationally renowned voice teacher, singer and innovator of this approach, have joined together to bring the reader through a process of utilizing archetypes in performance.

Armstrong has focused on fourteen archetypes ranging in diversity from Lucifer (the devil) to the Innocent Child. Each archetype is individually outlined with instruction on how to approach cross gender exploration and development for the individual artist.

The work is based on a combination of vocal and physical activities and applied research by Frankie Armstrong. Armstrong's source material is wide ranging from Plato to Carl Jung, but the practical work is a result of many years of collaboration between Armstrong and numerous voice specialist including Rogers.

Throughout the book, the personal investment of Ms. Rogers's zeal for the material is apparent, as she takes great care in providing firsthand accounts of each stage of character development. Rogers relates to her first impressions as she examined her first archetype, Lucifer. Advice and instruction on each archetype covers a wide range of techniques, suggestions and caveats providing helpful hints to meet needs ranging from the novice performer to the seasoned professional.

The CD provides vocal samples and instruction on the explorations of Ms. Armstrong's tribal and rhythmic songs designed to broaden the scope of performance choices, while the book has many helpful suggestions on how to best use the CD during the work, creating a balance between physical and vocal gesture with instruments and text.

The Foreword, by Kristin Linklater, speaks to the potential impact of the book's exercises when she writes "A wide audience can now benefit from their adventures in storytelling and archetypal song-making and sounds (ix)."

Through songs, storytelling and activities a ritualistic progression is established which serves as a gateway to entering and exiting each archetypal examination. The investigation

Book Review *by Scott Nice*

Acting and Singing with Archetypes
by Janet B. Rogers and Frankie Armstrong; foreword by Kristin Linklater

for each archetype includes a clear beginning and ending as participants literally go through the motion of stepping into the work as an ensemble and stepping out of the work at closure. The coined phrase of *stepping in* and *stepping out* are only part of the ritual of exploration which is established through the process. The combination of pedagogy and ritual for each archetypal investigation provides a comprehensive guide on a personal level serving as a gateway to one's discovery of the essence of the archetype in each of us.

Limelight; Pap/Com edition (November 1, 2009)

Book Review *by Erik Singer*
Filthy Shakespeare: Shakespeare's Most Outrageous Sexual Puns by Pauline Kiernan

Erik Singer teaches and coaches voice, speech and accents. He has taught speech, phonetics and accents at the Mason Gross School of the Arts at Rutgers University, and voice, speech and accents at HB Studio in New York. Erik has also provided the voice for numerous television and radio commercials, documentaries, animated shows, and best-selling audiobooks. He is the Associate Editor for the "Pronunciation, Phonetics, Linguistics, Dialect/ Accent Studies" section of the *Voice and Speech Review*. He is a graduate of the Webber Douglas Academy of Dramatic Art in London and of Yale University.

Pauline Kiernan's 2006 work of popular scholarship, *Filthy Shakespeare*, sets out to decode Shakespeare's sexual puns and wordplay. The book is great fun, but it is also stuffed with illuminating passages. In a number of cases, Kiernan's gloss on a scene is truly revelatory, sometimes making sense of a seemingly incomprehensible passage, occasionally revealing a meaning opposite to the surface one, or, often, intensifying the moment by adding a completely unexpected dimension. Much of this goes beyond mere titillation (though there is plenty of that). As one layer among many in these richly multivalent texts, the puns and double meanings often serve to heighten or refract a particular theme or theatrical effect. Kiernan's excellent explication of *Hamlet's* "Get thee to a nunnery" scene, to take one example, serves to underline the ways in which sexual puns can "express profound and complex feelings." (Kiernan 191)

The Puritan and Victorian eras that interposed themselves between Shakespeare's time and ours still cast a long and prudish shadow, and often make it difficult to grasp the full, multifarious, earthy, smelly, gruesome, violent, bodily, sweaty, and yes, *sexual* nature of the language, images, characters, and themes of the plays and poems. This is why Kiernan is at such pains to demonstrate and describe the frankness of sexual wordplay and suggestion between men and women—high-born no less than low. (Whether it's the Countess of Rosillon bantering obscenely with her clown about his monstrous penis or the ladies of *Love's Labour's Lost* trading outrageous sexual innuendos with their male counterparts and attendants, Shakespeare's high-born ladies invariably come out on top.) Kiernan emphasizes the point:

> There is plenty of evidence that in Shakespeare's day men and women spoke freely about sex with one another, and that women actively instigated talk about it. Plays by Shakespeare's fellow writers all have female characters talking about fucking, pricks, cunts, ejaculation and buggery. There was certainly no concession, then, to any notion of a 'female sensibility' which might have taken offence at the vulgar puns of the plays. (Kiernan, 26-27)

Kiernan also offers that the clitoris was "rediscovered" in 1559. (The book is stuffed with such intriguing tidbits.) Apparently, it was "known to Greek medical writers but then somehow got forgotten." (Kiernan, 22) She suggests that its rediscovery, five years before Shakespeare's birth, "showed that a woman's pleasure could be outside the control of a man." (Kiernan 22) One can imagine the anxiety.

A particularly good example of frank co-ed banter may be found in *Othello*. I don't have space to quote the scene, or Kiernan's gloss, in full, but it ends with the following lines:

Book Review *by Erik Singer*
Filthy Shakespeare: Shakespeare's Most Outrageous Sexual Puns by Pauline Kiernan

<u>Iago</u> …If she be fair and wise, fairness and wit,
The one's for use, the other useth it.
<u>Desdemona</u> Well praised! How if she be black and witty?
<u>Iago</u> If she be black and thereto have a wit,
She'll find a white that shall her blackness fit.
<u>Desdemona</u> Worse and worse.

Which Kiernan glosses as:

<u>Iago</u> …if she is fair and wise, there will be a vagina and a prick – the one's for being fucked, the other fucks it.
<u>Desdemona</u> Well praised! What if she's black and witty?
<u>Iago</u> If she's black, and has a cunt, she'll find a cock that will fit her cunt.
<u>Desdemona</u> Your lewdness gets worse and worse.
(Kiernan 86-87)

Among the puns this gloss depends are *fairness* as *vagina* (as in "fair parts"), and *wit* as either *prick* or *cunt* (derived from the similarity to *wight*, meaning *man*, or punning on the *white* in archery, "a white patch of cloth at the center of the target").

This is helpful. It's clear enough, listening to the scene, that something dirty is being said. But without a knowledge of the specific puns—knowledge Shakespeare's audience was intimately acquainted with—it's hard to know exactly what. The puns are crucial.

Even more significantly, however, and central to an understanding of Desdemona, is the way Kiernan's gloss brings our attention to the fact that she is actively instigating and encouraging the dirty talk. Rather than being a fainting, frail, proper and virtuous rose, as she is so often imagined and played, this is a feisty, adventurous, sexual woman who ran off with an exotic man her father disapproved of. And she can hold her own with Iago (at least in sexual banter). This is crucial to understanding her character and her function in the play.

In addition to the invaluable glosses and etymologies, Kiernan also offers, in an erudite, readable introduction and in sidebars throughout, a wealth of detail about life in Elizabethan and Jacobean London. Like E.M.W. Tillyard's essential *The Elizabethan World Picture*, the portrait she paints gives the reader crucial insight into what it was like to actually walk the streets of Shakespeare's London. On almost any day of the year, a Londoner might go to see a public disembowelment, beheading, dismemberment or burning at the stake. Heads on pikes lined London Bridge; corpses on the streets were common sights, even outside of plague years. The Thames, in addition to being the city's water supply, was also its sewer—when citizens bothered to dump their wastes there, rather than directly in the streets. Disease—from cholera and plague to venereal disease—was rife. Life for Shakespeare's contemporaries was nasty, brutish, and short (average life expectancy was 30-35 in the wealthier parts of London and 20-25 in the poorer parts). An active imaging of these and other circumstances is essential for an understanding of the plays and the lives they portray.

One major weakness of the book, it must be said, stems from its attempt to be, as a cover blurb from *The Spectator* has it, "A work of scholarship dressed up, with brilliant design, as titillation." It succeeds at both, but not without cost. It is fun, attractive and readable; it is clearly aimed at a popular audience. This in itself, of course, is not a problem. Casual readers, surreptitious secondary students and eager playgoers will clearly enjoy the eye-opening accounts of the Bard's bawdiest moments. But as a work of scholarship, which it undoubtedly is, the book frustratingly lacks detailed accounts of provenance and derivation for many of its glosses. Kiernan does provide an account of her sources, among them bilingual dictionaries like Randle Cotgrave's *A Dictionarie of the French and English Tongues* (1611) and John Florio's *A Worlde of Words, or Most copious, and exact Dictionarie in Italian and Englishe* (1598), often overlooked by the *Oxford English Dictionary*. These and other dictionaries and contemporary sources provide a "gold-mine of details for sexual puns," (Kiernan 39) often recording usage centuries before the Oxford English Dictionary. Very occasionally, Kiernan will cite a specific source for a gloss, such Cotgrave's explanation of several senses of the word 'dewlap': "The deaw-lap in a womans Privities….An ouglie nickname for an overridden Hackney (or Harlot)." (Kiernan, 131) But this is a rarity. The vast majority of the time, Kiernan simply asks us to take it on faith that she has uncovered contemporary authority for her explanations and glosses, even those that seem like they might be a bit of a reach. These omissions are unfortunate, and induce in the evidence-minded reader a lot of distracting speculation about provenance.

This is a quibble, however, and does not greatly lessen the practical usefulness of the book. Along with Tillyard, Harley Granville-Barker's *Prefaces to Shakespeare*, Harold Goddard's two-volume *The Meaning of Shakespeare*, and a handful of others, Kiernan's book belongs in that first rank of Shakespearean criticism—works that offer genuinely practical, playable insights, and that therefore belong in the library of every actor, director and student of Shakespeare.

Gotham; Reprint edition (October 7, 2008)

THE ELOQUENT SHAKESPEARE: A Pronouncing Dictionary for the Complete Dramatic Works with Notes to Untie the Modern Tongue by Gary Logan

Krista Scott is an Assistant Professor of Voice and Acting at Texas Christian University in Fort Worth, TX, as well as a certified Associate Teacher of Fitzmaurice Voicework and an associate editor of the International Dialects of English Archive. She currently serves on the VASTA board of directors, and is a frequent book review contributor to *The Voice and Speech Review*. She has coached voice/text/dialects at Trinity Shakespeare Festival, Illinois Shakespeare Festival, Connecticut Repertory, Kitchen Theatre, Dallas Theater Center, and others. Prior to her teaching career, Krista was Co-founder and Associate Director of The New Tradition Theatre Company in St. Cloud, MN.

THE·ELOQUENT
SHAKESPEARE
A·PRONOUNCING
DICTIONARY·FOR
THE·COMPLETE
DRAMATIC·WORKS
WITH·NOTES
TO·UNTIE·THE
MODERN·TONGUE
GARY·LOGAN

In the previous millennium, American practitioners of Shakespeare had scant reference sources for the pronunciations of Shakespeare's arcane terms, proper nouns and other anomalies of his texts. The Brits have had the aid of the *OED* (*Oxford English Dictionary*) and Helge Kokeritz's *Shakespeare's Pronunciations* for decades, but American actors relying on those pronunciation guides often sound so... well, un-American. All that changed, however, within a span of ten years with the publications of four different dictionaries for the American speakers of Shakespeare. Among them, *The Eloquent Shakespeare: a Pronouncing Dictionary for the Complete Dramatic Works with Notes to Untie the Modern Tongue*, by Gary Logan, is the lexicon that comes the closest to encompassing everything a voice and text coach would ever want in a pronouncing dictionary.

Actors, directors, stage managers, teachers, readers, and especially vocal coaches dealing with Shakespeare's texts will find that *The Eloquent Shakespeare* isn't merely a vast repository of answers to pronunciation questions; it also offers generous and concise tutorials in IPA narrow transcription and diacritic notation, prosody, verse and linguistic structures, the evolution of Standard American Stage Dialect (SASD) in actor training, and the historical sources of Shakespeare's words and their various interpretations. Within the forty brief pages of the Preface and the Introduction, Logan provides an immense amount of interpretive information with depth, breadth and clarity. Citing the tried-and-true glossary resources of the past and present, he addresses the need for a companion lexicon that goes beyond definitions, orthography and etymology, providing a guide for the appropriate American pronunciations of each word in every context it appears.

Beginning with "The Pronunciation Paradigm," Logan explains the ancestry of the model of SASD he espouses: "Current SASD pronunciation bears a resemblance to its grandsire [William Tilly's "Mid-Atlantic"dialect], and even more so to its immediate predecessor (what Edith Skinner (1902-1981) called *Good Speech for the American Stage*), but significant generational changes have occurred in response to modern proclivities in American English pronunciation warranting some subtle (and some not so subtle) modifications" (Introduction 1.2, p.2). Logan's practical modifications begin to bridge the gap between Skinner's interpretation of neutral pronunciation patterns and other paradigms of non-localized American speech. Post-vocalic "R-coloring", or rhoticity, is given its due credit in words such as *nurse** [nɜˑs], and *letter** [lɛɾɚ] as well as in the rhotic diphthongs and triphthongs, and a succinct explanation of when the post-vocalic "R-vowel" becomes a linking consonant [ɹ] is included in the Consonants section (Introduction 3.8, p.9). Other welcomed recognitions are a devoiced alveolar tap, [ɾ̥], as the allophone for a medial "t" sound (as

THE ELOQUENT SHAKESPEARE: A Pronouncing Dictionary for the Complete Dramatic Works with Notes to Untie the Modern Tongue by Gary Logan

vowel [i] replaces the RP/Skinnerian [ɪ] in words such as *happy** [hæpi]. For those of us who love the specificity that diacritical usage offers, this is extremely valuable detail. The acknowledgement of the "dark" (velarized) terminal /L/, as in "*fool*" [fuɫ], would be a useful inclusion in the next edition.

The Eloquent Shakespeare is a particularly ancillary tool for those who teach or have trained in a Skinner-based method of speech and IPA. The "Ask List" words (those assigned a vowel placement between the British low back vowel of *bath** [bɑθ] and the American low front vowel [bæθ], producing the Good Speech [baθ]) have been retained. Similarly, Logan's choice of rounded back vowels in words such as *cloth** [klɒθ] and *thought** [θɔt] maintains the Skinner Mid-Atlantic distinction from a non-localized, unrounded American pronunciation, and the "Liquid U", as in *duke* [djuk], is still applied, though perhaps less strictly than in the preceding generation of Standard American Stage Dialect.

Beyond dialectical systems of pronunciation, however, those who aren't Skinner-based in their training may find some of the SASD transcription choices confusing. Though the Skinnerian cursive notations are abandoned for a more state-of-the-science IPA font and updated diacritics, there are some interchanges and omissions in phonemic symbol assignments in relation to the established determinations of the International Phonetic Association. Specifically, Logan's usage of [ɛ] and [e] most closely resembles what one finds in Skinner's *Speak with Distinction*, which is contradictory of current American interpretations outside of Skinner's holdover from British transcription traditions. The vowel of *dress** is denoted as the close-mid front vowel [e] throughout, while the lower, open-mid front [ɛ] is relegated to what would be a higher front placement in foreign words and derivatives, such as the French "crêpe" and the first syllables of "prelude" and "deluge"; the diphthongs of *face** [eɪ] and *square** [ɛɚ], however, oppose this phonemic assignment, and are more consistent with a Detailed American Speech interpretation. To say the on-glide of the *face** diphthong is allophonic to the monophthong in *dress** seems rather fuzzy in logic and creates ambiguity among the front mid-vowels; moreover, it contradicts the specificity and precision in pronunciation the author seeks to establish with the narrow transcription and diacritical details. This shouldn't be a deal-breaker, though; once one wraps his/her mind around this issue, the overwhelming benefits of this lexicon can be fully appreciated.

Logan's painstakingly careful and thorough research of every word is apparent in the special contextual notes many entries include: deviations in pronunciation due to scansion, explanations of Folio and Quarto discrepancies, brief definitions of proper nouns, Latin or foreign phrases,

orthographical and etymological background information on arcane or questionable words verify his rationale for the pronunciation offered, and confirm his prodigious expertise in Shakespearean text interpretation. *The Eloquent Shakespeare* is an engrossing, impeccably organized, sensitively written, highly accessible, academically sound and supremely useful font of knowledge that has set the new standard for pronunciation dictionaries. The hardcover edition is reasonably priced at under $40 US; gracing the back cover of its elegant jacket are quotes of praise from some of today's most highly esteemed professionals in the field. The acclaim is well deserved.

* Denotes a key word used in J.C. Wells' "Lexical Sets", a common reference for IPA phonemes in dialect and accent study introduced in Accents of English I. (Cambridge University Press, 1982).

Book Review *by Marlene Johnson*

Thinking Shakespeare by Barry Edelstein

Marlene Johnson was named a 2011 National Teaching Artist by the Kennedy Center American College Theatre Festival—one of six such awards in the country for 2011. She acts and directs for City Equity Theatre recently playing Mrs. Gabor in Spring Awakening. She has vocal directed shows at Pennsylvania Shakespeare Festival, Orlando Shakespeare Theatre, Alliance Theatre, Theatre Virginia among others. Marlene has taught Acting Shakespeare at University of Westminster, London. Training includes American Repertory Theatre with Bonnie Raphael, National Theatre with Patsy Rodenburg, Kristin Linklater, Frankie Armstrong, Alexander Technique certification work. Marlene has served on the boards of VASTA and SETC. She teaches at University of Alabama Birmingham.

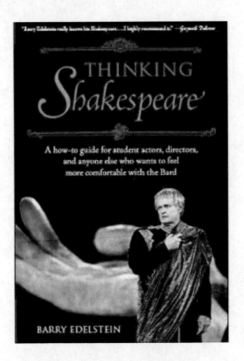

Barry Edelstein's *Thinking Shakespeare* exudes a vigorous voice and is among a small group of tomes on acting Shakespeare in which a director clarifies fundamentals. Edelstein's words jump off the pages with strength and humor almost as if he were in the room leading a seminar with you, which he has been doing for several years in addition to directing.

Edelstein cogently and succinctly argues that in order to do Shakespeare, the actor must learn to think, to process, to discover actively onstage in the moment as he speaks. By claiming and using formal elements, the actor is able to create more immediacy in this thinking. The key question for the actor "Why am I using these words now?" acknowledges that "words do things" (21) and invites the actor to keep discovering how he is using the words as tools "at this moment" (23) to drive home an argument and thus persuade himself or another to action. Although he mentions his debt to John Barton and to Cicely Berry, as well as to Kevin Kline, Edelstein focuses on the actor's necessity to keep his thinking active by using five main Shakespearean elements. It is this--along with an active style, humor, easy-to-follow, eye-friendly layout--that makes the book unique.

The book is organized into five "Acts." Act I lays out his theme and then overviews basic techniques of method acting including personalization and given circumstances and how words work in acting. "One speaks in order to get a desired result...which right now at this moment he can't otherwise obtain. That's acting in a nutshell." (23) Following a brief review of key Method acting concepts in the first two chapters, Edelstein persuades that Shakespeare requires more than simply filling in a role with the usual Method techniques.

Act II explores five fundamental formal elements: Scansion, argument, antithesis, changes in "height" of the language (individual character's styles of voice as well as the shifting voice of a single character from moment to moment), and phrasing with the verse line. "Scansion exists as a rhythmic framework not as a straitjacket. It is a guide, a roadmap."(57) Edelstein urges the actor to use his instincts while still testing the meter: "Trust your instincts about which words need stress, but verify those instincts by comparing them with what the meter says....Trust, but verify" (57)

An "intermission" chapter hammers home the necessity of using the five formal elements explained in Act II as a means to "think" and to act Shakespeare. He provides sample texts to demonstrate ways in which actors can remain active in playing their choices. Edelstein offers advice on the verse structure: "The verse structure makes the argument. You may choose to ignore this and phrase with the punctuation. Just know that to do so is to lose some of the uncanny subtlety in the way Shakespeare presents ideas, and to deny the characters the chance to do their thinking in front of us, to find the terms of their arguments under the pressure of real time and in the heat of the here and now. To ignore the verse structure is to take the thinking out of Shakespeare. That's no fun at all." (234-5)

Act III looks at: the musicality of the language—"sound sense", (i.e. meaning contained within the sounds) rhythm, tempo; the power of verbs; point of view. Act IV delves into areas that impact the actor's active thinking onstage. Act V offers some conclusions.

The "Epilogue" provides an excellent annotative list of resources, including a discussion of authoritative editions of the texts, acting and directing texts, and critical works. The ability to answer "Why am I using this word now?" depends on the accuracy of the word.

Like Shakespeare's language, Edelstein's style moves the reader forward. Overall, this actor-friendly book invigorates with a concise method for acting and directing Shakespeare. It would make an excellent text for a Shakespeare Acting class.

Book Review *by Julio Agustin Matos, Jr.*
Get the Callback: The Art of Auditioning for Musical Theatre by Jonathan Flom

Julio Agustin has been featured on Broadway in *Chicago*, *Bells Are Ringing* (revival), *Women on the Verge of a Nervous Breakdown*, and performed in the original companies of *Fosse*, *Steel Pier*, and *Never Gonna Dance*. A recent appointee to the Shelfer Scholar of the College of Music at the Florida State University, Julio runs a weekly audition studio in New York City (www.TheTransitionWorkshop.com) teaching his Transition Strategies to students transitioning from student to professional. He is a full-time lecturer at The City College of New York, CUNY, where he teaches Acting, Speech for the Stage, and Audition Techniques.

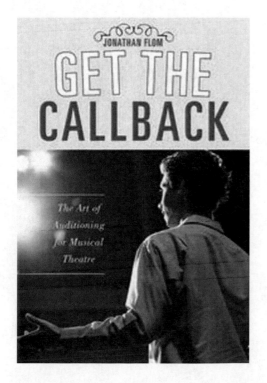

Very few books on the business of acting contain the type of practical and useful information that is offered in Jonathan Flom's new book, *Get the Callback: The Art of Auditioning for Musical Theatre*. He contends that "there are too many variables involved in final casting decisions that are completely out of [the actor's] control" (67). Therefore, the actor must focus on one goal only: *To earn a callback*. Flom's no-nonsense yet compassionate writing style is informed by his experience as a working director as well as an educator. He uses his relationships with his own mentors and collaborators as sources of inspiration and in forming his conclusive point of view. From Ed Linderman he instructs the reader to "convince the people behind the table that putting *you* in their show will help *them* look good" (2). From David Rodenberg, "Act like you're happy to be [at the audition]," and "you are only as good as your reputation" (viii). This combination point of view of director/educator offers student readers the perspective of a professional who also understands their particular needs and can guide them in a language with which they are familiar.

Flom structures the book based on the premise that a working actor will spend the majority of his/her time auditioning. Sequential chapters guide the performer through each stage of the audition process: "Before the Audition," "Walking through the Audition," "Callbacks," and "Job Offers." The specific needs of high school performers are addressed in his chapter "Auditioning for Colleges" in which Flom details how to research and audition for high-quality training programs.

Get the Callback is written predominantly for a student audience but the beginning to mid-career performer will also find a great deal of the information useful. In the chapter on "Headshots, Resumes, and Cover Letters," Flom walks the reader through the creation of a standout resume, for example, and even provides three sample resumes at various career stages to help illustrate his recommendations. In addition, he also includes one of the strongest cover letters I have ever encountered. Thus, Flom's perspective as a director serves to augment similar information currently offered by some college training programs.

The most useful part of the book, in my view, is left for the end: "Appendix A: Repertoire List." This unique guide breaks down both songs and monologues into genres useful to the actor/singer who understands the benefit of being prepared for any and all types of auditions. In my experience, this is one of the only song *and* monologue compilations of its kind, one that even acting and vocal coaches will find useful.

Working directors will likely disagree with one or more opinions offered by Flom. For example, he encourages performers to audition with material from the musical for which they are auditioning, a suggestion some would counsel against doing. Such is the creative and artistic part of our industry. Yet I strongly believe that few will disagree that this book is a very reliable resource whose detailed information and suggestions are relevant in today's market. *Get the Callback* is a must-read for students of college musical theatre programs and their instructors, as well as a useful resource for early professionals who have yet to reach their potential.

Scarecrow Press (2009)

Book Review *by Deborah Garvey*

What Every Singer Needs to Know About the Body
by Melissa Malde, MaryJean Allen and Kurt-Alexander Zeller

Deborah Garvey trained as an actress and singer and has worked extensively in theatre and broadcasting. She holds a music degree from Goldsmith's College, London and an MA in Voice Studies from Central School of Speech and Drama where she lectures on the BA Acting and MA Music Theatre programmes. Deborah is particularly interested in the links between singing and speech and her teaching work reflects this interest. She also teaches voice at Urdang Academy and singing at London School of Musical Theatre and has provided vocal support for Spontaneous Productions open-air events and student productions at Central.

What Every Singer Needs to Know About the Body

Melissa Malde
MaryJean Allen
Kurt-Alexander Zeller

What Every Singer Needs to Know About the Body offers a fascinating insight into how body mapping can enhance vocal production. So what is body mapping and why should it be of interest to the singer? It was first articulated by Barbara Conable, and is practiced by each of the authors who received their training with her. In the first chapter MaryJean Allen defines it as "a mental representation of your body's size, structure and function (2)." The book offers succinct anatomical descriptions, generously illustrated with clear diagrams. These are just some of the tools that guide the singer towards the embodiment of anatomical knowledge. Added to this are multi-sensory methods: Palpate the area to be mapped; Sketch it then relate it to the entire body; Use a mirror to determine size and shape and study accurate anatomical descriptions or models.

Conable presents singing as movement through the process of kinesthesia and states that singers have an inbuilt sensory system to feel movement. This sensory skill helps a singer to determine the amount of effort required for a particular movement, resulting in more efficient muscle use. Body mapping can only be fully effective when combined with kinesthetic awareness and a second sensory skill, inclusive awareness, or the ability to perceive self and world simultaneously. Thus, the singer can develop these combined skills to achieve a refined awareness of both the body's role in singing and one's external environment in performance.

Chapters 2-6 follow the logical progression of voice production: Alignment; Breath; Phonation; Resonance and Articulation. They begin with an overview of each process leading into an illustrated account of relevant anatomical structures. Practical exercises are included to help the singer map and develop kinesthetic awareness of these structures. The chapters close with a section on frequently asked questions. Throughout the book, references are made to body alignment by way of the 'six places of balance', the areas which collectively allow the skeleton to fulfill its role of supporting and distributing weight.

Kurt-Alexander Zeller provides a highly informative chapter on artistry entitled 'Physical Expression for Singers' with a section on the use of body mapping for characterisation. Conable's extensive Appendix on performance anxiety includes the appropriate acronym FEAR: the letter F stands for feel the fear; the letter E represents embody the fear; the letter A stands for arrive (in the performance space); and the letter R stands for relate (to the space, music, audience). FEAR employs inclusive awareness skills as a remedy for dealing with nerves.

This book's practical focus on body mapping, kinesthetic

Book Review *by Deborah Garvey*
What Every Singer Needs to Know About the Body
by Melissa Malde, MaryJean Allen and Kurt-Alexander Zeller

and inclusive awareness to support craft and artistry offers a commonality between singers based on [the unquestionable facts of] human anatomy. Reading through this book I gained a strong sense that these skills can be employed by the singer to produce a desired sound, replicate it and troubleshoot if necessary. Its clearly illustrated descriptions and exploratory exercises make it a highly accessible reference companion for singing teachers and students alike.

Plural Publishing, Inc.; 1 edition (October 1, 2008)

Book Review *by Anne Schilling*
Voice: Onstage and Off (2nd ed.), by Robert Barton and Rocco Dal Vera

Anne Schilling, Assistant Professor, Voice and Speech, Southern Methodist University. Previously taught at California State University-Long Beach, Cincinnati's College-Conservatory of Music, Ohio University, and in the UK at Guildford School of Acting. Voice, text, and dialect coach for numerous professional productions, in addition to private coaching. Graduated with Distinction in Voice Studies, Central School of Speech and Drama and a certified Associate Teacher of Fitzmaurice Voicework®. Currently serving on the VASTA Board of Directors. Publications include "An Introduction to Coaching Ritualized Lamentation" for VSR 2007 and "Bringing Lamentation to the Stage" for VSR 2009.

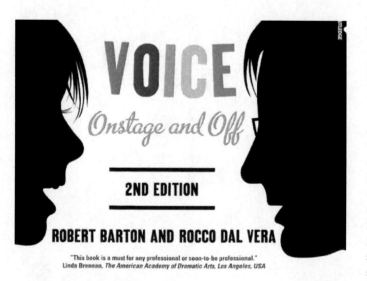

"This book is a must for any professional or soon-to-be professional."
Linda Brennan, *The American Academy of Dramatic Arts*, Los Angeles, USA

In voice and speech, with a tradition of master teacher as self-contained expert, many don't use a textbook. *Voice: Onstage and Off* is a powerful argument to question that model. How much more effective could we be if we had a foundational book that allows our students to self tutor, read and practice on their own and then bring their work to the classroom? How many teachers have the breadth of experience and time to cover as wide a range of material as they could with a text like this?

Few voice books are comprehensive, and almost none merge the many angles of training into a straightforward path. Now, here it is. Actually, here it is again and even better this time. Teachers and students will find this new edition a welcome revision that targets current demands in teaching and training. Various corporate mergers made the first edition of *Voice: Onstage and Off* occasionally hard to find, especially outside the USA. Routledge has now acquired the rights for this fresh edition, which is even more all-inclusive and more international.

Barton and Dal Vera are among the most influential writers in the field. Between them they have written over a hundred articles and published twelve books. Barton: *Acting: Onstage and Off*, *Style for Actors*, *Acting Reframes*, *Theatre in Your Life*, *Life Themes*, and *A Voice for the Theatre*. Dal Vera: *Acting in Musical Theatre* plus he founded this journal and edited the first three in the series.

Written in a playful, accessible, yet rigorous voice, the book takes the student through an eight-chapter process of (1) Owning your voice, (2) Healing your voice, (3) Mastering your language, (4) Expanding your voice, (5) Refining your voice, (6) Releasing your other voices, (7) Selecting your system, (8) Your voice future. There is a solid progression from self-awareness through remediation and expansion to long-term planning. And it is eminently adaptable. There is enough material here for 4 years of conservatory training, yet it is flexible enough for an introductory single term or even self-study.

All approaches to voice are honored, as exemplified through a comparison of the major teaching systems and emerging methodologies, providing a chance to "window shop" various techniques for further specialization. Teachers in training will find it an invaluable resource for their orientation to the field. The website (a particularly exciting new feature) includes the full audio text plus individual recordings of exercises, syllabi, rubrics, and a goldmine of support material. Students will love the interactive online activities and expanded dialect/accent resources. IPA is taught from a world-English viewpoint, including more in-depth explanations and details on pronunciation and transcription differences between North American English and UK models. There is even a side-by-side comparison of General American, Elevated Standard and Received Pronunciation.

The preface rightly states, "The book begins with the reader's vocal past and ends with their projected future (xxviii)." Essentially, this book is an encompassing perspective on all dimensions of voice and speech, and a welcome revision to what was already a voice text staple.

Routledge (2011)

Book Review *by Rena Cook*

Verbal Arts Workbook: A Practical Course for Speaking Text
by David Carey and Rebecca Clark Carey

Rena Cook is Professor of Voice at the University of Oklahoma. She holds an MA in voice from the Central School of Speech and Drama and an MFA in Directing from OU. She has coached such productions as *Beauty Queen of Leenane, The Real Thing,* and *Cosi*. She was Editor-in-chief for the *Voice and Speech Review* 09 issue and co-edited *Breath in Action* with Jane Boston. Her new book *Voice in Action: A Young Actor's Guide to Vocal Expression* is set for publication by Methuen in 2012. She has presented workshops throughout the US and the UK.

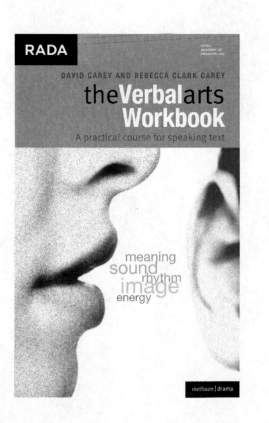

Following the success of their first book, *Vocal Arts Workbook*, which is an excellent sequential voice skills manual, David Carey and Rebecca Clark Carey have published a second book that focuses on the expressive potential of language and how through explorations and exercises teachers and actors can bring the power of spoken text to the stage. They have divided this well organized book into subheadings of "*Sound,*" "*Image,*" "*Sense,*" "*Rhythm,*" "*Argument*" and finally "*Putting it all together.*" The feature that distinguishes this work from other seminal books on classical text is its exemplary pedagogy which is deliberate and specific. The book bears an unparalleled depth and range of substance as it speaks to both students and their teachers in a clear and easy voice.

Each section follows a similar format, an organizing matrix, which facilitates the reader's journey through the book. Starting with the "*Framework,*" the authors lay the foundation for each chapter which includes background information, theory, definition of terminology, and appropriate examples. "*Teacher Tips*" are placed throughout each chapter which give advice, clarifications or words of encouragement to the educator who may be guiding a group of students through the exercises. The actual exercises and explorations are clearly laid out in language and format that is clear and easy to follow with thoughtfully chosen samples of text. The authors also provide suggestions for the amount of time needed to fully explore each exercise.

A unique feature of this book is the inclusion of additional suggested texts that bear similar features to the topic in question. Further, Carey and Clark Carey have not limited themselves to Shakespearean or classical text but offer a wide range of contemporary suggestions as well. This feature alone attests to a great deal of research and reading, a broad knowledge of dramatic literature, on the part of the authors. To give a more clear illustration of this feature, for an exercise called "*Who's Doing What,*" seven other playwrights are listed, including title, act, scene, name of character and stating line, options ranging from Tony Kushner's *Angels in America* to John Ford's *'Tis Pity She's a Whore.*

The final chapter, "*Putting It all Together*" confronts the fact that monologue study only takes an actor so far; ultimately text must be put into an acting context, characters battling it out with other characters. This chapter offers ways to explore dialogue using the previous topics of rhythm, image etc. to energize the dynamic between characters.

The addition of six *Appendices* provides an invaluable resource, including a vocal warm up; an explication of the work of Rudolf Laban, whose approach underpins some of the exercises in the book; punctuation and parts of speech, which illuminate how punctuation can provide interpretive clues; curriculum choices, suggestions on how the book

Book Review *by Rena Cook*

Verbal Arts Workbook: A Practical Course for Speaking Text
by David Carey and Rebecca Clark Carey

might be used throughout a term or semester of study; personal histories of the authors; and bibliography and resources, seven pages of titles and authors referenced within the book.

It is, of course, the exercises themselves that are the heart of *Verbal Arts Workbook*. Each has been given a succinct and clever title, "*You Can't Always Get What you Want,*" "*Here's the Deal,*" "*Minefield,*" all designed to open aspects of text, in order to help actors organically integrate intellectual understanding with spontaneous, authentic discoveries that put the words deeply in the body. Though many of the exercises come from the long British voice training tradition of working with text, most of the exercises described here feel fresh, current, alive and inventive. For example, an exercise called "*Twitter*" appeals to students' love of social networking. After working with a partner to discover the two or three keys words in each line, each actor then creates a "*Tweet*" that conveys the essence of the message contained in the speech.

An exercise that I have already used multiple times in a professional coaching situation is called "*Lists.*" Many classical and contemporary speeches, as we know, are structured on lists of ideas or images that build one upon the other, many may incorporate several lists, each having their own intrinsic build. The heart of this exercise is physically building the lists up the wall, the actor placing the first image low on the wall with each successive image going higher.

For "*Carry the Bag*" in the chapter entitled "*Sense,*" students are asked to place book bags randomly around the space. Done singly or as a group, the actor lifts a bag high over his head on the first word of each line and holds it high until the last word of the line when it is dropped and the energy of a new thought propels the actor to a new bag which again is lifted high over head. In this way, energy and clarity of each new thought is organically highlighted.

It must finally be noted that Carey and Clark Carey remain generous to their mentors and numerous influences throughout the book, meticulously citing where an idea came from or whose work inspired their version. The practitioners who have influenced them come from both sides of the Atlantic, their roots are deep and they acknowledge them proudly.

The Verbal Arts Workbook is a must have for the voice practitioner, text coach, actor or director. It should easily take its place with the other canonical texts written about the expressive power of language on the stage.

Methuen Drama and Royal Academy of Dramatic Art
(2010)

Book Review *by Erika Bailey*
Voice Work: Art and Science and Changing Voices by Christina Shewell

Erika Bailey teaches vocal production, text, speech, and dialects for the MFA program at University of Missouri, Kansas City. Among her projects as a dialect coach, Professor Bailey has coached *Syringa Tree*, *To Kill a Mockingbird*, and *Bus Stop* with Kansas City Repertory Theatre, and *A Christmas Carol* with Princeton, New Jersey's McCarter Theatre. Professor Bailey also served as dialect coach on the Broadway production of *Mary Stuart*. She received a BA in Theatre from Williams College, and an MA in Voice Studies from Central School of Speech and Drama. She is an Associate Teacher of Fitzmaurice Voicework®.

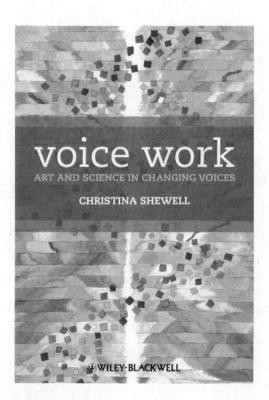

Christina Shewell's comprehensive and valuable reference book assembles theoretical and practical voice work from across the voice care spectrum, offering 'a meeting point for all those whose work is the repair, improvement and exploration of the voice' (xi). Her background as a certified speech language pathologist with an Advanced Diploma in Voice Studies from Central School of Speech and Drama creates the text's framework, combining scientific and artistic, theatrical explorations of voice.

While Shewell assumes an audience of professional voice users, coaches and therapists, she maintains an accessible style as she translates terminology and exercises between these varied fields. The majority of the book's five hundred pages lie in the chapters entitled Voice Work Foundations and Practical Voice Work. In Voice Work Foundations, Shewell provides her reader enough voice science to 'carry out voice exercises with a basic understanding of structure and function' (103). This information comes under nine headings: bodywork, breath work, channel work, phonation, resonance, pitch, loudness and articulation. The practical voice work section follows these same subjects but turns to a hands-on exploration of these elements and methods to create a free and efficient voice. Coming from a theatre voice background, I found many new exercises presented in a refreshingly quick and clear style. Some of the exercises have helpful accompanying recordings that can be found online. These online recordings, however, are not available at the web page listed in the book. Look for them under www.wiley.com/WILEYCDA/WileyTitle/productCd-0470019921,descCd-DOWNLOAD.html.

Shewell's encyclopedic look at voice exercises holds a vast quantity of useful information. For me, however, the book feels most original and groundbreaking in its introduction of Shewell's Voice Skills Perceptual Profile. She reminds us that voice teachers and SLPs are increasingly asked to 'prove' the effectiveness of their work. This requires a level of specific, quantifiable analysis that those of us on the artistic end of the voice spectrum may not have practiced. With the Voice Skills Perceptual Profile, Shewell provides voice teachers with a useable format within which to analyze the vocal functioning of new students and clients. The form takes the eight vocal areas explored in the practical voice work section, subdivides them further and asks for a numerical rating from 0 to 3 on each quality, 0 being no problems and 3 being severe problems with that area. For instance, the Body section is divided into a) posture/movement, b) shoulder, neck and extrinsic laryngeal muscle tension, c) vocal tract sensation, and d) overall physical/emotional tension. Space is then included for notes on steps to address the vocal difficulties heard and observed in the session. A copy can be given to the student or client, creating a written basis for future work. Further profiles can be collected later in the training to allow comparative study and mark client progress. Shewell suggests training in the use of the form will increase the coach or therapist's ability to score clients accurately and create more uniform responses when several practitioners profile one client. Even without this training, however, the form itself is an effective tool for any voice teacher or coach and I intend to make it an important part of my future diagnostic work.

In this compilation of approaches to exploring free and effective voice use, Christina Shewell has given her readers a treasure-trove of useful voice exercises and diagnostic tools. This book is an essential resource for voice practitioners from all parts of the art-science continuum.

Wiley; New edition (February 24, 2009)

Book Review *by Rebecca Root*

The Thought Propels the Sound *by Janet Madelle Feindel*

Photo © 2006 Steve Lawton

Rebecca Root is the recipient of the 2010 Clyde Vinson Memorial Scholarship bestowed by VASTA and holds MA Voice Studies (MAVS) from Central School of Speech and Drama. Her workshop on transgender voice was presented at the 2010 VASTA/Ceuvoz Conference in Mexico City; her earlier paper *There and Back Again: Adventures in Genderland* is published in *The Moving Voice* (VASTA 2009). Ms Root is a guest lecturer on MAVS; is Professional Consultant for the International Centre for Voice; and is principal voice instructor at Performers College, Essex. Ms Root continues her performance career.

Janet Feindel is a voice teacher, actor, playwright, and certified Alexander Technique teacher. Drawing on her extensive pedagogical experience at Carnegie Mellon School of Drama, UCLA School of Theatre, Film and Television, and countless professional productions, Ms Feindel has written *The Thought Propels the Sound* in order to share her knowledge on more than one level. Though certainly a book that will appeal to every voice coach and actor, it is clear from the start that the prime audience is the theatre director, who "often … [does] not know how to communicate or reinforce principles of healthy voice usage," (xviii).

Feindel is adamant that the audience will only be moved "to the core" (xxi) if actors connect mental stimulus to vocal liberation and stamina. "The thought propels the sound" thus becomes a ubiquitous catchphrase for the author. The concept of the spoken voice existing as the result of thought processes may not be new, but Ms Feindel is at pains to emphasise the link between acting and voicing. The creative intellect may be either blocked or free, and Ms Feindel has witnessed both on various productions as actor and voice coach. It is her objective to illuminate the reasons why certain actors lose their voice (and the audience's attention); while other performers have the ability to vocalise efficiently and safely, engaging the audience in the world of the play for hours at a time.

Ms Feindel begins by addressing voice work – the how, why and what of speech training for actors, within both conservatoire and professional environments. Healthy, expressive voice use and its opposite are considered alongside examples of notable performances that demonstrate each. A review of contemporary and traditional models of voice training (including Linklater, Fitzmaurice and Skinner) is followed by a discussion on the benefits of the Alexander Technique.

The meat of the book lies in the large, central chapters of "Vox Explora: What is it?", "Resonex", and "Voice and Text Explorations". It is here that Feindel most eloquently amplifies her practise, much of it inspired by the work of Berry, Linklater and Rodenburg, to whom she pays due credit. Not without first-hand experience, Feindel articulates her tenet that the voice coach can be an underused – and undervalued – member of the production team. This furnishes the reading director with great insight into the nature of voice work, and so fosters a closer relationship between him and his production voice coach.

Yet *The Thought Propels the Sound* is an invaluable tool not only for directors. Feindel considers practical matters that the voice coach grapples with: etiquette in the rehearsal room, note-giving and cast tutorials. The Resources section lists contact details for voice and performance-related organisations, and suggested further reading. The Appendix provides a limpid review of vocal anatomy and discusses a variety of vocal health issues present in contemporary theatre, from smoke and fog effects to vocal considerations for character choices.

Written with warmth and generosity, *The Thought Propels the Sound* represents a lifetime's work of teaching and performance, and is highly recommended.

Plural Publishing (2009)

Book cover Image sourced (at 27-09-10) at publisher's website: http://www.pluralpublishing.com/publication_tpts.htm

Selected Thesis and Dissertation Abstracts *Edited by Tara McAllister-Viel, Associate Editor*

Title: **Giving Autism a Voice: An Investigation into the use of a theatre-based approach to improving vocal skills in people with autism**

Author: Christian David Fellner
Type: MA Thesis, Voice Studies
Year: 2010
Institution: Central School of Speech and Drama, University of London
Supervisor: Rebecca Root

Abstract

This study investigated ways by which a theatre-based approach to voice teaching could be used to improve prosodic skills in people with autism. Lack of prosodic awareness has been shown to be an area of significant difficulty for this population and impedes the development of social and communication skills. Approaches to improving prosody in autism have to date been under-researched. In the present study, a scheme of work based on exercises drawn from theatre voice training was applied to two young adult males with diagnoses of high and low-functioning autism. The results suggested that this approach could facilitate significant improvements to prosodic awareness in high-functioning autism and showed potential promise in developing these skills in a low-functioning individual.

Key words: Autism, Asperger's Syndrome, prosody, speech, voice, voice-training

Title: **An evaluation of the effectiveness of using a spoken voice workshop to improve the performance of a song**

Author: Liz Flint
Type: MA Thesis, Voice Studies
Year: 2010
Institution: Central School of Speech and Drama, University of London

Abstract

Until now there has been very little research to investigate the positive effects that spoken voice exercises can have on the sung voice, and the performance of a song. This enquiry seeks to fill a gap in current research and evaluates the effectiveness of spoken voice exercises on the performance of a song, measuring in particular its efficacy at improving pitching/tuning, articulation/clarity and connection to the lyric.

Four participants' performance of a song was evaluated before and after a two-hour spoken voice workshop. Quantitative and qualitative methods were employed to assess each performance. The results revealed that there was significant improvement in pitching/tuning, clarity/articulation, connection to the lyric, and overall performance post-workshop, providing positive evidence that spoken voice exercises may be useful in improving the performance of a song. Further research is recommended to provide a larger sample evidence base.

Title: **Developing a Responsive Relationship Between Sound, Motion, and Text**

Author: Thrasivoulos Petras
Type: MFA Thesis, Theatre Voice Pedagogy
Year: 2010
Institution: University of Alberta, Department of Drama
Faculty Advisor: Betty Moulton

Abstract

Using a production of *The Good Woman of Setzuan* the voice, speech, and text coach (VSTC) takes advantage of Brecht's oft-debated theories to provide avenues of opportunity in investigating the responsive relationship between voice and movement in revealing meaning from the text.

Physical theatre methodologies based on the work of Jerzy Grotowski, Joseph Chaikin, Rudolf Laban, Linda Putnam and Kathleen Weiss were incorporated into the creative research. This helped performers develop unexpected Brechtian characters based on the impulse-driven responses to their own sound and movement. The research includes an inquiry into the misunderstood Brechtian paradigm and the challenge it poses in its translation from theory to practice. A coaching journal logs the actors' progress and the VSTC's preparation and collaboration with the creative team.

The role of the VSTC in exploring the connections between identity, breath, and text analysis is discussed. Maintaining a conscious sound-motion responsiveness provides the performer with a self-generating source. This fuels the clarity of meaning required by the text, without sacrificing the unexpected discoveries that are the privilege of the actor who is attuned to impulses through his breath. The result supports a gestic or archetypal voice: authentic, human, and surprising.

Surprise carries the possibility of unpremeditated physical and vocal response—the sounds and gestures we make when we're surprised do not lie. This connection to archetypal authenticity defines Brecht's practice of what he termed *gestus*. Exploring the integration of voice and movement training offers combinations of methodologies in both disciplines allowing for ongoing creative discovery in the rehearsal room as well as in performance.

Title: **Is the acquisition of the British RP accent necessary, desirable or achievable for Cantonese-speaking Hong Kong migrants entering the UK, speaking English as a second or foreign language?**

Author: Wing-Hong Li
Type: MA Dissertation
Year: 2010
Institution: Birmingham School of Acting
Faculty Advisors: Alex Taylor, Simon Ratcliffe

Abstract
Objective:
To investigate and analyse the Hong Kong accent of native Cantonese speaking migrants in London, focusing on issues of adjustment or compromise in relation to the various factors migrants encounter in a predominantly English speaking environment, and a consideration of the issue of individual identity in relation to the Hong Kong accent.
Participants:
15 Hong Kong migrants, aged from 17 to 63.

Method
Subjects were required to read out a set of reading materials and interviews were undertaken.

Results
Subjects speak with various degrees of the Hong Kong accent, of which differences are under the influence of various factors: age of arrival, length of residence, overall experience of the English language, their motivation and sense of identity. Early migrants who arrived in the UK aged 12 – 16 speak with less Hong Kong accent than later migrants. Subjects who have settled longest in the UK have a greater degree of Hong Kong accent remaining in their speech due to low motivation to change and strong views of their Chinese identity. However, significant changes of accent were noticed in all early migrants and some later migrants who have acknowledged strong motivations to change their accent.

Conclusion
Hong Kong migrants speak with various degrees of Hong Kong accent with some features of localised accent. It was clear that the early migrants who arrived in the UK aged 12-16 could acquire RP or nearly RP if resources were accessible. RP is not necessarily a desirable accent for Hong Kong migrants as a foreign accent has its own value in reflecting individual experience and background. Hong Kong migrants generally have limited knowledge about accents and tend to adapt to any accents around them. Therefore other British accents in London are relatively more desirable than RP for Hong Kong migrants due to their availability.

Title: The Moving Voice: The Integration of Voice and Movement Studies presented by the Voice and Speech Review.
Editor: Cook, Rena
Date: 2009
ISBN: 978-1-934269-55-8
Publisher: Voice and Speech Trainers Association, Incorporated, Cincinnati, OH
Description: *The official journal of the Voice and Speech Trainers Association containing 55 articles on a wide variety of issues in professional voice and speech use and training, many centered on the integration of voice and movement studies as they relate to training actors and working with clients. 474 pages, 8.5"X 11", paperback.*

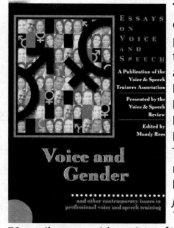

Title: Voice and Gender and other contemporary issues in professional voice and speech training presented by the Voice and Speech Review.
Editor: Rees, Mandy
Date: 2007
ISBN: 978-0-9773876-1-8
Publisher: Voice and Speech Trainers Association, Incorporated, Cincinnati, OH
Description: *The official journal of the Voice and Speech Trainers Association containing 78 artciles on a wide variety of issues in professional voice and speech use and training, many centered on the topic of voice and gender as they relate to training actors and working with clients. 410 pages, 8.5"X 11", paperback.*

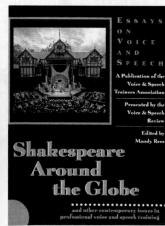

Title: Shakespeare Around the Globe and other contemporary issues in professional voice and speech training presented by the Voice and Speech Review.
Editor: Rees, Mandy
Date: 2005
ISBN: 0-9773876-0-7
Publisher: Voice and Speech Trainers Association, Incorporated, Cincinnati, OH
Description: *The official journal of the Voice and Speech Trainers Association containing 78 artciles on a wide variety of issues in professional voice and speech use and training, many centered on the topic of coaching actors to speak Shakespeare. 397 pages, 8.5"X 11", paperback.*

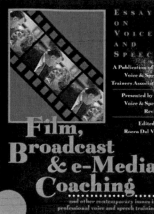

Title: Film, Broadcast and e-Media Coaching and other contemporary issues in professional voice and speech training presented by the Voice and Speech Review.
Editor: Dal Vera, Rocco
Date: 2003
ISBN: 1-55783-522-5
Publisher: Voice and Speech Trainers Association, Incorporated, Cincinnati, OH
Description: *The official journal of the Voice and Speech Trainers Association containing 67 articles on a wide variety of issues in professional voice and speech use and training, many centered on the topic of coaching actors for performances for the camera and microphone. 334 pages, 8.5"X 11", paperback.*
Library of Congress Catalog Card Number: 00-106487

Title: The Voice in Violence and other contemporary issues In professional voice and speech training presented by the Voice and Speech Review.
Editor: Dal Vera, Rocco
Date: 2001
ISBN: 1-55783-497-0
Publisher: Voice and Speech Trainers Association, Incorporated, Cincinnati, OH
Description: *The official journal of the Voice and Speech Trainers Association containing 61 articles on a wide variety of issues in professional voice and speech use and training, many centered on the topic of vocal use in staged violence. 338 pages, 8.5"X 11", paperback.*

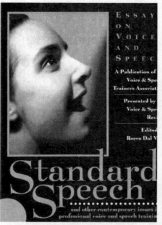

Title: Standard Speech and other contemporary issues in professional voice and speech training presented by the Voice and Speech Review.
Editor: Dal Vera, Rocco
Date: 2000
ISBN: 1-55783-455-5
Publisher: Voice and Speech Trainers Association, Incorporated, Cincinnati, OH
Description: *The official journal of the Voice and Speech Trainers Association containing 55 articles on a wide variety of issues in professional voice and speech use and training, many centered on the topic of standardized theatrical dialects. 332 pages, 8.5"X 11", paperback.*